The Editor, Professor Kurt Engemann, along with the effort of contributing authors, has created an important resource for scientists, practitioners and students by producing *The Routledge Companion to Risk, Crisis and Security in Business*. This quality book provides a thorough exploration of numerous significant issues and methods, not commonly covered in textbooks in this vital field.

*– Terje Aven, PhD, Professor of Risk Analysis and Risk Management, University of Stavanger, Norway*

This book is a comprehensive and authoritative source of the state-of-the-art in risk, crisis and security, from both a conceptual and a practical perspective. It is a must-read for business leaders, policy analysts, technicians and academics who seek innovative approaches and solutions for this exponentially growing complex field.

*– Giampiero E.G. Beroggi, PhD, Professor and Director Center for Business Innovation, University of Applied Sciences in Business Administration Zurich, Switzerland*

# The Routledge Companion to Risk, Crisis and Security in Business

Aware that a single crisis event can devastate their business, managers must be prepared for the worst from an expansive array of threats. *The Routledge Companion to Risk, Crisis and Security in Business* comprises a professional and scholarly collection of work in this critical field. Risks come in many varieties, and there is a growing concern for organizations to respond to the challenge. Businesses can be severely impacted by natural and man-made disasters including: floods, earthquakes, tsunami, environmental threats, terrorism, supply chain risks, pandemics, and white-collar crime. An organization's resilience is dependent not only on their own system security and infrastructure, but also on the wider infrastructure providing health and safety, utilities, transportation, and communication.

Developments in risk security and management offer a path towards resilience and recovery through effective leadership in crisis situations. The growing body of knowledge in research and methodologies is a basis for decisions to safeguard people and assets, and to ensure the survivability of an organization from a crisis. Not only can businesses become more secure through risk management, but an effective program can also facilitate innovation and afford new opportunities.

With chapters written by an international selection of leading experts, this book fills a crucial gap in our current knowledge of risk, crisis and security in business by exploring a broad spectrum of topics in the field. Edited by a globally-recognized expert on risk, this book is a vital reference for researchers, professionals and students with an interest in current scholarship in this expanding discipline.

**Kurt J. Engemann**, PhD, is Professor of Information Systems and Director of the Center for Business Continuity and Risk Management, Iona College, USA.

## Routledge Companions in Business, Management and Accounting

Routledge Companions in Business, Management and Accounting are prestige reference works providing an overview of a whole subject area or sub-discipline. These books survey the state of the discipline including emerging and cutting edge areas. Providing a comprehensive, up to date, definitive work of reference, Routledge Companions can be cited as an authoritative source on the subject.

A key aspect of these Routledge Companions is their international scope and relevance. Edited by an array of highly regarded scholars, these volumes also benefit from teams of contributors which reflect an international range of perspectives.

Individually, Routledge Companions in Business, Management and Accounting provide an impactful one-stop-shop resource for each theme covered. Collectively, they represent a comprehensive learning and research resource for researchers, postgraduate students and practitioners.

### Published titles in this series include:

THE ROUTLEDGE COMPANION TO ACCOUNTING INFORMATION SYSTEMS
*Edited by Martin Quinn and Erik Strauss*

THE ROUTLEDGE COMPANION TO AIR TRANSPORT MANAGEMENT
*Edited by Nigel Halpern and Anne Graham*

THE ROUTLEDGE COMPANION TO THE GEOGRAPHY OF INTERNATIONAL BUSINESS
*Edited by Jonathan Beaverstock, Gary Cook, Jennifer Johns, Frank McDonald and Naresh Pandit*

THE ROUTLEDGE COMPANION TO RISK, CRISIS AND SECURITY IN BUSINESS
*Edited by Kurt J. Engemann*

For more information about this series, please visit: www.routledge.com/series/RCBMA

# The Routledge Companion to Risk, Crisis and Security in Business

*Edited by*
*Kurt J. Engemann*

LONDON AND NEW YORK

First published 2018
by Routledge
2 Park Square, Milton Park, Abingdon, Oxon OX14 4RN

and by Routledge
711 Third Avenue, New York, NY 10017

*Routledge is an imprint of the Taylor & Francis Group, an informa business*



*British Library Cataloguing-in-Publication Data*
A catalogue record for this book is available from the British Library

*Library of Congress Cataloging-in-Publication Data*
Names: Engemann, Kurt J., 1950– editor.
Title: The Routledge companion to risk, crisis and security in business / edited by Kurt J. Engemann.
Other titles: Routledge companion to risk, crisis and security in business
Description: 1st Edition. | New York : Routledge, [2018] | Series: Routledge international handbooks | Includes bibliographical references and index.
Identifiers: LCCN 2017046181 | ISBN 9781138643109 (hardback) | ISBN 9781315629520 (ebook)
Subjects: LCSH: Risk management. | Crisis management. | Business enterprises—Security measures.
Classification: LCC HD61. R675 2018 | DDC 658.15/5—dc23
LC record available at https://lccn.loc.gov/2017046181

ISBN: 978-1-138-64310-9 (hbk)
ISBN: 978-1-315-62952-0 (ebk)

Typeset in Times New Roman
by Apex CoVantage, LLC

Printed in the United Kingdom
by Henry Ling Limited

# Contents

# Figures

# Tables

# Contributors

**Eirik B. Abrahamsen** is Professor of Risk Management at the University of Stavanger, Norway.

**Mitchell J. van den Adel** is PhD student of Operations Management at the Faculty of Economics and Business at the University of Groningen, the Netherlands.

**Benigno E. Aguirre** is core faculty member of the Disaster Research Center and Professor in the Department of Sociology and Criminal Justice at the University of Delaware, USA.

**Giuseppe Aliperti** is Research Fellow at the Management Institute of Scuola Superiore Sant'Anna–Pisa, Italy.

**Shaya (Isaiah) Altschuller** is Corporate Controller at Arch Reinsurance Company, USA.

**Shoshana Altschuller** is Associate Professor and Chair of Information Systems at the Hagan School of Business, Iona College, USA.

**Frank Asche** is Professor of Resource Economics at the University of Florida, USA, and the University of Stavanger, Norway.

**Nijaz Bajgoric** is Professor of Business Informatics and Information Technology Management at the University of Sarajevo, School of Economics and Business in Sarajevo, Bosnia-Herzegovina

**Mark Billington** is Fellow Chartered Accountant (FCA) of the Institute of Chartered Accountants in England and Wales (ICAEW) and Regional Director of ICAEW South East Asia.

**Kate Boothroyd** is the Founding Director at KB Risk Consulting Limited, UK.

**Ricardo Colomo-Palacios** is Full Professor in the Computer Science Department of Østfold University, Norway.

**Roy E. Dahl** is Associate Professor of Industrial Economics, Risk Management and Planning at the University of Stavanger, Norway.

**Robert J. Darling** is President and CEO of Turning Point Crisis Management-USA.

**Natalie M. Dengler** is Adjunct Professor in the Hagan School of Business at Iona College, USA.

**Eric Di Carlo** is in the Information Systems Department at Iona College, USA.

**Dirk Pieter van Donk** is Full Professor of Operations Management at the Faculty of Economics and Business at the University of Groningen, the Netherlands.

**Krista N. Engemann** is PhD Candidate in Organizational Science at the University of North Carolina–Charlotte, USA.

**Kurt J. Engemann** is Professor of Information Systems and Director of the Center for Business Continuity and Risk Management at Iona College, USA.

**Marco Frey** is Full Professor of Management at the Scuola Superiore Sant'Anna–Pisa, Italy.

**Barbara Gaudenzi** is Associate Professor of Supply Chain Management and Risk Management at the University of Verona, Italy.

**Jutta Geldermann** is Full Professor for Production and Logistics at the Georg-August-University of Göttingen, Germany.

**Petter Gottschalk** is Professor in the Department of Leadership and Organizational Behavior at BI Norwegian Business School, Oslo, Norway.

**Bingurath Ingirige** is Professor and Chair of Project Management and Resilience at the Global Disaster Resilience Centre (GDRC), University of Huddersfield, UK.

**Phil Kelly** is Senior Lecturer on the post-graduate team at the Liverpool Business School and Principal Examiner for risk assessment with the IRM, UK.

**Matthew Lagana** is Director and Chief Information Security Officer at MBIA Inc., USA.

**Haibing Lu** is Assistant Professor of Operations Management and Information Systems at Santa Clara University, USA.

**Cesar Marolla** is Senior Sustainability Manager at Deutsche Telekom/T-Mobile US and Advisory Committee Member for Sustainability at Harvard University, USA.

**Nirmita Mehrotra** is Head of the Department of Architecture and Planning, Gautam Buddha University, Greater Noida, India.

**Holmes E. Miller** is Professor of Business and Chair, Department of Accounting, Business, Economics and Finance at Muhlenberg College, USA.

**Manuel Mora** is Professor of Information Systems the Autonomous University of Aguascalientes, Mexico.

**Roy Nersesian** is Professor in the Department of Management and Decision Sciences, Leon Hess Business School at Monmouth University, USA.

**Rory V. O'Connor** is Professor of Computing at Dublin City University, and a Senior Researcher with Lero, The Irish Software Research Centre, Ireland.

**Gloria Phillips-Wren** is Professor and Chair of Information Systems/Operations Management Department at Loyola University Maryland, USA.

**Francesco Rizzi** is Associate Professor of Business Management at the University of Perugia, Italy.

**Kirstin Scholten** is Assistant Professor of Operations Management at the Faculty of Economics and Business at the University of Groningen, the Netherlands.

**Yossi Sheffi** is Elisha Gray II Professor of Engineering at MIT and Director of the MIT Center for Transportation and Logistics, USA.

**Jianping Shi** is Partner at Instramax, Singapore.

**Heechang Shin** is Associate Professor of Information Systems at Iona College, USA.

**Fen Wang** is Associate Professor of Information Technology and Administrative Management at the Central Washington University, USA.

**Gayan Wedawatta** is Lecturer at the School of Engineering and Applied Science, Aston University, UK.

**Wei Ning Zechariah Wong** is Business Continuity Management Lead at Horizon Nuclear Power, UK.

**Jarunee Wonglimpiyarat** is Professor of Technology Management at the College of Innovation, Thammasat University, Thailand and Visiting Professor at Boston University, USA.

**Ronald R. Yager** is Professor of Information Systems and Director of the Machine Intelligence Institute at Iona College, USA.

**Stephen Young** is Founder and Managing Director of Turning Point Crisis Management, Australia.

**George A. Zsidisin** is Professor of Supply Chain Management at Virginia Commonwealth University and co-editor emeritus of the *Journal of Purchasing and Supply Management*, USA.

# Part I

# Developing, implementing and maintaining risk strategies

# 1

# Developments in risk security

*Kurt J. Engemann*

## Understanding risk

Unanticipated crises can lead to immense negative consequences for businesses. Analyzing these risks and making appropriate decisions regarding them is very challenging but necessary to generate requisite security. A framework for risk management suggests that threats can lead to crisis events which can result in significant losses.

An important principle of risk management is that while risks cannot be eliminated, they can be controlled, thus organizations benefit from effective crisis management that should cover their entire enterprise. The most important goal of risk management is to preserve life and to provide safety, and failure to plan properly can not only be detrimental to humans but can also affect the entire system's operation. Choosing a risk management strategy is, in part, an economic decision, based on losses and costs. Specific risk events arise from threats such as hurricanes, fire, earthquakes, cyber-attacks, floods, power outages, strikes, crime and terrorism.

Risk management encompasses assessing risks, appraising alternatives and applying solutions. Identification of threats requires understanding what events can occur, what their likelihoods of occurrence are, and what the losses that they can generate are. Management must be involved at the outset to provide direction regarding threats, events, controls and the level of risk they are prepared to incur.

Collecting and evaluating information is a central activity during a crisis. The availability of timely, pertinent and accurate information will affect the course of actions as the crisis unfolds. Information analysis necessitates system understanding. If decision makers are unversed with the system they are dealing with, information can be misunderstood and needless time can be spent on bringing the decision makers up to speed regarding the matter being considered. Clearly defined roles with solid leadership is an effective way to reach a timely, correct decision; in addition, many decisions would need to be done in a decentralized mode.

Fundamental values manifest themselves in crisis decisions. Crisis situations do not lend themselves to the time for explicit discussions about values, however, they do illustrate how the core values of organizations and decision makers manifest themselves in decisions made under pressure. Crises lend themselves to systemic solutions. An institution in a crisis will be willing to take a risk, but given the option, only up to a certain level. Whenever possible, it will try to redefine the problem and share the risk among other stakeholders in the system.

Business organizations consider risk as a source of potential crisis events and as a basis of potential reward. The media generally place greater emphasis on negative events and the news overflows with reports of disasters which endanger people and organizations.

While viewpoints regarding risk and its treatment have transformed considerably over the last century, managing risk is a huge challenge that all businesses encounter. This development generally advanced from a narrow emphasis on risk transfer, to expanded organizational expertise to reduce losses, and more recently, to enterprise-wide risk management using a holistic approach. Businesses not only require comprehensive internal risk management processes but also need to manage extra-organizational risks.

There is a substantial body of knowledge regarding managing risk within organizations, from which risk professionals draw guidance. Scholars developed fundamental principles and the theories on the subject. Over time, the sense of risk and risk management has evolved. Traditionally, risk professionals viewed risk from a negative perspective which could be calculated objectively. More recently there is more of an inclusion of the positive aspects that risk may yield, while not neglecting the potential negative consequences. Moreover, while the early viewpoint focused on risk to physical properties, now risk professionals also place emphasis on organizational goals.

Myriad definitions of risk have been proposed: as uncertainty, an event, a probability, a consequence, a probability of loss, and as an effect of uncertainty on objectives. Essentially, risk may be defined as the possibility of experiencing an event characterized by probability and impact (Engemann and Henderson, 2012). Some definitions treat risk in an objective way while others consider it subjectively. Risk can be a quantitative or a qualitative concept. The risk perspective chosen clearly influences the means with which risk is analyzed and thus has important implications for risk management and decision making (Aven, 2012). All approaches add value to our discernment of risk, with a goal of qualitative insight, preferably through quantitative analysis.

Judgment and intuition play a vital role in crisis decision making. Effectiveness depends upon the decision maker's experience in the domain, the time constraints, and on the decision maker's task expertise. Relying on intuition in decision making is juxtaposed with the analytical processes that are powered by algorithms and data. Intuitive decision making often is viewed as more natural and may be given more credence than it deserves, and decisions that turn out right often do so more by chance than by intention.

The role of intuition in making decisions for crisis events may be unavoidable, especially when urgent actions are needed and insufficient data are available (Kahneman and Klien, 2009). The necessity for an intuitive decision should not be conflated with the predilection for intuitive decisions over analytical decisions, as the drawbacks of trusting too deeply on intuition, especially when other options are available, are profound.

Intuition, although frequently inexplicable by those using it, is a manifestation of identifying and acting on patterns. This recognition often encompasses the subconscious processes of assembling and evaluating previous information, and subsequently determining future decisions. Intuition is most valuable when data is unavailable and time restrictions necessitate instant action. Nevertheless, the choice of depending on intuitive decision making exclusively is not an assurance that the intuitive decision will be reliable. Intuition may be reasonably successful when a decision maker has both expertise in the task and experience in the domain in which the decision is being made. Progress in business analytics and artificial intelligence promise to modify intuition's role for crisis managers, and increasingly decision makers will need to refine their skills in using data and algorithms even in immediate decision environments.

Business continuity management has developed in response to the volatility of the business environment. The role of this profession in corporate governance has transformed from a technological role into a holistic business service. Although its value is generally recognized, its role predominantly remains process-driven, focusing on operational issues as to opposed strategic initiatives. Usually business continuity professionals focus on the physical and economic issues such as rapid recovery of critical services, information technology, and supply chain. This mindset is drawn from the early developments in technical advances to ensure reliability in the performance of essential activities. This is particularly the case in industries such as finance, energy and healthcare, which have significant impact on the public and substantial regulatory requirements.

Increasingly, practitioners and managers are endeavoring to pursue broader goals when applying business continuity at the corporate level. One definition of business continuity management is that it is a holistic management process that identifies potential threats to an organization and the impacts to business operations those threats, if realized, might cause, and which provides a framework for building organizational resilience with the capability of an effective response that safeguards the interests of its key stakeholders, reputation, brand and value-creating activities (International Organization for Standardization, 2014). Organizations that certify professionals in the field mutually promote the significance of business continuity management to an extensive range of activities across all organizational levels. At its core, the discipline offers a range of perspectives, from anticipative, managing the availability of business activities, to strategic, focusing on strengthening an organization's market position.

Accidents occur because those who manage complex systems are not sufficiently able to anticipate the problems generated by those systems (Weick, 1993). Safety may be considered as the minimization of risk, and correspondingly, significant breaks in safety may lead to disaster. Safety may also be viewed as a social construct; thus, safety climate is a socially constructed understanding of what is perceived to be valued in terms of safety and safe behavior. Where the environment is dynamic and the potential for loss is great, such as for high reliability organizations, it is imperative to engage knowledge that permits coordinated action. Members of a high reliability organization recognize what is expected and rewarded in terms of supporting knowledge. By facilitating collaboration, a high reliability organization has the capacity to succeed.

Knowledge is critical for the individual and the organization. For the individual, knowledge improves decision making; for the organization, knowledge is a key factor of overall viability. The conceptualization of knowledge has been advanced by many theoretical viewpoints (Engemann, 2017). Whether knowledge creation is encouraged to become a prescribed activity in a high reliability organization or it remains an unarticulated ongoing process, it must be remembered that knowledge can enable coordinated action.

Safety climate may improve understanding of emerging threats and vulnerabilities. Strategies to mitigate the risks are aspects of larger investments and involve technologies that affect systems and other organizations. These investment decisions are complicated by uncertainties involving costs and benefits because of rapid changes in the underlying technologies.

Organizations are reliant on each other and coordinate with partners who can provide critical products and services, even when crisis events occur. Risk management provides an approach to enable that the business functions, both in the short term and long term.

## Emerging crises

Events such as hurricanes, tornadoes, winter storms, earthquakes, tsunamis and power outages have underscored business organizations' vulnerability to natural disasters. Add to this list accidents, man-made disasters, terroristic activities, cyber-attacks, failing infrastructure, financial crises, crime, energy shortages and so on, and it is obvious that organizations need to identify threats and employ mitigating strategies. Furthermore, due to the inter-connectedness of business enterprises, even minor crisis events, if occurring in an exposed link, can be systemically devastating. In response, organizations are implementing risk management programs, utilizing structured management processes.

Given the increasing vulnerability, risk managers are confronted with the challenges of preventing and preparing for disasters, protecting life and safety, protecting the environment, minimizing asset destruction and providing continuous service to customers. Organizations need to have a have a plan to recover from disaster and resume operations in what may be a degraded operating environment. Risk assessment involves estimating the likelihood of crisis events, nevertheless, determining event probabilities is difficult because of the relatively small probabilities of event occurrences, and estimating potential losses is also challenging given the hypothetical nature of the task.

To be effective, the risk management must be business driven; business managers must frame priorities and provide overall guidance and support. Once the business priorities have been determined and risks assessed, structured methodologies can be used to develop the overall risk management plan.

Business continuity planning improves the likelihood of continuous business operations, as well as more broadly, emergency management in the region. Catastrophic events as well as localized events such as power outages and fires affect business operations. There is an increasing mindfulness of the need for systematic enterprise risk management, with organizations implementing prescribed risk management procedures necessitating a top-down risk assessment and enhanced internal risk controls. Enterprise risk management is becoming more standardized through the efforts of professional groups and international standards organizations. This has led to an increased awareness in protecting the environment, indisputably seen as a crucial resource for the economy. However, there is limited attention given to the connection between ecological degradation and the increased risk of disasters. Various levels of resources are available to governments, and those that are part of larger areas usually have access to more resources. Regulations regarding resource utilization as well as infrastructure development set the framework for promoting resiliency and sustainability.

Enterprise risk management mainly concentrates on risks to the organization's resources, including compliance, environmental, financial, governance, safety and security risks. Risks encountered by business include overall business risks that can disturb supply chains, such as product recalls or supplier bankruptcy, or the risks intrinsic in the operation of the supply chain due to financial, operational or strategic exposures

As businesses strive for increased market share, reduced costs and improved economies of scale, their dependence on more complex supply chains have created unintended risk consequences. Dependency on raw materials from distant suppliers creates risks of supply disruption. Businesses address supply disruption risks with familiar strategies, such as alternate suppliers and surplus inventories. However, modern global supply chains create new categories of risks that are outside the perimeter of the organization and its direct business partners (Sheffi, 2007). Consolidation and the growth of dominant suppliers, which then provide large proportions of global demand for numerous commodities, pose a risk of demand interruption outside the influence of the organization, and exceeding the capacities of enterprise risk management of separate organizations.

Globalization has created supply chains that are more efficient but are also now further disposed to serious disruption from distant events. Worldwide competition drives businesses to outsource more operations, thus increasing complexity and risk. Centralization of production capacity creates vulnerabilities as single points of failure arise outside a company's controlling capability. Thus, distant disruptions can now spread further along supply chains and can disrupt organizations in related industries. Risk exposures are linked to suppliers, customers and competitors, and supply chain risks ensue at a deeper industry level because of organizations' increasing interdependence. Thus, businesses expand risk management practices through their supply chains to manage risk linked to the global supply chains upon which they depend. Because risks lie outside the business, organizations are pushing enterprise risk management deep into the supply chain and are collaborating to create industry-wide risk management strategies.

Miller and Engemann (2008) present a model that simulates the effects of natural disaster risks for a hypothetical three-tier supply chain. Drawing on concepts from reliability theory and capacity analysis, the model is structured such that diminutions of service capacity at nodes lower in the supply chain can affect higher tier nodes. The model is used to examine various scenarios, including examining correlation among node locations, the effectiveness of disaster recovery plans and dual sourcing. In addition, the size of the lower tier of the supply chain is expanded and the ensuing results are compared to those for leaner supply chains.

A crisis requires a direct and decisive response from the leadership of an organization. During a crisis, all aspects of leadership are subject to intense scrutiny, thereby challenging an organization's viability. A crisis is a unique negative event for which there is no suitable prearranged response (Leonard, 2009). It is outside the bounds of a standard emergency response because of its complexity and magnitude. A routine emergency has an element of predictability because of its frequency of occurrence and because of extensive preparation and training.

Effective resolution of a crisis requires the involvement of decision makers, operations managers, specialists and senior leaders. Regardless of the type of crisis, an appropriately managed crisis can significantly benefit a senior leader by drawing attention to his or her leadership ability. Successful crisis leaders are decisive, intelligent and dependable, and are frequently recruited by other organizations to help lead them through their crisis. Conversely, a mishandled crisis can expose a weak leader who is incapable of functioning under pressure. The characteristics that make someone an executive are not always beneficial in leading through a crisis. Crisis leaders need to know how to initiate a crisis response, how to organize, who to call upon for assistance, how to delegate, how to interact with the media and how to lead an organization through to survive the event. Crises include natural disasters, technological crises, or cyber-attacks, organizational misdeeds, financial crises, workplace violence, rumors, product failures, terrorist attacks and other forms of man-made disasters, including white-collar crime.

White-collar crime is a crisis event that can challenge an organization's viability. White-collar crimes include bribing government officials, corruption, embezzlement and fraud. Numerous recent white-collar crime events have led to an increased awareness that white-collar crime is a crisis for which organizations must be alert and be prepared for. Victims of white-collar crime include the organizations themselves, employees, banks, customers, shareholders and suppliers. White-collar crime can lead to organizations being punished with substantial fines and executives being prosecuted criminally. If organizations survive serious white-collar crime, they need to go through a complete renovation of organizational structure and culture.

Not all organizations survive white-collar crime. Numerous executives involved in white-collar crime are aware that they were violating the law, but act to benefit themselves and their organization. The violation of integrity at the organizational level can lead to a crisis of the organization's legitimacy and has strong negative effects on stakeholders' trust in the organization.

Some businesses collapse when the organization is hit by a white-collar crime crisis in terms of detection and prosecution (Soltani, 2014). Some companies can recover after white-collar crime detection and prosecution. Recovery of collapse depends on numerous issues including the relationship between the perceived circumstances and applied actions. If senior management perceives the situation realistically and implements actions consistent with the situation, then recovery is likely. If senior management has an inaccurate perception of the situation, then collapse becomes a more likely outcome.

## Infrastructure risks

Infrastructure refers to the basic framework on which society operates. Critical infrastructures are telecommunications, electrical power systems, gas and oil storage and transportation, banking and finance, transportation, water supply systems, emergency services (including medical, police, fire and rescue) and continuity of government. Infrastructure's purpose is to facilitate commerce, travel, education, health care, security and so on. Infrastructure is usually taken for granted and comes into the spotlight only when things go wrong. There are challenges involved with building, operating and maintaining infrastructure so that it is effective, efficient and safe.

Modern civilisation depends upon electricity, whose availability is mostly taken for granted. Electricity is used by commerce, industry, households and transportation. The electric grid is a network for transporting electricity from its source to consumers. Threats exist that can substantially impact the grid's operation and performance over extended periods of time. The consequences of these events can be extreme and even catastrophic. Measures involving securing the entire grid are beyond the scope of any one organisation, however organisations can still act, even though the mitigating effects may be limited (Miller and Engemann, 2015).

Infrastructure for an organization also includes buildings, building systems and equipment. The starting point for the construction of a disaster resilient building is location. Nevertheless, site selection is only the beginning of the decision sequence that also includes building structure and layout. Every location is susceptible to threats which can disrupt a business. In selecting a new site location, those threats need to be determined along with the organization's tolerance level.

For natural disasters, such as blizzards, cyclones, dust storms, earthquakes, hurricanes and tornadoes, data regarding their frequency and magnitude may be available. These natural disasters can damage an organization's infrastructure and disrupt operations for some period. Some of these events may provide warnings and therefore allow time to prepare. Other natural events will occur with no or very limited notice, as in the case of an earthquake or tornado. Information regarding natural disasters may be obtained from various governmental and private sources. Once obtained, expertise is required to make informed decisions regarding the level of risk to accept.

Infrastructure outages may also be caused by man-made events, that is accidents or malicious acts. Oil spills, train derailments and fires are a few examples of events that may be caused by human error. Proximity to transportation lines may provide benefits to a business, however the possibility of a hazardous material spill needs to be assessed in making a site location decision.

Deliberate man-made events, such as civil unrest, also need to be addressed. Social issues and the political climate may have negative implications for a location. In addition, possible assistance from the local government and other external agencies needs to be assessed.

The type of building construction should be based upon the potential disasters. Recent innovations in earthquake resistant construction may allow a building to survive the resultant shaking from certain magnitude earthquakes. Buildings need to withstand not only the wind associated with a storm but also the associated rainfall and resultant flooding. To minimize risk, engineers need to determine the appropriate building construction to mitigate potential disasters.

Infrastructure risk is inherent in the construct of the megacity, defined as such because of the enormous population. The density and complexity of urban processes increases the vulnerability of megacities to disruption of utilities, communication, power and transportation. The interdependence of various urban functions increases risk substantially. Megacities typically have an extremely dense building infrastructure and the consequential high level of air pollution. Inadequacy and worsening of the infrastructure pose a risk, especially as the population increases. Harmful effects of chemicals, air pollution and ecosystem deterioration to which humans are being increasingly exposed, present potential risks to human health (Marolla, 2016). The stability of the economy and society are dependent on megacities and public health. Epidemics in one megacity can rapidly spread to other parts of the world, leading to widespread public health concerns.

Occurrences of crises in megacities are inevitable, thus the megacities' infrastructures must be resilient enough to endure these events. An effective response to a sudden event will determine if there will be disorder with significant losses or recovery with mitigated losses. The health care sector is fundamental to the general well-being of the population and in the suppression of pandemics. Disruptions to the health care infrastructure would be devastating to the health of the community, while innovative technologies can support its function and are pivotal to dynamically safeguard the population. The transportation system is at risk of disruptions in many ways, whereas intelligent transportation systems can aid in preparedness. Public safety in megacities is enhanced through intelligent systems, providing a dynamic resource management system and rapid emergency response. Megacities continue to be a dominant feature of society and can be secure with proper risk management.

As is evident when disaster strikes at the infrastructure, local groups and individuals need to respond immediately, often without the direction and assistance of centralized authorities. There is a need to address the role of these emerging groups in the process of response and recovery from catastrophic events. Lalonde (2004) pointed to emergence of new leaders at the level of local community as a disaster unfolds over time. The framework for assessment of resilience is deduced from self-organization in complex chaotic environments. These emerging leaders may not be part of a hierarchical response system, yet they drive the redesign of the organization. Cutter et al. (2010) points to the shift from vulnerability to disaster resilience as a more proactive and positive expression of community engagement. The challenges are a mixture of local issues and global dynamics in a period when nature can activate technological disasters and technology can stimulate natural disturbances.

A paradigm change in risk management in urban planning and governance is evolving. Disaster management systems which deal only with limited uncertainty need to be improved to handle events which cannot be so easily compartmentalized. Simple categorizations and disjointed methods are not effective any longer and crisis events increasingly validate that the current approach is ineffective. Innovative institutional changes are required to integrate sectoral issues of disaster management and make it sustainable.

Robust energy production is a key component of a strong infrastructure. The economy is principally driven by fossil energy resources, although there are avid proponents promoting the switch from fossil energy resources to renewable resources. The goal of reducing greenhouse gas emissions is driving the search for alternative energy sources. To reduce dependency on fossil energy resources, industry is increasing its use of sustainably produced biomass for fuel. The potential for using plants for energy is motivating their cultivation in recent years, and strategies to improve resource efficiency can also result in limiting environmental impact. To further protect the environment, multiple utilization of the same resource prior to the end of its life cycle is being practiced, leading to more complex production networks (Kircher, 2012). An important strategy for economic competitiveness of biomass inputs is to increase their utilization efficiency by applying the cascade utilization principle. However, this cascade utilization creates further complexity and additional risk.

These changes impact nearly all facets of industrial production. Organizations in this developing bioeconomy are experiencing new risks in addition to inherent risks. Specific to biomass inputs, there are risk associated with fluctuations in quality and availability and changes in material properties that occur as materials cascade through the production network. Although there is growing social pressure to promote sustainability, prudent risk management remains a prerequisite for sustainable development. Managing risks, nevertheless, is a difficult task and requires input from science, government, industry and society (Renn, 2015). To manage this complex risk environment, decision makers rely on a variety of decision analytical techniques.

New risks are associated with new technologies and increased complexity, suggesting that risk increases with more economic activity. This relationship between risk and economic activity is of great concern, as it relates to the safety of workers. In particular, the association between the accident risk a person is exposed to and the prosperity of a country is suitable for risk analysis. Increased economic activity generates new risks that may reduce safety levels. However, economic development leads to a structural transformation in what is produced and how, and with increased wealth there is stronger incentive to improve safety and thereby limit risk. With ample resources, societies are projected to apply more resources to reducing risk. There is evidence that societies with higher economic activity are safer, but that economic activity increases at a faster rate than safety, as predicted by the law of diminishing returns.

Finally, consider the infrastructure risk associated with flooding. Flooding is a threat to businesses in many areas, especially to small and medium-sized enterprises. Their vulnerability to disruptions arises because of the small scale of their human and financial resources and because of their insufficiency of preparation (Bannock, 2005). Some forecasts indicate that flooding is expected to further increase in severity in the future, due to climate change impacts. Damage to business infrastructure and the subsequent business closures may result in loss of jobs, hindering recovery efforts of local communities affecting the society at large (Tierney, 2007). Because social impacts, as opposed to physical damages, are not normally accounted for in monetary terms, it is difficult for policy makers to address the overall consequences of infrastructure risks.

Developing infrastructure necessitates both vision and resources. Vision identifies the technological advances to be created and resources enable their development. Security depends upon the critical infrastructure being in place to provide the foundation for business success.

## Systems security

An important area of interest in risk management is information technology (IT), with cost relationships governing IT being dynamic and benefits often uncertain. Vulnerability is exacerbated by most organizations' growing reliance on computing and telecommunications technologies, and with trends toward integrating suppliers and business partners into everyday business operations (Miller et al., 2006). Disaster recovery for IT focuses on maintaining or restoring the systems and communication capabilities of the organization after a disaster.

Ongoing trends for increasing computing services have amplified the requirement that data centers always be operating, and spotlighted the rapid technological change and uncertainty that characterize IT investments (Engemann et al., 2005). A key tenet of risk management is that while risks cannot be eliminated, they can be controlled. The appropriate level of control depends both on the likelihood of the risk occurring and the magnitude of the loss if the risk does occur. The principles and procedures of risk management apply to both disaster recovery and information security, and because disaster recovery and information security deal with improbable events, analyzing these risks as part of the investment decision analysis is challenging. The appropriate strategy to implement depends both on the likelihood of events occurring and the magnitudes of the losses if the events occur, however, controls to mitigate these risks may cause processing inefficiencies and increase capital and ongoing operational costs. Moreover, because measures to address disaster recovery and information security events are aspects of larger IT investments, they are themselves technologies that affect systems, operations, and other internal and external organizations.

Any organization that depends on computer processing needs an effective disaster recovery plan that covers the entire service delivery system. Ultimately choosing a disaster recovery strategy is an economic decision, based on risks, losses and costs. Often overlooked as a cost of a disaster recovery investment is the plan's ongoing maintenance and testing after implementation. Because of interdependencies between organizations and technology, changes by one area of an organization can affect other areas. These changes include implementing new technologies, implementing new procedures, changing capacities or just normal turnover of personnel familiar with the plan.

The role of disaster recovery and information security risk must be viewed in the context of the larger IT application. Disaster recovery and information security directly affect hardware, telecommunications and applications software, and indirectly affect the larger business system including the linkages between the application and other applications and business processes. Failure to adequately address these issues when evaluating IT alternatives can lead to significant losses; avoiding or mitigating these losses is a benefit of controlling IT risk.

The pervasive presence of software systems, interwoven into every facet of progress, invariably forces security to become a significant matter. The complexity of software, coupled with the immense interconnectivity of systems and the growing intricacy of applications, creates grave concerns regarding security threats. Not merely presenting a risk of financial loss, the consequences of a security failure may, in fact, be life threatening. Non-secure software can negatively impact a business organization's employees, customers and investors, and can damage an organization's reputation. Failures diminish services and increase costs; additionally, unprotected software can be altered and cause damage to other functional software. Moreover, compromised software can migrate through vast networks and harm other far-reaching systems.

Effective security can protect a business from the difficulties connected to crashes and allow the business to be more responsive and effective. Organizations benefit from robust security, thereby reducing the probability and impact of exploitation of weaknesses. By enhancing the application of security throughout the software development life cycle, secure software can be designed. Consequently, security should be an essential part of planning, design, development, testing and maintenance of all software systems. Strong software security enables an organization to achieve its goals and to enhance its reputation. By employing security concepts throughout the software development life cycle, the integration of security into the system will be seamless and effective.

Fundamental to the mission of information security is that of providing availability, integrity and confidentiality of an organization's information assets. The components and methods within the field of information security have transformed over the years as the threats confronting organizations have evolved and become more complex and insidious. Traditional security approaches, with heavy emphasis on boundaries, are outdated and no longer effective. As the perimeters for organizations and software systems continuously morph, modern security defenses must recognize threats from anywhere. Nevertheless, the proper blend of awareness, policies, practices, professionals and technology can effectively guard against the multitude of threats.

Threats continue to evolve and can only be effectively treated by adequately incorporating the components that comprise complete security. Information security is a synchronization of people, process and technology, each of which is integral to successful security. Security teams must continually develop their knowledge by collaboration with the broader security community; organizational policies, protocols and procedures must adapt to evolving threats; and finally, security platforms and analytics must effectively be applied. The strength of the alignment among these three components determines the success of an organization's overall security program.

Business computing has progressed through transaction processing systems, management information systems, decision support systems, office automation and personal productivity systems, with the benefits of improving the efficiency of operations and enhancing the effectiveness of decision making. Information systems were developed around traditional centralized computer centers, responsible for running business applications using a blend of batch and online applications. With the introduction of enterprise servers, client server computing, internet technologies and cloud computing, businesses became more IT dependent. In today's e-business world, the whole business is IT-dependent and data-driven. Business computing has evolved into an organizational engine that drives business and provides a powerful source for competitive advantage.

From the very first years of the e-business era, the availability of information system platforms has determined significantly e-business success. Downtime costs are tremendously high for businesses of all sizes and across all industries. Businesses can lose millions of dollars in failures lasting less than an hour, and cannot tolerate the same levels of downtime that they could in previous years. While transaction systems once characterized the critical aspects of an organization, today, systems of engagement are equally important; employees need access their productivity tools and communication channels. A major goal is to transform modern business into an always-on e-business by identifying and implementing continuous computing technologies.

Location-based services are an increasingly growing market in which companies can market to nearby users. Location-based services provide useful information about the area around a user and provide services based on the user's current location. Location-based services are used for mobile workforce management, store locations, location-awareness, travel information, proximity-based marketing, local news and weather. Due to these useful features, and because of the increase in the number of smartphone devices, location-based services have had tremendous growth all around the world, with continued growth expected (Basiri et al., 2016).

However, there are major privacy threats because an adversary can track a user, which can lead to a leak of personal information about the user. An adversary can find out a person's location through a location-based service provider. Users have valid concerns about their personal safety and privacy. To address these threats, the location of the user can be made less specific in a generalized region, making the user indistinguishable from other users. By implementing this control, it is harder for an adversary to distinguish between users within the generalized region, and thus, a user's location privacy is protected (Shin et al., 2011).

## Business sectors

There are many challenges facing all organizations regarding risk management. These challenges exist in every industry, whether it is banking, manufacturing, healthcare, education, transportation, energy, insurance, retail, agriculture, entertainment and so forth. The board of directors is an organization's uppermost management authority and has final responsibility for the organization's performance. The board of directors must support policies to ensure the organization's survival and fulfillment of its mission. Senior management is responsible for the organization's resiliency and it is the obligation of all employees to know their role and to participate as directed. All employees should appropriately be trained in the risk program and know the emergency response actions.

All organizations are comprised of the three primary functions of operations, finance and marketing. Operations is responsible for producing the goods and services of an organization. The finance function is responsible for managing an organization's financial assets. The marketing function is responsible for selling an organization's goods and services. Organizational support functions include information technology, human resources and communications. Because of interdependencies between organizations and technology, changes in one area of an organization can affect other areas.

Advances in technology have caused organizations to reconsider the implications that these fast-paced changes have on their business operations. This is especially pertinent regarding the risks and opportunities surrounding the use of information systems for the processing of accounting and financial data.

Accounting information systems are important to the proper functioning of all organizations. While risk management includes the analysis of a wide gamut of sources of risk, this comes at a time when accounting information systems are transforming business processes. Accounting information systems have been implemented to process data and transactions through an organization's operations. Investment in these systems has benefitted businesses by facilitating efficient cost saving procedures and by adding value through innovative data analysis. As accounting information systems continue to advance, they get more entrenched into the fabric of the organization's operations and simultaneously increasingly complex.

With these changes comes exposure to a multitude of risks. If the data provided to the system are not accurate, the value of the output is compromised. There is the risk that the programmer who designed the system did not accurately understand the calculations and introduced a logic error in the program. There is the risk that the output of an accounting information system is not appropriately understood by the user, as well as the risk that external auditors introduce control risk which involves the material misstatements of the firm's internal controls. A host of other risks related to an organizations' accounting information systems include access risk, business interruption risk, change management risk, control risk, legal risk, reliability risk and perhaps most significantly, cyber-security risk. Developments in accounting information systems will continue to generate significant changes in the way business data is collected and analyzed. These shifts have resulted in great opportunities for businesses but also significant risks.

Organizations have also experienced extraordinary benefits and substantial risks because of global supply chains. In addition to the opportunities connected to global markets, there are risks that businesses need to address. The cost of products in global supply chains are impacted by financial markets; therefore, organizations must effectively manage foreign exchange risk. Currency rate volatility poses both risks and opportunities for business involved in global supply chains.

Foreign exchange risk is defined as the risk of an investment's value fluctuation due to the changes in currency exchange rate. It can significantly affect profitability, organizational cash flow and the ability to competitively price products (Burnside, 2012). Foreign exchange risk management requires contracting and operating strategies encompassing customers and suppliers. Negotiations with customers and suppliers are influenced by foreign exchange dynamics and should be considered as factors in a foreign exchange risk management. Foreign exchange risk should be managed beyond the financing function of a business, and instead, be addressed in a more holistic manner by including purchasing and marketing, as well as the risk management expertise of legal professionals.

Now consider, as another example of business sector risk, the inherent risk of financing oil fracking in a free market. The free market permits great volatility in price depending on supply and demand. Although price may be a good signal on when to expand capacity, it does not indicate how much to expand. Invariably, excess capacity is generated which eventually distresses the industry. Oil frackers additionally face the risk created by the very short length of time their wells produce compared to conventional oil wells. The conventional oil well can profit even through fluctuations of oil prices, however, a fracked well does not usually recover after the market turns down.

If oil fracking investors consider the impermanence of business conditions, then they would make decisions which include contingencies for a market reversal and dampen the temptation of unwarranted overexpansion. Banks insisting on swaps to protect revenue is an example of risk mitigation. Simulation models can be used to determine the degree of swap coverage to reduce risk without overly diminishing profits. Some oil fracking business have successfully used swaps to remain solvent despite a sudden onset of low oil prices.

Another sector of interest regarding risk is in cause-related marketing. Disasters produce a multitude of negative effects, including loss of life and economic losses reaching into the hundreds of billions of dollars. Cause-related marketing is a form of fundraising that contributes to the recovery of communities struck by disaster. An increasing number of organizations are adopting cause-related marketing campaigns through promoting disaster-related causes. The tourist industry is engaged in this area, however, the links between cause-related marketing, tourism and disaster management remain weak. Some organizations are using disasters to enhance their brand image and influence the consumers' perception regarding their corporate social responsibility through promoting cause-related marketing campaigns.

Supply chain resilience evolves around the concept that all risks cannot be predicted; therefore, supply chains need to be capable of absorbing the impact of unforeseen disruptions. Risk management plays a vital role in effectively operating supply chains in the presence of a variety of uncertainties (Ho et al., 2015). Collaborative relationships in supply chains help partners achieve success by facilitating social capital. Appropriate levels of social capital foster teamwork and improves behaviour among partners, as underlying mechanisms aid organizations to deal with supply chain disruptions.

To be resilient a supply chain must prepare for unexpected events, maintain continuity, and recover from disruptions. Facing a disruption, a supply chain needs to have the flexibility to exploit multiple sources of capacity to ensure appropriate speed of recovery. Supply chain collaboration involves a long-term partnership where partners work closely together to achieve mutual advantages.

Technology incubators and science parks play an important role to support economic growth and sustainable development. Policy makers around the world create them to advance entrepreneurship and innovation and to improve national economic capacity. Technology-based start-up firms often benefit from technology incubators; however, these ventures are high-risk. Risk analysis tools are used to perform risk assessments across all aspects of entrepreneurial development, including product innovation, production, marketing, management, finance and investment. These dynamic tools are innovation enablers that optimize the likelihood of success of emerging businesses.

## Risk modeling

A decision model is a representation of reality. The decision maker determines the purpose and scope of the model, and selects the variables and relationships to be included. Analytics play a vital role in understanding a risk situation and in shaping the best strategy to implement. A strategy can be to implement controls that reduce the rate of occurrence of crisis events or mitigate losses if events do occur. Data analysis tools can help clarify relationships in an uncertain environment and decision models can supplement the decision-making process. The decision process can be viewed as consisting of: defining the problem frame, defining the objectives, identifying the alternatives, developing a decision model, collecting and processing information and implementing the solution (Hammond et al., 1999). The problem frame governs how the decision maker perceives the decision.

The framework for developing risk models is grounded in the way information is communicated. How words are used to portray risk is central to the successful and effective application of risk management. The term risk is used in several ways. Risk is frequently connected with a form of negative outcome. Risk is also thought of as related to uncertainty, or likelihood. The International Standard on Risk Management, ISO 31000, defines risk as the 'effect of uncertainty on objectives' (ISO, 2009), which covers both ideas above; outcome and uncertainty. Risk analysis can be defined as the process of identifying events, determining causes, and estimating probabilities and impact (Engemann and Henderson, 2012).

If an uncertain event were to arise, but would not affect the organization's objectives, it may not be thought of as a risk by some. A risk can be generalized to be an opportunity as well as a threat. Many people consider risk only as a negative term and do not associate it with a positive payoff. Accordingly, organizations typically associate the term risk with a negative outcome and not an opportunity.

Risk management is comprised of the following phases: risk framing, risk assessment, risk responses and risk monitoring (NIST, 2012). Risk framing establishes a high-level context of a risk management process. Risk assessment identifies risks through a detailed analysis of threats, impacts and likelihoods. Risk responses are the controls recommended from the risk assessment process. Risk monitoring is ongoing evaluation risk mitigation measures. Decision support systems are computer-based tools used to assist in the decision-making process; they are particularly valuable in risk assessment and may employ both qualitative and quantitative models.

In risk modeling, there is a need to represent the uncertainty associated with the selection of an alternative, expressed as an uncertainty profile. Making decisions yielding uncertain outcomes requires some depiction of our knowledge of uncertainties associated with the possible outcomes. Frequently this information is impossible to obtain precisely. A feature that may distinguish a risky alternative from one that is merely uncertain is that at least one of its possible outcomes is undesirable. The concept of undesirable is fuzzy and often includes aspects of perception.

A decision function needs to be modeled, including the decision maker's attitude regarding different uncertain risky circumstances. Moreover, these types of information are multifaceted, vague and inexact, and cannot be convincingly modeled by conventional methods. Nevertheless, technologies of computational intelligence, using fuzzy rule-based formulations, show potential. Perception based granular probability distributions are valuable in modeling the uncertainty profiles of alternatives, and new techniques are available for assessing rule based decision functions while incorporating perception based uncertainty profiles.

A risk decision model is often useful to provide support to a decision maker. Decision analysis is a method commonly used to determine the risk profile of strategies and to support the decision maker in selecting the preferred risk strategy (Engemann and Miller, 1992). To be most useful, the methodological approach should integrate the attitude of the decision maker and enable sensitivity analysis of the decision to this attitudinal construct. Immediate probabilities are a useful vehicle to accomplish this. Immediate probabilities amend typical probabilistic knowledge with information about the payoffs, mediated through dispositional information (optimism/pessimism) of the decision maker. The resulting probabilities are a revised formulation of the perception of probabilities in effect at the time of the current decision. This transformation is based upon a subjective component involving the decision maker's disposition (Yager et al., 1995; Engemann et al., 1996). Risk decision approaches are available that include using attitudinal summary measures for both central tendency and dispersion (Engemann et al., 2005, 2006). These models utilize a computational intelligence methodology, using attitudinal and fuzzy modelling, in the selection of risk strategies that incorporates sensitivity analysis of the decision maker's attitude (Engemann and Miller, 2009, 2015).

Evaluating risks is a challenging endeavor because of the difficulty involved in analyzing rare events with unknown impacts. Risk strategies are used to treat risk, particularly those risks which are potentially very damaging. To be most beneficial, the assessment of risk strategies should reflect the attitude of the decision maker, which in turn is influenced by the safety climate of the organization that the decision maker is a part of. A methodology based on the *Risk Attitude Chain* is promising because of the integration of the organization's safety climate and the capability to analyze sensitivity to risk attitude (Engemann and Engemann, 2017). Through the paradigm of the *Risk Attitude Chain*, safety climate can be viewed as influencing risk attitude. A high safety climate is reflective of a cautionary approach and is consistent with a risk attitude that places more weight on potential negative outcomes. A low safety climate reflects an uncritical view of unsafe behavior and is consistent with a risk attitude that, perhaps unjustifiably, predicts that things will go very smoothly.

Simulation models are also very useful tools to analyze risk, for example, in studying how disasters affect supply chains. Using simulation modeling creates the opportunity for a business to study their specific supply chain to determine strategies to best provide for security from potential crises (Miller and Engemann, 2014). Managers who use simulation models in their organizations can perform experiments, to give them insight into risks associated with their supply chains. Using simulation modelling, organizations can analyze complex strategies that are specifically designed to a firm's supply chain. For example, one case that might be examined would be how outsourcing supply to other countries affects the supply chain, where the probabilities of various types of events from outsourcing arrangements might be significantly higher than those of more locally sourced products. The essential advantage of a simulation model is that it affords a full distribution of outcomes, not simply a single bottom-line result. The benefits further extend to being able to provide more information to managers through the development of distributions of probabilities and downtime evaluations that are more comprehensive.

## Conclusion

An effective risk management program is essential for a business to enjoy security from crises. A critical benefit of the program is that it raises awareness of risks. A risk management program also provides an overall approach to identifying risk and developing alternatives, and the capability to evaluate those alternatives. Risk decision making is challenging, particularly for those situations involving human life and safety. Even though underlying threats may be known, how those threats manifest themselves in a complex system often is practically unpredictable. The central task in decision making is to compare alternatives and decide upon a best alternative. An option to consider is to focus on choosing strategies that are robust, regardless of the crisis event.

A methodology for risk management should include a framework to explore the relationship among threats, events, control alternatives and losses. Risk management provides the overall process of identifying, analyzing and monitoring risks as well as designing and implementing mitigation strategies. Including senior managers in the process yields important benefits: first, tapping their expertise creates a perspective that frames the decision process more realistically; and second, educating the managers on risk issues and obtaining their support, is necessary when resources are to be allocated. A consistent approach should be used across an organization to analyze how crises may cause losses, and to select strategies to treat risk effectively and provide for security.

## References


Aven, T. (2012). "The Risk Concept – Historical and Recent Development Trends," *Reliability Engineering & System Safety*, Vol. 99, pp. 33–44.

Bannock, G. (2005). *The Economics and Management of Small Business: An International Perspective*, London: Taylor & Francis Routledge.

Basiri, A., Moore, T., Hill, C. and Bhatia, P. (2016). "The Non-Technical Challenges of Location Based Services Markets: Are the Users' Concerns Being Ignored?", *Localization and GNSS (ICL-GNSS), 2016 International Conference on* (pp. 1–5), IEEE, June.

Burnside, C. (2012). "Carry Trades and Risk", In: James, J., Marsh, I., and Sarno, L. (Eds.), *Handbook of Exchange Rates*, Vol. 2. Hoboken, NJ: John Wiley & Sons, Inc.

Cutter, S. L. et al. (2010). "Disaster Resilience Indicators for Benchmarking Baseline Conditions", *Journal of Homeland Security and Emergency Management*, Vol. 7, No. 1, pp. 1–22.

Engemann, K. N. (2017). "Knowledge Management," In: Rogelberg, S. G. (Ed.), *The Encyclopedia of Industrial and Organizational Psychology* (2nd Edition), Vol. 2, pp. 844–849. California: Sage Publishing.

Engemann, K. N. and Engemann, K. J. (2017). "Risk Attitude Chain: Safety Climate, Risk Attitude and Risk Decisions", *International Journal of Business Continuity and Risk Management*, Vol. 7, No. 3, pp. 211–221.

Engemann, K. J., Filev, D. P. and Yager, R. R. (1996). "Modeling Decision Making Using Immediate Probabilities", *International Journal of General Systems*, Vol. 24, No. 3, pp. 281–294.

Engemann, K. J. and Henderson, D. M. (2012). *Business Continuity and Risk Management: Essentials of Organizational Resilience*, Brookfield, CT: Rothstein Associates Inc.

Engemann, K. J. and Miller, H. E. (1992). "Operations Risk Management at a Major Bank", *Interfaces*, Vol. 22, No. 6, pp. 140–149.

Engemann, K. J. and Miller, H. E. (2009). "Critical Infrastructure and Smart Technology Risk Modelling Using Computational Intelligence", *International Journal of Business Continuity and Risk Management*, Vol. 1, No. 1, pp. 91–111.
Engemann, K. J. and Miller, H. E. (2015). "Risk Strategy and Attitude Sensitivity", *Cybernetics and Systems*, Vol. 46, No. 3, pp. 188–206.
Engemann, K. J., Miller, H. E. and Yager, R. R. (1996). "Decision Making With Belief Structures: An Application in Risk Management", *International Journal of Uncertainty, Fuzziness, and Knowledge-Based Systems*, Vol. 4, No. 1, pp. 1–25.
Engemann, K. J., Miller, H. E. and Yager, R. R. (2005). "Disaster Management of Information Resources Using Fuzzy and Attitudinal Modeling", *International Journal of Technology, Policy and Management*, Vol. 5, No. 4, pp. 388–406.
Engemann, K. J., Miller, H. E. and Yager, R. R. (2006). "Computational Intelligence for Risk and Disaster Management", *Proceedings of the IEEE International Conference on Fuzzy Systems at the World Congress on Computational Intelligence*, Vancouver, pp. 6900–6906.
Hammond, J. S., Keeney, R., L. and Raiffa, H. (1999). *Smart Choices: A Practical Guide to Making Better Decisions*, Boston: Harvard Business School Press.
Ho, W., Zheng, T., Yildiz, H., and Talluri, S. (2015). "Supply Chain Risk Management: A Literature Review", *International Journal of Production Research*, Vol. 53, No. 16.
International Organization for Standardization (ISO) (2014). 22301:2014, *Societal Security Business Continuity Management Systems – Requirements*, London: British Standards Institute.
International Standard Office (2009). ISO 31000:2009 *Risk Management Principles and Guidelines*, Geneva: ISO.
Kahneman, D. and Klien, G. (2009). "Conditions for Intuitive Expertise: A Failure to Disagree", *American Psychologist*, Vol. 64, No. 6, pp. 515–526.Kircher, M. (2012). "The Transition to a Bio-Economy: National Perspectives", *Biofuels, Bioproducts and Biorefining*, Vol. 6, No. 3, pp. 240–245.Lalonde, C. (2004). "In Search of Archetypes in Crisis Management", *Journal of Contingencies and Crisis Management*, Vol. 12, No. 2, pp. 76–88.
Leonard, A. M. (2009). *Managing Crisis; Responses to Large-Scale Emergencies*. Washington, DC: CQ Press.
Marolla, C. (2016). *Climate Health Risks in Megacities: Sustainable Management and Strategic Planning*. Vol. 1. Boca Raton: CRC Press.
Miller, H. E. and Engemann, K. J. (2008). "A Monte Carlo Simulation Model of Supply Chain Risk due to Natural Disasters", *International Journal of Technology, Policy and Management*, Vol. 8, No. 4, pp. 460–480.
Miller, H. E. and Engemann, K. J. (2014). "Using Reliability and Simulation Models in Business Continuity Planning", *International Journal of Business Continuity and Risk Management*, Vol. 5, No. 1, pp. 43–56.
Miller, H. E. and Engemann, K. J. (2015). "Threats to the Electric Grid and the Impact on Organizational Resilience", *International Journal of Business Continuity and Risk Management*, Vol. 6, No. 1, pp. 1–16.
Miller, H. E., Engemann, K. J. and Yager, R. R. (2006). "Disaster Planning and Management", *Communications of the International Information Management Association*, Vol. 6, No. 2, pp. 25–36.
NIST (2012). *Guide for Conducting Risk Management* – NIST Special Publication 800–30 R1. National Institute of Standards and Technology Gaithersburg, MD, USA.
Renn, O. (2015). "Stakeholder and Public Involvement in Risk Governance", *International Journal of Disaster Risk Science*, Vol. 6, No. 1, pp. 8–20.
Sheffi, Y. (2007). *The Resilient Enterprise*, Cambridge, MA: MIT Press.
Shin, H., Vaidya, J. and Atluri, V. (2011). "A Profile Anonymization Model for Location-Based Services", *Journal of Computer Security*, Vol. 19, No. 5, pp. 795–833.
Soltani, B. (2014). "The Anatomy of Corporate Fraud: A Comparative Analysis of High Profile American and European Corporate Scandals", *Journal of Business Ethics*, Vol. 120, pp. 251–274.

Tierney, K. (2007). "Businesses and Disasters: Vulnerability, Impacts, and Recovery", In: Rodriguez, H., Quarantelli, E.L. and Dynes, R.R. (Eds.), *Handbook of Disaster Research*, pp. 275–296. New York: Springer.

Weick, K.E. (1993). "The Collapse of Sensemaking in Organizations: The Mann Gulch Disaster", *Administrative Science Quarterly*, Vol. 38, No. 4, pp. 628–652. https:/doi.org/10.2307/2393339

Yager, R.R., Engemann, K.J. and Filev, D.P. (1995). "On the Concept of Immediate Probabilities", *International Journal of Intelligent Systems*, Vol. 10, No. 4, pp. 374–397.

# 2

# The evolution of risk management thinking in organizations

*Phil Kelly*

---

> It is a world of change in which we live, and a world of uncertainty. We live only by knowing something about the future. We often act then on partial knowledge when making decisions about the future. Conscious life can react to a situation before that situation materialises; it can "see things coming." The role of consciousness is to give "knowledge" of the future. We perceive the world and make inferences before we react to it. The universal form of conscious behaviour is thus action designed to change a future situation inferred from a present one. It involves perception and, in addition, inference. We must infer what the future situation would have been without our interference. Unfortunately, none of these processes is infallible, or indeed ever accurate and complete. We do not perceive the present as it is and in its totality, nor do we infer the future from the present with any high degree of dependability, nor yet do we accurately know the consequences of our own actions.
>
> *Source*: Knight (1921, pp. 199–200)

In light of comments made almost a century ago by the influential classical writer Frank Knight, We start this chapter by asking, has our thinking about risk and its management changed much over the last century? Through a story about risk, indeed an account of the history of risk, told from the perspective of the organization, we will attempt to answer this question. In doing so, we hope to provide a foundation for the rest of this book and insights that may help the reader to think critically when considering risk. The aim of this chapter is to trace the historical foundations of our risk discourse; to document where risk thinking has been and where it is going. We will also consider a selection of major historic factors and events that have influenced such thinking significantly. Knight's (1921) insights into one of the fundamental challenges facing contemporary organizations (planning and acting with the future in mind), despite being written almost a century ago, could be applicable for many contemporary organizations today! We might therefore ask whether and, if so, how risk thinking, theory and practice and indeed the discipline and profession have evolved over the past century. How have our methods, theories, risk vocabulary and processes developed, if at all, to understand the future and the risks or uncertainties it may hold?

This chapter is about risk-thinking, the process of considering or reasoning about *risk* and how to manage it within the organization. Thinking describes what the conscious mind does and includes a range of cognitive processes such as perception, calculating and problem-solving. We tend to think using words and an inner dialogue; language and thought become integrated. Thought can refer to the ideas or arrangements of ideas that result from thinking. From a risk perspective, thought can be considered as a single idea, product of mental activity, process of thinking, judgement, opinion or belief. Thinking and thought are therefore about conceiving and considering risk in the mind, underlying organization action. Thinking enables organizational members to make sense of, interpret and to make predictions about their world. It helps organizations to plan and accomplish goals. Consequently, if we are to understand risk behaviour in the organization, we have to consider how organizations think about risk. When answering the fundamental question of 'how do we come to know about risk?', we need to consider not only cognitive processes and the conscience but also philosophy and its 'rules' that may govern the creation of risk knowledge. Throughout this chapter we explore risk philosophy, discussing the evolution of viewpoints and implications for risk theory. We also consider the evolution of organizations and management theory and implications for risk thinking. Furthermore, we consider how the concept of risk itself has evolved. More than a century ago Willet (1901, p28) declared the word risk "is by no means free from ambiguity." Over a century later we ask whether we are any closer to a shared meaning. The many faces of risk and its obscure origins are testament to its elusive character as a conceptual phenomenon (Althaus, 2005, p570). As was highlighted earlier, we think in a language and thinking drives action. Consequently, if the risk thinker thinks using terms of different meaning to other thinkers, they are likely to make different inferences and pursue different actions. It becomes important for groups confronting the same risk challenges to share meaning in the language they use with each other. In this sense, language can be a source of conflict and disagreement over action. Finally, we also consider the evolution of risk management, the risk discipline, function and profession within organizations. For simplicity, we have structured this chapter in three parts: risk-thinking (1) pre-mid-20th century; (2) the second half of the 20th century; and (3) the 21st century.

## 1 The 'insurance era' – modernity and pre-mid-20th century risk-thinking

### *Risk etymology*

The origins of the English word "risk" date back thousands of years to classical Greek, where the word 'rhizikon' was used as a metaphor for "difficulty to avoid in the sea" (a danger); in Latin "riscus" has similar meaning, passing into Arabic as "rizk" denoting "fate" or uncertain outcome. In the 1500s, in Germany, the meaning of the word "rysigo" developed to include an upside (benefit): to dare, to undertake, enterprise, or hope for economic success (Skjong, 2005). It can also be traced to the mid-17th century, from the French *risque* and Italian *risco* ('danger'). Risk in the Middle Ages was about the possibility of danger, an act of God or *force majeure* – seen as a natural event rather than a man-made one. In medieval times religion served as a belief system by which threats and dangers were dealt with conceptually and behaviourally, allowing people to feel as if they had some sense of control over their world (Lupton, 1999). In the enlightened and industrialised world (with the advent of modernity) science dominated thinking which became more rational and objective in pursuit of "laws." The science of probability and statistics was developed as a means of calculating normal and identifying deviations from it; paving the way for a belief that risk could be measured, calculated and predicted (Bernstein, 1998). As noted by Lupton (1999, p6), "during the 18th century, the concept of risk had begun to be scientised." Furthermore, she argues the development of statistical calculations of risk coincided with the expansion of the insurance industry. By the 19th century, the notion of risk was extended beyond natural events to include human action. The invention of "risk" enabled people to eliminate uncertainty, transforming an indeterminate cosmos into a manageable one (Reddy, 1996, p237). In modernity, risk relied on conditions in which the probability estimates of events are able to be known or knowable. Uncertainty, in contrast was used as an alternative term when these probabilities were inestimable or unknown (Lupton, 1999, p7). Modernist notions of risk also included the idea that risk could be both "good" and "bad"; though less emphasis was placed on the "good" aspect of risk from the beginning of the 19th century (Althaus, 2005, p570).

### *Early organizational efforts to manage risk: insurance*

The first half of the 20th century was marked with radical change throughout the world. During this time, economists in particular theorised about risk, with around 1,000 journal articles evident, entitled "risk." Aven (2012, p39) argues that a 20th century person was likely to be ruled by the "risk equals probability of a loss" perspective; however, he argues other risk meanings developed from this. Those adopting this definition, for example, may describe the risk of a theft or of fire and so forth. In this case the word "risk" can be substituted for the word "probability." However, an emerging criticism of this definition was that it failed to appreciate difference in the consequences. For example, this definition would not distinguish between how much was stolen, focusing mainly on the chance that something would be stolen. Thinking about risk and future loss or harm drove organizations to seek protection through insurance, providing a guarantee of compensation for specified loss or harm in return for payment of a premium. Gallagher (1960, p78) states insurance was in operation in AD 1100 in a form very similar to that used today. Employer's liability insurance was introduced in England in 1880; products liability insurance became available in 1910. "By this time, the countries' larger employers were forced to give separate attention to their insurance problems; clerks were assigned. . . [and] the new profession of risk management developed during this period" (Gallagher, 1960, p78). As insurance management demanded more and more time and knowledge, "executives handed it over to staff, some of whom already had or acquired a formal education with emphasis on insurance." According to Gallagher (1960, p79), "although no one consciously applied the term 'risk management', certain principles had begun to evolve."

### *Early developments: the economists and actuarial thinking*

One of the first 20th century books to address risk theory was arguably, *The Economic Theory of Risk and Insurance* by Allan Willett (1901). Discussing the nature of risk, he suggests that "to live and labour in uncertainty is the common lot of all men" (1901, p25). He noted it was only at the turn of the century that attempts had begun to isolate the phenomena of risk and risk-taking and to determine the laws which govern them. Early risk-thinking was contingent upon guidance from contemporary philosophers: "all the activities of the universe are obedient to law" (Willett, 1901, p26). In relation to probability, he argues, "as the degree of probability of loss increases from 0 to 100%, the degree of risk may be said to increase" (1901, p28). He discussed insurance, considering "the devices that have been adopted by society to counteract the unfavourable influence of risk" (Willett, 1901, p86). Furthermore, he discusses, "avoidance, prevention and assumption" and "transfer" (1901, p95). However, managing insurance at the time was problematic, with earlier writers noting the problems associated with an absence of data and statistics. For example, Barlow (1897), discussed industrial accidents and perils, noting that industrial injury statistics to compute risk, whilst available in Germany, were not available in the UK. Such figures were not available in England, where there was "no uniform and compulsory system of notification of accidents, figures must be more or less guesswork" (Barlow, 1897, p356). This problem, of how to think about risk in the absence of historical data, became a fundamental issue and challenge to risk professionals for the remainder of the century. Risk problems may be approached differently when we know or could know (knowable) something about them; where we have experience. This is different from new situations where we have no experience. In the 18th and 19th centuries, the actuarial profession was established to deal with the measurement of risk and uncertainty, developing methods to construct and use tables to facilitate timely, accurate and manual calculations of premiums. Over time, actuarial organizations were founded to support and further both actuaries and actuarial science.

During the first half of the 20th century, the insurance profession developed as a forerunner to risk management, founded in 1932, the American Risk and Insurance Association (ARIA) came together to advance the study and understanding of the field. The risk and insurance literature also developed in this period as books or journal articles. In the first half of the 20th century the business risk literature was arguably dominated by the "more scientific" disciplines of mathematics and economics. An influential risk thinker of the first half of the 20th century was American economist Frank Knight, best known as the author of the book *Risk Uncertainty and Profit*. Knight made a clear distinction between risk and uncertainty. Situations with risk were those where the outcomes were unknown but governed by probability distributions known at the outset. In his view, "we judge the future by the past" (Knight, 1921, p204) and that "It is evident that a great many hazards can be reduced to a fair degree of certainty by statistical grouping" (the application of experience data; Knight, 1921, p215). However, his bias toward statistics and frequency tables as tools for computing probability was evident in several of the comments he made throughout the book. Aside from statistical probabilities there are estimates, "this form of probability is involved in the greatest logical difficulties of all . . . We know that estimates or judgments are 'liable' to err'" (p225) and "the striking feature of the judging faculty is its liability to error" (p230).

## Organizations in the Insurance Era: Management 1.0

Risk was invented before management. Risk thinking occurs within the context of and, like management generally, is contingent upon the organization. An organization is a social arrangement for achieving controlled performance in pursuit of collective goals (Cole and Kelly, 2015). There has been a growth trend in the number of organizations around the world, as can be seen from an analysis of the situation in Great Britain as example, see Figure 2.1. Most organizations share a goal to be efficient, keeping costs (and threat) to a minimum, resulting in a shared interest in pure risk and its treatment. Profit-maximising business organizations will often have the additional goal to generate revenue, seizing opportunity, resulting in speculation and risk taking goals. Within the organization, management will organise and structure human resources (people) to

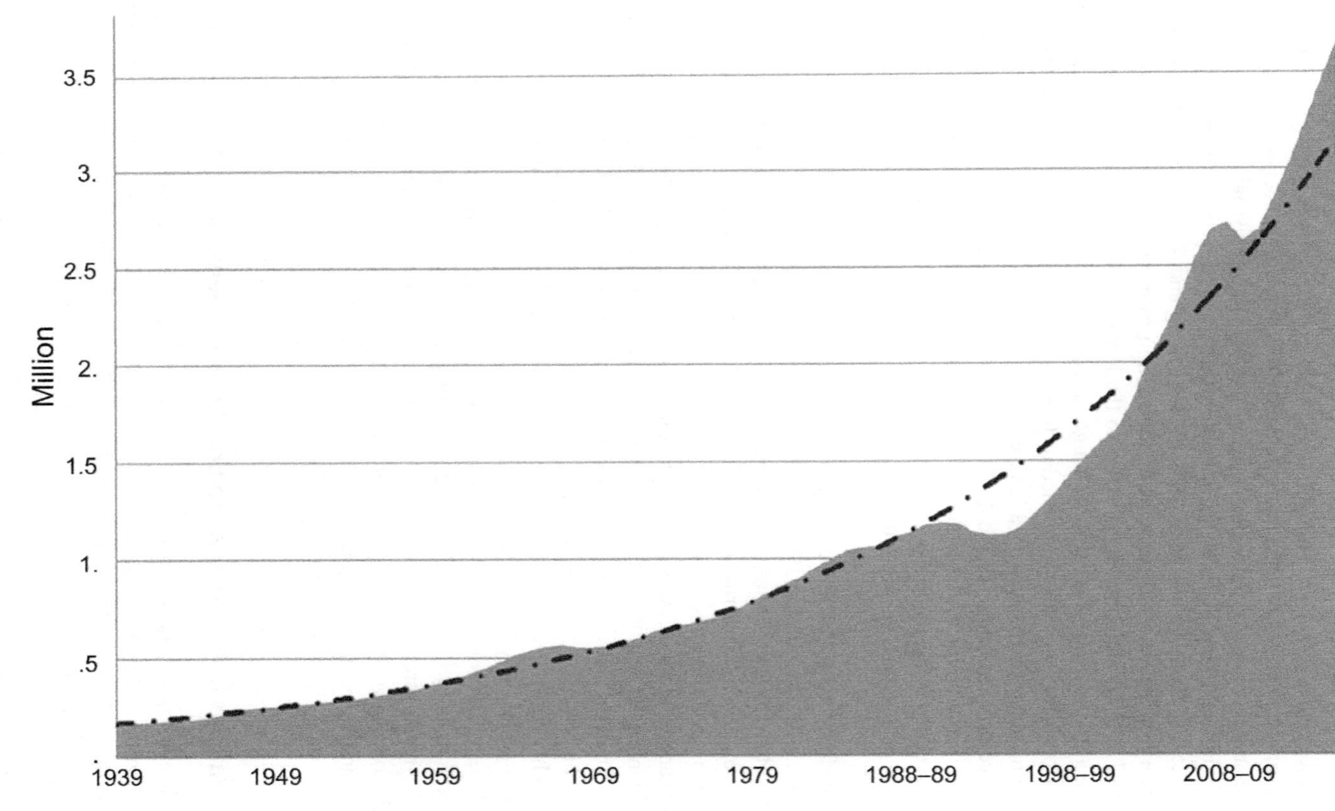


*Figure 2.1* Total register of UK companies 1939 to 2016

*Source*: Data from Companies House, www.gov.uk/government/statistics/incorporated-companies-in-the-united-kingdom-may-2016

enable goal attainment. Organizations are open systems which are continually dependent upon and influenced by their environments, driving managers to make attempts to anticipate the future and act in a manner that increases the likelihood goals will be attained. In short, managers seek to understand and control future uncertainties and risks. Not only is this done in the belief that it will help the organization function as planned but also to protect its assets.

Gary Hamel of London Business School outlines the 'invention' and evolution of management (Kelly, 2017). Starting around 1890 he notes the average manufacturing company had fewer than four employees. One generation later, by 1915 the Ford Motor Company was making over 500,000 cars per year and in the intervening period, Hamel argues that 'almost all of the tools of modern management get invented'. He refers to this as 'Management 1.0'. Similarly, McGrath (2014) argues there was little management prior to the Industrial Revolution (18th and 19th centuries). With the new means of production, organizations gained scale. The focus moved wholly onto execution of mass production, and managerial solutions such as specialisation of labour and the standardisation of processes (see for example the scientific management and bureaucratic management of the early 20th century in particular, see Taylor, 1911 and later, Weber, 1947). In addition, organizations of this era were influenced by the traditional theory of the firm which assumes that profit maximisation is the goal of the commercial organization. McGrath (2014) labels organization as machines in this era, characterised by a short-term orientation; the exploitation of existing advantages (i.e. efficiency was valued more than creativity) and a narrow focus on shareholders. Firms faced little competition and many industries were nationalised, operating as monopolies or within oligopolies. The first half of the 20th century was arguably dominated by the (domestic) "bureaucratic organization" managed impersonally and rationally through "command-and-control." A number of business schools were established and management became recognised as a discipline.

Risk thinking and action was contingent on the organizational context and management thinking of the time. The goals of the organization drive the goals of risk management (they are congruent) and the activities of the organization shape vulnerabilities and risk exposure. The first half of the 20th century was dominated with efficiency goals which drove incremental as opposed to radical change, favouring the status quo. The organization benefited from learning and experience which was then used to deliver economies of scale advantage. This experience also helped risk management method, providing historic data from which to base objective risk calculation. The future was seen more as an extrapolation of the past.

Early 20th century risk thinking and knowledge were swayed by philosophy which influences the way we come to know things. Philosophy, through scientific method, has therefore shaped the evolution of risk knowledge and thought. The way risk knowledge has been created has been contingent on our beliefs about how we should create knowledge. Easterby-Smith, Thorpe and Lowe (2000, p22) identify two main "traditions" (philosophies, paradigms of fundamental viewpoints) and their associated assumptions. First, and the most dominant in the earlier part of the 20th century, they discuss positivism which operates on the basic belief that science is value free, the observer is independent and the world is external and objective. Researchers focus on facts, searching for causality and fundamental laws and reduce phenomena to simple statements. A key emphasis of positivism is measuring things (using objective methods). Positivists operationalise concepts in a way that enables them to be measured quantitatively. Throughout much of the 20th century many held the view that positivism provided the best way of investigating human and social behaviour (Easterby-Smith, Thorpe and Lowe, 2000, p23). An attachment to scientific method in the early part of the 20th century not only influenced management but also risk theory. For example, Hardy (1923, p205) discusses the, "the application of scientific methods in the elimination of risk." Positivism and how risk is defined or understood led to belief in risk as a forensic concept, something that can be measured and on the basis of which predictions can be made (Walklate, 1999).

## 2 Risk thinking in the second half of the 20th century: risk management and the corporate era

Organizations became more sophisticated during this era where we witnessed a proliferation of specialisms within the organizational chart and hierarchy. Initially organizations favoured corporate specialists and centralised decision making for consistency and control, making use of formal mechanisms to coordinate employees and ensure efficiency goals were attained, that is scientific management continued to dominate organizational management thinking. The second half of the 20th century was somewhat different from a scholarly perspective, with around a quarter of a million journal articles written having the term "risk" in the title. Short (1984, p712) utilises studies that show the use of the term risk (in academic journal titles) increasing, exponentially, between 1966 and 1982. In addition, we witnessed the formation of a number of new professional bodies such as the Risk and Insurance Management Society, Inc. (RIMS) founded in 1950. From the 1950s to the 1970s, risk managers began to realise it was not only too expensive to manage every risk with insurance but also that many of their risks were uninsurable, so the discipline began to seek alternative risk treatments. As the era progressed, the term risk management gained in popularity and the scope of the professions' work broadened. For many risk professionals, in the mid-20th century, risk was viewed as both consequence and probability (a combination of the two). In other disciplines, risk evolved to incorporate uncertainty (Aven, 2012, p40).

### Organizations in the Corporate Risk Era: Management 2.0

McGrath (2014) suggests the next major era of management emphasised expertise. The mid-20th century was a period of remarkable growth in theories of management which were imported from other fields (sociology and psychology) to apply to management (McGrath, 2014). Statistical and mathematical insights were imported, forming the basis of the field that would subsequently be known as operations management. Later attempts to bring science into management included the development of many well-known theories. New theories of management arose placing far more emphasis on motivation and engagement of workers and on the management of knowledge. As a consequence, for many managers, the mind-set of command and control was replaced with a more participative style. This coincided with the rise of personnel management as an administrative function, later evolving into human resource management (HRM), with a more strategic role. Organizations from this era remained formal, typically embracing hierarchical, functional structures. Whilst the first management era emphasised efficiency and scale this second era began to emphasise effectiveness. As a consequence, organizational leadership and teamwork became more important.

Throughout this era the functional structure (e.g. departments for finance and marketing etc.) was most popular amongst organizations. Employees who perform similar functions or work or who bring similar knowledge and skills to bear, are grouped together. Functions arose from principles of scientific management (1920s), which favoured specialisation. The degree of specialisation is contingent upon organizational size and it is often larger organizations that have a specific risk function. Throughout much of the 20th century organizations grew in size thus enabling higher degrees of specialisation (and to some extent bureaucracy). Whilst the term "risk function" has been in use for much of the 20th century, its popularity began in the 1940s, peaking in the 1970s. The term "risk manager," as head of that function, was not really used until the 1950s but has witnessed increased use since. At the beginning of this era, organizations grappled with problems regarding the name of this function and which specialists (health and safety, security etc.) should report into it. As we entered the first half of the 20th century, Johnson (1952, p807) noted risk management to be a rapidly developing but still incomplete field of interest. Risk management began to be studied after World War II. Many dated the origin of modern risk management to a period between 1955 and 1964 (Dionne, 2013). Snider (1956) cited in Dionne (2013) observed that there were no books on risk management at the time, and no universities offered courses in the subject. The first two academic books were published by Mehr and Hedges (1963) and Williams and Heins (1964). Their content covered pure risk management. Gallagher (1956, p75) stated that "in the post-war battle for tighter cost control, many managements have been making great efforts to cut down the effects of accidents or damage to the company's physical assets." He argued there to be little or no published literature in the area of risk management and that few organizations were allocating sufficient effort to the problem despite organizations becoming more liable. New forms of pure risk management emerged during the mid-1950s ("Modern risk management started after 1955") as alternatives to market insurance when certain types of insurance coverage became very costly and incomplete (Dionne, 2013).

### *Emerging roles and responsibilities: from (insurance) technician to (risk) manager*

Organizations operating in the early part of the 20th century wanted knowledgeable technicians who could purchase insurance professionally, in a cost effective manner, to protect the organization from the costs of externally inflicted harm. Mid-20th century academics and practitioners began to refine discussions on the meaning of risk and explore risk management activities in more detail in order to develop risk knowledge and thinking. Risk practitioners repeatedly questioned and developed their role within the organization. For example, Gallagher (1956, p76) considered the aim of risk analysis "to discover through inspection and research, the full extent of possible loss." However, his definition of loss was limited to accident or damage through natural causes or arising from negligent acts; it did not include business loss resulting from managerial judgements for example. He emphasised the need to "seek out the underlying causes of risk and to pinpoint sources of possible serious loss for the company." Gallagher (1956, p77) strongly believed that the person in charge of risk analysis and its related functions – the "Risk Manager" – should be an executive in the company (reporting into the insurance function, p79). Only such a person would have the appropriate access to create a true picture of the hazards involved in a wide variety of company activities. In justifying the role of the risk manager, Gallagher argued that they could reduce insurance premiums through risk abatement (which could be accomplished through training, safety engineering, plant protection, quality control and plant location). Gallagher (1956, p80) added that "when analysis has proved the existence of hazard, and study has revealed no means by which the exposure can be averted or abated, there are three basic ways in which the risk may be treated": assumed, self-insured or commercially insured. Gallagher also drew attention to unique aspects of the risk manager's job. "Since the important function of risk abatement involves every department of the business, one of the Risk Managers' principal tasks is getting cooperation agreement from all line executives in analysing risks and taking action" (Gallagher, 1956, p85). Finally, he adds, "a good Risk Manager will help executives to avoid needless hazards in their plans and decisions. And he will see to it that, when the inevitable losses and accidents do occur, the corporation as a growing enterprise has as much protection as possible at the lowest possible cost" (Gallagher, 1956, p86). Four years later, in an article he wrote for *Business Horizons*, Gallagher (1960, p86) stated that "many Risk Managers report that they now occupy a much more responsible position in their companies than they did four years ago." Apparently risk managers, in 1960, "have been able to go more fully into the analysis and abatement phases of their programs." According to Dionne (2013) during the 1960s, contingent planning activities were developed, and various risk prevention or self-protection activities and self-insurance instruments against some losses were implemented. Gallagher (1960, p86) also commented on risk management education, arguing, "our colleges and universities educate [people] to become insurance company executives, salesmen, and actuaries, but not Risk Managers." Gallagher (1960) declares that "the Risk Manager, in a few years, will have been educated rather than trained in his profession."

Denenberg and Ferrari (1966) focused on the term "risk management" in order to help define the area of responsibility of the risk manager. They discuss two different viewpoints: risk manager as technician or as manager. They argue many see the risk manager as technician (expert) and in support of this they review a number of recent textbooks on the subject, noting how they failed to employ management theory; "up to this point, the risk management textbooks have evidently ignored (management) . . . Risk management academicians have ignored the literature of management, but the literature of management has also ignored risk management" (Denenberg and Ferrari, 1966, p649). "Risk is currently fashionable as a substitute term for insurance (for example, Risk Manager versus Insurance Manager) " (Denenberg and Ferrari, 1966, p653). "One major problem is that risk implies too much. All members of the managerial team are involved with risk and it is not hard to understand why the title of Risk Manager, which alludes to a rather pervasive managerial responsibility for risk, lacks general acceptance" (Denenberg and Ferrari, 1966, p657). Whether or not the term "Risk Manager" becomes generally accepted, there is need to put management into the risk management process, argued Denenberg and Ferrari (1966, p660). Despite many developments surrounding the risk manager's role, there remained considerable variation from organization to organization. The transition from technician (insurers) to risk manager was still in its infancy during the 1960s, as can be seen from the comments of Todd (1969): "The risk management speciality has yet to emerge from the role of part-time insurance purchasing."

## *The risk curricula: what should managers and risk professionals be taught?*

The first major effort to define a risk curriculum arguably occurred in the 1960s when the ARIA created a Committee to examine the place of risk and insurance in collegiate (academic) curricula. They attempted to articulate a body of concepts, publishing a booklet titled "Curricular Concepts in Risk and Insurance." At the outset, they considered it important to recognise risk as an ambiguous construct, with an up and downside (p257). There was clear evidence of the dominance of positivism within the thoughts of the committee, when they declared, "In recent years, Association members and others have attempted to analyse scientifically the risk which confronts individuals and Organizations in a variety of circumstances." They also considered the emerging role of 'risk managers' charged with "(1) identification and analysis of the risk to which the respective Organizations are exposed, particularly the pure or negative aspects of the risk, and with (2) proposals for Organizational action which is most nearly in consonance with such risk" (p258). In discussing the treatment of risk, they argued, "the ultimate justification of any attempt by an individual to understand the nature and significance of risk is that such understanding may be used to avoid or reduce loss," thus emphasising the importance of risk knowledge and education. It was clear insurance was considered the most prominent device for treatment of risk at that time, but that "Loss prevention, assumption of risk, and non-insurance transfer of risk are other devices" (p258). They argued students should be able to identify risk situations, understand consequences and develop a familiarity with probability theory and quantitative techniques. They recognised a distinction between generalist and specialist and that the specialist requires additional depth of knowledge in these areas. In particular, the specialist should be able to analyse hazards which threaten organizations; be able to apply qualitative analysis to decision making; appreciate alternative ways of treating risk and so forth. The committee discussed two main approaches: (1) the traditional approach – where the primary emphasis is on the mechanism of insurance as a device for treatment of risk; and (2) the decision-making approach – an alternative approach, "which is receiving increasing attention" involving the study of risk and insurance within the framework of management decision making; an approach which, "gives considerable leeway for emphasis to be placed on the various ways of treating risk" (ARIA, 1962, p261). The committee's thoughts reinforce the argument that the risk discipline was initially dominated by positivism, a reactive approach, the insurance industry and a focus on pure risk.

The same year (1962) a practising risk manager (James Cristy) offered his thoughts. He recounted two basic problems inherent in risk management: "(1) acceptance of senior management that risk and its management deserves careful and studied attention, and (2) a source of competent personnel." Cristy (1962) argued these to be persistent problems. His account is of interest as it shows the continued struggle to establish risk management as a credible and much-needed business function, able to make a significant contribution to the Organization. He noted that, "all but the most articulate Risk Managers still have trouble educating their management associates to take a broad approach to treatment of risks of accidental loss." He moves on to discuss the need for management (risk) education. "Before there can be a climate conducive to best results in risk treatment, managers generally must come to understand risk. They must appreciate the importance of controlling the risk of accidental loss so as to permit maximum assumption of speculative risk." Providing insights into the industry more broadly, he argues "industry's reluctance to adopt the term 'Risk Manager' is a sign of this need for management education. Speakers at AMA Conferences began using the term about 1955," but at that time Cristy claimed he knew of only two companies where anything like 'Risk Manager' appeared in job titles. According to Cristy, (1962, p567) "Executives well accustomed to titles like 'Controller' and 'Director of Personnel' which have recognised special meanings, continue to take issue with 'Risk Manager' saying, in effect, the Risk Manager in this firm is the General Manager." Thus, ARIA, with contributions from practicing risk managers, began to shape a risk curricular for risk professionals and for other types of functional managers who needed to be more aware of risk management.

## *The rise of risk decision-making theory and alternative risk treatments and controls*

As the 20th century progressed, risk professionals broadened their repertoire of risk treatments as alternatives to the risk problems they identified. Faced with (treatment) choices, academics and professionals began to place greater emphasis on the importance of decision-making theory: how risk problems were structured and solutions (treatments and risk controls) selected in the most rational manner. Around this time the influential Herbert Simon proposed his theory of corporate decision making in his book *Administrative Behaviour*; he recognised multiple factors that contribute to quality decision making (Simon, 1955). Cristy (1962, p567) believed we needed "considerably more than insurance technicians . . . the emphasis has shifted from insurance buyer to Insurance Manager to Risk Manager. The horizons have been correspondingly broadened, and the need is now for managers rather than clerks." According to Cristy (1962, p568),

> Scholars have been studying both risk and insurance for some years. But the traditional approach in university courses of insurance has been to meet the needs of those headed for the insurance business. Only lately have these courses given a sidelong glance at corporate insurance buyers. Hence, it is gratifying to risk managers to see university teachers of insurance becoming teachers of risk and insurance and increasing the curricular emphasis on the broad study of risk as a fundamental aspect of business.

The risk manager emerged as an entity capable of rational evaluation of risk-treating alternatives but there are indications insurance is still considered the device of first resort. Cristy (1962, p568) suggests that practitioners in management are also interested in using other risk-treating devices when insurance is adequate but not economical.

> While insurance may be the dominant risk-treating device for most of industry, it is, in the consumer's logic, the device of last resort, not first . . . Management needs to treat risks of accidental loss (pure risks) in the most economical way available. This points up the importance of educating the generalist in the various risk-treating techniques.

Referring back to the committee's two approaches (traditional or decision making) he argues that, "the 'Decision-Making Approach' is much more attractive." Three years later, Horn (1965 p645) discusses possible course titles of "insurance" or "risk and insurance" or "risk management" or "even simply risk." The University of South Carolina offered four courses: (1) principles of risk and insurance; (2) fundamentals of life and health insurance; (3) fundamentals of property and liability insurance; and (4) business risk management. This latter course examined the role of the risk manager in treating non-speculative risks. The course was taught from an insurance industry standpoint on the assumption that most of the students would be employed in some phase of insurance following graduation. Much of the course was designed from the standpoint of "the professional Risk Manager." However, the influence of positivism was strikingly evident in the language of "principles" in the way the course was described. This was reiterated by Hall (1969) who stated, "one of the most fundamental problems facing an instructor of students at every level of the academic ladder is the identification and clear definition of 'principles' which are basic to a given discipline."

### *The continued search for a widely accepted definition and principles of risk*

Curricular developments and the associated increased attention from academics resulted in more risk research. Of all the decades of the 20th century, the search for risk principles and a clear risk definition probably dominated the 1960s and 1970s. Whilst no agreed-upon answers came from this intensive risk thinking and debate, we did witness the evolution of the profession, with many moving from technician to manager. In 1966 the bulletin of the commission on insurance terminology of the ARIA proposed a definition of risk as either "an uncertainty as to the outcome of an event when two or more possibilities exist" or "a person or thing insured." The committee considered risk as being essentially tantamount to uncertainty and sparked a significant debate amongst academics and practitioners. Head (1967) wrote a paper declaring he was not willing to accept risk as being essentially tantamount to uncertainty. His first reason for objection was based on the use of a vague word (uncertainty) to define another vague word (risk). Second, he felt that the proposed risk definition would make risk "very difficult to measure and express quantitatively" (p206). Uncertainty is not a self-explanatory term, notes Head (1967), pointing to at least two important meanings in scholarly writing. Uncertainty, from decision theory, denotes a condition where it is impossible to assign any probabilities to possible outcomes of an event. By this definition uncertainty is contrasted with risk where probabilities can be assigned. Second, in psychology, uncertainty denotes a state of mind characterised by doubt, or a conscious lack of knowledge about the outcome of an event. Head (1967, p210) proposed an alternative definition, arguing risk is a probability and therefore a risk is a number, a result of a mathematical operation, making risk demonstrably verifiable. He also adds clarity about the type of probability that should be used, noting it can be a subjective belief or relative frequency but favoured the latter. He argued the second important point about the suggested definition "is that risk is an objective probability. This means that the relevant probability is based on the best scientific knowledge available, and not on a more or less uninformed or unverifiable subjective estimate of the probabilities of the possible outcomes of an event . . . this scientific knowledge can be drawn from . . . observed relative frequencies." Over the following years we observed numerous contributions and discussions on the matter (see for example Table 2.2 Definitions of "Risk").

Practitioners and academics also continued with the call and search for general risk theories, principles and laws. According to Gahin (1967, p122), "one of the major problems facing risk management practitioners [in the 1960's] is the lack of an appropriate theory or a finite set of guiding principles." He adds that valuable scientific principles exist in all the other social sciences which enable better decision making. Interestingly, he adds,

> there is a common agreement that risk management, like all other fields of business management, is both an art and a science. As an art, risk management needs personnel with considerable background in many fields . . . as a science, risk management should be based on scientific principles derived from a consistent body of knowledge . . . To date, risk management has been more of an art than a science.

He argued, "The literature on risk management has been preoccupied with insurance principles and practices" (1967, p124). He is not alone in his call for more basic research into risk and its management, citing Mehr and Hedges (1963, p257):

> the management of risk by scientific formulas, based on the mathematics and statistics, could remove much of the human element from risk management . . . Certainly there is

room for more scientific risk management than is currently practised but not enough to replace artful risk management.

## *The 1970s and 1980s: the developing scope of risk management*

McCahill (1971), an insurance manager, adds to the discussion on risk management, aiming to dispel the prevalent notion that a risk manager's main contribution to the company is his sagacious purchase of insurance policies. He argued that, "the term "risk management" encompasses primarily those activities performed to prevent accidental loss" (1971, p58). His article was influential in bringing risk management theory to the attention of a wider management audience. Caswell and Wilkens (1975, p41) traced the evolution of the role of the risk manager: "Today a new managerial role is emerging as a result of consumer and social movements in the 1960s, and subsequent laws and government regulations enacted in the early 1970s." Historically, the risk manager's corporate position was primarily that of insurance purchaser they argued. "Consequently, Risk Managers concerned themselves solely with pure risks" (Caswell and Wilkens, 1975, p41). They conclude by stating, "the role of the Risk Manager has begun to emerge as one of the most important management positions within an Organization . . . this role will continue to expand" (Caswell and Wilkens, 1975, p48). The use of derivatives as instruments to manage insurable and uninsurable risk began in the 1970s and developed very quickly during the 1980s (Dionne, 2013). The concept of risk management in the financial sector was revolutionised in the 1970s, when financial risk management became a priority for many companies, including banks, insurers, and non-financial enterprises exposed to various price fluctuations, such as risk related to interest rates, stock market returns, exchange rates, and the prices of raw materials or commodities. The late 1970s marked a period of rapid growth in the use of the term "Risk Management" (see Figure 2.3). Much of 1980s management theory and literature was dominated by strategy, quality management and later business processes. This found its way into the risk literature which started to emphasise the risk management process (RMP) and the search for risk knowledge and methods that would improve the quality of risk decision making.

During this era the 'expert 'or 'professional' risk-discourse was influenced by post-modernity (the questioning of established thought, deconstruction of tradition and breakdown of norms). There was still no general agreement on where the boundaries of the subject lay, and a satisfactory definition of risk management remained notoriously difficult to formulate (Crockford, 1982, p170). In 1982, Crockford wrote:

> Operational convenience continues to dictate that pure and speculative risks should be handled by different functions within a company, even though theory may argue for them being managed as one. For practical purposes, therefore, the emphasis of risk management continues to be on pure risks.
>
> *(Crockford, 1982, p171)*

According to Douglas and Wildavsky (1992) cited in Lupton (1999), the word risk now means danger.

> Risk is now generally used to relate only to negative or undesirable outcomes, not positive outcomes . . . In everyday lay people's language, risk tends to be used to refer almost exclusively to a threat, hazard, danger or harm . . . risk and uncertainty tend to be treated as conceptually the same thing.
>
> *(Lupton, 1999, pp8–9)*

There was a significant focus on financial risks, credit risk in particular during the 1980s. Earlier we noted the role of institutes in delivering education in support of professional development. Within the UK, the Institute of Risk Management (IRM) was founded in April 1986 to meet growing demand for a diploma course in risk management.

### *Multiple risk perspectives, the rise of qualitative methods and fall of the risk expert*

One of the consequences of postmodernism is the embracing of multiple perspectives. Throughout the latter part of the 20th century many perspectives on risk developed and are evident in specific disciplines: statistical analysis (including the actuarial approach), toxicology/ epidemiology, probabilistic risk analysis, economics of risk, psychology of risk, social theories of risk and cultural theory of risk, other scholars distinguish between logic and mathematics, science and medicine, social sciences (anthropology, sociology, economics, law, psychology, linguistics), history and humanities (history, the arts), religion and philosophy. Drawing on this risk discourse are professions such as health and safety, security, insurance, IT and cyber security, audit and broader areas of management. In some disciplines risk is viewed as a calculable phenomenon in logic and mathematics, an objective reality in science and medicine, as a societal phenomenon in sociology and as a concept in linguistics (Aven, 2012, p34). These disciplines and areas have different needs, and this has contributed to various differing views that exist on risk. A brief summary of risk perspectives can be seen in Table 2.1. Easterby-Smith, Thorpe and Lowe, (2000, pp22–24) argue, "There has been a trend away from positivism towards phenomenology." This is the second philosophical tradition and paradigm which

> has arisen during the last half century, largely in reaction to the application of positivism to the social sciences, and stems from the view that the world and reality are not objective and exterior, but that they are socially constructed and given meaning by people.

The phenomenological paradigm focuses on meanings (not facts) and tries to understand what is happening, looking at the totality of each situation. The phenomenologist is more likely to embrace qualitative methods and rather than search for external causes and fundamental laws to explain behaviour they assume human action arises from the sense that people make of different situations. The phenomenologist is likely to attack positivism on the notion of "scientism" which holds that the only knowledge of any significance is that derived from the use of objective measures. Another is the view that science itself should be based only on data that can be observed and measured directly. One of the strongest attacks on positivism has been on its assumptions of value-freedom.

The move from positivism and objective methods not only paved the way for qualitative approaches but raised the issue of the fallibility of the risk expert, questioning whether it is indeed possible to be an expert of risk management (see for example Walklate, 1999 and Kelly, 2009). This issue gained prominence throughout the 1990s and into the millennium. Expert status has implications for the way organizational professionals approach risk management. Those who believe in expert status are more likely to adopt the doctor-patient model in a way that they singularly deliver their counsel and services to others. This is often described as a centralised approach. Those who recognise the fallibility of experts are more likely to embrace broad participation in risk decision making. Whereas the 20th century organization arguably relied on the single risk expert these organizations are now more likely to embrace broad

*Table 2.1* Risk perspectives and discourses

| |
|---|
| PHILOSOPHICAL PERSPECTIVES ON RISK |
| Risk can be defined philosophically in different ways. Rooted in these definitions is a distinction between risk defined as a reality that exists in its own right in the world (e g., objective risk and real risk) and risk defined as a realty by virtue of a judgment made by a person or the application of some knowledge to uncertainty (e.g., subjective risk, observed risk, perceived risk). Whereas the former considers the metaphysical properties of risk, the latter is what can be termed an epistemological approach to risk; risk comes to exist by virtue of judgments made under conditions of uncertainty. Philosophy sees risk with metaphysic, epistemic, and moral eyes and tells us that risk exists and that it is difficult to understand, (Althaus, 2005, p578). |
| MATHEMATICS, LOGIC, AND RISK AS A CALCULABLE PHENOMENON |
| The aim is to turn uncertainties into probabilities argues A thaus (2005, p571).The mathematical and logic literature on risk can be divided into three strands consisting of probability, statistics, and game theory.<br>Overall, probability, statistics, and game theory are tools by which uncertain events and behaviour can be modelled and calculated. Risk is a function of probability, which can be derived from statistics. What the mathematical literature brings to the notion of risk is therefore a notion of its calculability; "everyone indisputably applies the calculable concepts unconsciously" (Althaus, 2005, p572). |
| SCIENCE AND RISK AS AN OBJECTIVE REALITY |
| Science and medicine understand and define risk as an objective realty that can be measured, controlled, and managed, (Althaus, 2005, p572). However, as people do not react rationally to risk in the same scientific way, psychology is closely linked with the "scientific" approach to risk, as it helps explain some of the reasons why people do not tend to respond rationally and logically – scientifically – to risks. Conceptually, every science employs its own characteristics, abstractions, terminology, and techniques of interpretation and explanation Science and its ability to objectify risk remains relevant, largely because the scientific methodology has yet to be dislodged as a valid and accepted way of obtaining reliable information, (Althaus, 2005, p573). |
| ECONOMICS AND RISK AS A DECISIONAL PHENOMENON |
| Althaus (2005, p573) suggests the general concept of risk in economics is a mix of challenge and security; entrepreneurs voluntarily take on risks in the belief that a reward will ensue; conversely involuntary risks should be insured against. The economic theory of risk management is closely tied to the scientific and mathematical world- view, as it defines risk as an objective and measurable phenomenon, although I does recognise value issues and is thustied to psychology. |
| PSYCHOLOGY AND RISK AS A BEHAVIOURAL AND COGNITIVE PHENOMENON |
| Psychologists entered the risk debate by exposing the subjective nature of risk vis-a' -vis the objective scientific view of risk and were preoccupied with determining why there is disparity between expert and lay risk perception, (Althaus, 2005, p574). They also assess what makes people risk-averse, risk-indifferent, or risk- takers. Thus, psychology divides into studies of risk action and risk perception. The psychological literature featured in the 1970s with the publishing of. for example, prospect theory, (Kahneman and Tversky, 1979) or Slovic, Fischhoff and Lichtenstein (1981); the latter group were responsible for the psychometric paradigm and for introducing the notions of perceived versus actual risk, which in turn has produced interest in "acceptable risk" and in risk communication. |
| CULTURAL AND SOCIOLOGICAL PERSPECTIVES ON RISK |
| For discussion about anthropology and risk as a cultural phenomenon see Douglas and Wildavsky (1982); the sociological literature on risk is diverse; dominant works include Beck (1998) and Giddens (1984) for example. The definition of risk used in sociology is that of the people defining it. That is, therefore if people define risk we must turn to people and the societies within which they live to understand risk. The sociological literature argues that the world is currently going through a period of societal change and the dominant scientific paradigm is eroding and creating a malaise in the definition and treatment of risk, (Althaus, 2005, p575); "Suddenly, there are no "experts" and the scientific definition of risk has become nebulous and rubbery." |

participation. This is often accompanied by a move from centralised risk decision making (a throwback of scientific management) to one where each and every manager and employee has some recognised responsibility for risk and its management. This approach tends to emphasise a need for risk professionals to adopt an "assurance" model of risk management, embracing a need to understand and manage risk culture. Developments in management theory at this time were also responsible for changes in risk thinking. Towards the end of the 20th century, management thinking emphasised effectiveness (creativity, innovation and entrepreneurialism) as a source of competitive advantage. This led to more change, often radical change. Consequently, the organization's environment became more turbulent and less predictable. Organizations were more likely to engage in new activities for which they had no experience and therefore no historic data on which to base risk thinking calculation. In the absence of objective data, risk professionals tended to rely on their own intuition and judgement to determine risk subjectively in a given situation. Associated risk methods (risk estimates) were not only driven by data limitations but also by the organization's need to be more responsive, that is the pursuit of faster decision making. In many cases it was possible for the risk professionals to make a faster subjective judgement than pursuing objective alternatives. Thus whereas risk method in the early 20th century was able to make use of historic data (the known and knowable) many risk professionals towards the end of the 20th century were confronted by the unknown and often unknowable. Consequently, risk academics became more interested in how risk professionals made their judgements and decisions and how risk information was recorded and communicated throughout the decision-making process. For example, Sitkin and Weingart (1992) presented their conceptual model, placing risk propensity and risk perception in a more central role in models of risk decision making.

Towards the end of the 20th century organizations recognised a need to be more responsive. The traditional functional silo approach to management came under attack; organizations delayered, empowered employees, outsourced more activities and made use of database and communication technologies to enable autonomous employees to make speedy decisions wherever they were working. Management then focused on integration. Companies were internationalising and creating global supply chains. This created a new context for risk management. Many organizations implemented jobs with the title "chief risk officer" to provide risk leadership, acting as integrative and coordinating mechanisms. Additionally, the role of the board developed. In 1992 the UK's Cadbury Committee suggested board responsibility for setting risk management policy and taking a risk oversight role, ensuring organizations understood all their risks. At the end of the 20th century, distinctions between risk and uncertainty and "good risk" and "bad risk" tended to be somewhat lost (see Figure 2.2). The concept of risk became widely used to explain deviations from the norm. "Risk" is a word whose use in organizations and society is on the rise as can be seen in Figure 2.3; in the late 1960s, "risk" became a 'hot topic'; the frequency of its usage increasing dramatically, peaking in 2006. Similarly, the term "corporate disaster" peaked around the same time, see Figure 2.4. In response to the new risk context of increased turbulence and uncertainty, organizations recognised the need to build resilience, favouring thinking that emanated from business continuity management and disaster planning. Participative risk methods resulted from several related developments in management theory. The strategic goal of greater responsiveness led to increased empowerment. Motivation theory and change management theory both argued for increased involvement of employees. Furthermore attacks on bureaucracy and a shift from both formal and centralised control emphasised a greater need for informal control, that is culture as control (see Ouchi, 1980).

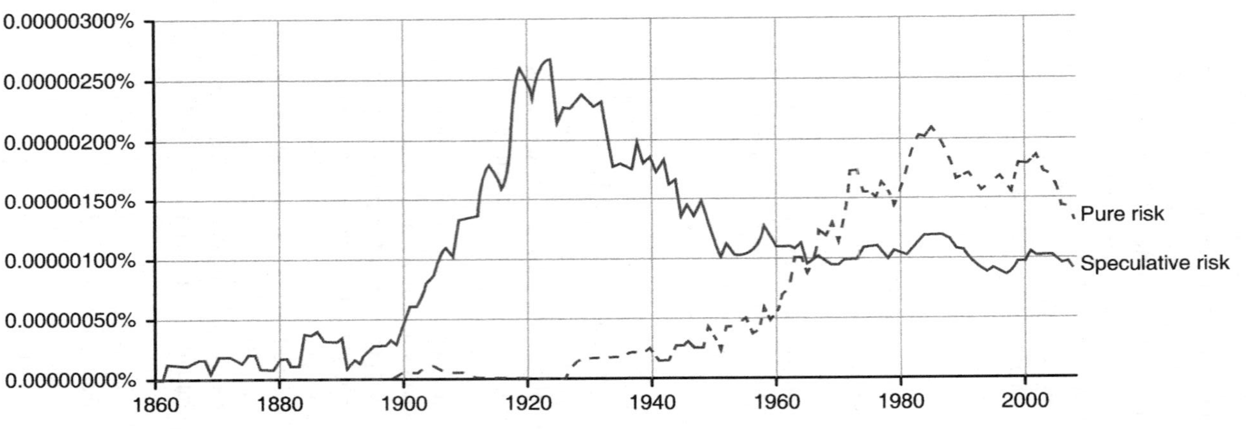


*Figure 2.2* Ngram 'pure risk, speculative risk' 1930–2008

*Source*: © 2013 Google

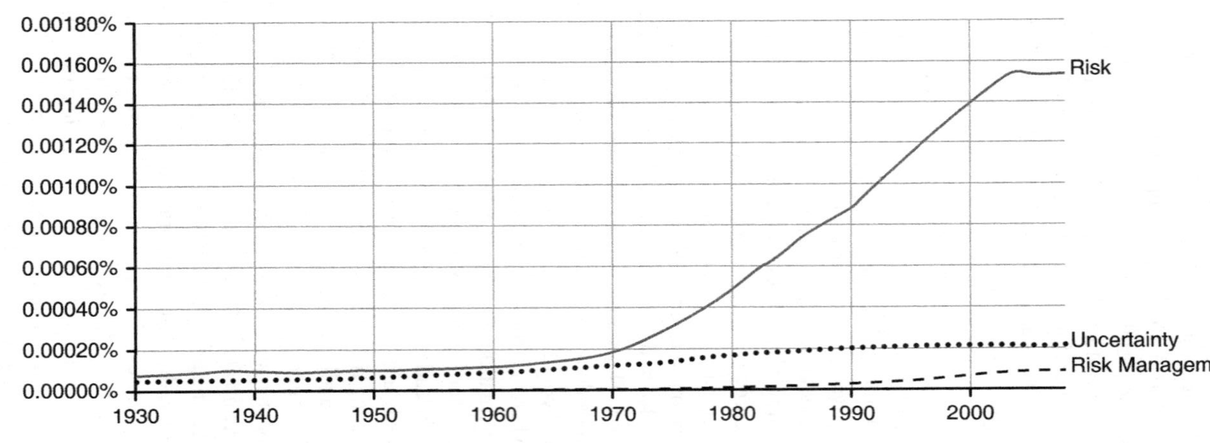


*Figure 2.3* Ngram 'risk, risk management, uncertainty' 1930–2008

*Source*: © 2013 Google

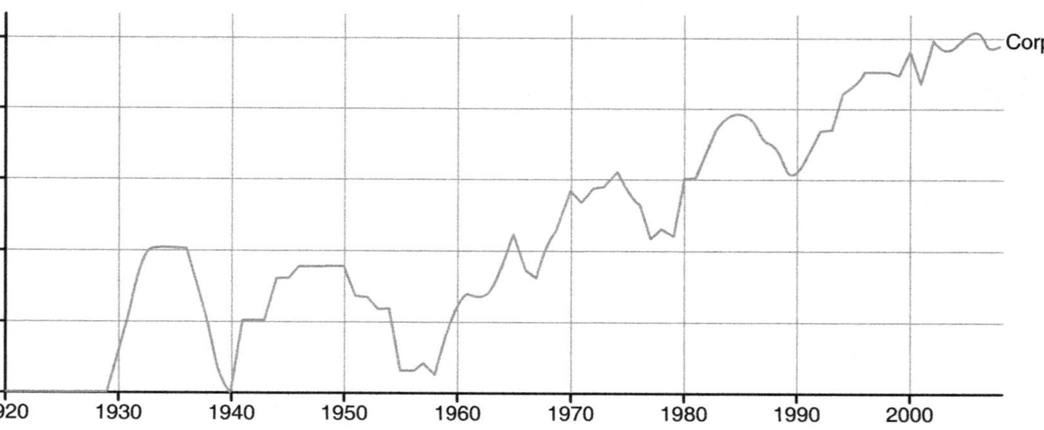


*Figure 2.4* Ngram 'corporate disaster' 1930–2008

*Source*: © 2013 Google

## 3 21st century risk-thinking: the ERM, governance and resilience era

### 21st century organizations: management 3.0

Within this new era organizations are influenced by the concept of the triple bottom line (TBL) with performance measurements aligned with people, the planet and profit. This demands company responsibility to stakeholders rather than simply shareholders. The era is typified by work done through networks rather than through lines of command; organizations emphasise values and corporate social responsibility (CSR); they are more international in outlook (see Figure 2.5) and virtual in organization and tend to be less formal, leaner and flatter, more flexible and agile, empowering employees, seeking to engage them. Managers reward creativity, innovation and entrepreneurial behaviours whilst retaining efficiency goals. Organizations of this era are seen as boundaryless and nearly all significant business processes and relationships are digitally enabled and key corporate assets are managed through digital means (Cole and Kelly, 2015).

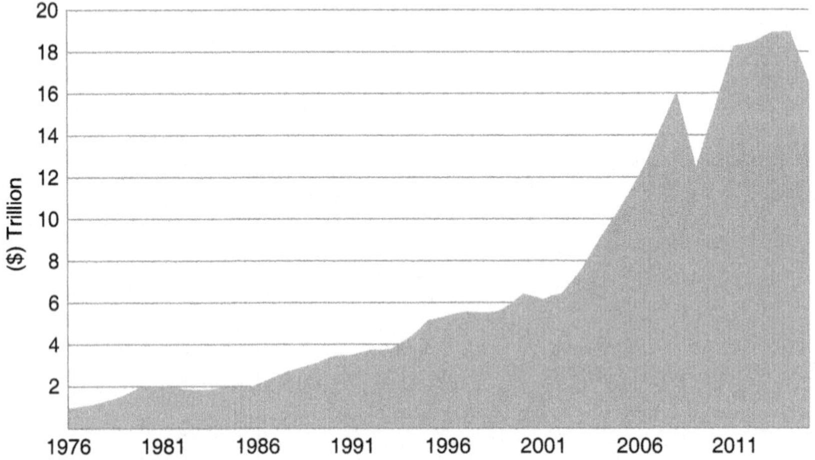


*Figure 2.5* Merchandise: total world trade, 1976–2015
*Source*: UNCTAD

The 21st century started in the wake of a number of high-profile business failures and scandals which resulted in a loss of confidence in business by investors. Whilst in the 20th century many held the view that the application of risk management was limited to the field of pure risks, thinking changed dramatically at the end of the 20th century. The scope of risk management developed to include speculative and goal-oriented risk. The ISO 31000 standard on risk management (2009) and the ISO guide 73 on risk terminology defined risk as the effect of uncertainty on objectives. However, in the 21st century there remains no widely agreed upon definition of the concept of risk, there never has been one, and there are many different definitions within the literature (Aven, 2012, p33). The way we define our terms both reflects and affects our thinking, (Athearn, 1971). Classifying risk definitions into two broad areas he suggests that, "some consider risk as subjective . . . whereas others grant risk an ontological status." For some it is defined into existence (based on judgments and knowledge of a person) whilst others it is "real," existing whether we choose to think about it or not. Risk thinking became more holistic and more integrated within the organization. Furthermore, risk management seemed to get "more teeth" with new legislation (the Sarbanes-Oxley regulation was introduced in the United States in 2002, stipulating governance rules for companies), codes (such as the UK's Combined Code of 1998) and standards (for example, the AS/NZS 4360 Risk Management Standard and the IRM 'Risk Management Standard' originally published in 2002. This was followed by the publication of ISO 31000, the Global Risk Management Standard).

### *Risk management scope: from central function (narrow) to enterprise wide (broad)*

Insurance is a means for dealing with the vagaries of fate (Lupton, 1999, p96). Traditionally it was used by organizations to protect from loss caused by some external or natural event. However, towards the latter part of the 20th century, organizations realised increasingly that risk exposures were driven by the actions of employees and partners; therefore many of their risks were uninsurable. Operational risk emerged in the 1990s (see for example Smallman, 2000) – the risk of loss resulting from inadequate or failed internal processes, people and systems or from external events. In the mid-1990s, enterprise risk management (ERM) arose as a concept and as a management function within corporations. ERM is a systematic and integrated approach to the management of the total risks that a company faces, (Dickinson, 2001). Fraser and Simkins (2010) believe ERM is a natural evolution of risk management. They draw upon the committee of Sponsoring Organizations of the Treadway Commission (COSO) definition. ERM is

> a process, affected by an entity's board of directors, management and other personnel, applied in a strategy setting and across the enterprise, designed to identify potential events that may affect the entity, and manage risk to be within its risk appetite, to provide reasonable assurance regarding the achievement of entity objectives.

ERM differs from earlier perspectives of risk management in that it has a strategic and future (goal) orientation, takes a broad view and holistic approach.

> Some sources have referred to ERM as a new risk management paradigm. As in the past, many Organizations continue to address risk in 'silos' as a narrowly-focused and fragmented set of activities. Under ERM, all risk areas function as part of an integrated, strategic, and enterprise-wide system. And whilst risk management is coordinated, with senior-level oversight, employees at all levels of the Organization using ERM are encouraged to view risk management as an integral and ongoing part of their jobs.
>
> *(Fraser and Simkins, 2010, p3)*

Furthermore, in the 21st century, "Risk management is part of corporate governance" (Dionne, 2013, p164). In this era, many professionals have adopted the ISO definition of risk, that is the effect of uncertainty on objectives (ISO, 2009). Whereas the 20th century started with a bias toward quantitative and objective method, towards the end of the 20th century qualitative and subjective method gained importance in the risk community. Saunders, Lewis and Thornhill (2012, p129) ask whether it is necessary to adopt one position. They recognise the pragmatist

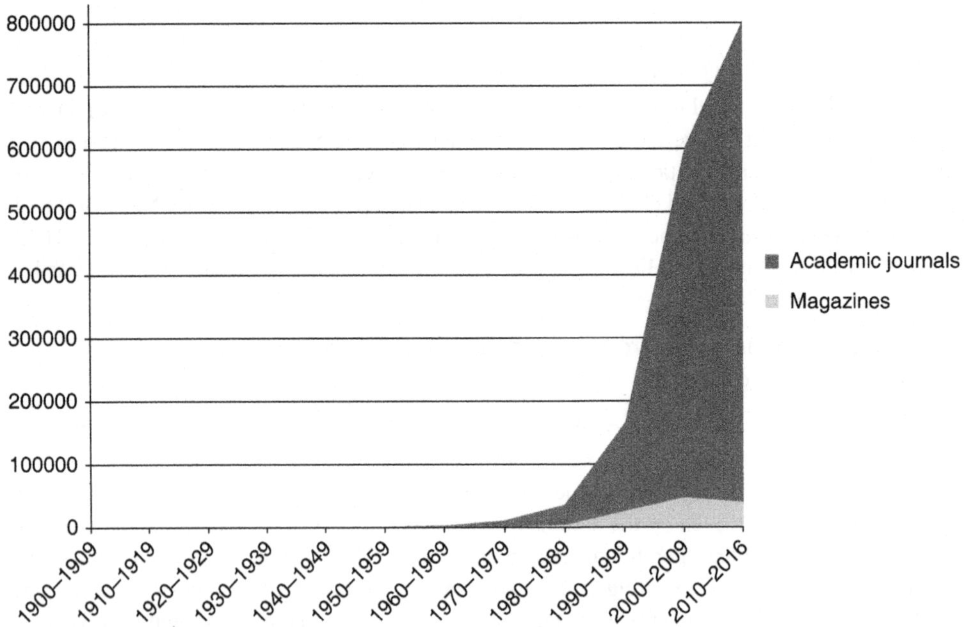


*Figure 2.6* Academic journal articles with "risk" in title by decade

*Source*: EBSCO Discovery Service (university databases)

view that it is possible to work with different philosophical positions and that multiple methods are possible. Pragmatists recognise there are many different ways of interpreting the world and that no single point of view can ever give the entire picture.

The scholarly interest in risk continued to intensify with over 1.3 million academic journal articles containing "risk" in their title and over 100,000 magazine and news articles written in the first 15 years; creating a wealth of risk knowledge for the academic or practitioner to embrace. From Figure 2.6 we can deduce the risk scholar at the turn of the 20th century could keep up comfortably with the one article a month published, whilst the risk scholar of the 21st century faces information overload.

## Summary and closing comments

Understanding risk is one of the "eight great challenges every business faces" (Conner, 2013). Bernstein (1998) argues that as organizations have progressed we have become increasingly dependent upon risk management. We opened this chapter by asking whether our thinking about risk and its management has changed much over the last hundred years. As with management generally, risk thinking and risk management in organizations is something of an eclectic affair. Risk thinking is contingent on management thinking, itself contingent on the environment, philosophical thinking and influenced by a wide variety of academic disciplines. Consequently, an understanding of how these have changed can help us to understand how risk thinking has evolved. This evolution can be explored from multiple perspectives and we have summarised these, making reference to three key eras, for simplicity, as shown in Figure 2.7. Whilst merely an approximation to aid understanding, for many organizations, the

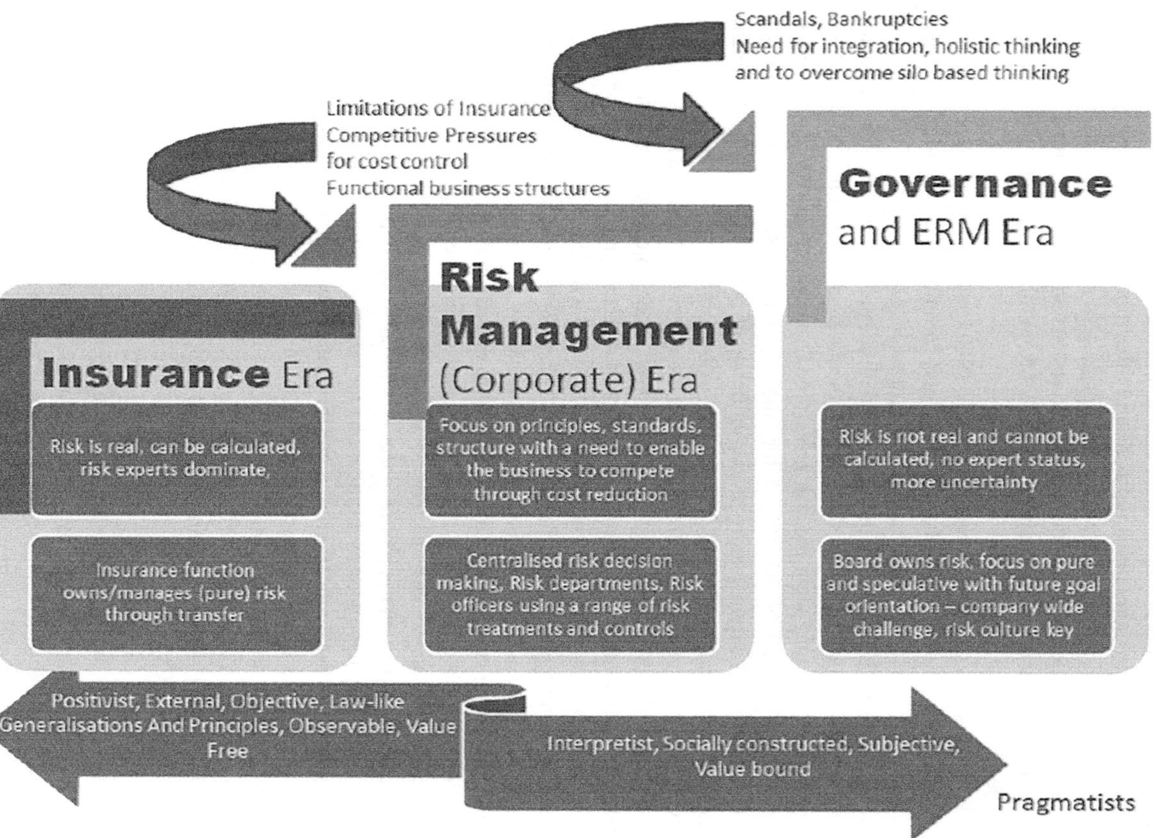
Limitations of Insurance
Competitive Pressures
for cost control
Functional business structures
Scandals, Bankruptcies
Need for integration, holistic thinking
and to overcome silo based thinking
Insurance Era
Risk is real, can be calculated, risk experts dominate,
Insurance function owns/manages (pure) risk through transfer
Risk Management (Corporate) Era
Focus on principles, standards, structure with a need to enable the business to compete through cost reduction
Centralised risk decision making, Risk departments, Risk officers using a range of risk treatments and controls
Governance and ERM Era
Risk is not real and cannot be calculated, no expert status, more uncertainty
Board owns risk, focus on pure and speculative with future goal orientation – company wide challenge, risk culture key
Positivist, External, Objective, Law-like Generalisations And Principles, Observable, Value Free
Interpretist, Socially constructed, Subjective, Value bound
Pragmatists

*Figure 2.7* Eras of risk-thinking in organizations

first half of the 20th century may be described as the "insurance era" with its narrow focus on risk, simply transferred as somebody else's problem. In the second half of the 20th century corporate expertise grew and Organizations developed their capabilities to identify and reduce losses using a variety of treatments and controls. Finally, in the governance and ERM era risk management was given a broader, holistic and companywide role, empowered through the board. There are many ways of thinking about and managing risk within organizations. Old ideas and thoughts remain, sometimes replaced and other times enhanced by new ideas and risk thinking. There are no universal laws, rules or principles with regard to risk yet there is a significant body of knowledge which has grown and is constantly aggregating. Contemporary managers and risk professionals, as pragmatists, select from this body of knowledge what they consider to be relevant.

At the defining points of risk management, in the 1960s and 1970s, scholars pursued principles and a shared definition of risk. Crowe, Horn and Hall (1967), for example suggest that scholars in several other disciplines have demonstrated increased interest in the concept of risk, a development which has further muddied the definitional waters. A review of a selection of "risk" definitions (Table 2.2) shows that people associate varied meanings to the term. With the passage of time it would seem the risk professionals' meaning of risk and risk management has evolved. For much of the 20th century many risk professionals viewed risk from a downside only perspective (pure) and with the influence of positivism and the dominance of economics and the insurance industry, viewed risk to be something that could be calculated objectively. Towards the end of the 20th century this view seemed dated and many emphasised the upside as well as the downside, the subjective as well as the objective aspects to it. Furthermore, whilst the early insurance industry focused on risk to tangible assets, later risk professionals, towards the end of the 20th century also considered a need to focus on the company's goals (a future and intangible orientation). Aven (2012, p37) notes a range of definitions that view risk as probability, event or consequence, the probability of loss, a combination of likelihood and outcome, as uncertainty and more recently as the effect of uncertainty on objectives. Some definitions treat risk as real and calculable (ontological/objective) and others treat it as a personal judgement (subjective); risk can be a quantitative or qualitative concept. Finally, Aven (2012, p42) remarks that the risk perspective chosen strongly influences the way risk is analysed and hence may have serious implications for risk management and decision making. If risk is considered as the application of some form of knowledge to the unknown (future) in an attempt to confront uncertainty and make decisions, then each discipline can be said to apply its own form of knowledge to uncertainty that uniquely "creates" varying types of risk (Althaus, 2005, p580). As a result, all the disciplines have something valuable to add to our understanding of risk. The way we think about and seek to manage risk is contingent on the situation. Bernstein (1998) states that

> our lives teem with numbers, but we sometimes forget that numbers are only tools . . . to judge the extent to which today's methods of dealing with risk are either a benefit or a threat, we must know the whole story, from its very beginnings. We must know why people of past times did-or did not-try to tame risk, how they approached the task, what modes of thinking and language emerge from their experience, and how their activities interacted with other events, large and small, to change the course of culture. Such a perspective will bring us to a deeper understanding of where we stand, and where we may be heading.

We hope that this chapter will act as a foundation for the chapters that follow.

*Table 2.2* Definitions of "risk"

| | |
|---|---|
| Willett, A. H. (1901) *The economic theory of risk and insurance*, New York: Columbia University Press. | The objectified uncertainty regarding the occurrence of an undesirable event |
| Knight, F. H.. (1921) *Risk, uncertainty and profit*, Ed. 1964. Boston: Houghton Mifflin. | Measurable uncertainty |
| Mehr, R. I. and Hedges, B A. (1962) *Risk management in the business enterprise*, Homewood, Illinois: Richard D. Irwin, Inc. | Uncertainty regarding a loss (No definition of uncertainty provided. Their discussion of uncertainty referred clearly to predictability.) |
| Head, G. L. (1967) 'An alternative to defining risk as uncertainty', *Journal of Risk & Insurance*, 34 (2), pp. 205–214. | The objective probability that the actual outcome of the event will differ significantly from the expected outcome |
| Gahin, F. S. (1967) 'A theory of pure risk management in the business firm', *Journal of Risk & Insurance*, 34 (1), pp. 121–129. | The maximum potential loss of a specific event |
| Williams, C. A. and Heins, R. M. (1971) *Risk management and insurance*, 2nd ed. New York: McGraw-Hill Book Co. | The variation, in the possible outcomes that exist in nature in a given situation |
| Ratcliffe, D. T. (1971) 'Teaching the meaning of risk', *Journal of Risk and Insurance*, 38 (3), pp. 455–461. | Danger |
| Short, J. F. (1984) 'The social fabric at risk: Toward the social transformation of risk analysis', *American Sociological Review*, 49 (6), pp. 711–725. | The probability of some future event |
| Vaughan, E. and Vaughan, T M. (1995) *Essentials of insurance: A risk management perspective*, John Wiley & Sons. | A condition in which there is a possibility of an adverse deviation from a desired outcome that is expected or hoped for |
| Dickson, G C. (1995) *Corporate risk management*, Witherby & Co. | The unwanted future event |
| Bozeman, B. (1998) 'Risk Culture in Public And Private Organizations', *American Society for Public Administration*, 58 (2), pp. 109–118. | The exposure to the chance of loss from one's actions or decisions |
| Stock, M., Copnell, T. and Wicks, C. (1999) *The combined code: A practical guide*, Gee Publishing Ltd. | Real or potential events which reduce the likelihood of achieving business objectives. |
| British Standards. (1999) 'BS ISO/IEC TR 13335–1:1996 Information technology Guidelines for the management of IT Security Part 1: Concepts and models for ITSecurity', BSI. | The potential that a given threat will exploit vulnerabilities of an asset or group of assets to cause loss or damage to the assets |
| Hodges, A. (2000) Emergency risk management, *Risk Management: Perpetuity Press Ltd.*, 2 (4), pp. 7–18. | The chance of something happening that will have an impact upon objectives. It is measured in terms of consequences and likelihood. |
| Knight, D., Durham, C. and Locke, E. (2001) 'The relationship of team goals, incentives, and efficacy to strategic risk, tactical implementation, and performance', *Academy of Management Journal*, 44 (2), pp. 326–338. | The possibility of suffering harm or loss in pursuit of a desired outcome |

(*Continued*)

*Table 2.2* (Continued)

| | |
|---|---|
| Huczynski, A. and Buchanan, D. (2001) *Organizational behaviour: An introductory text,* 4th ed. Financial Times/Prentice Hall. | A condition in which managers have a high knowledge of alternatives, know the probability of these being available, can calculate the costs and know the benefits of each alternative and have a medium predictability of outcomes. |
| Barton, T. L., Shenkir, W. G. and Walker, P. L. (2002) *Making enterprise risk management pay off: How leading companies implement risk management,* Financial Times/Prentice Hall. | Any event or action that will adversely affect an organisation's ability to achieve its business objectives and execute its strategies successfully |
| ISO/IEC. (2002) 'GUIDE 73', Ed. 1. ISO/IEC. | Combination of the probability of an event and its consequence |
| Johnson, G., Scholes, K. and Whittington, R. (2006) *Exploring corporate strategy enhanced media edition,* FT Prentice Hall. | The probability and consequences of the failure of a strategy |
| Huczynski, A. and Buchanan, D. (2007) *Organizational behaviour,* 6th ed., FT Prentice Hall. | A condition in which managers have a high knowledge of alternatives; know the probability of these being available; can calculate the costs and know the benefits of each alternative; and have a medium predictability of outcomes. |
| ISO. (2009) *Risk management – Principles and guidelines ISO 31000:2009∊,* ISO. | Effect of uncertainty on objectives |
| ISO/IEC. (2013) *PD ISO Guide 73:2009 Risk management Vocabulary,* BSI Standards Limited. | Effect of uncertainty on objectives |
| Blunden, T. and Thirlwell, J. (2013) *Mastering operational risk – A practical guide to understanding operational risk and how to manage it,* 2nd ed. Pearson. | An occurrence that may cause damage or loss through preventing or hindering the achievement of a firm's objectives |
| Boothroyd, K. (2014) *Study guide module 3: Risk assessment,* Institute of Risk Management. | Effect of uncertainty on objectives (an effect is a deviation from the expected – positive and/or negative) |
| Hopkin, P. (2014) *Fundamentals of risk management,* 3rd ed. London: Kogan Page. | Effect of uncertainty on objectives |
| Cole, G. A. and Kelly, P. P. (2015) *Management theory and practice,* 8th ed. Cengage EMEA. | Combination of the probability of an event and its consequence |

## References

Althaus, C. E. (2005), 'A Disciplinary Perspective on the Epistemological Status of Risk', *Risk Analysis: An International Journal,* Vol. 25, Issue 3, June 2005, pp. 567–588.

ARIA Committee on Curricular Concepts in Risk and Insurance (1962) 'Curricular Concepts in Risk and Insurance', *Journal of Risk & Insurance,* 6 January 1962, Vol. 29, Issue 2, pp. 256–264.

Athearn, J. L. (1971), 'What Is Risk?', *Journal of Risk & Insurance,* Vol. 38, Issue 4, December 1971, pp. 639–645.

Aven, T. (2012), 'The Risk Concept – Historical and Recent Development Trends', *Reliability Engineering & System Safety*, Vol. 99, March 2012, pp. 33–44.

Barlow, M. (1897), 'The Insurance of Industrial Risks', *The Economic Journal*, Vol. 7, Issue 27, pp. 354–367.

Beck, U. (1998), 'Risk Society', Sage.

Bernstein, P. L. (1998), *Against the Gods: The Remarkable Story of Risk*, Wiley, Hoboken, NJ.

Caswell, J. W. and Wilkens, P. L. (1975), 'Emerging Role of the Risk Manager', *Business Horizons*, Vol. 18, Issue 6, December 1975, pp. 41–48.

Cole, G A. and Kelly, P. (2015), *Management Theory and Practice*, Ed. 8. London: Cengage EMEA.

Conner, C. (2013), 'The "8 Great" Challenges Every Business Faces (And How to Master Them All)', Forbes on-line March 4, 2013, available from www.forbes.com/sites/cherylsnappconner/2013/03/04/the-8-great-challenges-every-business-faces-and-how-to-master-them-all/#5b14a8f71eb9, accessed 20 July 2016.

Cristy, J. (1962), 'A Risk Manager Looks at Curricular Concepts in Risk and Insurance', *The Journal of Insurance*, 12 January 1962, Vol. 29, Issue 4, pp. 567–569.

Crockford, G. N. (1982), 'The Bibliography and History of Risk Management: Some Preliminary Observations', *The Geneva Papers on Risk and Insurance*, Vol. 7, pp. 169–179, available at www.genevaassociation.org/media/219919/ga1982_gp7(23)_crockford.pdf.

Crowe, R. M., Horn, R. C. and Hall, C. P. (1967) 'The Meaning of Risk', *Journal of Risk & Insurance*, September 1967, Vol. 34, Issue 3, pp. 459–474.

Denenberg, H. S. and Ferrari, J. R. (1966), 'New Perspectives on Risk Management: The Search for Principles', *The Journal of Risk and Insurance*, 12 January 1966, Vol. 33, Issue 4, pp. 647–661.

Dickinson, G. (2001), 'Enterprise Risk Management: Its Origins and Conceptual Foundation', *The Geneva Papers on Risk and Insurance*, July 2001, Vol. 26, Issue 3, pp. 360–366.

Dionne, G. (2013), 'Risk Management: History, Definition, and Critique', *Risk Management & Insurance Review*, Fall 2013, Vol. 16, Issue 2, pp. 147–166.

Douglas, M. and Wildavsky, A. (1982), *Risk and Culture*, University of California Press, Berkeley.

Easterby-Smith, M., Thorpe, R. and Lowe, A. (2000), *Management Research – An Introduction*, Sage, Thousand Oaks, CA.

Fraser, J. and Simkins, B. J. (2010), *Enterprise Risk Management: Today's Leading Research and Best Practices for Tomorrow's Executives*, Ed. 1, Wiley, Hoboken, NJ.

Gahin, F S. (1967), 'A Theory of Pure Risk Management in the Business Firm', *Journal of Risk & Insurance*, March 1967, Vol. 34, Issue 1, pp. 121–129.

Gallagher, R. B. (1956), 'Risk Management: New Phase of Cost Control', *Harvard Business Review*, September/October 1956, Vol. 34, Issue 5, pp. 75–86.

Gallagher, R. B. (1960), 'A Practical Approach to Risk Management', *Business Horizons*, June 1960, Vol. 3, Issue 2, pp. 78–86.

Giddens, A. (1984), 'The constitution of society', Polity Press, Cambridge.

Hall, C. P. (1969), 'Curricular Concepts in Risk and Insurance', *Journal of Risk & Insurance*, June 1969, Vol. 36, Issue 2, pp. 296–296.

Hardy, C. O. (1923), 'Risk and the Management of Capital', *The University Journal of Business*, 2 January 1923, Vol. 1, Issue 2, pp. 205–220.

Hawley, F. B. (1893), 'The Risk Theory of Profit', *Quarterly Journal of Economics*, July 1893, Vol. 7, Issue 4, pp. 459–479.

Head, G. L. (1967), 'An Alternative to Defining Risk as Uncertainty', *Journal of Risk & Insurance*, June 1967, Vol. 34, Issue 2, pp. 205–214.

Heins, C. A. and Williams, R. M. (1964), 'Risk Management and Insurance', McGraw-Hill.

Horn, R. C. (1965), 'Curricular Concept in Risk and Insurance', *Journal of Risk & Insurance*, December 1965, Vol. 32, Issue 4, pp. 645–648.

ISO/IEC. (2013), *PD ISO Guide 73:2009 Risk management Vocabulary*, BSI Standards Limited, London.

Johnson, G. L. (1952), 'Handling Problems of Risk and Uncertainty in Farm Management Analysis', *Journal of Farm Economics*, 12 January 1952, Vol. 34, Issue 5, pp. 807–817.

Kahneman, D. and Tversky, A. (1979), 'Prospect Theory: An Analysis of Decisions Under Risk', *Econometrica*, Vol. 47, pp. 262–291.

Kelly, P. (2009), 'Conceptualising Business Risk Culture: A Study of Risk-Thinking and Practice in Contemporary Dynamic Organizations', *International Journal of Business Continuity and Risk Management*, Vol. 1, Issue 1, pp. 19–37.

Kelly, P. (2017), *Business Management in Practice*, Ed. 2. London: ICSA Publishing Limited.

Knight, F.H. (1921), *Risk, Uncertainty and Profit*, Ed. 1964, Houghton Mifflin, Boston.

Lupton, D. (1999), 'Risk', Routledge.

McCahill, F.X. (1971), 'Avoid Losses Through Risk Management', *Harvard Business Review*, May/June 1971, Vol. 49, Issue 3, pp. 57–65.

McGrath, R. (2014), 'Management's Three Eras: A Brief History', *Harvard Business Review Digital Article*, available from hbr.org/product/managements-three-eras-a-brief-history/H00X83-PDF-ENG.

Mehr, R.I. and Hedges, B.A. (1963), *Risk Management in the Business Enterprise*, Richard D. Irwin, Homewood, IL.

ONS. (2016), 'Statistical Bulletin: UK Business: Activity, Size and Location: 2015', available at www.ons.gov.uk/businessindustryandtrade/business/activitysizeandlocation/bulletins/ukbusinessactivitysizeandlocation/2015-10-06, accessed 15 July 2016.

Ouchi, W.G. (1980), 'Markets, Bureaucracies, and Clans', *Administrative Science Quarterly – Ithaca*, Vol. 25, Issue 1, pp. 129–141.

Reddy, S.G. (1996), 'Claims to Expert Knowledge and the Subversion of Democracy: The Triumph of Risk Over Uncertainty', *Economy and Society*, May 1996, Vol. 25, Issue 2, pp. 222–254.

Saunders, M., Lewis, P. and Thornhill, A. (2012), *Research Methods for Business Students*, Ed. 6, Pearson, Boston, MA.

Short, J. F. (1984), 'The Social Fabric at Risk: Toward the Social Transformation of Risk Analysis', *American Sociological Review*, 12/1/1984, Vol. 49, Issue 6, pp. 711–725.

Simon, H.A. (1955), 'A Behavioral Model of Rational Choice', *The Quarterly Journal of Economics*, February 1955, Vol. 69, Issue 1, pp. 99–118.

Sitkin, S B. and Weingart, L R. (1992), 'Reconceptualizing the Determinants of Risk Behavior', *Academy of Management Review*, January 1992, Vol. 17, Issue 1, pp. 9–30.

Skjong, R. (2005), 'Etymology of Risk', available at research.dnv.com/skj/papers/etymology-of-risk.pdf, accessed 14 July 2016.

Slovic, P., Fischhoff, B. and Lichtenstein, S. (1981), 'Perceived Risk: Psychological Factors and Social Implications', *Proceedings of the Royal Society of London. Series A, Mathematical and Physical Sciences*, Vol. 376, Issue 1764, pp. 17–34.

Smallman, C. (2000), 'What Is Operational Risk and Why Is It Important?', *Risk Management: Perpetuity Press Ltd*, Vol. 2, Issue 3, pp. 7–14.

Snider, H.W. (1961), 'Teaching Risk Management', *The Journal of Insurance*, June 1961, Vol. 28, Issue 2, pp. 41–43.

Taylor, F. (1911), *The Principles of Scientific Management*, Ed. 1. London: Harper & Brothers.

Todd, D.J. (1969), 'The Risk Management Function in Municipal Government', *Journal of Risk & Insurance*, June 1969, Vol. 36, Issue 2, pp. 285–295.

Walklate, S. (1999), 'Is It Possible to Assess Risk?', *Perpetuity Press: Risk Management – An International Journal*, Vol. 1, Issue 4, pp. 45–53.

Weber, M. (1947), *The Theory of Social and Economic Organization*, Free Press, Glencoe, IL.

Willett, A.H. (1901), *The Economic Theory of Risk and Insurance*, The Columbia University Press, New York

3

# Intuition and decision making for crisis situations

*Holmes E. Miller*

## Introduction

Moments before the Apollo 11 lunar landing in 1969, a yellow warning light appeared at the NASA Houston mission control center indicating an error, which would mean aborting the landing. In an obituary of Jack Garman, one of the participants, Sam Roberts (2016) described the sequence of events:

> The alarm appeared to indicate a computer systems overload, raising the specter of a breakdown. With only a few minutes left before touchdown on the moon, Steve Bales, the guidance officer in mission control, had to make a decision: Let the module continue to descend, or abort the mission and send the module rocketing back to the command ship, Columbia.
>
> By intercom, Mr. Bales quickly consulted Jack Garman, a 24-year-old engineer who was overseeing the software support group from a back-room console.
>
> Mr. Garman had painstakingly prepared himself for just this contingency – the possibility of a false alarm.
>
> "So I said," he remembered, "on this backup room voice loop that no one can hear, 'As long as it doesn't reoccur, it's fine.'"

While the decision to continue clearly depended in Bales' and Garman's intuition, the phrase "painstakingly prepared himself for just this contingency" illustrates intuition's proper role in crisis decision making. Intuition is not just an uninformed gut feeling, but rather results in actions that are informed by the experience, expertise, and the domain knowledge of the decision maker. Certainly for something as critical as a moon landing, NASA officials would not ask and act on a 24-year-old's recommendation without first knowing that the recommendation, intuitive though it may appear, was informed by prior analysis.

In Garman's case it was. Roberts continues:

> As a result, (Garman) said, Gene Kranz, the flight director, "had asked us to write down every possible computer alarm that could possibly go wrong and what could happen, what might cause it."

> Rather than pose a serious problem, it proved to be a self-correcting signal indicating that the mission's relatively primitive guidance computers were struggling to keep up with the tide of data they were receiving.
>
> "Quite frankly," Mr. Bales said, "Jack, who had these things memorized, said, 'That's O.K.,' before I could even remember which group it was in."
>
> Four similar alarms followed within a minute.
>
> "I remember distinctly yelling – by this time yelling, you know, in the loop here – 'Same type!'" Mr. Garman said.
>
> The message was relayed to Armstrong: "We're go. Same type. We're go."

Though crisis decision making may employ the logical procedures of the decision analysis literature (e.g., Raiffa, 1968; Keeney, 1992; Hammond et al., 1999), in a time constrained crisis environment intuition often augments and even replaces analytical procedures. Garman's split-second intuitive recommendation was based on hours of simulating crisis scenarios and his ability to recognize a pattern. Intuition can also be employed in the longer term, such as when fire behavior specialists – sometimes called "fire whisperers" – use their intuition to augment sophisticated computer models (Lacey, 2011). In this chapter, we will address how intuition can contribute to making decisions for crisis events. We will examine what intuition is and how researchers have assessed its role in decision making, and we will present a taxonomy, informed by the work of others, regarding how to view intuition's role in decision making in a crisis.

## *Intuition and systems 1 and 2*

What do we mean by intuition? A dictionary definition of intuition is *a natural ability or power that makes it possible to know something without any proof or evidence: a feeling that guides a person to act a certain way without fully understanding why* (Merriam-Webster, 2016). Cholle (2016) defines intuition as *a process that gives us the ability to know something directly without analytic reasoning, bridging the gap between the conscious and nonconscious parts of our mind, and also between instinct and reason.* Kahneman (2002) refers to intuition as *thoughts and preferences that come to mind quickly and without much reflection.*

Though often used interchangeably, intuition and instinct are not identical. Whereas instinct is innate, intuition is developed through experience. Later, we shall see that prior experience is important in discussing intuition and that one's intuitive decision-making abilities may be strong in one domain, yet lacking in other domains where the decision maker has less experience and expertise.

Daniel Kahneman has done groundbreaking work on the role of intuition in decision making. In his Nobel Prize lecture (Kahneman, 2002) he discusses intuition as System 1 and System 2:

> The operations of System 1 are fast, automatic, effortless, associative, and difficult to control or modify. The operations of System 2 are slower, serial, effortful, and deliberately controlled; they are also relatively flexible and potentially rule-governed. . . . the operating characteristics of System 1 are similar to the features of perceptual processes. On the other hand, the operations of System 1, like those of System 2, are not restricted to the processing of current stimulation. Intuitive judgments deal with concepts as well as with percepts, and can be evoked by language.

In further discussion, he notes that System 1's perceptual and intuitive operations generate impressions of the attributes of objects of perception and thought, which are neither voluntary nor necessarily verbally explicit. In contrast System 2, which involves rational analysis, leads to judgments that are always explicit and intentional, even when not overtly expressed. He concludes, "System 2 is involved in all judgments, whether they originate in impressions or in deliberate reasoning."

Decision making in crisis situations clearly involves both System 1 and System 2. System 2 is required for the planning and preparation stages for responding to crisis events, but even there, System 1's intuitions may be part of the process. In the immediate time frame when a crisis event occurs, and when there is no time for analysis, the intuitive operations of System 1 dominate.

In his discussion, Kahneman discusses accessibility:

> A defining property of intuitive thoughts is that they come to mind spontaneously, like percepts. To understand intuition, then, we must understand why some thoughts are accessible and others are not. The concept of accessibility is applied more broadly in this treatment than in common usage. Category labels, descriptive dimensions (attributes, traits), values of dimensions, all can be described as more or less accessible, for a given individual exposed to a given situation at a particular moment.

Analyzing *accessible thoughts* in relation to crisis events helps to inform the discussion below. Generally, thoughts are accessible if they are based on some prior experience and also some expertise in interpreting that experience. For example, a person experiencing a major fire for the first time would perceive the magnitude of the flames, the roar of the fire, the intense heat, and perhaps aspects of what is happening to the building on fire, but would be unable to articulate many thoughts beyond those. On the other hand, and experienced fire captain, who has seen many such fires before, would be able to integrate these perceptions with knowledge of fires and structures and experiences and in doing so have access to more profound thoughts that – even in a System 1 environment – may inform decisions and actions.

## A model for short-term decision making in a crisis

In the 1980s and after, Gary Klein and a team of researchers at MIT (Klein, 1998) did extensive observational research on fireground commanders. Initially they had assumed that the commanders would follow procedures spelled out in classical decision analysis – develop several options and then after analysis, choose the best. Because of the immediacy of the decisions the commanders faced, Klein and his team hypothesized that rather that considering a group of options, the commanders would just consider two. Even this hypothesis was conservative. In practice the commanders just considered one. In fact, one commander denied that he even made decisions at all! He argued that at each step of the process the choice was obvious.

This led Klein to develop the "recognition primed decision model." In this model, based on the situation and the constraints that he faces, a *decision* maker generates a course of action and modifies it as the situation evolves. Klein notes, "It was not that the commanders were *refusing* to compare options; rather, they did not *have* to compare options. I had been so fixated on what they were not doing, that I had missed the real finding: that the commanders could come up with a good course of action from the start. Even when faced with a complex situation, the commanders could see it as familiar and know how to react." The fireground commanders relied on their experience and expertise to recognize and act on patterns. If the course of action they were considering seemed appropriate, they would implement it. If not, they would modify it and if modification was impossible, they would consider the next most plausible option. This iterative procedure would be followed until an acceptable course of action was found.

In discussing Klein's findings, Kahneman (2002) notes that, "The options that were rejected are not represented. Doubt is a phenomenon of System 2, a meta-cognitive appreciation of one's ability to think incompatible thoughts about the same thing." The key characteristic about the situation the Klein describes is that there is no time for analysis – the decision must be made immediately and made under pressure. This leads us to highlight several attributes of the decision makers. For the fireground commanders this includes both the professional expertise that led to their being promoted to commander, and also experience fighting fires similar to one that they encountered.

To illustrate this last point, Klein mentions another case where a commander of a fire company in a small Texas town was confronted with a massive fire involving oil storage tanks. Although he had many years of experience fighting fires one would encounter in small towns, and had a great deal of expertise, he never had encountered a fire of this magnitude or of this type. In this case the experience and expertise that may have informed intuitive decisions for people experienced fighting oil fires was absent.

## *Two decision making approaches*

Making decisions intuitively based on recognizing patterns and acting on this information is referred to as *naturalistic decision making* (NDM). An alternative approach is based on *heuristics and biases* (HB). Whereas the NDM approach reflects Klein's findings for fireground commanders – which are replicated for nurses and others making decisions in time constrained environments – the HB approach is Kahneman's System 2 procedures operationalized. Kahneman and Klein (2009) discuss both of these approaches in a joint paper.

HB researchers are skeptical when considering "experts." They would posit that even "expert intuitive performance" – if analyzed in detail – would do poorly when compared with performance generated by formal models and rules. HB researchers are inclined to recommend that informal judgment be replaced by algorithms whenever possible. Indeed, in the field of medical care, protocols are replacing physicians' intuitive decisions and increasingly, health care organizations are opting for evidence based medicine, which illustrates the HB rather than in the NDM approach (Leonhardt, 2009). HB approaches often require universal structures and rules on judgments and on choices that often must be made in complicated, time-constrained environments. NDM researchers have little faith in these approaches, in part because of their impracticality. Indeed, in general NDM researchers rely on field research with professionals whereas HB researched rely on laboratory research that can be replicated.

Both approaches recognize that intuitive judgments and preferences have the characteristics of System 1 activity, and arise effortlessly, without immediate justification. Yet the two approaches focus on different types of intuition. NDM proponents opt for intuitive judgments arising from experience and skill, whereas HB researchers are concerned with intuitive judgments that arise from simplifying heuristics rather than from specific experiences.

Just as there is a place for both System 1 and System 2 in human decision making, so the principles behind the NDM and the HB approaches can be employed in analyzing the various decisions facing crisis manager in various time frames. In the following sections we present a model and a taxonomy that can help inform decision makers.

## The model

Many authors describe intuition as recognizing patterns and then acting on them. Perhaps the most accessible example are chess grandmasters who recognize tens of thousands of patterns of arising in chess matches and use this information to make, to the uniformed observer, what appears to be intuitive decisions that are highly effective (Simon, 1996). As we will see, recognizing these patterns is the result of both task and domain knowledge.

Dane and Pratt (2007) claim that intuition involves a decision maker consciously aware of the "logical connections supporting a particular answer or solution." They proceed to argue that intuition involves both domain knowledge and task characteristics. This leads to the two intertwined schema involving domain attributes and task attributes. Whereas insight is unconscious and may result in outcomes whose success of failure essentially depends on chance, a decision maker's domain and task knowledge forms a rational basis for evaluating how effective intuition may be applied in various decision situations.

Our model involves both domain and task attributes. By domain we mean the environment in which a crisis event occurs. Although many variables exist, we reduce these to two dimensions. Time is the first dimension. Various times frames are associated with decision making for crisis events. FEMA – the Federal Emergency Management Administration – lists four phases of disaster management (FEMA, 2016): Mitigation (Preventing future emergencies or minimizing their effects); Preparedness (Preparing to handle an emergency); Response (Responding safely to an emergency); and Recovery (Recovering from an emergency). Other methodologies break these tasks down into other components such as risk assessment and strategy development, but for our purposes the time constraints on some phases such as mitigation and preparedness are looser than others such as response and recovery.

Experience in the domain is the second dimension. Later we will discuss experience with elements of the decision itself, but we distinguish between the two. Domain experience is an individual's experience in the environment where the event occurs. For example, a New York firefighter may have domain experience in skyscraper fires, but little domain experience in fighting large forest fires. Conversely, his twin out west who is experienced with forest fires may have little domain knowledge regarding skyscraper fires. Klein's oil tank fire in a small Texas town illustrates this point well. The town's firefighters "had never seen anything like this before in their lives. As one commander described it to us, 'Our heads turned to stone.'" They had "no resources for fighting the fire and no understanding of what to do."

## Domain attributes

Figure 3.1 gives a schema regarding domain attributes and the two dimensions described above. The horizontal axis contains the time frame for the event's decision environment, and the vertical axis contains the decision maker's level of domain experience. The northeast quadrant, where the time frame is extended and the domain experience is extensive, is characterized by a high potential for applying intuition in the decision process. In this case the intuition would not be the type that Klein identified as taking one course of action and amending it as the decision process evolved, but more like employing intuition in the System 2 processes discussed by Kahneman and others. Examples here might include identifying variables to include in decision models, sources of data, analyzing results, developing scenarios, and developing strategies.

Conversely the southwest quadrant is characterized by an immediate time frame and little experience in the event domain. Here intuition should be avoided, as the effectiveness of

| EXPERIENCE | Extensive | High Intuition Potential | High Intuition Potential |
|---|---|---|---|
| | Little | Avoid | Develop Experience |
| | | *Immediate* | *Extended* |
| | | *TIME FRAME* | |

*Figure 3.1* Domain attributes

whatever recommendations would arise would be governed primarily by chance, and the most likely the outcomes would be negative since the decision maker would essentially be a novice, regardless of his expertise in the decision tasks.

The southeast quadrant is defined by an extended time frame and little experience in the domain. Here, while immediately applying intuition would be ineffective in the process, the looser time constraints allow for developing more domain experience. This would involve some form of training, for example experiential or even exposing the individual to various forms of simulations or gaming. The objective would be to move that person up toward the northeast quadrant.

Finally, the northwest quadrant involves an immediate time frame and extensive experience in the domain. As with the northeast quadrant, this quadrant too has a high potential for applying intuition in the decision process. However, rather than the more analytical System 2 processes being used, the immediate time frame would require more of the System 1 intuitive thinking which might manifest itself in Klein's "ongoing amending of the one option" strategy discussed earlier.

Yet the overall effectiveness of the outcome cannot depend on the domain expertise alone and the decision maker also must have expertise in the decision tasks at hand. A firefighter with a great deal of experience fighting forest fires may not have the deep knowledge and experience of a fireground commander; a national guardsman might have experience rescuing people in floods, but not have the analytical and organizational experience to develop larger response and recovery plans required for flood events.

Domain attributes indicate a decision maker's familiarity with the domain in which an event occurs, task knowledge also is important. Dane and Pratt (2007) discuss how intuition is most effective when dealing with unstructured problems. They note that "the holistic, associative properties of intuition involve recognizing patterns or other linkages among disparate stimuli. Hence, philosophers have linked intuition with 'seeing' or 'recognizing' an answer." While the process of intuitive thought may appear to be non-rational and more from the heart or gut than from the head, Dane and Patt note that "the individuals most capable of making the associations that trigger accurate intuitive judgments are those who possess complex, domain-relevant cognitive structures within a particular domain. . . . the holistic and associative properties of intuition may help to integrate the disparate elements of an ill-defined, or judgmental, problem into a coherent perception of how to proceed. Experts may be especially well-suited to draw these holistic associations on judgmental tasks because the sophistication of their cognitive structures may permit them to integrate the components of an ill-structured problem with relative ease."

## *Task area attributes*

To best inform decision making, domain knowledge and experience needs be augmented by task area expertise and experience. Figure 3.2 presents a schema for such knowledge.

Since intuition depends on individuals using their System 1 skills to recognize patterns, experience and expertise in the subject area is necessary to form patterns from what may seem to be unrelated stimuli. Recognizing patterns is part of the overall process of "sense-making." Moynihan (2012) says that "A first step of sensemaking is developing an accepted interpretation of external events." The challenges are significant when these events border on the catastrophic and involve many people. Coordinating large networks consisting of many actors is critical, and Moynihan uses Hurricane Katrina as an example: "Nevertheless, it is clear that better coordination among the network of responders, a greater sense of urgency, and more successful management of related risk factors would have minimized some of the losses caused by Katrina."

Intuition plays a large role both in sensemaking and in the overall coordination of responders in a crisis. For Hurricane Katrina, New Orleans mayor Ray Nagin and FEMA director Michael Brown were criticized for their untimely and ineffective responses. The nature of the event and the time pressure required crisis managers with intuitive skills that neither Nagin nor Brown possessed. In this crisis, General Russel Honoré took charge and reversed many earlier decisions concerning mistreatment of people affected by the disaster and logistical failures, finally heading up an effective response. His experience leading soldiers in the military informed his decisions and his approach to dealing with the disaster. As a New Orleans native, his "domain" experience was helpful, but even more important was his experience and expertise in crisis situations. This experience made him able to make better decisions than Nagin or Brown, who had neither task experience nor task expertise.

The northeast quadrant of Figure 3.2 indicates a high potential for effectively applying intuition to the decision-making process. The combination of a decision maker's high expertise and experience creates a foundation for effectively intuiting courses of action. System 1 processes occur in all time frames but when the decision maker has more time – such as in cases where one plans for events and develops strategies – System 2 and the associated intuitive processes come into play. Referring to Hurricane Katrina, Bluestein (2006) discusses General Russel Honoré's actions when he assumed command of the response efforts:

| *EXPERIENCE* | *Extensive* | Develop Expertise | High Intuition Potential |
|---|---|---|---|
| | *Little* | Avoid | Develop Experience |
| | | *Low* | *High* |
| | | *EXPERTISE* | |

*Figure 3.2* Task attributes

> His mission came with incredible pressure. At stake were the fates of thousands of New Orleans residents and, perhaps, the future role of the military in domestic disasters. At its peak, the military's joint task force had 22,000 military personnel, one of the largest military deployments in the South since troops returned home from the Civil War. No one knew how the contingent would respond when faced with restive residents, but many worried it could set a dangerous precedent. Honore' took pains to treat the residents like civilians, not criminals. He ordered weary police officers to keep their guns pointed down and reminded his troops they were in an American city, not war-torn Iraq. He refused to command his troops to forcibly remove the thousands of residents who refused to evacuate.

These actions regarding the civilians not only paved the way for orderly logistical evacuations but provided a sense of order and calm that reigned in a situation spinning out of control with no leadership. How did he do this? Surely he used his military training and experience, and his decisions reflected the intuitions based on this. It is interesting to hypothesize that his sequence of decisions was not unlike Klein's fire commander who rather than analytically choosing an optimal option from among many, took incremental actions that were the "best" at each step along the way.

The ability to meld experience and expertise effectively means that intuition can be applied to situations where, if more time were available, more analytical methods might be employed. Or intuition can be used to augment existing analysis. In a CNN interview (Fantz, 2011) General Honoré in discussing a possible evacuation of prisoners from New York's Rikers Island in 2011 in response to a coming hurricane said, "Mayor Bloomberg said that it (Irene) wasn't a threat to that area where Rikers is located, so I have to defer to him and the others who made that call. The way the storm has panned out, I can't say that it was a terrible decision. One has to weigh the massive amount of money that it takes to evacuate prisoners and the likelihood that that area will be hit. There wasn't an assessment of the latter (in New Orleans during Katrina), and here (in New York) you apparently had that."

Conversely, the southwest corner of Figure 3.2 indicates that intuition be avoided. Here the decision maker has neither expertise nor experience and what "intuitions" he may have regarding the unfolding event will most likely be more like guesses than System 1 processes that recognize patterns because here there would be not patterns to recognize. The ensuing decisions would be right or wrong with the same accuracy as decisions made by rolling dice or flipping coins.

The northwest and southeast quadrants are both labeled "develop expertise" and "develop experience", respectively. Here, either experience or expertise is well developed but the other is not. We will further discuss methods for doing this below, but in general expertise arises from study and training coupled with hands-on exercises. Experience is gained on the job, where an individual absorbs various seemingly unrelated scenarios, problems, and resolutions day in and day out. Both expertise and experience can be enhanced through gaming, where the games can be simulation exercises such as drills, extended scenario-based role play exercises, computer games constructed to mimic scenarios and situations, or possible applications of virtual reality technologies. While there is some overlap between task experience and domain experience, the difference lies in that task experience involves doing a task in one domain while domain experience involves experience in the domain where the event occurs and may or may not be related to specific tasks.

### *Combining domain and task attributes*

In January 2009 Chesley "Sully" Sullenberger landed a USAirways jet in the Hudson River after a massive flock of Canada geese disabled both of his plane's engines. In an interview with the *Wall Street Journal* (2016), Sullenberger described the sequence of events that involved life and death decisions made in a matter of seconds:

> I reported the damage to air-traffic control, telling them I planned to return to LaGuardia or land at New Jersey's Teterboro Airport. That's when I realized we weren't going to make it. I decided the Hudson River would be our best and only landing option.
>
> Even though I had never done anything like this before, I was confident I could do it. The solution was to have a mental paradigm for solving the emergency: Force calm, fly the plane and set priorities to achieve the landing.
>
> I never even had time to talk to my co-pilot, Jeff Skiles, about how to handle the situation. There would be only 208 seconds from hitting the birds to reaching the water. We collaborated instinctively, with few words.

Although Sullenberger had never landed a plane in a river, in the interview he discussed a childhood incident when his father received a serious cut from a pane of glass. His father remained calm. Sullenberger said, "I had been taught that if you panicked in life, you'd be ineffective and you couldn't help anyone or yourself."

Sullenberger's reaction to the plane event illustrates the importance of melding domain and task intuition: outstanding experience and expertise create an intuitive skill as much as practice creates the muscle memory of an athlete or a dancer. But this alone is not enough. To meet an event's challenges domain skills, including the ability to react quickly and effectively, are needed.

After the geese disabled his engines, Sullenberger's first intuitive response was to head to an airport to land the plane at an airport and realizing that he could not, to attempt to land in the Hudson River. This "airborne pilot's intuition" can be viewed as domain intuition that was informed by his years of flying experience and experiences, such as with his father of remaining calm in a crisis. The steps involved in actually landing the plane in the river drew on his expertise and experience as a pilot – his task intuition. He had never landed a plane on water, but in the interview his description of the actual landing illustrated is his ability as a pilot and his intuitive grasp of the situation and the immediate task confronting him:

> As we came down, Jeff began calling out airspeed and altitude so I could judge the height off the water before pulling up the nose. At 100 feet, traveling at 150 mph – four seconds before touchdown – I began raising the nose.
>
> The rear hit first, then the main body with a jolt and we coasted to a rest. The plane was afloat. The flight attendants got everyone out into the slide rafts or onto the wings, where the temperature was 21 degrees. Less than four minutes later, the rescue began when the first ferry arrived.

Figure 3.3 classifies decisions and intuition as a function of task and domain requirements, that is the requirements defined by the domain, that is the site of the decision, and the task, that defines what the decision maker will do. The four quadrants illustrate the four classes of decisions defined by the task and domain combinations. For each class, we can establish how effectively using intuition can add value to the decision process. By "effectively use," we mean that the decision maker needs extensive domain and task experience and also a high level of task expertise. For lesser levels of these attributes, a decision maker can certainly act intuitively but the outcomes will depend more on chance than System 2 responses developed and informed by experience and expertise.

Achieving good outcomes using intuition in decision making is especially needed for the northeast quadrant in Figure 3.3. Here domain and task requirements are high. Because decisions are complex and time constraints are tight, a decision maker must formulate and implement strategies quickly. This involves developing and implementing one course of action in real time as Klein observed with fireground commanders, or as Kahneman prefers (Kahneman and Klein, 2009) to the extent possible, applying System 2 thinking and algorithmic methods.

As one goes toward the southeast or northwest quadrants, intuition is less needed. For the southeast quadrant, domain requirements are looser and the decision is not immediate, yet the task requirements are high which means the decision maker can better employ System 2 thinking. Here intuition would inform and analytical and algorithmic decision-making processes. For the northwest quadrant, where the decisions are immediate but the task requirements (and hence the impact of the decision maker) are lower, decisions need less intuitive thinking. As intuition involves recognizing and acting on patterns, here the patterns are more easily recognized or are not that complex. Either case better lends itself to System 2 and algorithmic thinking.

In the southwest corner, both the domain and task requirements create lots of slack and reduce the need for intuition in the decision-making process. While intuition has a place, any value that intuitive thinking adds to the decision-making process can be augmented by further data collection and analysis.

Kahneman and Klein quote Simon (1992) as concisely defining what skilled intuition is. "The situation has provided a cue: This cue has given the expert access to information stored in memory, and the information provides the answer. Intuition is nothing more and nothing less than recognition." Kahneman and Klein then define two conditions that must be satisfied for an intuitive judgment to qualify as "skilled": "First, the environment must provide adequately

| *DOMAIN REQUIREMENTS* | | | |
|---|---|---|---|
| | *High* | Low impact, normal, varied decisions that are immediate | Complex, consequential decisions that are immediate and require task expertise |
| | *Low* | Decisions with extended time frames with less task expertise required | Decisions with extended time frames that require task expertise |
| | | *Low* | *High* |
| | | *TASK REQUIREMENTS* | |

*Figure 3.3* Decisions and intuition

valid cues to the nature of the situation. Second, people must have an opportunity to learn the relevant cues." This implies that the environment be one of regularity that gives the decision maker or expert the ability to practice his skill. This is why the combination of both domain and task attributes is so important. By creating opportunities for practice and recognition, the decision maker experiences more cues and hence recognizes more patterns, which enhances skills and quickens response. To do this require both working in the domain and also requires working on the substantive elements associated with the decision problem.

### *Developing intuition*

The decision's domain and the decision maker's expertise and experience are critical in developing how a decision maker can use intuition to more successfully contribute to the decision-making process. Domain experience is a necessary but not sufficient condition for developing overall intuitive decision-making capability. The difference between an athlete and a coach in a sport such as football or basketball illustrates this relationship. The athlete, while playing the sport, becomes intimately familiar with the sport's domain. He also develops task expertise and experience *in his position*, which may allow him to use his intuition to its fullest while playing the sport. This intuition however, often is restricted to his performance at his position as an athlete. The coach, on the other hand, also needs the experience in the domain (as a participant or as an acute observer) but also needs broader experience and expertise in the theory of the game and demands of coaching, which requires looking at a broader picture than just mastering one position. This may be one reason why star athletes, who may successfully apply intuition to their performance on the field, often falter as coaches.

While a decision maker's experience refers to time spent in a domain and on a task, developing expertise has both learning and experiential components, both in actual environments, classroom environments and simulated environments. Klein (McKinsey Quarterly, 2010) discusses the importance of the domain itself on how successfully intuition may be applied. He holds that a decision situation first must be characterized by a certain structure and predictability for intuition to work. If that is not present, applying intuitive thought is illusory. Turbulent environments with low "validity" are not good candidates for intuitive thinking. Naturally, when confronted with a turbulent environment with immediate time requirements, one may need to lean on intuition, but these constraints may mean that the result might be unsatisfactory. Experience in a domain also may define what is "turbulent" – in many sports a novice who observes the game for the first time may find the pace and flow incomprehensibly fast and even random. Yet after more observation, the game "slows down" and what was incomprehensible becomes structured and regular.

Klein also claims feedback also must be present because developing an expert's expertise – in this case the decision maker's – requires feedback on judgments. This again implies environments where similar events occur over and over again. Unfortunately, many business and crisis environments do not have this high "validity," in that the events and the decisions are one-time occurrences. This immediately creates barriers for developing successful intuitive thinking.

Kahneman is even more skeptical, claiming that an expert's intuition only is effective for things they have dealt with repeatedly before. Further, expertise is domain specific, which creates boundary issues where an expert with intuitive success in one domain makes be overconfident about applying it in others. Here, examples would include an orthopedic surgeon applying intuition in diagnosing neurological disorders, or a financial industry analyst picking individual stocks in the entertainment sector. In the McKinsey article, Kahneman also cautions about overconfidence in low validity environments involving elements that one cannot see. He discusses business environments where the actions of competitors are hidden, which may cause using one's intuition to be even less reliable that where making a decision in an environment that is more deterministic. For crisis environments, an analogy would be a situation where there is an opponent, such as in a hostage or conflict situation.

That said, strategies to better develop intuition do exist. Such strategies match individuals and environments such that the decision domain is structured and feedback is possible. Domain design involves both physical and process-based aspects. This may include regularizing architectural and process design. For example, nurses working in hospitals would encounter rooms designed similarly where equipment was also similarly organized, and processes were articulated even to the extent of following protocols. In this regard Kahneman is particularly fond of using checklists.

Developing expertise in both domain and task environments follows traditional educational patterns such as classroom, case and experiential learning, coupled with feedback and exercises. Expertise development can occur in four ways (Klein, 1998):

- Deliberately practicing, setting specific goals, and establishing evaluation criteria;
- Compiling extensive experience banks;
- Getting accurate, timely feedback;
- Reviewing prior experiences to derive new insights and lessons from mistakes.

While traditional methods of classroom and case study can lead to achieving overall task expertise, hands-on scenario-based experiential approaches often are equally effective in developing decision-making expertise in a specific domain as well as enhancing task expertise. Examples of these approaches include: role-playing exercises such as police and fire drills; "war gaming," which may involve testing disaster recovery plans for a scenario-based event; technical devices, such as flight simulators to replicate potential disaster events; video games possibly augmented by virtual reality technologies; and "apprentice-type" experiences where one learns from the experiences and reactions of a veteran in the field.

Technology, data, and information processing and retrieval are germane, as they affect a decision and a decision maker's approach and how much intuitive thought need be applied. Indeed, increases in technology may reduce the need for intuition in decision making because any "intuitive" solution becomes inferior to decisions resulting from applying the technology. For example, consider a driver in her car going from New York to Philadelphia. Before the age of cell phones or other communications devices she would know many routes would be possible although some would be preferred. She would have a mental map of her route. Suppose that she encountered a traffic jam and threatening skies. Based on her "intuition" flooding might be possible too. What should she do?

Without further information, her intuition might cause her to change her route. She might choose a series of roads and highways based on past experiences. Additional information could be obtained from a map. This information might expand the list of alternatives and lessen intuition to some extent, but the decision regarding the final choice of routes would still be intuitive.

Fast forwarding to today, her cell phone and GPS app (e.g., Waze) would provide a route based on crowdsourced information for traffic and weather conditions and give her turn-by-turn instructions. Rather than use her intuition, she would rely on technology and the embedded information within that technology and the verbal interface between the cellphone and driver. The need to use intuition in decision making would disappear.

In the age of big data and artificial intelligence, as more and more data is collected, catalogued, analyzed, and immediately retrieved, our need to use our intuition in decision making may decrease. Whereas today fireground commanders lean on their intuition when ordering their crews to evacuate a building that may collapse, having information from drones and even sensors in the building would enable them to decide more on a data-driven basis than an intuitive basis. Given the ubiquitous nature of data in many domains, data-driven decision making is supplanting decisions that are intuitive yet when analyzed, less effective.

An example relating to consumer behavior appears in McKinsey Quarterly (2010) regarding Duncan Watts, a principal research scientist at Yahoo! Prior to the availability of big data, designers would design web pages based on their intuition regarding what attributes would most attract users. With the ability to conduct many experiments and collect vast amounts of data (often real time) regarding which aspects of web design actually attract the most "clicks," Yahoo! researchers found that intuitions invariably are wrong, and other designs are superior. This reality is repeating itself in many other domains as well and while they may be some role for intuition as we move forward, as more data and information processing capability becomes available, intuition's role in the decision-making process may diminish.

## Conclusion

Intuition in decision making is an example of System 1 behavior, as contrasted with the more analytical System 2 processes that are driven by data and algorithms. Intuitive decision making often is viewed as more "natural" and "human" and may receive more credence that it deserves. Decisions that turn out right often do so more by luck than design and those who make them, especially if they are charismatic and self-assured, often rise to positions of corporate power.

The role of intuition in making decisions for crisis events may be unavoidable, especially when the decisions need be immediate and are make with little available data. The need for an intuitive decision should not be conflated with the preference for intuitive decisions over data-based, analytical decisions. The work Daniel Kahneman and others has shown the pitfalls of relying too heavily on intuition, especially when other options are available.

Intuition itself, while often unexplainable by those exercising it, is a manifestation of recognizing and acting on patterns. This recognition often involves the subconscious processes of collecting and analyzing past information and events and from these results, deciding on future courses of action. Intuition is most useful when data is unavailable and time constraints require immediate action, but even then, the option of reverting to intuitive decision making is not the same as the guarantee that the intuitive decision will be any good.

Klein's work with fireground commanders presents an interesting model for immediate, intuitive decisions because here the decision maker does not analyze many options but rather selects one course of action and tweaks it based on incoming information and results as the event evolves. Recognizing this decision model is useful for training decision makers faced with crisis events because the process of choosing and eliminating and developing options in real time is an element that can inform training, and can also inform processes of processing data from experiences.

Because of the dependence of intuition of the domain and the experience of the decision maker, intuition can be viewed through both domain and task lenses. Perhaps the only combination where intuition has a relatively good chance of being successful (beyond success due to chance) is when a decision maker has both expertise and experience in the task being performed and also experience in the domain in which the decision is being made. These facts should also inform both the selection and the training of those who have decision-making power.

Because of the relationship of intuition to pattern recognition, technology and data can support and even replace intuition. A classic example occurs in chess, where early studies by Simon and others noted the congruence with chess grandmasters' intuitive abilities with their ability to recognize many patterns of various chess configurations. Since these early studies, IBM's Deep Blue program has repeatedly defeated grandmasters, not by intuitive thought but by its ability to rapidly process all the possible decision trees evolving from any chess position presented. Although chess is more structured than many decision situations, advances in data collection, analysis, presentation, and artificial intelligence promise to alter intuition's role for crisis managers. While one may argue that we never will reach a time where every decision can be made algorithmically, as time evolves more and more decisions will fall in this category.

The implications are just as machines created a need for man-machine interfaces to perform manual work, increasingly decision makers will need to hone their skills in using data and algorithms even in immediate decision environments. While future automated pilot technology may not have chosen to land Sully Sullenberger's plane in the Hudson River and then actually done so, the confluence of advances in decision technology and also advances in data reporting from decision domains may significantly alter how we view intuition and decision making in a crisis.

## References


Bluestein, G., (2006) *Army General Recalls Katrina Aftermath*; The Associated Press; Washington Post; www.washingtonpost.com/wp-dyn/content/article/2006/09/07/AR2006090700163.html; (accessed June 29, 2017).

Cholle, F., (2016) What Is Intuition and How do We Use it?; www.psychologytoday.com/blog/the-intuitive-compass/201108/what-is-intuition-and-how-do-we-use-it; (accessed June 29, 2017).

Dane, E., and Pratt, M., (2007) Exploring Intuition and Its Role in Managerial Decision Making; *Academy of Management Review*, Vol. 32, No. 1, 33–54.

Fantz, A., (2011) *A General Talks Storm Lessons Since Katrina, CNN*; www.cnn.com/2011/US/08/28/honore.qanda/; (accessed June 29, 2017).

Federal Emergency Management Agency, (2016) *The Four Phases of Emergency Management*; https://training.fema.gov/emiweb/downloads/is10_unit3.doc; (accessed June 29, 2017).

Hammond, J. S., Keeney, R., L. and Raiffa, H., (1999) *Smart Choices: A Practical Guide to Making Better Decisions*; Boston: Harvard Business School Press.

Kahneman, D., (2003) Maps of Bounded Rationality: A Perspective on Intuitive Judgment and Choice; *Les Prix Nobel. The Nobel Prizes 2002*, Edited by Tore Frängsmyr, [Nobel Foundation]; Stockholm; pp. 449–489.

Kahneman, D. and Klien, G., (2009) Conditions for Intuitive Expertise: A Failure to Disagree; *American Psychologist*, Vol. 64, No. 6, 515–526.

Keeney, R. L., (1992) *Value Focused Thinking*; Cambridge: Harvard University Press.

Klein, G., (1998) *Sources of Power: How People Make Decisions*; Cambridge, MA: MIT Press.

Lacey, M., (2011) Fighting Wildfires With Computers and Intuition; *New York Times*; www.nytimes.com/2011/06/24/us/24wildfires.html?mwrsm=Email&_r=; (accessed June 29, 2017).

Leonhardt, D., (2009) Making Health Care Better; *New York Times Magazine*; (Nov. 3).

McKinsey Quarterly, (2010) *Strategic Decisions: When Can You Trust Your Gut?*; (March).

Merriam-Webster, (2016) Simple Definitions of Intuition; www.merriam-webster.com/dictionary/intuition; (accessed June 29, 2017).

Moynihan, D. P., (2012) *The Response to Hurricane Katrina, IRGC Report "Risk Governance Deficits: An Analysis and Illustration of the Most Common Deficits in Risk Governance"*; http://irgc.org/wp-content/uploads/2012/04/Hurricane_Katrina_full_case_study_web.pdf; (accessed June 29, 2017).

Phillips, J. K., Klein, G. and Sieck, W. R., (2004) Expertise in Judgment and Decision Making; *Blackwell Handbook of Judgment and Decision Making*; Edited by Derek J. Koehler and Nigel Harvey; Malden, MA: Blackwell Publishing; pp. 297–315.

Raiffa, H., (1968) *Decision Analysis: Introductory Lectures on Choices Under Uncertainty*; New York: Random House.

Roberts, S., (2016) Jack Garman, Who Saved Moon Landing, Dies at 72; *The New York Times*; (September 25); p. 29.

Simon, H. A., (1996) *The Sciences of the Artificial* (3rd ed.); Cambridge, MA: MIT Press.

*Wall Street Journal*, (2016) 'Sully' Sullenberger's Serene Texas Home; *Real Estate Section*; (August 30).

# 4

# Business continuity management organizations

## The models of implementation

*Wei Ning Zechariah Wong and Jianping Shi*

### Introduction

The discipline and profession of business continuity management (BCM) emerged strongly over the past decade in response to the volatility of the business environment, increased global competition and the effect of customer choice. These forces are driving organizations in every sector to reinvent themselves and compete on the basis of flexibility, speed and customer responsiveness. The pervasive influence of technology and the concepts of lean management have further revolutionized how organizations conduct their business.

The recognition of the role BCM in corporate governance along with the growing understanding of the need to safeguard interests of key stakeholders has eased its introduction in management activities. While it emerged in the '90s with its root in disaster recovery – a subject which primarily focuses on the recovery of vital technology infrastructure and systems – over the years BCM has transformed the subject from a technological-oriented specialist function into a multidisciplinary vocation and business service.

Though the value of BCM is widely understood, its function is still process-driven, that is, the practice predominantly focuses on the operational side of business continuity in relation to its strategic possibilities. In most cases, practitioners' perspective of BCM focuses on the physical and economic factors such as swift recovery of critical services, information technology (IT), workplace and supply chain continuity. Drivers for such corporate state of mind can be traced to its early developments as a strong technical capability governed by regulatory requirements to ensure reliability in the performance of essential activities that it supports, particularly in industries with systemic impact on the community, notably finance, energy, public agencies and such like.

The BCM discipline is currently in something of a state of flux, with a growing number of managers and practitioners attempting to break new boundaries when implementing business continuity at the corporate level. However, such aspirational effort is bound to have limited effect unless the current challenges of implementing BCM along with its varied levels of integration throughout the organization are established.

As such, this chapter begins with an outline of the management issues when pursuing business continuity in organizations. This is followed by a review of the current state of BCM development based on three types of BCM organizations. Next, it proposes three models of implementation according to the types of BCM organizations and explores their key attributes when incorporating at different levels of the corporate structure. Then, it sets out a progressive approach to BCM implementation – using the three models to define the critical enablers (CEs) for achieving effective implementation, leading to desired successful outcomes (DSOs) at each level. Finally, the chapter ends by suggesting three key factors that need to be adopted in order to realize the value BCM contributes to organizational success.

## Challenges of implementing business continuity management

The universally agreed definition of BCM is a holistic management process that identifies potential threats to an organization and the impacts to business operations those threats, if realized, might cause, and which provides a framework for building organizational resilience with the capability of an effective response that safeguards the interests of its key stakeholders, reputation, brand and value-creating activities (International Organization for Standardization, 2014). Given the all-compassing nature of this definition, it is adopted by the Disaster Recovery Institute and the Business Continuity Institute, which collectively advocate the relevance of BCM to a wide range of activities across all levels of the organization. In essence, the discipline offers two levels of management perspective: on one level it adopts an anticipative approach to managing and underpinning the availability of corporate activities (Barnes, 2001; Norrman & Jansson, 2004; Zsidisin et al., 2005; Engemann & Henderson, 2012), whilst on another level it focuses on stakeholder interests in order to strengthen an organization's position in the marketplace (Sheffi & Rice, 2005; Elliott et al., 2010; Low et al., 2010; Wong & Shi; 2010).

Many organizations predominantly operating in sectors such as finance, manufacturing, utilities and health care, establish the BCM capability to secure the confidence of customers, shareholders and the public. This in turn could strengthen organizational resilience whilst transforming the way business products and services are managed and delivered. Business continuity is one of many critical success factors (CSF) that can be pursued and generated a source of competitive advantage for an organization. In contrast to other factors such as revenue, productivity, cycle time and product/service quality, to establish a case for business continuity as a CSF is particularly challenging for several reasons:

- Return on investment: the implementation of the BCM initiative requires time to integrate into the organizational system of processes. Its return on investment along with its long-term value may only be realized over an extended period of time. Due to an increasingly volatile business climate, the focus of many senior managers has become ever more short term, expecting quick gains for shareholders whilst improving their revenue growth. Against such a backdrop, the justification for business continuity often meets with corporate resistance.
- Support function: unlike "frontline" services and income-generating activities that have direct impact (e.g. financial, operational and reputational) on the organization and its business, business continuity is considered as a support function that provides resilience to the core operations. Ensuring that this support is adequate requires making continual and often invisible incremental improvement to the BCM programme that may be difficult to identify.
- Competing business priorities: organizations have a list of business priorities to support key corporate strategies and objectives. In the absence of BCM leadership, the function

along with its activities are likely to relegate to an administrative role and may encounter management antagonism during resource allocation.
- Management complacency: as resilience level increases, the decreasing frequency of incidents may result in management complacency and diversion of business continuity focus and resources.
- Awareness and commitment: as in most cases when business is in a constant state of availability, business continuity becomes taken for granted and drops out of corporate awareness. This eventually leads to the "built to last" mentality that senior managers may reluctant to commit further to the initiative.
- Corporate mindset: the historical origin of business continuity goes back to the recovery of information technology. Without adequate support, particularly from the senior leadership team, to raise the awareness of BCM as a mainstream management discipline and how it contributes to business success, it will remain predominantly as a technology-driven function.

## Current state of implementation

The implementation of BCM or as an integral part of wider risk management in organizations is recognized as good business practice (Gallagher, 2002; Musgrave & Woodman, 2013; Wong & Shi, 2015). Key motivations for adopting the management discipline are varied, ranging from corporate governance, experience of an actual incident and customer requirements (Musgrave & Woodman, 2013). Though key government policies, regulations and business-driven objectives have each had an influence on the creation of the conditions in which BCM has emerged and is gaining ground, the level of implementation is largely depended on how the organizations perceive the role of BCM in business management. According to Wong (2010), there are three types of BCM organizations, namely, process organizations (POs), business continuity management organizations (BCMOs) and strategic resilient organizations (SROs), which are defined by the extent BCM is integrated with corporate activities.

POs predominantly adopt BCM at service level. The primary focus of implementation is on planning to safeguard the continuity of the organization's critical products and services (e.g. disaster recovery, business resumption and workplace recovery). POs are characterised by the emphasis on planning rather than management since plans and procedures, that are process driven and time bound, are developed according to specific recovery requirements. According to Smith (2003) "planning" is deliberate since the process implies a duration to completion whilst "management" entails a dynamic, proactive and ongoing process. The responsibility for implementing and maintaining BCM primarily lies with process specialists and IT/service functions (Swartz et al., 2003; Snedaker & Rima, 2014).

BCMOs, on the other hand, adopts the view that BCM is a management programme that provides resilience to safeguard the organization's assets (Higgins et al., 2018). It forms a subset of enterprise-wide risk management (Sheffi, 2009). In this level of implementation, BCM is a series of planned phases (Barnes, 2001; McManus & Carr, 2001; Elliott et al., 2010; Higgins et al., 2018) that encapsulate the major activities of development, management and maintenance of resilience capability. It underpins the oversight capabilities that ensure controls are in place to protect key assets and earning capacity. According to Rössing (2007), being a subset of all organizational processes and controls BCM requires a well-defined set of criteria for measuring success or failure, and for establishing good corporate governance. The BCM programme lead is usually a director or a manager while a board member assumes the ownership of the programme (O'Hehir, 2007).

In SROs, BCM as a value-added discipline is incorporated in board-level activities. The principles of resilience are adopted to support strategy formulation and executive decision-making process. As stated by Sheffi and Rice (2005), building a resilient enterprise should be a strategic initiative that changes how an organization operates and increases its competitiveness. In this level of implementation, business continuity is adopted as part of an organization's long-term planning to optimize management capability in dealing with uncertainty. For instance, it challenges business assumptions about threats and uncertainties by introducing "what-ifs" and uses probable scenarios in the strategic management process, with particular emphasis on corporate survival (Wong & Shi, 2015). It also reviews the life cycle of a strategy by identifying and assessing vulnerability by means of the business impact analysis methodology. Such an approach helps to determine various dynamics that could threaten strategy formulation and implementation whilst identifying issues that require management attention. According to Wong (2010), the central tenet of SROs lies in the ability to generate competitive advantage through the incorporation of business continuity in strategic planning. As such, it is an enabler that minimize vulnerability in management capability whilst providing greater confidence in business decisions and strategies, thereby generating superior performance. Due to its long-term focus, BCM has become an integral part of board-level activities and requires the ongoing effort of the senior leadership team to ensure that it continues to add value to management success.

This taxonomy provides two dimensions of BCM, namely, its *role* and *implementation* in organizations. First, it offers the management interpretation of business continuity as a discipline and how it supports existing activities. Second, it highlights the levels of BCM integration in the corporate structure, which in turn reflects the relationship between the organization's perception of BCM and its implementation in activities contributing to business performance.

Though there will not be a single approach that is "ideal" for all organizations, we believe that for business continuity to become a CSF it needs to form an integral part of strategic planning. A common developmental sequence is when an organization first embarks on the BCM initiative, it is one which starts with a specialist operational function (POs) and then progresses toward a corporate-level activity (SROs) that supports strategy formulation and implementation.

This "incremental" approach is highly attractive to managers, practitioners and others who strive to position BCM as a mainstream discipline that sits alongside board-level planning, which directly contributes to strategic initiatives and business performance of the organization. This, however, requires strong BCM leadership and the support of the senior management team.

Due to the dynamics of individual organizations, the most appropriate approach is one that aligns BCM with business priorities. If organizations are able to adopt a fresh perspective of BCM by opening its boundaries, that is, role and purpose, rather than confining it to the narrow focus on information technologies and workplace recovery, they have a higher possibility of transforming a recovery-focused service into a systemic process of strategic nature.

In following discussion about BCM integration, we propose three models of implementation and describe their individual characteristics along with the challenges when introducing the discipline at each level of the organizational structure. We enlist a number of critical enablers (CEs) that could influence the desired success outcomes (DSOs) of each model based upon the analysis of various research articles and from our own consultation projects. Though every organization is unique in context and differs in the state of development, it is important to adequately address these enablers to establish business continuity as a CSF as well as to elevate the discipline as an organization-wide initiative. In essence, these suggested CEs serve as a "blueprint" for design possibilities that transforms BCM from a process-centric approach to a board-level activity with strategic focus.

It is important to note that designing and implementing business continuity at different levels is a process in its own right. Progressing to a next level of implementation does not mean giving up the essential features or activities of the previous level, but rather enhancing to and integrating new capabilities with those already functioning.

## Levels of integration

### *Process-centric model*

The implementation of the process-centric model is primarily piecemeal and confines to particular services – predominantly client-facing and income-generating activities. For most organizations BCM serves as a recovery activity that can be employed to provide greater confidence that the outputs of processes and services can be delivered in the face of risks (Gibb & Buchanan, 2006). This level of implementation predominantly deals with the delivery aspect of business. The ability to manage the continuity of key services and operations has become the lifeblood of business success. This is an ongoing challenge for every business since swift recovery from any type of interruption, whether natural or man-made, is critical to a company's survival (Cerullo & Cerullo, 2004; Borodziez, 2005). Being an offshoot of ITDR (information technology disaster recovery), the fundamental aim of this level of implementation is to build resilience in critical processes and systems to ensure that the organization is capable to withstand the undesired impact of an incident – by initiating comprehensive disaster recovery plans and procedures to re-establish the performance of the process or service. The principles of business continuity are embedded in processes designed to deliver value to customers. Staff responsible for business continuity are predominantly technologists and process specialists who possess specific skills and knowledge in their areas of expertise.

While process-centric approach is the basic model to introducing business continuity to key processes along with the benefits such as fostering specialization, resource consolidation, and cost effectiveness, it can also serve as a barrier to further BCM as a mainstream function. Since business continuity is implemented and managed at local level, corporate learning in designs and management of the discipline emerged from specialist groups and expertise is not widely shared across the organization, which could result in "reinventing the wheel" and incur additional resources, time and effort.

Creating a knowledge-rich setting for generating new ideas and continuous improvement plays an essential part of BCM. As discussed earlier, this model of implementation contributes to greater resilience of key processes; however, the lack of synergies between various teams coupled with the absence of a far-sighted view (from senior managers) fail to generate the subject beyond its current role. From a management point of view, adopting BCM at the process level confines the discipline as a specialist activity with operational focus rather than recognizing its potential as a "critical success factor," a management tool that could help to generate opportunities to maximize superior business performance. Though process-centric model is often the start of an attempt to introduce business continuity in organizations, senior leaders should recognize the discipline as a fully fledged management programme in order for the organization to align with internal and external forces of change. As Sheffi and Rice (2005) point out that those that are responsive will have the opportunity to gain market share in competitive environments as well as underpin their leadership position in areas they already dominate.

## *Suggested tactics of implementation*

To enable POs to be first emerged, the organizations need to recognize the role business continuity as a loss mitigation process that supports the continuation of operations to a state of business as usual following a disruption. In essence, it seeks to reduce impact and restore critical activities by ensuring alternative business continuity capability is available during an incident (Hiles, 2007). The CEs that are necessary to implement the process-centric model include:

- BCM skills and knowledge: according to Burtle (2007), staff need to have the right set of abilities, skills and knowledge to undertake in the necessary tasks in the BCM programme as well as under difficult conditions. As stipulated in the international standard, ISO 22301 (2014), when embarking on BCM the organization is required to determine the necessary competence of individuals on the basis of appropriate education, training, and experience. The collection of staff's managerial competencies and knowledge have a significant impact on how BCM activities are planned, conducted and managed, which in turn influence the effectiveness of the developed plans and processes.
- Defined user requirements: organizations are composed of a wide range of processes to achieve their intended purpose. Processes consist of sets of activities which are designed to deliver value to customers (Gibb & Buchanan, 2006). In order to design an appropriate and fit-for-purpose BCM strategy key business requirements should be to be clearly defined. Successful BCM addresses these requirements (determined by business impact analysis) by establishing a shared knowledge with the process owners; and using this information to formulate business continuity responses and plans (Naujoks, 2002; Sikdar, 2011).
- Recovery resources: this critical enabler has a major influence on the design and selection of business continuity strategy options (Wong & Shi, 2015), which is based on the availability and adequacy of resources. It dictates the recovery capability in terms of speed and duration of recovery. Resource requirements should be addressed throughout the life cycle of incident. As stated by Gibb and Buchanan (2006), it is essential to determine the required resources to achieve a minimum level of continuity in order to enable the full recovery of an incident.
- Controls: this refers to the establishment of a range of validation processes to assess the adequacy of staff's BCM competencies along with their plans and procedures. Review mechanisms are also required to ensure that the change management component is established in the process-centric model to maintain the efficacy of arrangements and to comply with the corporate governance, thereby meeting business and relevant regulatory requirements.
- Management support: though the responsibility of BCM at the service level is assumed by process managers, it requires executive support to ensure the discipline effectively integrated in key processes. As Gallagher (2003) notes, the knowledge of senior executives about business continuity can affect the status of the activity within their organizations. As such, it is important to present how BCM can add value to business performance through organizational resilience.

Though process-centric model is concerned with maintaining continuity of key products and services, that is, optimising operational availability, it seeks to achieve a number of desired successful outcomes (DSOs):

- Credible responses: the establishment of appropriate business continuity responses coupled with adequate controls enable the affected products and services to effectively recover within the required timescale. These responses collectively establish the capability to maintain continuity whilst minimizing the duration of a disruption and its impact to business; this is also extended to key suppliers that contribute to the organization's goals and strategies (including business continuity objectives) (Kildow, 2011), thereby safeguarding organizational performance.

- Increased productivity: the ability to achieve business continuity reduces downtime and associated cost of alternative work arrangements; this in turn improves staff productivity and consumer confidence. This also increases reliability of production and service delivery which could underpin corporate stance and secure future opportunities in the marketplace. According to Krell (2006), business benefits of effective BCM include retaining customers following an incident as well as building staff morale through successful management of an incident.
- Proactive approach: the implementation of BCM at process level enables the discipline to form as an integral part of day-to-day activities in key products and services. With its defined whole life cycle framework (see examples such as ISO 22301 and Good Practice Guidelines), it is capable of determining critical requirements as well as identifying threats and impacts to those requirements, which then devises targeted risk controls and business continuity strategies to address delivery issues.

## *Programme-centric model*

In contrast to the process-centric approach, this level of implementation adopts BCM as an independent function or as an integral part of the enterprise risk management. According to Sheffi (2009), business continuity is the recovery component of risk management. This is an enterprise-wide programme attempts to consolidate a BCM process across all levels within the organization, and focuses not only on specific functions or processes, but also co-ordinates and consolidates all business continuity activities. Due to its corporate-wide nature, the programme implementation should be led by a member of the senior leadership team (Gibb & Buchanan, 2006; Burtle, 2007). As such, dedicated resources could be readily dispensed to ensure that the programme achieved its objectives.

Typical to this model is the establishment of a framework that sets out a common business continuity approach that is usually adopted at the project-centric level. This helps to ensure that the planning is consistently managed across the organization – examples of guidelines that support the development of such framework include ISO 22301 – Business Continuity Management System (International Organization for Standardization, 2014) and Good Practice Guidelines (Higgins et al., 2018). Being a mainstream programme, BCM forms an essential part of an organization's overall approach to governance compliance. It helps organizations assess their business continuity risks, develop appropriate responses, and address management requirements as well as regulations imposed by authorities.

Though programme-centric model enables the principles of BCM to be embedded in the organization, it poses a number of underlying challenges which could affect its effective integration within the corporate structure. First, as BCM grows in terms of profile and influence, the ownership of the programme and where it should reside within the organization become management issues for the senior leadership team. This in turn could result in "identity crisis" for BCM along with its function in business activities. As mentioned by McCrackan (2005), poor positioning of business continuity within the organization can result significant impact to corporate success.

Second, like any major programmes in the organization, there are drivers to introduce a series of improvements to underpin the management effectiveness of the discipline, which could lead to the creation of overly "engineered" processes. A potential detrimental outcome is a more robust and unwieldly programme than its original intent. Third, another challenge to this model is being one of many functions within the organization, key individuals responsible for key programmes compete with a broad spectrum of business and management disciplines in terms of priorities and resources. Conflicts inevitably become an additional source of pressure as key individuals strive to preserve their areas of influence. This could inadvertently affect investment in the BCM programme since it is neither a client-facing function nor made up of income-generating activities.

### *Suggested tactics of implementation*

The programme-centric model adopts an organization-wide approach of implementing BCM. The BCM programme provides ongoing management and governance to ensure that functional level business continuity activities are conducted and implemented in a co-ordinated and consistent manner in order to achieve the objectives stipulated in the organization's BCM policy. A number of CEs are required to establish a sustainable BCM programme as part of the corporate governance.

- Critical interdependencies: a holistic approach should be adopted when implementing the programme-centric model. Organizational functions and their dependencies (internal and external) that directly support or contribute to business strategies and goals should fall within the scope of the BCM programme. This determines which business functions must be restored in the order of priority (Elliott et al., 2010; Snedaker & Rima, 2014); and enables the BCM programme to establish the necessary resilience in value-creating processes and to safeguard the organization's market position during an incident.
- Staff support: this enabler entails staff awareness and commitment to the effectiveness of the organization's BCM capability. As stated by Morwood (1998), the effectiveness of business continuity plan is highly dependent upon on staff knowledge about the plan and assigned activities. Though board-level leadership is critical to spearhead the BCM initiative across the organization, it is the collective staff effort that ensures BCM is adequately implemented and integrated as part of day-to-day business as usual activities. In order to strengthen ongoing acceptance and support for the BCM programme, briefings and training should be conducted at planned intervals. According to Wilson and Hash (2003), to achieve a successful programme an awareness and training program is crucial and should focus on the organization's entire population.
- Resource allocation: as stipulated in ISO 22301 (2014), appropriate resources should be determined and assigned for the management of the BCM activities. The presence of resource recovery strategy is a precondition of developing the BCM capability (Wong & Shi, 2015). Apart from allocating resources to address strategy and response formulation, the availability of critical knowledge and skills, budget and external support are also required to maintain and achieve the objectives of the BCM programme.
- Team capability: the selection and formation of the BCM central team is one of the essential enablers for a successful BCM programme. It should comprise a diverse group of expertise who can contribute to the management effectiveness of the programme. The experience and competence of those responsible for the BCM programme are reflected in the organization's ability to recover during an incident. As such, it is advised that

organizations focus on the competence levels of staff in order that they can adequately apply the necessary skills and knowledge (Hillson, 2001). Such attributes also shape the continual improvement of the programme in the long term.

- Management commitment: though recognized as a mainstream programme, the corporate longevity of the BCM programme requires board-level commitment and support in terms of time, budget and resources. This requires the recognition of the ongoing role and value the discipline add to organizational processes. One crucial element that reflects management attitude towards BCM is the appointment of a champion, who assumes BCM leadership of the programme and leads the establishment of business continuity as a management priority within the organization. As mentioned by Elliott et al. (2010), to incorporate BCM as a priority includes the involvement of senior board members to provide symbolic support to effect an organizational cultural change.

The intent of an established programme-centric model is to provide an ongoing management and improvement of BCM activities to support the organization's changing business requirements. Along with enterprise risk management and other cognate disciplines, this corporate-wide initiative underpins the organization's resilience capability. The DSOs of an effective implementation include:

- Good management practice: BCM enables the senior leadership team to fulfil their organizational responsibilities of safeguarding assets, earning capacity and business confidence. According to Gallagher (2003), good management puts BCM as a priority and it forms an integral part of good corporate governance. In addition, the planning process of the BCM programme supports the compliance with legal, regulatory and governance (Higgins et al., 2018; Engemann & Henderson, 2012).
- Cross-collaborative approach: the programme-centric model firmly establishes a cross-disciplinary effort to managing the organization's BCM capability. The programme of activities involves the close collaboration between a broad spectrum of management and technical disciplines. According to Fasolis et al. (2013), organizations become more competitive when using collective intelligence to acquire knowledge to create collective solutions for BCM. This holistic effort ensures that key threats are identified and calls for shared ownership of strategies to address business challenges, thereby preserving the well-being of the organization and its stakeholders.
- Mainstream management programme: as an organization-wide initiative endorsed by the senior leadership team, BCM becomes an embedded discipline alongside risk management, health and safety, emergency and security. This ensures business continuity is adopted seriously and is part of staff awareness that the resilience-based approach should remain firmly within the business line. Being an integral part of the programme-centric model, structured staff awareness and training campaigns are developed to maintain the ongoing interest and capability of general staff along with those with roles in the BCM programme. Furthermore, planned regimes such as maintenance, plan review or audit and testing all present opportunities to raise awareness of BCM (Hiles, 2007) and could hone the skills of those with BCM responsibilities.
- Management of uninsurable risks: as defined in the international standard, ISO 22301 (2014), BCM safeguards the interests of its key stakeholders, reputation, brand and value-creating activities. The programme-centric emphasis creates the framework to underpin the organization's resilience capability to protect its "intrinsic" value, namely, business performance, stakeholder confidence and statutory compliance, during unexpected

events. Though often recognized as a process-driven discipline to safeguard the continuity of physical assets, this model adopts a wider perspective to minimize impact and loss to intangible assets – through its strategic-level plans and procedures (Higgins et al., 2018).

- Clearly defined role and responsibilities: as mentioned by Snedaker and Rima (2014), a range of expertise in several areas are required in business continuity and disaster recovery planning. The programme approach provides a clear definition of roles, responsibilities and autonomies of individuals, which collectively form the BCM team of the programme. Tasks pertaining to programme management as well as incident management are adequately assigned to appropriate managerial and operational individuals based on the required levels of business and technical expertise.
- Continual improvement: the introduction of review and continual improvement – in accordance with ISO 22301 – fosters the commitment to maintain an ongoing effectiveness of the BCM capability. Being a proactive management discipline, BCM strives to align with the changing dynamics of the organization. This forward-looking driver enables the incorporation of new management concepts into the programme, thereby aligning to business requirements and strategies. Continual improvement should be established for constant change, flexibility, and always striving to achieve best practice in order to minimize vulnerability to organizations (Porter, 1996).
- Established supply chain continuity management programme (SCCM): supply chain management covers a full range of activities concerned with the direct and/or indirect provisions and supports to the organization's key products and services. Due to the vulnerability of supply chains, it is important to integrate this network of businesses in all aspects of risk management and business continuity (Kildow, 2011). Being a DSO of the programme-centric model, an established SCCM determines and adequately addresses those critical factors pertaining to supply chain (including value chain) which contribute to the organization's business performance. It also sets out the requirements to ensure suppliers actively seek out their continuity risks in order to minimize impact to product or service delivery. As mentioned by Norrman and Jansson (2004), apart from the inward focus of risk and business continuity on the host organization's process networks, emphasis should also extend to suppliers and their networks in the management of risk and business continuity as well as encouraging them to implement a holistic approach.

## *Strategic resilient model*

The implementation of the BCM initiative reaches the board-level level when key aspects of the process- and programme-centric models are synthesized with corporate planning. The central tenet of strategic resilient model is to strengthen the organization's strategic management capability. It is essentially built on two levels. At the first level, business continuity is firmly established at process and programme levels in order to create the desired setting, namely, optimized service/product availability and business resilience, for the formulation and implementation of strategies. At the second level, it integrates business continuity in the organization's strategic planning process. Principal activities used in BCM, such as impact analysis and desktop exercise, are adopted to evaluate the criticality of a given strategic option – in terms of time and impact of implementation – in simulated scenarios. Such an approach helps to uncover management issues not previously considered, which in turn improves the quality of planning.

Organizations that implement strategic resilient model tend to encounter the following challenges when introducing business continuity in board-level planning. First, amongst board members the knowledge of BCM is perceived as a technical discipline along with its specialist nature limits the role business continuity plays in strategic management. Such an implicit assumption is due to the combined assumptions, beliefs, values and patterns of behaviour that are shared by members of an organization (Higgins et al., 2018) and created the corporate mindset in which how tasks are designed and managed. As Talke (2007) states the corporate mindset is an inherent element of a firm's disposition towards innovating activities. Many senior leaders have a mindset developed for different times, they see no reason to change the one that has served them well so far (Grayson et al., 2008). In the absence of recognizing its systemic characteristics as a tool that supports the formulation of strategies and key decisions, BCM remains predominantly as a process-driven activity.

Second, the missing link between BCM and strategic planning inhibits the subject from taking a foothold at board level. This is due to the lack of active participation amongst members in the senior leadership team. The supervisory responsibilities for BCM are mainly assigned to a member of middle management. Though a survey conducted by Continuity Insights and KPMG (2014) shows 71.2% of the participating organizations have some form of steering committee to support the organization's business continuity activities, their primary focus is on the day-to-day aspects of planning, implementation and management of the BCM programme – *programme-centric model*. Majority of those responsible for the programme assume either the role of a director or a manager, who reports to a C-level executive. Though the ultimate responsibility resides with a member of the senior leadership team and who also acts as the figurehead for BCM, the individual is not necessarily involved in the management of the programme (as the results have shown). In such instance, the knowledge and value of the BCM remains grounded at programme-level.

## *Suggested tactics of implementation*

At this level business continuity pervades across the organization as a mainstream initiative that supports board-level activities. Building on the successes achieved at process and programme levels, three crucial enablers are required for the implementation of strategic resilient model.

- Management appreciation: as discussed earlier in this chapter, the main challenges of recognizing BCM as a mainstream activity and its role within the organization are rooted on its historical origin as well as the difficulty of determining the incremental improvement and benefits to business. These factors coupled with the organization's current context shape executive management's perception of its corporate value, which in turn affects the investment decision in the discipline. As such, from the outset, the benefits and objectives of BCM need to be communicated to staff (Gibb & Buchanan, 2006; Hamilton, 2007; International Organization for Standardization, 2014; Wong & Shi, 2015); in this case, senior executives at board level.
- Board-level champion: this enabler helps to instil business continuity amongst members of the senior leadership team, which in turn galvanizes the support for the strategic resilient model. To maintain an ongoing appreciation of BCM at board level, a member of the senior leadership team with adequate subject knowledge should be nominated. As Wong and Shi (2015) puts it, the individual should have sufficient influence to engender support for the BCM team and programme as well as to overcome the organizational obstacles

for the initiative. In essence, this individual assumes two roles, namely, to advocate the relevance of BCM in long-range planning, and to lead and directly participate in the organization's BCM initiative.

- Management leadership: this enabler requires board-level leadership to drive the BCM initiative as an integral part of the organization's long-term success. As stated by Higgins et al. (2018), top management should demonstrate positive leadership with respect to BCM in the organization. Such an approach ensures that business continuity has a higher possibility of transforming into a proactive management activity that contributes to business excellence. Though staff commitment has been secured for the BCM programme, the vision and ongoing steer from the senior leadership team has a significant influence on its status across the organization.

In this level of integration, BCM is recognized as a systemic approach that could be flexibly adapted to address management challenges faced by the leadership team – from the formulation of long-term strategies to the consolidation of market position.

- Enhanced reputation and market position: ongoing leadership and commitment to the BCM initiative reflects good business management. Policies and systems designed at board level encapsulate resilience concepts, which is one of fundamental approaches to strengthening the organization's corporate governance. In time of an incident, value-creating assets, notably brand and reputation, are safeguarded whilst undesired impact to the interests of key stakeholders are effectively mitigated.
- Strong management capability: this DSO refers to the establishment of crisis leadership during an incident. As quoted by Lucero et al. (2009), crisis leadership comprises five critical tasks, namely, sense-making of the crisis, making decisions to deal with the crisis, framing and making meaning of the crisis to stakeholders, terminating the crisis to restore normalcy to the organization, and steering the organization to learn from the crisis (Boin et al., 2005). Such essential activities demonstrate management competence of the senior leadership team – the ability to make timely decisions and actions to galvanize an effective recovery effort to business normality. Effective leadership has direct impact on organizational value during an incident, that is, to recover business faster and more effectively, thereby reinforcing corporate position in the marketplace (Garcia, 2006).
- Effective strategy planning: principles of BCM are adeptly applied in different aspects of strategic management. During the process of planning, underlying assumptions are challenged with resilience criteria – such as the availability and/or vulnerability of resources to implement a given strategy, which helps to foster a creative approach to problem solving. According to Wong and Shi (2015), the incorporation of the concept of "continuity" improves the quality of planning and ensures the devised strategies are not incapacitated by unforeseen circumstances.
- Competitive advantage: crisis response, being an integral part of BCM, is an essential activity during an incident. According to Garcia (2006), effective crisis response is a competitive advantage whilst an ineffective crisis response is detrimental to the business and could jeopardise an organization's existence. Though minimizing downtime, securing market confidence and winning future opportunities are advantages over competitors, it is the integration of business continuity principles in board-level planning helps to generate these superior performances. As Sheffi and Rice (2005) put it, resilience can be achieved by increased flexibility; this in turn can create competitive advantage in day-to-day activities, that is, arrangements and options that are adaptable to the situation at hand.

*Table 4.1* Features of the three BCM models

| *Features* | *Types of business continuity management models* | | |
|---|---|---|---|
| | *Process* | *Programme* | *Strategic Resilient* |
| Main characteristics | • Driven by product and services<br>• Process and procedure oriented<br>• Process-level ownership<br>• Ad-hoc implementation<br>• Integral part of products and services<br>• Procedural and systematic | • Driven by corporate governance<br>• Programme oriented<br>• Organization-wide ownership<br>• Holistic implementation<br>• Integral part of Enterprise Risk Management (or as a separate initiative)<br>• Oversight and compliance | • Driven by long-term competitiveness and goals<br>• Strategic oriented<br>• Board-level ownership<br>• Dynamic and wide-ranging<br>• Management instrument to aid board-level planning<br>• Planning and review |
| Challenges | • Functional isolation<br>• Knowledge confinement<br>• Lack of synergy<br>• Barrier to collaboration | • Ownership issue<br>• Complex and multi-layered programme and process<br>• Conflicts of priorities and resources | • Board-level mindset and ownership<br>• Lack of active senior participation |
| Enablers | • BCM skills and knowledge<br>• Defined user requirements<br>• Recovery resources<br>• Controls<br>• Management support | • Critical interdependencies<br>• Staff support<br>• Resource allocation<br>• Team capability<br>• Management commitment | • Management appreciation<br>• Board-level champion<br>• Management leadership |
| Desired outcomes | • Credible responses<br>• Increased productivity<br>• Proactive approach | • Good management practice<br>• Cross-collaborative approach<br>• Mainstream management programme<br>• Management of uninsurable risks<br>• Clearly defined role and responsibilities<br>• Continual improvement<br>• Established supply chain continuity management programme | • Enhanced reputation and market position<br>• Strong management capability<br>• Effective strategy planning<br>• Competitive advantage |

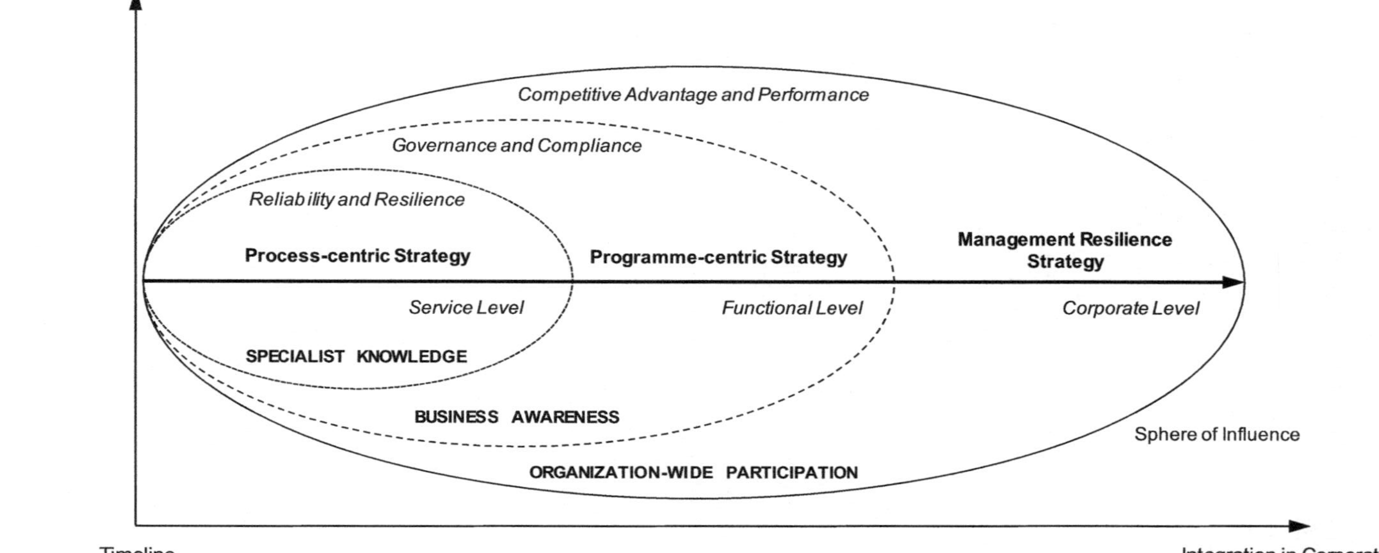
BCM Awareness & Participation
Competitive Advantage and Performance
Governance and Compliance
Reliability and Resilience
Process-centric Strategy
Programme-centric Strategy
Management Resilience Strategy
Service Level
Functional Level
Corporate Level
SPECIALIST KNOWLEDGE
BUSINESS AWARENESS
Sphere of Influence
ORGANIZATION-WIDE PARTICIPATION
Timeline
Integration in Corporate Structure

*Figure 4.1* Incremental development of BCM

## Conclusions

This chapter has set out to provide a snapshot of the types of BCM organizations and to propose three implementation models – according to the level of integration in organizational activities. It then explored the main characteristics of the individual models and how critical enablers (CEs) and desired successful outcomes (DSOs) of each model can help to set the pace to elevate the BCM initiative up the management structure. In order to fully recognize business continuity as an integral part of organizational activities the three models need to be viewed as an incremental approach and systemically established across all levels of the organization.

Designing and implementing BCM requires balancing varied and often conflicting priorities. As discussed at the beginning of this chapter, establishing business continuity as a CSF requires overcoming a series of challenges. This would also require an adequate understanding of the management issues described in each model of implementation along with the establishment of the appropriate enablers to realize the DSOs bring to business. Whilst every organization differs in management culture and context, we outline three factors that could help to incrementally integrate the models in the corporate structure.

### *Leadership*

The objective to secure future business success is an ongoing priority for every organization. However, current business drivers, whether external or internal, can affect how the organization plans and conducts its activities. In times of uncertainty along with growing emphasis on sustainable growth, seeking new dynamics in planning and managing corporate performance will continue to dominate board-level agenda. Within organizations, BCM must exert greater influence in the business and management arena. Given its emphasis in optimising service availability at the process level, it is important for senior business managers to take advantage of its role in bringing positive changes to business – using appropriate DSOs to further the discipline in other parts of the organization. This, however, would require the creation of conditions in which business continuity can be effectively introduced and integrated into mainstream activities.

### *Business influence*

The climate for the acceptance of BCM and the opportunities for its influence in the organization are often based on its perceived benefits in safeguarding business performance. As a business discipline, BCM is concerned with underpinning operation and management resilience through assimilating its principles across the corporate structure. This would require an intimate knowledge on how it can best shape the way organizational activities are conducted. For instance, in the planning and development phase BCM can be adopted to assess threats and impacts in the product/service life cycle, which in turn informs decisions about potential resilience strategies in key processes. Such an influence enables a greater role the discipline contributes to organizational success.

### *Role and purpose*

BCM should be viewed as a multi-disciplinary activity which entails the implementation of a generic range of management and technical skills across traditional, functional and professional spheres within the organization. Though there is a widely recognized definition available to define its role, it is ultimately for the organization which adopts the BCM initiative to decide the function and objectives according to its business context. As such, it is useful to consider four interrelating factors prior to the design and implementation of BCM. This in turn will sufficiently define what its *role* and *purpose* are. First, the potential benefits the discipline brings the existing processes – this determines the level of commitment and support for BCM. Second, the ownership and implementation responsibilities – this defines the management emphasis of BCM along with the required skills for implementation. Third, the structure of BCM – this refers to how BCM is adopted, that is, piecemeal versus holistic, within the organization. Finally, the motivations of BCM – this defines the focus of intent: operational versus board-level priorities.

To improve resilience, organizations will need to adopt a step change in management thinking and view BCM as an enabler that helps to maximize opportunities and performance. Such a shift in mindset would need to be embraced by members of the senior leadership team as well as local-level managers and staff who assume the design and implementation responsibilities for BCM. Depending on the state of BCM development in an organization, the three models discussed in this chapter intend to set the foundation of embedding the principles of BCM in a defined and incremental modus operandi. Once having gained the momentum of implementation, further commitment and effort are necessary to establish BCM as a day-to-day business as usual activities across all levels of the organization. We argued that an adaptable framework aligned to business requirements should be used in the design of BCM model as opposed to a standardised rigid approach. Such an approach ensures BCM remains relevant according to the corporate context and has a higher chance of adding value to key business areas whilst strengthening organizational capability during an unexpected scenario.

## References

Barnes, J. C. (2001), A *Guide to Business Continuity Planning*, John Wiley & Sons Ltd, Chichester.

Boin, A., Hart, P., Stern, E. and Sundelius, B. (2005), *The Politics of Crisis Management: Public Leadership Under Pressure*, Cambridge University Press, Cambridge.

Borodzicz, E. (2005), *Risk, Crisis and Security Management*, Wiley, Chichester.

Burtles, J. (2007), *Principles and Practice of Business Continuity: Tools and Techniques*, Rothstein Associates Inc., Brookfield, CT.

Cerullo, V. and Cerullo, M. J. (2004), "Business continuity planning: A comprehensive approach", *Information Systems Management*, *21*(3), pp. 70–78.

Continuity Insights and KPMG (2014), *The 2013–2014 Continuity Insights and KPMG LLP Global Business Continuity Management (BCM) Program Benchmarking Study*, US, available at: https://abm-website-assets.s3.amazonaws.com/continuityinsights.com/s3fs-public/newsletter-ads/Final Results_CI-KPMG2013-2014.pdf [accessed 10 October 2016].

Elliott, D., Swartz, E. and Herbane, B. (2010), *Business Continuity Management: A Crisis Management Approach*, 2nd edition, Routledge, London.

Engemann, K. and Henderson, D. M. (2012), *Business Continuity and Risk Management: Essentials of Organizational Resilience*, Rothstein Associates Inc., Brookfield, CT.

Fasolis, E., Vassalos, V. and Kokkinaki, A. I. (2013), Designing and developing a business continuity plan based on collective intelligence, in Douligeris, C., Polemi, N., Karantjias, A. and Lamersdorf, W. (Eds), *Collaborative, Trusted and Privacy-Aware e/m-Services: 12th IFIP WG 6.11 Conference on e-Business, e-Services, and e-Society, I3E 2013, Athens, Greece, April 25–26, 2013, Proceedings*, Springer, Heidelberg, pp. 278–285.

Gallagher, M. (2003), *Business Continuity Management: How to Protect Your Company From Danger*, Financial Times and Prentice Hall, London.

Garcia, F.H. (2006), "Effective leadership response to crisis", *Strategy & Leadership*, *34*(1), pp. 4–10.

Gibb, F. and Buchanan, S. (2006), "A framework for business continuity management", *International Journal of Information Management*, *26*(2), pp. 128–141.

Grayson, D., Jin, Z., Lemon, M., Rodriguez, M.A., Slaughter, S. and Tay, S. (2008), *A New Mindset for Corporate Responsibility*, British Telecommunications Plc and Cisco Systems, UK, available at: https://dspace.lib.cranfield.ac.uk/bitstream/1826/4161/1/A_new_mindset_for_corporate_sustainability.pdf [accessed 10 October 2016].

Hamilton, D.C. (2007), "Multilateral continuity planning", in Hiles, A. (Ed), *The Definitive Handbook of Business Continuity Management*, John Wiley & Sons Ltd, Chichester, pp. 59–71.

Higgins, D., Grimes, L. and Greenish, A. (Eds) (2018), *Good Practice Guidelines 2018 Global Edition: A Guide to Global Good Practice in Business Continuity*, Business Continuity Institute, Caversham, UK.

Hiles, A. (2007), "An introduction to business continuity planning", in Hiles, A. (Ed), *The Definitive Handbook of Business Continuity Management*, John Wiley & Sons Ltd, Chichester, pp. xxiii–xxvii.

Hillson, D. (2001), "Benchmarking organizational project management capability", *Proceedings of the 32nd Annual Project Management Institute 2001 Seminars and Symposium*, Project Management Institute, Newtown Square, PA.

International Organization for Standardization (ISO) (2014), *22301:2014, Societal Security – Business Continuity Management Systems – Requirements*. British Standards Institute, London.

Kildow, B.A. (2011), *Supply Chain Management: Guide to Business Continuity*, AMACOM, New York.

Krell, E. (2006), *Management Accounting Guidelines: Business Continuity Management*, Society of Management Accountants of Canada (CMA), Canada, available at: www.cimaglobal.com/Documents/ImportedDocuments/Tech_mag_business_continuity_sept06.pdf [accessed 10 October 2016].

Low, S.P., Liu, J. and Sio, S. (2010), "Business continuity management in large construction companies in Singapore", *Disaster Prevention and Management: An International Journal*, *19*(2), pp. 219–232.

Lucero, M., Tan, T.K.A. and Pang, A. (2009), "Crisis leadership: When should the CEO step up?", *Corporate Communications: An International Journal*, *14*(3), pp. 234–248.

McCrackan, A. (2005), *Is Business Continuity a Subset of Risk Management?* Continuity Central, UK, available at: www.continuitycentral.com/feature0178.htm [accessed 10 October 2016].

McManus, D.J. and Carr, H.H. (2001), "Risk and the need for business continuity planning", in Doughty, K. (Ed), *Business Continuity Planning: Protecting Your Organization's Life*. CRC Press, Auerbach, Boca Raton, pp. 3–10.

Morwood, G. (1998), "Business continuity: Awareness and training programmes", *Information Management & Computer Security*, *6*(1), pp. 28–32.

Musgrave, B. and Woodman, P. (2013), *Weathering the Storm: The 2013 Business Continuity Management Survey*, Chartered Management Institute, London, available at: www.bcifiles.com/CMI-Weatheringthestorm.pdf [accessed 10 October 2016].

Naujoks, U. (2002), "Business continuity planning (BCP) in a globalised bank", in Wieczorek, M., Naujoks, U. and Bartlett, B. (Eds), *Business Continuity: IT Risk Management for International Corporations*, Springer, Heidelberg, pp. 99–117.

Norrman, A. and Jansson, U. (2004), "Ericsson's proactive supply chain risk management approach after a serious sub-supplier accident", *International Journal of Physical Distribution and Logistics Management*, *34*(5), pp. 434–456.

O'Hehir, M. (2007), "What is a business continuity planning (BCP) strategy?", in Hiles, A. (Ed), *The Definitive Handbook of Business Continuity Management*, John Wiley & Sons Ltd, Chichester, pp. 27–45.

Porter, M. (1996), "What is strategy?", *Harvard Business Review*, November/December, pp. 61–78.

Rössing, R. (2007), "BC audit", in Hiles, A. (Ed), *The Definitive Handbook of Business Continuity Management*, John Wiley & Sons Ltd, Chichester, pp. 339–367.

Sheffi, Y. (2009), "Business continuity: A systematic approach", in Richardson, H. W., Gordon, P. and Moore II, J. E. (Eds), *Global Business and the Terrorist Threat*, pp. 23–41. Cheltenham, UK: Edward Elgar Publishing.

Sheffi, Y. and Rice, J. B., Jr. (2005), "A supply chain view of the resilient enterprise", *MIT Sloan Management Review*, *47*(1), pp. 41–48.

Sikdar, P. (2011), "Alternate approaches to business impact analysis", *Information Security Journal: A Global Perspective*, *20*(3), pp. 128–134.

Smith, D. (2003), "Business continuity and crisis management", *Management Quarterly*, *44*(1), pp. 27–33.

Snedaker, S. and Rima, C. (2014), *Business Continuity and Disaster Recovery Planning for IT Professionals*, Syncress, Waltham, MA.

Swartz, E., Elliott, D. and Herbane, B. (2003), "Greater than the sum of its parts: Business continuity management in the UK finance sector", *Risk Management*, *5*(1), pp. 65–80.

Talke, K. (2007), "Corporate mindset of innovating firms: Influences on new product performance." *Journal of Engineering and Technology Management*, *24*(1), pp. 76–91.

Wilson, M. and Hash, J. (2003), *Building an Information Technology Security Awareness and Training Program*, NIST Special Publication 800–50, National Institute of Standards and Technology (NIST), US, Gaithersburg, MD, available at: http://citadel-information.com/wp-content/uploads/2012/08/nist-sp800-50-building-information-security-awareness-program-2003.pdf [accessed 10 October 2016].

Wong, W.N.Z. (2010), "A taxonomy of 'business continuity organisations", *Continuity*, March/April, pp. 128–141.

Wong, W.N.Z. and Shi, J. (2010), "The role of business continuity management in organisational long range planning", *International Journal of Business Continuity and Risk Management*, *1*(3), pp. 247–258.

Wong, W.N.Z. and Shi, J. (2015), *Business Continuity Management System: A Complete Guide to Implementing ISO 22301*, Kogan Page, London.

Zsidisin, G.A., Melnyk, S.A. and Ragatz, G. L. (2005), "An institutional theory perspective of business continuity planning for purchasing and supply management", *International Journal of Production Research*, *43*(16), pp. 3401–3420.

# 5

# Knowledge in high-reliability organizations

## A review of interrelated perspectives

*Krista N. Engemann*

### Introduction

Organizational knowledge, hereinafter referred to as knowledge, is difficult to define, problematic to access, and difficult to manage. Not only is there is limited consensus with respect to its definition and operationalization, but the methodology associated with empirically assessing this topic area is only just emerging from nascence. It is nonetheless presumed that knowledge-based resources are valuable to the organization and that knowledge may be readily created, captured, codified, shared, and applied. This chapter adopts a post-modern perspective of risk and uncertainty and, accordingly, conceptualizes and explores the role of knowledge in organizations that function in these dynamic environments.

### Conceptualizing knowledge

A great deal of literature about knowledge and knowledge management relies on Polanyi's (1967) distinction between tacit and explicit knowledge. Most scholars refer to some variation of this dichotomy in terms of explicit knowledge as "know-what" and tacit knowledge as "know-how." Explicit knowledge is also characterized by declarative content that has been captured in a tangible format, such as manuals, models, and other documents that are accessible through databases and other forms of media. Tacit knowledge, on the other hand, is characterized by content that is more difficult to consciously access or verbalize. This form of knowledge exists exclusively within the brain of the knower and may include mental models and personalized insights.

Knowledge is nonetheless personal. As such, Polanyi maintains that knowledge can be applied like a tool, where the tool becomes an extension of ourselves. Just as we learn to use a tool, we gradually become unaware of how we are using it to achieve our desired result. To this end, Polanyi asserts that all information and insights are mediated by personal judgment, and accordingly, no knowledge is fully explicit or tacit.

Knowledge may also more so be a reflection of the knower than of the content itself. That which is difficult to articulate by one knower may be readily articulated by another. For instance, expert individuals can struggle to articulate an aspect of their extensive and rich insights about a particular topic, while novice individuals can readily verbalize the process of a newly learned task. This paradox again reflects the personal quality of knowledge, but also implicates the action of knowledge, or know*ing*, as the active engagement and shaping of one's experience in the pursuit of meaning.

This distinction between knowledge and knowing is subtle, but critical. Knowing is an ongoing social accomplishment, such that it is constituted and reconstituted in everyday practice. On the other hand, knowledge is represented by the prescriptive rules that inform behavior. For instance, you could have knowledge of grammar and syntax at a point in time, the basis of which was formed by your participation in English or writing courses, the publication process, and the like. Although your knowledge of grammar and syntax does not enable you to write, your 'knowing' is displayed in how you use those rules as you are writing. That is, your writing suggests that you use your knowledge of grammar and syntax as a tool, like Polanyi suggests. However, prescriptive rules must be continually abstracted in practice, oftentimes leading to their update. Interactions between yourself and your English teacher, your journal editor, or any other writing resource not only afford you knowledge about grammar and syntax at one point in time, but also provide insight as to how to continue to use these rules in the future. This suggests that knowledge is a function of collaborative and complex social processes.

Knowledge is also informed by meaning, and such meaning is drawn from a particular group context. Moreover, knowledge is distinct from a simple aggregation of the knowledge of each individual member of a group. Orr's (1996, 2006) ethnography of Xerox photocopier technicians demonstrates these characteristics. Though not formally established by their organization's description of their role, these technicians collectively and informally established that a requisite skill for their position was an ability to create, trade, and understand highly ambiguous technical situations. When the situation at hand presented information that was otherwise indeterminable, and when one individual failed to successfully put into place what he or she knew, they could share stories and construct new options all with others technicians. The ethnography also suggested that Xerox photocopier technicians relied more so on practical insights that emerged from conversation than on detailed product manuals and formal training to assist them in repairing machines. Not only did storytelling, collaboration, and social construction allow for increased understanding, but it also supported any newfound understanding to become a part of the community's collective knowledge. This knowledge could then be used and further modified by the group upon encountering ambiguous technical situations in the future.

In this example, knowledge is represented by the blend of experiences, values, contextual information, and expert insight which inform a framework for evaluating and incorporating new input. However, this knowledge is static and, as such, could become obsolete when the technical situation is deemed indeterminable. Alternatively, knowing is represented by the dynamic, relational work that is performed as part of the practice of solving these technical problems. To this point, authors like Cook and Brown (1999) and Orlikowski (2002) have asserted that one's ongoing engagement in social practices is how one reconstitutes knowledge overtime. That is, when a group changes their practices, their knowing (or their way of using their knowledge) changes. For instance, Cook and Brown's explanation of knowing is grounded in what they see as the dynamic interaction of the 'knowledge' possessed by the individual and the 'knowing' that is an aspect of the individual's work. This interaction affords more than an exchange in which the net sum of knowledge is the same, but rather sustains a "generative dance" (1999, p. 383), where sense is made and new knowledge is maintained. Similarly, Orlikowski asserts that we effectively learn to know differently as we interact and improvise with others.

This chapter's conceptualizations argue for knowledge as a tool and knowing as the use of this tool. Moreover, this conceptualization halts excessive emphasis on knowledge as dichotomized into tacit and explicit parts. This conceptualization suggests that knowledge is inseparable from its constituting practice, making the sharing of knowledge not a problem of a direct transfer or a disambiguation of insight from one individual to another, but rather a process of enabling others to learn to act and improvise in a variety of ways and in a variety of contexts. As such, knowledge is an organized process which supports a group of individuals to align their cognition and organize for collective action.

## Distinguishing knowledge

This chapter's conceptualization of knowledge is evoked in related literature, but it is often confounded by other emphases. Scholars tend to conceptualize knowledge in terms of its equivalence to other concepts like information, organizational assets, or networks, and these equivalents inform a variety of theories. Rather than conceptualize knowledge as that which is possessed in the mind of the knower, bound in values and experiences of the knower, and as that which influences the actions of the knower, these perspectives distinguish knowledge in terms of the content, structure, accuracy, abundance, or utility of the insights themselves.

When knowledge is treated as roughly equivalent to information, the question becomes how to best store, retrieve, and transmit it. Some scholars thus assert that organizations have different types of knowledge (e.g., explicit and tacit), and that identifying and examining these will lead to more effective means for generating, sharing, and managing knowledge. An example of this is Nonaka's (1994) theory of organizational knowledge creation. Nonaka identified information as a flow of messages, while knowledge is created and organized by this flow and is anchored in the commitment and beliefs of the individual. The theory situates organizational knowledge as an outcome that emerges from a complex process of knowledge conversion. Knowledge becomes organizational knowledge by amplifying that which individual members know and then crystallizing it as part of a larger network. The author identifies several modes of knowledge conversion, where each relies on, contributes to, and benefits from other modes, and where knowledge – an object in the head of an individual – is acquired, modeled, and expressed most accurately and in the most objective and explicit terms to as many members of the organization as possible. Nonaka equates knowledge with both an outcome of a complex process and with an enhanced capacity to act, define, and solve problems.

Other scholars explore the idea that organizations consist of particular strategic processes that create value through the deliberate manipulation of resources – like knowledge – for new value-creating strategies. For instance, Nahapiet and Ghoshal (1998) frame knowledge as that which can be converted for organizational advantage. The authors theorize that social integration mechanisms facilitate the sharing and eventual exploitation of knowledge by the organization through structural, cognitive, and relational dimensions. That is, the combination and exchange of knowledge is facilitated when individuals are motivated to engage in its exchange, there are structural links or connections between individuals (i.e., structural capital), individuals share a common language which helps them understand and use each other's contributing insights (i.e., cognitive capital), and their relationships have strong, positive characteristics like trust, cooperation, and a shared identity (i.e., relational capital). Each of these are forms of social capital that make up an aspect of the organization's social structure, facilitating the combination and exchange of knowledge between individuals within that structure. This suggests that wherever we may see organizations with these forms of capital, we would expect to also see these organizations emerge with both a shared corpus of knowledge and the capability to access and wield that knowledge. Organizations subsequently build and retain their advantage by managing these capabilities.

Overall, these theories discuss how knowledge acquired by individuals in an organization is associated with organization-level learning, how a group's mastering of explicit routines is contingent upon the depth of organizational memory (i.e., knowledge which resides in such forms as written documentation, information stored in electronic databases, and relationships), and how the tacit skills of an individual can be tapped for the benefit of the organization. Knowledge is an object to be exploited, and doing so requires the sharing of relevant knowledge among members of the organization and promoting mutual understanding and comprehension.

However, these perspectives do not necessarily clarify how knowledge is connected to action, and subsequently – and more fundamentally – what knowledge actually is. Specifically, it is unclear as to whether organizational knowledge is viewed as equal to the knowledge of individuals or as a derivative of these individuals' insights. In addition, framing organizations as generating a competitive advantage by tapping into a pool of existing knowledge leaves important collaborative practices underspecified. Moreover, there is little specification about concrete outcomes, and this lack of precision complicates empirical observation and measurements. There is also ambiguity about the goal of the study of knowledge – competitive advantage, shaping routines and practices that enable the organization to be resilient in the face of change, forestalling error, maintaining reliable operations, and so on. This, however, may likely depend on disciplinary preferences. Finally, while these perspectives acknowledge the organization as a repository of socially complex, distinctive, and inimitable organizational knowledge and as a body that can potentially affect positive, competitive development to the organization's operations, the management of knowledge is implied to abide by exact, systematic processes that are guided and informed by explicit organizational goals. These perspectives suggest an exact transferability and manipulation of knowledge toward strategic use, such that knowledge is subsequently removed from the lived experience of the knower.

Alternatively, this chapter's conceptualization of knowledge illustrates more clearly how knowledge that is distributed among individuals and embedded in their work practices can be integrated and shared with others. This conceptualization attempts to balance an information-based approach, where knowledge is deemed manageable, and an interactional approach, where knowledge is bound to the knower, is difficult to transfer, is digested (and not merely stored), requires context, and is one aspect of a larger system. This view of knowledge places it in a specific social context where it is reified as functional and applicable in concrete scenarios. Moreover, knowledge is conceptualized in a way that suggests that it is an outcome of practices, but is also embedded in the practices themselves. Knowledge here is both an outcome and a process.

## Contextualizing knowledge: the high reliability organization

The conceptualization of knowledge put forth in this chapter both adheres to Polanyi's thesis and presumes characteristics that are critical to an organization. The notion that knowledge is a process whereby cognition is organized for collective action centralizes the communicative mechanisms by which rich, situated insight is constructed and shared. As Orr's ethnography demonstrates, there are also circumstances in organizations which may encourage us to seek more emergent knowledge resources in order to address problems and implement change. A particular setting where knowledge plays a critical, if not a life-saving, role is the high reliability organization. A high reliability organization is one that functions in the regular maintenance of safe operations in light of error-prone surroundings (Roberts, 1990; Weick & Roberts, 1993). In doing so, the high reliability organization, which spans such professions as firefighters, nuclear aircraft carriers, air traffic controllers and emergency medical treatment teams, develops and maintains complex adaptive systems in support of safe and error-free operations.

The theory that guides present understanding of this unique organizational context contends that errors are systemic, dynamic workplace conditions (e.g., Rochlin, 1999; Weick, Sutcliffe, & Obstfeld, 1999). Moreover, errors are not consequences of failed coupled system structures, but are inherent and always to be expected. As such, routines are seldom stable in a high reliability organization; each time a routine is enacted, it will ultimately unfold in a slightly different manner. Reliability is thus a reflection of the organization's management of its fluctuating, dynamic environment.

Weick and colleagues (2005) articulate that we typically do not notice reliability until it has lapsed. In other words, we often do not notice the influence of what sustains safe, error-free operations until it has disappeared. For example, we may not readily acknowledge the lifesaving quality of the habitual practice of buckling up a seatbelt before driving, but when we hear of a tragic accident in which someone was flung from a car and we learn that they were not wearing their seatbelt at the time, we recall the capability for buckling up to keep us safe from a similar fate. While this conceptualization in some ways complicates the study of what is seemingly an indiscernible event, it also focuses our attention on the ongoing processes which manage the environment for sustained reliable outcomes.

How the high reliability organization operates and, ultimately, manages error is complicated by the ambiguity of its surrounding environment. The continually changing and oftentimes hazardous environment is such that any event could presumably result in substantial failure or loss. While failure may be expected in any organization, high reliability organizations are distinct in that the "consequences and costs associated with major failures . . . are greater than the value of the lessons learned from them" (LaPorte & Consolini, 1991, p. 19). Because the hazardous operations and surrounding conditions of the high reliability organization do not afford the flexibility of trial and error learning, the organization is not without routine. A high reliability organization may have specific operational procedures, extensive training, comprehensive debriefings, and other deliberate safety measures. High reliability organizations may also attempt to document and codify lessons from failures into standardized rules and abstracted insights in order to fit a wider variety of events. Such preoccupation with failure (Weick, Sutcliffe, & Obstfeld, 2008) effectively permeates the high reliability organization, such that all levels of the organization act appropriately for the situation at hand.

While these rules and routines might suggest that the high reliability organization will apply them directly and perpetually to counter emergent crises, crises are just that: emergent. Events may culminate in a manner that ultimately renders current rules and routines obsolete. Moreover, these unexpected events create uncertainty and are perceived to threaten such prioritized goals as the security and well-being of life, community, and property (Seeger, Sellnow, & Ulmer, 1998). In order to maintain reliable operations, the high reliability organization requires the continual generation of new knowledge, thereby stimulating the creation and application of new rules, insights, and routines.

Just as crises engage action, action helps the high reliability organization identify the distinctions and anomalies of the crisis scenario. In particular, mindfulness gives order to a high reliability organization by providing latitude for unique action. Weick and Sutcliffe (2006) characterize mindfulness as a psychological state grounded in patterns of analyzing, categorizing and making distinctions about that which is around us, resulting in focus, stability, and a vivid recollection of the scene. These mindful processes might include devoting more time to examining error, resisting the urge to simplify assumptions about the scene, observing operations and their effects, locating local expertise, and creating a climate of deference to those experts (Weick & Sutcliffe, 2007). These processes form a basis for members of the high reliability organization to interact continuously and to develop, refine, and update a shared understanding of the situation they face and their capabilities to act on that understanding.

## Evaluating knowledge

Although action guided by explicit rules and routines is essential to the maintenance of reliability, this does not dismiss the importance of alertness and sensing that something is just "not right." Emergent events effectively render useless the same prescriptive rules and routines that enabled success at a point in time, and this triggers the process of new discovery and new knowledge. However, knowledge that is created as errors are detected, corrected, and analyzed may also precariously sustain the chance for disaster in a high reliability setting. For instance, Weick (1993) asserts that knowledge was destructive rather than constructive as smoke jumpers struggled to put their standard operating procedures into use and quell the now-famous wildfire at Mann Gulch. The process of new discovery and new knowledge has the capacity to enable shared insights among the group, but new knowledge can also become tightly coupled with operations and, when deemed obsolete in a moment of action, can quickly become perilous. When in a setting in which trial and error is dangerous, yet present knowledge may at any time become obsolete, the paradox of the high reliability organization emerges (Milosevic, Bass, & Combs, 2018).

A reorientation about the in-the-moment communicative processes that guide knowledge in high reliability organizations may illuminate opportunities to resolve this paradox. Jahn (2016) observes how these processes might work in a study of wildland firefighters. The author asserts that prescriptive rules and routines for safety should be used as tools for creative action, and that these safety rules are helpful for negotiating meaning of a scene when members "ventriloquize," or speak on behalf of these rules and make them present in conversation. This practice of ventriloquizing was best supported in debriefings, where the group retrospectively discussed their actions, articulating for everyone important activities and cues during the event in question while either explicitly or abstractly drawing safety rules into the discussion. For example, members of the wildland firefighting crew might have spoken on behalf of an organization's mission or its policy documents to remind each other of the overarching goals of their work. These efforts helped members to learn about and anticipate common hazards. However, the author contends that rule adaptation was not necessarily a spontaneous act. Rules were adapted according to interpersonal relationships and took place in a group setting, or they were adapted through deference to experts and took place in more private, reflective spaces.

Evaluating knowledge ultimately requires some degree of autonomy. This approach presumably allows problems to be detected and solved more quickly and effectively as well as enables decision makers to learn from experience. This is best articulated by Eisenberg (1990), who argues that organizations should not only create a "structure for surrender" in order to facilitate improvisation, but also establish guidelines with which to base improvised action. Eisenberg also emphasizes that there should be sufficient representation of experts, but also a blurring among them in order to increase ease of interaction among expert and non-expert individuals.

In essence, an organization can evaluate its needs and preparedness by "letting go." Procedures might be used to standardize operations under routine conditions to ensure consistency and facilitate coordination among different individuals. However, individuals should also be given the autonomy to manage disturbances locally. For instance, these local individuals would be encouraged to improvise where necessary and do what is needed to respond to threats and disruptions effectively. While this process is generative, there are some qualities that sustain it, including a joint commitment to a temporarily shared social reality that is both established and continually modified. Eisenberg (1998) likens this to playing ball on running water, where you commit to keeping the game going, despite the context constantly changing. Therefore, evaluating knowledge requires a commitment to living both within and beyond the current context.

## Creating knowledge

Given that knowledge is defined here as an organized process which supports a group of individuals in aligning their cognition for collective action, it is important to take a closer look at the complexities of that conceptualization. First, this conceptualization presumes that one's initial inquiry about the routine nature of the scenario at hand "acts as impetus for coordination processes, [whereby] individuals open up space for multiple interpretations of what is happening by interweaving their insights with that of others" (Milosevic et al., 2018, p. 15). This conceptualization also suggests that such interactions within the group not only serve as a search for ways with which to assign meaning to the scenario, but also as a reinforcement and challenge of the group's grasp of its knowledge base. Finally, this conceptualization suggests that these coordinated actions expand the base of knowledge with which the group will work.

Not only does this conceptualization implicate the importance of requisite variety in this knowledge creation process, where organizations with access to more varied insights will engage their environment in a more adaptive manner than those with comparably limited insights (Weick, 1995), but it also reveals patterns of "heedful interrelating" (Weick & Roberts, 1993). Where 'heed' implies a set of cognitive qualities that emphasize rich and discriminatory awareness to detail (Weick & Roberts, 1993; Weick & Sutcliffe, 2007), heedful interrelating then describes how an individual's own contribution, representation, and modification of their actions with respect to others influences how they learn and adapt in a dynamic environment. In this instance, the individual – aware of themselves, the people around them, the potential for error in the operations that they oversee or contribute to, and their attribution to resulting outcomes – is capable of coordinating their opinions and behaviors with that of others in order to respond swiftly and effectively in emergent situations. Much like how knowledge is conceptualized in this chapter, this perspective emphasizes coordination among individuals, rather than the individual's cognition and decisions alone (e.g., Jeong & Brower, 2008), to maintain performance in settings that require ongoing reliability.

How knowledge is created from these "heedful" patterns of interaction may also be explained by processes of sensemaking. Sensemaking theory (Weick, 1979, 1995) emphasizes the processes by which a group communicates and interprets shifts in the organizational environment. By focusing the group's attention toward a particular set of events or details of a situation, imposing some finite set of interpretations on that bracketed portion of the situation, and then drawing upon previous knowledge that is somewhat analogous to the situation at hand to inform and shape their action, the members of the group are incited to reflect upon their own behavior and their attribution to particular outcomes. In turn, the group collectively maintains attention to detail as a means of preventing minor errors from becoming larger-scale failures. In other words, by jointly (or, intersubjectively) interpreting their environment, the group creates accounts that allow them to comprehend their environment and act collectively. This sensemaking perspective also informs how meaning – and, ultimately, knowledge – of new or ambiguous events or experiences are sustained over time.

Critically, the form of knowledge evoked in this chapter should not be one that forms as the group intersubjectively engages the *same* interpretations. This distinction is perhaps best articulated by Weick and Roberts (1993) as they describe the complex but nonetheless deliberate interactions they observed among crewmembers of an aircraft carrier:

> We avoid the phrases "group mind" and "organizational mind" in favor of the phrase "collective mind." The word "collective," unlike the words "group" or "organization," refers to individuals who act as if they are a group. People who act as if they are a group interrelate their actions with more or less care, and focusing on the way this interrelating is done reveals collective mental processes that differ in their degree of development. Our focus is at once on individuals and the collective, since only individuals can contribute to a collective mind, but a collective mind is distinct from an individual mind because it inheres in the pattern of interrelated activities among many people.
>
> *(p. 360)*

This insight can be further clarified from a perspective of diversity. Given a group comprising of individuals with similar experiences, its members may offer similar interpretations, whereby limiting the collective, intersubjective processes with which the group will attempt to organize their dynamic environment. The knowledge that emerges in this setting may not harbor the requisite variety with which to ultimately cope with a changing environment. Thus, the knowledge discussed in this chapter emerges from the "collective" that intersubjectively engages an array of interpretations.

Furthermore, the knowledge that emerges from such coordination among the "collective" described by Weick and Roberts (1993) is deliberate. This characteristic is particularly important to the processes that inform knowledge and its management in high reliability organizations. Moreover, this characteristic is perhaps critical for Weick and Roberts's distinction of the "collective" from the "group." That is, the "group acting like a group" acknowledges our colloquial tendency to use the term "group" in order to evoke an interdependent set of people who engage one another with or without a particular sense of interconnected responsiveness. Furthermore, this colloquial interpretation ignores our capacity to act in spite of apparent differences to meet similar goals through coordinated action. This caveat is ultimately what makes those groups of individuals operating within high reliability organizations distinct, and is perhaps what makes the knowledge that is created as errors are detected, corrected, and analyzed sufficiently complex to solve problems in the future.

## Promoting knowledge

The more individuals of a group interpersonally act with "heed," the more developed the "collective" becomes (Weick & Roberts, 1993), particularly in terms of the knowledge that guides members' coordinated action and decision making during unanticipated scenarios. Given that the high reliability organizations function on the basis of continuous evaluation and improvement through interaction, this suggests that communication and learning from frontline employees must be ongoing for these practices to critically impact the organization's functioning. Overall, it is important to develop a context for richer interactions that improve cross-functional relationships and coordination.

It is important to note that the discussion of knowledge thus far in this chapter has essentially assumed that interaction unvaryingly accomplishes the requisite meaning that will sustain reliable organizational outcomes. There are nonetheless exceptions to this notion. For instance, Weick (1987) asserts that "smart people who don't talk" (p. 115) may complicate whether the high reliability organization attains the rich insights necessary to develop meaning toward safe and reliable operations. Furthermore, when performance boundaries in high reliability organizations become obfuscated, pressures like operational efficiency may influence the extent to which accidents, injuries, and near misses are discussed. For instance, Collinson's (1999) ethnographic case study of events on an oceanic oil rig revealed that employees, having been incentivized to primarily act efficiently, ultimately engaged in fewer discretionary and compulsory safe behaviors. The author suggested that as employees collectively made sense of the values, practices, and procedures of their organization, their actions undermined prescribed safety practices and, in turn, reinforced new behavior. This resulted in a strained relationship between acknowledging, discussing, and learning from error and proceeding safely.

High reliability organizations can nonetheless support, consolidate, and reconcile diverse concerns about safety through social processes. Supervisors are often conceived as the source around which concerns about operations are brought together and then disseminated to the group. Supervisors are particularly important in a high reliability organization because policy and procedure rarely cover the innumerable situations that could emerge from interactions among humans, machines, and the environment. If we conceive of the supervisor's role as more of a social process, this suggests that it involves recognizing when guidelines and formal policy no longer fit the environment. As such, supervisors that foster direct attention to safety are able to disseminate safety information as well as demonstrate how commitment to safety and reliability is practiced in daily work (Zohar & Luria, 2010). Moreover, supervisors create and sustain the conditions within which employees act, establishing a psychologically safe environment for behaviors like seeking feedback, sharing information, experimenting, asking for help, and talking about errors (Edmondson, 1999).

In addition, organizations can support the consolidation and reconciliation of safety concerns by creating structured, psychologically safe forums for issues to be identified and solved as a group. This practice is particularly important for high reliability organizations because they are likely to become more vulnerable to error when their attention is scattered, distracted, and dominated by abstractions. After-action reviews are a particular location for such strategic, deliberate discussion. After-action reviews are feedback procedures often used in military contexts, although similar approaches are abstracted to others fields like medicine (e.g., post-fall huddles). After-action reviews help these organizations engender learning from both successes and failures by guiding participants to construct a comprehensive representation of their individual interpretations of the event in question. After-action reviews are also a site where supervisors reaffirm the importance of safety and safe practices. It is thought that the frequency of these meetings will serve to reinforce norms and create a setting where the group can better understand specific incidents that they encounter (e.g., Dunn, Scott, Allen, & Bonilla, 2016). Notably, these reviews are distinct from other types, like post-incident critiques, because they are not necessarily organization-wide or formal and, as a result, eschew some problems of political maneuvering or blame in discussion. After-action reviews are either formal or informal, specific to the group using the technique, and occur soon after an incident or a training exercised is concluded. Such elaborating is most fruitful when feedback is exchanged without defensiveness and when the review is continued until a shared understanding is achieved. These sessions serve to set the stage for what can be learned from the event at hand for application in the future.

In organizations that continuously struggle to detect and correct misunderstandings that pose threats to safety, practices which support supervisor-employee relationships or group discussion are effective ways in which the group can combat complexity and reduce the effects of their organization's tightly coupled system structure. Weick (1988) argues that because crises engage human action, and human action helps us identify what may have set the crisis in motion, individuals can more readily capture the anomalies of the scene by maintaining and supporting practices which sustain mindfulness. Overall, these practices should help individuals see the importance of expertise, understand how formal structures can accelerate or decelerate responsive action to crises, and identify causes of lapses as well as where interventions are possible. Organizations can effectively prevent larger crises by more mindfully managing error.

## Conclusion

The definition and conceptualization of knowledge and its related constructs have been developed by many theoretical perspectives. While this has contributed to a varied and rich supporting literature domain, it has also engendered a fair amount of conceptual, empirical and practical ambiguity. This chapter conceptualizes knowledge as both an inherently social process and as an outcome of this process. In turn, this chapter discusses how a group might organize for reliable outcomes and distinguishes the high reliability organization as one that maintains operations within highly ambiguous and oftentimes dangerous settings. High reliability organizations are unique because they maintain a self-conscious dialogue among members, which captures collective learning from success and failure. Such dialogue is maintained by the belief that learning cannot be exhaustive and knowledge is inherently non-permanent and imperfect. Whether knowledge creation is incentivized to become a prescribed activity in an organization or it remains an unarticulated, yet ongoing process, knowledge remains a valuable resource capable of enabling coordinated action and change.

## References

Collinson, D.L. (1999). 'Surviving the Rigs': Safety and surveillance on North Sea Oil installations. *Organization Studies*, 20(4), 579–600.

Cook, S.D., & Brown, J.S. (1999). Bridging epistemologies: The generative dance between organizational knowledge and organizational knowing. *Organization Science*, 10(4), 381–400.

Dunn, A.M., Scott, C., Allen, J.A., & Bonilla, D. (2016). Quantity and quality: Increasing safety norms through after action reviews. *Human Relations*, 69(5), 1209–1232.

Edmondson, A. (1999). Psychological safety and learning behavior in work teams. *Administrative Science Quarterly*, 44(2), 350–383.Eisenberg, E.M. (1990). Jamming: Transcendence through organizing. *Communication Research*, 17(2), 139–164.

Eisenberg, E.M. (1998). Flirting with meaning. *Journal of Language and Social Psychology*, 17(1), 97–108.

Jahn, J.L.S. (2016). Adapting safety rules in a high reliability context: How wildland firefighting workgroups ventriloquize safety rules to understand hazards. *Management Communication Quarterly*, 30(3), 362–389.

Jeong, H.S., & Brower, R.S. (2008). Extending the present understanding of organizational sensemaking: Three stages and three contexts. *Administration & Society*, 40(3), 223–252.

LaPorte, T.R., & Consolini, P.M. (1991). Working in practice but not in theory: Theoretical challenges of "High-Reliability Organizations." *Journal of Public Administration Research and Theory: J-PART*, 1(1), 19–48.

Milosevic, I., Bass, A.E., & Combs, G.M. (2018). The paradox of knowledge creation in a high-reliability organization: A case study. *Journal of Management*, 44(3), 1174–1201.

Nahapiet, J., & Ghoshal, S. (1998). Social capital, intellectual capital, and the organizational advantage. *Academy of Management Review*, 23(2), 242–266.

Nonaka, I. (1994). A dynamic theory of organizational knowledge creation. *Organization Science*, 5(1), 14–37.

Orlikowski, W.J. (2002). Knowing in practice: Enacting a collective capability in distributed organizing. *Organization Science*, 13(3), 249–273.

Orr, J. (1996). *Talking About Machines: An Ethnography of a Modern Job*. Ithaca, NY: Cornell University Press.

Orr, J.E. (2006). Ten years of talking about machines. *Organization Studies*, 27(12), 1805–1820.

Polanyi, M. (1967). *The Tacit Dimension*. London: Routledge and Kegan Paul.

Roberts, K.H. (1990). Some characteristics of one type of high reliability organization. *Organization Science*, 1(2), 160–176.

Rochlin, G.I. (1999). Safe operation as a social construct. *Ergonomics*, 42(11), 1549–1560.

Seeger, M.W., Sellnow, T.L., & Ulmer, R.R. (1998). Communication, organization, and crisis. *Annals of the International Communication Association*, 21(1), 231–276.

Weick, K.E. (1979). *Social Psychology of Organizing*. Reading, MA: Addison Wesley.Weick, K.E. (1987). Organizational culture as a source of high reliability. *California Management Review*, 29(2), 112–127.

Weick, K.E. (1988). Enacted sensemaking in crisis situations. *Journal of Management Studies*, 25(4), 305–317.

Weick, K.E. (1993). The collapse of sensemaking in organizations: The Mann Gulch disaster. *Administrative Science Quarterly*, 38(4), 628–652.

Weick, K.E. (1995). *Sensemaking in Organizations*. Thousands Oaks, CA: Sage.

Weick, K.E., & Roberts, K.H. (1993). Collective mind in organizations: Heedful interrelating on flight decks. *Administrative Science Quarterly*, 38(3), 357–381

Weick, K.E., & Sutcliffe, K.M. (2006). Mindfulness and the quality of organizational attention. *Organization Science*, 17(4), 514–524.

Weick, K.E., & Sutcliffe, K.M. (2007). *Managing the unexpected: Resilient performance in an age of uncertainty*. San Francisco, CA: Jossey-Bass.

Weick, K., Sutcliffe, K., & Obstfeld, D. (1999). Organizing for reliability: Processes of collective mindfulness. *Research in Organizational Behavior*, 21, 81–123.

Weick, K.E., Sutcliffe, K.M., & Obstfeld, D. (2005). Organizing and the process of sensemaking. *Organization Science*, 16(4), 409–421.

Weick, K.E. Sutcliffe, K.M., & Obstfeld, D. (2008). Organizing for high reliability: Processes of collective mindfulness. *Crisis Management*, 3, 81–123.

Zohar, D., & Luria, G. (2010). Group leaders as gatekeepers: Testing safety climate variations across levels of analysis. *Applied Psychology*, 59(4), 647–673.

# Part II

# Natural and man-made disasters

# 6

# A retrospective account of the impacts of the 1960 Valdivia, Chile, earthquake and tsunami and the lack of business continuity planning

*Benigno E. Aguirre*

This chapter examines retrospectively the impact on the businesses in the city of Valdivia, Chile, of the earthquake and tsunami on "El Día de Los Santos Inocentes" (April Fools Day), Sunday afternoon, May 22, 1960. The setting is Chile, a modern society justly proud of its many achievements. Almost all the observations made during field work are limited to the city of Valdivia. They also reflected conditions in 2007, and the situation may be different today. Still, it is useful to share with others the result of my observations.

The chapter shows that business recovery from a disaster is a complex and uncertain social outcome. It has sections on the extent and effects of the hazards; their impacts on the businesses of the city; and the puzzle, despite the occurrence of similar risks, of the continued lack of business continuity planning and programs in the region almost half a century afterward. Ignored are the well-known principles of business continuity planning in disasters that improve the chances of continuous business operations, as well as more broadly, emergency management and the social science study of disasters. The absence of a connection between cause and effect, between the prolonged human suffering produced by the disasters (and the well-known hazardousness of the region) and the lack of culturally subscribed approaches about how to minimize their effects, is a surprise to this writer. The city is not a stranger to the upheavals brought about by natural and technological hazards. Before the 1960 earthquake, Valdivia had experienced earthquakes and fires that caused very significant damage in 1575, 1633, 1737, 1835, 1837, and 1907. In 1754 the town was attacked by the hostile Araucano Indians and entirely destroyed by fire. More than a century later, in 1909, at a time of thriving economic and social development spurred by German immigration, another massive fire destroyed more than 18 squares (manzanas) in the center of the city, and with them its most important buildings (Guarda, 1993; 2001.) The conclusion speculates, in the absence of other tested explanations, about reasons why these patterns are taking place and why the prevailing consensus accepts Divine Providence and the truthfulness of fatalistic beliefs about people's inability to mitigate the risk of disasters.

## The extent and effects of the 1960 hazards

The Valdivia, Chile earthquake of 1960 is considered one of the two largest earthquakes on the historical record, rated 9.5 on the moment magnitude scale and X on the Mercalli scale, nearly matched only by the recent earthquake and tsunami that brought about the Japanese catastrophe of March 11, 2012. The Chilean earthquake generated almost unbelievable, yet visible changes to the landscape. Its effects covered an area 800 kilometers long, from the island of Chiloé in the south to the town of Chillán in the north (Canisius, 1960.) In the impacted zone the land rose 1 meter on average (3.3 feet), while it dropped an average of between 1.5 meters (4.92 feet) and 2.2 meters (7.2 feet) in Valdivia. Mountains collapsed and rivers changed their courses. Urban fires spared Valdivia, but in a repeat of what occurred in the 1575 earthquake, the River San Pedro was clogged upstream at its confluence with Lake Riñihue. The water level of the lake went up 20 meters (65.61 feet). The immediate effect of this obstruction is that the water level of the Valdivia River also gained more than 3 meters (9.84 feet) and flooded vast areas of the city, destroying some buildings, other structures, and roads. The threat of a sudden, destructive mass of water flooding the city remained for more than two months (Serrano, 2002) and was obviated only through by the heroic efforts of hundreds of men who had been working on a nearby construction site.

The effects in the landscape of the city of Valdivia were conspicuous. Some of these persist to this day. Permanently flooded and lost to agriculture are 13,000 acres of fertile farmland surrounding the town that now is a valuable wetland area; 7,000 acres of land in the city proper experienced temporal flooding, and the ground dropped on average 2.2 meters (7.23 feet). Nevertheless, despite these changes, the overall geologic shifts caused by the earthquake altered hydrological patterns and made Valdivia less prone to regular flooding. Another positive result is that the bed of the Valdivia River dropped quite a bit, making it more navigable (Doyel et al., 1963).

### *The importance of the impacted zone to Chile*

Affected by the earthquake was 31% of the population of the country, or 2,509,402 people out of a total population of close to 7.7 million inhabitants. The damage in the region amounted to $500 million, or 12% of gross national product (GNP). The economy of the area impacted was based primarily on agriculture, livestock, and energy generation. The region raised half of the country's cattle and other livestock. It produced all of Chile's condensed and dry milk and more than 90% of the country's cheese, wood, and paper products; 80% of wool products and tiles; and all of the window glass, pig iron, and iron sheets produced in the country. The impacted zone accounted for 30% of the national labor force, 49% of the people employed in agriculture and livestock, and 24% employed in manufacturing industries. It had 48% of all rural housing. Concentrated in the impacted region was 40% of all capital invested in the agricultural sector and 28% of all capital invested in industrial enterprises. Before the catastrophe, it produced 38% of the national output of agriculture and livestock and 31% of all electric energy. Fifty percent of all livestock raised in Chile came from the impacted region. The earthquake and tsunami destroyed 58,622 houses and nearly two million people were left homeless. Approximately 5,700 died and 3,000 were injured (see Figure 6.1). Tsunamis also struck Hawaii (61 deaths and $75,000 in damage), Japan (138 fatalities and $50,000 in damage), the Philippines (32 deaths), eastern New Zealand, southeast Australia, the Aleutian Islands, and the West Coast of the United States ($500,000 in damage).

In Valdivia, the ground dropped 2.2m on average. The bed of the Valdivia River also dropped, while the changes in hydrological patterns made Valdivia less prone to flooding. 13,000 acres of surrounding farmland were permanently flooded. The next paragraphs examine

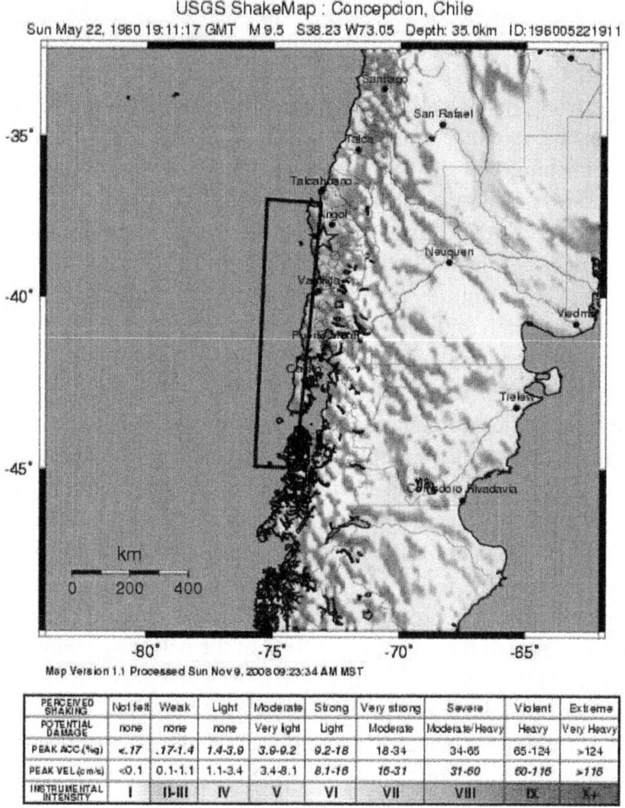


| PERCEIVED SHAKING | Not felt | Weak | Light | Moderate | Strong | Very strong | Severe | Violent | Extreme |
|---|---|---|---|---|---|---|---|---|---|
| POTENTIAL DAMAGE | none | none | none | Very light | Light | Moderate | Moderate/Heavy | Heavy | Very Heavy |
| PEAK ACC.(%g) | <.17 | .17-1.4 | 1.4-3.9 | 3.9-9.2 | 9.2-18 | 18-34 | 34-65 | 65-124 | >124 |
| PEAK VEL.(cm/s) | <0.1 | 0.1-1.1 | 1.1-3.4 | 3.4-8.1 | 8.1-16 | 16-31 | 31-60 | 60-116 | >116 |
| INSTRUMENTAL INTENSITY | I | II-III | IV | V | VI | VII | VIII | IX | X+ |

*Figure 6.1* USGS map of the area impacted by the 1960 Valdivia earthquake

the broad impact of the earthquake and tsunamis on Valdivia's substantial agglomeration of businesses and manufacturing industries.

## *The effects on businesses in Valdivia*

While the heaviest damage occurred in Valdivia, also impacted by the hazards were the towns of Puerto Montt, Rio Negro, Lebu, Concepcion, Alerce, and Riñihue. Roughly half an hour after the earthquake, a tsunami destroyed the low-level areas of Valdivia's port town of Corral and its steelworks industrial complex (Altos Hornos). Corral is 12 kilometers (7.456 miles) from Valdivia, where the mouth of the Valdivia River meets the Pacific Ocean. The tsunami traveled inland from the coast through the Valdivia River, reversing for a while its natural flow towards the sea. It destroyed the buildings of most if not all of the industries in Valdivia, for they operated on the river's banks. Ironically, they had used the river to carry out many essential business tasks, among them to receive needed inventories and transport their products by the sea for distributions to their clients.

There is scant information available about the economic effects of the earthquake on small business firms. Before the quake, Valdivia's industrial park was second in importance in the entire zone of impact. Five months after the date of the disaster, reportedly 4,000 workers were on emergency government assistance, and 12,000 were residing in shelters. Later on, reportedly there was an attempt by the national government to provide the owners of the destroyed manufacturing companies low-cost disaster loans and advantageous repayment options to encourage them to reopen their businesses, as part of a government effort to assist the entire zone impacted by the hazards. However, the hoped-for results did not materialize. Instead, Valdivia lost the two most important pillars of its economy: industry and agriculture. Arguing against reopening was the loss of the port facilities in the town of Corral and the regional railway services facilitating local business activities in the national and international markets. To this day, the city depends on road transportation, which is a poor substitute for the efficient system in place before the earthquake.

Valdivia's recovery was painfully slow, aggravated by the consequences of the 1973 military takeover. In the aftermath of this event, the new government brought about an administrative reorganization of the country that resulted in Valdivia losing its status as the capital of the "Region de Los Lagos" to the nearby city of Puerto Montt. This change meant that almost all employees of the national government moved out of the town with their families. Their move signified a loss of the direct and multiplicate effects of their economic activity and social capital. It also meant the emergence of Puerto Mont as the principal city in the economy of southern Chile. The political and cultural decline of Valdivia was reversed symbolically only in March of 2007 when President M. Bachelet signed a law designating Valdivia as the capital of the "Regi6n de Los Ríos."

Overall, it took more than 40 years from the day of the earthquake for the city of Valdivia to regain its prosperity as part of the ongoing uplifting of the national economy and the development of the forestry, cellulose, and tourist industries. This reverse shows by the relative size of the population of Valdivia during nearly three decades, an unrefined and yet useful indicator of the drawn-out turmoil it experienced. According to Chile's national censuses, the size of Valdivia's population was 45,128 people in 1952, and by 1960, the year of the disaster, it had grown very rapidly by 36%, to 61,334 inhabitants. In the aftermath of the disaster, it dropped a whopping 28% in 10 years to 47,623 by 1970 – very close to what it had been 20 years earlier. Afterward, it yet again reversed course and by 1982 had more than doubled in size to 101,126 residents for a 48% gain!

According to the West German government report about the effects of the earthquake in Chile (Canisius, 1960), before the quake there were 89 firms in Valdivia, and 30 had nationwide economic significance. One, Empresas Navieras, a maritime transportation company, was judged to be a vast enterprise. The report includes a nearly complete list of the lost large businesses in the city. They included a furniture factory, a shipyard, a transport company (Compañía Naviera), two manufacturers of shoes and other leather products, the local brewery, and a sugar refinery. A large paper factory was also heavily damaged, but its ultimate fate was unclear at the time of the report. The findings of field work conducted in Valdivia in 2007 reproduced these results. We obtained the assistance of a family of long-term adult residents of Valdivia who inspected the list of the local companies in the German report and told us which had in fact disappeared in the aftermath of the disaster. These were Anwandter (a brewery), Rudloff (a shoe manufacturer), Perez (a shoe manufacturer), Hoffmann (producer of corn meal and refined sugar), Stonzelbach (processing of leather products), Weiss (processing of leather products), Lunicke (processing of leather products), Altos Hornos (processing of steel in Corral), Astillero Naval Alberto Daiver y Compañía Limitada (ship maker), and Boeckemeyer (processing of wood for building construction.) Two corporations survived: Hoffman (a sugar refinery and producer of the raw meal) and Collico Flour. Regrettably there is no information available on small businesses that would help determine their differential ability to survive the disaster.

## The puzzlements of the Chilean case

During a stay in the field of approximately four months, not observed were processes of public remembrance and commemoration of the suffering produced by the disasters that dot the corporate history of the people in Valdivia. There were no remembrances of the destruction and the suffering of the victims of the 1960 earthquake and tsunami.

Beyond the risks of the frequent earthquakes and tsunamis impacting the region, probably the most ever-present threat that is part of the hazards facing the residents of Valdivia are the risks emanating from numerous building fires produced by overheating of electric currents, and by self-construction. Importantly, there is an excellent, modern electrical code regulating electric use in Chile, but widespread violations of the law are common. In the typical case, a building constructed of wood, the most common material used, goes up on fire due to the increased demands for electricity from recent additions such as electronic printers and computers, as well as from up-to-date refrigerators, furnaces, and other electric systems in the home that render the average number of electric circuits and resistors in use insufficient in many cases, producing the overheating and short-circuiting of the electrical currents and in some cases fires. Here again we did not observe a public outcry demanding the solution to this problem.

The other hazard is the practice of self-construction of houses. In the typical case, a person adds space to her home or builds a house without following the established procedures which incorporate first-rate building practices and official approval. Then at some point in the future, the home is added to the housing inventory of the city and the risk is "covered or disappeared" as it were, even if in this manner the collective risk accumulates. These two main risks have an interactive effect, creating higher risks of fire for wooden houses that are constructed by their owners, many of them of limited economic means, sometimes lacking the proper number of electric circuits and other safeguards. As far as could be ascertained, the press, other fora, and the public did not discuss these matters during the period of fieldwork.

Chile's national disaster program reflects current understanding of risks. It is an impressive document that includes the involvement of citizens in committees that are part of the program. However, we were able to ascertain that in Valdivia and in many other areas of the country, the citizen's panels that are a central part of the national plan do not exist. It makes the plan a phantom document. How to solve these pressing issues should be the subject of future research efforts.

## Business continuity

To our knowledge, business continuity planning and practice in the business corporations of the city of Valdivia and surrounding areas do not exist. The Department of Business Administration of the local Universidad Austral de Chile does not offer courses on the topic. There was also widespread unawareness of the specialty of disaster management and disaster science among its students, faculty members, and the general public, who were surprised when told that it was common in other countries. One graduate student in the program at the end of a talk by this author declared that the topic was not germane to his studies of business management!

Unfortunately, the lack of business continuity and disaster management practices were revealed most starkly by the building fire that destroyed the then relatively new multistory engineered building housing the College of Science on the campus of the Universidad Austral de Chile in December 2007. Lost were unique collections of fish and other animals dating to Charles Darwin's explorations in southern Chile and ongoing investigations by faculty and research projects by graduate students. Even though the Universidad Austral is on the island of Teja, surrounded by water, it had not constructed stations to pump the water from the nearby rivers for use by the university campus. Thus, the local fire department, which is in dire need of new equipment and training, had to let the building burn to the ground. The university response was ad hoc and showed widespread bureaucratic confusion. It had no emergency manager, and no adequate procedures to organize the response to the fire and coordinate the activities of university personnel, Carabineros (national police), local, and later on, national firefighting organizations, and other agencies and students. Neither the city nor the school, the largest business enterprise in the region, had preexisting plans and training to respond to the fire. Soon after the fire, the university closed, followed by student strikes and civil disturbances on campus protesting the emergency arrangements and decisions by the administration. Two years later, a new building became available to replace the one lost to the fire. Auspiciously, the university also inaugurated a new emergency brigade.

## Conclusion

The case of Chile is puzzling in that it is the most advanced economy in Latin America. It handles some risks adequately, from public health and medicine to the risks generated by industrial production. Other local hazards, such as environmental degradation, have elicited much public nationwide concern. In Valdivia, there is an active interest in protecting the local environment, seen as an enormous resource for attracting tourists. The region's environmental movement has succeeded to some degree in protecting the waterways and fauna such as the *cisne de cuello negro* (black-necked swan, *Cygnus melancoryphus*), which are an essential feature of the ecology of the region. However, to our surprise, the connection between ecological degradation and the increased risk of disasters, as the socialization of nature continues apace, has not received sustained consideration. The generalized view found during field work is that disasters are acts of God and the absence of the newer understanding that disasters are primarily acts of humans and that the best public policy is one of mitigation of vulnerabilities.

Valdivia is not entirely representative of other cities. There are different levels of resources available to the municipal governments, and those that are part of the bigger metropolitan cities like Santiago, the capital, probably obtain greater resources. Perhaps laws guiding the function of the town architects in the regulation of the housing stock are applied less strictly in smaller cities than in larger ones, due in part to the lack of resources and the higher dependence of the offices of the city architects on regular elections by the same populations that they are supposedly regulating.

Yet another part of the problem may be that while the successful handling of the public relations and rhetorical aspects of disasters (as acts of God) is a key prerequisite of successful politicians in Chile, they can more or less ignore the long-term consequences and requirements of a successful policy of mitigation and reduction of the vulnerability of the society. For it requires long-term efforts in transforming the culture of the society to make risk management an integral part of its functioning. Unfortunately, disasters often do not have organized and persistent political constituencies, and politicians can safely ignore them. Hopefully, future studies may provide answers to many of these questions..

## References

Canisius, Peter, editor. 1960. Resultados de las investigaciones hechas por la comisión de expertos alemanes enviada a Chile después del terremoto de 1960. Available from the E. L. Quarantelli Collection, Disaster Research Center, University of Delaware.

Doyel, W. W., Moraga, B. A. and Eduardo Falco, M. 1963. The relation between the geology of Valdivia, Chile and the damage produced by the earthquake of 22 May 1960. *Bulletin of the Seismological Society of America*, vol. 58, no. 6, 1331–1345.

Guarda, Gabriel. 1993. *Una Ciudad Chilena del Siglo XVI: Valdivia: 1552–1604, urbanistica, res pública, economía, Sociedad.* Santiago: Univ. Católica de Chile.

Guarda, Gabriel. 2001. *Nueva Historia de Valdivia*. Chile, Santiago: Ediciones Universidad Católica de Chile.

Serrano, Gustavo. 2002. *450 Años de Valdivia*. Chile, Temuco: Imprenta. Austral. Niños.

# 7

# What lurks beneath

## Deep supply chain risks

*Yossi Sheffi*

The past decade has seen a growing awareness of the need for systematic enterprise risk management (ERM) practices. In the wake of the 2001 Enron accounting scandal in the US, the Sarbanes-Oxley Act of 2002 pushed companies to adopt more formal risk management procedures by requiring a top-down risk assessment and improved internal risk controls. ERM is becoming more standardized, too, through the efforts of groups such as COSO (Committee of Sponsoring Organizations of the Treadway Commission)[1] and ISO (International organization for Standardization).[2] ISO, for example, maintains a host of related standards that address specific categories of risks such as ISO 31000 (overall risk management), ISO 28000 (security risk management systems for the supply chain), ISO 27001 (information security), ISO 26000 (social responsibility), ISO 14000 (environmental management), and ISO 9000 (quality management).[3] The ERM Initiative at North Carolina State University has traced the rising adoption of ERM with annual surveys beginning in 2009.[4] In 2009, only 8.8% of companies claimed to have "a complete ERM process." By 2015, the number had risen to 25%.

Much of the maturing discipline of enterprise risk management focuses on risks to the company's facilities, personnel, and resources. These include risks in categories that span environmental, health, and safety; site security; business process integrity; regulatory compliance; financial controls; and governance. Companies address supply disruption risks with well-known strategies, such as second-sourcing and stockpiled inventories of crucial materials. Yet a series of examples from the new millennium shows how modern global supply chains create new categories of risks that are far outside the four walls of the company and its direct business partners.

Using examples of natural and man-made disruptions, this chapter enumerates many of the types of risks intrinsic to complex, deep, broad supply chains to provide a case-driven multi-organizational view of enterprise risk. These examples cover deep-tier supply chain risks; indirect risk exposures linked to suppliers, customers, or competitors; and supply chain risks that occur at a broader industry or regional level due to companies' increasing mutual interdependence within the global economy. The chapter also illustrates how companies map and manage these risks to push sound risk management practices out into their industries or through the tiers of their supply chains. The chapter assumes that the company already has sound internal risk management and crisis management processes but needs to understand and manage these extra-organizational risks.

## 1 Risks beyond the four walls

Three trends – the increasing globalization of suppliers and customers, the widespread use of lean manufacturing, and the increasing sophistication of materials and technologies in products – give rise to a growing category of business risks that occur outside the four walls of an organization and beyond that organization's direct control.

The leading driver of this growing vulnerability is the explosion of global trade. Global merchandise exports surged from $7.38 trillion in 2003 to $18.49 trillion in 2014.[5] Rapidly declining costs of communications and growing efficiency of logistics are enabling all this trade, with the resulting lengthening of supply chains. Digital communications mean companies can more readily work with facilities, suppliers, and distribution centers on the other side of the world.

Global competition motivated companies to hunt for the best price and performance in global supplier markets. As companies outsourced their manufacturing operations to distant lands and distant suppliers, lead time from order to delivery lengthened, meaning that there were more opportunities for things to go wrong. More actors were involved – from suppliers to service providers to multiple governments and regulatory regimes – thereby further increasing complexity and the probability of failure.

With product complexity comes the need to use more suppliers, who in turn may use more suppliers, leading to more complex supply chains. For example, car seats of the past were like pieces of furniture in that they depended only on suppliers of cloth, leather, stuffing, and some metal or plastic framing. But modern car seats are technological gizmos that also include switches, motors, heating elements, sensors, and the ubiquitous microprocessor to control the seat. Even the seat materials themselves are more advanced, with high-tech foams, more durable, fashionable, and sustainable textiles, and high-strength steel alloys that reduce the weight of the seat to improve fuel economy.[6] Although all of these changes improve the average performance of the products and companies, they also create increased risks as exemplified by the following examples.

### *1.1 Disruption in the deep tiers*

At 2:26 p.m. local time, Friday, March 11, 2011, some 72 kilometers off the coast of the Tohoku region of Japan, the Pacific plate broke its locked fault line and began to shear downward and westward while the Okhotsk plate beneath northern Japan thrust upward and eastward. More than 1,000 years of accumulated tectonic strain broke free, sending a seismic shock wave racing at over 7,000 kilometers per hour through the solid rock of the floor of the Pacific.[7] In less than a minute, the first earthly shudders reached Japan. And after the shaking came an enormous tsunami that inundated much of the northeast coast of Japan and flooded the nuclear reactor complex at Fukushima.

General Motors' Detroit headquarters lay a comfortable 6,400 miles from Japan. The quake and tsunami struck around 1 a.m. Detroit time. When GM's executives learned of the disaster in the morning, they were somewhat worried about their Japanese Tier 1 suppliers but did not think that they faced a corporation-wide crisis. A scant 2% of GM vehicle parts came from Japan, and only 25 of GM's 18,500 Tier 1 suppliers were in Japan. Yet GM's experience with the 2011 quake shows just how deeply interconnected companies have become, and how unknown risks can vastly outweigh known ones.

GM's purchasing department worked through the weekend, trying to get information from Japanese suppliers. However, like many other companies, GM had a difficult time reaching these suppliers. Power and telecommunications were down in the affected area. Japanese roads and railroads were closed pending inspection for damage, so workers could not get to suppliers' work sites. By Monday, GM received some initial reports of the severity of the damage and which suppliers had been impacted.

By Tuesday, March 15, GM estimated that 30 suppliers and 390 parts were affected by the quake and tsunami. Although 390 parts out of a total of about 30,000 parts for an average car seems minor, GM can only ship cars that have all their parts. Initial estimates based on available inventories showed that outages of these parts would halt production at many GM assembly plants in only 8 days. More ominously, the initial estimate was that by the end of March, all of GM's factories worldwide would be down. Worse, initial estimates suggested that production might be disrupted for at least seven months. That's when alarm bells rang throughout GM.

The deeper GM's team dug, the bigger the problems they found. Some of GM's non-Japanese suppliers had Japanese suppliers. And some of GM's non-Japanese suppliers had other non-Japanese suppliers who had Japanese suppliers. Although an anti-lock brake module or dashboard assembly might be made in the US by an American Tier 1 supplier, the electrical components may have come from Japan, which has a long history of making these devices. Like many products, automobiles have become more complex through the addition of dozens of microprocessors, sensors, and actuators that boost fuel efficiency, performance, and driver conveniences.[8] All of GM's cars had computer chips, sensors, displays, radios, and navigation systems made with electronic parts from Japan.

"The list kept growing. And every day, it went up. It was a moving target for us," said Rob Thom, Manager, Global Vehicle Engineering Operations.[9] Electronics weren't the only concern. GM soon discovered that almost every type of part on many different vehicles required something from Japan. Xirallic, a sparkly additive in the paint used on the Corvette, came from Japan. Special plastics for the body trim came from Japan. Rubber seals and gaskets came from Japan. High-tech chrome plating on turbochargers came from Japan. Cooling fans, radiator caps, air-conditioner compressors, and many more parts had some tie to Japanese suppliers.

From the known 390 affected parts on March 14, the number grew to 1,551 parts on March 24, 1,889 on March 29, and to a staggering 5,329 by April 13. During the month after the quake, GM discovered an average of 160 disrupted parts each day. Nor was the problem helped by the ongoing crisis with the Fukushima nuclear plant and the persistent power shortages in Japan. In the end, it took more than two months to even know how many parts were impacted. The final figure of 5,830 affected parts was nearly 15 times higher than the initial estimate of 390 parts associated with the Tier 1 suppliers in Japan. And each missing part raised the specter of halting production somewhere in GM's system.

## *1.2 Dangerous diamonds in the supply chain*

Some of the individual supplier disruptions during the 2011 Japan earthquake illustrate a more serious category of deep supply chain risk. Silicon chips may get all the glory as the premiere technology that powers smartphones, tablets, laptops and almost every electronic product, but the less glamorous plastics used in chip substrates and printed circuit boards are just as essential. Current-day microchips can have over 500 connections using a tiny grid of solder balls embedded in a thin substrate.[10] That inscrutable density of connections requires extremely specialized materials such as bismaleimide triazine (BT), an epoxy resin that is strong, thermally conductive, and able to hold extremely tight tolerances over time and temperature variances.

Until the quake, Mitsubishi Gas Chemical's (MGC) Fukushima facility supplied most of the world's BT.[11] A prolonged shutdown of MGC's factories after the earthquake caused bottlenecks in the worldwide integrated-circuit (IC) assembly industry supply chain.[12] "Our contacts in Asia suggest one of the bigger problems may actually be the growing shortage of BT," said Craig Berger, an analyst with investment bank FBR.[13] Lead times for IC substrates grew to the 75- to 125-day range.[14] A company such as Apple or Samsung might buy chips from more than a dozen different chip makers, including second sources or second fabs for many components. Yet all of those different chip makers and alternative suppliers depend on BT, most of which came from that one MGC facility.

Whereas the typical supply chain diagram shows fans of interconnections by which every company has many suppliers – shaped like a pyramidal hierarchy – the BT/MGC example shows that sometimes those lines converge to a single dominant supplier deep in a lower layer – a diamond-shaped interconnection structure. BT/MGC wasn't the only diamond structure disruption of specialized materials exposed by the Japan quake. Disruptions in the supply of Xirallic, the pigment made in Japan by Merck, affected manufacturing of certain colors of luxury cars at Toyota Motors, Chrysler LLC, GM, Ford Motor, BMW, VW, Audi and other car makers.[15] Lithium ion batteries require PVDF (polyvinylidene fluoride), and 70% of the global supply came from one factory in Fukushima province. Although the plant survived the quake, the tsunami devastated the nearby port that was critical to supplying raw materials to the plant.[16] Other supply chain diamond structures revealed by the Japan quake included high-purity hydrogen peroxide used in chip making, and EPDM (ethylene propylene diene monomer) used by car makers in rubber gaskets and seals.[17] "What we've found is that in Tiers 3 and 4, the convergence of underlying raw material supply starts to become really significant," said Jackie Sturm, Intel's Vice President and General Manager of Global Sourcing and Procurement.[18]

Other examples of deep diamond risks occur at the country level. Japan makes 100% of the world's supply of protective polarizer film for LCD displays, 89% of aluminum capacitors, and 72% of silicon wafers.[19] Four companies in Japan have a near monopoly on digital compasses: the tiny magnetic field sensors that sit inside almost every new phone, tablet, laptop, and navigation system device.[20] "Many organizations are more or less forced to put all eggs in one basket because of the clusters of suppliers for various goods around the globe," said Damien Pang, Regional Manager, Claims, at Allianz Global Corporate & Specialty Asia/Pacific.[21]

## *1.3 Lateral disruptions of customers*

Moreover, some supply chain risks can have indirect, lateral effects on companies that don't even buy materials from the disrupted suppliers. For example, hard disks would seem to be extremely easy items to procure and to second-source. They adhere to well-known mechanical, electrical, and software standards. Although drives do vary somewhat in performance and reliability, most are generally interchangeable for most applications. Further, in 2011, the hard disk industry had five large competitive suppliers to handle the volume.[22] But then the rains came.

Between late June and early October 2011, above-normal monsoons plus five tropical cyclone systems struck Southeast Asia and dumped heavy rains in the highlands of Thailand. Over a period of weeks the waters rose, displacing more than two million people, flooding 7,510 factories, and damaging 1,700 roads, highways, and bridges. Some factories were underwater for more than five weeks.[23]

The floods proved that second sourcing doesn't always mitigate risks. The industrial parks in central Thailand had become an economic cluster for making hard disks and their components. Four of the five top suppliers of drives (Western Digital, Seagate Technologies, Hitachi Global Storage Technologies, and Toshiba) all had facilities or key suppliers in Thailand. And all four suffered substantial capacity disruptions during the Thai floods.[24] In aggregate, Thailand provided 45% of worldwide hard-drive production. The flood disrupted much of it,[25] creating a 35% shortfall in disk supplies for the PC industry.[26]

The floods in Thailand did not directly affect Intel nor its suppliers. In fact, Intel stood to gain from the disruption because the company sold SSDs (Solid State Drives), which compete with hard disks for mass storage solutions in PCs, laptops, and servers. "We'll be using this as an opportunity" to increase sales of solid-state drives, Intel's Chief Financial Officer Stacy Smith told analysts.[27]

But the 35% shortfall in disk supplies hit PC production, which meant that PC makers curtailed purchase of all PC components, including Intel products. "We've seen a drop in orders for microprocessors in the fourth quarter," said Smith.[28] Intel lost about $800 million in revenue for the fourth quarter 2011 relative to expectations.[29] "We found with Thailand that for want of a nail a kingdom can be lost. So for us, even though our production might continue, if other critical components to our customers can't ship, like a hard drive, then everybody stops," said Intel's Jackie Sturm.[30]

Unlike many other classic disruption risks, lateral disruptions impact demand: customers curtail purchasing. Traditional supply chain risk strategies such as second sourcing or added inventory offer no mitigation. In fact, the inventory stockpiling strategy actually increases the risks of obsolete inventory.

## *1.4 Industry-wide risks from economic clusters*

The Intel Thailand example shows how a supplier disruption can disrupt customer companies which, in turn, disrupts other unrelated suppliers. The reverse can occur with a disrupted customer company that disrupts suppliers and, in turn, disrupts other customers. It's not every day that the CEO of one major company pleads for a government bailout of his fiercest competitors. Yet that's exactly what Ford CEO Alan Mulally did in front of the Senate banking committee on November 18, 2008. He said:

> If any one of the domestic companies should fail, we believe there is a strong chance that the entire industry would face severe disruption. Ours is in some significant ways an industry that is uniquely interdependent – particularly with respect to our supply base, with more than 90 percent commonality among our suppliers. Should one of the other domestic companies declare bankruptcy, the effect on Ford's production operations would be felt within days, if not hours. Suppliers could not get financing and would stop shipments to customers. Without parts for the just-in-time inventory system, Ford plants would not be able to produce vehicles.[31]

"Our dealer networks also have substantial overlap. Approximately 400 of our dealers also have a GM or Chrysler franchise at their dealership. The failure of one of the companies would clearly have a great impact on our dealers with exposure to that company." Mulally concluded, "In short, a collapse of one of our competitors here would have a ripple effect across all automakers, suppliers, and dealers – a loss of nearly three million jobs in the first year, according to an estimate by the Center for Automotive Research."[32]

Yet Mulally may have been wrong in his belief of being "uniquely interdependent." The contaminated peanut scare and German *Escherichia coli* cases (described in the next section) show the interdependence of food producers in which quality failures at one producer can severely disrupt the sales of all producers. The acetonitrile/acrylonitrile case (described in the following section) shows the interdependence between housing and pharmaceuticals industries. It also demonstrates the fragility of coupled production, in which a manufacturing process creates two or more different commodities simultaneously. If demand for one commodity drops, then supply of the other commodity falls, too. Issues such as rare earths, conflict minerals, and RoHS-obsolete[33] parts create interdependence among many companies, industries, and regions.

Finally, the economic events of 2008 proved that the global financial system was the biggest diamond of them all. Most companies discovered just how dependent they were on their suppliers of capital – the banks – to support themselves, their suppliers, and ensure customer demand. Ultimately, government bailouts did avert a systemic cascading failure in the banking system and major industries.

## *1.5 Lateral co-supplier disruptions*

During a 2-month period beginning in May 2011, some 3,100 German residents and European tourists suffered from bloody diarrhea, 850 developed hemolytic uremic syndrome, and 53 people died.[34] The frantic search for the cause depended on very sick people's fuzzy memories for where they had eaten and what they had eaten. "Our absolute first priority is to clarify the source of the outbreak because, if we can't do that, we're not going to win back consumer confidence," said Roger Waite, a spokesman for Dacian Ciolos, the European agriculture commissioner.[35]

Based on victims' reports, salad in Germany topped the menu of suspects. The Robert Koch Institute advised consumers to avoid raw vegetables.[36] European supermarkets drastically cut orders for tomatoes, lettuce, and cucumbers, causing European farmers significant losses. On May 26th, the Hamburg Institute for Hygiene and the Environment found three Spanish cucumbers that tested positive for *Escherichia coli*,[37] causing eight countries to ban Spanish cucumbers.[38]

The effects were swift and devastating. Spanish farmers lost €200 million a week as some 150,000 tons of unwanted Spanish fruit and vegetables (not only cucumbers) piled up each week, according to FEPEX, Spain's fruit and vegetable export body.[39] Asked about the scope of the slump in demand, Jorge Brotons, FEPEX president said: "Almost all Europe. There is a domino effect on all vegetables and fruits."[40]

When further tests showed that Spanish cucumbers did not have the outbreak's particular strain of *E. coli*,[41] the German agriculture secretary Robert Kloos admitted: "Germany recognizes that the Spanish cucumbers are not the cause."[42] Yet German officials continued to advise avoidance of raw tomatoes, lettuce, and cucumbers, causing the slump to hit farmers in other countries, too. Victor Miranda, a grocer in Paris, said, "Even if the cucumbers are from France and not from Spain, nobody wants to eat them."[43] Koos De Vries, a Dutch cucumber grower, said, "From a business point of view, it's a catastrophe for us."[44]

Ultimately, neither Spanish produce nor any kind of cucumbers, tomatoes, or lettuce proved to be the cause. Instead, the contamination was traced to Egyptian fenugreek seeds[45] used by a small German producer of organic sprouts.[46] Yet vindication was cold comfort for all the cucumber and salad ingredient producers in Spain and across Europe who were brought to the edge of bankruptcy by the scare and erroneous government warnings.

A similar case occurred when Sunland Inc., a processor of organic peanuts and other nuts, had a salmonella contamination that sickened 42 people in 20 US states.[47] Although Sunland Inc. was only a $55 million company, its nuts and the subsequent recall encompassed over 300 products from 36 brand-name companies. The recall hit a number of "healthy" food and retail brands, such as Trader Joes, Whole Foods, Earth Balance, Newman's Own Organics, and Cadia All Natural,[48] as well as more mainstream brands such as Harry and David, Target, and Stop & Shop. And it wasn't just jars of peanut butter but also cookies, snack crackers, brownies, nut mixes, and even ice cream that were recalled.

The direct costs of the recall were $78 million, yet the estimated costs to American peanut-containing product makers was $1 billion, including growers and product makers unaffiliated with Sunland.[49] Deep-tier diamond structures reside in many industries, and a small problem with a niche supplier can reverberate far and wide. As with the Thailand-Intel example, the food contamination events can operate laterally and disrupt demand for many customers and supplier companies beyond those directly hit.

## *1.6 Lateral disruption of other customers of suppliers*

Disruptions can zigzag through one supply chain to disrupt other supply chains. Acrylic and ABS (acrylonitrile-butadiene-styrene) are very popular plastics used in carpet, cars, electronic housings, and small appliances. When the financial crisis struck in 2008, demand for acrylic and ABS plummeted, affecting plastics makers and suppliers of the ingredient chemicals used to synthesize these plastics. One key ingredient is acrylonitrile, a colorless liquid with a garlic-like odor made by reacting ammonia with propylene gas. As demand for these plastics dropped, global acrylonitrile production dropped by 40%.

Acrylonitrile synthesis also creates a sister chemical, acetonitrile, as a by-product. For every 100 liters of acrylonitrile produced, the chemical maker also typically gets about 2–4 liters of acetonitrile. Some chemical plants simply burn the by-product as fuel for the factory. But a few companies extract the acetonitrile, purify it, and sell it for a host of minor applications, including as a solvent used in research labs and in quality assurance testing in the pharmaceutical industry.

When acrylonitrile production plummeted, the acetonitrile supply went with it. At the same time, the Chinese restricted production in order to reduce air pollution for the Beijing Olympic Games, and Hurricane Ike knocked out a Texas supplier.[50] "The market is beyond short," said Jerry Richard of Purification Technologies, a Chester, Connecticut-based firm that buys acetonitrile in bulk, purifies it, and sells it to laboratory chemical suppliers. "You have people scrambling around trying to get material. My phone is ringing off the hook," Richard said.[51] Risks such as these are a side effect of companies' quests for efficiency and utilization – to the extent that companies in one industry produce by-products that can be sold to another industry, the risks of supply or demand disruptions become coupled between the two industries.

## *1.7 The dark underbelly of supply chains*

Much farther down in all supply chains for material goods lies one more layer of suppliers of basic commodities such as oil, minerals, and agricultural products. Many of these commodities – such as oil, gasoline, diesel, natural gas, steel, copper, wheat, and cotton – have very broad production and distribution networks around the world. Aside from local distribution disruptions (e.g., the scarcity of gasoline in New York City after hurricane Sandy[52]), these commodities are available at all times on world markets, although the prices can be volatile.

And because companies can manage price volatility risks of common commodities using hedging or vertical integration, the risks of true disruptions seem minimal. Yet companies face two serious exceptions to this general rule of mitigatable risks for base commodities.

High technology supply chains, especially, depend on a very large number of commodities, many of which either don't come from broad supply bases or lack adequate hedging instruments in the financial markets. This risk has risen with the increasing use of obscure elements in electronic products. "Twenty or thirty years ago electronics were being made with 11 different elements. Today's computers and smartphones use something like 63 different elements," explained Thomas Gradael, a professor of geology and geophysics at the Yale School of Forestry & Environmental Studies.[53]

Of special importance are 17 metals known as rare earth elements (REE) that go into a wide range of technology products such as iPhones, wind turbines, solar cells, jet engines, fiber optics, hard disk drives, and compact fluorescent bulbs.[54] The average Ford car, for example, contains about half a kilogram of REE scattered in the vehicle's sensors, electric motors, displays, and catalytic converter. In 2002, those REE cost only about $10 per car. In 2012, they cost $100. New electric cars require even larger amounts of rare earth materials in their batteries and electric motors – about $1,000/car (in 2012 REE prices).[55] In 2007, the metal europium (an REE) cost $300/kg.[56] By 2010, that price had more than doubled to $625/kg. In 2012, it surged to $3,800/kg.[57] Yet unavoidable price volatility is least of the risks.

China produces 95% of the world supply of REE and in July 2010, China restricted exports of REE – cutting off many companies that make products using these materials.[58] In response, the US lodged a formal protest with the World Trade Organization (WTO). EU Trade Commissioner Karel De Gucht said, "China's restrictions on rare earths and other products violate international trade rules and must be removed. These measures hurt our producers and consumers in the EU and across the world, including manufacturers of pioneering high-tech and 'green' business applications."[59] Whether China's rationale for this action was environmental[60] or economic[61] is beside the point. Such actions – dubbed "resource nationalism" – can disrupt raw material supplies on which so many products and global companies depend.

An EU Commission study of 54 materials identified 20 as being of both of global economic importance and having supply risks, including concentration of supply, instability of the producing countries, and difficulty of substitution.[62] Besides REE, the study found potential supply risks in materials such as silicon, chromium, magnesium, graphite, phosphates, and others. An analysis of risks in the mining industry ranked "resource nationalism" as the #1 risk in both 2011 and 2012.[63] Some 33% of companies in a 2011 World Economic Forum survey ranked "export/import restrictions" as "most likely to provoke significant and systemic effects on supply chain or transport networks."[64]

A second category of commodity-related deep supply risks comes from the other end of the supply chain and is actually exacerbated by breadth of supply. For example, to protest the destruction of tropical forests for the farming of palm oil, Greenpeace attacked Nestle with a video parody of the company's KitKat "give me a break" candy bar ads.[65] The video implied that Nestle was killing orangutans by buying palm oil from suppliers who were destroying Indonesian rain forests.[66] Greenpeace raided Nestle's annual meeting in 2010. Activists dressed as orangutans stood outside Nestle's headquarters in Frankfurt, Germany, while other activists unfurled a banner inside the meeting itself.[67]

Consumer-facing companies are especially sensitive to brand reputation issues, which is why activists typically attack consumer brand companies rather than the deeper tier suppliers who may be the ones directly guilty of perceived environmental or social responsibility misdeeds. Greenpeace attempted to disrupt demand for Nestle products despite the fact that Nestle does not directly buy palm oil from any specific plantation and, in the words of Jose Lopez, who was responsible for Nestle's manufacturing of KitKat, "you would have to 'look through a microscope' to find the palm oil in the snack."[68]

In another example, Forest Ethics has a long-running campaign to force companies to avoid buying diesel fuel derived from Canada's tar sands.[69] Although many of the targeted manufacturers and retailers buy no diesel fuel directly because they rely on trucking companies to move their wares, consumer-facing companies are more susceptible to public pressure, demonstrations, and boycotts. "The trucking companies care more about what their customers want than what we want," explained Forest Ethics' U.S. campaign director Aaron Sanger.[70]

## *1.8 Knots in the network*

Although most disruptions hit the manufacturing nodes in the supply chain, a crucial category of deep supply chain hazards affect the transportation links that connect all those nodes together. For example, in April 2010, a modest-sized ice-capped volcano named Eyjafjallajökull in southern Iceland roused from a 187-year slumber. When blazing hot lava hit the volcano's ice and water-filled caldera, the mixture flashed into ash-laden steam that blasted high into the atmosphere. The prevailing winds carried the thick gray-brown ash cloud southeast.

The ash cloud's potential threat to aircraft caused European aviation authorities to close portions of European airspace, starting with Norway. The closures expanded and shifted over a 6-day period as the eruption continued and capricious winds pushed the ash in different directions. Major air freight hubs such as Heathrow, Amsterdam, Paris, and Frankfurt were closed for up to five days.[71]

Although volcanoes, primarily in the Pacific Rim, had in the past caused trouble for individual aircraft and particular air routes, they had been localized incidents easily handled by detouring around the affected area.[72] Companies, however, weren't prepared for an event that shut down every airport and every carrier over a large, economically vigorous region. For example, FedEx's contingency plan for a closure of Paris was to use Frankfurt, but Frankfurt was closed, too.[73]

"There's a major disruption of the supply chain," said Paul Tsui, Vice Chairman of the Hong Kong Association of Freight Forwarding and Logistics."[74] In the UK alone, air freight provides 25% of all imports[75] and 55% of exports to non-EU countries.[76] Although some air freight might not be particularly time-sensitive (e.g., jewelry), many categories of freight are (e.g., perishable goods, vaccines, emergency spare parts, surgical instruments, and components for just-in-time manufacturing).[77] The closures hit supply chains in both upstream and downstream directions.

Migros, the Swiss supermarket chain, noted disruptions in supplies from the U.S. (green asparagus), Iceland (cod), and Southeast Asia (tuna). UK grocery stores ran out of pre-sliced fruit and tropical fruits like pineapple.[78] Hotels and restaurants in Hong Kong had shortages of French cheese, Belgian chocolates, and Dutch fresh-cut flowers.[79] In many cases, the declared value of the air freight belied the importance of the shipments to the recipient. Nissan's inability to fly $30 air pressure sensors from Ireland to Japan kept the car maker from producing $30,000 Nissan Murano SUVs.[80] Three BMW plants in Germany couldn't get inbound parts from Asia.[81] And an inability to ship transmissions out of Europe disrupted production at BMW's U.S. factory.[82]

"It's a terrible nightmare," said Stephen Mbithi, the chief executive officer of the Fresh Produce Exporters Association of Kenya.[83] During the 6 days of airport closures, thousands of tons of fresh flowers rotted in storage units and warehouses, representing a loss to the Kenyan economy of $3.8 million per day,[84] which represents about 3% of Kenya's daily gross domestic product (GDP).[85] "Cow food, that's about all we can do with it now," concluded Kenneth Maundu, general manager for Sunripe produce exporters.[86] Italian exporters of mozzarella and fresh fruits lost about $14 million each day during the closures.[87] For many purveyors of time-sensitive goods, air freight to or from Europe was a diamond in their supply chain structure – a chokepoint in transportation that impacted all of them.

The International Air Transport Association (IATA) estimated that the Icelandic volcano crisis cost airlines more than $1.7 billion in lost revenue in the 6 days after the initial eruption. At its worst, the ash cloud grounded 29% of the world's scheduled air travel – some 107,000 flight cancellations – over an 8-day period.[88] The disruption of passenger air travel would seem to mean little to the air freight industry, except for the fact that most air freight actually comes in the bellies of passenger aircraft.[89] In total, global cargo flights were down over 15% in April, proving that the post-disruption rebound did not make up for the losses.[90]

Air freight isn't the only vulnerable mode, and volcanoes aren't the only hazard that causes disruption to bottlenecks in transportation systems around the world. On the Rhine River, which carries 16% of Germany's trade,[91] recurring droughts,[92] an overturned barge in 2011,[93] and unexploded bombs from WWII[94] have all created constrictions in freight volume. In the U.S., drought in the Mississippi River basin caused a 2-month disruption in the winter of 2012–2013 and resulted in an estimated $6 billion in losses.[95] A quarter of all U.S. rail traffic and half of all intermodal rail traffic passes through Chicago, which was disrupted by a 1999 blizzard. "We basically waited for the spring thaw," said David Grewe, a supervisor for Union Pacific Railroad.[96] In November of 2012, 400 office clerks walked off their jobs at the ports of Los Angeles and Long Beach, thereby halting the movement of $760 million a day worth of goods.[97]

These logistical network risks are a paradoxical result of the success of the logistics industry to create high-speed, high-reliability, low-cost movement of goods around the world. As more companies, suppliers, and suppliers' suppliers build manufacturing and distribution strategies around high-performance global logistics, they expose themselves to risks that a disruption in logistical networks can ripple through the supply chain.

## 2 Managing deep supply chain risks

"I have 14,000 suppliers. I guarantee that with 14,000 suppliers, at least one of them is not performing well today," said Tom Linton, chief procurement and supply chain officer at Flextronics.[98] As companies realize they are exposed to deep and broad supply chain risks, they seek ways to identify, prevent, and mitigate those risks. And because those risks lie far outside the span of control of the enterprise, these deep supply chain risk management activities sometimes depend on third parties who may have better visibility or better influence over the deeper parts of the supply chain.

### *2.1 Mapping the supply chain*

"We're trying to understand the sub-supply chain wherever it's possible and where our suppliers will share that information," said Intel's Sturm. One major challenge is the natural reticence of suppliers, because the identity of a supplier's suppliers, the materials they procure, and the relationships between the companies are proprietary and are part of the supplier's competitive advantage. A second challenge is the dynamic nature of supply chains, with constant turnover in the supply base as well as the locations used by suppliers for any particular part. Moreover, as more companies attempt to map their supply chains, suppliers face administrative costs for responding to multiple requests for information.

Resilinc Inc.[99] exemplifies a new generation of supply chain software and services companies addressing these mapping issues. Resilinc surveys a client company's suppliers to map them and keeps suppliers' proprietary business data secure. The surveys cover risk management issues such as supplier facility locations, sub-supplier locations, business continuity planning, recovery times, emergency contact data, conflict minerals, and other concerns. Resilinc uses the client's bill-of-material data and value-at-risk estimates (a measure of the potential loss to the company) for each product to cross-reference parts with mapped locations and identify high-risk parts. The software uses data on the supplier locations producing each part, the parts in each product, and the financial contributions of each product to estimate the value-at-risk of each supplier location. Other companies offering similar services include Razient Inc.[100] and MetricStream.[101]

Some companies, such as IBM, Cisco, and ATMI, created in-house supplier mapping applications. However, third-party services such as Resilinc and its competitors can reduce the costs of supplier mapping and updating because the survey data can be pooled among multiple customer companies, which often have overlapping sets of suppliers. Such a "network effect" reduces the costs of information collection as well as the compliance burden on suppliers. Whichever way it is done, geographic mapping of the supply chain helps find concentrations of risk at the product, supplier, industrial cluster, and commodity level.

## *2.2 Monitoring the supply chain*

"Information and visibility are the backbones of incident response, and these tools have to be in place prior to the crisis," said John O'Connor, Cisco's Senior Director of Supply Chain Transformation.[102] Detecting deep-tier disruptions quickly is essential. It gives the company time to assess the problem and mitigate the disruption – by finding alternative suppliers, qualifying new materials, or helping the deep-tier supplier to recover. It also gives the company a leg up on competitors in securing supplies. Monitoring world events, detecting potentially disruptive ones, and creating alerts can be handled by companies like Resilinc or by the company itself.

Although a company's emergency operations center may be monitoring 24-hour TV news channels, these sources of breaking news only cover the largest of stories of a more general interest. Event monitoring services such as NC4,[103] Anvil,[104] IJet,[105] OSAC,[106] or CargoNet[107] offer more fine-grained monitoring, sometimes with a specialized purpose such as travelers' security (Anvil), socio-political threats (OSAC),[108] or cargo security (CargoNet). In a representative week, a service such as NC4 might issue 1,700 alert messages covering 650 events around the world.[109] Many events seem quite localized, such as a shooting in a mall in Omaha, student demonstrations in Colombia, or the crash of a small plane in Mexico City.[110]

The raw event feed is then filtered by the event monitoring service, a company like Resilinc, or by the company's own incident management systems. The filters remove non-supply-chain disruptions (e.g., residential house fires) and then cross-compare the distances of potential disruptions with the locations of mapped facilities. Most alert-software tools offer customization, allowing companies to specify alert thresholds for each type of facility based on event severity and distance from the facility.[111] If an event potentially affects a supplier and thus affects one or more of their clients' companies, Resilinc determines which parts and products may be affected as well as the potential value-at-risk and sends an alert about the event to each affected company. During the 2011 Thailand floods, Resilinc helped Flextronics gain about a week's warning regarding the threat posed by the rising waters.

## 2.3 Supplier code of conduct

Supply disruptions are not the only enterprise risks lurking in deep supply chains. On April 24, 2013, horrific images saturated news outlets as over 1,100 bodies were pulled from the collapsed eight-story Rana Plaza garment factory in Bangladesh.[112] Rana Plaza wasn't an isolated incident. Six months before, a fire at a different Bangladeshi garment factory, Tazreen Fashions, killed 112.[113] These events put a tragic human face on repugnant conditions deep within some companies' global supply chains.

Paralleling the gruesome search for bodies under the rubble was the search for the Western companies whose garments were made in these death-trap factories. Most companies denied using suppliers operating in the structurally unsafe buildings. In the case of Rana Plaza, name-brand companies such as Benetton, Mango, Bonmarché, Primark, The Children's Place, and others acknowledged their current or past use of the suppliers operating there.[114]

Many companies simply didn't know which suppliers they were using, given the murky web of brokers, contractors, and subcontractors operating in countries like Bangladesh. For example, in the case of the Tazreen Fashions factory fire, Walmart believed it was not involved because the retailer had banned Tazreen Fashions more than a year prior to the fire after Walmart's hired auditors had declared Tazreen to be "high risk." But one of Walmart's other authorized suppliers subcontracted with another authorized supplier and then that subcontractor shifted the work to Tazreen.[115] Nor was worker safety in a few unsafe buildings the only social concern in Bangladesh. When Pope Francis learned that Bangladesh's minimum wage was only $40 per month, he said, "This is called slave labor."[116]

Revelations of substandard working conditions or environmental transgressions can disrupt a company's operations in at least three ways: consumer revulsion disrupts demand, local unrest disrupts supply, and regulatory changes impact costs. "Companies feel tremendous pressure now," said Scott Nova, the executive director of the Worker Rights Consortium, a factory-monitoring group based in Washington, DC.[117] He added, "The apparel brands and retailers face a greater level of reputation risk of being associated with abusive and dangerous conditions in Bangladesh than ever before."[118] The earlier example of Greenpeace's attack on Nestle over palm oil shows that environmental practices of suppliers deep in their supply chains create risks for consumer brand companies.

Companies typically rely on supplier codes of conduct enforced by audits. Such codes define expected or prohibited behavior, with some being prohibitions considered "zero-tolerance" requirements (e.g., child labor, toxic waste dumping). Yet the Walmart-Tazreen example shows that compliance is not always guaranteed, especially in the deeper tiers. Non-compliance incidents per audit are 18% higher at Tier 2 suppliers and 27% higher at Tier 3 suppliers compared to Tier 1 suppliers, according to data from the non-profit supply chain auditing group Sedex.[119]

Disney may be one of the most reputation-sensitive companies in the world, with a corporate unit devoted to developing and protecting a worldwide brand that is synonymous with happy families, the innocence of childhood, and wholesomeness. "Our goal is to have a supply chain that mirrors Disney's own desire to operate as a responsible business," said John Lund, Disney's senior vice president, integrated supply chain management.[120] Nearly two months before the Rana Plaza collapse, Disney ordered an end of sourcing from Bangladesh and four other countries (Pakistan, Belarus, Ecuador, and Venezuela) based on audits and personal visits by senior executives.

## 2.4 Cascading ERM into the supply chain

As large companies implement ERM, they start encouraging or requiring suppliers to do the same. For example, Medtronic expects suppliers to create and maintain Medtronic-specific business continuity plans (BCPs) and to show their BCPs to Medtronic on request. The company expects each supplier's planning to include a plan of action, checklist of activities, communication plans, escalation procedures, and the organization of teams, roles, and responsibilities.[121] Similarly, Cisco expects suppliers to use BCP and asks them about specific continuity assets such as backup generators (and fuel), fire protection and sprinkler systems, IT recovery strategies, and overall site recovery plans. Cisco surveys about 700 of its top suppliers and partners twice a year on BCP issues.[122] If Cisco finds gaps in a supplier's BCP, it works with the supplier via Cisco's supplier commodity managers.[123]

Rather than try to extract sensitive commercial information about the deeper-tier suppliers, some companies are helping their Tier 1 suppliers to manage their Tier 2 risks with the intent that Tier 2 suppliers will, in turn, manage the Tier 3 risks and so on. For example, Boston Scientific trains Tier 1 suppliers on its supplier risk scorecard system so they can use the system for their own suppliers.[124] Similarly, Tanya Bolden, Program Manager for the Auto Industry Action Group, said that "auto makers are relying on their large, direct suppliers to 'cascade training on safety and other workplace issues to their subcontractors.'"[125] Tim Hendry, Intel's Vice President, Technology and Manufacturing Group and Director of Fab Materials said, "We're trying to get our suppliers to work with their sub-suppliers on their resiliencies, sitting down and discussing their business continuity plans."[126]

## *2.5 Finding a locus of risk control*

In April 2009, John Prendergast, a human rights activist who had worked for the Clinton White House, the US State Department, and UNICEF prior to founding the Enough Project,[127] sent a letter to leading electronics firms, including Intel, HP, Motorola, and AT&T.[128] The letter warned that four metals (gold, tantalum, tin, and tungsten) used in electronic products could be akin to blood diamonds. Militants and terrorists in the eastern region of the Democratic Republic of Congo (DRC) were using violence, rape, and other atrocities to force citizens to mine the ore to help finance wars. The Enough Project sought to cut off indirect Western funding of the conflict by convincing companies not to buy so-called conflict minerals. The reputational threat to the companies receiving the letter was clear.

As a first step, Intel attempted to assess if it was using conflict minerals. But no one at the company knew because Intel itself didn't buy these metals or their ores directly. Next, the company asked suppliers about the issue: some didn't know, some didn't respond, and some said they didn't use conflict minerals but lacked supporting evidence.[129] Intel realized it would need to map these metals' supply chains down to the mine level to understand whether conflict minerals were getting into Intel's products and how Intel might control this risk.

Because the electronics industry consumes 60% of the world's tantalum supplies, Intel picked this metal as its first supply chain to map. The company mapped over 90% of its microprocessor supply chain, with employees visiting 13 countries in person to gain a firsthand understanding of the issues. Company employees toured mines with non-governmental organizations (NGOs) and followed the journey of the minerals as the ore went through a series of intermediaries to the smelters. The employees conducted more than 50 on-the-ground smelter reviews to understand ore sourcing practices. From the smelters, tantalum went to refiners for reprocessing into other forms, such as electronic-grade tantalum powder that is used by makers of electronics components that eventually make their way into Intel's products.

Controlling the risks of conflict minerals would be hard because "putting a de facto ban on materials out of the Congo means that good people might starve," said Gary Niekerk, Director of Global Citizenship at Intel. A ban would impact the 100,000 legitimate artisanal miners in the country, harm the economy, and fuel further unrest. The mapping effort helped Intel see that the relatively small number of smelters could be the logical focal point for controlling conflict minerals. Smelters were the last stage in the supply chain where the source of the ore could be identified. "Once it's turned into a bar of something, you can't trace the source," Niekerk said. "But as an ore, you can trace it. So we focused on smelters."[130]

Getting the cooperation of the smelters in managing conflict mineral risks was another challenge. These smelters sat six to seven layers deep in Intel's supply chain, which is far outside the usual span of influence that buyers have on their suppliers. Why would a Brazilian tantalum smelter care about Congolese ore or about an American chip-maker that's not the smelter's customer? As large as Intel might be, it represents a minuscule fraction of the demand for conflict minerals, especially tin, tungsten, and gold. As such, Intel, by itself, couldn't drive change.

Intel realized it would need to work with other companies in the electronics industry to create a critical mass of buyers who could cascade conflict mineral avoidance practices down through the many layers of the supply chain. To this end, Intel helped found the Electronic Industry Citizenship Coalition (EICC), which grew to encompass dozens of chip-making equipment suppliers, chip-makers, contract manufacturers, and electronics original equipment manufacturers (OEMs).[131] Intel and the EICC worked to create a simple, standardized Conflict-Free Smelter (CFS) certification process and reimbursed some of the costs of certification.

Intel set a 2013 goal to eliminate conflict-sourced tantalum in all its microprocessors. Next, Intel tackled gold, tin, and tungsten. In January 2014, Intel announced that its entire 2014 line of microprocessors would be conflict-free for all four minerals.[132] In August 2012, the U.S. Securities and Exchange Commission implemented rules outlined in the 2010 Wall Street Reform and Consumer Protection Act (aka "Dodd-Frank") to require public companies to disclose whether they use conflict minerals.[133]

## 2.6 Industry-level incident management

On March 31, 2012, a tank filled with highly flammable butadiene exploded in a chemical factory in Marl, Germany. Intense flames and thick black smoke billowed from Evonik Industries' cyclododecatriene (CDT) plant at the 7,000-worker chemical complex in the heavily industrialized Ruhr River valley. Roughly 130 firefighters fought the blaze for 15 hours to prevent its spread to the rest of the facility and to ultimately extinguish it. The explosion and fire killed two workers and severely damaged the plant.[134]

Cyclododecatriene sounds like an obscure chemical, but it is a key ingredient in making a high-performance plastic called nylon-12 or PA-12 that is especially prized for its chemical resistance, abrasion resistance, and fatigue resistance. PA-12 is a favorite of the auto industry, which uses it for fuel lines, brake lines, and plastic housings. The average light vehicle in 2011 used over 46 pounds of nylon, up from just 7 pounds in 1990.[135] PA-12 also goes into solar panels, carpets, athletic shoes, ski boots, optical fibers, cable conduits, and flame-retardant electrical insulation. CDT is a key precursor for making many other chemicals, such as brominated flame retardants, fragrances, hot-melt adhesives, and corrosion inhibitors.[136]

Whereas Japan's 2011 earthquake, tsunami, and nuclear reactor disaster devastated a region, directly impacted thousands of businesses, and dragged on for weeks, the Evonik fire was tiny and strictly localized by comparison. One part of one factory in one town had a fire. Less than a day later, the fire was out. But the explosion and fire destroyed almost half the world's production capacity for CDT. Worse, at the time of the explosion, CDT supplies were already tight due to its use in the booming solar panel industry.

Because Evonik was so deep in the supply chain, automakers weren't initially aware that the fire occurred. Not until a maker of fuel lines and brake lines – TI Automotive – raised the alarm about the dire implications of the Evonik fire did the automotive industry spring into action. The effect of the Evonik fire would prove to be very large – at GM, for example, supplies of 2,000 parts were jeopardized, which was one-third the number of parts that were disrupted by the far larger Japanese disaster. The impact of Evonik was so large because every car made by GM and every other automaker required nylon-12 plastic, which became scarce because of the Evonik fire. Dual- or multi-sourcing couldn't help in the case of the Evonik chemical plant explosion because no second source in the world had the capacity to make up for the loss at Evonik.

The auto industry convened an emergency summit on April 17 because no single automaker or supplier could address the problem. Two hundred people attended the summit, representing eight automakers and 50 suppliers.[137] All tiers of the affected sectors of the automotive supply chain came, including the big OEMs, their Tier 1 suppliers, component makers, polymer resin makers, and on down to chemical makers such as Evonik and BASF.[138] The summit was moderated by a neutral third party, the Automotive Industry Action Group (AIAG).[139] The AIAG is a volunteer-run, non-profit organization that provides shared expertise, knowledge, and standards on quality, corporate responsibility, and supply chain management to a thousand member firms in the automotive industry.[140]

The summit participants had three incident management objectives that required the collective expertise of the entire industry. First, they wanted to understand and quantify the current state of global PA-12 inventories and production capacities throughout the automotive supply chain. Second, they wanted to brainstorm options to strategically extend current PA-12 capacities and/or identify alternative materials or designs to offset projected capacity shortfalls. Third, they wanted to identify and recruit the necessary industry resources required to technically test and approve the alternatives.

The group formed six committees to help quickly create action plans to lessen any impact of shortages on component and vehicle production.[141] Each committee tackled an assigned task, such as managing remaining inventories, boosting production at existing suppliers, identifying new firms to produce resins, and finding replacement materials.[142] The group hosted multiple technical follow-up meetings during the subsequent weeks on these issues.[143]

This multifaceted collaboration was key to overcoming the challenge. Within a week of the meeting, the top OEMs had jointly drafted a plan to expedite their parts validation processes.[144] Harmonized validation processes ensured that a supplier didn't need a different validation process for each customer OEM. Suppliers from other industries lent their capacity to automotive applications. For example, carpet maker Invista Inc. released capacity for production of CDT.[145] In the end, cars continued to roll off the line even though the Evonik factory was offline for 9 months after the explosion and fire.[146]

## *2.7 Managing broad and deep risks beyond the four walls*

This chapter's examples illustrate both the risk exposures and risk management elements of organizations that are operating in a context of global suppliers and global customers. The combined quests for cost reductions, economies of scale, and market share drive consolidation and the development of dominant suppliers and supplier clusters, which then provide large fractions of global demand for a myriad of obscure but essential commodities. Companies' dependence on many different petrochemical, mineral, and agricultural raw materials creates risks of both supply disruption and demand disruption that arise far outside the normal span of influence of the organization and transcend the ERM capacities of individual companies. These concentrations in suppliers reduce the effectiveness or even the possibility of second sourcing as a risk management strategy. Furthermore, the rise of lean manufacturing, shorter product life cycles, and demand-disrupting risks makes extra inventory an unpalatable risk management strategy.

By taking a broader and deeper view of risk, companies can go beyond enterprise risk management to manage exposures and incidents linked to the deep and broad supply chains upon which virtually all companies depend. A more holistic understanding of the supply base, customer base, and lateral connected industries helps companies understand over-the-horizon risks such as hidden sole sources, lateral risk exposure, geographic chokepoints, and vulnerable commodities that are uncommon (REE) or contentious (palm oil). And because deep risks lie outside the enterprise, the risk management methods often lie outside the enterprise in using third-parties, cascading ERM deep into the supply chain, and collaborating to create industry-level risk management solutions. The economic forces that have driven globalization, innovation, and lean optimization are not likely to abate, which implies that as companies come to control their internal enterprise risks and proximate supply chain risks, they will find that further progress on enterprise risk management will increasingly entail managing broad and deep supply chains.

## Notes

1 www.coso.org/documents/coso_erm_executivesummary.pdf
2 www.iso.org/iso/home/standards/iso31000.htm
3 www.iso.org/iso/home/standards.htm
4 https://erm.ncsu.edu/library/article/current-state-erm-2015
5 www.wto.org/english/res_e/statis_e/its2015_e/its2015_e.pdf
6 www.automotive-textiles.de/
7 www.geonami.com/tohoku-earthquake-geophysical/
8 Robert Charette, This Car Runs on Code, *IEEE Spectrum*, February 1, 2009. http://spectrum.ieee.org/green-tech/advanced-cars/this-car-runs-on-code
9 Interview with Rob Thom, Manager, GM Global Vehicle Engineering Operations, August 2012.
10 www.intel.com/content/dam/www/public/us/en/documents/packaging-databooks/packaging-chapter-14-databook.pdf
11 www.docstoc.com/docs/88638192/Japan-Earthquake---Related-Industry-News-Update-Compiled-by; "Japan Earthquake Aftermath – Related Industry News Update" Compiled by Advanced MP Technology www.docstoc.com/docs/88638192/Japan-Earthquake---Related-Industry-News-Update-Compiled-by
12 "Japan Earthquake Aftermath – Related Industry News Update."
13 Mark LaPedus. "Quake to Cause Prices Hikes, Shortages." March 15, 2011. www.eetimes.com/document.asp?doc_id=1258944
14 www.researchinchina.com/news/NewsInfo.aspx?Id=18292
15 www.paintsquare.com/news/?fuseaction=view&id=5329&nl_versionid=859
16 Mariko Sanchanta, "Chemical Reaction: iPod Is Short Key Material," *Wall Street Journal*, March 29, 2011.
17 www.advisorperspectives.com/commentaries/gmo_112612.php
18 Interview with Jackie Sturm, VP and GM of Global Sourcing & Procurement at Intel, July 31, 2012.
19 Peter March, "Industry Left High and Dry," *Financial Times*, April 12, 2011.
20 www.emsnow.com/npps/story.cfm?pg=story&id=45416
21 Allianz, *Managing Disruptions*. www.agcs.allianz.com/assets/PDFs/white%20papers/AGCS%20Managing%20disruptions%20Nov2012.pdf
22 http://press.ihs.com/sites/ihs.newshq.businesswire.com/files/2011-09-06_HDD_Market_Share_0.jpg

23 http://thoughtleadership.aonbenfield.com/Documents/20120314_impact_forecasting_thailand_flood_event_recap.pdf
24 www.digitimes.com/news/a20111117PD210.html
25 http://news.techworld.com/personal-tech/3320401/thailand-floods-hard-drive-shortage-makes-small-pc-makers-hike-prices/
26 www.digitimes.com/news/a20111127PD201.html
27 Quentin Hardy, "Intel Sees Opportunity in Storage Drives," *New York Times*, December 12, 2011.
28 Eric Smally, "Thai Flood Sink Intel Chip Orders," *Wired*, December 12, 2011.
29 www.bloomberg.com/news/2011-12-12/intel-reduces-forecast-for-fourth-quarter-sales-on-hard-disk-drive-supply.html; Charles Arthur, "Intel Cuts Revenue Forecast as Thai Floods Hit PC Sales," *The Guardian*, December 12, 2011.
30 Interview with Jackie Sturm, VP and GM of Global Sourcing & Procurement at Intel, July 31, 2012.
31 www.gpo.gov/fdsys/pkg/CHRG-110shrg50418/html/CHRG-110shrg50418.htm
32 www.gpo.gov/fdsys/pkg/CHRG-110shrg50418/html/CHRG-110shrg50418.htm
33 http://ec.europa.eu/environment/waste/rohs_eee/events_rohs1_en.htm
34 European Food Safety Authority, E. Coli: Rapid Response in a Crisis. www.efsa.europa.eu/en/press/news/120711.htm
35 Joshua Chaffin, "Source of E. Coli Eludes Experts," *Financial Times*, May 31, 2011.
36 "New epidemiological data corroborate existing recommendation on consumption by BfR." Bundesinstitut für Risikobewertung.
37 www.bbc.co.uk/news/world-europe-13605910
38 www.thejournal.ie/spanish-cucumbers-not-responsible-for-e-coli-outbreak-146922-Jun2011/
39 www.theguardian.com/uk/2011/may/31/e-coli-deaths-16-germany-sweden
40 www.bbc.co.uk/news/world-europe-13605910
41 http://metro.co.uk/2011/06/01/1500-now-hit-by-e-coli-bug-as-spain-sues-for-damages-30231/
42 www.thejournal.ie/spanish-cucumbers-not-responsible-for-e-coli-outbreak-146922-Jun2011/
43 http://english.cntv.cn/program/newsupdate/20110601/103130.shtml
44 http://english.cntv.cn/program/newsupdate/20110601/103130.shtml
45 www.bfr.bund.de/cm/349/ehec-outbreak-2011-updated-analysis-as-a-basis-for-recommended-measures.pdf
46 Peter Walker, Abby D'Arcy Hughes and Adam Gabbatt, "E. Coli Outbreak "Trail" Leads to German Bean Sprouts, Authorities Say," *The Guardian*, June 6, 2011.
47 www.cdc.gov/salmonella/bredeney-09-12/index.html
48 http://concord-ca.patch.com/groups/politics-and-elections/p/peanut-butter-recall-expands-as-salmonella-outbreak-worsens
49 Associated Press, "Peanut Industry: Recall Price Tag $1 Billion," March 11, 2009. www.msnbc.msn.com/id/29634279/
50 www.zurich.com/internet/main/SiteCollectionDocuments/products-and-services/SCI_Risk_Insight_WSJ_articles.pdf
51 www.dailykos.com/story/2008/12/01/668305/-Side-Product-of-the-Economic-Meltdown-160-Important-Research-Chemical-in-Short-Supply
52 www.nydailynews.com/new-york/gas-nightmare-drags-new-yorkers-article-1.1198150
53 http://science.time.com/2013/12/20/rare-earths-are-too-rare/
54 http://blogs.ei.columbia.edu/2012/09/19/rare-earth-metals-will-we-have-enough/
55 Randolph Kirchain, presentation at the MIT CTL conference, "Crossroads 2012: "Supply Chains in Transition," held on June 28, 2012 in Cambridge, Massachusetts.
56 Marc Humphries, "Rare Earth Elements: The Global Supply Chain." Congressional Research Services, June 8, 2012. www.fas.org/sgp/crs/natsec/R41347.pdf
57 Marc Humphries, "Rare Earth Elements."
58 www.forbes.com/sites/larrybell/2012/04/15/chinas-rare-earth-metals-monopoly-neednt-put-an-electronics-stranglehold-on-america/
59 Eric Martin and Jennifer Freedman, "Obama Says China Rare-Earth Case Is Warning for WTO Violators," *Bloomberg*, March 13, 2012. www.bloomberg.com/news/2012-03-13/eu-joins-u-s-japan-in-challenging-china-s-rare-earth-export-restrictions.html
60 http://www3.weforum.org/docs/WEF_SCT_RRN_NewModelsAddressingSupplyChainTransportRisk_IndustryAgenda_2012.pdf
61 www.kitcometals.com/charts/copper_historical.html

62 http://eur-lex.europa.eu/legal-content/EN/TXT/?uri=CELEX:52014DC0297
63 Ernst and Young, Business Risks Facing Mining and Metals 2012–2013. www.ey.com/GL/en/Industries/Mining---Metals/Business-risks-facing-mining-and-metals-2012–2013
64 http://www3.weforum.org/docs/WEF_SCT_RRN_NewModelsAddressingSupplyChainTransportRisk_IndustryAgenda_2012.pdf
65 www.greenpeace.org/kitkat
66 Jeremiah Owyang, "Greenpeace vs. Brands: Social Media Attacks to Continue." *Forbes*, July 19, 2010. www.forbes.com/2010/07/19/greenpeace-bp-nestle-twitter-facebook-forbes-cmo-network-jeremiah-owyang.html
67 Greenpeace, Greenpeace Protests at Nestle Shareholder Meeting, 2010. Retrieved from: www.youtube.com/watch?v=s8kwVU5pujg
68 *The Economist*, "The Other Oil Spill," June 24, 2010. www.economist.com/node/16423833
69 http://forestethics.org/tar-sands
70 www.forbes.com/sites/amywestervelt/2011/08/17/the-big-pr-lesson-companies-still-need-to-learn-about-facebook/
71 http://en.wikipedia.org/wiki/Air_travel_disruption_after_the_2010_Eyjafjallajökull_eruption
72 http://pubs.usgs.gov/ds/545/DS545.pdf
73 http://blog.van.fedex.com/blog/business-unusual-flight-planning-and-iceland-volcano-eruption
74 http://in.reuters.com/article/2010/04/20/idINIndia-47840520100420
75 Richard Wray and Graeme Wearden, "Flight Ban Could Leave the UK Short of Fruit and Veg." *The Guardian*, April 16, 2010.
76 Bernice Lee and Felix Preston, with Gemma Green, "Preparing for High Impact, Low Probability Events: Lessons from Eyjafjallajokull," *Chatham House Report*, January 2012. www.chathamhouse.org/sites/default/files/public/Research/Energy,%20Environment%20and%20Development/r0112_highimpact.pdf
77 Bernice Lee and Felix Preston, with Gemma Green, "Preparing for High Impact, Low Probability Events."
78 Richard Wray and Graeme Wearden, "Flight Ban Could Leave the UK Short of Fruit and Veg," *The Guardian*, April 16, 2010. www.guardian.co.uk/business/2010/apr/16/flight-ban-shortages-uk-supermarkets
79 http://news.bbc.co.uk/2/hi/8631676.stm
80 http://news.bbc.co.uk/2/hi/8631676.stm
81 http://news.bbc.co.uk/2/hi/8631676.stm
82 www.thestate.com/2010/04/20/1251405/volcano-disrupts-bmw-supply-chain.html; http://news.bbc.co.uk/2/hi/8631676.stm
83 Jeffrey Gettleman, "With Flights Grounded, Kenya's Produce Wilts," *New York Times*, April 19, 2010.
84 Bernice Lee and Felix Preston, with Gemma Green, "Preparing for High Impact, Low Probability Events: Lessons From Eyjafjallajokull," *Chatham House Report*, January 2012. www.chathamhouse.org/sites/default/files/public/Research/Energy,%20Environment%20and%20Development/r0112_highimpact.pdf and Airmic Technical, "Supply Chain Failures" www.airmic.com/report/supply-chain-failures
85 www.cia.gov/library/publications/the-world-factbook/geos/ke.html
86 Jeffrey Gettleman, "With Flights Grounded, Kenya's Produce Wilts."
87 www.worldtradewt100.com/blogs/14-wt100-blog/post/iceland-s-volcano-does-a-number-on-global-supply-chains
88 www.science20.com/planetbye/volcanic_eruptions_science_and_risk_management-79456
89 Richard Wray and Graeme Wearden, "Flight Ban Could Leave the UK Short of Fruit and Veg."
90 www.science20.com/planetbye/volcanic_eruptions_science_and_risk_management-79456
91 www.toponline.org/books/kits/welcome%20to%20germany/WTGpdf/Handout%204.pdf
92 www.handyshippingguide.com/shipping-news/more-misery-for-rhine-shippers-as-drought-continues_626; www.hellenicshippingnews.com/News.aspx?ElementId=1c36a1ec-edf3-4a27-a8c5-d107b0a268c2
93 www.csmonitor.com/World/Latest-News-Wires/2011/0113/Acid-tanker-capsizes-on-Rhine-in-Germany
94 Mathew Day, "War Bombs Cause Chaos on the Rhine," *The Telegraph*, November 23, 2011.
95 Darryl Fears, "Drought Threatens to Halt Critical Barge Traffic on Mississippi," *The Washington Post*, January 6, 2013. www.washingtonpost.com/national/health-science/drought-threatens-

to-halt-critical-barge-traffic-on-mississippidrought-threatens-to-halt-critical-barge-traffic-on-mississippidrought-threatens-to-halt-critical-barge-traffic-on-mississippi/2013/01/06/92498b88–5694–11e2-bf3e-76c0a789346f_story.html
96 www.nytimes.com/2012/05/08/us/chicago-train-congestion-slows-whole-country.html?pagewanted=all
97 www.commercialappeal.com/news/2012/dec/04/la-mayor-says-both-sides-in-west-coast-port-have/
98 Interview with Tom Linton, chief procurement and supply chain officer at Flextronics, on July 30, 2012
99 www.resilinc.com/index.aspx
100 www.razient.com/
101 www.metricstream.com/solutions/supply_chain_risk_management.htm
102 www.usresilienceproject.org/pdfs/USRP_Priorities_Final_020112.pdf
103 www.nc4.us
104 www.anvilgroup.com
105 www.ijet.com
106 www.osac.gov/Pages/Home.aspx
107 www.cargonet.com/ſ
108 www.osac.gov/Pages/Home.aspx
109 www.nc4.us/RiskCenterStats.php
110 www.nc4.us/FI_Archived.php
111 www.nc4.us/riskcenter_security.php
112 www.bbc.co.uk/news/world-asia-22476774
113 http://abcnews.go.com/Blotter/fire-kills-112-workers-making-clothes-us-brands/story?id=17807229
114 www.bbc.co.uk/news/world-asia-22474601
115 http://online.wsj.com/article/SB10001424127887323401904578159512118148362.html?google_editors_picks=true
116 www.nytimes.com/2013/05/02/business/some-retailers-rethink-their-role-in-bangladesh.html?_r=0
117 www.nytimes.com/2013/05/02/business/some-retailers-rethink-their-role-in-bangladesh.html?pagewanted=all
118 www.nytimes.com/2013/05/02/business/some-retailers-rethink-their-role-in-bangladesh.html?_r=0
119 www.sedexglobal.com/wp-content/uploads/2011/06/Sedex-Transparency-Briefing-Nov-2013.pdf
120 www.gscreview.com/feb10_john_interview.php
121 www.medtronic.com/wcm/groups/mdtcom_sg/@mdt/@corp/documents/documents/019-g034.pdf
122 Kevin Harrington and John O'Connor, "How Cisco Succeeds," *Supply Chain Management Review*, July/August 2009. www.imperiallogistics.co.za/documents/06.HowCiscoSucceeds_.pdf
123 Kevin Harrington and John O'Connor, "How Cisco Succeeds."
124 MIT CTL Crossroads conference: Managing Supply Chains During Turbulent Times. Presentation by Mike Kalfopoulos, Senior Manager, Global Sourcing at Boston Scientific, March 26, 2009, in Cambridge, Massachusetts.
125 Colum Murphy, Joseph White and Jake Maxwell Watts, "GM Doesn't Plan to Change Supply-Chain Safety Process," *Wall Street Journal*, August 5, 2014.
126 https://supplier.intel.com/static/bc/considerations.htm
127 See www.enoughproject.org/
128 www.enoughproject.org/publications/can-you-hear-congo-now-cell-phones-conflict-minerals-and-worst-sexual-violence-world
129 Interview with Gary Niekerk, Director of Global Citizenship at Intel, July 23, 2012.
130 Interview with Gary Niekerk, Director of Global Citizenship at Intel, July 23, 2012.
131 www.eiccoalition.org/about/members/
132 http://thinkprogress.org/security/2014/01/07/3126271/intel-announces-launch-conflict-free-microprocessors/
133 Jim Low, "Dodd-Frank and the Conflict Minerals Rule," *KPMG Directors and Boards*, 4th Quarter, 2012, pp. 44–45.
134 Marc Reisch, "Explosion at German Chemical Plant Kills Two," *Chemical and Engineering News*, April 2, 2012. http://cen.acs.org/articles/90/web/2012/04/Explosion-German-Chemical-Plant-Kills.html

135 www.plastics-car.com/lightvehiclereport; http://plastics.dupont.com/plastics/pdflit/americas/markets/nylon_under_hood.pdf

136 www.daicel-evonik.com/english/products/manufacture/C12,C8/index.html

137 Melissa Burden, "Auto Group Looks for Ways to Work Around Resin Shortage," *Detroit News*, April 19, 2012.

138 www.aiag.org/staticcontent/press/releases/GENERAL/AIAG%20Post%20Summit%20UPDATE%20-%20FINAL4-18.pdf

139 www.bloomberg.com/news/2012-04-13/auto-supplier-warns-of-resin-shortage-disrupting-output.html

140 www.aiag.org/staticcontent/about/index.cfm

141 Melissa Burden, "Auto Group Looks for Ways to Work Around Resin Shortage."

142 Jeff Bennett, "Nylon-12 Haunts Car Makers," *Wall Street Journal*, April 17, 2012. www.crainsdetroit.com/article/20120417/STAFFBLOG12/120419913/auto-industry-tries-to-head-off-resin-shortage-but-what-can-it-do

143 www.businessweek.com/news/2012-04-19/dupont-sees-boost-to-polymers-from-automakers-seeking-resins

144 Criag Trudell, "Automakers to Speed Part-Validation Process," *BloombergBusinessweek*, April 24, 2012.

145 www.plasticsnews.com/headlines2.html?id=25223

146 http://ei.wtin.com/article/T4Ellxyt6c/2013/02/26/polyamide_12_production_restarts_without_limitations_at_germ/

# 8

# Crisis leadership

## A leader's new normal

*Robert J. Darling and Stephen Young*

For centuries, academics and experts have been saying, "Nothing tests a leader like a crisis and nothing defines an organization like a senior leader in a crisis". During a crisis, all aspects of a leaders' leadership knowledge, skills, abilities, and other characteristics are under the microscope and subject to intense scrutiny and judgment, often influencing an organization's viability and good standing after such an event.

But just what constitutes a crisis? How is it different from an emergency? According to Leonard (2009, pp. 4–5),

> a crisis is a negative event that is "*sui generis*," meaning no suitable prescribed response can be found. It has grown beyond the standard emergency response repertoire and because of its novelty, scale and complexity, successful handling will now require the involvement of a range of managers and decision makers, not just operating managers, but political leaders and technical specialists as well.

The term, "novelty," as it is written above, refers to those emergencies that are not "routinely" prepared for in advance. A routine emergency has an element of predictability due to years of experience, lessons learned, or extensive on-the-job training. As an example, firefighters responding to a house fire are not dealing with a crisis but rather a routine emergency where they fully know what to expect, have defined roles and responsibilities when they arrive, and have spent countless hours training and preparing for this type of emergency or event. However, should that house fire suddenly be found to contain an unknown toxic chemical, or illegal or improperly stored high explosives, or some other, unforeseen, unplanned complexity in which the firefighters have neither the ability to properly identify it, the expertise to safely contain it, or the resources to recover from it, then the routine house fire has just become a "novel" or unique crisis event that will now require an "out of the box" solution, new talent, and a large coordination effort with other jurisdictions to properly deal with it. The types of crisis could include natural disasters, technological or cyber crises, organizational or economic misdeeds, workplace violence, rumors, terrorist attacks, or other forms of man-made disasters.

Regardless of the type, a properly handled crisis can greatly benefit a senior leader by drawing attention to his or her leadership abilities and strengths. Successful crisis leaders are courageous, decisive, intelligent, and reliable, and are often called upon by other agencies or organizations to help lead them through their crisis. Conversely, a mishandled crisis can expose a weak leader who is unable to operate under pressure, lacks courage, character, intestinal fortitude, is unreliable, self-centered, and/or uncaring, most likely ending their career as the organizational leader. Research has also shown that the day-to-day skills that make someone a great executive are not always conducive to leading through a crisis. History is littered with high-profile executives who have found themselves "put to the sword" or having severely damaged their professional reputations due to their mishandling of a corporate crisis. But why did these leaders perform so poorly? Why weren't they prepared? Why couldn't they adjust their leadership style to accommodate the deteriorating situation and anticipate the potential negative ramifications of their actions or, in some cases, inactions? Even today's finest business schools are only just beginning to address the subject of crisis management and crisis leadership as a necessary skill in today's tumultuous and uncertain world, leaving many corporate and government leaders simply unable to properly detect, make decisions, and successfully lead their organizations through extreme situations.

So what are the very first steps a leader should take when a crisis occurs? How should they organize? Where should they go? Who is the first person they should call? How do they activate their crisis response plans? How much time do they have until the media shows up and demands answers? Do they themselves have to be the crisis leader, or can they delegate that leadership role to another senior member of the organization with more experience? And finally, how will they know when the crisis is over, and that their organization has survived the event?

All great questions. For that reason, this chapter on crisis leadership is dedicated to exploring the first thoughts and immediate actions of the crisis leader. The crucial steps taken in the first 30 minutes to an hour, once one realizes that something has changed, something terrible that requires an immediate and decisive response from the leadership. A decision that may ultimately define the rest of their career as being a successful leader or corporate failure. This discussion, by design, is not about the contents of a well-written business continuity plan (BCP), a cybersecurity or disaster recovery plan (DRP), or the technological importance of having an emergency communication plan (ECP). Rather, this chapter is about you, the leader, and what you need to do to get your organization through a truly significant crisis event: protecting your people, reputation, and corporate bottom line. The goal of this chapter is to get you mentally out of the corner office, away from the boardroom, or your daily *Wall Street Journal* article and into a new, perhaps unfamiliar space. This is an opportunity to help you understand the enormity of your position as a corporate leader, and your responsibilities to your employees and stakeholders in a new light. Finally, you will discover why your integrity, character, competence, and ability to influence those around you *in the immediacy of the moment* might be your best hope for a successful outcome. How will *you* perform in the "fog" of a crisis? How will you measure up against ill-defined and unrealistic "standards"? Finally, how can you stack the odds in your favor? Starting with the end in mind often determines how you end up. This is one of the first things a crisis leader should learn.

To support our ideas and opinions on successful and unsuccessful crisis leadership, we collectively draw on specific examples from our personal experiences being a military helicopter pilot who served inside the White House bunker on September 11, 2001, and having over three decades of professional experience as both a firefighter and crisis leader and trainer in Australia, the Middle East, and Asia. We will also use some well-known, highly publicized corporate crisis events that occurred over the last few years.

## Crisis management versus crisis leadership

Crisis management (CM) is known as the process by which an organization deals with a disruptive and unexpected event that threatens to harm the organization, its stakeholders, or the public. It can be thought of as the short-term tactical response to a crisis event. Successful crisis management is important; however, it is narrow in its scope and tends to focus on the actions necessary during the crisis only and not the actions of the leaders at the center of the crisis itself. Crisis leadership (CL) is multifaceted: it's part art and part science, encompassing more thought, more preparation, and more learning. A crisis leader is best described as someone who is guided by corporate principles and values, able to comprehend and communicate the formation of multifaceted and complex events, a person of integrity, with courage and accountability for the outcome of the crisis itself, and is strategic by nature.

Crisis leaders today are challenged with asking themselves new questions from a new perspective, often from a completely new field of vision. What could and should they do to prevent or mitigate a crisis from ever occurring in the first place? Is that indeed possible? What processes are needed to help the organization recognize a looming or developing threat? What procedures are in place to help the workforce organize, respond, sustain ongoing operations, and communicate if normal communication means are no longer available? What special training is needed? What do they need to learn?

A post-9/11 world means the role of the CEO has become exponentially more difficult than it was a few decades ago. Our new normal involves understanding the terrorism threat, the insider threat, the activities and techniques of cyber thieves, the risk to corporate operations and sales due to geopolitical turmoil and the unrest around the globe. Today's CEOs must now find ways to continue to generate shareholder value and profits while also creating innovative ways to secure their facilities and protect their workforces. Some have invested and developed comprehensive crisis plans and procedures while others have not. As a result of 9/11, our societal needs have also changed; the next wave of newly minted, sought-after graduates seeking desirable positions with great companies will surely be looking at those organizations that not only care about the environment, offer great health care benefits and competitive starting salaries, but also invest in and value personal privacy, a healthy work-life mix, and have taken concerted steps to protect them from active shooters, cyber thieves, disgruntled employees, or other forms of external or insider threats. These future employees will certainly be asking their interviewers what kind of comprehensive crisis management plans, safeguards, and training are in place to protect them as they work to benefit the company.

Crisis leadership also requires a level of maturity, experience, and confidence in oneself to accept the fact that despite your education, management style, and previous corporate resume, you must be willing to accept that you too, will someday face a crisis. It's inevitable. It's also important to know that you shouldn't be consumed with trying to prevent all forms of crisis from happening, but rather, you should be dedicated to preparing the organization and workforce to successfully manage any type of crisis. This is commonly called the "all hazards" approach. This notion of preparedness includes how to recognize the type of crisis, when to activate the crisis response plan, steps to isolate impact(s), mitigate damage, make decisions, terminate the crisis plan, and document and learn from the event. A properly equipped CEO can meet stakeholder expectations *and* protect the workforce and business from catastrophic financial loss or reputational damage from a crisis.

As mentioned earlier, this chapter is dedicated to helping those seeking to expand and enhance their abilities as crisis leaders. The next generation of CEOs looking to learn the skills, knowledge, and attributes required to lead their workforces into the new reality of global competition and worldwide unrest, need to balance these demands with the needs of employees seeking secure environments from which to live and work. This new generation of corporate leaders must possess the unique ability to do it all: to protect the workforce while producing results.

According to Arjen Boin, Paul 't Hart, Eric Stern, and Bengt Sundelius, the authors of *The Politics of Crisis Management*, this new breed of corporate leaders must possess the following skills: *sensing*, or how to determine and recognize when a crisis is happening; *decision making*, or the ability to rapidly form multiple courses of action; *meaning making*, or understanding and communicating the full effect of the crisis; *terminating*, or the transition back to normal operations; and *learning*, or the documenting, learning, and exercising of the workforce to prevent the same similar crises from happening again.

## Sense making

> Sense making is a motivated, continuous effort to understand connections (which can be among people, places, and events) in order to anticipate their trajectories and act effectively.
>
> —Gary Klein, Brian Moon, and Robert R. Hoffman, IEEE Intelligent Systems,Vol. 21, No. 4, July/August 2006

According to Karl E. Weick, author of *Sense Making in Organizations*, sense making is *retrospective*. "It is greatly influenced by our personal experiences or past recollections" (1995, p. 17).

During 9/11, Vice President Dick Cheney, influenced by personal experiences, immediately recognized United Flight 93 not for what it originally was prior to the terrorists taking over the aircraft, but rather what it had become: essentially a 150-ton missile traveling toward Washington D.C., at nearly 500 miles per hour.

### *9:52 a.m., September 11, 2001, the White House bunker*

> The call was from the upstairs Situation Room, and the news was heart-stopping. Departing from the businesslike and neutral language used in communications in and around the Executive Office, the staffer on the other end of the line, clearly agitated, just blurted it out: "We have a hijacked plane sixteen miles south of Pittsburgh, inbound to Washington DC."
>
> "Major, what have you got?" the Vice President asked.
>
> I then responded, "Mr. Vice President, the Situation Room is reporting another hijacked airliner approximately sixteen miles south of Pittsburgh, inbound for Washington DC."
>
> Without any hesitation, Cheney ordered the Pentagon, "We have a hijacked plane approximately sixteen miles south of Pittsburgh, inbound to Washington DC. I want two F-15s out of Otis Air National Guard Base. Let me know when they're airborne, and stand by to shoot this plane down!"
>
> From the Pentagon, National Military Command Center (NMCC) came the reply, "Copy all, sir."
>
> *(Darling, 2010, pp. 52–53)*

According to Boin et al. (2005), cognitive research also supports the view that "experience" or mental representations is the basis for human *sense making* in everyday life as well as extreme situations. When it comes to situational awareness, comprehension, or mental modeling, one's lifelong learning has much to do with their ability to process small bits of critical information. Professional military commanders and emergency managers have been known to also have this innate ability to rapidly "sense" what may be happening in their fast-paced, deadly environments more quickly than a novice officer due to their career experiences and "repertoire" from which they can draw upon. Collectively, they seem to develop a wider capacity or discipline for understanding and resist the temptation to cling to the first interpretation or thought, avoiding timely and sometimes costly mistakes.

As the CEO, drawing on your own experiences, along with the time you may or may not have available, you must do your best to properly assess the unfolding crisis. If time is available, it may be prudent to consult others who have been around longer, or call on a trusted advisor who may have seen or experienced something similar in size, scope, and complexity in their previous positions, before claiming too quickly you understand what it is you may think is happening. An incorrect assessment leading to an incorrect response may prove costly and dangerous. However, once a crisis is in process, and time is not on your side due to the nature of the event, it is vitally important that you, the crisis leader, do your best to immediately sense or understand what you think is happening, and take action. Anything less, by most standards, would be considered a dereliction of duty and may have severe consequences either during or after the crisis. In the next section, we will discuss decision making and offer some techniques and tools for developing various courses of action in support of a crisis response.

A key to getting the sensing piece right is through gaining appropriate levels of "situational awareness" (SA), which is articulately described as "the pilot's internal model of the world around him at any point in time. It is derived from the aircraft instrumentation, the out-the-window view, and his or her senses. Individual capabilities, training, experience, objectives, and the ability to respond to task workload moderate the quality of the operator's SA" (Endsley, 1998, n.p.).

The question for the crisis leader is to figure out how you achieve this. How do you balance your internal model of the world when the crisis is unfolding? What do you use as your instruments, how do you get that out of the window view, and do you have enough confidence, training and experience to trust your senses?

However, being situationally aware might just be the first step; being able to anticipate what's next, and to conduct some analysis as to what the data is telling you are key steps towards effective sense making. Klein (2001, p. 127) is right when he makes this assertion, "Sense making is not just a matter of connecting dots. Sense making determines what counts as dots. Jumping to conclusions is sometimes the right thing to do even before all the dots have been collected." This is the ongoing challenge for the crisis leader.

## Decision making

It is often noted that decision making is the most difficult challenge for leaders during a crisis. Most successful leaders of large corporations can afford to surround themselves with the best talent money can buy to help them make the best choice for their organizations. These CEOs have access to sought-after, highly paid business and academic experts with decades of on-the-job experience analyzing corporate balance sheets, hiring and firing personnel, conducting mergers and acquisitions, managing and negotiating international business deals, with a Rolodex of other successful, like-minded professionals to back them up if the need arises. Their primary job is to make sure the CEO they are working for makes well-informed business decisions. These experts are helping the CEO with what is known as analytical decision making. It is the most common and comprehensive form of decision making. Many of us do it every day

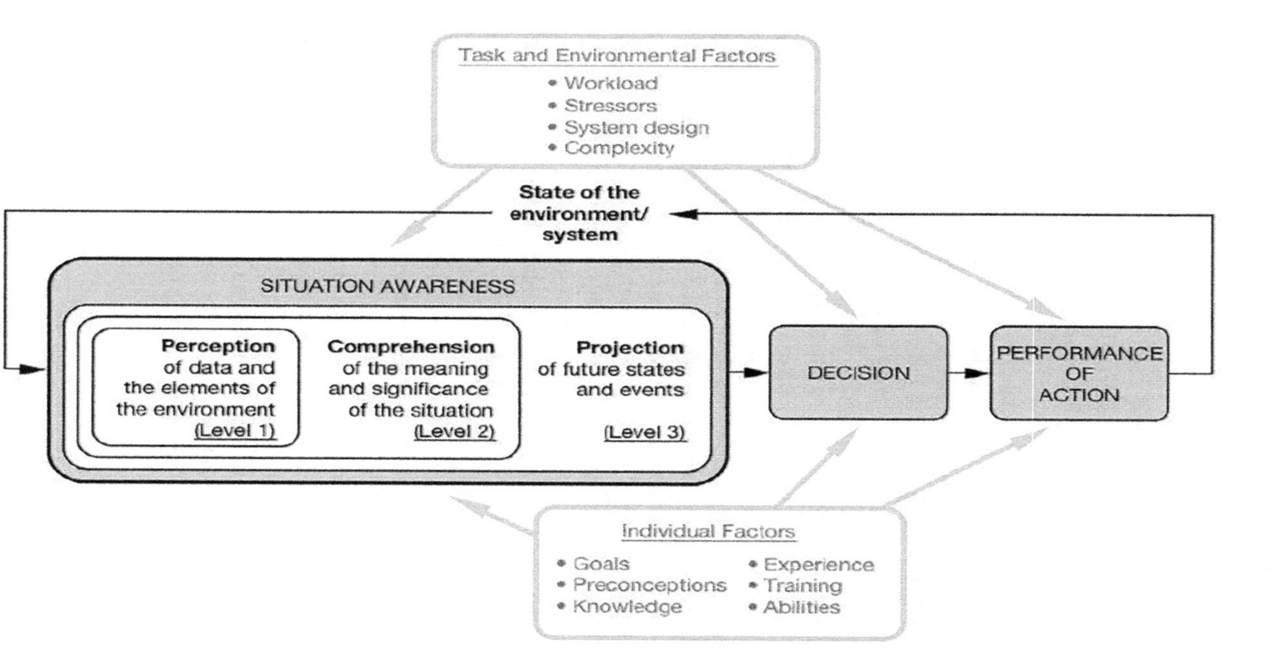


*Figure 8.1* Endlsey's model of SA in dynamic decision making

*Source*: Endsley (1995a) and Endsley (2000). Drawn by Dr. Peter Lankton, May 2007.

in the normal course of our personal and business lives. It is the type of decision making used when there is ample time and data available for a detailed review of the situation which leads to numerous options available to support sound and reasonable decision making.

However, when it comes to a crisis, when time is critical, when there's a high degree of chaos, uncertainty, risk, and conflicting goals and opinions, the best choice for rapid decision making isn't analytical decision making but rather recognitional decision making. Using recognitional decision making, the decision maker is forced to "sense" or accept what they think is happening in their environments as reality, and must rapidly move to formulate as many courses of action (COAs) as possible to consider, given the constraints of time, risk to life and/or property, and select the best COA available. A simple but effective initial decision-making tool that can be used by the crisis leader is a common emergency responders model, called the "size up." This model forces the decision maker to undertake a systematic mental or written process, identifying first the "facts," the things we know for certain. The model then assesses the "probabilities," those things we think using our sensing abilities are likely as a result of the fact-finding step. Following the assessment of the "facts and probabilities," the decision maker then looks at their "own capabilities," their organizational or individual capacity to do something. These three steps then guide the decision maker to the final step, which are the "courses open" or in simple terms the "options open" to the crisis leader: the decision to act or not.

According to Gary Klein (1998, pp. 1–30), there are three variations to recognitional decision making: Variation 1, decision makers properly "sense" or grasp the situation ***and*** fully understand the resources and courses of action they have available to them to deal with the crisis. This is common of more experienced decision makers that are well educated on crisis leadership skills and techniques and have comprehensive crisis response plans in-place. Variation 2, when the decision maker is unable to fully "sense," grasp, or ascertain what is exactly unfolding ***and*** yet is well versed of the resources and courses of actions available to them. This often occurs when the CEO or leader is unable to connect the "right dots" and yet has the Business Continuity, Cyber Security, and Disaster Recovery programs in-place, but remains unsure which one to implement only because they are unsure what type of crisis they are actually facing. In Variation 3, the decision maker is knowledgeable of the situation and recognizes the threat, but is unaware of the tools, resources, plans in place and therefore lacks a proper course of action. The decision maker therefore implements a mental trial and error simulation to develop the most effective course of action. Variation 3 takes the form of "I know the threat, but remain skeptical we have the right contingency plans or any contingency plans in-place to deal with it properly and fully.

On 9/11, President Bush made a recognition primed decision, Variation 1, when he fully understood the terrorists were targeting our financial, military, and political capital, and therefore ordered the enactment of two classified programs: Continuity of Government and Continuity of Presidency, designed to preserve the sanctity and functions of the U.S. government and the Office of the President, in times of national emergency.

## *10:11 a.m.*

> As the Vice President reached to pick up the handset to take the President off the speaker, the Situation Room called again to report that a section of the Pentagon had just collapsed.
>
> The Vice President, still using the phone's speaker, forwarded the message: "Mr. President, we just got word that a portion of the Pentagon has collapsed. We haven't yet confirmed the casualty figures, but it could be as high as eight hundred to a thousand dead or wounded."

> The President seemed to pause momentarily before acknowledging the latest news. And with that, the speaker went silent as the Vice President picked up the handset and he and the President continued their conversation in private.
>
> Seconds later, Major Tom Sharpy, on orders from the deputy national security advisor, called for everyone's attention and announced, "By executive order of the President of the United States, Continuity of Government and Continuity of Presidency programs are now in effect."
>
> By those words, the President had established the defined procedures that made it possible for the government to continue its essential operations during catastrophic events. Key individuals from the executive, legislative, and judicial branches were separated to take up their positions at the now-famous "undisclosed locations." Similarly, he ensured that the executive branch put into effect the established succession plan, should the President and Vice President be killed or unable to fulfill his duties.
>
> *(Darling, 2010, pp. 56–57)*

The vice president then made a recognition primed decision, Variation 2, when moments later it was reported that an unidentified, high-speed, low-level aircraft was discovered heading for the White House. The vice president, unsure about the exact nature of threat but confident the military could intercept it in time, ordered the Pentagon to take offensive, lethal military action against this threat.

## *10:13 a.m.*

> It was the Situation Room again. This time to relay a message from the Secret Service that a high-speed, low-level aircraft was approximately eight miles out, coming down the Potomac in the direction of the White House.
>
> The Vice President, along with Secretary of Transportation Mineta, turned to the speaker box with the FAA representative on the other end and asked for confirmation that there was an inbound aircraft headed toward the White House.
>
> "We can't see him, sir," was the reply. "He's too low for us to pick up on radar."
>
> The Vice President asked, "Don, are you up?"
>
> For the first time that day, Secretary Rumsfeld responded, "I'm here."
>
> Rumsfeld had just returned from the west side of the Pentagon, doing what he could to help wounded employees who had either streamed out or been carried out from the burning wreckage that had earlier in the day been the south side of the building.
>
> Cheney told Rumsfeld that the Secret Service was tracking an aircraft over the Potomac, heading toward the White House.
>
> "It's eight miles out, coming down the Potomac. Do you have an asset in the air that can take a shot at this guy?"
>
> "We're checking."
>
> I turned to the Vice President with an update. "Mr. Vice President, the aircraft is now six miles out."
>
> Cheney said, "Don, I'll authorize a long-range shot at this guy."
>
> "We're still checking."
>
> I continued my tracking report. "Mr. Vice President, the aircraft is now four miles. Now three miles. The aircraft is – "
>
> The Vice President wheeled around, his face flushed with concern. "Stop!" he commanded me.
>
> The room went quiet. To me, it seemed as if the White House had just succumbed to the inevitable. If the Defense Department didn't have an asset in the Washington area capable of engaging this aircraft – either airborne, as in a fighter, or ground-based, as

> in a surface-to-air missile – and if the Secret Service couldn't deal with it on the roof, there was nothing left for anyone in the room to do except wait for the impact.
>
> *(Darling, 2010, pp. 57–58)*

This unknown aircraft was eventually identified to be a friendly, medical evacuation helicopter (medevac) from Fort Belvoir Army base located just south of Washington, DC. This helicopter crew was merely trying to respond to the Pentagon's call for additional helicopter support to evacuate the seriously burned victims from the impact of American Airlines Flight 77. However, when the helicopter pilots called Ronald Reagan Airport Tower for clearance through the DC airspace, there was no one left to answer them. The tower crew had evacuated due to the nearby attack on the Pentagon. Instead of turning around and returning to Fort Belvoir, the helicopter crew made the decision to enter the airspace without authority, in the hope of reaching the Pentagon safely. This decision nearly cost them their lives as the White House and Pentagon were desperately searching for an armed, nearby fighter jet to shoot them down. Fortunately for all involved, the Pentagon did not have a fighter jet in the area at that time and the medevac helicopter was properly identified as a friendly aircraft, making it to the Pentagon safely.

Finally, the vice president, along with the Secretary of Transportation, Norman Mineta, made another recognition primed decision, this time Variation 3, when they began to "sense" the threat involving hijacked aircraft might be larger than they first realized as numerous commercial airliners were reported not to be following the orders of local air traffic controllers, creating the concern that they too may be hijacked. Feeling as if the scope of threat may be larger than first thought, and yet unsure about the air traffic controllers' ability to handle a larger more complex event, took the unprecedented action of ordering every aircraft flying over the United States to land immediately. If you were not a military aircraft, you were no longer authorized to be operating in our nations' airspace. The magnitude of the threat wasn't fully understood, however, the military might of our nation's air force was, and the decision was made for them to take action and clear the skies.

### *10:15 a.m.*

> The Vice President and the Secretary of Transportation were engaged in a private conversation. Secretary Mineta's department included the FAA and, given the still unknown scope of the air attacks, a series of decisions were made to clear American airspace immediately. At the secretary's recommendation, Cheney returned to the room and ordered the FAA to get every civilian airliner on the ground immediately. The FAA's first response was to remind the Vice President that at that moment, there were still more than two thousand airliners in the air coast to coast.
>
> The Vice President said he understood and then reiterated his order: "I want them all on the ground immediately."
>
> *(Darling, 2010, pp. 59–60)*

### *10:16 a.m.*

> The NMCC announced that at the direction of the President, the North American Aerospace Defense Command (NORAD) had assumed control over all North American airspace, meaning that all aircraft, whether an American Airlines Airbus, a corporate jet, or a Piper Cub at the local flying school, now came under the control of the U.S. Air Force.
>
> *(Darling, 2010, p. 59)*

> This was the first time in our nation's history that NORAD and the United States military had direct, operational control of the entire airspace over North America.
>
> *(Darling, 2010, p. 60)*

As previously stated in the previous section on "sense making," there most likely won't ever be perfect information or an abundance of time available in a crisis from which to make these important critical decisions. Leaders must do their best to avoid waiting too long to act. By understanding the variables of chance, risk, information, time, uncertainty, and experience, you must allow yourself the ability to weigh options against your own intuition and experience and execute the best course of action you can in uncertain situations. This is often referred to as your "70% solution."

## Decision-making support models

In addition to the "size up" model and Klein's three variations to recognitional decision making, there are a few common decision-making support models used today in both business as well as the military to aid in the process of determining how to gather information, analyze data, and make decisions. Below, we have provided a very brief description of these models, who primarily uses them, and the steps they take to process data. Each tool, despite being slightly different, has the same purpose; assist the decision maker in making better, more reasonable, scientific and timely decisions.

The first model is known as the Boyd cycle, or commonly referred to as the "the OODA loop." It is a concept developed by USAF Colonel John Boyd, used to describe a re-occurring decision-making cycle. The goal is to process the cycle quickly and continuously, allowing the individual to react to the changing environment more quickly than his opponent.

The acronym OODA stands for the four elements of decision making: observe, orient, decide, and act. The OODA loop is applicable to the decision-making process and is a useful tool for any leader, whether working in business or the military, and for making both analytical or recognitional decisions.

Another decision support tool commonly used in business, specifically, the scientific community is known as the Plan, Do, Check, Act model (PDCA).

It was originally developed by Dr. W. Edwards Deming, considered the father of modern quality control, who later changed the acronym of the model from "Plan, Do, Check, Act" to "Plan, Do, Study, Act." Dr. Deming did so because he felt "check" didn't properly capture the notion that true quality control requires a willingness to seek constant improvement, not merely "checking" ones' hypothesis for accuracy. "Study" highlighted the need to make this model a repeatable process. Figure 8.3 depicts the model in its original form.

Finally, we have found another decision support tool that is popular among marine corps military planners, deployed on navy vessels in warzones, as well as joint staff officers working in the Pentagon in support of the Chairman of the Joint Chiefs of Staff and the National Military Command Center (NMCC). The military model is known as the Rapid Response Planning Process (R2P2) or simply, the Crisis Action Plan (CAP). The CAP military model was originally designed in the 1960s and updated in the early 2000s to enable our military planners to more quickly assess and determine if and when to inform our military commanders when crisis situations are developing, requiring their immediate attention. According to the *Joint Operation Planning and Execution System (JOPES), enclosure (E), Crisis Action Planning, 14 July 2000*, there are six phases to this crisis action plan. These phases include

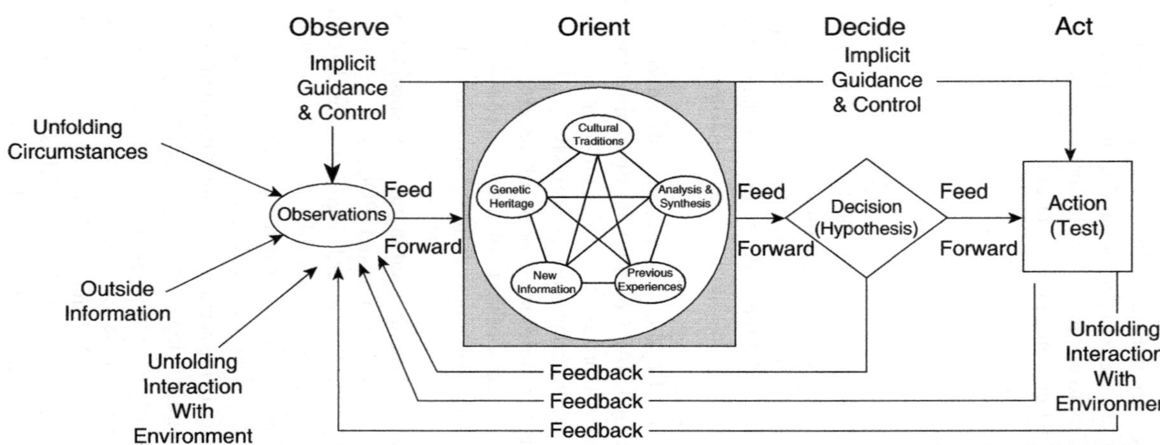


*Figure 8.2* Colonel John Boyd's OODA loop model for decision making

*Source*: Drawn by Patrick Edwin Moran, April 2008

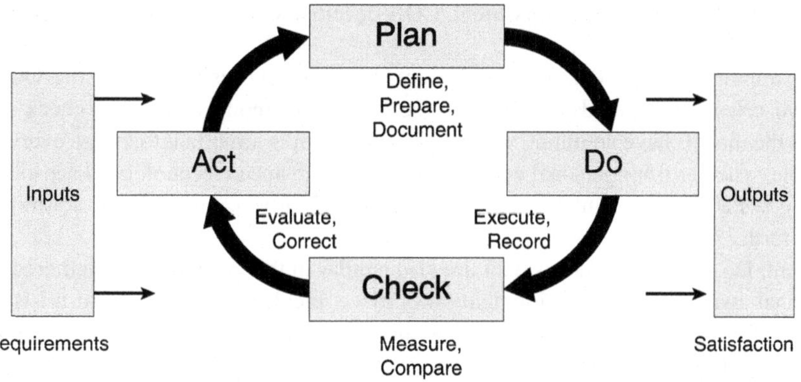


*Figure 8.3* Dr. W. Edwards Deming model for scientific decision making

| *Phase I* | *Phase II* | *Phase III* | *Phase IV* | *Phase V* | *Phase VI* |
|---|---|---|---|---|---|
| Situation Development | Assessment | Course of Action Development | Course of Action Selection | Execution Planning | Execution |
| **Action** | | | | | |
| • Monitor world situation<br>• Recognize problem<br>• Submit CINC's ASSESSMENT<br>• Monitor reporting from other agencies. | • Increase awareness<br>• Increase reporting<br>• Assesses situation<br>• Advises on possible military action<br>• NCA-CJCS evaluates | • Develop COAs<br>• CINC assigns tasks to sub-ordinates by evaluation request message<br>• CINC reviews evaluation response messages<br>• Create/modify TPFDD<br>• USTRANSCOM prepares deployment estimates<br>• Evaluate COAs | • CJCS advises NCA<br>• CJCS may send **PLANNING ORDER** to begin execution planning before formal selection of COA by NCA | • CINC develops **OPORD**<br>• Refine TPFDD<br>• Force preparation | • CJCS sends **EXECUTE ORDER** by authority of SECDEF<br>• CINC executes OPORD<br>• JOPES database maintained<br>• JPEC reports execution status<br>• Begin redeployment planning |
| **Outcome** | | | | | |
| • **Assess** that event may have national implications<br>• **Report** the event to NCA/CJCS | • NCA/CJCS decide to develop military COA | • CINC sends Commander's Estimate with recommended COA | • NCA select COA<br>• CJCS releases COA selection by NCA in **ALERT ORDER** | • CINC sends **OPORD** | • Crisis resolved<br>• Redeployment of forces |

*Figure 8.4* Flow diagram of the crisis action procedures

*Source*: CJCSM 3122.01 JOPES Vol. 1

situation development, crisis assessment, COA development, COA selection, execution planning, and execution.

The military CAP model, at its very core, is similar in design to both the OODA loop (observe, orient, decide, and act) as well as the Dr. Deming model of plan, do, check/study, and act. All the models have an initial "sense" phase where it is important to utilize every resource available, whether from personal experience to more advanced technological sensors or other warning systems such as intelligence, space systems, early warning radars, seismic sensors, and so forth.

Orient, Do, and Crisis Assessment are also similar in that resources are gathered together, situational awareness and development takes place, incident management or crisis planning teams are formed, leadership is alerted, and the process of monitoring and analyzing the deteriorating situation or event takes place. The Decide, Do, and Crisis Assessment, are all part of determining the proper next steps, course of action development and course of action selection. Finally, act: the action of issuing orders, tasking individuals, or in some cases, releasing of weapons. In this phase, all the models stress the importance of following through with the decision until either the crisis is abated or more information becomes available which could lead to another course of action and executive decision. This process should continue until the crisis is resolved or escalated to a higher level of command and control due to the failure to contain or control the crisis.

In summary, decision-making models are important for the crisis leader, not only do they provide a process to obtain the best decision possible given the time pressures of the crisis, but they also serve as a highly defensible process in the post-crisis analysis that can provide substance and justification for why you made the decisions you did.

Whether you're in the corporate boardroom considering how to handle an active shooter situation within one of your facilities, working through a catastrophic product failure or recall at a major industrial manufacturer, or determining whether to shoot down an aircraft threatening our nation's capital, the process for gathering awareness, identifying resources, developing courses of action, and taking action are the same. The key to effective crisis decision making hinges on the leader's ability to accept what your "senses" are telling you, the wisdom to begin planning and rapidly formulate as many courses of action (COAs) as possible given the constraints of time, risk to life and/or property, and the courage to take repeated action until the crisis is resolved.

It is the job of the crisis leader to recognize that moment in time when the crisis appears to be moving into its next phase. The decisive courses of action have been implemented, the immediate threat is waning. It is now time for the CEO to address the internal and external stakeholders of the company and explain what happened and why, providing a clear picture of how the crisis has been resolved and what it means for the workforce and company moving forward. This critical crisis leadership process is called "meaning making."

## Meaning making

Meaning making can simply be described as "an attempt to reduce public and political uncertainty and inspire confidence in crisis leaders by formulating and imposing a convincing narrative" (Boin, 2013, p. 79). formulating an authoritative definition of the situation". It is an attempt by leadership and other stakeholders to reduce the overall internal and external uncertainty caused by the crisis. This is done by shaping the narrative, developing the storyline for the media, the public at large, local politicians, and most importantly, your employees, equity owners and stakeholders who need to hear from their leader. They deserve to know why the crisis happened, how can it be prevented from happening again in the future, the state of the company and leadership team, and whether the community still has confidence in their collective ability to operate in a safe, reliable manner. Former New York City Mayor Rudy Giuliani is credited during his messaging to the city after the 9/11 attacks with deploying the following technique for mass meaning making and crisis communications. The model Giuliani used is brilliant in its simplicity. It is a method that the crisis leader should adopt. It is a four-step method, "what we know; what we don't know; what we're doing about it; and what we need you to do." It has become the gold standard in crisis communications. President George W. Bush accurately framed the events of 9/11 as attack on the United States that demanded an immediate response; however, he wasn't able to create a compelling message to the public during the events of Hurricane Katrina.

It is also important to know that meaning making is a time-sensitive event; the longer it takes to develop your message, the greater the risk that a local reporter seeking a front-page story, or an aspiring or adversarial politician or government official, or the public in general may shape the story from their vantage point only and create even more confusion and uncertainty than currently exists.

Failure to communicate your message clearly, consistently, truthfully, and as often as necessary could create yet another crisis that could result in your employees losing confidence in your ability as their leader, potentially damage the corporate brand, or maybe even jeopardize the future of the company. Figure 8.5 is a pictorial reminder that crisis leaders must manage the entire meaning making process. Failure to address one stakeholder or group without the same intensity of effort for the others, will only incite them to take it upon themselves to do it for you. And as the saying goes, "nature abhors a vacuum." This vacuum will often be filled with misinformation not favorable to the crisis leader or the crisis leadership effort.

According to Boin et al. (2005, p. 72), "the mass media are a pivotal force in discovering, conveying, and (de)escalating crisis." The authors go on to state that the role of the media in creating and modulating crisis isn't new. For decades, it has been known that sensationalism sells, the truth is debatable, and anonymous sources tend to prevent the media from being held accountable for their lack of facts when quoting an unknown source or printing misleading articles. Couple this with the technological advances of the internet, social media, mobile phones, and the instantaneous news cycle, and it is more important than ever to have a crisis communication plan in place to address critical issues before losing control of the message. When dealing directly with the public, the responses could be mixed. If the interviewee has recently been promoted, recognized as a top performer, a member of a generational employed family, then the message about the conduct and abilities of the leadership might be positive

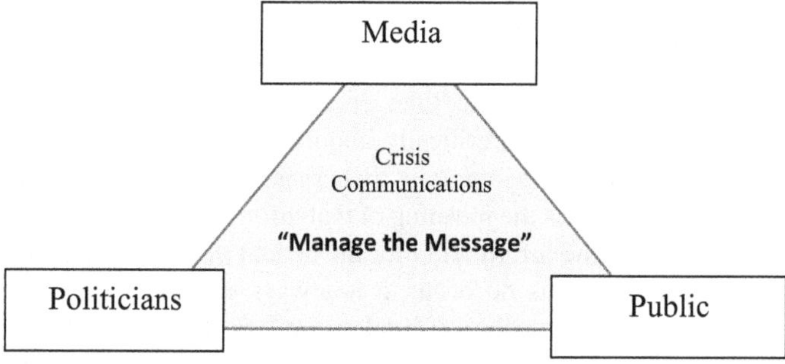


*Figure 8.5* Triangular relationship: media, public, and politicians during crisis communications

and uplifting. However, if the employee or a member of the public was affected by the crisis or the company in the past in a negative way, then the desire to speak to the media or a reporter as a way to tell their side of the story could merely be a ploy to either bring pressure against the company to compensate them for their past losses, a way to gain short-term notoriety as an important member of their community, or a way to attempt to permanently damage the brand and create widespread negative feelings about the actions or competence of the corporate leadership team. A notable and high-profile example was the error made by former BP CEO Tony Hayward during the early stages of the response to the Deepwater Horizon crisis. When questioned about how long the response would take, Hayward delivered the crisis-P.R. sound bite from hell: "I'd like my life back" (Reed, 2012).

Crisis communication is an important tool for every crisis leader to understand and master, before a crisis occurs. According to *the Harvard Business Review*, (2002, pp. 103–109), crisis leaders must "handle the media with care and choose their channels carefully." The media can be friend or foe, they don't care which side they're on. It is also critically important to get your messages out as early as possible to "frame" the crisis from your point of view to shape the narrative and public opinion.

Strategists and experts in the field of crisis communications exist to train and help prepare corporations to handle their crisis responses. Here are a few of their suggestions to properly prepare for media inquiries and deliver your corporate message. Anticipate the questions you may be asked by the news outlets. Use an articulate and well-trained spokesperson to deliver the message. This is normally the CEO or crisis leader; however, it doesn't always have to be. The CEO could be in the background, ready to step up to answer questions once the spokesperson has completed the corporate statement. But at the very minimum, the CEO must be present, show empathy for any victims, be accountable for the crisis as the leader, and be willing and able to handle any negativity that comes their way. Other strategies include segmenting your audience and using matching media for each of the segments. For example, using the press conference is a great way to get wide exposure over a large population to get your initial corporate message out to the public. Using print ads to reach the older, working-class segment of the community, social media for the younger adults, radio for another. The intent is to think of your crisis communication plan as you would your marketing plan and find innovative ways to reach as many members of the public as you can. Finally, be systematic – meaning that the best time to develop and train for a crisis is before a crisis occurs. Along with the development of a comprehensive crisis communication plan, create multiple messages, in multiple media formats, to handle multiple types of crises.

The experts go on to recommend additional tips: be factual, candid, and timely with your message. Never speak off the record. Invite the media to central location and "tell it all, tell the truth, and tell it fast." When it comes to crisis communications, the longer it takes to get your message out, the more time you're allowing for the rumors to grow and the confusion and concern to circulate. Finally, don't be pessimistic but be realistic. Preparing people for the worst and having a good outcome is better than letting them down twice.

In summary, meaning making is a critically important part of your comprehensive crisis response and management plan. It is important that crisis communication is designed to manage both the information as well as the meaning of that information. The term "framing" refers to controlling the meaning of the information for the benefit of the crisis leader, the company, and the public. When crisis events do occur, it is always beneficial to the company to get their message out as quickly as possible. If it takes too long, it will create a void for misinformation, chaos, and confusion. And finally, crisis leaders must learn to harness the power of social media by integrating it into the corporate periphery to monitor public sentiment and perceptions. When organizations take the proactive steps to keep social media in their daily operations, they are better able to detect and respond to threats before they manifest into a crisis.

At some point, a leader must declare an end to the crisis. The outcome has been determined, the crisis has been resolved, and it is time to get back to work. Other signs include your customers and suppliers are ready to place new orders, the media stops requesting interviews, and the sales are improving to pre-crisis levels, as your business performance is the major concern or topic of the boardroom. This process is known as *terminating.*

## Terminating

Terminating is defined as ending the crisis and moving the company back to normal operations, or indeed as many organizations discover, a move to the new normal. It's worthy of consideration that there are often different finishing lines for the various actors involved in the crisis.

> Some actors may find it expedient to move back to normalcy – however defined – as soon as possible, whereas other may seek to stretch the life span of an ongoing crisis as much as they can. How, may we ask, do crises in fact evolve over time? And how do they come to an end?
>
> *(Boin et al., 2005, p. 93)*

This phase could be a challenging process given the nature of the crisis that took place. There will be legitimate questions as to why this happened, how can it be prevented from happening again, is the workplace and workforce safe, is the company financially secure, is the leadership competent, do the stakeholders and community still have confidence in the leaders' ability to operate safely in their community. These reviews can be formal, such as a legal inquiry to determine any criminality or fault, they can even be a parliamentary inquiry to determine if laws need to be changed, as was recommended by the 9/11 Commission. The reviews can also be informal and internally driven to identify cause and areas for improvement. They are an important element to the end of any crisis. Remember to start with the end in mind.

The following section will address the process of moving from a crisis back to normal operations. The "end of a crisis" on its very surface means the incident is over; you've fended off the potentially hostile actors, such as the labor union, you've survived the lawsuit, weathered the storm, kept or lost your job. It is worthy of note that former BP CEO Tony Hayward was replaced less than three months after the Deepwater Horizon crisis started.

You may have successfully negotiated the process of sense making, decision making, and meaning making, and feel you will soon be getting that welcomed relief from the crisis, and yet, the worst may be yet to come. According to Boin et al. (2005, p. 92), "Crises often come with aftermath complexities." For example, the mortgage meltdown of 2008 ended in 2013, with the return of property values, the stock market to pre-crisis levels, along with an improving unemployment rate, only to be overshadowed by the irreplaceable loss of millions of dollars in retirement accounts, thousands of homes lost due to foreclosure, the loss of higher paying jobs, and the complete lack of trust in our financial and political system. For many, the crisis of 2008 will continue and be personally and financially felt for many years to come.

The loss of trust in our elected leaders, financial institutions, our news organizations, and each other, is an aftermath of that crisis, with no end in sight. "*To end a crisis, closure must be achieved on both the operational and political dimensions of crisis management*"

(Boin et al., 2017, p. 107). They also refer to the "fast burning crisis" versus the "long shadow crisis." The fast burning crisis is characterized as an event where the operational and political (internal or external) response and interest in the crisis is short. We usually see this with tornados, fires, mudslides, tsunamis and other types of natural disasters where accountability is difficult, resources to rebuild are abundant, and politically, it's difficult to find fault or negligence in someone or something for it happening. The long shadow crisis, however, can last years after the operational or political work is done. These types of crisis can be characterized as "endemic," meaning unmanageable or too large to solve, such as global warming, deforestation, overpopulation, and of course, terrorism. Other types of long shadow crises could be the result of deeper issues. These could include the continued struggle to effectively combat terrorism, race relations, equal pay for equal work, or the high cost of health care for workers.

In each of these cases, the crisis will only end when the operational as well as the political aspects of crisis management has been satisfied. Declaring an end to the crisis as a leader when lawsuits are pending against the company, the public is outraged, the government is investigating, is a futile attempt to make it all go away, when the reality is it's probably only going to getting worse. Similarly, declaring an end to the crisis without addressing your employees as to its cause, or avoiding taking responsibility for it happening, or ignoring the importance of investing in new equipment or safety systems to prevent it from happening again, will also lead to an employee and community backlash, resulting in negative repercussions and ramifications as well. A good example of this occurred on May 1, 2003, the day President Bush declared the operational aspect of the war on terror over, while aboard the USS *Abraham Lincoln* off the coast of San Diego. It was to be a great moment for the president. He flew onto the deck of one of America's mighty warships, having just returned home from the Persian Gulf where its crew was engaged in combat operations, only to proudly declare, at that moment, an end to combat operations in Iraq.

Essentially, America had won the war, the troops were coming home. The problem was, the president completely missed the fact that a new form of combat operations involving asymmetric warfare against guerilla forces was just beginning. America had hundreds of thousands of its military members still deployed in harm's way, and it was about to get worse for them. He was immediately attacked by all sides for his mis-characterization of combat operations. This example illustrates the importance of and consequences of ignoring the model, as the president hadn't properly satisfied either the *operational* or the *political* aspects of his constituents and as a result, suffered politically for his mistake.

## "Mission accomplished"

> They had a sign that said, "Mission Accomplished." It was a sign aimed at the sailors on the ship, but it conveyed a broader knowledge. To some it said, well, Bush thinks the war in Iraq is over, when I didn't think that. But nonetheless, it conveyed the wrong message, he said. The speech the president made under the banner became a symbol of his poor choice of words and overconfidence about Iraq, which from that point on deteriorated into a bloodbath.
>
> —Macy Hurwitz, *The Telegraph*

As was mentioned, the key to "ending" a crisis is accountability. Everyone respects a leader that avoids the blame game and is seen taking responsibility for the good, bad, and the ugly that happens on their watch. The public is usually impressed with their courage, moral conviction, ethics and values. CEOs who accept responsibility are often forgiven at some point and survive to lead another day. On the other hand, it can be a double-edged sword to admit culpability in any crisis. This act of taking accountability and responsibility may invite serious scrutiny into the leader's policies, preparedness, and into almost every management decision ever made. Depending on the size, scope, and political mood of the public and the stakeholders, taking accountability may see the leader being found culpable in failing to protect and serve the workforce and the community. Further, this act of accountability may result in the perception of "negligence," which could create a long shadow crisis resulting in their termination, a lawsuit against the company, or some other form of criminal action which could affect them for years to come. The mass media also tend to "swarm" if they believe the leader or a company could be found negligent due to their own admission about the crisis. Such an admission could make for sensational headlines on the front page of the newspaper, especially if the negligent confessions lead to other more serious perceived crimes. The media prides itself on its ability to help its readers understand complex issues simply by simply asking the question: do you think the crisis leader is a villain or a hero?

A good example of the risk of taking total responsibility for a crisis is the famous case involving Captain "Sully" Sullenberger, the pilot-in-command of the doomed US Airways Flight 1549, which struck a flock of Canada geese while on takeoff from New York's LaGuardia Airport on January 15, 2009. The good news is that all 155 people on board that aircraft survived because of the "miracle on the Hudson" landing he performed on the Hudson River that day. However, the initial reports from the National Transportation Safety Board (NTSB) initially ruled that Captain Sullenberger had taken responsibility for his actions and was in fact negligent as the pilot in command of the damaged aircraft because he failed to "sense" the situation in a timely fashion, and failed to "decide" on the proper course of action, which according to the NTSB, resulted in him having to land his aircraft in the Hudson River.

The media immediately pounced on the rumor that the NTSB would find him negligent in his handling of the crisis. The investigative reporters went to great lengths to attempt to show him as a villain rather than a hero by interviewing all sorts of people who claimed to know the Sullenbergers. They inquired into the health of his marriage, his drinking habits, mental state, and professionalism as a pilot. They wanted to be the first with the breaking news on why Sully was not what he seemed to be and should be held accountable. When it was later proven that Sully did in fact make the right decision and was exonerated by the NTSB, those same news outlets quickly changed the narrative and wrote countless articles on his skills as a leader and pilot, hailing him a national hero. When it comes to a crisis and the media, there's a fine line between success and failure! It's important to note that the media more than often don't care which side they take.

In summary, "a crisis may end, but it doesn't just fade away into the distance" (Klann, 2003, p. 59). Leader's terminate the crisis by rebuilding and reassuring their internal and external stakeholders that they are safe, and that you will conduct an extensive review into all causes of the crisis to answer their questions as to why it happened, and what you'll be doing to insure it won't happen again. These actions are captured in our final step on crisis leadership. It is known as "Learning." It is the best way to help the company heal as it prepares for the next crisis.

## Learning

Treat this crisis as practice for the next crisis.
—John Parenti

The Spanish-American philosopher George Santayana is credited with the saying, "Those who cannot remember the past are condemned to repeat it." This is equally true when recovering from a crisis. Crisis learning is an excellent opportunity for any company or organization to take the time necessary to re-examine, re-assess, and re-think about their existing processes, procedures, and training techniques to better prepare and re-assure the workforce that they are better prepared to handle their next crisis. A well-designed learning program involves at least three types of learning. These include experience-based, explanation-based, and competence or skill-based learning.

Experience-based learning is learning by surviving the crisis. There's no greater form of learning than firsthand experience. Vivid memories of loss, chaos, fear, and confusion, along with images of courage, resiliency, and inspirational moments, all combine to make a powerful argument for attentive learning. This type of learning occurs naturally within professions that routinely deal with crisis. The military is an excellent example of this: the best instructors are combat proven and battle-hardened officers. When they talk, you listen. They speak with firsthand knowledge and authority. They are especially effective because they tend to avoid subjects or topics of little relevance and focus on those items that literally just might save your life. Unfortunately, these types of instructors are rare and not always available outside of the military to teach and share their life lessons with others; therefore, the second, more common type of learning is explanation-based learning. This type of learning is focused on cause and effect. This is research-based, machine type learning. It involves a detailed review of the corporate or organizational processes, operational processes, maintenance procedures, decision-making steps to be followed, along with the expected outcomes from each of those steps. It is then analyzed and compared to other industry standards to determine where in the process the deviation or breakdown occurred. NASA and other scientific firms use this type of learning. And finally, there is competence or skill-based learning, a review into the corporate capability of a company to handle risks, at all levels, compared to the types of risks they made be required to handle. If it is determined that a capability gap exists between corporate capabilities and the threats they face, skill-based learning supports the idea that it may be necessary to acquire new systems or hire new people with the needed skills and competencies required to improve the overall effectiveness of the company moving forward. Examples of this include a hospital hiring doctors with experience dealing with pandemics, buying new equipment to prevent workplace mishaps, improving facilities to deal with extreme weather, hiring a security force to protect sensitive assets, or any other equipment or experts to fill the capability gap needed to prevent a similar crisis.

Another common challenge in learning after a crisis involves whether the crisis leader feels they did well or poorly in handling the crisis. Naturally, if the leader did poorly, they tend to feel threatened or lack the confidence necessary to have their decisions or actions scrutinized for the sake of crisis learning. If they were recognized as doing well, they are more apt to allow a detailed review of their plans and actions. To add to this complexity, whether the lessons learned are ever implemented depend on the management strategy that is was adopted to deal with the crisis. Corporate leaders tend to take two viewpoints when implementing necessary change: the conservative approach and the reformist approach. The conservative approach aims to defend and maintain current policies and procedures rather than completely change the how business is done. And if it does decide to implement change, it is usually not widespread or sweeping change, but merely an incremental approach to change. The conservative approach leader believes that anything more than a minor change in policy or procedure will be perceived as too extreme and may reflect poorly on their leadership ability and style. The reformist approach supports more extensive change to bridge the exposed capability gap and restore faith of the stakeholders and public that substantial changes have been made. It requires bold leadership to implement, and there is often resistance from both internal as well external forces to perhaps slow down and to adopt a more conservative strategy. Whichever strategy the crisis leader selects, it is imperative that it be accepted by their employees, be properly implemented, and that it restore confidence in the company or organization. And as a final point regarding change, the crisis leader must avoid being perceived as only doing this to appease the public or their stakeholders for the purpose of seeking short-term relief from further scrutiny. They must believe in the change they propose and realize they must "sell" it rather than mandate it to their employees and stakeholders.

## "Identify your blind spots"

One of the most significant issues to address within your management team is to adequately account for every possible scenario which could negatively influence or affect ongoing operations in the form of operational risk, or in other words an understanding of your vulnerabilities.

There are many approaches to managing risk; one involves use of a "vulnerability assessment" model. A vulnerability assessment conducted by an impartial, outside professional can truly help an organization identify the threats and potential hazards that could negatively affect the health and continued operations of the company. Once it is determined what types of hazards or threats exist, the leadership team must convene a planning session and carefully assess the impact each of those identified risks, should they occur, on the continued operation of the business, as well as their internal abilities to handle each of the crisis events. A high probability of occurrence risk with only a low or minimal effect on the people, facilities, or profits of the business might not need to be addressed or planned for as much as a low to medium probability risk which could have a devastating effect on the overall health of business. A well-conducted vulnerability assessment considers both internal and external risks to the business to include economic, informational, physical, human resources, reputational, high-risk or psychopathic employee or former employee or family member, and of course natural events such as acts of weather. The assessment will identify and assign a score to each of them as to their probability of occurrence, their economic or political impact on the company and community, as well as the company's internal or external ability to handle and overcome each.

## Developing the crisis management team

Crisis management is the application of priorities, strategies, and procedures designed to help a company or organization deal with a sudden and significant negative event. For this to happen, a company must have a dedicated crisis management team identified and composed of people with a solid understanding of the business and its operations, the authority to make critical decisions, the ability to deploy and move resources quickly, and creative in developing innovative solutions for leadership to make timely decisions to overcome any critical event. Additionally, the crisis management team must have the training required to perform in their duties as members of the team, the support of leadership, be collaborative and willing to work together to improve the safety and well-being of the workforce, conduct exercises, and able to recommend to leadership when it's time to acquire new equipment or hire new personnel with the skills necessary to fill any gaps in capability, experience or expertise that the company may need to maximize workplace safety or to better deal with a crisis should it occur. A well-written, understood, and exercised crisis management plan can increase the safety and well-being of employees and the public, minimize downtime, increase productivity, and provide leadership the peace of mind that a well-trained workforce is a happy workforce.

## Writing the crisis management plan

The crisis management plan is a compilation of all available information about your organization, including all hazards and emergencies identified by the vulnerability assessment, or other potential risks deemed important by the leadership team. The British Standard for Crisis Mmanagement – Guidance and Good Practice (BS 11200:2014) is considered one of the best guides available and suggests that an effective crisis management plan should be as concise as possible to ensure that it is read and exercised before it is needed, and that it can be understood and actually used when a crisis breaks out. It also suggests that this plan should include the following key information: a) who has authority and responsibility for key decisions and actions in a crisis (the crisis leader); b) key contact details: how staff are to be contacted in the event of a crisis; c) crisis communications (internal and external); d) activation mechanism for a crisis and how it works in practice; e) details of the levels of response across the organization (i.e. who is to be contacted for what level of problem) and a flow chart showing the sequence of actions; f) the structure and role of the CMT and what is expected of it; g) where the CMT is to meet (with alternate locations) and what equipment and support are required; h) key templates (such as CMT meeting agenda and logbook); i) log-keeping guidance; j) a situation report template which is to be used across the organization.

In many organizations, the most common forms of plans found are either business continuity plans (BCP) and/or disaster recovery plans (DCP). These should be children of the parent plan, that is the crisis management plan. The BCP is, according to the British Standard for Business Continuity BS 25999–2:2007, a "documented collection of procedures and information that is developed, complied and maintained in readiness for use in an incident to enable an organization to continue to deliver its critical activities at an acceptable level." These include risks to critical elements such as people, property, corporate reputation, business operations to include financial, supply chain, and logistics. The next most common plan is the disaster recovery plan (DRP) or cybersecurity plan, and is generally focused on the technology and infrastructure that supports your organization's operations. The two most important factors you should consider with the disaster recovery planning are the recovery point objective (RPO), the point in time (history) to which you are recovering your data, and the recovery time objective (RTO), the maximum time the IT system will not function or be available to use before it is restored.

The goal of the crisis management plan is to provide the leadership team and their employees with a blueprint or roadmap to help them perform in a systematic and orderly manner during a crisis. This roadmap identifies the first steps necessary once a crisis has occurred. This guidance includes how to activate and organize, where to go should the workplace be affected, how to communicate via multiple means with supervisors and other staff, roles and responsibilities of each department, points of contact and other emergency numbers, and how to know when the crisis has ended and it's time to return to normal operations.

## The importance of testing the plans

Given the world we live in today and the enormity of the types of crisis we are facing, it is imperative that organizations not only have a crisis management plan in place, but that they regularly test and exercise that plan extensively. The seamless and coordinated response to the 2005 London Bombings by the London Emergency Services is credited to their exercising regime, affectionately known as the "Hanover Series" (Government Office for London, 2006). For years before the 2005 attacks, the anti-terrorism branch of the London Metropolitan Police Service host[ed] quarterly joint exercises, known as the Hanover Series, to practice their response in the event of a major incident. Partner agencies and other stakeholders meet in the outskirts of London for weekend tabletop exercises that increase everyone's knowledge of roles and responsibilities. According to emergency service personnel, the practice sessions also increase familiarity with other key personnel, provide the opportunity to test procedures and rehearse the standardized emergency panel command and control system, and help agencies learn how to respond and react collectively. More mature organizations ensure that they also practice with their network to ensure the same levels of understanding, cooperation, and coordination.

Additionally, these exercises provide you and your staff with an opportunity to practice, develop competence, build understanding of your arrangements, their roles and responsibilities, enabling you the crisis leader to build trust and confidence with your employees and other stakeholders, that the company is well managed and prepared for the inevitable first or next crisis. Exercising the plan is also a great way to evaluate your leadership capability to effectively implement the plan. And finally, we'd like to make the point that it is critical that every member of the organization or company participate in the crisis management training and exercise. It simply cannot be overstated. There have been countless examples in our history when the highest leaders of an organization are simply not prepared to lead in a crisis. In a crisis, an untrained leader is nothing more than a liability.

> An untested plan is only a strategy.
>
> —Richard Gagnon

## Summary

Over the years, significant events have depicted that a crisis can test a leader and an organization unlike any other event. Leadership is not given, but earned through one's ability to make sense of the multiple aspects influencing a unique situation while being able to make sense of all the different aspects of a crisis affecting an organization. During a crisis, all aspects of a leader's leadership knowledge, skills, abilities, and other characteristics are on full display and are subject to stakeholder criticism and judgment. These leadership and decision-making attributes are normally made public and influence an organization's viability and good standing immediately during and after such an event or crisis. An organizational crisis can greatly benefit a senior leader by drawing attention to his or her leadership strengths and conversely, it can also expose serious leadership skill deficiencies such as an inability to operate under pressure or the inability to handle an organizational crisis.

As stated earlier, the purpose of writing this chapter was for the crisis leader. It was our intent to provide you with some of the countless tools necessary to help organize your thoughts and get your crisis team moving so that you can successfully lead your organizations safely out of a crisis. We discussed the framework and skills a leader must possess to include sensing, or how to determine and recognize when a crisis is happening; decision making, or the ability to rapidly form multiple courses of action; meaning making, or understanding and communicating the full effect of the crisis; terminating, or transitioning back to normal operations; and learning, or the documenting, learning, preparation, and exercising of the workforce to prevent the same similar crises from happening again. These are proven steps from the greatest minds in crisis leadership.

We discussed the Boyd cycle, commonly referred to as the "the OODA loop." The model developed by USAF Colonel John Boyd is used to describe a reoccurring decision-making cycle. Dr. Deming's model of "Plan-Do-Check-Act," designed to properly capture the notion that true quality control requires a willingness to seek constant improvement, and finally, the military's Crisis Action Plan: situation development, crisis assessment, course of action development, course of action selection, execution planning, and execution.

These models were developed and designed for one reason: to help leaders make better decisions while under the pressure and strain of the crisis. During a crisis, as information becomes available and is "fed" into these models, our situational awareness begins to improve where we can develop sound and reasonable courses of action and ultimately, turn them into decisions. As more information becomes available, we either stay the course, change direction by modifying our initial decision, or completely start over by making a new decision to support the new data we just received. We discussed meaning making, or crisis communication. With the rapid advancement of personal cell phones to support our constant need to communicate, with as many people as possible, simultaneously, it is critical that leaders be technologically savvy enough to "control the message" before, during, and after a crisis has occurred, and to prevent outside forces such as the media or political operatives from distorting the facts, creating even more chaos and corporate damage in the process. We then discussed terminating and the importance of re-building the trust and confidence we need in our leaders to accept accountability and responsibility for what went wrong, along with their willingness to make the right changes to improve the organizations ability to safely operate into the future. And finally, we discussed learning. The importance of identifying, planning, training, exercising, and preparing the entire workforce to better handle any crisis into the future. This Sensing, Decision Making, Meaning Making, Terminating and Learning model was developed by Arjen Boin, Paul 't Hart, Eric Stern, abd Bengt Sundelius, the authors of *Politics of Crisis Management*, and is the crisis leadership model we think is best suited to the corporate leaders, department heads and supervisors we work with. It can easily be remembered by the acronym S-D-M-T-L or simply, *Start Doing More To Live*!

We hope this chapter has provided you with essential tools you can use in a crisis that will make you a more confident, effective, accountable, and responsible crisis leader. We wish you best on your lifelong journey of leadership learning and stand ready to assist you should you need any help along the way!

## Bibliography

Argenti, P. (2002). Best Practice Crisis communication: Lessons from 9/11. *Harvard Business Review*. 80(12), 103–109.

Beringer, D.B. (1989). Summary of the various definitions of Situation Awareness. Exploring situational awareness: A review and the effects of stress on rectilinear normalisation, 646–651.

Boin, A., 't Hart, P., Stern, E., & Sundelius, B. (2005). *The Politics of Crisis Management: Public Leadership Under Pressure*. Cambridge: Cambridge University Press.

Boin, A. (2013). Orchestrating Joint Sensemaking across government levels: Challenges and requirements for crisis leadership. *Journal of Leadership Studies*, 41–46.

Boin, A., 't Hard, P., Stern, E., & Sundelius, B. (2017). *The Politics of Crisis Management: Public Leadership Under Pressure*, Cambridge: Cambridge University Press.

British Standards Institution. (2007). *Business Continuity Management – Part 2: Specification BS 25999–2:2007*. London: BSI Standards Limited.

British Standards Institution. (2014). *Crisis Management – Guidance and Good Practice BS 11200:2014*. London: BSI Standards Limited.

Darling, R. J. (2010). *24 Hours Inside the President's Bunker: 9/11/01: The White House*. Stafford, VA: iUniverse.

Endsley, M. R. (1988). Situational awareness global assessment technique (SAGAT). National Aerospace and Electronic Conference (NAECON), Dayton.

Endsley, M. R. (1995). Measurement of situation awareness in dynamic systems. *Human Factors*. 37(1), 65–84.

Endsley, M. R. (2000). Theoretical underpinnings of situation awareness: A critical review. In M. R. Endsley & D. J. Garland (Eds.), *Situation awareness analysis and measurement*. Mahwah, NJ: LEA.

Government Office for London. (2006). Looking Back, Moving Forward: The Multi-Agency Debrief. Retrieved from London: Government Office for London.

Klann, G. (2003). Crisis Leadership: Using Military Lessons, Organizational Experiences, and the Power of Influence to Lessen the Impact of Chaos on the People You Lead. Greensboro, NC: Center for Creative Leadership.

Klein, G. (1998). *Sources of Power: How People Make Decisions*. Cambridge, MA: The MIT Press.

Klein, G. (2011). *Streetlights and Shadows – Searching for the Keys to Adaptive Decision Making*. Cambridge, MA: Massachusetts Institute of Technology.

Klein, G., Moon, B., & Hoffman, R. R. (2006). Making Sense of Sensemaking 1: Alternative Perspectives. *IEEE Intelligent Systems*. 21(4).

Leonard, A. M. (2009). *Managing Crisis; Responses to Large-Scale Emergencies*. Washington, DC: CQ Press.

Reed, S. (2012, September 1). Tony Hayward Gets His Life Back. Retrieved from New York Times: www.nytimes.com/2012/09/02/business/tony-hayward-former-bp-chief-returns-to-oil.html

States, T. R.-2. ((1854–1919)).

Strom, K. E. (2008, July 15). Interagency Coordination: A Case Study of the 2005 London Bombings. Retrieved from NIJ National Institute of Justice: www.nij.gov/journals/260/pages/interagency-coordination.aspx

Weick, K. E. (1995). *Sensemaking in Organizations*. California: Sage Publications, Inc.

# 9

# Internal investigations of white-collar crime

*Petter Gottschalk*

## Introduction

White-collar crime is a crisis event that can challenge an organization's viability (Piquero, 2012). Numerous white-collar crime events in the last decade have led to an increased awareness of the need to be prepared for the worst. When white-collar crime suspicions arise, a feasible action is to initiate an internal investigation by fraud examiners to establish whether or not wrongdoings have occurred (Gottschalk, 2015). Victims of white-collar crime include organizations themselves, banks, revenue services, customers, shareholders, employees, and suppliers. When white-collar crime is prosecuted, organizations are punished with substantial fines, while executives are sent to prison (Podgor, 2007).

Not all organizations survive white-collar crime. Enron in the United States is a classic example (Williams, 2008). When organizations survive white-collar crime, they have to go through a complete overhaul of both organizational structure and organizational culture. Siemens in Germany is a classic example. German police raided Siemens headquarters in Munich and the homes of leading executives. Siemens had been bribing government officials to secure contracts and to gain favorable conditions for more than three decades. Eberl et al. (2015: 1209) argue that most of the executives involved "were clearly aware that they were violating the law, but they acted out of a sense of loyalty to and for the benefit of their company." The severe violation of integrity at the organizational level at Siemens led to a substantial crisis of the organization's legitimacy and had strong negative effects on stakeholders' trust in the organization.

Early initiatives of internal investigations by fraud examiners can potentially reduce the harm from white-collar crime. Private investigators will reconstruct the past as well as provide suggestions for corrective actions. Examples in the United States include General Motors (Valukas, 2014) and Wildenthal (Breen and Guberman, 2012).

The purpose of this chapter is to describe white-collar crime, internal investigations, and characteristics of successful fraud examinations that can potentially reduce the consequences of a crisis event. While this chapter is concerned with the action of internal investigation when a possible crisis in terms of fraud is emerging, my other chapter in this book on "Collapse or Recovery After White-Collar Crime" is concerned with the later stage of organizational collapse or recovery after the fact of white-collar crime detection.

## White-collar crime

Ever since Sutherland (1940) coined the term white-collar crime, there has been a debate as to who to include in and who to exclude from this category of criminals. However, it is generally accepted that white-collar crime is financial crime committed for personal or organizational profits based on privileged opportunities (Benson and Simpson, 2015). Convenience in white-collar crime relates to savings in time and effort by the elite to reach a goal, such as new telecom licenses, new construction contracts, or establishing new subsidiaries. Convenience is an attribute of white-collar crime. Convenience comes at a potential cost to the offender in terms of the likelihood of detection and future crisis. In other words, reducing time and effort now entails a greater potential for future cost.

Convenience is a key characteristic of white-collar crime. Convenience represents a time and effort component related to the complete illegal transaction process or processes (Collier and Kimes, 2012). People differ in their temporal orientation, including perceived time scarcity, the degree to which they value time, and their sensitivity to time-related issues. Facing strain, greed, or other situations, an illegal activity can represent a convenient solution to a problem that the individual or the organization otherwise find difficult or even impossible to solve.

The desire for convenience varies among people. Convenience orientation is a term that refers to a person's general preference for convenient solutions to problems. A convenience-oriented individual is one who seeks to accomplish a task in the shortest time with the least expenditure of human energy (Farquhar and Rowley, 2009).

Three main dimensions to explain white-collar crime have emerged. All of them link to convenience. The first dimension is concerned with economic aspects, where convenience implies that the illegal financial gain is a convenient option for the decision maker to cover needs. The second dimension is concerned with organizational aspects, where convenience implies that the offender has convenient access to premises and convenient ability to hide illegal transactions among legal transactions. The third dimension is concerned with behavioral aspects, where convenience implies that the offender finds convenient justification.

White-collar criminals have convenient access, and financial crime saves them time and effort to solve a problem related to making a personal or organizational profit. Convenience is a relative concept, where the ease of problem solving can cause future costs for the offender. Crime is committed if found suitable by the offender, and especially when no alternative is in sight.

The economic dimension implies that white-collar crime is profit-driven crime based on favorable economic circumstances. As argued by Naylor (2003), transfers of property occur by free market exchange or fraud, and these transfers involve redistribution of wealth and distribution of income. Fraud is illegal procurement of a private asset or means of advantage through deception or through the neglect of care for the interests of an asset required by duty. In particular, fraud includes heterogeneous forms such as misappropriation, balance manipulation, insolvency, and capital investment abuse (Füss and Hecker, 2008).

The organizational dimension implies that white-collar crime opportunity is a distinct characteristic and varies depending on the kinds of criminals involved (Michel, 2008). An opportunity is attractive as a means of responding to desires (Bucy et al., 2008). It is the organizational dimension that provides the white-collar criminal an opportunity to commit financial crime and conceal it in legal organizational activities. While opportunity in the economic dimension of convenience theory is concerned with goals (such as sales and bonuses), opportunity in the organizational dimension is concerned with crime (such as corruption and embezzlement).

Aguilera and Vadera (2008: 434) describe a criminal opportunity as "the presence of a favorable combination of circumstances that renders a possible course of action relevant." Opportunity arises when individuals or groups can engage in illegal and unethical behavior and expect, with reasonable confidence (Haines, 2014), to avoid detection and punishment.

Most theories of white-collar crime develop along the behavioral dimension. Researchers introduce numerous suggestions to explain white-collar individuals such as Madoff, Rajaratman and Schilling. Along the behavioral dimension, we find strain theory (Langton and Piquero, 2007), deterrence theory (Comey, 2009; Holtfreter et al., 2008), self-control theory (Gottfredson and Hirschi, 1990; Holtfreter et al., 2010; Piquero et al., 2010), obedience theory (Baird and Zelin, 2009), fear of falling (Piquero, 2012), negative life events (Engdahl, 2015), slippery slope (Welsh et al., 2015), and the American dream of economic success (Pratt and Cullen, 2005; Schoepfer and Piquero, 2006) – just to name a few. These theories suggest motives for committing white-collar crime, and they make crime a convenient option according to convenience theory. It is convenient for the criminal to be deceitful and breach trust to cause losses to others and gain for oneself (Pickett and Pickett, 2002).

In recent years, neutralization theory seems to increase in importance as a source of explanation. By applying neutralization techniques, white-collar criminals think they are doing nothing wrong. They deny responsibility, injury, and victim. They condemn the condemners. They claim appeal to higher loyalties and normality of action. They claim entitlement and they argue the case of legal mistake. They find their own mistakes acceptable. They argue a dilemma arose, whereby they made a reasonable tradeoff before committing the act (Siponen and Vance, 2010).

## Internal investigations

To handle an emerging crisis because of white-collar crime suspicions, a business enterprise may initiate an internal investigation by fraud examiners. By initiating an investigation, the corporation may find out what actually happened, and the corporation may stay in control over information about negative events. Also, private investigators may come up with recommendations how to emerge viable out of the crisis.

Convenience theory suggests that white-collar crime is stimulated when there is a need for profits, when the organization provides ample opportunities for misconduct, and when professionals in important and trusted positions find it acceptable to commit crime. In such organizations, suspicions of crime will occur more frequently than in organizations where people are less concerned with profits, where criminal opportunities are almost not present, and when the potential offender finds crime unacceptable.

When suspicion arises that crime has occurred, it can either be ignored or investigated. If the organization decides to investigate crime suspicions, then internal and/or external experts might get involved. Internal private investigations examine facts, the sequence of events, and the causes of negative events as well as who are responsible for such events. Pending what hiring parties ask for, private investigators can either look generally for corrupt or otherwise criminal activities within an agency or company, or look more specifically for those committing white-collar crime. In other situations, it is the job of the private investigators to look into potential opportunities for financial crime to occur, so that the agency or company can fix those problems in order to avoid misconduct down the road.

Internal investigations include fact-finding, causality study, change proposals, and suspect identification. Recent years have seen an increasing use of private internal investigations in terms of the assessment of financial irregularities. The form of inquiry aims to uncover unrestricted opportunities, failing internal controls, abuse of position, and any financial misconduct such as corruption, fraud, embezzlement, theft, manipulation, tax evasion, and other forms of economic crime (ACFE, 2014; CFCS, 2014).

Characteristics of a private investigation include a serious and unusual event, an extraordinary examination to find out what happened or why it did not happen, develop explanations, and suggest actions towards individuals and changes in systems and practices. A private investigator is someone hired by individuals or organizations to undertake investigatory law services. They often work for attorneys in civil cases. A private investigator also goes under the titles of a private eye, private detective, inquiry agent, fraud examiner, private examiner, financial crime specialist, or PI (private investigator) for short. A private investigator does the detailed work to find the answers to misconduct and crime. Financial crime has become a major offense that clients hire private investigators to find the solutions to, in order to bring justice to the individuals affected, as defined by the client paying for the investigation.

Criminal investigation is a goal-oriented procedure for reconstructing the past. It is a method of creating an account of what has happened, how it happened, why it happened, and who did what to make it happen or let it happen. Criminal investigation is a reconstruction of past events and sequence of events by collecting information and evidence (Osterburg and Ward, 2014). An investigation is designed to answer questions such as when, where, what, how, who, and why, as such questions relate to negative events in the past. Internal private investigations typically have the following characteristics:

- Extraordinary investigation of suspicions by goal-oriented data collection
- Based on a mandate defined by and with the client
- Clarify facts, analyze events, identify reasons for incidents
- Evaluate systems failure and personal misconduct
- Independent, careful and transparent work
- The client is responsible for implementation of recommendations.

White-collar crime investigations are a specialized knowledge industry. Williams (2005) refers to it as the forensic accounting and criminal investigation industry. It is a unique industry, set apart from law enforcement, due to its ability to provide "direct and immediate responsiveness to client objectives, needs and interests, (unlike police) who are bound to one specific legal regime" (Williams, 2005: 194). The industry provides flexibility and a customized plan of attack according to client needs.

Investigations take many forms and have many purposes. Carson (2013) argues that the core feature of every investigation involves what we reliably know. The field of evidence is none other than the field of knowledge. There is an issue of whether we can have confidence in knowledge. A private investigator accumulates knowledge about what happened.

## Successful examinations

To reconstruct the past successfully in a professional manner, there is a need for knowledge management, information management, systems management, configuration management, and ethics management. Criminal investigation is based on a foundation of increasing knowledge over time, where knowledge is defined as information combined with interpretation, context, and reflection. A private investigation into financial crime suspicion needs to interpret and reflect on numbers in financial documents. One primary factor in financial documents that distinguishes fraud from error is whether the underlying action that results in the misstatement of financial accounts is perceived as intentional or unintentional. The ability to understand documents such as invoices, bank and other financial records, and the individuals who updated the records is a critical skill in financial crime and asset recovery work (CFCS, 2014).

The client defines a mandate for the investigation, and the investigation has to be carried out according to the mandate. The mandate tells investigators what to do. The mandate defines tasks and goals for the investigation. The mandate is an authorization to investigate a specific issue or several specific issues by reconstructing the past. The mandate can be part of the blame game, where the client wants to blame somebody while at the same time diverge attention from somebody else (Eberly et al., 2011). Some are too powerful to blame (Pontell et al., 2014). The mandate can be part of a rotten apple or rotten barrel approach, where attention is either directed at individuals or at systems failure (Ashforth et al., 2008). Anchoring of suspicion can be unintentionally or purposely be misplaced in the mandate. The blame game is often part of unsuccessful examinations.

A badly formulated mandate can be misleading for investigators and also represent possible avenues for opportunistic behaviors by investigators. Rather than getting to the core of the matter, an investigation may end up avoiding touching on inflamed issues. Rather than spending resources on difficult issues, investigators may end up solving the simple issues, thereby completing the assignment quickly and making a business profit on the project. Investigators can take advantage of positions of professional authority and power as well as opportunity structures (Kempa et al., 2009).

An important task of private investigators is protection against self-incrimination. A witness or suspect has no obligation to pass on information that may reveal that he or she was involved in crime. Investigators should provide interviewees a complete protection against disclosure of information that could reveal own offenses. However, lack of integrity on the part of the investigator may cause a breach of this protection mechanism.

Generally, there are two steps of looking for causal explanations in internal investigations where integrity is at stake. The first step is concerned with the mandate, where examiners define and develop the investigative focus. The second step is concerned with findings, where reconstruction of the past leads to potential suspects. Individuals suspected of financial crime can often perceive this as a blame game. Suspects tell investigators: "You should not blame me for what happened!"

Research on organizational justice and social accounts focuses on how actors publicly communicate explanations of negative events to others. Explanations affect outcomes such as trust in the organization, feelings of anger, dissatisfaction, frustration, and stress. Suspects find it unfair, especially when suspicions develop into more or less grounded accusations. Of course, this can happen in police investigations as well.

The term "blame game" can describe a phenomenon that happens in groups of people when something goes wrong. Blaming others is typically attractive when a negative event has occurred (Lee and Robinson, 2000). The blamers in our context are the private investigators, who receive financial reward for successfully affixing blame on targeted individuals. Blame can have varying degrees of impact on the blamed person. In the extreme, it can cause considerable harm, such as miscarriage of justice, public prosecution without evidence, humiliation in the media, and job loss.

A bias can occur among private investigators based on client mandate and available resources in fraud investigations, where anchoring of suspicion can be misplaced. If the client has strong beliefs one way or the other, this will manifest itself both in the mandate and in expectations.

Bias is an inclination to hold a partial perspective, often combined with a refusal or reluctance to consider other potential perspectives. Investigators may have bias toward or against certain leads, individuals, hypotheses, and facts. Investigation bias is the bias of examiners in their selection of which evidence they select and report. While an unbiased investigation is a true reconstruction of the past, a biased investigation is a distorted reconstruction of the past. Practical limitations to investigation neutrality include the inability of investigators to report all available stories and facts. Therefore, an investigation report tends to have biased characteristics in the selection of which events and stories investigators pay attention to, and how they are covered. Since it is impossible to report everything, selectivity is inevitable.

## Key investigation issues

Fraud examiners, financial crime specialists and counter fraud specialists are in the business of private internal investigations for their clients. Six problematic issues related to their roles have to be emphasized: privatization of law enforcement, secrecy of investigation reports, lack of disclosure to the police, competence of private investigators, limits by investigation mandate, and the issue of regulation of the investigation business. We have already touched on the investigation mandate linked to the blame game.

A number of issues, dilemmas, problems, and challenges in private investigations are important to explore in order to understand the business of financial crime specialists. Their hidden world is problematic. It was Williams (2005) and Schneider (2006) in the journal *Policing & Society* who first described and discussed problems related to privatizing economic crime enforcement and governance of private policing of financial crime. Since their research a decade ago, few of the problems they identified have been solved. Rather, the forensic accounting and corporate investigation industry has grown rapidly without any signs of effective regulation or self-regulation. Exceptions include the emergence of the counter fraud specialist in the United Kingdom (Button and Gee, 2013) and the works of voluntary organizations such as ACFE (2014) and CFCS (2014).

A *Privatization of law enforcement.* Ever since Schneider (2006) wrote his classic article on privatizing economic crime enforcement, the potential threat to criminal justice from private rather than public investigation, prosecution and sentencing of individuals in white-collar crime cases has steadily increased. In our context of private investigations, we apply the term "private policing" to capture similarities and differences with law enforcement. Private policing of economic crime can be detrimental to an open and democratic society where the rule of law is to be transparent. Privatization of law enforcement and criminal justice, as is currently a trend in many countries, represents a potential threat to democratic societies as all powers towards citizens in a state should be organized and managed by public authorities under democratic government control, and not by private business firms.

B *Secrecy of private investigation reports.* Very often, clients and their investigators deny researchers and journalists insight into private internal investigation reports. Investigators argue that reports are the property of their clients, while clients argue that there are circumstances that prevent them from disclosing reports. In my search for private investigation reports, I met a variety of reasons why clients and their investigators denied me access to investigation reports. The reasons for secrecy fall into three main categories. First, there were reasons important to the investigated organization. Second, there were reasons important for the investigating firm. Finally, there were reasons important for the relationship between the investigated and the investigator.

Reasons important for the investigated company include:

1. *Damage*. The private investigation report includes business secrets that might be damaging to disclose to competitors.
2. *Disagreement*. Executives in the client organization disagree how to interpret the investigation report.
3. *Protection*. Many key individuals in the organization have provided sensitive information to the investigators. They need protection.
4. *Workload*. Before possible disclosure, someone needs to black out a number of words, such as names of suspected but innocent persons, which represents too much work.
5. *Discretion*. Top executives who initiated the investigation do not like to see text about themselves leaking to the external environment.
6. *Property*. The client has paid investigators for the report and feels no obligation to disclose it to others.

Reasons important for the investigating firm include:

7. *Confidentiality*. Lawyers and other investigators have to respect the client-attorney privilege, similar to medical doctors and psychologists.
8. *Error*. There are serious flaws, mistakes, errors, and shortcomings in the investigation report, which investigators do not want others to find out and learn about.
9. *Accusation*. The investigation report documents a number of unfounded accusations against individual persons.
10. *Failure*. Investigators were unable to answer the questions formulated by the client in the mandate.
11. *Misconduct*. Investigators ignored or violated protection against self-incrimination and other ethical guidelines.
12. *Criticism*. Investigators do not like the report to become a victim of criticism by researchers and commentators in the media.

Reasons important for the investigator-client relationship:

13. *Suspicion*. The investigation report describes suspicion towards individuals, which the client did not choose to follow up nor to report to the police.
14. *Packaging*. The investigation report is impossible to read because of lack of clarity in its presentation.
15. *Termination*. The internal investigation was never completed.
16. *Evidence*. Findings from a private investigation can lose its value as evidence in a following police investigation and prosecution in the criminal justice system.
17. *Sensitivity*. Both client and investigator are afraid of breaking privacy law because of sensitive personal information in the report.

In addition, there is a problem of data protection legislation in some countries, which complicates the sharing of information.

C *Lack of disclosure to the police*. The rule of law and criminal justice works in constitutional states by public prosecution and courts that are open to everyone to observe. If there are suspicions of violations of criminal laws in a country, it is important that knowledgeable sources communicate information about suspects to public authorities such as police investigators and public prosecutors. Disclosure of investigation reports is a necessity in cases of criminal offences. Preferably, investigation reports should not only reach the attention of the police but also reach citizens through the media. However, many financial crime specialists consider their reports as the sole property of their clients, since clients pay for the job and the result in the shape of investigation reports. They consider their work as a piece of consulting assignment or legal advice, which might be protected by the client-attorney privilege (Schechtman, 2014). As a key issue in private investigations, disclosure is required to ensure criminal justice by avoiding privatization of prosecution and conclusion (verdict). Therefore, all reasons for secrecy are indeed questionable in cases of obvious crime suspicions. Reasons for lack of disclosure to the police include control, reputation, exclusion, effort, penalty, protection, bargaining, passivity, competence, capacity, failure, and trifle.

D *Competence of private investigators*. The competence of financial crime specialists and fraud examiners is varying to an extent that it represents a threat to the rule of law, privacy, and democracy. Some private investigators seem very professional, while others are not. Especially lawyers seem to suffer the danger of making many mistakes in private investigations, since they are not trained detectives. The institute of counter fraud specialists (ICFS) was founded as a result of the UK government's initiative to professionalize public sector fraud investigation. The institute exists to further the cause of fraud prevention and detection across all sectors of the UK and abroad. The membership of the ICFS is made up of accredited counter fraud specialists who have successfully completed the government's professionalism in security training (Button and Gee, 2013). In the accredited counter fraud specialist handbook by Tunley et al. (2014) mandatory elements of the accreditation are covered.

E *Limits by investigation mandate*. The client defines a mandate for the investigation, and the investigation has to be carried out according to the mandate. The mandate can be part of the blame game, where the client wants to blame somebody while at the same time divert attention from somebody else. Investigators with some integrity should deny acceptance of such assignments.

F *Regulation of the investigation business*. Regulation implies the presence of formal, direct mechanisms of control established with the stated intention of preventing or reducing injustice and incompetence in investigations. Most jurisdictions have some self-regulation by means of voluntary industry associations. Associations such as ACFE (2014) and CFCS (2014) play this role in the United States by providing guidelines and certification for fraud examiners and financial crime specialists. In Norway, the association of lawyers has developed some guidelines for private internal investigations (Schiøtz et al., 2011). Button et al. (2007) describe new directions in policing fraud in the UK in terms of counter fraud specialists. In Canada, guidelines resulted from consultations with security industry representatives (O'Connor et al., 2004). Burbidge (2005) argues that there is a governance deficit and lack of accountability in private policing in Canada. The standard applied is often public policing, which is subject to oversight both from a legislatively mandated governance authority with the mandate to give policy direction to the force, and from a public complaints authority, which has the mandate to investigate and prosecute cases of alleged police misconduct and abuse of authority. However, this standard can be an unfair basis for comparison, since private policing is subject to oversight in a number of other ways. For example, private investigators can be accountable to courts just like other potential criminals, and they are bound by contractual liability to clients in the private or public sector. In addition, there is self-regulation, as well as the pressures for good performance imposed by the competitive market for fraud examination services.

## Business self-regulation

Businesses and other organizations have a perspective on white-collar crime that has to do with the management of risk to make a profit. The criminal justice system has a perspective on white-collar crime that has to do with law enforcement and punishment. Therefore, privatization of law enforcement implies a paradigm shift from the penal system to the market system.

Larsson (2012) argues that inside corporations and other organizations there are no sharp distinctions between crime, misconduct, and risk. Most corporations share a managerial approach to crime, rather than a law enforcement approach to crime. The main question when industry itself is talking about white-collar crime is the cost of it, the risk, how to deal with it practically and reduce the loss, and maybe even get some compensation. In this perspective, a private internal investigation is an investment to reduce costs of crime, to recover the loss from crime, and to avoid loss from future crime. The investigation serves to help managers run the organization with reduced risk of white-collar crime. This way of dealing with crime is far from the traditional law and order approach stressing the moral and normative aspects of violations.

Therefore, privatization of law enforcement leads to a different perspective from the public police perspective. It is the harm caused by the offense that is at the core of attention, not the prosecution and conviction of the offender. Larsson (2012) suggests that the privatization of policing causes the role of public police to change. The role of the public police will increasingly be policing the private police and other collaborators such as private investigators.

Larsson (2012: 41) finds the modern language of crime prevention and control quite interesting:

> The last decades have witnessed a growing use, also in the Nordic countries, of economic, market, and consumer terminology. Security is a commodity that can be bought and has a price in the market place. There are partnerships in crime prevention and problem owners. All of these are terms from the private industry.

Larsson (2012) found that criminal law and the business world in some respect represent two different systems of logic. The penal system is primarily occupied with morals and guilt. Punishment is part of the system's toolbox. The business world is concerned with making a profit by managing risk. Therefore, a transition from public regulation to self-regulation in organizations will imply a paradigm shift from law enforcement to business success.

Schneider (2006) found that law enforcement officials are concerned with some aspects of the private policing sector: poor training, a lack of minimum standards or accreditation, and unethical and illegal tactics. Criticism is also based on the private investigation industry's for-profit nature, which has been blamed for placing results and efficiency over ethics, and the pursuit of the private interests of the client at the expense of the greater public good.

Regulation implies the presence of formal, direct mechanisms of control established with the stated intention of preventing or reducing injustice and incompetence in investigations.

Most jurisdictions have some self-regulation by means of voluntary industry associations. Associations such as ACFE (2014) and CFCS (2014) play this role in the United States by providing guidelines and certification for fraud examiners and financial crime specialists. In Norway, the association of lawyers has developed some guidelines for private internal investigations (Schiøtz et al., 2011). Button et al. (2007) describe new directions in policing fraud in the UK in terms of counter fraud specialists. In Canada, guidelines resulted from consultations with security industry representatives (O'Connor et al., 2004).

Burbidge (2005) argues that there is a governance deficit and lack of accountability in private policing in Canada. The standard applied is often public policing, which is subject to oversight both from a legislatively mandated governance authority with the mandate to give policy direction to the force, and from a public complaints authority, which has the mandate to investigate and prosecute cases of alleged police misconduct and abuse of authority. However, this standard can be an unfair basis for comparison, since private policing is subject to oversight in a number of other ways. For example, private investigators can be accountable to courts just like other potential criminals, and they are bound by contractual liability to clients in the private or public sector. In addition, there is self-regulation, as well as the pressures for good performance imposed by the competitive market for fraud examination services.

Williams (2005) finds that one problem with self-regulation is corporate executives' eagerness to avoid the embarrassment and negative publicity associated with white-collar crime cases. From time to time, crime cases will occur, in the form of corruption, embezzlement, or other kinds of financial crime. The issue is how such incidents are handled. If disclosed, allegations of fraud could have a potentially devastating impact on the reputation and share value of a company. One of the primary reasons corporate executives fail to report cases of financial wrongdoing to the police is that they lose control over the matter and thus sacrifice secrecy and discretion.

Regulatory policy provides the frameworks used by government agencies developing regulations rules that implement and give meaning to laws. Regulatory policy sets forth the guidelines for developing, promulgating, implementing, and enforcing systems of public protections. For example, regulatory policy gives guidance on how to prioritize rulemaking agendas, defines constraints to agencies' rulemaking ability, and determines the breadth and depth of information necessary for an agency to proceed with a rulemaking. Regulatory policy guides agencies' rulemaking agendas (CEG, 2015).

A regulation is a legal norm intended to shape conduct by prescribing and proscribing conduct. In 2015, the state of Colorado in the United States introduced a regulation that made licensure for private investigators mandatory. The Office of Private Investigator Licensure in the Divison of Professions and Occupations is now licensing private investigators in Colorado. The office's activities include licensing, investigation of complaints, determination of discipline, and enforcement of discipline for those who violate Colorado statues and licensure rules. The application fee for mandatory private investigator licensure was $330 in 2015 for both Level I and Level II private investigators (Colorado, 2015).

Ever since Williams (2005) wrote his classic article on the governability of the private policing of economic crime, the threat to criminal justice from private rather than public investigation, prosecution, and sentencing of individuals in white-collar crime cases has steadily increased. Similar to the private policing sector in general, the private forensic sector is only loosely regulated in countries like Canada (Schneider, 2006) and not regulated at all in many other countries.

Williams (2005) argues that there is a need for governance of the private investigation industry. However, he finds that the governability of the industry is inscribed within the features and properties of its legal, political, and cultural environment. Therefore, legal regulation might be necessary. The possibility of industry reform is inevitably complicated by the secrecy and low visibility of private investigations and their existence in the shadow of the law. This is in sharp contrast to the public's access to court proceedings, where everything is open and shared.

Weissmann and Block (2010) argues that the self-regulatory model of corporate governance in the global business environment has failed. The model rests on the theory of self-regulation as the most effective and efficient means to achieve corporate self-restraint in the marketplace for professional services firms engaged in private investigations. The model seems to fail in achieving regular compliance with basic ethical and legal behaviors as evidenced by a series of firm debacles. The self-regulation model is premised on self-control with regulatory oversight. As argued by James and Seipel (2010), an important element of government and client confidence in private investigators is the perceived strength of firms' corporate governance.

Firm governance is the systems and structures through which each entity is directed and run (Goldschmidt, 2004). Governance is an established and agreed structure in which the goals for private investigations are to be met. The concept of governance deals with several normative principles including accountability, transparency, participation, responsiveness, equity, and the rule of law. The concept is based on an assumption that all organizations have the need to benchmark their activities against governance standards (Jones, 2009).

Firm governance has to do with the allocation of rights and obligations among financial crime specialists in the organization. Without firm governance, people in the organization tend to count on others to do what is necessary such as instructing and monitoring financial crime specialists when they are working for clients.

## Conclusion

When crisis of white-collar crime suspicions emerges in business emerge, such as fraud, corruption, or embezzlement, the business needs to act to clarify the situation and to recover from the situation. A feasible option is to hire private investigators to conduct financial crime examinations. However, as pointed out in this chapter, several issues have to be addressed before, during and after the investigation to make sure the examination contributes to organizational viability.

## References


ACFE (2014). *Report to the Nations on Occupational Fraud and Abuse, 2014 Global Fraud Study*, Association of Certified Fraud Examiners, Austin, Texas.

Aguilera, R.V. and Vadera, A.K. (2008). The Dark Side of Authority: Antecedents, Mechanisms, and Outcomes of Organizational Corruption, *Journal of Business Ethics*, 77, 431–449.

Ashforth, B.E., Gioia, D.A., Robinson, S.L. og Trevino, L.K. (2008). Re-Reviewing Organizational Corruption, *Academy of Management Review*, 33 (3), 670–684.

Baird, J.E. and Zelin, R.C. (2009). An Examination of the Impact of Obedience Pressure on Perceptions of Fraudulent Acts and the Likelihood of Committing Occupational Fraud, *Journal of Forensic Studies in Accounting and Business*, Winter, 1–14.

Benson, M.L. and Simpson, S.S. (2015). *Understanding White-Collar Crime – An Opportunity Perspective*, New York, NY: Routledge.

Breen, K.M. and Guberman, P. (2012). *Special investigative report regarding allegations of impropriety by Dr. C. Kern Wildenthal relating to travel and entertainment expenses paid for by University of Texas Southwestern Medical Center*, Hastings law firm.

Bucy, P.H., Formby, E.P., Raspanti, M.S. and Rooney, K.E. (2008). Why Do They Do It?: The Motives, Mores, and Character of White Collar Criminals, *St. John's Law Review*, 82, 401–571.

Burbidge, S. (2005). The Governance Deficit: Reflections on the Future of Public and Private Policing in Canada, *Canadian Journal of Criminology and Criminal Justice*, January, 63–86.

Button, M. and Gee, J. (2013). *Countering Fraud for Competitive Advantage – The Professional Approach to Reducing the Last Great Hidden Cost*, Chichester: Wiley & Sons.

Button, M., Johnston, L., Frimpong, K. and Smith, G. (2007). New Directions in Policing Fraud: The Emergence of the Counter Fraud Specialists in the United Kingdom, *International Journal of the Sociology of Law*, 35, 192–208.

Carson, D. (2013). Investigations: What Could, and Should, be Taught? *The Police Journal*, 86 (3), 249–275.

CEG (2015). Basic Overview, *Center for Effective Government*, www.foreffectivegov.org/node/3460

CFCS (2014). *CFCS Certification Examination Study Manual*, 4th Edition, Certified Financial Crime Specialist, Association of Certified Financial Crime Specialists, Rivergate Plaza, Miami, FL 33131.

Colorado (2015). Office of Private Investigator Licensure, Division of Professions and Occupations, *Department of Regulatory Agencies*, Colorado, http://cdn.colorado.gov/cs/Satellite?c=Page&childpagename=DORA-Reg/DORALayout&cid=1251632358945&pagename=CBONWrapper

Collier, J.E. and Kimes, S.E. (2012). Only If It Is Convenient: Understanding How Convenience Influences Self-Service Technology Evaluation, *Journal of Service Research*, 16 (1), 39–51.

Comey, J.B. (2009). Go Directly to Prison: White Collar Sentencing After the Sarbanes-Oxley Act, *Harvard Law Review*, 122, 1728–1749.

Eberl, P., Geiger, D. and Assländer, M.S. (2015). Repairing Trust in an Organization After Integrity Violations: The Ambivalence of Organizational Rule Adjustments, *Organization Studies*, 36 (9), 1205–1235.

Eberly, M.B., Holley, E.C., Johnson, M.D. and Mitchell, T.R. (2011). Beyond Internal and External: A Dyadic Theory of Relational Attributions, *Academy of Management Review*, 36 (4), 731–753.

Engdahl, O. (2015). White-Collar Crime and First-Time Adult-Onset Offending: Explorations in the Concept of Negative Life Events as Turning Points, *International Journal of Law, Crime and Justice*, 43 (1), 1–16.

Farquhar, J.D. and Rowley, J. (2009). Convenience: A Services Perspective, *Marketing Theory*, 9 (4), 425–438.

Füss, R. and Hecker, A. (2008). Profiling White-Collar Crime: Evidence From German-Speaking Countries, *Corporate Ownership & Control*, 5 (4), 149–161.

Goldschmidt, L. (2004). The Role of Boards in Preventing Economic Crime, *Journal of Financial Crime*, 11 (4), 342–346.

Gottfredson, M.R. and Hirschi, T. (1990). *A General Theory of Crime*, Stanford, CA, Stanford University Press.

Gottschalk, P. (2015). Private Investigations of White-Collar Crime Suspicions: A Qualitative Study of the Blame Game Hypothesis, *Journal of Investigative Psychology and Offender Profiling*, 12, 231–246.

Haines, F. (2014). Corporate Fraud as Misplaced Confidence? Exploring Ambiguity in the Accuracy of Accounts and the Materiality of Money, *Theoretical Criminology*, 18 (1), 20–37.

Holtfreter, K., Beaver, K.M., Reisig, M.D. and Pratt, T.C. (2010). Low Self-Control and Fraud Offending, *Journal of Financial Crime*, 17 (3), 295–307.

Holtfreter, K., Slyke, S.V., Bratton, J. and Gertz, M. (2008). Public Perceptions of WhiteCollar Crime and Punishment, *Journal of Criminal Justice*, 36, 50–60.

James, K.L. and Seipel, S.J. (2010). The Effects of Decreased User Confidence on Perceived Internal Audit Fraud Protection, *Journal of Forensic & Investigative Accounting*, 81, 1–23.

Jones, M. (2009). Governance, Integrity, and the Police Organization, *Policing: An International Journal of Police Strategies & Management*, 32 (2), 338–350.

Kempa, M., Carrier, R., Wood, J. and Shearing, C. (2009). Reflections on the Evolving Concept of 'private policing', *European Journal on Criminal Policy and Research*, 7, 197–223.

Langton, L. and Piquero, N.L. (2007). Can General Strain Theory Explain White-Collar Crime? A Preliminary Investigation of the Relationship Between Strain and Select White-Collar Offenses, *Journal of Criminal Justice*, 35, 1–15.

Larsson, P. (2012). Regulating Corporate Crime: From Punishment to Self-Regulation, *Journal of Scandinavian Studies in Criminology and Crime Prevention*, 13, 31–46.

Lee, F. and Robinson, R. J. (2000). An Attributional Analysis of Social Accounts: Implications of Playing the Blame Game, *Journal of Applied Social Psychology*, 30 (9), 1853–1879.

Michel, P. (2008). Financial Crimes: The Constant Challenge of Seeking Effective Prevention Solutions, *Journal of Financial Crime*, 15 (4), 383–397.

Naylor, R. T. (2003). Towards a General Theory of Profit-Driven Crimes, *British Journal of Criminology*, 43, 81–101.

O'Connor, D., Lippert, R., Greenfield, K. and Boyle, P. (2004). After the "Quiet Revolution": The Self-Regulation of Ontario Contract Security Agencies, *Policing & Society*, 14 (2), 138–157.

Osterburg, J. W. and Ward, R. H. (2014). *Criminal Investigation – A Method for Reconstructing the Past*, 7th Edition, Anderson Publishing, MA: Waltham.

Pickett, K.H.S. and Pickett, J. M. (2002). *Financial Crime Investigation and Control*, New York: John Wiley & Sons.

Piquero, N. L. (2012). The Only Thing We Have to Fear Is Fear Itself: Investigating the Relationship Between Fear of Falling and White Collar Crime, *Crime and Delinquency*, 58 (3), 362–379.

Piquero, N. L., Schoepfer, A. and Langton, L. (2010). Completely Out of Control or the Desire to Be in Complete Control? How Low Self-Control and the Desire for Control Relate to Corporate Offending, *Crime & Delinquency*, 56 (4), 627–647.

Podgor, E. S. (2007). The Challenge of White Collar Sentencing, *Journal of Criminal Law and Criminology*, 97 (3), 1–10.

Pontell, H. N., Black, W. K. and Geis, G. (2014). Too Big to Fail, Too Powerful to Jail? On the Absence of Criminal Prosecutions After the 2008 Financial Meltdown, *Crime, Law and Social Change*, 61 (1), 1–13.

Pratt, T. C. and Cullen, F. T. (2005). Assessing Macro-Level Predictors and Theories of Crime: A Meta-Analysis, *Crime and Justice*, 32, 373–450.

Schechtman, J. (2014). Are Internal Bribery Probes Private? Attorney-Client Privilege Protections Over Corporate Investigations Led By Outside Law Firms Are Eroding, *The Wall Street Journal*, October 11, http://online.wsj.com/articles/are-internal-bribery-probes-private-1413157700

Schiøtz, C., Helsingeng, A. and Mo, P. H. (2011). *Retningslinjer for Private Granskinger* (*Guidelines for Private Investigations*), Advokatforeningen (Attorney Association), Oslo. www.advokatforeningen.no/PageFiles/19999/Retningslinjer_for_private_granskinger.PDF.

Schneider, S. (2006). Privatizing Economic Crime Enforcement: Exploring the Role of Private Sector Investigative Agencies in Combating Money Laundering, *Policing & Society*, 16 (3), 285–312.

Schoepfer, A. and Piquero, N. L. (2006). Exploring White-Collar Crime and the American Dream: A Partial Test of Institutional Anomie Theory, *Journal of Criminal Justice*, 34, 227–235.

Siponen, M. and Vance, A. (2010). Neutralization: New Insights Into the Problem of Employee Information Security Policy Violations, *MIS Quarterly*, 34 (3), 487–502.

Sutherland, E. H. (1940). White-Collar Criminality, *American Sociological Review*, 5, 1–12.

Tunley, M., Whittaker, A., Gee, J. and Button, M. (2014). *The Accredited Counter Fraud Specialist Handbook*, Chicheester: Wiley & Sons.

Valukas, A. R. (2014). *Report to the board of directors of General Motors company regarding ignition switch recalls*, Jenner & Block law firm, 325 pages.

Weissmann, A. and Block, J.A. (2010). White-Collar Defendants and White-Collar Crimes, *Yale Law Journal*, 116, 286–291.

Welsh, D. T., Oronez, L. D., Snyder, D. G. and Christian, M. S. (2015). The Slippery Slope: How Small Ethical Transgressions Pave the Way for Larger Future Transgressions, *Journal of Applied Psychology*, 100 (1), 114–127.

Williams, J. W. (2005). Governability Matters: The Private Policing of Economic Crime and the Challenge of Democratic Governance, *Policing & Society*, 15 (2), 187–211.

Williams, J. W. (2008) The Lessons of Enron: Media Accounts, Corporate Crimes, and Financial Markets, *Theoretical Criminology*, 12 (4), 471–499.

# 10

# Collapse or recovery after white-collar crime

*Petter Gottschalk*

## Introduction

Some corporations collapse when the organization is hit by a white-collar crime crisis in terms of detection and prosecution. Classic examples include Enron and WorldCom (Soltani, 2014). Enron (and their auditing firm Andersen) went bankrupt because of a white-collar crime crisis in 2001 (Powers et al., 2002), while WorldCom went bankrupt because of a white-collar crime crisis in 2002 (WilmerHale and PwC, 2008). Some companies are able to recover after white-collar crime detection and prosecution. A classic example is Siemens, which has faced the greatest bribery scandal in the history of German business. In 2004, Siemens faced a series of bribery and money laundering allegations in more than a dozen countries (Eberl et al., 2015).

Collapse or recovery depends on a number of factors. We argue that the relationship between perceived situation and implemented actions will determine whether the outcome will be successful. If reality is denied and top management has a distorted perception of the situation, then collapse becomes a much more likely outcome. If the perceived situation is consistent with the actual situation, and implemented actions are consistent with the needs of the situation, then recovery becomes a more likely outcome.

## The collapse of Enron

Powers et al. (2002) wrote a report of investigation about the Enron scandal. In the economical dimension, the threat of corporate collapse made crime a convenient option. The crime consisted of restating financial statements for the period from 1997 to 2001. Furthermore, Enron employees were enriched by tens of millions of dollars they should never have received – Andrew Fastow by at least $30 million and Michael Kopper by at least $10 million. Some accounting transactions were implemented to offset losses. They allowed Enron to conceal from the market very large losses resulting from Enron's merchant investments by creating an appearance that those investments were hedged – that is, that a third party was obligated to pay Enron the amount of those losses – when in fact that third party was simply an entity in which only Enron had a substantial economic stake. Thus, in the organizational dimension, Enron was able to report earnings that were almost $1 billion higher than should have been reported. In the behavioral dimension, top executives found that they could justify deviant financial statements, and they found that they personally deserved large payments. Executives included Kenneth Lay, Jeffrey Skilling, Richard Causey, and Richard Buy, in addition to Fastow and Kopper.

Enron was an American energy, commodities, and services company based in Houston, Texas. The company employed 20,000 people in the areas of electricity, natural gas, communications, and pulp and paper. In the 1990s, the company ran into financial problems. Enron was in need of a rescue plan. One alternative for the rescue operation was to sell off subsidiaries and close down unprofitable business. Another alternative was to let a competing business enterprise take over Enron to restructure it and merge it with similar activities. A third alternative was to replace top management with new skills to change product lines, marketing strategy, and organizational structure. A fourth alternative was for the failing top management team to commit white-collar crime.

The top management team consisted of Kenneth Lay, Jeffrey Skilling, and Andrew Fastow. They decided to implement alternative four. This alternative was considered the most convenient one. By committing white-collar crime, they believed that they could rescue Enron. They thought the financial problems were temporary and would disappear after some years. They thought they might be able to correct their crime when profits would be flowing in again. They were convinced Enron would recover.

Alternatives one to three were less attractive to them. They had built an empire that was associated with success, status, and influence. Ken Lay was a close friend of the Bush family, including the president. Enron made large campaign contributions to Bush and headed several important committees in the Republican Party. In their prestigious positions, it was unacceptable to Lay, Skilling, and Fastow to hand over the business to others. It was unacceptable to reveal to the environment that Enron was performing poorly.

White-collar crime was thus a convenient option. By presenting financial results far more favorable than the real situation told them, they were able to stay on top of a seemingly successful, expanding, and profitable business enterprise. It was the threat of collapse and bankruptcy that made white-collar crime a seemingly convenient way out of performance problems. If the white-collar crime had been successful, then Enron would recover and probably nobody would have learned about the offense. It would serve to protect Enron's interests.

Some quotes from the internal investigation report by Powers et al. (2002) illustrate convenience in the economical dimension:

- "Enron used this strategy to avoid recognizing losses for a time" (page 14).
- "One perceived solution to this finance problem was to find outside investors willing to enter into arrangements that would enable Enron to retain those risks it believed it would manage effectively, and the related rewards" (page 36).
- "On June 18, 1999, Fastow discussed with Lay and Skilling a proposal to establish a partnership, subsequently named LJM Cayman. Fastow would serve as the general partner and would seek investments by outside vendors" (page 68).
- "Fastow and Glisan developed a plan to hedge the Rhythms investment by taking advantage of the value in the Enron shares covered by the forward contracts" (page 78).
- "In late 1999, at Skilling's urging a group of Enron commercial and accounting professionals began to devise a mechanism that would allow Enron to hedge a portion of its merchant investment portfolio" (page 99).
- "It is particularly surprising that the accountants at Andersen, who should have brought a measure of objectivity and perspective to these transactions, did not do so" (page 132).

- "The Board of Directors was denied important information that might have led it to take action" (page 148).

Powers et al.'s (2002) investigation report reveals that not only a threat motive made white-collar crime a convenient option. Also greed was present, especially as it relates to Fastow:

- "Andrew S. Fastow, Executive Vice President and Chief Financial Officer of Enron, is the managing member of LJM1's general partner. The general partner of LJM1 is entitled to receive a percentage of the profits of LJM1 in excess of the general partner's proportion of the total capital contributed to LJM1, depending upon the performance of the investments made by LJM1" (page 184).
- "The failure to set forth Fastow's compensation from the LJM transactions and the process leading to that decision raise substantial issues" (page 187).

Unfortunately for Lay, Skilling, and Fastow, their white-collar crime was not successful. It did not solve the problem. Enron went bankrupt, and the executives went to prison.

While the economical convenience of white-collar crime in the Enron case is mainly characterized by the need for success and the fear of falling (Piquero, 2012), the organizational convenience is characterized by opportunities of advanced manipulation techniques that are available to top executives (Benson and Simpson, 2015). The behavioral convenience can be found in a corporate culture dominated by Lay, Skilling, and Fastow focusing on goals that justify (illegal) means (Jonnergård et al., 2010) and neutralization of potential guilt feelings (Stadler and Benson, 2012).

## The collapse of WorldCom

WilmerHale and PwC (2008) wrote a report of investigation about the WorldCom scandal. CEO Bernard Ebbers had to go to jail. Other involved top executives at WorldCom included Scott Sullivan, David Myers, Buford Yates, and Mark Abide. In the economic dimension, Ebbers personally acquired real estate ventures, hotels, and other kinds of property. He had purchased the largest working cattle ranch in Canada and approximately 540,000 acres of timberland in four southern U.S. states. The total scope of Ebbers's non-WorldCom businesses was summarized to include a Louisiana rice farm, a luxury yacht building company, a lumber mill, a country club, a trucking company, a minor league hockey team, an operating marina, and a building in downtown Chicago. To buy all these properties, he had accumulated substantial debts with a number of banks. Ebbers took out more and more loans from commercial banks. Many of these loans were margin loans secured by shares of Ebbers's WorldCom stock. Although the terms varied among various margin loans, each required that the value of Ebbers's stock remained greater than or equal to some multiple of the amount of the loan.

Therefore, CEO Ebbers had to make sure that WorldCom stock prices were high, and much higher than real accounting justified. The massive indebtedness left Ebbers exposed to decline in the price of WorldCom stock. Ebbers initiated more than $9 billion in false or unsupported accounting entries in WorldCom's financial systems in order to achieve desired reported financial results to boost the WorldCom stock value. Most of WorldCom's people did not know it was occurring. In the organizational dimension, Ebbers was able to initiate and conceal the false entries. The fraud was the consequence of how Ebbers ran the company. He was the source of the culture, as well as much of the pressure, that gave birth to the fraud. That the fraud continued as long as it did was due to a lack of courage to blow the whistle on the part of others in WorldCom's financial and accounting departments.

In the behavioral dimension, Ebbers had strong narcissistic tendencies. He had grand images of himself both as an executive and as a private businessman. He found he deserved to spend a lot of money on himself. Ebbers had a very expensive lifestyle. WorldCom had tremendous success under the leadership of Ebbers in the past. When things got bad, Ebbers presented a substantially false picture to the market, which he felt entitled to do.

Ebbers directed significant energy to building and protecting his own personal financial empire, with little attention to the risks these distractions and financial obligations placed on the company that was making him one of the highest paid executives in the country. It was when his personal financial empire was under the greatest pressure – when he had the greatest need to keep WorldCom's stock price up in order to avoid margin calls that he could not meet – that the largest part of the fraud occurred (Soltani, 2014). And it was shortly after he left that it was discovered and disclosed.

The fraudulent corporate culture began at the top. Ebbers created the pressure that led to the fraud. He demanded the results he had promised, and he appeared to scorn the procedures (and people) that should have been a check on misreporting. When efforts were made to establish a corporate code of conduct, Ebbers reportedly described it as a "colossal waste of time." He showed little respect for the role lawyers played with respect to corporate governance matters within the company (Yeoh, 2016). While we have heard numerous accounts of Ebbers's demand for results – on occasion emotional, insulting, and with express reference to the personal financial harm he faced if the stock price declined – we have heard none in which he demanded or rewarded ethical business practices.

Ebbers was autocratic in his dealings with the board, and the board permitted it. With limited exceptions, the members of the board were reluctant to challenge Ebbers even when they disagreed with him. They, like most observers, were impressed with the company's growth and Ebbers's reputation, although they were in some cases mystified or perplexed by his style. This was Ebbers's company. Several members of the board were sophisticated, yet the members of the board were deferential to Ebbers and passive in their oversight until April 2002.

An example of the board's deference was its failure to challenge Ebbers on the extent of his substantial outside business interests (and the resulting claim on his time and energies). Those interests included a Louisiana rice farm, a luxury yacht building company, a lumber mill, a country club, a trucking company, a minor league hockey team, an operating marina, and a building in downtown Chicago. Most properly run boards of directors would probably not permit a chief executive officer to pursue an array of interests such as these, certainly not without careful examination of the time and energy commitments they would require. Yet there seems to be no evidence of any such challenge.

Ebbers dominated the board meetings, which followed a consistent format. Each meeting opened with a prayer. A series of presentations – generally done fairly quickly – followed. Typically, the chairmen of the audit committee and compensation and stock option committee, Bobbitt and Kellett, respectively, each reported to the board. Michael Salsbury, general counsel, reported on legal and regulatory issues.

The fragmentation of the legal department was Ebbers's choice. None of the company's senior lawyers was located in Jackson. He did not include the company's lawyers in his inner circle and appears to have dealt with them only when he felt it necessary. He let them know his displeasure with them personally when they gave advice – however justified – that he did not like. In sum, Ebbers created a culture in which the legal function was less influential and less welcome than in a healthy corporate environment.

WorldCom marketed itself as a high-growth company, and revenue growth was clearly a critical component of WorldCom's early success. In the 1990s, WorldCom was often cited as a top "growth stock." Analysts marveled at WorldCom's ability to "outgrow an industry that was outgrowing the overall economy," and Ebbers repeatedly trumpeted the company's impressive record on revenue growth during his quarterly conference calls with analysts. As Ebbers stated in 1998, "[WorldCom's] industry leading and accelerating revenue growth, combined with a demonstrated track record of margin expansion, are cause for optimism as we continue our relentless pursuit of increasing shareholder value." This growth was both critical to WorldCom's stock market valuation, and to its ability to use its stock as currency for compensation and expansion.

Beginning in September 2000, the compensation committee extended to Ebbers a series of loans and guaranties that, by April 29, 2002, reached approximately $408 million (including interest). These loans and guaranties enabled Ebbers to avoid selling most of his WorldCom stock in response to the demands of those banks from which he had borrowed substantial sums of money. The loans from WorldCom provided Ebbers the funds with which to conduct his personal business affairs at advantageous interest rates. In making these loans and guaranties, WorldCom assumed risks that no financial institution was willing to assume. The company did not have a perfected security interest in any collateral for the loans for most of the time period during which they were outstanding.

The price of WorldCom stock continued to decline during 2000, and Ebbers continued to face margin calls from his lenders. By September 6, 2000, the day of a scheduled meeting of the compensation committee, the stock price was down to $30.27 a share. Shortly before the meeting, Ebbers told Stiles Kellett, the committee's chairman, about the margin calls he was facing and they discussed the possibility that the company would give him a loan. There is conflicting evidence whether it was Ebbers who first suggested the loan. Kellett agreed to take the matter to the committee. At the meeting that followed, the committee directed the company to give Ebbers a $50 million loan and – as part of the retention bonus program then being applied to many WorldCom employees – pay him a $10 million bonus.

At some point, in-house counsel to the compensation committee discovered that Ebbers was withdrawing money from the direct loans for use in connection with his other companies' operating expenses. When confronted with this fact, Ebbers justified the use of the money for these other businesses as necessary in order to avoid impairing the value of these assets. Instead of objecting and demanding that Ebbers use the loans only for their intended purpose, however, the committee accepted this rationale, concluding it was in the company's interest that these assets remain unimpaired so that Ebbers could sell them, if necessary, and repay WorldCom.

After discovering Ebbers's other uses of the loan proceeds, the company characterized the purpose of the loans more neutrally in its filings with the Securities and Exchange Commission:

> We have been advised that Mr. Ebbers has used, or plans to use, the proceeds of the loans from WorldCom principally to repay certain indebtedness under loans secured by shares of our stock owned by him and that the proceeds of such secured loans were used for private business purposes.

## The recovery of Siemens

Eberl et al. (2015) discuss the recovery at Siemens. Siemens might have collapsed if German authorities had been as tough on the company as United States authorities were on Enron,

Andersen, and WorldCom. Siemens faced the greatest bribery scandal in the history of German business. In 2004, Siemens faced a series of bribery and money laundering allegations in more than a dozen countries.

Historically, Siemens was known not only for innovative products, but also for high integrity. The company has been mentioned as a best practice model for its ethical standards and its anti-corruption programs. But it turned out to be all about window dressing. CEO Heinrich von Pierer, who one year later had to resign and was prosecuted because of the corruption scandal, wrote in 2003 (Eberl et al., 2015: 1208):

> There is no reason why moral or legal value orientation concerning corruption should be overridden outside the company's home base or home country. . . . In the recent past, Siemens has had to suffer a lot in single cases as well – and has learned. Today corruption amongst employees is prohibited in all forms.

One year later, in 2014, the homes of Pierer and other top executives at Siemens were raided. German police and public prosecutors uncovered more than 2.3 billion euros' worth of suspicious payments used to secure foreign contracts, mainly in the telecommunication and IT industries. Investigators revealed that Siemens had been bribing governmental officials to secure contracts and to gain favorable conditions for more than three decades. Most of the top executives involved where clearly aware that they were violating the law, but they acted out of a sense of loyalty to and for the benefit of their company.

Eberl et al. (2015) studied the recovery process in terms of repairing trust in an organization after integrity violations. Their findings suggest that tightening organizational rules is an appropriate signal of trustworthiness for external stakeholders to demonstrate that the organization seriously intends to prevent integrity violations in the future. However, such rule adjustments were the source of dissatisfaction among employees since the new rules were difficult to implement in practice.

Eberl et al. (2015) argue that different impacts of organizational rules result from their inherent paradoxical nature. One paradox is that strict rules are implemented from the top to lower levels of management, while crime itself occurred at the top. To prevent white-collar crime from happening again at Siemens, new rules and procedures should be implemented at the board and executive level, rather than at the middle management level. Consistency between actual situation and relevant actions implies that degrees of freedom should be reduced and new controls should be installed among board members and chief executives at Siemens. But this was and is no priority at Siemens. Siemens thought that by replacing fired executives by new similar executives white-collar crime would disappear by itself in corporate top management. They have introduced a tone from the top that seems similar to the previous tone from the top. If white-collar crime at the very top of an organization is to disappear, then new rules and procedures at the top have to be introduced.

Another paradox can be found in organizational rules. Eberl et al. (2015: 1220) suggest that organizational rules implemented with the intention to preempt future corruption practices are perceived as difficult to implement by Siemens employees: "Employees had severe problems following the tightened rules in an appropriate way." The complaints triggered new rounds of rule adjustment within Siemens with the intention of making them more applicable. Therefore, middle managers still have a challenge in distinguishing between rule following and rule breaking. To be on the safe side, some middle managers do as little as possible to avoid rule breaking.

Eberl et al. (2015) argue that because rules have to be formulated in abstract terms, they cannot precisely prescribe behavior in any specific situation. To act in novel situations sometimes requires bending or even breaking rules in order to fit it to the circumstances at hand.

Despite these shortcomings, Eberl et al. (2015) find some strength in the recovery procedures at Siemens. Tightening organizational rules seems to be a successful signal of trustworthiness for external stakeholders to demonstrate that the organization seriously intends to prevent integrity violations in the future.

## Governance and compliance

White-collar crime is sometimes attributed to the defects and failure of corporate governance practices by key players in the business. For example, executive compensation schemes can induce extreme risk-taking without punishing failures while focusing on short-term interests without aligning with the long view of risk. Yeoh (2016) suggests that decision makers should be held more accountable for criminality resulting from their negligence. Corporate governance refers to the mechanisms, processes, and relations by which corporations are controlled and directed.

Compliance with organizational rules is seen as a key mechanism to ensure integrity and prevent organizational members from engaging in inappropriate behavior. Consequently, organizations first have to punish rule breaking, which in turn reinforces the rule and signals to external stakeholders that rule violations are not tolerated. Eberl et al. (2015) suggest that punishment – as far as external stakeholders are concerned – re-establishes trust. Compliance is the act or process of doing what is expected to be done.

Unfortunately, rules frequently serve the main purpose of window dressing in organizations. Ethical guidelines, control procedures, and auditing manuals mainly serve the purpose of impressing stakeholders. Consequences do seldom occur for top executives when they break the rules. Window dressing is a strategy used to improve the appearance of a company.

Today, companies are expected to take on responsibilities beyond regulatory compliance and posting profits (Ditlev-Simonsen, 2014: 117):

> How companies engage the environment, human rights, ethics, corruption, employee rights, donations, volunteer work, contributions to the community and relationships with suppliers are typically viewed as components of CSR.

There are several links between CSR and crime prevention. One link is the company's responsibility towards society if crime occurs, as mentioned above. Another link is the effect of CSR on organizational members. Ditlev-Simonsen (2015) studied this effect in terms of affective commitment among organizational members from active CSR. Her study explored the relationship between employees' CSR perception and employees' affective commitment. Affective commitment is defined as an employee's duty or pledge to the company. Results indicate that CSR perception is a significant predictor of affective commitment, although how employees feel that the company cares about them has a stronger explanatory power on affective commitment.

Ditlev-Simonsen and Midttun (2011) phrased the question: what motivates managers to pursue corporate responsibility? Branding, stakeholders, and value maximization were found to be key motivators. Branding is concerned with building a positive reputation and brand image. Stakeholders are about satisfying different stakeholders, while value maximization is concerned with creating long-term value for shareholders.

Corporate social responsibility is defined as a leadership task. Board members and chief executives in an organization have a particular responsibility to make sure that they themselves are in compliance with laws and regulations, and that the organization makes contributions to society wherever relevant. Chief executives should make the organization accountable, compensate for negative impacts, contribute to societal welfare, operate business ethically, take responsibility for society, and manage in relation with society.

But what happens then when such trusted persons in important leadership positions in business enterprises and other organizations abuse their positions for illegal gain? (Gillespie et al., 2014). That is what white-collar crime is all about: either it is for personal gain or it is for company gain. Crime is completely opposite of corporate social responsibility. Criminal activity is to abuse a privileged position for a purpose detrimental to CSR. White-collar crime is financial crime by privileged, powerful, and influential people when they occupy positions in business enterprises, public agencies, and political governance.

Osuji (2011) argues that corporate social responsibility is a relatively underdeveloped concept despite its increasing importance to corporations. One difficulty is the possible inexactness of CSR. Another is the apparent reluctance by regulatory authorities and policy makers to intervene in the area. Corporate involvement in unethical secrecy in cases of misconduct and crime has emerged as a component of CSR debate and agenda. In recent years, corporate operations and impact in areas such as criminal justice, human rights, and the environment have grown hand in hand with governmental and public concern for firm misconduct, and privatization of law enforcement and criminal justice (Schneider, 2006), particularly in relation to outsourcing of crime investigations to professional services firms. A critical question is how corporate misconduct and crime and the associated detection by financial crime specialists from professional services firms can be contextualized within the CSR agenda.

## Corporate responsibility

In this section, we suggest that the powerful concept of stages of growth is extremely important in management research. Stages of growth models have been used widely in both organizational research and information technology management research. According to King and Teo (1997), these models describe a wide variety of phenomena. These models assume that predictable patterns (conceptualized in terms of stages) exist. The stages are (1) sequential in nature, (2) occur as a hierarchical progression that is not easily reversed, and (3) involve a broad range of organizational activities and structures.

Researchers have struggled for decades to develop stages of growth models that are both theoretically founded and empirically validated. Two decades ago, Kazanjian and Drazin (1989) found that the concept of stages of growth was already widely employed. Later, a number of multistage models were proposed which assume that predictable patterns exist in the growth of organizations, and that these patterns unfold as discrete time periods best thought of as stages. These models have different distinguishing characteristics. Stages can be driven by the search for new growth opportunities or as a response to internal crises. Some models suggest that an organization progresses through stages, while others argue that there may be multiple paths through the stages. Therefore, a stages of growth theory needs to allow for multiple paths through stages as long as they follow a unidirectional pattern.

Maturity models can have varying number of stages, and each stage can be labeled according to the issue at hand. Here we suggest the following four stages of growth for CSR:

1 *Business stage of profit maximization for owners within the corporate mission.* At this basic maturity level, the company is only concerned with itself and its owners. In addition, the company seeks to please its customers so that they will continue to buy its goods and services. The sole responsibility corporations have is that of maximizing profits to shareholders while engaging in open and free competition, without deception or fraud (Adeyeye, 2011). To make decisions that serve other interests at the expense of shareholders would constitute a breach in trust and loyalty (Gillespie et al., 2014). It would be like taking money away from owners and resemble a kind of theft. According to this perspective, corporate executives do not have the right to behave like modern Robin Hood types, taking money from the rich and giving it to the poor.
2 *Function stage of establishing a function for corporate social responsibility in the company.* At this second maturity level, business executives have understood that they need to address company relationships with the outside world in a professional manner. Out of necessity and external expectations, a CSR function is established within the company staffed with individuals who have a business perspective. The function here is to survey implications of business activities in the external environment; to develop intelligence to learn about external reactions to business practices; and to conduct risk assessments in terms of effects on corporate reputation. Here, Basu and Palazzo (2008) define corporate social responsibility as a process. The process implies that corporate leaders in the organization reflect over, and discuss, relationships with stakeholders and partners. The process also implies that corporate leaders identify their own and the organization's roles in relation to societal conditions and societal utility. This kind of reflection and discussion will cause them to endow their roles with relevant content and action.
3 *Resource stage of resource mobilization for potential threats and opportunities.* At this level, we find a complete, yet passive form of corporate social responsibility. It represents a reactive strategy where the company has mobilized resources for cases of emergency. The company is prepared for crisis management, as well as opportunity exploration and exploitation. Opportunities may emerge where corporate executives will implement opportunistic behavior to benefit from opportunities in terms of strengthening corporate reputation. CSR, at this level, is a concept that causes the company to integrate principles of social and environmental responsibility and induces engagement in the company's activities, both internally and externally. Two perspectives emerge from this definition. First, CSR implies a strong link to internal business processes; second, interactions with stakeholders and the society at large also require the involvement of stakeholders and the society at large, in terms of their relationships to the company (Zollo et al.,. 2009).
4 *Contribution stage of proactive involvement in society.* At this final maturity level, corporate executives as well as all other organizational members perceive their business as part of a greater course in society. They adopt a comprehensive and active responsibility in both the local and the global society, and they look for opportunities in society where the company can make a difference. At this level of CSR, short-term loss to the company can be acceptable when weighed against the long-term good to society. CSR at this level is a long-term commitment to society (Mostovicz et al., 2009). Evidence is emerging that long-term citizen commitment on the part of the company by no means has to harm corporate profitability, in either the short term or the long term.

One example might be the Norwegian insurance company Gjensidige. Gjensidige had a claim in the clubhouse of Hell's Angels (Gottschalk, 2013): although the claim involved an insignificant amount of money, which was almost impossible to retrieve, the claim had a greater value in that it could nevertheless help both the municipality and the police in fighting organized crime in society.

## Organizational dimension

Recovery after white-collar crime has to occur in the organizational dimension. Situation-focused theories explain crime in terms of opportunity structures. Piquero and Benson (2004) proposed a middle-ground explanation of white-collar crime, which they call the punctuated situational theory of offending. This theory assumes that white-collar criminals start offending when they reach their thirties or forties. External factors, such as personal or occupational crisis, and opportunities that result from a certain occupational status are claimed to explain crime. Situational opportunities – such as a more influential job and more important contacts – give access to legitimate means to obtain desirable goals.

The opportunity perspective in the situation has also been stressed by Benson and Simpson (2015). They emphasize legal access to premises and resources, distance from victims, and manipulation within regular transactions.

The situation is not only characterized by opportunities in the organization, but also by the organizational environment. Criminogenic conditions in the environment make white-collar crime even more accessible. Alibux (2015) exemplify the environment by the attitude towards banks that are considered too powerful to fail, which thus may protect wrongdoings of bank executives. This is in line with institutional theory, which suggests that opportunities are shaped by individuals, groups, and other organizations, as well as society at large.

Opportunity is a distinct characteristic of white-collar crime and varies depending on the kinds of criminals involved. An opportunity is attractive as a means of responding to desires. It is the organizational dimension that provides the white-collar criminal an opportunity to commit financial crime and conceal it in legal organizational activities. While opportunity in the economic dimension of convenience theory is concerned with goals (such as sales and bonuses), opportunity in the organizational dimension is concerned with crime (such as corruption and embezzlement).

Aguilera and Vadera (2008: 434) describe a criminal opportunity as "the presence of a favorable combination of circumstances that renders a possible course of action relevant." Opportunity arises when individuals or groups can engage in illegal and unethical behavior and expect, with reasonable confidence, to avoid detection and punishment. Opportunity to commit crime may include macro and micro level factors. Macro level factors encompass the characteristics of the industries in which the business finds itself embedded, such as market structure, business sets of an industry, that is, companies whose actions are visible to one another, and variations in the regulatory environment.

Benson and Simpson (2015) argue that many white-collar offences manifest the following opportunity properties: (1) the offender has legitimate access to the location in which the crime is committed; (2) the offender is spatially separate from the victim; and (3) the offender's actions have a superficial appearance of legitimacy. Opportunity occurs in terms of those three properties that are typically the case for executives and other individuals in the elite. In terms of convenience, these three properties may be attractive and convenient when considering white-collar crime to solve a financial problem. It is convenient for the offender to conceal the crime and give it an appearance of outward respectability.

Opportunity is dependent on social capital available to the criminal. The structure and quality of social ties in hierarchical and transactional relationships shape opportunity structures. Social capital is the sum of actual or potential resources accruing to the criminal by virtue of his or her position in a hierarchy and in a network.

The organizational dimension of white-collar crime becomes particularly evident when financial crime is committed to benefit the organization rather than the individual. This is called corporate crime as opposed to occupational crime for personal benefit. Hansen (2009) argues that the problem with occupational crime is that it is committed within the confines of positions of trust and in organizations, which prohibit surveillance and accountability. Heath (2008) found that individuals who are further up the chain of command in the firm tend to commit bigger and more severe occupational crime. Corporate crime, sometimes labeled organizational offending, on the other hand, is resulting from offenses by collectivities or aggregates of discrete individuals. If a corporate official violates the law in acting for the corporation, we still define it as corporate crime. However, if he or she gains personal benefit in the commission of a crime against the corporation, we regard it as occupational crime. A corporation cannot be subject to imprisonment, and therefore, the majority of penalties to control individual violators are not available for corporations and corporate crime.

An organization is a system of coordinated actions among individuals and groups with boundaries and goals. An organization can be a hierarchy, a matrix, a network, or any other kind of relationships between people in a professional work environment. Rule breaking and law breaking seem sometimes necessary to ensure organizational flexibility and reach business goals. Because rules and laws are formulated in abstract terms, they cannot precisely prescribe behavior in any situation. To act in novel situations sometimes demands breaking rules and laws in order to fit it to the organizational circumstance at hand.

The organizational dimension of white-collar crime also becomes particularly evident when several persons in the business participate in crime, and when the organization generally is dominated by misconduct and an unethical culture, either it is occupational crime or corporate crime that is occurring. When several participants and sleeping partners are involved in crime, and the corporate culture almost stimulates violation of the law, then we label the organization as a rotten apple barrel or rotten apple orchard, as Punch (2003: 172) describes them:

> The metaphor of "rotten orchards" indicate that it is sometimes not the apple, or even the barrel that is rotten but the system (or significant parts of the system).

White-collar crime is illegal and unethical actions by agents of organizations. Agency theory is a management theory often applied to crime, where normally the agent, rather than the principal, is in danger of committing crime. Problems arise in the relationship because of diverging preferences and conflicting values, asymmetry in knowledge about activities, and different attitudes toward risk. Agency theory describes the relationship between the two parties using the concept of work-based interactions. The agent carries out work on behalf of the principal in an organizational arrangement. Principal-agent theory holds that owners (principals) have different interests from administrators (agents), such that principals must always suspect agents of making decisions that benefit themselves, to the cost of the principals. For example, chief executive officers (CEOs) are suspects for cheating the owners (WilmerHale, 2008), and purchasing managers are suspects for cheating their CEOs.

In general, agency models view corruption and other kinds of financial crime a consequence of the principal's inability effectively to prevent the agent from abusing power for his or her personal gain. However, the principal can just as well commit financial crime in the principal-agent relationship. For example, the chief financial officer (CFO) as an agent provides a board member with inside information on which the principal acts illegally.

## Conclusion

Collapse or recovery after white-collar crime depends on a number of factors. Collapse is inevitable if fines and other costs lead to bankruptcy. Recovery is possible if the market still exists and stakeholders are willing to give the company a second chance. An element of recovery is corporate responsibility combined with enhanced self-regulation.

## References

Adeyeye, A. (2011). Universal Standards in CSR: Are We Prepared?, *Corporate Governance*, 11 (1), 107–19.

Aguilera, R.V. and Vadera, A.K. (2008). The Dark Side of Authority: Antecedents, Mechanisms, and Outcomes of Organizational Corruption, *Journal of Business Ethics*, 77, 431–449.

Alibux, A.N.R.N. (2015). Criminogenic Conditions, Bribery and the Economic Crisis in the EU: A Macro Level Analysis, *European Journal of Criminology*, 12 (1), 1–21.

Basu, K. and Palazzo, G. (2008). Corporate Social Responsibility: A Process Model of Sensemaking, *Academy of Management Review*, 33 (1), 122–136.

Benson, M.L. and Simpson, S.S. (2015). *Understanding white-collar crime – An opportunity perspective*, New York, NY: Routledge.

Ditlev-Simonsen, C.D. (2014). Are Non-Financial (CSR) Reports Trustworthy? A Study of the Extent to Which Non-Financial Reports Reflect the Media Perception of The Company's Behaviour, *Issues in Social and Environmental Accounting*, 8 (2), 116–133.

Ditlev-Simonsen, C.D. (2015). The Relationship Between Norwegian and Swedish Employees' Perception of Corporate Social Responsibility and Affective Commitment, *Business & Society*, 54 (2), 229–253.

Ditlev-Simonsen, C.D. and Midttun, A. (2011). What Motivates Managers to Pursue Corporate Responsibility? A Survey Among Key Stakeholders, *Corporate Social Responsibility and Environmental Management*, 18, 25–38.

Eberl, P., Geiger, D. and Assländer, M.S. (2015). Repairing Trust in an Organization After Integrity Violations: The Ambivalence of Organizational Rule Adjustments, *Organization Studies*, 36 (9), 1205–1235.

Gillespie, N., Dietz, G. and Lockey, S. (2014). Organizational Reintegration and Trust Repair After an Integrity Violation: A Case Study, *Business Ethics Quarterly*, 24 (3), 371–410.

Gottschalk, P. (2013). Limits to Corporate Social Responsibility: The Case of Gjensidige Insurance Company and Hells Angels Motorcycle Club, *Corporate Reputation Review*, 16 (3), 177–186.

Hansen, L.L. (2009). Corporate Financial Crime: Social Diagnosis and Treatment, *Journal of Financial Crime*, 16 (1), 28–40.

Heath, J. (2008). Business Ethics and Moral Motivation: A Criminological Perspective, *Journal of Business Ethics*, 83, 595–614.

Jonnergård, K., Stafsudd, A. and Elg, U. (2010). Performance Evaluations as Gender Barriers in Professional Organizations: A Study of Auditing Firms, *Gender, Work and Organization*, 17 (6), 721–747.

Kazanjian, R.K. and Drazin, R. (1989). An Empirical Test of a Stage of Growth Progression Model, *Management Science*, 35 (12), 1489–1503.

King, W.R. and Teo, T.S.H. (1997). Integration Between Business Planning and Information Systems Planning: Validating a Stage Hypothesis. *Decision Science*, *28*(2), 279–308.

Mostovicz, I., Kakabadse, N. and Kakabadse, A. (2009). CSR: The Role of Leadership in Driving Ethical Outcomes, *Corporate Governance*, 9 (4), 448–60.

Osuji, O. (2011). Fluidity of Regulation-CSR Nexus: The Multinational Corporate Corruption Example, *Journal of Business Ethics*, 103 (1), 31–57.

Passas, N. (2007). *Corruption in the procurement process/outsourcing government functions: Issues, case studies, implications*, Report to the Institute for Fraud Prevention, shortened version by W. Black, 33 pages, www.theifp.org/research-grants/procurement_final_edited.pdf

Piquero, N. L. (2012). The Only Thing We Have to Fear Is Fear Itself: Investigating the Relationship Between Fear of Falling and White Collar Crime, *Crime and Delinquency*, 58 (3), 362–379.

Piquero, N. L. and Benson, M. L. (2004). White Collar Crime and Criminal Careers: Specifying a Trajectory of Punctuated Situational Offending, *Journal of Contemporary Criminal Justice*, 20, 148–165.

Powers, W. C., Troubh, R. S. and Winokur, H. S. (2002). *Report of investigation by the special investigative committee of the board of directors of Enron corporation*, published February 1, http://news.findlaw.com/wsj/docs/enron/sicreport/, 218 pages.

Punch, M. (2003). Rotten Orchards: "Pestilence", Police Misconduct And System Failure. *Policing and Society*, 13, (2) 171–196.

Schneider, S. (2006). Privatizing Economic Crime Enforcement: Exploring the Role of Private Sector Investigative Agencies in Combating Money Laundering, *Policing & Society*, 16 (3), 285–312.

Soltani, B. (2014). The Anatomy of Corporate Fraud: A Comparative Analysis of High Profile American and European Corporate Scandals, *Journal of Business Ethics*, 120, 251–274.

Stadler, W. A. and Benson, M. L. (2012). Revisiting the Guilty Mind: The Neutralization of White-Collar Crime, *Criminal Justice Review*, 37 (4), 494–511.

WilmerHale and PwC (2008). *Report of Investigation submitted by the Council of the District of Columbia*, Wilmer Cutler Pickering Hale and Dorr LLP (Councel) and PricewaterhouseCoopers LLP (Forensic Accounting Advisors), www.dcwatch.com/govern/otr081215.pdf, downloaded February 8, 2015, 126 pages.

Yeoh, P. (2016). Corporate Governance Failures and the Road to Crime, *Journal of Financial Crime*, 22 (1), 216–230.

Zollo, M., Minoja, M., Casanova, L., Hockerts, K., Neergaard, P., Schneiderand, S., Tencati, A. (2009). Towards an Internal Change Management Perspective of CSR: Evidence From Project RESPONSE on the Sources of Cognitive Alignment Between Managers and Their Stakeholders, and Their Implications for Social Performance, *Corporate Governance*, 9 (4), 355–372.

# Part III
# Infrastructure risks

# 11

# Business resiliency considerations

## In the site selection and construction of a new facility

*Natalie M. Dengler*

---

As in real estate, the starting point for building a disaster resilient building is all about location, location, location; but it does not stop there. There is a myriad of components that need to be considered: from where to build (i.e., site selection) to how it is built (i.e., structure) to what it will include (i.e., layout). The purpose of this chapter is to identify the various components which should be considered, reviewed, and analyzed when a business decides to relocate or expand. Each component provides the starting point for analysis and risk evaluation as you progress through the design, construction, and relocation to a new building location. This is not meant to be the how-to for building your new location, but as guidance for identifying trouble spots.

### Site selection

The site selected for the new location must be carefully analyzed. There is no such thing as a perfect location. Every location, no matter where in the world, is susceptible to some type of event which will impact it and disrupt your business. In selecting the new site location, you need to identify those events and determine your acceptable level of tolerance. So your first step is to identify the various potential threats and events for every site you are considering.

The easiest events to identify are the natural ones such as earthquakes, hurricanes, cyclones, blizzards, tornadoes, and dust storms. Each of these natural events has the possibility of impacting your business and disrupting it for some period of time. Some of these natural events may provide warnings and give your company time to prepare for impact, as in the case of hurricanes and blizzards. Other natural events will occur without notice, as in the case of an earthquake. Whether with or without warning, natural events may also impact your workforce and their home life. When your employees' families are impacted, your ability to recover your business in a timely fashion may be limited. Your employees' first priority will be their families.

There are other outages caused by nature which also might be a cause of concern. These situations are associated with the actual plot site. They will not impact your employees or their families, but they could impact and disrupt your business.

- Is the property high on the edge of a cliff where erosion over time is possible?
- Is the property down lower than the surrounding area (e.g., in a valley)?
- Is the property within a floodplain?[1] How frequently is it expected to flood: every year, every 100 years, or every 500 years?

Information and data regarding these situations may not be easy to obtain. It may require obtaining data from various federal or local governmental sources, independent surveyors, insurance providers, and general observations of local citizens. Once obtained, it may also require expertise to decipher and then draw conclusions regarding risk. It is then up to you to make an informed decision: Can you accept the risk? What level of risk can you accept?

Other outages may be caused by man-made events, such as accidents or malicious acts. Oil spills, train derailments, and wildfires are just a few examples of events that may be the result of human error. Would any of these accidental events impact the location and thus limit your ability to continue to conduct business? For example, does a rail line or an interstate highway run alongside or near the property? Are these lines used to transport toxic or hazardous waste? The need for your business to be near a rail line or interstate may offset this exposure. If this is the case, then you would want to assess the risk against the benefits associated with being near these transportation lines.

But what about the deliberate man-made events, such as civil unrest? These events are somewhat difficult to assess. The site may have no exposure today, yet by the time a building is completed, social issues or the political climate may have changed and events may be more common. On the other hand, the site may be in an area where unrest is common today, yet the local government is working to clean up the area and bring in businesses and the associated jobs. In this case, you need to decide if your business wishes to be part of the solution and accept the risk. Under circumstances such as this, it may cost you more to protect your staff and your building now, but over time the value of your investment may increase. So once again, you need to identify the risks associated with each site and select the best fit for your company's needs.

## Building structure

Now that you have evaluated property sites and their environs and have selected your location, it is time to determine what type of building will be constructed.

### *Limiting impact of natural disasters*

The type of building you will construct should be based upon the potential natural disasters. If you are in an earthquake-prone area, you will want a building that is earthquake resistant and able to survive the intensity and magnitude associated with major earthquakes. Will the building withstand the resultant shaking? Here it pays to research and review the latest innovations in earthquake resistant construction. Japan is considered a leader in research and preparedness in this area.

We have all seen the pictures of an apartment building or office building flattened out like a pancake after an earthquake, no matter where it occurred in the world. These buildings were most likely made of unreinforced brick, adobe, cement slab, or concrete block. This type of construction is considered the most dangerous because the lateral movement of the ground during an earthquake, which is similar to an ocean wave, can cause floors to shift off their ledges. One way to make a structure more resistant to the lateral forces is to tie the walls, floor, roof, and foundations into a rigid box that holds together when shaken by a quake. Here is a sample (see Figure 11.1) taken from the ReidSteel website[2] which shows the basic ideas.

The same is true if you are in an area prone to hurricanes, cyclones, or tornadoes. You will want a building that can withstand sustained winds upward of a category 5 hurricane (157 mph or 252 km/h). Building damage is the result of wind finding a way into your building, ripping off the roof or breaking a window, and causing the wind to whip through the building and blow it apart. As Figure 11.2 shows, the enclosed building, constructed properly will equalize the pressure and sway and bend with the wind, while the building on the right will allow the wind to enter and will eventually yield to the pressure and pop through the other side.[3] With the proper anchoring and today's technology, it is possible to build wind-resistant buildings. They may be more expensive to build, but you may find the cost justified in what it saves you vis-à-vis the cost of recovery and reconstruction after a storm.

If the building withstands the wind, it may not be able to withstand the rainfall associated with the storm or the resultant flooding due to lack of drainage or failed dams. To minimize your risk, buildings in these locations should be aboveground and preferably raised to prevent damage from water entering the building. Water that enters a building and sits for some time will cause significant damage from mold and mildew. This may leave the building uninhabitable for a significant period of time, leaving you with a substantial bill for cleanup and reconstruction. If it is important for your business to have facilities underground, then you need to spend additional time with engineers to understand the water table and drainage and then allocate the funds required to make the basements waterproof.

## *Designing building interior*

After reviewing the structure and determining that it meets your needs, you now need to lay out the building interior. This includes interior elements such as elevator shafts, utility risers, HVAC (heating, ventilation, and air-conditioning) ducting, plumbing, raised floors, and staircases for emergency egress or to just move people between floors. The issue here is that these various elements take up precious space both in terms of the square footage of a floor and in the height of each floor and the total building.

Therefore, the desire is to limit the size or the number of each element required. Keep in mind that having one of anything can become the cause of a future outage which may require you to activate your business recovery plan at a significant cost in terms of time and money. Also, combining some of these elements may be an opportunity for a disaster. After all, water and electricity in the same riser do not mix well. Having your emergency exit stairs wrapped around the elevator shafts may make the stairs useless during a fire, especially if the elevator shaft has become a conduit for flames and smoke. Another consideration is to allow for future growth which may eat up space. Adding additional cabling in a riser for increased power demand should be easy and accessible and, therefore, not an event that causes the existing power to be interrupted.

So, let's look at the risers that carry services vertically through the building. There should be multiple risers for each element, two at a minimum. Those two risers should not abut each other: they should be distributed, preferably on opposite sides of the building. This design will be of benefit as you develop the grid for distributing power, communications, technology, and

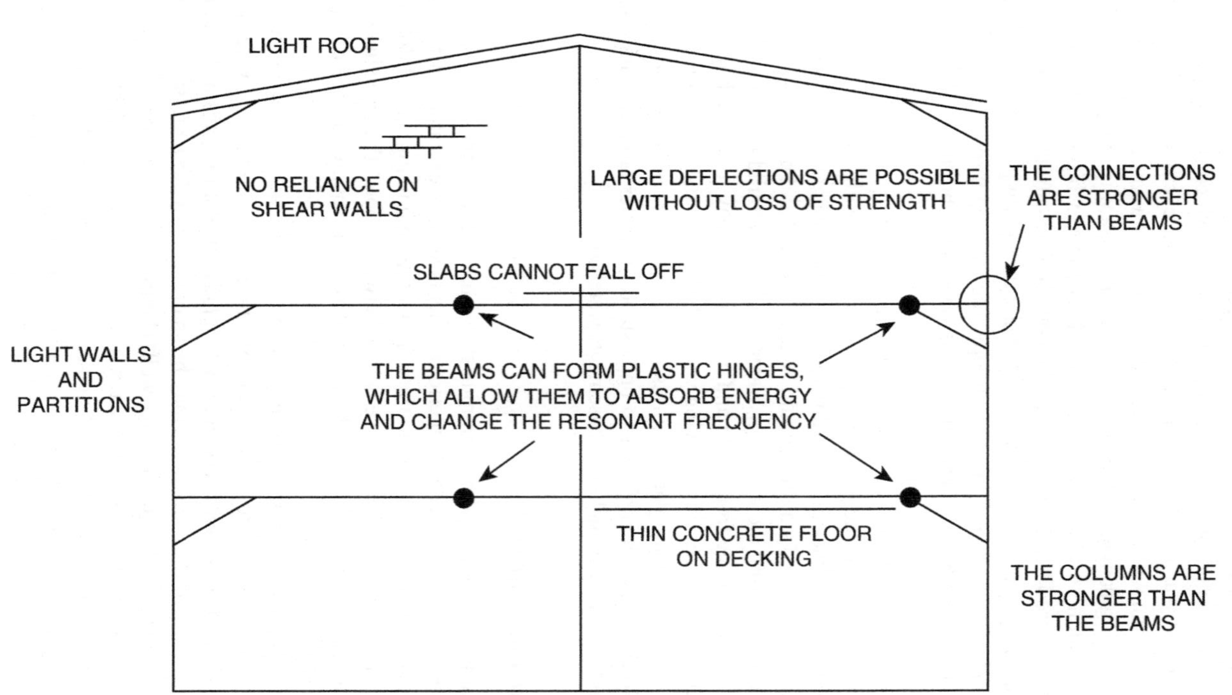


*Figure 11.1* Resisting frame to prevent earthquake damage

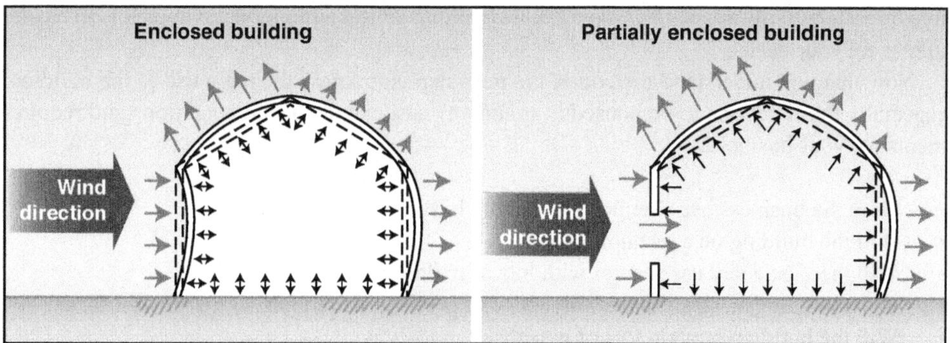


*Figure 11.2* Internal pressurization and resulting building failure due to wind

so forth throughout each floor. Having power or communications servicing half of a floor is better than nothing, and may help you to continue performing critical business services while repairs are made in the damaged riser.

## *Looking good*

Now that you have analyzed and determined the internal structure and layout of your building, it is time to review the exterior. Everyone wants the building they design or work in to look good. But looks may not provide the needed security for the building. Here, it is important to understand the various construction materials for the building shell. The various materials used to provide the façade for the building include, but are not limited to cement, brick, aluminum, steel, and glass. Then, you need to understand how these elements would be used, integrated, and connected for your building façade.

For example, in a high-rise building, the façade is usually clipped and hung from the cement slab floors and is called a curtain wall. First, have an engineer review the design and mechanisms being used to attached the curtain wall to the building. Second, have the material, being considered for the curtain wall, assessed and rated by fire safety engineers as to the potential for a fire to travel up the curtain wall creating a wall of flames. These are important steps to provide safety and minimize damage.

## Fire prevention

When designing the fire safety systems for the building, the primary considerations are the safety of people as well as limiting business losses. The starting point is understanding the fire safety codes for the jurisdiction responsible for your building. Each jurisdiction has established well-defined specifications. Reach out to the local expects to help you interpret these codes and install systems that achieve their purpose. Most of these specifications are taken from the National Fire Protection Association (NFPA), a standards association that develops codes and standards to address fire, electrical and other related hazards. NFPA was used as the basis of the International Code Council (ICC) fire safety standards.

Remember, though: standards are the minimum requirements. You can always install more than what is required by law. Fire safety systems have many components that need to work in unison with each other. These components can be obtained from various manufacturers, and it is important to always review the reliability ratings of the equipment components to ensure they meet your needs.

Now that you understand the codes, the next step is to know the main use of the building, especially the functions to be housed in it and any associated special conditions and requirements for your business:

- Does the business use chemicals or handle hazardous materials?
- Will the building be a technology hub?
- Will there be a day care center with lots of children in the building?
- Is the building an open space warehouse or is it segmented into lots of small offices?
- Will the building contain lots of paper?
- Will your building contain all of these components and more?

Knowing the purpose, people load, equipment, and chemical contents of the building helps to provide for the proper design of key safety features such as emergency building evacuation, smoke and carbon monoxide detection systems, and fire suppressant systems.

### Emergency building evacuation

The emergency evacuation design is based upon the number of people in the building. It would include the number and locations of emergency exit doors, the egress routes to those doors within the building and upon exiting the building, and the ability to notify personnel and visitors at the time of an emergency. Egress routes will impact how you lay out each floor in terms of walls, offices, storage, and so forth.

### Detection systems

Detection systems for smoke or carbon monoxide are considered the primary notification systems of an imminent problem. They send out an audible alarm to notify the inhabitants of the building and they send notification to the building's fire safety team and to the local authorities. Smoke detection and water detection systems should be installed in all raised floor areas to alert people of hidden problems. The smoke detection system may also be linked to the building HVAC systems to manage the flow of air within the building as to damper oxygen to some locations and ensure continued air flow to emergency egress routes. Smoke detection systems might also be linked to the fire suppressant systems in order to activate the system (e.g., with water).

### Fire suppressant system

Fire suppressant systems are used, as the name implies, to suppress flames by separating the heat source from oxygen. They consist of pipes and sprinkler heads to deliver the suppressant onto the fire; they are connected to the smoke or fire alarm systems; and they are usually activated through a computerized system which limits and reduces water or chemical damage to the affected areas only. Although there are many variations to the fire suppressant systems, basic and distinct types of systems include:

- A wet pipe system. This system tends to have water in the pipes all the time. The sprinkler heads in this system act as a regulator. When the temperature of the fire melts the coating on the sprinkler head, water begins to flow to douse the flames.

- A dry pipe or pre-action system. This system has nothing in its pipes until a smoke or fire alarm goes off. Then valves are activated and the water fills the pipes. Here the sprinkler heads act as the regulator described above.
- A deluge system. This system is like the dry pipe system described above, but the sprinkler heads are always open. So, as the water enters the pipes it immediately begins to douse the flames. A system like this would be used in high hazard areas where the density and combustibility of the material in the area require high volume suppression to prevent fire spread.
- A chemical system. Chemical fire suppressant systems for the purpose of this discussion include foam and $CO_2$ systems. These systems tend to operate like a pre-action system where an alarm triggers the loading of the system and is based upon the type of extinguishing agent the system discharges. Most of these types of systems are selected for use in the areas and industries such as flammable liquid storage areas, loading docks, data processing facilities, warehouses, manufacturing plants, and aircraft hangers, to name just a few.

As can be seen, fire safety is complicated in its design. Besides consulting fire safety engineers, an excellent source for assistance is your insurance underwriter. Your insurer has a vested interest in ensuring that your building is well protected against the most likely event: fire. And the upfront costs spent in the design and implementation may result in annual savings in terms of lower premiums.

## Power

Power is a major component in keeping your business going. However, you cannot depend only on one source or supplier. You need to evaluate every potential source of power.

The place to start is by looking at the power utility and the main generation plant that supplies your building location. Follow the power distribution route from the plant to the building.

- Is it susceptible to trees taking out a power line?
- Is it buried under ground where it is susceptible to backhoes?
- Does it run along the railroad tracks and is it susceptible to a train derailment?

In other words, you need to know and follow the path of the power and understand all the risks along that path.

### *Utility power*

A better approach is to work with the utility company to determine if the power distribution can take two completely separate and different routes to the location. Understand each of these routes and their risks. Then look to see if those different routes could come from two different power generation plants. Finally, dig even deeper to see it those different generation plants are truly independent. This type of analysis requires working very closely with the power company. It's important to have a group of people from both your company and the power company understand why this analysis is being done and what, if any, are the residual risks.

No matter what the results (i.e., one power generation plant with one route or multiple generation plants with multiple routes), if the business conducted in the building is so critical that a minimal power outage or any power outage is unacceptable, then the next decision point is developing internal power generation requirements.

### *Private generation*

Generating your own power can be expensive. The largest consumer of power within a building is the air-conditioning and ventilation system, or HVAC. Given the construction of today's buildings, where the windows are sealed and the building is a self-contained environment, the continuous circulation and purification of air is important. In addition to this, other requirements include the power needed for life safety systems, security systems, and all the technology and computers. And then finally, the power needed for the general lighting and miscellaneous equipment, like charging phones. It is extremely important to size your generator needs appropriately. This requires you to know the power load for each floor and special work areas of the building. Which of these areas will need power? How much power will they need?

Knowing your power requirements for today can help you determine your requirements for tomorrow. Will you provide generators to supply a subset of today's power usage, or should it provide 150% of today's usage? What are the peak usage requirements? Once you have made the decision as to how much power generation is sufficient for today's needs and have sized the generators, you should then decide upon future needs and at least provide the space required for future growth in power demand. This would include allocating space in the building design for generator pads, power distribution panels, and of course, riser space for future wiring.

One final feature of your generator system is the fuel source to run it. Your options will tend to be oil or natural gas. In the case of oil, you need to size the storage tanks, which includes understanding replenishments requirements (i.e., timing and capacity) when the generators are in use. Sizing for oil tanks should also address future growth needs. Next you need to determine a safe location to place the tanks. They may be located within or outside the building, but much of this decision will be based upon understanding the environmental impact and complying with all regulatory requirements. An alternate fuel source might be natural gas. If you choose natural gas, you need to understand the pipeline routes to your site and apply the same single point of failure analysis you did with the utility power source.

In some cases, such as a data processing facility, an uninterruptible power supply (UPS) is required. The purpose of a UPS is to protect your computer equipment or any electronic equipment susceptible to power surges. It also provides backup power during a power outage for a limited time period (e.g., about 15 to 20 minutes). This limited period of time provides the opportunity to save data and safely shut down the equipment. A UPS system should also be used in conjunction with generators to smooth power. Also, just in case the generators do not kick in immediately, the UPS will again provide the opportunity for a smooth shutdown.

A key component in designing the power generation backup is to incorporate separate and distinct components from the utility power components and equipment in your design (wiring, distribution panels, switches, etc.). You do not want one piece of electrical equipment taking out both the utility and generator power to your building. The same will be said for designing the sustainable energy system.

### *Sustainable energy*

You may want a Leadership in Energy and Environmental Design (LEED) certified building. LEED is a rating system developed by the U.S. Green Building Council (USGBC) to evaluate the environmental performance of a building and encourage sustainable design.[4] One of the major LEED building components is related to renewable energy systems, such as wind or solar to offset power generated by fossil fuels.

These alternate sources may contribute up to 30% of your daily required power requirements. They provide a way to reduce your daily dependency on the utility companies and may even provide a means to generate power back to the utility company. However, you may not be able to use these renewable energy sources after a disaster because they may be damaged (e.g., a fallen wind turbine or smashed solar panels). Additionally, the expertise and parts and material to repair them may not be readily available. Another issue is how the alternate power supply is connected to the utility. In many cases, restrictions are placed by the utility companies on using these sustainable systems during a power outage. This is because your sustainable building power system may not be designed to be truly isolated from the utility's power grid. Electricity is like water: if it finds an opening, it will take it, and in the case of electricity it could travel along wiring being repaired by the utility and cause serious harm, and even death, to people and workers.

Remember, renewable energy systems need to be designed with the same due diligence as any engineering project; ensure the design engineer understands your requirements in terms of business resiliency. Evaluate the reliability of the material and parts being recommended and review the final design for any single points of failure and, if any are found, eliminate them.

## Telecommunications

The ability for a company to communicate inside and outside its organization is essential in today's business climate. Communications is also the key to a good recovery. Maintaining that business presence to your customers in times of adversity is essential. A company needs to communicate with its clients, vendors, employees, regulators, and especially with the media. There is no time to lose during an event in getting out your message.

### *Telecommunications services*

So how do you determine telecommunications requirements? Planning is similar to the other utilities discussed earlier.

- Where is the central office?
- Can multiple offices provide you service?
- How are lines routed to your building?
- Is it a single route or multiple routes?
- Are the routes diverse or follow the same path?
- Do they all enter your building in one place and travel through same building riser?
- Do they enter at opposite sides of the building, travel up through the building, never really intersecting except to feed each floor or portion of each floor?

Remember, the last section of the route into your building is the most susceptible to an outage.

Are there multiple providers of telecommunications serving this new location? If yes, then it may be useful to contract several of these providers. However, just because you have multiple providers, it may not mean you have diverse routing of services. They may actually be using the same central office or routing along the same pathway. You need to check this out. Knowing the paths of the services will allow you to make the appropriate decisions for your business.

There are many variations of technology available for communication today. The original copper wire, which has been or is being eliminated in many areas, did have one advantage: there would always be phone service as long as the central office did not lose power. This was because the power for the tethered plain-old-phone (POP) line was supplied by the telephone company. With the newer technologies of fiber optics, cable, and voice over internet protocol (VOIP), this is no longer the case. You, the telecommunications client, must ensure that you have the power needed to continued phone, data, and internet service. That alternate power, which you supply, is then provided through a battery backup or a generator. If you are depending only on battery backup, then the battery capacity needs to be sized to meet your expected outage needs and duration. However, if the telecommunications utility is not up and running by the time the battery backup is drained, then you have no telephone or internet service. As to the generator, you must remember to include the telecommunications power requirements into your analysis for the needed generator power capacity.

But what if the fiber cable that provides communications to or in your location is cut? Well the good news is that fiber is faster to repair than the old copper wire, but the bad news is that you will not have any phone or data service until the entire fiber cable is repaired. So, what do you do in the meantime? Look up. You may be able to use cellular or satellite.

### *Alternate telecommunications services*

Let's first look at satellite. Due to cost, this might not be considered a replacement for your entire telecommunications network. It may, however, be a stopgap measure. You may be, at the very least, able to get critical messages to key customers, vendors, employees, regulatory agencies, and the media. You might also use satellite phones to connect key business areas around the world, such as your crisis command centers.

As to cellular, this may be an excellent alternative to continue to remain in contact with all your clients. You may be able to continue taking orders, tracking production, resolving issues, answering questions, and so forth. The issue to consider with cellular is that significant and sustained damage to the cell towers may result in a dead zone. During an area-wide outage, it may not have sufficient capacity to support your business needs and the local community's recovery needs. Also, power is needed to recharge phones, so it's important to remember to include this requirement in the generator calculations.

Remember that telecommunications outages may happen to you or any utility provider during natural events such as hurricanes, tornadoes, or earthquakes, where equipment is aboveground and exposed to the elements. So even though you have alternate services, they will never replace the need for robust business resiliency plans.

## Mechanical systems

The HVAC system is the key to the comfort design of the building. The design will be based upon the business activities performed within the building complex.

- What is the major purpose for the building: Office? Warehouse?
- Will it contain a data processing center?
- Does it contain a restaurant or cafeteria?
- Is the building open to the public 24 hours a day?

- Does it contain lots of people during the day but limited staff in the evening?
- Are there large open areas or many smaller private offices?
- Where is the building located: is it in a snow belt or a tropical zone?

All of these, and more, determine the design, capabilities, and capacity of the HVAC system for the building.

Now that you know the day-to-day HVAC requirements, you need to determine what will make that system resilient. A fully redundant system may be cost prohibitive; therefore, a risk and cost benefit analysis must be conducted. Similar to the review for power, you need to review what are the critical business functions conducted in the building and what are their HVAC needs. Do you need the entire building up and running 24 hours a day, 7 days a week, 52 weeks of the year? Or is it only a subset of select critical areas in the building that needs this year-round environment? Functions that fall into this category may be in the area of scientific research where a consistent climate is mandatory. It could also include a company's data processing facility. It may be a 24-hour customer service function, such as 911 emergency services, that needs to continue throughout any disaster. The HVAC system is expensive to install, takes up a lot of building space, and the costs of providing backup power are expensive. Therefore, it's important to conduct this type of analysis, going through each processing function of your business and each physical area of your plant and determine what is needed and for how long.

In addition to the energy sources previously discussed, another way to provide the heating and cooling environment for a building is through steam generated by a power utility or through a geothermal exchange system. The process for designing and installing these systems is the same as discussed previously for power, communications and the HVAC systems. You work with the design engineer and review the design for single points of failure. If any are found, eliminate them to ensure your HVAC system is resilient.

## Water

Water is a necessity of life. It is also essential in your building design. Functioning fire suppressant systems, cooling systems, and most important of all, plumbing systems use water. All must be operational to allow the building to be occupied.

We addressed the fire suppressant and cooling systems in previous sections. Now we will look at the plumbing system, which is made up of water and waste. Unfortunately, both these components occasionally leak. That leaking can cause significant damage to your building and shut it down for a substantial period of time. Therefore, in designing the plumbing system you want to minimize the size of the area through which the piping runs over and through. This will minimize your exposure to leakage.

If you need to cover a large area, such as an entire floor, with water pipes, then consider placing drainage pans and water detection alarms underneath the pipes. This will help to contain the water and to resolve the issue before significant damage occurs.

One of the features of the modern-day bathroom is automation – the faucets, soap dispensers, towel dispensers, and toilets all use electric eyes to work. It saves water and paper, but did you include these features in the calculations for the generator design? This is a simple example of how complex designing a resilient building is. Every component interrelates to another.

## Transportation access

In selecting the location, you analyzed what and where the risks were as associated with the location. This included access to freight railroad lines and interstate highways. Both of these had the potential for carrying hazardous and flammable materials. Now you need to look at the various transportation facilities that will allow your staff easy access to the site. This is the true sense of risk assessment and decision making, that is, offsetting the risk of one selection with the benefits of another selection.

Your staff needs to be able to access the site. This access should match your business needs. If your company is open only 5 days a week, then what are the various modes of transportation on those days? If your staff only needs to work at the site during the night and evening shifts, then transportation needs must address the off-hours availability of commuting services. Ideally a location should provide access 24 hours a day, 7 days a week, and 52 weeks a year, because you never know when your staff will need to access the building.

When analyzing the access to your location, you need to look at where your workforce resides. How does your workforce tend to move around: Public transportation? Do they drive? Do they take a car service? Are they more inclined to walk or bicycle? Understanding their needs will help in determining the transportation requirements of your new location.

Let us look at each of various modes of transportation individually. Your workforce may use one or more of these modes of transportation.

### *Bike or walk*

If the workforce can walk or bike to work, then this means your workforce lives close to your business location. Having a work force that can easily get to work is great. However, it also means that their home can be impacted by the same types of events, such as a power outage, as their workplace. This might limit the ability for them to work from home during a business disruption. Another key thing to remember is that it is human nature to take care of those closest and dearest to them – their family – first. They will need to be sure that their family is safe and secure before they think about helping your business.

### *Public transportation*

If the workforce travels mostly by public transportation, what are the choices? If there is only one train or single bus line, then that particular line can be crippled by problems such as a strike, storm, or accident. Your workforce may not be able to arrive at work, and if they do make it, they may not arrive on time. This may not be an issue if you operate a multiple shift operation. You may be able to keep the previous shift until the staff arrives. However, this may incur an additional expense due to overtime. If, however, you run a '9 to 5' type of operation, will opening up later really work? And how often will customers accept a delayed opening before moving to the competition? Therefore, your building should be accessible by multiple public transportation services as provided by different companies, where available. As has been said many times – you need multiple access routes, multiple vendors, and a plan to help your staff get to work when any of these services fail.

### *Car*

If the workforce drives, then you need to look at both the various routes to your building and the parking facilities at your building. Similar to public transportation, your building needs to be accessible by several different roads. A single road will limit access to your building when that road is closed due to an accident or weather conditions. It will also impede the ability to evacuate your site. A variety of roads, major highways, and local streets would be ideal. This will not only allow for faster travel but also for backup routes if the major road is closed.

Once at the site, there is then a need to look at parking facilities. Will it be a parking garage that is attached to your building? The risks here are easy to determine. Would a fire or bomb easily damage your building? You can mitigate the risk of a fire by insuring that the garage structure has a robust fire suppressant system. However, with a bomb, how would your staff vacate the building? How would they get home if the garage is damaged and closed?

When parking is a large open area, there is an opportunity to use this expanse as assembly locations for the staff if the building is evacuated. The design concern here then is the access roads and entry points into the parking lot. Is it a single entry/exit point? This will limit the ability for emergency services to access your building, especially if your workforce is in a panic trying to leave the building, get in their cars, and exit the parking lot. You need to give serious consideration to the parking lot layout and all access and egress points. As stated earlier when discussing utilities, multiple routes from each side of the building, in this case the parking lot, are required.

So in selecting your location, a component to consider is where your workforce lives. Map this out and then determine all the various modes of transportation they may take. The more variety the better. Determine the quality and reliability of each mode of transportation and then develop the requirements needed to address each mode. This would include bicycle racks, parking spaces, and shuttles to public transportation hubs.

## Security

There are few locations in the world today where you do not need to be concerned with physical and cybersecurity. In terms of business resiliency, you want your building to have state-of-the-art physical security. This starts with perimeter security. Designing a building with lots of hidden corners limits your line of sight and provides an opportunity for people and objects to hide. Along this same theme, you need to decide how much open access to the general public you want to provide or may be required to provide by law. Will providing free and open access to the building limit the business functions and services you can offer and perform from that location? If you limit access, where will the checkpoints be established: at the front door or the edge of the property? Will the perimeter security include motion sensor cameras or 24-hour continuous surveillance? What type of internal building security system will you install: a badge, a fingerprint, or a voice recognition system? How do you handle visitors to the building? No matter what you choose, security must be available and functioning 24 hours a day, 365 days of the year. This requires a design that has built-in redundancy, no single point of failure, state-of-the-art cybersecurity, and continuous power.

## Business components

A key issue for any building is what it will house, meaning what business will be conducted and what functions will be performed. Some of the building components are very straightforward. If it will be a manufacturing plant, you know what equipment you need. If it will be an office building for medical, legal, or financial organizations, then a list of the standard office requirements is easy to identify.

However, there may be many other components that your business needs or wishes to provide to your staff, your customers, or your community. These components run the gamut from a print shop that may require special chemicals, to an emergency day care center for children of the staff, to a gym for use by anyone who wishes to join – employee or not, near or far.

Each one of these components brings special requirements in term of business resiliency. Whether it be in the requirements for backup power, a plan to shelter in place, or in the cleanup procedures of hazardous materials, it is important to know in the early stages of the building design exactly what will be in your building.

Adding some service components to the building may be a result of asking your staff and customers. For example, your customers may want a place to eat and talk while they wait for business to be transacted. Should that be a restaurant, a coffee shop, or a vending machine? Satisfying your customer will bring in more business, but guessing what they want will not.

For your staff, you may want to provide a full-time day care center, but your employees may only want a facility for emergency day care services to be used when their regular service is not available or schools are closed. If you do provide day care services, remember that there may be special regulations or legal requirements. This area should be one of the first areas to have a well-documented and well-tested emergency plan for evacuation and for sheltering in place.

In developing a new location, it may be an opportunity to obtain new equipment and new furniture. New equipment may be more energy efficient, which would then impact your power requirements. New office furniture may take up a smaller footprint and therefore require a change in the fire suppressant system because now more people fit in the space. No matter what the changes, it helps if you involve your staff in the selection and design of the new equipment and furnishings. After all, they are the ones who use the equipment or who will sit at the desk for 8 hours a day.

## Layout

After you know all the components which the building will house, you now need to lay them out. Significant time will be spent on this endeavor. You will need additional information such as:

- What is the square footage requirement for each business component?
- What are your short-term plans for expansion and growth for each area?
- What areas need to be adjacent to other areas?
- What areas are sensitive and require significant security to gain access?

And the list goes on.

Let's look at some sample placements of the business components within the facility.

### *Data center*

Where should you place the data processing center? Equipment does not need a window. Equipment does not need a nice view. Historically, a data processing center would be placed in the basement where the building's water and waste pipes run above it. This placement will make your data processing susceptible to water damage and flooding – either from an internal event (e.g., broken pipe) or an external one (e.g., hurricane).

You may also find data processing centers on the ground floor because of the ease to move heavy equipment into place and not have to hoist it. The ground floor might also be reinforced to support the equipment. The issue with this type of placement is exposure to physical damage, either accidentally or intentionally by an errant car or truck. In some cases, your building may only be a single story; then consider placing the data processing equipment in the center of the building to limit damage and eavesdropping.

If you are fortunate enough to be developing a multi-story building, then you need to pick the least risky location for your data processing equipment – high above the ground floor; not immediately above or below a cafeteria; not on a high pedestrian traffic floor with lots of staff or a walk-through for customers; not visible from the street or adjoining buildings; but easily accessible for installing equipment and responding to emergencies. Finding the perfect location may sound impossible, but you will find it if you look for it.

### Mechanical rooms

Another key component to any building is the mechanical room, which houses your power and generator equipment, your HVAC systems, and other critical building services. Ideally, you should have at least two mechanical rooms, designed in such a way as to supply services evenly distributed throughout the building. This will allow the building to continue to function if one mechanical room encounters some problems. Unless there is a particular reason for some services to be in the basement or on the ground floor, mechanical rooms should be dispersed throughout the upper floors of the building. For example, if the building has 12 floors, then place the mechanical rooms on the fourth and ninth floors.

### Human resource department

The human resource department is an example of a business function that may be placed on the ground or first floor. It is an area that may have a lot of pedestrian traffic daily as people apply for jobs, come for interviews, or are leaving their positions. You would not want all these people roaming through your building.

### Conference center

The conference center can be placed anywhere within the building. You may, however, want to provide it with its own special entrance and elevator service if it will be open for use by other/external organizations. Another consideration may be to design the conference center to be used as a recovery facility for one of your other work locations. In this case, you should include these requirements in your power and communications design.

### Cafeteria/dining room/restaurant

Cafeterias, dining rooms, and restaurants carry the same risk: a potential fire. Therefore, you would not want to place any one of these immediately above or below a highly critical business area. Another issue to consider in designing the kitchen for these services is the location where the stove vents exit the building. You want the ductwork to be accessible for cleaning and the distance to be as short as possible. This will help reduce the likelihood of a grease fire.

The key in developing the layout for the building is to understand each business component and its potential risks when placed near other components.

## Moving day

The building is now constructed: the exterior has been completed. The electrical, plumbing, heating, cooling and fire suppressant systems have been installed throughout the building. The individual floors are starting to be outfitted with walls, floors, and furniture. However, you don't have to wait until the entire building's interior is completed. You can start to move in to select areas.

But where do you start? You start slowly with the least critical functions for your business. Statistics show that the most likely time for a building to have a problem, such as a fire, water, or smoke damage, is during construction or renovation. So as long as there are construction workers still in the building and building systems still being tested, then there is a high potential for problems to occur, resulting in the building being evacuated and/or closed.

Once building workers have completed all interior construction and system testing, you can begin to move in the most critical business functions, including data processing centers. The move of these services should be carefully orchestrated and pre-tested before you 'flick the switch' and begin full operations at the new location.

## Summary

There is no perfect location or building. Every site selected will have some risk associated with it. The purpose of the information provided here is to provide a starting point for understanding various areas of potential risks and things to consider when developing and selecting a new office building, manufacturing plant, data processing center, or even a business disaster recovery site. This should allow for a site selection where one is aware of the potential risks and can, therefore, develop better business resiliency plans in order to maintain continuous business services, thus serving its customers and its workforce.

## Notes

1 FEMA's National Flood Hazard Data from Flood Insurance Rate Maps (FIRMs) https://fema.maps.arcgis.com/home/item.html?id=cbe088e7c8704464aa0fc34eb99e7f30
2 How to Make Buildings & Structures Earthquake Proof at www.reidsteel.com
3 *Safe Rooms for Tornadoes and Hurricanes*, FEMA P-361 Third Edition, March 2015.
4 U.S. Green Building Council.

## References

Bøllingtoft, A. and Ulhøi, J.P. (2005), 'The networked business incubator – leveraging entrepreneurial agency?' *Journal of Business Venturing*, 20(2), pp. 265–290.

Clinton, S.B., Pinello, A.S. and Skaife, H.A. (2014), 'The implications of ineffective internal control and sox 404 reporting for financial analysts', *Journal of Accounting and Public Policy*, 33(4), pp. 303–327.

Committee of Sponsoring Organizations of the Treadway Commission (COSO) (2013), 'COSO Internal Control – Integrated Framework', the Institute of Internal Auditors (IIA) Research Foundation, the Institute of Internal Auditors, Lake Mary, FL.

Lee, C., Miller, W., Hancock, G.M. and Rowen, H. (2000), *Silicon Valley Edge: The Habitat for Innovation and Entrepreneurship*, Stanford University Press, Palo Alto.

Rittenberg, L.R. (2018), 'COSO Internal Control – Integrated Framework: Turning Principles into Positive Action', Institute of Internal Auditors, Lake Mary, FL.

Wright, R. A. (2013), 'The Internal Auditor's Guide to Risk Assessment', Institute of Internal Auditors, Lake Mary, FL.

# 12
# Megacities at risk

*Cesar Marolla*

A megacity is a metropolitan area with a total population of more than 10 million people. The definition was expanded by Spanish sociologist Manuel Castells in response to economic and social shifts. Castells defines megacities as large urban areas in which some people are connected to global information flows while others are disconnected and information poor (Marolla, 2016). Natural and man-made disasters are the cause of loss of life, financial collapse, and migration and public health risks among other issues.

## Climate change impact on urban dwellers

The stability of the global economy and political order are critically dependent on two inextricable factors: megacities and public health. Protecting the public health of these urban areas has more far-reaching repercussions than protecting the health of individuals in those densely populated areas. A health problem in one megacity can spread rapidly to other parts of the world (Pappas and Khan, 2011), leading to widespread public health concerns and destabilizing the megacity's operations. The effects are felt not just in the health sector but throughout the entire system (Marolla, 2016). The complexity of urban processes increases the vulnerability of megacities to severe climatic events, disruption of communication networks, energy resources, and transportation halts. Consequently, the interdependence of different urban functions and of the various districts increases the risks dramatically. More than half of the world population currently lives in densely populated areas; therefore, they are considered highly potential risk zones. Thirteen of the world's 20 major cities are situated on the coastal zones, and more than a third of the world's people live within 150 km of seashore. Low-lying coastal areas account for 2% of the world's land area, but include 13% of urban inhabitants (Mcgranahan et al., 2007). Further studies illustrate that much of the increase in exposure of population and assets to coastal flooding is likely to be in cities in developing countries, especially in East and South Asia. By the year 2070, approximately 9 out of the top 10 cities in terms of population exposure are expected to be in Asian developing countries (Nicholls et al., 2008).

Urban environments have implications – both positive and negative – for almost every phase of human health and well-being. Megacities can offer a wide range of public health services and innovations in addition to the networks necessary to inform and educate the public on disease prevention, risks, and treatments. These benefits can drastically improve the quality of life in urban areas (Marolla, 2016). However, megacities are also areas of deteriorated physical and social environments. These megacities frequently have high levels of air pollution, high building densities, and loss of social connections, which all have negative impacts on the health of urban residents (Harpham, et al., 2009; Stephens, et al., 2008). This deterioration is especially common in the megacities of developing countries, where rapid urbanization has growing numbers of people living in slums and unhealthy environments. Furthermore, harmful effects of chemicals, air pollution, and ecosystem deterioration to which humans are being increasingly exposed present potential risks to human health (Marolla, 2016).

## Better management of urban environments

Changes in climate have an effect in the well-being of the urban dwellers. Climate-related risks should be considered as an essential component of the megacity strategic planning with a priority in developing and implementing infrastructure investments, zoning, and ecosystem-based strategies. The types of environment most vulnerable to severe climatic events are summarized below:

- Effects of sea-level rise in coastal cities
- Effects of extreme events on built infrastructure
- Effects on health
- Effects on energy use
- Effects on water availability and resources.

*(Shrestha et al., 2015)*

Disaster recovery and business continuity planning is important preparation for coping with major disruptions. Many cities seek to create their own unique sustainability or continuity programs. They are using the people resources that need to be helping the organizations in the city to become more sustainable and responsive to the climate change challenges.

The challenge for megacities is to implement and develop an effective urban risk management framework to adapt and mitigate impacts and deliver essential services to deter climate change effects. Cities need to consider the issues of climate change and urban health by conducting evaluations of related risks to identify feasible measures in their planning and management processes (Dickson et al., 2011).

Additionally, susceptibility to climate variability and change and subsequently its health effects are increased as the concentration of economic activity and population density exacerbates the health issues faced by the world's major cities. Therefore, climate change impacts on health intensify their effects on urban populations (Feiden, 2011). The capacity of the urban poor to adapt is weak in comparison with the rest of the population because the poor settle into inadequate facilities and are exposed to poor nutrition, overcrowded living conditions, and displacement. Resources and information are scarce and the urban poor cannot respond efficiently to take actions to mitigate climate change effects, and this situation creates a gradual exposure to health risks. The poor population's vulnerability will be exacerbated by exposure to severe weather effects and lack of ability to adapt to climate change (Marolla, 2016). Hence, linking risk management to the megacity strategy, processes, and operations reduces the potential losses compared to the base case. The impact of a crisis depends upon its extent and duration. The net benefit of a strategy is obtained by subtracting the total annual cost of the alternative from its benefit. Sensitivity analysis as a method to determine the strength of an assessment (by examining the extent to which results are affected by changes in methods, models, values of unmeasured variables, or assumptions) should be used to determine how changes in the estimates of costs, losses, and probabilities would affect the selection of a strategy. A comprehensive strategic planning approach examines how successful models can be scaled up and accelerated through appropriate policy action and position leaders to understand that, without evolution and improvement, nothing survives (Marolla, 2016).

## Role of information and communications technology

The design and planning of megacities is an important aspect to consider when diminishing the effects of any type of disruptions such as severe weather events, earthquakes, power outages, and so forth. The loss of life, infrastructure, telecommunications, and transportation interruptions can exacerbate the consequences of any detrimental impact and put the megacity's leaders in a threatening situation to minimize the hazards and plan a recovery strategy to go back to "normal operations." The concept of sustainable development has been largely missing in our design culture and that translates into the need to be sustainable through the cycle of planning, design and construction.

Information and communications technology (ICT) is a critical connective infrastructure that supports the global flow of information. As megacities are a complex system with interdependent systems, ICT systems support and connect an increasingly large and complex range of urban systems including social networks, commerce, and emergency response. The importance of utilizing ICT to detect, minimize, and/or prevent catastrophic events plays a main role. Nevertheless, failure of a single ICT system may cause disproportionally large impacts across other systems. Hence, ICT networks are a critical addition in disaster response and support the delivery of information regarding evacuation, mobilization of vulnerable sectors of the population, and shelter, and in coordinating the health and emergency responders and low-capacity backup systems supporting disaster response (Maynard and Stanbrough, 2017).

## Resilient megacities

Can megacities be resilient? The threat of climate change, natural disasters, terrorism, cyberattacks and other disruptive events put mayors, policy makers, and decision makers in a leading position to understand and proactively use ICT tools to cope with the likelihoods and consequences of impacts. A geographic information system (GIS) is a system designed to capture, store, manipulate, analyze, manage, and present spatial or geographic data (University of Wisconsin, 2016). Integrating GIS databases and ICT applications for the design of energy circulation systems, understanding current and potential future impacts of climate change, and options for resiliency and contingency planning and disaster resistant community planning and design have been used extensively to aid in responses to nearly every major natural disaster since the early 1990s (Sorensen, 2013).

## The new era of megacities

In regards of disaster management approaches, a dynamic and quick response to unexpected events will make a difference between a complete chaos and an effective recovery process with minimum losses. Intelligent technologies can help to limit the impact of these events and maximize resources in a coordinated and effective way. City management systems must be flexible and adaptable to the geographical, environmental, social, and financial situation and consequently be tailored and applied in megacities around the world. Therefore, ICT presents an opportunity to improve the quality of life, sustainable socio-economic development, lessen environmental impacts, and build the capacity for a proactive risk management and strategic planning to minimize and/or deter disruptions. The health care sector is the foundation of a megacity's function and reinforces and unifies public health efforts aimed at combating diseases and building healthy societies. New technologies support its function and inform the public of safety measures to actively safeguard their communities. Therefore, remote systems help diagnosis and treatment procedures, enhance patient experience and penetration of direct care, and improve the response of the emergency crew. In chaotic situations, the transportation system can suffer disruptions and intelligent transport systems can be tailored to the preparedness plan, such as direct traffic flow based on real-time information in addition to automatic systems for reducing congestion to improve the mobility flow in times of emergency, which are crucial components for resilience. Public safety and security are maintained and assessed through intelligent systems, citywide monitoring, sensor tracking, alerting controls constituting a comprehensive and dynamic resource management system and quick emergency response. Overall, megacities are in a position to embrace ICT with practical solutions to confront global risks and validate the significance of sustainability.

## References

Eric Dickson, Judy Baker. Daniel Hoornweg and Asmita Tiwari. Understanding urban risk: an approach for assessing disaster & climate risk in cities. *The World Bank*, 2011, 1: 9–11.

Feiden, Peter. Adapting to climate change: Cities and the urban poor. *International Housing Coalition*, 2011.

Harpham, et al. 2009. Urban health in developing countries: what do we know and where do we go? *Health & Place*, 2009, 15: 107–116.

Krishna, Shrestha, Hemant Ojha, Phil McManus, Anna Rubbo, and Krishna Kumar Dhote. *Inclusive Urbanization: Rethinking Policy, Practice and Research in the Age of Climate Change*. 1st ed. Vol. 1. Abingdon, UK: Routledge, 2015. ISBN-13: 978–0415856027

Mapping and Geographic Information Systems (GIS). University of Wisconsin, 2016.

Marolla, Cesar. *Climate Health Risks in Megacities: Sustainable Management and Strategic Planning*. 1st ed. Vol. 1. Boca Raton: CRC Press, Taylor & Francis Group, 2016. ISBN 9781498767743

Maynard, Trevor, and Lucy Stanbrough. "Future Cities: Building ICT infrastructure resilience." *Emerging Risk Report 2017 Society and Security*, March 2017.

Mcgranahan, G., D. Balk, and B. Anderson. "The rising tide: assessing the risks of climate change and human settlements in low elevation coastal zones." *Environment and Urbanization*, 2007, 19, no. 1: 17–37. https:/doi.org/10.1177/0956247807076960.

Nicholls, R. J., P. P. Wong, V. Burkett, C. D. Woodroffe, and J. Hay. Climate change and coastal vulnerability assessment: scenarios for integrated assessment. *Sustainability Science*, 2008, 3: 89–102.

Pappas, Gregory, and Omar Khan. Megacities and Global Health, 2011. http://ajph.aphapublications.org/doi/pdf/10.2105/9780875530031fm03.

Shrestha, A., et al. *Inclusive Urbanization: Rethinking Policy, Practice and Research in the Age of Climate Change*. New York: Routledge.

Sorensen, Mark. "The Strategic Use of Spatial Data for Urban Resilience." ICLEI Resilient Cities, May 2013. Accessed June 19, 2017. http://resilient-cities.iclei.org/fileadmin/sites/resilient-cities/files/Resilient_Cities_2013/Presentations/F1_Sorensen_RC2013.pdf.

Stephens, C., D. Satterthwaite, and H. Kris. *Urban Health in Developing Countries, International Encyclopedia of Public Health*. Oxford: Academic Press, 2008, pp. 452–463.

# 13

# Self-organization and its role in building disaster resilience

*Nirmita Mehrotra*

## Introduction

The emphasis of this chapter is that crisis management must reinvent its foundations to be truly operational, particularly to address the role of emerging groups in the process of recovery from catastrophic events. This concept relates to the work of Lagadec and Topper (2012). Lalonde (2004) pointed to emergence of new leaders at the level of local community as a disaster unfolds over time. Resilience is an attribute of emergence, enacted through local actors and individual organizations. The framework for assessment of resilience is deduced from the phenomenon of self-organization in complex, chaotic environments. These new leaders may not be part of a hierarchical response system; however, they drive the reconfiguration of the organization, pushing for nonlinear interaction to seek order. Cutter et al. (2010) point to the shifts from vulnerability to disaster resilience as a more proactive and positive expression of community engagement. This is done through implementation of a program of change through institutional flexibility and by absorbing technological, economic and social changes.

With the increasing frequency and magnitude of disasters, resilience thinking is essentially bringing a paradigm shift in urban planning and governance of our evolving cities (Mehrotra 2010). Lagadec and Topper (2012) questioned 'why do we continually appear disaster behind?' in the context to Hurricane Katrina. They see the need for the reinvention of crisis management. Regarding this paradigm shift, where outcome disasters have changed the scale of demographic trends, the challenges are a mix of local problems and global dynamics. Predominance of nonlinearity and feedback loops has shown evidence of systematic collapses in the world, as in the case of the catastrophic devastation of Japan's 2011 tsunami, causing the Fukushima nuclear reactor disaster. The concept of natural disaster management should be revised in a time when nature can trigger technological disasters and technology can spark off natural upheavals. The application of various tools for disaster management has shown a pattern of change in the last 50 years. Some of the lessons summarized by Mileti (1999), Comfort, Godschalk (2003), Folke (2006), Raschky (2008) and Bosher and Dainty (2011) have been used in this chapter to formulate a systematic framework for assessment of urban resilience. Mileti (1999) argued that disaster losses are the result of interaction among multi-agents of systems and subsystems which may be the earth's physical system, the human system and the constructed system. Lagadec and Topper (2012) indicates the cause for the necessity of a new conceptual framework; linear disaster management systems only consider limited and marginal uncertainty, in which the events and the contexts in which they occur can be only be clearly compartmentalized. Yet, as he states and as many researchers also believe, this is not the situation in which disasters emerge today or will occur in the future. Simple categorizations and fragmented approaches are not valid anymore. Cases increasingly demonstrate that something is wrong with the current approach. Some mitigation activities do not prevent damage but merely postpone it. Innovative institutional changes are required to integrate sectoral issues of disaster management and make it sustainable.

Resilience thinking is an approach for the management of socio-ecological systems that aims to develop an integrated framework for consolidating the often fragmented, diverse research on disaster risk management. After decades of research on disaster management, hazard researchers agree to view disasters as window of change and look forward for a new approach which is open to social innovation. The systems approach has been used to understand and maintain heterogenity and variability of attributes where the cumulative effect of a system varies from its collective output. This chapter's goal is to advance this discussion and to promote operationalization of resilience through the analysis of key components of the city.

## Complexity theory of cities

Complexity has been a central construct in many paradigms. This chapter first examines the complexity of cities and their operation in interdependent subsystems and sub-subsystems. The second perspective is the disaster process as directly interlinked in a cyclical phenomenon to development. The third perspective views the complexity of disaster and emergency management, where intra-organizational collaboration is essential and dependent on the cognitive ability of the organizations. The concept of disaster resilience is characterized by its complexity and interconnectedness, where uncertainty plays important role in creating networks (Eiser et al. 2012). Complex systems are characterized with several phenomena such as chaotic change, emergence, self-organization and strange attractors. Complexity science, as a scientific endeavour used to explain large systems, utilizes complex adaptive systems where multiple interconnected elements operate and engage in continuous learning. This shift in the worldview is from rational, to where technical, social, economic environments are rationally viewed, to an interconnected evolving one. The Santa Fe Institute has been undertaking research on complex adaptive systems since 1984. The institute's research pursues the mechanism which leads to an evolutionary process of adaptation and interaction in nominally distinct physical, biological, social and technological systems. The institute's researchers derived six characteristics of complex system based on simulations of complex networks, which should be incorporated in city planning and governance. These are:

1. There is no central control.
2. There are inherent underlying structures within systems.
3. Feedback and feed-forward mechanisms modify the system's characteristics and operation.
4. Nonlinear behaviour is common because things do not happen in a simple cause and effect manner.
5. Emergence is an outcome of the system parameters which happens without planned intent.
6. The system is non-reducible. This means that system behaviour cannot be understood by looking at one part or element.

## Resilience and uncertainty

Among its many definitions, resilience is interpreted in terms as how well a system adapts its structure and functions in response to shocks, before changing its structure. Hazard mitigation planners continuously work in the environment of uncertainty and change. Rigid policies and task divisions can delay operation and prolong recovery from disruption. People bring key resources to the community that influence their capacity to confront adverse events (Paton 2014). Paton compared the preparedness of communities based on individualistic cultures and collective cultures and concludes that collectivistic cultures, like that of Japan, are better in achieving collective goals of safety and protection from perennial hazards. Collective actions are underpinned by culturally embedded beliefs and align with social norms. Paton states that faced with uncertainty, people turn to others who share their interests and values to find ways to manage their risk. There is evidence of people ignoring the official warnings and instructions to evacuate during the Indian Ocean tsunami in 2004, whereas in case of Cyclone Phailin in 2013, evacuation and warning was issued through the help of community groups, and inhabitants extended full support and relocated to evacuation shelters in time.

To understand disasters, Lorenz (2010) views a disaster as a failure of fundamental structures of expectation in an uncertain environment and an uncertain future. Resilience (social, physical, technical, economic) is framed as the internal ability of a system to prevent and mitigate a disastrous change. Wildavsky (1991) highlighted the connection between resilience and uncertainty, referring to Holling (1973) that if a system itself is a moving target, it cannot be predicted. Research is shifting from ad hoc, disaster driven and reactive policies to proactive, threat-driven and adaptation-focused approaches. Resilience, in a systems perspective, is an all-hazards proactive approach. As development is not merely growth, increased resiliency and robustness against environmental changes is essential. Recovery of a system depends on the status prior to the extreme event, the nature of the event, and how in place a self-organizing system is before and after the event. For institutions, recovery is not merely returning to what was before the event; it is to achieve viability in the newly emerging environment within which they exist, to the extent they can shape the environment. To understand the post-disaster recovery process of a complex system, regarding Ashby's law of requisite variety, an array of coping mechanisms is required at least equal to the array of challenges it faces. This necessitates demographic, social and economic linkages to remain viable.

## Institutional resilience

Risk management requires a control system (institutional structure) and an actuation system (public policies and actions) to implement the changes needed. Institutions are factors in determining safety and vulnerability in society. Robustness of institutions relates to their readiness to learn and act in intra-organizational coordination and interact with community networks. One of the central arguments of this research is that some vulnerability is created by institutions. Institutional vulnerabilities are hypothetically a matter of coping, and adapting to natural hazards, in an anticipatory approach with coordination of the local community.

The traditional hierarchical government model does not meet the demands of this complex, rapidly changing age. Rigid bureaucratic systems with command and control procedures, narrow work restrictions and inward-looking cultures and operational models are particularly ill-suited to address problems that often transcend organizational boundaries. Governments are confronted with challenges and are posed to work through community networks and allow for innovative roles in solving societal problems. Disaster risk reduction is not a single piece of legislation that cures all ills, but a system that needs to be woven into the societal fabric in a way that will make it invisible and acceptable. The participatory process itself may be as important as the outcome (Godschalk 2003). These arguments reveal the complexity of planning and incorporation of disaster management in the urban system, where lack of participation of people in the policy formulation has proven to be a major setback in its implementation. A compilation of 27 national progress reports on implementation of the Hyogo Framework of Action (HFA Priority 4) Planning and Management of human settlement incorporates disaster risk reduction elements, including enforcement of building codes. In the Philippines, limited progress has been achieved promoting systematic policy and institutional commitment to guide land use planners and policy makers in disaster risk reduction. Regarding systematic policy application, India displays weakness at the level of operational mechanism. These arenas may emerge as networks at all levels from individuals, to local community groups, to national governments and to international institutions and organizations. Governance scholars Duit and Galaz (2008) have studied issues of complexity and governance to cope with uncertainty and change. Systems evolve iteratively with uncertainties of events, exposure of population, physical population determinants and response to various interventions of recovery and relief. As the impacts of disasters are felt in varying proportions at different locations, newer models of inclusive governance, rather than the traditional top-down model, are required to handle the various phases of disaster management and recovery.

## Disaster resilient city

The capability of resilient cities to withstand severe shocks without either immediate chaos or without physical, social and economic damages is increasingly gaining importance. A resilient city is a sustainable network of physical systems and human communities (Godschalk 2003). A physical system is the constructed and natural components of the city. It includes roads, building infrastructure, communications and energy facilities, as well as waterways, soil topography, geology and other natural systems. Critical breakdowns in physical systems can result in major losses. Godschalk (2003) emphasized that a city without resilient communities is extremely vulnerable to disasters. For a resilient city, communities are not simply a group of individuals who happen to be categorized together, but a group of individuals who interact and communicate with one another creating a social system. The communities act as the brain of the city, directing its activities, responding to its needs and learning from its experiences. Thereby it is the responsibility of institutions to see that during the extreme and uncertain conditions of a disaster, community networks must be able to survive and function.

The concept of resilience emerged in the 1970s and 1980s in ecology and social studies reflecting the inherent dynamism of natural and social systems, respectively. Today resilience is referenced on a wide range of issues associated with social and ecological systems, including disaster management, economics, community planning, urban renewal, and development (Carpenter 2001). Involvement of communities in disaster risk management is essential to utilize capacities and knowledge that communities possess. Here capacities refer to institutional, technological, economic and social capabilities to plan and implement a program of change on vulnerabilities reduction. The collective capacity of a community or urban system to make informed decisions and take coherent actions in the face of danger is a measure of community resilience, constituting urban resilience at large. Individuals and organizations display a complex interplay of extrinsic and intrinsic values resulting in institutional changes. The concept of institutional change by emergence of local actors and individual organizations has led to the phenomenon of self-organization in complex chaotic environments. It implies that uncertainty and surprise are part of the environment and one must be prepared to live with it. This perspective is in stark contrast to equilibrium-centred command and control strategies that attempt to control variability. Resilience incorporates concepts of both outcome and process. Outcome is defined as the ability to bounce back or cope with a hazard, whereas process-related resilience is defined more in terms of continual learning and taking responsibility for improvement. Resilience has been defined by two qualities: inherent functions operating well during non-crisis periods, and adaptability and flexibility in response to disasters. Scope for social innovation, based on the understanding of system dynamics and emergence of new structures, is key to resilience. It is a relational concept (Lorenz 2010) that saliently marks the importance of the balance between a system and its environment, as well as the adjustment for a safe future. Far from a 'fix it forget it' approach, resilience is a balancing act between risk and resources, between vulnerabilities and escalating or unmanageable catastrophic impacts (Comfort et al. 2010).

## Types of resilience

There are many notions of resilience, for example, engineering resilience, ecological resilience, and socio-economic resilience. In engineering, resilience is the efficiency of a system's return to stability (Walker and Salt 2006). Ecosystem resilience is the capacity of an ecosystem to tolerate disturbance without collapsing into a qualitatively different state that is controlled by a different set of processes. Ecologist C. S. Holling's view has been particularly important. He proposed the concept that resilience determines the persistence of a system and is a measure of the ability of a system to absorb changes. Concepts of ecological diversity also took its roots to address institutional diversity and redundancy by scholars like Low et al. (2003) and Ostrom (2005). Resilience, as applied to ecosystems, or to the integrated systems of people and the natural environment, has three defining characteristics: first, the amount of change the system can undergo and still retain the same controls on function and structure; second, the degree to which the system is capable of self-organization: and third, the ability to build and increase the capacity for learning and adaptation.

Walker et al. (2006) gave special focus on institutions in exploration of resilience in socio-ecological systems and insisted that efforts to deliberately enhance adaptability can unintentionally lead to resilience. This should first come from all forms of capital (social, human, natural, manufactured and financial) and second from systems of institutions and governance. Resilience engineering acknowledges disasters as disruptions, where the initiating event leads to catastrophes, due to an intrinsic or external error, and results in cascading failures in operation and deliverance of services. In complex adaptive systems (CAS), resilience comprises different aspects of engineering and ecological resilience with another layer of complexity, that is human cognition and sense making. Control in CAS is highly dispersed and decentralised, where coherent behaviour amongst agents in CAS arises from communication, cooperation and collaboration. Overall behaviour of the system is the result of numerous decisions made each moment by many individuals. The basic four characteristic factors for CAS are self-organization, hierarchy, emergence and learning. Thus CAS should support a heterogeneous collection of individual agents that interacts locally. The literature survey undertaken for this research identifies a research gap for exploration of emergent groups, leaders and their influences on different phases of disaster mitigation: preparedness, planning, protection and recovery. The research also considers the phenomenon of self-organization, which can be sustained, to be utilized on a consistent basis in mainstreaming disaster management.

The different types of resilience also have varied methods of assessment. Resilience of ecological systems is influenced by factors such as biodiversity, redundancies, response, diversity,

*Table 13.1* Resilience perspectives

| *Resilience Perspective* | *Philosophical Background* | *Assessment of Resilience* |
|---|---|---|
| Engineering Resilience | Return to stability, maintain efficiency of function, resist change, vicinity to stable equilibrium. | Size of stability domain, resumption time. |
| Ecological Resilience (Folke et al. 2006) | Ability to have buffer capacity, withstand shock, maintain function. | Disturbance absorbed before control mechanism shifts to another set of variables. |
| Organizational Resilience (Lee et al. 2013) | Organizations train employees for continuity of operations. | Organizational learning, feedback loops for continued monitoring and evaluations. |
| Community Resilience | Social cohesiveness, bonding, collective efficacy and information sharing. | Strong social capital adds to robustness. |
| Institutional Resilience (Tierney and Bruneau 2007) | Formal and informal organization in stand alone or in collaborated partnership, increased accountability and awareness. | Flexibility and change management through operation of networks clusters. |
| Infrastructural Resilience (Yazidini 2010) | Heterogeneity for functional redundancy, fail safe technologies. | Robustness, redundancy. |
| Socio-ecological Resilience (Holling 1973) | Transformation, reorganization, sustaining development by learning. | Renewal, regeneration and self-organization capacity, connecting experts and motivated actors. |
| Economic Resilience (Rose and Krausmam 2013) | Micro-insurance, diversity, livelihood, business continuity. | Recoverability, rapidity. |
| Socio-technical System Resilience (Silva et al. 2013) | Uncertainty reduced by continuously learning and change management. | Human and social capital, institutional innovation, learning and Redundancy. |
| Complex Adaptive System | Feedback, heterogeneity, redundancy, continual adaptation, local interaction | Self-organization, evolution of the system, reformability for flexible institutions. |

spatial planning, governance and management plans (Folke 2006, Cutter et al. 2010). Social resilience can be enhanced through improvement in communications, risk awareness and preparedness, implementation of disaster plans, purchase of insurance and sharing of information in the recovery process (Paton and Johnston 2006). Resilience perspectives are presented in Table 13.1.

## Framework to assess resilience

Anderies et al. (2013) refer to resilience as broader system level attributes such as the ability to build and increase the capacity for learning and adaptation. Actual recovery depends on parameters such as vulnerabilities of institutions to restructure and reconfigure, and rapid decision making and policy implementation. Tierney (2002) and Madini (2009) studied the response of resilient systems to disasters and defined certain characteristics of resilient systems. Tierney and Bruneau (2007) stated four domains of resilience: technical, organizational, social and economic (TOSE), within the framework of robustness, redundancy resourcefulness and rapidity with varied attributes of assessment. Bruneau et al. (2003) gave an analysis of seismic resilience and application at four levels:

1 Technical: the performance of physical systems when subjected to earthquake forces.
2 Organisational: the ability to respond to emergencies and carry out critical functions.
3 Social: the capacity to collectively act to protect loss of critical services.
4 Economic: the capacity to reduce both direct and indirect economic losses.

Figure 13.1 portrays the centrality of institutional resilience in the overall resilience framework.

Resilience of urban system categorized in four components to cover different functional variations:

*Economic resilience*: Role of economic resilience in reducing monetary losses in disasters is achieved through the adoption of mitigation strategies that aim to lessen the probability of failure and reduce property losses and business disruption (Rose and Krausmam 2013).

*Institutional resilience*: This includes elements of the organizations, such as members, organizational structure, capacity to interact and make decisions through leadership, training and experience, and communication technology (Cutter et al. 2008, Tierney and Bruneau 2007). An organization which is hierarchical with a command and control mechanism is less flexible in the face of disaster than one with integrated management structures which encourages flexibility and adaptation to changing conditions.

*Infrastructural resilience*: Tightly coupled and interconnected infrastructure exhibits less resilience. A high degree of interdependence also reduces resilience since a disruption in one sector cascades into impacts on other sectors (Chang et al. 2007).

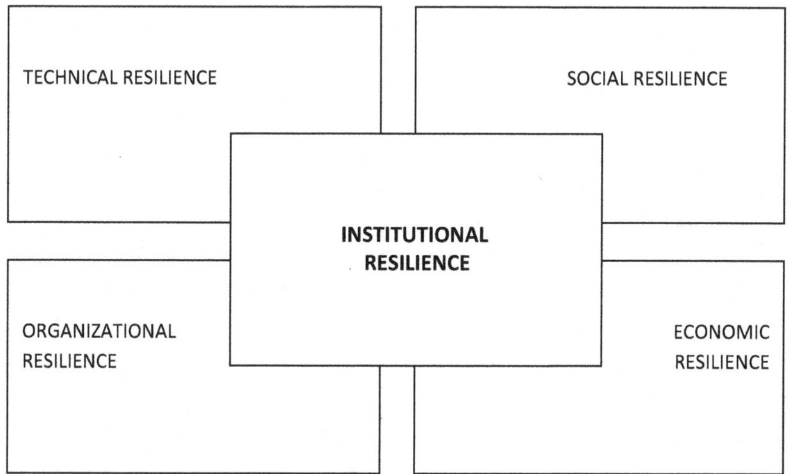


*Figure 13.1* Institutional resilience framework

*Community competence*: This is another form of resilience and highlights those attributes that promote population wellness, quality of life and emotional health. Silva et al. (2012) identify three networks as infrastructure network, institutional network and knowledge networks which help to operationalize resilience. These three networks are considered as socio-technical networks since they are composed of physical elements (technology and buildings) as well as social institutions (regulatory structures, formal and informal practices). Resilience perspective is used here to understand dynamics of cities within four networks as discussed below.

*Institutional networks* involve norms and cultures, regulations, rule of law and codes. Institutions have often been overlooked by the risk researcher community (Lassa 2010). Morehouse (2011) and Folke et al. (2006) present the concept of institutional resilience as a means of coping with changes and shocks. It is important to understand challenges of the uncertainties and complexities inherent in biophysical and human processes for environmental decision making and governance. Networks need to incorporate flexibility to meet unforeseen challenges of uncertainty.

*Infrastructure networks* are the key physical and technological assets of cities, which enable exchanges and dynamic relationships, between different actors representing capital and knowledge, embedded in the city. This includes networks which enable access to essential resources (food, water and energy), provisions of health, education, buildings and services for government, business, and access to markets and information.

*Knowledge networks* refer to structures and systems that regulate flow of information, as communication and sharing information is crucial for emergence of self-organization. Flows of information and technological development are critical to enable urban systems to learn and adapt to changing circumstances (Silva et al. 2012). Access to information happens on an everyday basis from local radio stations, the internet, newspapers, social network sites, community gatherings, and transnational professional networks. Continuous exchange of information is vital for self-organization to happen.

*Community networks*, as social capital, emphasize aspects of social structure, trust norms and social networks that facilitate collective action (Peacock et al. 2010). Social capital reflects the quantity and quality of social cooperation and may be measured by several variables including religious organizations, voluntary organizations, newspaper readership and non-profit organizations. These community networks could be as formal as a sport club or as informal as a group of friends.

Phillips Berkes (2003) defined system attributes of resilience as (1) the amount of disturbance a system can absorb and remain within the same state or domain of attraction, (2) the degree to which the system is capable of self-organization and (3) the degree to which the system can build and increase the capacity of learning and adaptation. Tierney and Bruneau (2007) defined a framework for components of resilient infrastructure as robustness, redundancy, resourcefulness and rapidity within technical, social, economic and institutional domains, as follows:

*Robustness*: strength to withstand a given level of stress without loss of function.

*Redundancy*: the extent to which alternate elements are available as a substitute to avoid disruption.

*Resourcefulness*: the extent to which a local community has access to resources including human resources to meet the needs of disaster victims and recover. This includes the capacity to identify problems, establish priorities and mobilize resources accordingly.
*Rapidity*: the capacity to meet priorities and achieve goals, so a system can be restored in a timely manner.

Resilience also emphasizes trying to build fail-safe and intelligent systems, which are capable of learning and self-organizing. Parameters of robustness and redundancy are not sufficient to assess resilience. Also important are opportunities that disturbances create in terms of recombination of evolved structures and processes, renewal of systems and emergence of new trajectories, referred to as adaptive capacity by Folke (2006). Bruneau et al. (2003) indicate that resourcefulness and redundancy are the fundamental means for achieving adequate robustness and rapidity. Adaptive capacity in resilience provides an interplay between sustaining versus incorporating changes, as too much change could lead to collapse. Here capacity to transform from the current state to a more desirable state depends on the self-organizing capacity of the system. Urban resilience is both a product and process of service deliverance to regain normalcy after an event of disturbance. Six indicators that contribute to the perception of urban resilience, both in the process of evolution and as an outcome, where the latter is assumed to be the capacity of self organization, are as follows:

*Robustness*: Anderies et al. (2013) related robustness to resilience in terms of performance measurement. Robustness focuses on the fundamental principle of the feedback and feed-forward behaviour of systems. The design of robust policies and fundamental robustness fragility trade-off is associated with different policy designs and governance structures, and focused on reducing sensitivity of the system output in a defined class of disturbances and uncertainties. Robustness provides concepts and tools to develop fundamental properties of feedback systems within clearly defined boundaries, to reduce sensitivity of a given system. It is also defined by the status of existing planning and incorporation of safety standards for continued operation after disturbances.
*Resourcefulness*: Diversity of resources, economic variability and available institutional structures are the key elements for resourcefulness. Loose coupling, flexibility and redundancy support provisions of resources. This parameter is categorized into 10 attributes, where respondents were asked to give ratings based on their actual utilization and usefulness. It is a basis to assess both technical and indigenous knowledge resources, to reduce damages, and to regain normalcy after a disturbance. Availability and accessibility to financial resource and status of social trusted networks and community groups are vital contributions to this parameter. Existing disaster management policies and the ability to procure resources in case of emergency, including reserves for emergency supplies, are essential.
*Redundancy*: These are the decentralised systems designed with multiple nodes to avoid cascading failure from one component to failure of the entire system. Redundant systems could simply have variability in elements and more connections to assure fault-free functioning of the system. Ostrom (2005) argues for polycentric and multilayered governance systems with overlapping units to have the capacity and diversity to compensate for failure. Low et al. (2003) argue that redundancy of institutions and their overlapping functions across organizational levels play a central role in absorbing disturbances and in spreading risk. Resilience is determined by the availability of backup systems to provide continuity when the primary systems fail (McEntire 2003).

*Table 13.2* Parameters of institutional resilience

| *Parameter* | *Description* |
|---|---|
| Robustness (Yazdani 2010) (Anderies et al. 2013) | Ability of the system to withstand stresses; continuity of operation and delivery of services after disturbance. |
| Redundancy (Ostrom 2005) | Variability in elements and connections to assure functioning; alternatives for machinery and supplies. |
| Resourcefulness (Tierney 2003) | Availability, distribution and accessibility to reduce damages and regain normalcy after a disturbance. |
| Recoverability (Bosher et al. 2007) | Enhance capacity to recover after disaster; failsafe design; knowledge-sharing network. |
| Reformability (Takeda and Helms 2006) | Institutional system restructures in response to damage; redistribute resources; flexibility to complete the tasks. |
| Rapidity (Bruneau 2003) | Optimize recovery time; capacity to meet priorities; contain losses; avoid future disruption. |

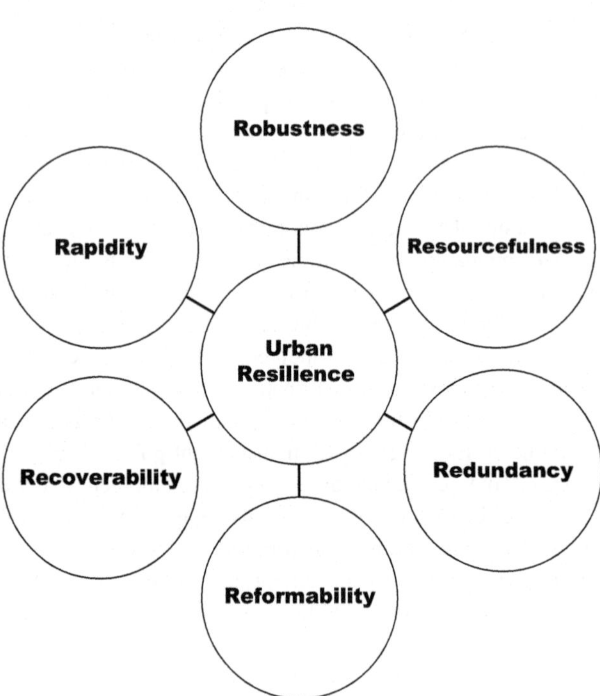


*Figure 13.2* Parameters for urban resilience

*Reformability*: Reformability is the ability of an institutional system in a rigid bureaucracy to restructure itself in response to external damage and to reprioritize distribution of staff or resources. Reformability is broadly an institutional attribute, which directly and indirectly influences all other aspects of building capacity and operations. This also refers to adaptability as the concept of resilience, that is to transform a system completely or partially in the case when the present system becomes untenable (Folke et al. 2010).

*Recoverability*: As a built environment cannot be disaster-proof (Bosher et al. 2007), focus is to incorporate elements that enhance capacity to recover after event of disaster. This also relates to threshold capacities and variable modes of recovery as strategies for adaptation, buffer resources and inclusion of community.

*Rapidity*: Rapidity is the capacity to meet priorities and achieve goals in a timely manner to prevent losses and avoid future disruptions (Bruneau 2003). It is based on an assessment of procedures and their effectiveness in reducing the time to gain normalcy, for example in livelihood opportunities and living conditions.

Table 13.2 provides additional descriptions of these resilience parameters, and Figure 13.2 portrays their linkage to urban resilience.

## Operationalization of resilience for assessment

The major challenge in the research for assessment of resilience is that it can be only assessed truly after people have experienced disaster and have been exposed to significant disruption. Paton et al. (2010) tried to identify proxy measures that will be indicative of what would allow people and communities to adapt to hazard consequences. First, the level of protective measures (adoption of seismic codes during construction), retrofitting of dilapidated buildings and so forth; second, level of resources and access to them in emergency, response plans and their execution; third, people's ability to cope within their community; and lastly, the capacity and accessibility to utilize services (health, welfare, business, emergency response, etc.) to meet local needs and to facilitate local recovery. Variables identified for the District of Gautam Buddha Nagar are based on its demographics, administrative setup, status of the built environment, and participative capacity of the community in overall decision-making process and actions. Cutter et al. (2010) provide an example to test the internal consistency of the Baseline Resilience Index for Communities (BRIC).

The multifaceted nature of resilience, including physical, social, institutional, economic and ecological dimensions, becomes a challenge in assessment. Resilience therefore will only be achieved through the cumulative contribution of multiple interventions and actions over time and the ability of individuals and institutions to internalize learning for improved future behaviour (Silva et al. 2012). Paton et al. (2005) identified social cohesion and participation in community activities as predictor of preparedness, for example, the duration residents stay in any neighbourhood and their participation in community organizations, use of technology to predict hazard and preparedness programs. People's perception of risk, and what actions can be taken to manage or reduce risk, is influenced by their immediate social groups. Information dissemination through social networks (e.g. social clubs, cultural festivals) assist them in decision making under threatening circumstances. Collective efficacy provides one means of assessing community members' ability to identify needs, assess their capabilities and formulate plans to use resources in both individualistic and collective cultures. Most assessment techniques are quantitative and use selected indicators or variables as proxies because it is often difficult to quantify resilience in absolute terms without any reference of validation. This diversity in the role of civil society, and formal and informal networks of community with professional bodies, needs to be an integral part of the institutional mechanism for building resilience. Gunderson (2010) compared ecological and human community systems for operation of resilience both in terms of recovery time and adaptability. In the age of networks, their role is measured through the social networking capacity, where networks are the building blocks to operate resiliently. In the light of the above facts, this research explores the existing role of community networks, leading to self-organization.

## Observation on status of resilience

The newly created Gautam Buddha district has been the highest gross domestic product (GDP) contributor in the state of Uttar Pradesh. Crises can unfold from industrial disasters, technological failures, natural disasters or other events of cascading failures in the operation of urban services. Greater Noida, a suburb of NCR Delhi, has in integrated urban complex with a robust infrastructure, six-lane road network, and interconnected green areas from city greens to local parks. The city has adequate resources but weak institutional mechanisms of knowledge transfer to support self-organization. There are no evacuation maps or resiliency guidelines for public buildings, commercial facilities and residential complexes. The large fluctuating population (e.g. student community, knowledge parks, international community) is a great challenge for systematic disaster management. Mock drills, which have been conducted at industrial complexes, do not include the local community. The entire mechanism is based on command and control, rather than synergizing communities to empower and strengthen themselves. The predominant Gurjar community maintains cultural values and higher social capital. With low density development, people prefer to develop a one-to-one relationship among themselves and connect on a day-to-day basis. Being the highest GDP contributor in the Uttar Pradesh state, the district would benefit from a comprehensive business continuity plan and institutional mechanisms to formally recognize the existing community networks and utilize their potential for building urban resilience.

Takeda and Helm (2006) explore the failure of the bureaucratic approach. Problems originate because of decentralized knowledge and centralized decisions. Other issues are ignoring outside information and committing to failed courses of actions. They discuss the bureaucratic system that relies heavily on group decision making within formalized roles and codified information sharing. Communication tools require large amounts of time and effort, and hinders the system's ability to take swift and decisive actions. They continue to argue that though large numbers of people have roles in the decision-making process, they do not have authority of action. Management of Cyclone Phailin's landfall on the Orissa coast (2013) is compared to the that of the 1999 cyclone, where the local community members lead campaigns of warning and evacuation at multi-layered plans of government and community shifted to emergency shelters on time.

In the aftermath of the Gujarat earthquake (2000), the persistent case of deliberate vulnerabilities pointed to the lack of the state's capacity to monitor and regulate housing construction. There have been perennial problems caused by low quality building material, deliberate non-compliance with building codes, regulations and safety norms, which have transformed the region's seismic hazard into a disaster of catastrophic proportions. Another example showing amplifying effects between different types of governance systems can be found in the case of Hurricane Katrina in New Orleans in 2005. A large part of the storm's devastating impact did not result from a lack of scientific information or failed meteorological predictions (Science

2005) but rather from the combination of a rigid federal emergency management system and an ill-prepared and disorganized fragile local governance system.

Baud and Nainan (2008) present the case of Mumbai, where advance locality management (ALM) groups from the residents of neighbourhoods, with the original mandate of monitoring and improving visible basic services at neighbourhood level, were instrumental in holding the local government accountable. Through ward committees of elected representatives, representing low income and vulnerable groups of society, dependent on political connections and authority, ALM representing middle-class residents dealt directly with the executive wing of local government to raise their point and ensure delivery of required services. Another example of women empowerment and poverty alleviation is named *Kudumbashree*, where 41 women joined the mission initiated by the Government of Kerala, India. These women form collectives and participate in various initiatives aimed at better health, better education, and better social and economic status of women in the state. "In collective functioning, if one person falls behind, the others will help her manage, Kerala's experience provides an innovative example of bridging the divide between planning and Local Action. It brings together the people and the government; long range planning and short range programs, synchronizes the planning with implementation. In 1994, an outbreak of plague epidemics in City of Surat, where India threatened to spread around the world after infecting around 300,000 people and killing 52. About 60% of the population fled the city and the industry suffered an estimated loss of Rs. 12 Billion. There emerged a model of community participation in the direct leadership of the Surat Municipal Corporation (SMC).

Horizontal and vertical restructuring may facilitate self-organization of communities in both bottom-up and top-down governance. The phenomenon of self-organization is deduced from illustrative examples of the Voluntary Disaster Preparedness Organization (VDPO) in Japan and other success stories like Patanka Navjivan Yojana (PNY), where government promoted resilience of the community. Devolution of finance and convergence of other schemes operating at grassroots levels, to Neighbourhood Groups (NHG) and Community Development Society (CDS) is discussed by Mehrotra (2015). Similarly, in Indonesia, multiple organizations emerged as agents exercising roles beyond the state, when the state government was unable to effectively respond. A few organizations have emerged as agents in driving governance and institutional change in disaster management. Namely, KOKAMI in Japan, has emerged as an agent in exercising a plan of community disaster preparedness.

## Conclusion

A framework for the assessment of resilience has been formulated in this chapter using a systems approach, where resilience is taken as a system attribute. From a theoretical perspective, a contribution of this research work is in the melding of the inputs from myriad fields, in a multidisciplinary perspective on disaster resilience and development of composite indicators for assessment of resilience. It provides information for researchers and practitioners to construct a resilience index that is theoretically grounded in a multidisciplinary perspective, and aims to develop an integrated framework for bringing together the often fragmented, diverse research on disaster risk management. This research suggests a relationship of resilience to self-organization, embarking on its institutional component and its strength in the process of recovery from disasters. An approach for assessment of resilience as a system output, is used through this framework. A model to operationalize resilience has been envisaged, highlighting its contribution to the community's capability of self-organization. Within the context of the newly planned industrial towns of the National Capital Region and the

Uttar Pradesh sub-region, hub of industrial, institutional and export investments, the model has been used to operationalize and check the hypothesis of institutional resilience contributing to self-organization. Findings from this research study point to the resilience deficit at level of institutions, which hinders the implementation of the Disaster Management Act 2005, for the protection infrastructure and the community from catastrophes. Recovery consists of those actions that aim to bring the disrupted areas back to an improved condition of normalcy. The main challenge of the recovery phase is to restore living conditions in the short term, and in the long term achieve sustainability and survivability of the community. These operational processes require effective coordination and cooperation of various agents, such as governmental agencies, non-governmental organizations, volunteer groups and private companies.

Self-organization is a complex phenomenon and emerges in uncertainty of the aftermath of disasters, discussed in detail through illustrated cases from the Uttrakhand flash floods, Sikkim earthquake 2011, Cyclone Phailin 2013 and the greater eastern Japan earthquake 2011. Qualitative as well as quantitative analysis of these events, together with deductive research, has been used to justify the research outcome. The concept of institutional resilience has been used to support the phenomenon of self-organization in a complex and variable environment. Government's role is as a network promoter, by supporting and encouraging networks enhances the capacity of a community to self-organize in the aftermath of a disaster. The role of community clusters like Gayatri Parwar, Shati Kunj in Uttrakhand and other similar local networks have been instrumental in providing rescue and relief. The Disaster Management Act of 2005 and devised institutional mechanism remain to be a theoretical construct in absence of guidelines pertaining to the complexity and uncertainty of unfolding disasters and behaviour patterns of people. Mainstreaming resilience into development requires the efforts of emerging local actors for sustained self-organizing efforts.

## References


Anderies, J.M., Folke, C., Walker, B., Ostrom, E. (2013); Aligning key concepts for global change policy; Robustness, resilience and sustainability; *Ecology and Society* 18(2): 8.

Aguirre, Ben, Russell, Dynes, James, Kendra, Rory, Conell (2005); Institutional resilience and disaster planning of new hazards: Insights from hospitals; *Journal of Homeland Security and Emergency Management* 2(2): Article 1.

Baud, Nainan, N. (2008); Negotiated spaces‖ for representation in Mumbai: Ward committees, advanced locality management and the politics of middle-class activism; *Environment and Urbanization*, October 2008, 20: 483–499, https:/doi.org/10.1177/0956247808096124

Berkes, Fikret (2007); Understanding uncertainty reducing vulnerability: Lessons from resilience thinking; *Natural Hazards* 41: 283–295.

Bosher L.S. and Dainty A.R.J. (2011), 'Disaster risk reduction and 'built-in' resilience: Towards overarching principles for construction practice', *Disasters: The Journal of Disaster Studies, Policy and Management*, 35(1), pp. 1–18.

Bosher, L. S., Dainty, A., Carrillo, P., Glass, J., Price, A. (2007); Realising a resilient and sustainable built environment: Towards a strategic agenda for the United Kingdom; *Disasters* 31(3): 236–255.

Bruneau, M. (2003); A framework to quantitatively assess and enhance the seismic resilience of communities; *Earthquake Spectra, Earthquake Engineering Research Institute* 19(4): 733–752.

Carpenter, S., Walker, B., Anderies, J. M., Abel, N. (2001); From metaphor to measurement: Resilience of what to what? *Ecosystems* 4: 756–781.

Chang, S. E. (2010); Urban disaster recovery: A measurement framework and its application to the 1995 Kobe earthquake; *Disasters* 34(2): 303–327.

Comfort, L.K. (1994); Self organization in complex system: Integrating theory and practice in dynamic system; *Journal of Public Administration Research and Theory* 4(3): 393–410.

Comfort, L. K. (1999); *Shared Risk: Complex Systems in Seismic Response*. Oxford: Elsevier Science.

Comfort, L.K., Boin, A. and Demchak, C. (2010), *Designing Resilience: Preparing for Extreme Eevents*. University of Pittsburgh Press, Pittsburgh.

Cutter, S.L., Burton, C.G., Emrich, C.T. (2010); Disaster resilience indicators for benchmarking baseline conditions; *Journal of Homeland Security and Emergency Management* 7(1): 1–22.

Da Silva, J., Kernaghan, S. and Luque, A. (2012). 'A systems approach to meeting the challenges of urban climate change', *International Journal of Urban Sustainable Development*, 4(2), pp. 125–145. http://dx.doi.org/10.1080/19463138.2012.718279

Duit, A., Galaz, V. (2008); Governance and complexity – Emerging issues for governance theory; *Governance: An International Journal of Policy, Administration, and Institutions* 21(3): 311–335.

Eiser, R., Bostrom, A., Burton, I., Johnston, D., McClure, J., Paton, D., Pligt, J., White, M. P. (2012); Risk interpretation and action: A conceptual framework for responses to natural hazards; *International Journal of Disaster Risk Reduction*. Oxford: Elsevier. October 2012, 1: 5–16.

Folke, C. (2006); Resilience: The emergence of a perspective for social-ecological systems analyses; *Global Environmental Change* 16: 253–267.

Godschalk, D. (2003); Urban hazard mitigation: Creating resilient cities; *Natural Hazard Review* 4(3): 136–143.

Holling, C. S. (1973); Resilience and stability of ecological systems; *Annual Review of Ecology and Systematic* 4: 1–23.

Holling, C.S. (2001); Understanding the complexity of economic, ecological, and social systems; *Ecosystems* 4: 390–405.

IPCC (2001); *Climate Change 2001. Proceedings of Third Assessment Report of the Intergovernmental Panel on Climate Change*. London: Cambridge University Press.

Lagadec, P. and Topper, B. (2012); How crises model the modern world; *Journal of Risk Analysis and Crisis Response* 2(1): 21–33.

Lalonde, C. (2004); In search of archetypes in crisis management; *Journal of Contingencies and Crisis Management* 12(2): 76–88.

Lee, et al. (2013), 'Resilience: A meta analytic approach', *Journal of counseling & Development JCD*, 91(3).

Lorenz, D. F. (2010); The diversity of resilience: Contributions from a social science perspectives; *Natural Hazards*, DOI 10.1007/s11069–010–9654-y.

Low, et al. (2003); *Redundancy and Diversity: Do They Influence Optimal Management; Navigating Socio- Ecological System; Building Resilience for Complexity and Change*. Cambridge: Cambridge University Press, pp. 83–114.

Madini, A., Jackson, S. (2009); Towards a conceptual framework for resilience engineering; *IEEE System Journal*.

Manyena, S.B. (2006); The concept of resilience revisited; *Disasters* 30(4): 433–450.

McEntire, D.A. (2003); Searching for a holistic paradigm and policy guide: A proposal for the future of emergency managementǁ; *International Journal of Emergency Management* 1(3): 298–308.

McEntire, D., Floyd, D. (2003); Applying sustainability to the study of disasters: An assessment of strengths and weaknesses; *Sustainable Communities Review* 6(1/2): 14–21.

Mehrotra, N. (2010); Disaster management: Need of revival in policy framework; *Institute of Town Planners India Journal* 7(2): 98–102, ISSN: 0537–9679.

Mehrotra, N. (2014); Research on emergence of self organization through resilience in cities with system perspective; *International Journal of Complexity in Leadership and Management* (IJCLM) 2(4).

Mehrotra, N. (2015); Disaster management: Role of transparency and disclosure, in *Transparency Disclosure and Governance*. A.K. Singh, Ravi Pandey (eds) CPC, pp. 170–188.

Mileti, D. (1999); *Disaster by Design*. Washington, DC: Joseph Henry Press.

Morehouse, B. J., Henderson, M., Kalabokidis, K. (2011); Wildland fire governance: Perspective from Greece; *Journal of Environment Policy and Planning*, December 13(4): 349–371.
Ostrom, E. (2005); *Understanding Institutional Diversity*. Princeton, NJ: Princeton University Press.
Paton, D. (2014); Disaster ready communities: A social-cognitive perspective; *Continuity* Q3–2014: 13–15.
Paton & Johnston (2006) *Disaster Resilience: An Integrated Approach. Charles Thomas.*
Peacock, et al. (2010); *Advancing the Resilience of Coastal Localities: Implementing and Sustaining the Use of Resilience Indicators*. College Station, TX: Hazard Reduction and Recovery Centre.
Pelling and High (2005); Understanding adaptation: What social capital offer assessment of adaptive capacity; *Global Enviromental Change*
Raschky, Paul (2008); Institutions and the losses from natural disasters; *Natural Hazard and Earth System Sciences* 8: 627–634.
Renn, O. (2005); White paper no.1 risk governance: Towards an integrative approach. Annexes by Peter Graham. International Risk Governance Council, Geneva
Rose, A., Krausmam, E. (2013); An economic framework for development of resilience index for business recovery; *International Journal of Disaster Risk Reduction* 5: 73–83.
Silva, Jo da, Kernaghan, S., Andrés, L. (2012); A systems approach to meeting the challenges of urban climate change; *International Journal of Urban Sustainable Development*, HTTPS:/DOI.ORG/10.1080/19463138.2012.718279
Simonovic, Slobodan (2011); *System Approach of Management of Disasters, Methods and Applications*. Singapore: Wiley Publications.
Stephenson, A., Vargo, J., Seville, E. (2010); Measuring and comparing organisational resilience; *Australian Journal of Emergency Management* 25(2): 27–32.
Takeda, M. B., Helms, M. H. (2006); Bureaucracy meet catastrophe, analysis of Hurricane Katrina efforts and their implication on Emergency Governance; *International Journal of Public Sector Management* 19(4): 397–411.
Tierney, K., Bruneau, M. (2007); Conceptualizing and measuring resilience: A key to disaster loss reduction; *TR News*, pp. 14–17.
Tierney, K. J. (2002). 'Not Again! Recycling Disaster Myths m the Aftermath of 9–11', Paper presented at the 9P mua~ meeting of the American Sociological Association, Chicago, IL, USA, August 16–19.
Walker, B. and Salt, D. (2006), *Resilience Thinking: Sustaining Ecosystems and People in a Changing World,* Island Press, Washington, DC.
Wildavsky, A. (1991); *Searching for Safety*. New Brunswick, NJ: Transaction Publishers.

# 14

# Risk management in the bioeconomy

*Jutta Geldermann*

## Introduction

Current industrial production is based largely on fossil energy resources. The twin goals of reducing greenhouse gas emissions and moving from finite fossil resources to sustainable renewable resources are driving the search for alternative energy inputs and feedstocks. The possibilities for using agricultural and forest plants for raw materials and energy are manifold, and their cultivation has increased accordingly in recent years. Cascade and by-product utilization are major strategies to increase resource efficiency, which can be a key economic advantage in competitive businesses and can also limit environmental impacts. These strategies are characterized by multiple, sequential utilization of the same input prior to its energetic conversion at the end of the life cycle. This approach leads to more complex production networks, however, since it requires companies from previously unrelated industries to collaborate and learn how to utilize residual and fresh biomass in new value chains (Kircher, 2012b). Moreover, innovative material developments significantly affect feedstock production, industrial processes, production sites, infrastructure and logistics, distribution network structures, and trade.

Against this backdrop, companies in this emerging bioeconomy are experiencing new risks and uncertainties. Fluctuations in the quantity and quality of harvested plants and changes in the material properties arising from multiple usage of resources are just two of the challenges to creating resource-efficient value chains in production processes. Both generate a need for careful and flexible planning. How the enterprises involved can quantify the desired resource efficiency is an open question, however, since efficiency and resilience are often at odds with one another. There is also increasing social pressure to promote sustainability, a factor that must also be accounted for in any evaluation. Prudent risk management is a prerequisite for sustainable development. Assessing and managing risks, however, is not a simple task and requires input from science, government, industry, and society (Renn, 2008, 2015; Renn et al., 2011).

Although there are numerous techniques for decision analysis available to help address current environmental issues, their appropriateness in the different contexts to which they might be applied needs further study (French and Geldermann, 2005). The aim of this chapter is to offer an analytic approach for structuring decision problems regarding the use of renewable resources for industrial feedstocks and fuels. First, some risks and uncertainties in the bioeconomy are briefly introduced. Then, the Cynefin framework, developed by Snowden (2002; Snowden and Boone, 2007) on the basis of concepts from knowledge management and organizational strategy is presented. This approach assigns situations to certain "domains" defined by cause-and-effect relationships, which helps to assess and classify decision situations more accurately and leads in turn to more appropriate responses (French and Niculae, 2005). Subsequently, the implications for decision makers operating in the bioeconomy are elaborated and put into context with risk management. Finally, some conclusions are drawn.

## 1 Risks and uncertainties in the bioeconomy

To address global climate change, fossil resource limitations, and geopolitical tensions and to exploit the economic opportunities inherent in new technologies for the bioeconomy, several countries are developing strategies to promote the change from finite fossil feedstocks to sustainable biomass resources (Kircher, 2012a, 2012b, 2015). The bioeconomy, as it is called in Germany and Finland, or biobased economy, as the Dutch call it, refers to the sustainable and innovative use of renewable resources to provide food, feed, and industrial products with enhanced properties. Besides economic growth, the bioeconomy also targets food security, climate protection, and natural resource conservation. It is characterized by networked value chains of products in different industrial sectors and by the high-quality utilization of by-products and residues.

What are some of the challenges for production planning in the bioeconomy? Most obviously, the utilization of by-products. Cascade utilization is a much-discussed option for the sequential use of biogenous resources for material and energy. Cascading uses products or their components comprehensively within the economic system via a sequence of multiple material and – at the end of the life cycle – energetic use (Sirkin and Houten, 1994; Haberl and Geissler, 2000). Here is a typical example for the cascade utilization of a tree trunk: solid wood beams (timber) and boards or other solid wood products are produced for the building and furniture industry from the core (Gärtner et al., 2013; Carus et al., 2014; Brosowski et al., 2015; Mantau, 2015). Wood-based panels (particleboard, fiberboard) or pulp and paper products are produced from the sawmill by-products (industrial waste wood). At the end of their lifetime, the original solid timber products are chipped and ground to particles and fibers for wood-based panel production. Eventually, these wood-based panel products can also be recycled to produce new panel products. Finally, at the very end of the cascade, all the wood-based panels and paper products can be burned for energy. By-products from the wood-based panel industry as well as the pulp and paper industry can also be used for energy production (Taskhiri et al., 2016). Figure 14.1 shows a biomass value pyramid that depicts where biomass could have the highest value added (Bosman, 2014). The residues from higher-value processes can be re-used lower in the pyramid.

Unrelated industries must form cooperative networks and learn how to create new value chains of global dimensions. Although the chemical industry has not in the past used bio-precursors delivered from bio-refineries in bulk volumes, refineries must learn to use residual biomass; farmers need economical logistics to exploit the value of residual biomass; and the forestry sector should shift its focus from bulk to high-end specialty products (Kircher, 2012b). Figure 14.2 illustrates the complexity and interdependency inherent in the value chains. For example, material innovations on the nanoscale, such as wood plastic composites, will broadly impact planning, even up to the highest strategic levels.

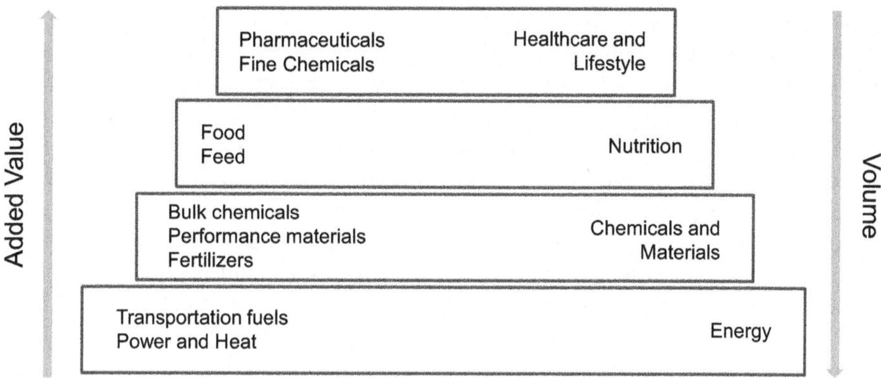


*Figure 14.1* Biomass value pyramid

*Source*: Bosman (2014)

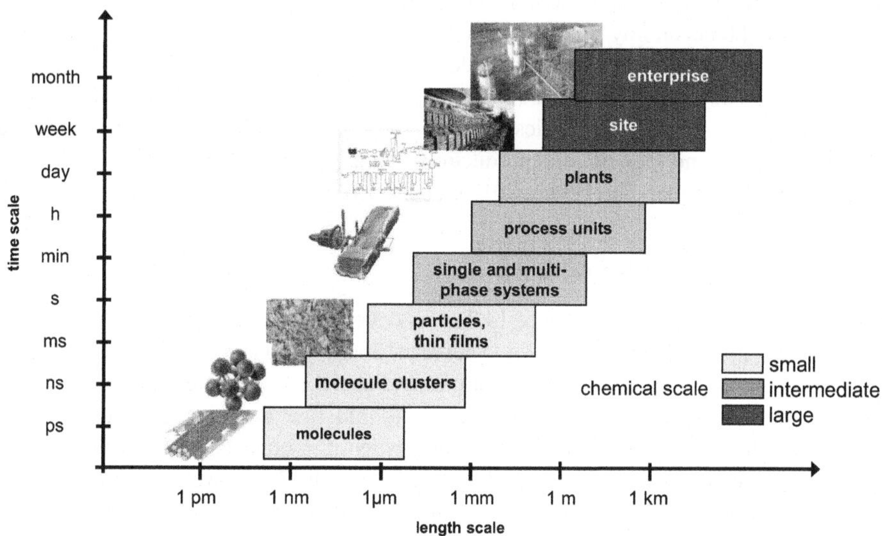


*Figure 14.2* Multiscale, interdisciplinary model and simulation approach across the entire value chain

*Source*: Charpentier (2002)

The new value chains connecting biomass, energy, and chemical production are challenging for three main reasons: First, the quality (in terms of chemical composition or content of extractive matter) and yields (harvesting and logging levels) of renewable resources fluctuate significantly. This, along with price fluctuations, can strongly influence operational planning. Increasing the use of renewable raw materials in industrial production networks thus requires more refined operational planning approaches. Second, the newly developing production-oriented value chains call for *completely new technologies and processes*. Academia and industry are investigating innovative theoretical concepts through research and development (R&D) and scaling up to commercialization. Some of these new concepts are quite radical (or even called disruptive) and aim at producing and doing things in an entirely new way, rather than doing the old things more efficiently. They may have a dramatic impact on global feedstock production, infrastructure and logistics, trade, industrial processes, and production sites, with industrial as well as emerging economies involved (Kircher, 2012b). However, radical innovations often face fierce resistance from vested interests in the energy, petrochemical, agriculture, and forestry sectors. And third, the growing industrial demand for bio-feedstock drives land acquisitions and raises land prices in biomass-producing areas.

Against this background, achieving *societal acceptance*, establishing legal frameworks, research and economic policies, and governmental measures, and making wise industrial investments become extremely difficult and complex goals. Kircher (2012b) concludes that

> translating strategy into industrial reality is challenging and complex. To achieve societal support, the strategy needs to be communicated to the public, politics, academia, and industry. A consensus-building process is necessary and should be initiated and moderated by independent and broadly accepted institutions.

In this chapter, we highlight the implications for managerial decision making in companies within networked bioeconomy supply chains. In this setting, entrepreneurs must balance many operational variables, which results in such decision problems as location planning (Karschin and Geldermann, 2015), capacity planning (Lauven et al., 2014), supply planning (Wiedenmann and Geldermann, 2015), logistics for new networks (Taskhiri et al., 2016; Mulyati and Geldermann, 2017), and logistics and production planning for bioenergy villages (Lerche and Geldermann, 2015; Eigner-Thiel et al., 2013), to name just a few.

## 2 Snowden's Cynefin framework

Snowden's Cynefin framework (Figure 14.3) was developed in the context of understanding knowledge and knowledge management (Snowden, 2002; Snowden and Boone, 2007). Cynefin is Welsh for "habitat" and includes cultural and social as well as environmental aspects in its meaning. Snowden divides decision contexts into four domains: obvious, knowable, complex, and chaotic. The fifth, disorder, applies when it is unclear which of the other four contexts predominates. French and Niculae (2005; French, 2013) were the first to put the Cynefin model into context with decision making in different decision situations. The Cynefin framework can help managers sort issues according to the relationship between cause and effect, in order to identify appropriate decision making.

Simple or known contexts prevail in the *obvious domain*, where all physical systems and behaviors are well understood and modeled. Relationships between cause and effect are known, and thus the consequences of actions may be predicted with confidence. In this domain of scientific knowledge, decision making tends to consist of recognizing patterns in the situation and responding with well-rehearsed actions, a process often referred to as recognition-primed decision making. Best practices and straightforward directives can be applied, and exhaustive communication among managers and others is not usually required, since disagreement about needed actions is rare.

Complicated contexts, unlike simple ones, may contain multiple right answers, so that not everyone can clearly see the relation between cause and effect. Thus, in the *knowable domain*, cause and effect relationships exist and are generally understood, but there is insufficient data available to immediately and firmly forecast the consequences of an action. Experts are needed to analyze and diagnose the problem. To make a decision, there is a need for data acquisition

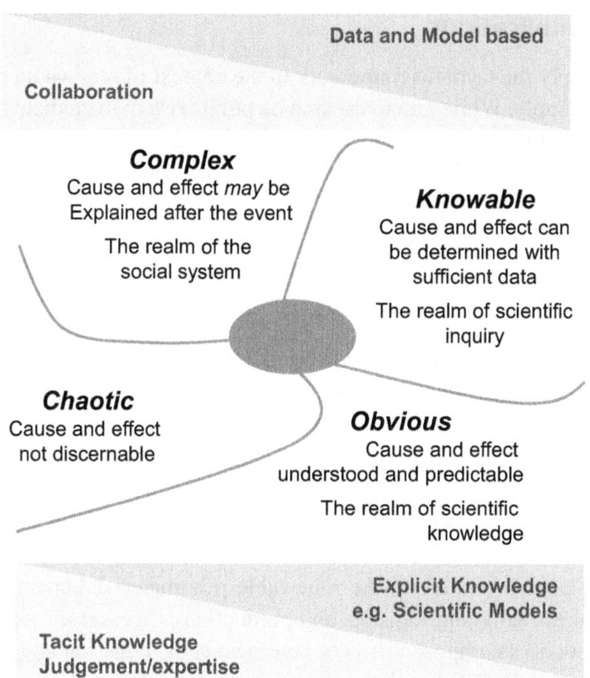


*Figure 14.3* The differing emphases on tacit and explicit knowledge in the Cynefin domains

*Source*: Snowden (2002) following (French, 2008; French, 2013; Stewart et al., 2013; French and Niculae, 2005)

and assimilation and for analysis rather than recognition. Decision support will include the fitting and use of models to forecast the potential outcomes of actions with appropriate levels of uncertainty.

In the *complex domain*, systems involve many interacting causes and effects, and understanding is often only possible in retrospect. Typically, such complexity arises in social systems, where knowledge is at best qualitative, since there are too many potential interactions to disentangle particular causes and effects. Therefore, there are no precise models to predict system behaviors. Analysis is still possible, but its style will be broader, with less emphasis on details. Decision support focuses more on exploring judgments and issues and on developing broad strategies that are flexible enough to accommodate changes as the situation evolves.

In the *chaotic domain*, things happen that are beyond common experience; relationships between cause and effect are impossible to determine, since they shift constantly. Thus, no manageable patterns exist. Decision support cannot be analytical because there is no concept of how to break things down into an analysis. Managers simply need to take probing actions and see what happens, until they can make some sense of the situation and thus gradually draw the context back into one of the other domains. Snowden and Boone (2007, p. 6) also highlight the danger that managers are not able to switch styles to match the shifting contexts.

Altogether, they conclude that simple, complicated, complex, and chaotic contexts all call for different managerial responses. Likewise, in dealing with renewable resources in industry and the energy supply, it is important to identify the governing contexts in order to choose the decision-making tools and style appropriate to the evolving business environment.

## 3 Managerial implications

We now want to apply the Cynefin framework to the context of renewable resources in industry and the energy supply. While much research on public risk management has been published in the scientific literature (Renn, 2008, 2015; French and Niculae, 2005), there is not much available to help managers in industrial companies. Therefore, the focus here is on the managerial implications of the different decision contexts under the risks and uncertainties typically associated with the evolving bioeconomy.

### 1 *Obvious domain*

In the obvious domain, causes and effects are understood and predictable. Decision making relies on scientific knowledge and tends to consist of recognition patterns in the situation and responding to well-rehearsed actions (French and Niculae, 2005). In the context of renewable resources in industry and the energy supply, where the raw material supply varies in space and time, countermeasures have been established, for example, in inventory management. Renewable raw materials are usually harvested within a short period, whereas a specific quantity and quality must be kept on hand for industrial processes throughout the year. During transport, storage, and post-harvest treatment, the renewable raw materials' chemical properties may change. This requires realigning logistics and production processes throughout supply chains and production networks composed of very heterogeneous industrial and non-industrial partners. Operations research (OR) has developed numerous models and solution methods for use in forestry and wood-processing (Rönnqvist et al., 2015; Taskhiri et al., 2016), many of which focus on uncertainties in quantity and time (cf. Table 14.1).

So-called linear (routine) risk problems are quite simple in structure, the probabilities of harm are well understood, and the risks and their reduction measures are noncontroversial, and thus do not require a sophisticated approach that involves all potentially affected parties (Renn, 2008, 2015). But Renn (2008, p. 9) also points out that one should be aware, however, that frequently risks that appear linear turn out to be more complex, uncertain or ambiguous than originally assessed. Figure 14.1 and Figure 14.2 illustrate the intertwining production processes in the bioeconomy, where very heterogeneous industries and economic

*Table 14.1* Uncertainties in cascading use of renewable resources (Geldermann, 2012)

| *Uncertainty concerning* | *Example* | *Countermeasure or consequence* |
|---|---|---|
| Quantity | Competition between energy and material usage<br>Stronger variability because of climate change → storm losses | Wood material substitutes (e.g. substitution by straw)<br>Disruptive innovations?<br>More efficient logistics |
| Quality | Changing chemical, physical or biological properties<br>Quality change due to substitution of wood by straw or miscanthus<br>Pest infestation, storm losses | Adjustment of production processes (e.g. reduction of proportion of silicon)<br>Energetic use |
| Time | Uncertain amounts of used raw-materials within the utilization cascade | Fast and comprehensive information of all network partners |

sectors – each with its own specific planning challenges – must cooperate with one another. Supposedly small deviations can pose industry-wide and global risks to the whole supply chain – as many recent examples in the automobile and computer industry have shown (see also Sheffi in this volume). Biomass is prone to infestations, for example, and it was relatively minor logistical mistakes in 19th century Ireland that caused the potato blight and the subsequent great famine. In former times, the petro-industry was hailed as a great advance, since it meant that agricultural and industrial production no longer depended on uncertain agricultural yields, but had access to reliable and plentiful sources of oil.

## 2 *Knowable domain*

In the knowable (or complicated) domain, cause and effect can be determined via scientific inquiry, given sufficient data. For instance, replacing fossil-based raw materials with biomass requires investigating changes in chemical, physical, and biological properties and modifying production processes. Currently, many researchers are studying innovative wood material development (Alfranca et al., 2014; Hansen et al., 2014; Roos et al., 2014). Engineering skills allow one to sense-analyze-respond and to find new process adaptations (French). Thus, changes in the quality of raw materials may demand a different decision-making toolbox than changes in quantity and time (see Table 14.1). In the knowable domain, there is more analysis than recognition, and one must learn from available data about the precise circumstances being faced. Decision support uses models and much explicit knowledge of cause and effect to forecast (with appropriate levels of uncertainty) the potential results of a given action (French and Niculae, 2005).

Because the bioeconomy deals with the sustainable and innovative use of renewable resources to provide food, feed, and industrial products, a verification of the positive effects would be desirable. Quantification of the positive environmental effects and the trade-offs with other consequences of cascade utilization, however, remains elusive both in theory and in practice, because of the manifold interdependencies in the bioeconomy supply network (see Figure 14.1 and Figure 14.2). At first glance, assessing the environmental impacts of a product or production service appears easy, since a suitable instrument (i.e., life cycle assessment, or LCA) is readily available. LCA traces the environmental consequences of products, services, and processes "from cradle to grave" in order to identify problematic parts of the life cycle and specify what gains can be made via alternative ways of fulfilling the function. Choosing between ecological profiles involves balancing different types of impacts and is typical of multi-criteria decision problems, where explicit or implicit trade-offs are needed to construct an overall judgment (French and Geldermann, 2005; Belton and Stewart, 2002; Seppälä et al., 2001). However, metrics for economic and environmental impacts and for resource efficiency are still missing (Watson et al., 2010; Malhotra et al., 2013; Bach et al., 2014). Moreover, choosing the right system boundaries for meaningful comparison with other products or production processes is not trivial. How should one compare bulk chemicals produced from crude oil with those from biomass, for example? Should indirect land use changes be taken into account? And how can one compare plastics, wood, and wood plastic composites without clear knowledge about their usage phase and future recycling modes?

Most environmental decisions have much in common. There are many stakeholders[1] and uncertainties involved; there are multiple, possibly conflicting criteria; and there are impacts that extend far into the future (French and Geldermann, 2005). In the case of bioenergy, the broad range of stakeholders and their preferences, viewpoints, and values can complicate seemingly easy decisions, such as location planning for a community biogas plant (Uhlemair et al., 2014; Eigner-Thiel et al., 2013). As soon as values and beliefs come into play, transparency regarding subjective judgments and the knowledge elements that have shaped the decision parameters becomes indispensable (Renn, 2008).

## 3 Complex domain

Systems with many interacting causes and effects form the complex domain, where tacit and explicit knowledge may be extensive, but is unlikely to be comprehensive (French/Nicola). According to Snowden and Boone (2007), much of contemporary business has shifted into this domain, since major changes have become part and parcel of the modern business environment and these introduce unpredictability and flux. For example, the shift towards more renewable resources has brought major changes to energy suppliers and other industries. The changing business environment is creating an incentive for management to adopt new approaches to improve resource efficiency along the entire value chain – from design, supply chain, and operations to consumer purchasing and end of life (Odenwald and Berg, 2014).

This complex domain is also the realm of social systems, where cause and effect may be determinable only after the fact. Ambiguity arises when individual actors or stakeholders value some input or output of the system differently (Renn et al., 2011). Decision support will focus more on exploring judgment and issues, and on developing broad strategies that are flexible enough to accommodate changes as the situation evolves. For example, first generation biofuels – biodiesel, bioalcohol, and syngas – were derived from starch, sugar, animal fats, and vegetable oil. After an initial positive ascription as environmentally friendly alternatives to fossil fuels, they were later much criticized because of many ethical and sustainability issues (e.g. Mohr and Raman, 2013). As a consequence, second-generation biorefineries have now been developed that use residual biomass as feedstocks (Lauven). Plant managers preoccupied with the technical challenges of substituting raw materials have been suddenly confronted with fierce public reactions. Especially when it comes to sustainability, decision problems are inherently complex. As (Renn, 2008) puts it: "At the foundation of sustainable development is the need for a well-rounded balance between effectiveness, efficiency, resilience and social cohesion." *Effectiveness* is the degree to which objectives are achieved and the extent to which targeted problems are solved. However, the comprehensive elucidation of the desired targets is a difficult task, given the manifold interdependencies, as indicated in Figure 14.1 and Figure 14.2. Effectiveness is determined without reference to costs (meaning "doing the thing right"), while *efficiency* (meaning "doing the right thing") describes the degree to which scarce resources are used to reach the intended goal (Renn, 2008). Many methods from OR have been developed to analyze whether the chosen option achieves the desired output with the fewest resources – within certain system boundaries and under a number of restrictions.

*Resilience* describes the ability of a system to remain functional even under severe stress or unfamiliar conditions. British Standard, BS65000(2014) defines "organizational resilience" as the "ability of an organization to anticipate, prepare for, and respond and adapt to incremental change and sudden disruptions in order to survive and prosper." When drawing renewable energy from wind or solar power, for example, the volatility of the energy sources makes obvious the need for backup systems to increase resilience.

Across organizational boundaries, *social cohesion* is gaining importance, since it acknowledges the need for social integration and collective identity despite pluralistic values and lifestyles (Renn, 2008). For example, social criteria for assessing different bioenergy paths' sustainability can be divided into four sub-categories: acceptance, participation, psychological consequences and employment. Eigner-Thiel et al. (2013) discuss whether a biogas plant has different consequences for rekindling village life, strengthening the democratic process, consolidating a region's economic potential, and strengthening rural development, depending on whether it is operated by an electric service provider, a farmer, or a village cooperative (as a bioenergy village). Here, multicriteria decision support can help distinguish between the subjective and objective preferences specified during the decision process.

In many countries of the world, stakeholders, experts, and the public are being invited to take part in decision making about management options to deal with environmental and health risks and facilitate a transition into a sustainable future (Renn, 2008). The popularity associated with public participation, however, obscures the challenge of how to ensure that risk management reflects the main goal of effectiveness, efficiency, and fair burden-sharing. From a managerial viewpoint, it is an open question how to incorporate public preferences, integrate public input into the management process, and assign the appropriate roles to technical experts, stakeholders, and members of the public. Renn (2008, p. 5) stresses that "reaching consensus and building-up trust on highly complex subjects such as global change is, however, much more difficult. Being inclusive and open to social groups does not, therefore, guarantee constructive cooperation by those who are invited to cooperate," and "that actors, along with developing faith in their own competence, start to place trust in each other and have confidence in the process of risk management. This is particularly true for the local level where the participants are familiar with each other and have immediate access to the issues" (as in the case of bioenergy villages, see Eigner-Thiel et al., 2013; Uhlemair et al., 2014).

## 4 Chaos domain

In the chaos domain, the relationships between cause and effect are not discernible, and there are the high levels of uncertainty, incomplete understanding, and imperfect data typical of dynamic open systems. Decision support cannot be analytical, since there is no concept of how to break things down into an analysis. Managers simply need to take some action and see what happens, probing until they can make some sense of the situation, gradually nudging the context into one of the other domains (French and Niculae, 2005).

Natural disasters, for example, are one source of chaos. Storms, floods, and earthquakes can have multiple effects on various parts of the supply chain and energy supply, and pest infestations can have severe consequences for human health. Increasing urbanization and industrialization, combined with the greater vulnerability (increasing susceptibility and high capital intensity) of new technologies and the rising complexity of supply chains, means that natural disasters will cause increasing future losses in industrial facilities. Although such emergency situations may differ in their causes and the dimensions of their impact, they all share the characteristic of sudden onset and the necessity for coherent and effective emergency management (French and Geldermann, 2005).

For strategic planning in the bioeconomy, it has to be taken into consideration that raw material cultivation may be subject to long-term changes, such as climate change, or irregularly recurring events, such as natural calamities. In forestry, calamities include severe wind damage or heavy infestations of fungi and insects, with high overall economic consequences. Extreme weather events, if they occur, also have a substantial influence on production planning. The most frequent collapses into chaos occur because of complacency in putatively simple contexts.

A *crisis* (or *emergency situation*) is a sequence of sudden, disturbing events harming an organization. It generally arises on short notice and triggers a feeling of fear and threat among the affected individuals. It can be caused by technological failure, machine malfunction, or problems with the internet, for example.

Modern industries can be economically affected by natural disasters in two ways (Geldermann et al., 2008). First, there may be *direct losses* from physical damage to buildings, industrial installations, and inventories. Second, there may be *indirect losses*, that is, losses that are not directly caused by the extreme event, but are spatially or temporally separated from it. In general, these indirect losses emerge from damages initiated by disruption of physical and economic linkages, for example, the interruption of production or a reduction in investment. Extra costs, such as emergency costs or the costs of remediation measures, can also be regarded as indirect losses and may add up to enormous amounts within the affected companies.

Neglecting minor issues at the beginning of an emergency can lead to a major crisis and a state of uncertainty. Crisis management prepares individuals to face unexpected developments and adverse conditions in the organization with courage and determination. It should help managers devise strategies to lead their organizations out of the uncertain circumstances and decide on a future course of action.

Initially, there is a need for urgent decisions under stressful circumstances. Subsequently, there is a need for decisions on remediation strategies to bring the affected area back to *a* – not necessarily *the* pre-existing – "normality" (French and Niculae, 2005). Often, the teams faced with handling the emergencies have not worked together before – although they may have rehearsed a bit during exercises within other teams. Most importantly, they need to balance the needs of many stakeholders. *Risk communication* becomes crucial to maintaining public and stakeholder trust (Renn and Levine, 1990; French and Niculae, 2005). There is the need to negotiate a shared meaning, which requires tacit knowledge and perspectives about aspects of complex behaviors from a variety of disciplines. Tacit knowledge is best shared through multidisciplinary discussion, such as group work and, particularly, decision conferencing and facilitated workshops (French and Niculae, 2005).

## 4 Conclusions for risk management

The bioeconomy is characterized by networked value chains for various products from biogenous raw materials in different industrial sectors and by a high-quality utilization of by-products and residues. Companies in this newly emerging sector are experiencing several risks and uncertainties. While research aims to reduce uncertainties, the primary purpose of adopting a risk-based approach to decision making is to ensure that uncertainty is acknowledged and treated rigorously in the decision-making process (Willows et al., 2003). Most people demand healthy and safe products and technologies and expect regulatory agencies to reduce risk to levels deemed tolerable by the majority of people (Renn, 2008). Therefore, public risk management (also called risk governance) is concerned with generating and collecting knowledge about risks and making decisions about how to mitigate, control, or otherwise manage them. However, companies in networked supply chains subject to risk and uncertainty also need suitable tools for risk management that are based on prudent judgment competence. Only in this way can managers make the necessary trade-offs between risk, benefit, and other important impact categories.

The Cynefin framework, developed by Snowden (2002) on the basis of concepts from knowledge management and organizational strategy, can help managers sort the various types of decision situations by the nature of the relationship between cause and effect, in order to identify appropriate decision making and respond accordingly.

In the *obvious and knowable domains*, explicit knowledge can be deployed through databases, knowledge bases and models (French and Niculae, 2005). Here, decision making is the act of choosing from among a set of alternatives. The decision-making process includes recognizing and defining the nature of a decision situation, identifying alternatives, choosing the "best" (according to the desired outcome) alternative and putting it into practice. Decision models under certainty assume that a decision maker knows the alternatives with reasonable certainty, as well as the conditions associated with each one.

Decision models under risk are used when a decision must be made under conditions in which the availability of each alternative and its potential payoffs and costs are all associated with probability estimates. Risk is then the product of the probability (frequency or likelihood) of a consequence and its magnitude. In risk management, risk analysis combines three elements: hazard, vulnerability (in terms of susceptibility of the affected element) and exposure of assets. Such decisions are often based on past experiences. However, the inherent uncertainty in such models is often grossly underestimated and poorly represented (Niculae et al., 2004; Shepherd et al., 2006). To summarize, the contexts in the obvious and knowable spaces are necessarily repeatable or commonly occurring in a certain sense, such that a sufficient understanding and scientific theories allow for predictive models (Stewart et al., 2013).

Contents the *complex and chaotic domains* tend to be novel, and the latitude for judgment is greater, tools that aid collaboration and build judgment are needed (French and Niculae, 2005; Stewart et al., 2013). Disagreement often arises because of different values (or even worldviews; Renn, 2015), leading to diverging or conflicting interests and preferences (Stewart et al., 2013). Suitable participative processes should be designed that encourage the various actors to contribute in those areas in which they are competent and can thus help improve the quality of the final outcome (Renn, 2008, p. 7).

Stewart et al. (2013, p. 680) suggest the use of scenarios to articulate discussion between different stakeholders, allowing each to explore their preferences between alternative strategies in the context of a range of future worlds, which are ideal from the various viewpoints of the different subgroups in society. This way, a well-chosen set of scenarios could capture gross uncertainties through the differences between the scenarios. It would also allow for working with deterministic models, if carefully structured sensitivity analyses are supplement. Rare, high impact events, however, are even more difficult to anticipate and thus require specific forecasting methods (Goodwin and Wright, 2010).

A state of uncertainty exists when a decision maker either does not know all of the alternatives or does not know the risks consequences associated with each one. Uncertainty describes the quality of our knowledge concerning risk and may affect both the probability and consequence components of the risk. Managers must secure as much relevant information as possible and approach the situation logically and rationally. Intuition,[2] judgment, and experience significantly influence decision making under these conditions. The behavioral aspects of decision making (Geldermann and Rentz, 2003; Franco and Hämäläinen, 2016; Hämäläinen, 2015) must also be taken into account. These aspects reflect subjective considerations, such as tastes, political forces, intuition, escalation of commitment (where a decision maker stays with a decision, even when it appears wrong), risk propensity (the extent to which a decision maker will gamble when making a decision), and ethics.

Because the bioeconomy claims to support sustainability, its managers must consider a broad range of stakeholders – each with unique preferences, viewpoints, and values – when making decisions. Thus, the following questions on sustainability, fairness, and public acceptance that have to date been discussed primarily in public risk management also become relevant for industrial managers (Renn, 2008, p. 6):

- Does the option contribute to the overall goal of sustainability? Does it assist in sustaining vital ecological functions, economic prosperity, and social cohesion?
- Does the option burden the subjects of regulation in a fair and equitable manner?
- Will the option be accepted by those individuals who are affected by it? Are there cultural preferences or symbolic connotations that have a strong influence on how the risks are perceived?

As in public risk governance (Renn, 2008, p. 6), two major challenges of risk management are (1) generating and collecting knowledge about the risk and (2) deciding how to mitigate, control, or otherwise manage it. Thus, companies should deliberate whether risk governance frameworks (e.g., the multi-stage model of stakeholder participation based on the risk governance framework published by the Geneva-based International Risk Governance Council (IGRC) in 2005) could be modified for managerial tasks. Risk governance applies the principles of good governance to the identification, assessment, management, and communication of risks. Industrial risk management takes a different perspective, however.

For example, a company's crisis management includes developing mitigation measures, structuring insurance protection, and planning emergency management. Estimating industrial asset values as part of the total vulnerability and risk assessment is also an important input for planning and relief decisions in industrial crisis management and allows judgments about acceptable expense levels for risk mitigation measures. Furthermore, industrial asset estimation helps identify exceptionally vulnerable points of the supply chain and thus shows where broad and consistent planning of emergency management and provisions is fundamental. These aspects are of special importance in the energy sector, for example, where securing a continuous supply of electricity or gas is essential. To ensure effective local emergency management, it is crucial that required emergency resources be available in appropriate places (for instance emergency power aggregate in a bioenergy village).

## 5 Summary

To reduce dependency on exhaustible fossil resources and decelerate climate change, industry will have to increase its use of sustainably produced biomass for feedstocks and fuel. An important strategy for economic competitiveness of biomass inputs is to increase their utilization efficiency by applying the cascade utilization principle. Cascade utilization inherently brings additional complexity into production, however, and with it, additional risk. Companies that previously operated independently must form networks and cooperate in planning and coordination tasks. New feedstocks must be integrated into existing value chains or new value chains must be developed to take advantage of new inputs. These changes impact nearly all aspects of industrial production, from process engineering to production siting to logistics, infrastructure, and marketing. On top of these inherent risks come risks specific to biomass inputs, such as fluctuations in quality and availability and changes in material properties that occur as materials cascade through the production network.

To manage this complex risk portfolio, decision makers can resort to a variety of decision analytical techniques. However, it would be useful for managers to have more clarity about which techniques are most suitable under which circumstances. This chapter helps provide such clarity by applying Snowden's Cynefin framework specifically to the decision-making context of the "bioeconomy." The model presented offers bioeconomy managers a practical first step toward making more effective planning decisions according to the prevalent decision context.

## Notes

1 Renn (2008, p. 3) makes a distinction between *stakeholders* (socially organized groups who are or will be affected by or have a strong interest in the outcome of an event or activity), the *directly affected public* (individuals and non-organized groups who will experience the positive or negative impacts of an event or activity), the *observing public* (the media, cultural elites, and opinion leaders), and the *general public* (all individuals who are not directly affected by the risk and are part of the emerging public opinion on the issue).

2 Intuition is often described as an innate belief about something, without conscious deliberation, which may be based on years of experience and practice in decision making in similar situations.

## References


Alfranca, O., Voces, R., Herruzo, A. C. and Diaz-Balteiro, L. (2014), "Effects of innovation on the European wood industry market structure", *Forest Policy and Economics*, Vol. 40, pp. 40–47.

Bach, V., Scheider, L., Berger, M. and Finkbeiner, M. (2014), "Methoden und Indikatoren zur Messung von Ressourceneffizienz im Kontext der Nachhaltigkeit", in Thomé-Kozminsky, K. J. and Goldmann, D. (Eds.), *Recycling und Rohstoffe: Band 7*, TK-Verlag, Neuruppin, pp. 87–101.

Belton, V. and Stewart, T. J. (2002), *Multiple Criteria Decision Analysis: An Integrated Approach*, Springer US, Boston, MA.

Bosman, R. (2014), "Benchmarking Finnish and Dutch bioeconomy transition governance", No. December.

Brosowski, A., Adler, P., Erdmann, G., Stinner, W., Thrän, D., Mantau, U., Blanke, C., Mahro, B., Hering, T. and Reinholdt, G. (2015), *Biomassepotenziale von Rest- und Abfallstoffen (Status quo in Deutschland), Schriftenreihe Nachwachsende Rohstoffe.*

Carus, M., Raschka, A., Fehrenbach, H., Rettenmaier, N., Dammer, L., Köppen, S., Thöne, M., Dobroschke, S., Diekmann, L., Hermann, A., Hennenberg, K., Essel, R., Piotrowski, S., Detzel, A., Keller, H., Kauertz, B., Gärtner, S., Reinhardt and Joachim (2014), *Mehr Ressourceneffizienz und Klimaschutz durch nachhaltige stoffliche Nutzungen von Biomasse,* Dessau-Roßlau: UBA-Texte, German Federal Environmental Agency.

Charpentier, J.-C. (2002), "The triplet "molecular processes – product – process" engineering. The future of chemical engineering ?", *Chemical Engineering Science*, Vol. 57 No. 22–23, pp. 4667–4690.

Eigner-Thiel, S., Schmehl, M., Ibendorf, J. and Geldermann, J. (2013), "Assessment of Different Bioenergy Concepts in Terms of Sustainable Development", in Ruppert, H., Kappas, M. and Ibendorf, J. (Eds.), *Sustainable Bioenergy Production – An Integrated Approach*, Springer, Dordrecht, New York, pp. 339–384.

Franco, L. A. and Hämäläinen, R. P. (2016), "Behavioural operational research. Returning to the roots of the OR profession", *European Journal of Operational Research*, Vol. 249 No. 3, pp. 791–795.

French, S. (2008), *Cynefin: Repeatability, Science and Values*, European Working Group "Multiple Criteria Decision Aiding". Series 3, no. 17, Spring 2008.

French, S. (2013), "Cynefin, statistics and decision analysis", *Newsletter for the European Working Group "Multicriteria Decision Aiding."* Brussels.

French, S. and Geldermann, J. (2005), "The varied contexts of environmental decision problems and their implications for decision support", *Environmental Science & Policy*, Vol. 8 No. 4, pp. 378–391.

French, S. and Niculae, C. (2005), "Believe in the model. Mishandle the emergency", *Journal of Homeland Security and Emergency Management*, Vol. 2 No. 1.

Gärtner, S., Hienz, G., Keller, H. and Müller-Lindenauf, M. (2013), *Gesamtökologische Bewertung der Kaskadennutzung von Holz. Umweltauswirkungen stofflicher und energetischer Holznutzung im Vergleich.*, Heidelberg: IFEU.

Geldermann, J. (2012), "Einsatz nachwachsender Rohstoffe in der Produktion und Konsequenzen für die Planung", in Corsten, H. (Ed.), *Nachhaltigkeit: Unternehmerisches Handeln in globaler Verantwortung; Wissenschaftliche Tagung des Verbandes der Hochschullehrer für Betriebswirtschaftslehre e.V. an der Technischen Universität Kaiserslautern 2011*, Springer Gabler, Wiesbaden, pp. 191–213.

Geldermann, J., Merz, M., Bertsch, V., Hiete, M., Rentz, O., Seifert, I., Thieken, A.H., Borst, D. and Werner, U. (2008), "The reference installation approach for the estimation of industrial assets at risk", *European Journal of Industrial Engineering*, Vol. 2 No. 1, pp. 73–93.

Geldermann, J. and Rentz, O. (2003), "Environmental decisions and electronic democracy", *Journal of Multi-Criteria Decision Analysis*, Vol. 12 No. 2–3, pp. 77–92.

Goodwin, P. and Wright, G. (2010), "The limits of forecasting methods in anticipating rare events", *Technological Forecasting and Social Change*, Vol. 77 No. 3, pp. 355–368.

Haberl, H. and Geissler, S. (2000), "Cascade utilization of biomass: Strategies for a more efficient use of a scarce resource", *Ecological Engineering*, Vol. 16, pp. 111–121.

Hämäläinen, R.P. (2015), "Behavioural issues in environmental modelling – The missing perspective", *Environmental Modelling & Software*, Vol. 73, pp. 244–253.

Hansen, E., Nybakk, E. and Panwar, R. (2014), "Innovation insights from North American forest sector research: A literature review", *Forests*, Vol. 5 No. 6, pp. 1341–1355.

Karschin, I. and Geldermann, J. (2015), "Efficient cogeneration and district heating systems in bioenergy villages. An optimization approach", *Journal of Cleaner Production*, Vol. 104, pp. 305–314.

Kircher, M. (2012a), "How to turn industrial biotechnology into reality", *New Biotechnology*, Vol. 29 No. 2, pp. 243–247.

Kircher, M. (2012b), "The transition to a bio-economy. National perspectives", *Biofuels, Bioproducts and Biorefining*, Vol. 6 No. 3, pp. 240–245.

Kircher, M. (2015), "Sustainability of biofuels and renewable chemicals production from biomass", *Current Opinion in Chemical Biology*, Vol. 29, pp. 26–31.

Lauven, L.-P., Liu, B. and Geldermann, J. (2014), "Determinants of economically optimal cassava-to-ethanol plant capacities with consideration of GHG emissions", *Applied Thermal Engineering*, Vol. 70 No. 2, pp. 1246–1252.

Lerche, N. and Geldermann, J. (2015), "Integration of prospect theory into PROMETHEE – A case study concerning sustainable bioenergy concepts", *International Journal of Multicriteria Decision Making*, Vol. 5 No. 4, p. 309.

Malhotra, A., Melville, N.P. and Watson, R.T. (2013), "Spurring impactful research on information systems for environmental sustainability", *Management Information Systems Quarterly*, Vol. 37 No. 4, pp. 1265–1274.

Mantau, U. (2015), "Wood flow analysis: Quantification of resource potentials, cascades and carbon effects", *Biomass and Bioenergy*, Vol. 79, pp. 28–38.

Mohr, A. and Raman, S. (2013), "Lessons from first generation biofuels and implications for the sustainability appraisal of second generation biofuels", *Energy Policy*, Vol. 63 No. 100, pp. 114–122.

Mulyati, H. and Geldermann, J. (2017), "Managing risks in the Indonesian seaweed supply chain", *Clean Technologies and Environmental Policy, 19*(1), pp 175–189.

Niculae, C., French, S. and Carter, E. (2004), "Emergency management: Does it have a sufficiently comprehensive understanding of decision-making, process and context?", *Radiation Protection Dosimetry*, Vol. 109 No. 1–2, pp. 97–100.

Odenwald, T. and Berg, C. (2014), "A new perspective on enterprise resource management", *MIT Sloan Management Review*, No. Fall 2014, pp. 7–9.

Renn, O. (Ed.) (2008), *Stakeholder Involvement in Risk Governance: Paper for the AAAS Meeting*, Boston, 18–22 February 2008.

Renn, O. (2015), "Stakeholder and public involvement in risk governance", *International Journal of Disaster Risk Science*, Vol. 6 No. 1, pp. 8–20.

Renn, O., Klinke, A. and van Asselt, M. (2011), "Coping with complexity, uncertainty and ambiguity in risk governance. A synthesis", *AMBIO*, Vol. 40 No. 2, pp. 231–246.

Renn, O. and Levine, D. (1990), "Credibility and trust in risk communication", in Kasperson, R.E. and Stallen, P.J.M. (Eds.), *Communicating Risks to the Public: International Perspectives, Technology, Risk, and Society, An International Series in Risk Analysis*, Springer, Netherlands, Dordrecht, pp. 175–217.

Rönnqvist, M., D'Amours, S., Weintraub, A., Jofre, A., Gunn, E., Haight, R.G., Martell, D., Murray, A.T. and Romero, C. (2015), "Operations Research challenges in forestry: 33 open problems", *Annals of Operations Research, 232*(1), pp 11–40.

Roos, A., Lindström, M., Heuts, L., Hylander, N., Lind, E. and Nielsen, C. (2014), "Innovation diffusion of new wood-based materials – reducing the 'time to market'", *Scandinavian Journal of Forest Research*, Vol. 29 No. 4, pp. 394–401.

Seppälä, J., Basson, L. and Norris, G.A. (2001), "Decision analysis frameworks for life-cycle impact assessment", *Journal of Industrial Ecology*, Vol. 5 No. 4, pp. 45–68.

Shepherd, R., Barker, G., French, S., Hart, A., Maule, J. and Cassidy, A. (2006), "Managing food chain risks: Integrating technical and stakeholder perspectives on uncertainty", *Journal of Agricultural Economics*, Vol. 57 No. 2, pp. 313–327.

Sirkin, T. and Houten, M. (1994), "The cascade chain. A theory and tool for achieving resource sustainability with applications for product design", *Resources, Conservation and Recycling*, Vol. 10, pp. 213–277.

Snowden, D. (2002), "Complex acts of knowing. Paradox and descriptive self-awareness", *Journal of Knowledge Management*, Vol. 6 No. 2, pp. 100–111.

Snowden, D. and Boone, M.E. (2007), "A leader's framework for decision making", *Harvard Business Review*, November, pp. 69–76.

Stewart, T.J., French, S. and Rios, J. (2013), "Integrating multicriteria decision analysis and scenario planning – Review and extension", *Omega*, Vol. 41 No. 4, pp. 679–688.

Taskhiri, M.S., Garbs, M. and Geldermann, J. (2016), "Sustainable logistics network for wood flow considering cascade utilisation", *Journal of Cleaner Production*, Vol. 110, pp. 25–39.

Uhlemair, H., Karschin, I. and Geldermann, J. (2014), "Optimizing the production and distribution system of bioenergy villages", *International Journal of Production Economics*, Vol. 147, pp. 62–72.

Watson, R.T., Boudreau, M.-C. and Chen, A.J. (2010), "Information systems and environmentally sustainable development: Energy informatics and new directions for the IS community", *Management Information Systems Quarterly*, Vol. 34 No. 1, pp. 23–38.

Wiedenmann, S. and Geldermann, J. (2015), "Supply planning for processors of agricultural raw materials", *European Journal of Operational Research*, Vol. 242 No. 2, pp. 606–619.

Willows, R., Reynard, N., Meadowcroft, I. and Connell, R. (2003), *Climate Adaptation: Risk, Uncertainty and Decision-Making*. UKCIP Technical Report. UK Climate Impacts Programme.

# 15

# SMEs defending their businesses from flood risk

## Contributing to the theoretical discourse on resilience

*Bingunath Ingirige and Gayan Wedawatta*

### Introduction

Evidence suggest that flooding has become a significant threat affecting small and medium-sized enterprises (SMEs) in the UK. Previous research has identified vulnerability of SMEs to various disruptions and challenges. Their vulnerability to disruptions arises virtually by definition because of the small scale of their human and financial resources (Bannock, 2005). For instance, research has found that SMEs suffer the most in times of crisis and are the least prepared of all organisations (Ingirige et al., 2008) hence an important proponent in crisis and security of business. Flooding in many forms is expected to further increase in frequency and severity in future due to climate change impacts (Environment Agency, 2005; Stern, 2007; Munich Re Group, 2008). Flooding can also cause both immediate and secondary impacts. SMEs can be severely affected not just by the immediate impact but also due to the sometimes 'slow burning' secondary impacts. Damage to business premises and resultant temporary and permanent business closures may result in loss of jobs, negatively affecting incomes and further hindering recovery efforts of local communities (Tierney, 2007) affecting the society at large. Such wider economic and social impacts are not normally accounted for in monetary terms, as opposed to direct physical damages in relation to flooding. Therefore, without a coherent strategy it is difficult for policy makers to address the overall consequences of flooding and improve their capacity of managing their risks better. This has become a growing problem and cannot be taken lightly. For example, a recent survey found that the financial cost of severe weather events to have been just under £7,000 on average for each affected SME out of a survey sample of 1,199 SMEs in the UK (FSB, 2015). This has necessitated that businesses, especially SMEs who are said to be highly vulnerable to flooding when compared with larger businesses (Crichton, 2006), implement various coping strategies in order to defend their businesses from flood risks and better prepare themselves to face the future flood risk. The aim of the chapter is to contribute to the theoretical discourse on resilience with specific reference to improving preparedness of SMEs against flood disasters in the UK. Thereby this chapter adds to the broader domain of crisis and security of business.

## Background literature forming the research problem

Adopting measures to avoid or to control flood disasters and disruption has received much attention from policy makers and scientists in the UK as revealed by the Strategic Defence and Security Review (HM Government, 2010). Due to significant impact on communities during the recent years and resultant public and media attention, flood risk management has emerged as a top agenda item for the relevant policy makers as having a significantly high risk in terms of economic, social and environmental consequences.

The UK government's view in terms of flood mitigation is not just about blanket solutions such as constructing flood defences in key risk areas, but also to set in motion a strategy of community participation in adopting measures of flood resilience so that the community displays adequate levels of participation in decision making. Within this context, DEFRA's (2011) report is an important landmark as it identifies that communities at risk of flooding should learn to live and adapt to flooding by implementing adjustments to their property rather than relying totally on insurance or the government to invest in expensive schemes. Despite this policy move, there have not been widespread measures or initiatives that have emerged to implement the policies in practice. Many cities and towns that are at risk of flooding are abundant with SMEs whose existence is central to the survival and vibrancy of communities living in those cities and towns, mainly due to their ability to generate employment (BIS, 2012). From a numerical standpoint, BIS defines an SME as "any enterprise with less than 250 employees" (BIS, 2010). Their vulnerability to various disruptions arises virtually by definition because of the small scale of their human and financial resources (Bannock, 2005). SMEs have been reported as one of the most vulnerable groups worst affected by the impacts of flooding (Crichton, 2006; Pitt, 2008; Wedawatta et al., 2012). Therefore it is important to investigate resilience measures that will enable SMEs to sustain their businesses. Blackburn and Smallbone (2008), who have reviewed SME behavior widely, argue that SMEs cannot be treated as scaled-down versions of large businesses. They have unique characteristics that determine how they respond to challenges and opportunities. Hence, it is pertinent to consider SME behavior, challenges and their impacts as unique in comparison with other types of businesses. Herbane (2015), for instance, identifies that in the context of SMEs their ability to respond to any acute business interruption such as that caused by a natural hazard such as flooding is less well understood. Some of the formal managerial tasks such as formal planning are not often the practice in SMEs, as such a sudden event that impacts an SME presents them with unique challenges that sometimes can eliminate them completely in the market. For example, the Centre for Economics and Business Research Ltd (CEBR) predicted an additional 2,000–3,000 business failures (in the UK) as a result of the disruptions caused by the heavy snowfall in 2009, with a significant proportion of these coming from the construction sector (McWilliams, 2009).

According to Ingirige et al. (2015), as SME owners are often based locally, they are likely to be affected by disasters in two fronts – as business owners and local residents – creating significant psychological stress and trauma. This view is prevalent in many countries and it is valid in most parts in the UK as SMEs dominate many local areas. Since their existence has been established in the local areas for a very long period of time (e.g. local bakeries, snack bars, retail outlets), it makes it difficult for SMEs to move to another area. Therefore, it is in their interest to increase their ability to be more resilient to flood events. Further, SMEs are an integral component in local community cohesion. As local businesses aiding community connectedness, SMEs can play a significant role in developing disaster resilience and recovery of local communities. For this to happen, it is vital that SMEs themselves are made resilient by integrating DRR in business planning; a practice that is seldom implemented as of now (Ingirige et al., 2015).

Resilience measures to protect from flooding can be grouped into structural (e.g. community flood defences and individual property protection measures) and non-structural (e.g. business continuity measures and adjusting and re-aligning business processes). Structural measures aim to reduce flood risk by controlling the flow of water, whereas non-structural measures seek to manage flood risk by building the capacity of people to cope with flooding in their environments (Jha et al., 2012). The Environment Agency has predicted that flood defences managed by them (structural measures) had protected about 100,000 properties from flooding in the case of the 2007 summer floods, which affected many parts of the UK (Environment Agency, 2009a). Still, over 55,000 properties were flooded due to that event (Pitt, 2008). The Environment Agency still believes that despite increased investment in flood risk management about 500,000 properties will still be left at high risk of flooding by 2035 due to various localised flood situations not covered by the main community flood defences (Environment Agency, 2009b). Surface water flooding, for instance, caused by the combined effect of heavy and prolonged rainfall and extreme ground saturation is difficult to prevent, and the community-wide structural flood defence schemes, which have been built to resist overflowing of rivers, do not prevent surface water flooding. Therefore, despite the high investment in community-based structural flood resilience schemes, it is inevitable that appropriate property level measures at a more micro level are taken to increases flood resistance and resilience of at-risk properties. Furthermore, some of the large community flood defence schemes located on river banks and coastal flood defence schemes might not have the flexibility to cater to changing climatic conditions such as sea level rise and the more intense and prolonged rainfall patterns that have been experienced recently in many parts of the world. Flood disasters in the past have shown that some of the older paradigms such as 'flood control' and 'flood defence' sometimes cause more problems than they solve (Ingirige and Wedawatta, 2014; Kelman, 2001). Instead, contemporary researchers argue that the modern communities from a sustainability and resilience point of view are learning to live with rivers (ICE, 2001) and emphasise continuity by 'living with risk' (UNISDR, 2004). This suggests that the current trend is to sustain business continuity despite any imminent threats of flooding rather than finding somewhat easier propositions to relocate.

It is practically very difficult based on expensive large-scale structural flood defence schemes to protect every property at risk of flooding as they have been designed to cater to larger regions. Smaller pockets within those regions can therefore still encounter flooding at an individual property level. It is therefore important to study adapting individual properties at risk of flooding utilising products such as door guards, airbrick covers and putting up sand bags to resist the effect of flooding, or by installing resilience measures such as installing concrete floors as opposed to carpets or timber floors so that the property owners can return quickly to the property and continue their respective business (Environment Agency, 2009a). For small businesses, returning to properties is extremely critical to their survival and sustainability (Wedawatta et al., 2012). This is also the case when looking at the problem from the point of view of local councils, whose main motivation is to get the businesses in the area up and running after the flood events to maintain the prosperity and vibrancy of small townships and to promote more footfall in high streets to maintain local economies. Business failure and disruption due to flooding can also translate to insurance claims of very high magnitude. For instance, in the case of the flooding in 2007, £1 billion was paid to businesses by the insurance industry (ABI, 2008a).

SME property owners can also consider adopting non-structural resilience measures for purposes of business continuity. These could include general measures such as obtaining property insurance and business interruption insurance, business continuity planning advice, and home or flexible working for some of the employees whose work could continue despite the business being affected by flooding (Wedawatta and Ingirige, 2012). Some of these are general measures adopted for the purposes of managing risk and are popular among some commercial enterprises. On certain occasions they are written rules in their business plans. Previous research conducted in this area added a new dimension to this knowledge by investigating specific non-structural measures which are flood risk-related and found that some SMEs, for instance, signed up for a flood warning system, and a few even carried out a detailed flood risk assessment of their premises and so forth (Kreibich et al., 2007; Kreibich et al., 2008; Ingirige and Wedawatta, 2011; Wedawatta et al., 2012). However, these examples are very few, and some of the micro sized businesses, which are found to dominate urban cities and towns, lack the necessary awareness, knowledge or resources to implement any of these measures. According to Ingirige and Wedawatta (2014), a study done on SMEs affected by flooding in Cockermouth in Cumbria found several non-structural measures being adopted. These included reviewing property insurance, relocating vulnerable/important stock to upper floors, obtaining property insurance, conducting a flood risk assesment on property, storage of stock/equipment above floor level. Of these measures 44% of those surveyed opted for reviewing of existing insurance, whilst a small percentage (11%) of those SMEs surveyed adopted the strategy of concentrating on storage and stock for the purpose of relocating them. These are non-structural or soft measures that are specific to a business. Due to the experience of facing up to flooding very frequently, SMEs tend to modify or adjust some of their strategies from one event to another.

It seems that a small adjustment such as keeping stock at a slightly higher level above the floor seems to have very few takers among the SMEs. Instead they tend to prefer safer options of insurance to recover losses after a flood event rather than trying to prevent flood impacts. Where storage and stock holding is key in an SME (e.g. groceries, cake shops, hardware stores), such minor adjustments could hold the key to minimizing of damage against flooding. Repeated flood events therefore seem to create a somewhat heightened awareness among the SME community with regard to insurance, where they review their existing policies and consider getting alternative policies, amendments to existing policies and new policies such as business interruption. But there was very little consideration of smaller adjustments (such as minor retrofits and business continuity measures) to protect their stock, which can be more cost effective and achieve quick wins as they can be perceived as 'low-hanging fruit'.

Wedawatta et al.'s (2014) study also showed that except in the case of a few SMEs, most of the SMEs studied adopted various generic coping strategies that aid business continuity, rather than those that are directly flood-related coping strategies. This is confirmed by Crichton's (2006) study, which found evidence of the measures adopted such as obtaining property insurance, having a business continuity plan, using a business data backup system, and obtaining business interruption insurance, which are general risk reduction measures that have been reported as good practice among the business community. Some of the trade organisations advocate these among their private sector counterparts.

Ingirige et al. (2015) contributing to the UNISDR's Global Assessment Report of 2015 found that some countries have already taken the initial steps towards substantially involving private sector businesses in disaster risk reduction (DRR) in general (not just against flood risk but a whole host of other disasters). These trends are likely to require private sector businesses to invest their financial and other resources in risk reduction initiatives (Edo et al., 2014). This is a challenging task unless businesses realise the business case for DRR. Whilst global businesses are now beginning to consider DRR, much of the businesses still do not consider disasters a major business risk (UNISDR, 2013). However, their willingness to engage with and implement DRR activities is likely to increase following experience of disaster events. Businesses that have been affected by one or more disaster events have been noted as more likely to implement DRR strategies than those without such experience (Kreibich et al., 2010). Whilst larger businesses could be in a position to implement DRR strategies, committing financial and other resources for DRR is likely to be challenging for SMEs. Therefore, policy initiatives will be required to be sensitive to the requirements and capacities of SMEs, which form the overarching majority of private sector businesses in many economies.

IFRC (2013) states that as a rule of thumb for each dollar spent on disaster preparedness, an average of four dollars is saved on disaster response and recovery. Therefore, the preparation phase of a disaster management cycle (see O'Brien et al., 2010; Ingirige, 2016 for a discussion on disaster management cycle) can often equip the SMEs with the appropriate tools to reduce the impact of a hazard later on in the cycle. According to Coffrin et al. (2011), the broad preparedness measures cover short-term emergency planning (that includes insurance), hazard warning (e.g. early warning systems as appropriate within the case of SMEs), procedures taken to meet any contingencies (in the form of documentation and guidance) and the stockpiling of any physical supplies (flood prevention products) that can mitigate the impact of flooding.

Any disaster risk reduction cycle can be customised to the context discussed in this chapter on SMEs and their resilience against flood events considering the broader goals of risk reduction. The longer phases of risk and vulnerability assessment and preparedness allow the policy makers and the community to intensify the existing resilience in a cost-effective way as pointed out by IFRC (2013). Places such as Cockermouth in Cumbria that have faced repeated flood events can utilise more resources during the phases before a flood event so that there is resilience built up in SMEs against any future flood events. The current awareness on insurance can be further extended with more of a flood-specific long-term risk management approach by considering both structural and other non-structural measures of coping measures against flooding that can be applied within the appropriate SMEs' contexts. These measures can be part of a broader mitigation and adaptation planning process (during the pre-event stage) to increase the SME capacity to meet the challenges of flooding (during the post-event stage).

The place based model of understanding community resilience to natural disasters considers 'place-specific multiscalar processes' (Cutter et al., 2008, p. 602), which are unique to a specific social, natural and built environment of a place. Hence Cutter et al.'s model is known as the Disaster Resilience of a Place (DROP) model, which involves not just the location characteristics but also social, natural and built environment specific factors that helps in building up coping measures. Although its primary focus is on understanding community resilience to natural disasters, the model can relate well to understanding of the coping behavior of SMEs as it is a key group within an overall community. The SME coping measures align well on another theoretical aspect according to Cutter et al. (2008), which is absorptive capacity. They define absorptive capacity of a hazard such as flooding as "the ability of the community to absorb event impacts using predetermined coping responses." The preparedness and the risk and vulnerability assessment phase as per the model allows space for the SMEs to develop the predetermined coping responses with a longer timescale given that there is appropriate resource investments and initiatives that add value in the long run. Paton and Hill (2006) for instance identified that resource constraints might inhibit developments of such capacity to cope but maintaining the functions of those SMEs amidst significant disturbances (Paton, 2007) such as a flood is an important consideration for business continuity. Initiatives such as private and public sector collaboration, government incentives for improvement of both structural and non-structural coping measures of SMEs are some of the examples that might work in building up the coping capacity as well as to ensure business continuity in this instance. Our review of literature suggest that SMEs display unique behaviours when facing flood events and this could be due to the variations in their developed coping measures, which allow them to differentiate their responses against the flood impacts. For example, in studies conducted in Cockermouth, Cumbria (Wedawatta et al., 2014), we saw wide disparities of flood impacts on individual SMEs although they were located on the same street. Sullivan-Taylor and Branicki's (2011) argument that no one size fits all in the case of creating resilient SMEs confirms this argument. Further, similarities in terms of the scale of business and industry sector did not necessarily mean that those SMEs in similar locales, industries and so forth displayed similar impact consequences, but rather their impacts/responses were found to be quite a disparate set. It seems that they were in most of the cases dependent on their developed coping measures and how they were able to display resilience against those flood impacts based on their degree of coping. The DROP model therefore can be used to understand the nature of this differentiation in terms of how SMEs face up to flood events. Although the DROP model and the attempt to have a longer preparedness phase seems to be a winning argument most of the time, it is a bleak picture that often emerges in practice. This clearly identifies an opportunity to develop coping measures against flooding, the reality in many parts of the UK tends to suggest just the opposite: a much weaker situation. For instance, the latest FSB (2015) survey identify that out of a sample of 128 SMEs related to the retail sector, 71% experienced cost and prevalence of severe weather impacts over the last 3 years. This was also accounted as a monetary value, which showed that their average cost of the impact was £10,522, which presents a bleak picture in the retail sector. Climate change is set to make things worse for the SMEs, in that according to IPCC (2007) and the United Nations Climate Change Conference in 2015 (Paris Summit), that there seem to be more widespread extreme weather events in the future. Therefore, it is important to understand what is hindering or preventing the SME coping measures to be developed, as identified in the discussion despite the potential opportunity for them to succeed and perform better in their industry or the sector. SMEs can then better defend their businesses from future flood risk.

The research problem of investigating the barriers for implementing and strengthening the coping measures of SMEs contributes towards the existing resilience discourse that adds a new dimension to the existing literature. This will be best explained by taking a small SME community, such as Braunton in North Devon, where the key coping measures against flooding can be investigated.

## Study of SMEs frequently encountering flooding

The chapter reports on a collection of SME cases conducted in Braunton, North Devon (see Ingirige and Russell, 2015), that developed further value into the developments in coping measures adopted by SMEs. SMEs in Braunton have experienced several flood events during the last few years. Of particular interest were the two recent episodes of flooding, once in 2009 and again in 2012. Both events occurred in the month of December with flood waters reaching a higher level and remaining standing for a longer period in the 2012 event. This event proved catastrophic to the small businesses in the Caen street in Braunton due to its low-lying locale (Ingirige and Russell, 2015). This winter flood completely overwhelmed the designed standards of an existing flood defence scheme, which was of an indicative standard of resisting a 1 in 100-year flood event. The resultant flood event was not only caused by overflowing of the river but lack of drainage and heavy rainfall combined with high levels of ground saturation during the winter that contributed towards building up of surface water flooding within the area.

Seven SMEs and their representatives were interviewed utilising a SME resilience toolkit produced as part of the Engineering and Physical Sciences Research Council (EPSRC) funded Community Resilience to Extreme Weather (CREW) research project in 2011 (Ingirige and Wedawatta, 2011). The process involved entering the raw data (the transcripts) into Nvivo10 software, which is a powerful tool for analysing qualitative data. The research also investigated views of other stakeholders of the flood mitigation problem facing SMEs. Two representatives one from the Braunton Parish Council and a representative of the Environment Agency in the area were also interviewed. These extended interviews provided a wider policy making angle to the research (Ingirige and Russell, 2015). The SMEs and their business types are given in Table 15.1.

All the above interviewees have personally encountered at least one flood event during the last few years. Hence their level of experience is quite varied and due to the differences in their context, the impacts that they have suffered as a result of flooding was different. For example, in the case of CS2, the business was purchased being fully aware of the previous flood events. CS3 was closed for approximately eight weeks due to damage to premises after the recent flood event. In the case of CS4, the 2012 flooding occurred during the busiest period in the year (the Christmas trading period) and they lost approximately 80% of the stock in hand due to the floods. CS5 is located in the lowest part of Caen Street, and following the 2012 flooding they were unable to occupy the building for 4 months. The estate agent at that time relocated to their main branch at Barnstaple and continued their business from that branch. However, they incurred a lot of additional costs due to travelling between Barnstaple and Braunton due to property viewings. CS6 was closed for over six months due to the recent flood event, but it received assistance from the head office during the period of the closure. CS7 owned both the business and the building and had his insurance excess increased from £500 to £10,000 after the flood event (Ingirige and Russell, 2015).

The main focus of the case studies was to identify how best the local policy makers, action groups or trade organisations can support SMEs (from the point of view of SMEs) to better cope with future flooding. Primarily, the findings revealed the various disparities in the levels of coping among the SMEs. Due to facing of repeated flood events in the area, most SMEs had sandbags in their possession (or at least knew where to get them in an emergency) as the first resort to a flood response. Similarly some of them possessed proprietary products such as door guards, air brick covers and so forth, which could potentially be used to prevent the flood waters entering the property. It was found that most of the SMEs tend to overly rely on these

*Table 15.1* SME case study details

| *SME Case* | *Business type* |
|---|---|
| CS1 | Sandwich shop |
| CS2 | Newsagent |
| CS3 | A shop selling surfing equipment and merchandise |
| CS4 | A card shop |
| CS5 | An Estate agent |
| CS6 | Bakery |
| CS7 | Optician |

basic flood prevention mechanisms without much of an understanding of their degree of vulnerability to a flood. Previous studies have shown that some members of the community living in flood affected areas perceive a 'sandbag' coping approach in a very simplistic fashion, without much of a deeper engagement with the likely flood scenario or the context. However, a few of the SMEs had gone a step further and assessed their business and their operations more closely and adopted methods such as moving the stock beyond the previous flood height, special mechanisms to prevent damage to targeted expensive equipment in their business (e.g. the 'fundus machine and expensive spectacle frames' of CS7), special mechanisms and processes of data backup and conducting small-scale retrofits to the properties such as raising electrical sockets to a higher level on the walls (CS3). These measures were predominantly of a non-structural nature and had a lot of thought processes behind them being implemented even when there was some element of a structural nature. The SMEs perceived that these measures would allow them to minimise the flood impacts and cope better (for CS7 this made a lot of sense, particularly due to their very high insurance excess). Further methods of support were explored directly with the SMEs and it was found that the guiding principle of support and collaborating with SMEs should be done with the understanding that SMEs are entities having specific needs, and that their levels of preparedness differed substantially. In the SMEs own words, what they valued most was more of a "practical and emotional assistance" (see Ingirige and Russell, 2015 for more details) to improve themselves to better prepare for future flood events as they were found to be at different scales in adopting coping measures against flooding. Therefore development of coping measures is something that needs to be carefully planned in a way that is sympathetic to the needs of SMEs.

One of the important findings was the consideration that in certain instances it was important that the whole community should pull together to make a difference. For instance, one of the case study representatives identified that flood protection needed to be a collective responsibility of the SMEs. The following comment identifies the sophistication of his understanding of flood resilience:

> The only [way] we can be [less] vulnerable would be if we could make this an island of security, which we can't because not everybody has put flood gates up. My next door neighbour hasn't, he doesn't own the building, he possibly can't afford to do it. For whatever reason he does not have any flood gates, which means when water comes in to him it will soak through to my wall.

Such understanding shows the main barrier sometimes faced by SMEs where a community living in flood affected areas often fails to pull together. Sometimes this results in some sort of a perceived disincentive to take up or improve the current coping measures and defend their business against flooding. The SME seems to understand that any measures that they take to cope will not realise in achieving the full value if the community fails to pull together. Therefore, among the SMEs and their disparate sets of coping measures there seems to be some pockets of good practice being followed by SMEs. Such an improved level of understanding compared with some of the basic measures proposed by the majority of SMEs seems to identify different degrees of coping measures among SMEs located in the same area. Paton (2007) terms these measures as indicators of resilience and groups them in a similar fashion. Braunton SME case studies identified barriers to improve the coping measures against flooding and therefore presented a very good opportunity to document the different practicalities faced by the SME community in facing up to the challenges of flooding. Such practicalities, measures and challenges that SMEs face will help documenting good practice across other similar contexts, considering the fact that Braunton is a typical village where there is a lot of potential to transfer good practice and learning to other similar areas in the UK as well as other parts of Europe. The Braunton study also adds value as it is in line with the current government policy of the communities being empowered to learn and live with the flooding so that small businesses are able to develop their coping mechanisms for preparedness and continuity of their businesses.

## Comment on the appropriate approaches undertaken

The study identifies several key issues in relation to the effect of flooding on SMEs and their role in defending their businesses against flooding. Primarily the review of literature identified the key role played by SMEs within a community and how an acute disruptive event such as a flood can create a crisis of innumerable proportion. The value that is generated by ensuring that SMEs' disruption is minimized or avoided and their demise is prevented is beginning to get appreciated by policy makers and the government stakeholders due to the very important role that they play within a community. Therefore, the issue of flooding and its impact on SMEs is gradually getting to the top of agendas in most societies. As explained earlier new public and private sector joint initiatives (as highlighted in the discussion) have emerged to maintain the sustainability of SMEs in managing their risks of facing up to weather events. As reported, in the UK, the very recent study undertaken by the Federation of Small Businesses shows a grim picture despite several mechanisms and initiatives that are in place. Hence this chapter investigates some of the root causes that inhibit SMEs taking up coping measures and adds to the theoretical discourse on resilience on the aspect of the role played by SMEs within a community.

First, both the review of literature and the SME case study identified some of the unique scenarios that result on SME flood impact. It is clear that many other factors beyond one's location needs to be considered when discussing the SME flood impacts. The effect of flooding on SMEs would have different impacts based on the type of ownership (tenant or owner occupier), previous flood experience, assistance and support from others, government incentives, personal motivation and so forth. The cases in particular demonstrates how SMEs located on the same street will have different impacts. The DROP model therefore can be widely used with additional perspectives or views by reviewing its influence on location specific intensity to cover further aspects.

It was interesting to find some consistency with the FSB (2015) survey and other survey data regarding the risk management approaches adopted by SMEs. Whilst the surveys in general highlight the point that SMEs approaches to risk management were predominantly generic risk management and business continuity approaches, the cases bring out the specific flood relevance in their risk management approaches. Some of the coping measures that were found in our SME cases in Braunton were specifically flood related (e.g. retrofits to premises, elevated storage areas above the flood height). The main reason behind this variation is due to the sampling in the case of the survey and the case study. Whilst the survey in general documented in literature include SMEs in many areas which have wide dispersions in the element of flood risk, the case studies of SMEs in general and the one that this chapter reported were generally located in areas that recently encountered flooding. Hence their level of awareness of flood damage and coping measures tend to rely on the very recent flood experience rather than the generic risk management approaches often encountered in surveys.

Whatever the above context (whether generic or specific to flood risk), key barriers seem to exist in SMEs developing and adopting coping measures against flooding. Those SMEs that once or twice faced flood events tend to perceive that flood damage was minimum, so no need to prepare. Some of the SMEs are overly optimistic that their businesses are 'extremely flexible' and hence they have a natural level of coping against any disaster event and it is only when the disaster is unprecedented that the coping capacity is breached and they are impacted. Hence our findings revealed quite a disparate number of measures and degrees of coping. It is important to note that SMEs do not have resources in abundance to engage in formal managerial activities such as risk management and planning, hence it is important that the support network targets their needs with coping measures in line with their requirements. Therefore, new innovative initiatives such as partnership approaches such as public-private partnerships and other partnership approaches with communities (such as the ones covered under Ingirige et al., 2015) tend to work well with SMEs to develop their coping mechanisms against flooding. The new concept of Area Business Continuity Management developed and piloted by JICA, where a "cooperative approach is undertaken by those who wish to improve capacity for continuity and/or early recovery of businesses in their area in the event of emergency such as natural disasters that affect the entire area" (AHA Centre and JICA, 2015), could be an effective way of promoting business continuity of all SMEs in an at-risk small town like Braunton or Cockermouth. This approach can also help individual SMEs to develop their own business continuity plans in tandem with that for their neighbourhood and benefit from resources allocated towards the Area Business Continuity Plan. Government incentives could be driven to fulfil some of these initiatives. Finally, it is important to note that funding on flood mitigation cannot be just on community flood defences but there should be good measures that will ensure business continuity at individual SME level. Therefore, SME operational patterns, their unique concerns should be communicated well to the emergency response teams well in advance of any anticipated flood events as well as their importance to the community in recovery processes should be emphasized so that flood recovery coordinators can get SMEs back in business sooner for the sustainability of the community.

## Conclusion

This chapter addressed SME flood impacts and their coping measures, which is an important aspect of crisis and security in business. Thereby this research will have an impact on modern society whilst adding value to the overall resilience discourse.

The chapter investigated the research problem of why small businesses are often impacted due to natural hazards such as flooding and unable to cope despite their importance within crisis and security in business. The chapter explored the existing coping measures of SMEs, what inhibits their developments and what key considerations should guide their developments. First, the researchers' interpretation of resilience and related concepts were reviewed based on extant literature and a case study was discussed to subsequently identify the key issues at a more local level. We then presented our findings on what is seemingly the current outlook within this field.

Accordingly, the starting point of our literature review identified the current coping measures and their degree of development amidst some of the policy making, government, public and private sector agendas focused on improving risk management in SMEs in many sectors. It was found that there is no crystal ball as such, but what is really important is to consider that SMEs are a unique set within business and hence an important aspect within crisis and security studies area. Their uniqueness is often underrepresented in literature, thereby the chapter is well positioned to study this area and to contribute knowledge into the overall resilience agenda and discourse. Whilst the conceptual underpinnings helped in arriving at the research problem, the short case study of Braunton helped in grounding this research within some of the practical SME scenarios that had wide disparities. So the unique SME behaviour could be well positioned both in theory and practice.

The study provided a novel way of representing the unique SME context as the guiding principle to develop the current coping measures of SMEs against flooding as opposed to following of any generic frameworks/models on resilience of businesses. The unique SME behaviours could set up the policy making in this area in the UK and other places in Europe and also in other countries. The government investments in flood resilience should therefore improve with a better balance in flood protection based on structural and non-structural coping measures, which will be the key to ensure a secure community. Further research in conducting more of an operational study into unique SME behaviours and their orientations when faced with a multitude of natural hazard events can emerge from this research.

## References

ABI (2008) *Insurance for Small Businesses: A Guide to Protecting Your Business*. London: Association of British Insurers.

AHA Centre and Japan International Cooperation Agency (2015) *Planning Guide for Area Business Continuity: Area BCM toolkits – Version 2 Main Volume*. Jakarta: AHA Centre.

Bannock, G. (2005) *The Economics and Management of Small Business: An International Perspective*. London: Taylor & Francis Routledge.BIS (2010) Small Business Survey 2010. Retrieved from www.gov.uk/government/uploads/system/uploads/attachment_data/file/32228/11-p74-bis-small-business-survey-2010.pdf (accessed on 23 June 2016).

BIS (2012) *Business Population Estimates for the UK and Regions 2012*. Sheffield: Enterprise Directorate Analytical Unit, Department for Business, Innovation and Skills (BIS).

Blackburn, R.A. and Smallbone, D. (2008) Researching Small Firms and Entrepreneurship in the U.K.: Developments and Distinctiveness. *Entrepreneurship Theory: Theory and Practice*, 32(2), 267–288.

Coffrin, C., Van Hentenryck, P. and Bent, R. (2011) Strategic Stockpiling of Power System Supplies for Disaster Recovery. *IEEE*, 1(8), 24–29.

Crichton, D. (2006) *Climate Change and Its Effects on Small Businesses in the UK*. London: AXA Insurance UK.

Cutter, S.L. et al. (2008) A Place-Based Model for Understanding Community Resilience to Natural Disasters. *Global Environmental Change*, 18(4), 598–606.

DEFRA (2011) *Understanding the Risks, Empowering Communities, Building Resilience: The National Flood and Coastal Erosion Risk Management Strategy for England*. London: The Stationery Office.

Edo, P.J.M., Morris, D. and Puutio, T. (2014) *Engaging Asia-Pacific Businesses in Disaster Risk Management*. Bangkok: The Asian Disaster Preparedness Center.

Environment Agency (2005) *The Climate is Changing: Time to Get Ready*. Bristol: Environment Agency.

Environment Agency (2009a) *Flooding in England: A National Assessment of Flood Risk*. Bristol: Environment Agency.

Environment Agency (2009b) *Investing for the Future: Flood and Coastal Risk Management in England*. London: Environment Agency.

Federation of Small Businesses (FSB) (2015) Severe Weather: A More Resilient Small Business Community. Retrieved from www.fsb.org.uk/docs/default-source/fsb-org-uk/pressroom/fsb-severe-weather-report-final.pdf (accessed on 01 June 2016).

Herbane, B. (2015) Threat Orientation in Small and Medium-Sized Enterprises: Understanding Differences Toward Acute Interruptions. *Disaster Prevention and Management*, 24(5), 583–595.

HM Government (2010) *Securing Britain in an Age of Uncertainty: The Strategic Defence and Security Review*. London: The Stationery Office.

ICE (2001) Learning to Live With Rivers. Institution of Civil Engineers.

IFRC (2013) Disasters Preparedness Saves Lives and Saves Money. Retrieved from www.ifrc.org/fr/nouvelles/nouvelles/common/disasters-preparedness-saves-lives-and-saves-money-61204/ (accessed on 12 July 2017).

Ingirige, B. (2016) Theorising Construction Industry Practice Within a Disaster Risk Reduction Setting: Is It a Panacea or an Illusion. *Construction Management and Economics*, 34, 592–607.

Ingirige, B., Amaratunga, D., Kumaraswamy, M., Liyanage, C., Perwaiz, A., Towashiraporn, P. and Wedawatta, G. (2015) Private Investment in Disaster Risk Management. The Global Assessment Report of 2015: Background paper, UNISDR Publications: Geneva. Retrieved from http://goo.gl/FrZsvh (accessed on 12 July 2017).

Ingirige, B. and Russell, R.C. (2015) Investigating SME Resilience to Flooding: The Braunton Report. Retrieved from www.arcc-network.org.uk/wp-content/pdfs/SME-resilience-Braunton-Dec2015.pdf (accessed on 12 July 2017).

Ingirige, B. and Wedawatta, G. (2011) Impacts of Flood Hazards on Small and Medium Companies: Strategies for Property Level Protection and Business Continuity. In: Proverbs, D., Lammond, J., Hammond, F. and Booth, C. (Eds.), *Flood Hazards, Impacts and Responses for the Built Environment*. London: Routledge.

Ingirige, B. and Wedawatta, G. (2014) Putting Policy Initiatives Into Practice: Adopting an 'honest broker' Approach to Adapting Small Businesses Against Flooding. *Structural Survey*, 32(2), 123–139.

Ingirige, B., Jones, K. & Proverbs, D. (2008). Investigating SME resilience and their adaptive capacities to extreme weather events: A literature review and synthesis *Proceedings of the Conference on Building Education and Research* (BEAR 2008). Kandalama, Sri Lanka.

IPCC (2007) Climate Change 2007: The Physical Science Basis. Contribution of Working Group I to the Fourth Assessment Report of the Intergovernmental Panel on Climate Change. [Solomon, S., Qin, D., Manning, M., Chen, Z., Marquis, M., Averyt, K.B., Tignor, M. and Miller, H.L. (Eds.)], Cambridge, UK and New York, NY, USA: Cambridge University Press, 996 pp.

Jha, A.K., Bloch, R. and Lamond, J. (2012). *Cities and Flooding: A Guide to Integrated Urban Flood Risk Management for the 21st Century*. Washington, DC: The World Bank.

Kelman, I. (2001) The Autumn 2000 Floods in England and Flood Management. *Weather*, 56(10), 346–360.

Kreibich, H., Muller, M., Thieken, A.H. and Merz, B. (2007) Flood Precaution of Companies and Their Ability to Cope With the Flood in August 2002 in Saxony, Germany. *Water Resource Research*, 43(3), 1–15.

Kreibich, H., Seifert, I., Thieken, A., Lindquist, E., Wagner, K. and Merz, B. (2010) Recent Changes in Flood Preparedness of Private Households and Businesses in Germany. *Regional Environmental Change*, pp. 1–13.

Kreibich, H., Seifert, I., Thieken, A.H. and Merz, B. (2008) Flood Precaution and Coping With Floods of Companies in Germany. In: Proverbs, D., Brebbia, C.A. and Penning-Rowsell, E. (Eds.), *Flood Recovery, Innovation and Response*. Southampton: WIT Press.

McWilliams, D. (2009) *Hit From the Big Freeze Will Be 2–3 Thousand Businesses Going Bust Earlier*. London: Centre for Economics and Business Research Ltd. Retrieved from www.cebr.com/Resources/CEBR/The_cost_of_the_big_freeze.pdf (accessed on 20 June 2017).

Munich Re Group (2008) *Topics Geo: Natural Catastrophes 2007 – Analyses, Assessments, Positions*. Knowledge series, München: Munich Re Group.

O'Brien, G., O'Keefe, P., Gadema, Z. and Swords, J. (2010) Approaching Disaster Management Through Social Learning. *Disaster Prevention and Management*, 19(4).

Paton, D. (2007) Measuring and Monitoring Resilience in Auckland, Institute of Geological and Nuclear Sciences Limited.

Paton, D. and Hill, R. (2006) Managing Company Risk and Resilience Through Business Continuity Management. In: Paton, D. and Johnston, D. (Eds.), *Disaster Resilience: An Integrated Approach*. Illinois: Charles C Thomas Publisher Ltd.

Pitt, M. (2008) *The Pitt Review – Learning Lessons From the 2007 Floods*. London: Cabinet Office.

Stern, N. (2007) *The Economics of Climate Change: The Stern Review*. Cambridge: Cambridge University Press.

Sullivan-Taylor, B. and Branicki, L. (2011) Creating Resilient SMEs: Why One Size Might Not Fit All. *International Journal of Production Research*, 49(17), 5565–5579.

Tierney, K. (2007) Businesses and Disasters: Vulnerability, Impacts, and Recovery. In: Rodriguez, H., Quarantelli, E. L. and Dynes, R. R. (Eds.), *Handbook of Disaster Research*, pp. 275–296. New York: Springer.

UNISDR (2004) *Living With Risk: A Global Review of Disaster Reduction Initiatives*. New York and Zurich: International Strategy for Disaster Risk Reduction.

UNISDR (2013) *Global Assessment Report on Disaster Risk Reduction: From Shared Risk to Shared Value: The Business Case for Disaster Risk Reduction. United Nations International Strategy for Disaster Reduction*. Geneva, Switzerland: UNISDR.

Wedawatta, G. and Ingirige, B. (2012) Resilience and Adaptation of SMEs to Flood Risk. *Disaster Prevention and Management*, 21(4), 474–488.

Wedawatta, G., Ingirige, B. and Proverbs, D. (2012) *Impacts of Flooding on SMEs and Their Relevance to Chartered Surveyors: Final Report of the Developing Flood Expert Knowledge in Chartered Surveyors – DEFENCES Project*. London: Royal Institution of Chartered Surveyors.

Wedawatta, G., Ingirige, B., and Proverbs, D. (2014) Small Businesses and Flood Impacts: The Case of the 2009 Flood Event in Cockermouth. *Journal of Flood Risk Management*, 7(1), 42–53.

# Part IV

# Systems security for business resiliency

# 16

# Security awareness in the software arena

*Rory V. O'Connor and Ricardo Colomo-Palacios*

## 1 Introduction

In modern society we are highly dependent on software systems in most aspects of our daily activities, such as financial services, telecommunications, electronics, transportation, home appliances and more. As the software system is involved in various aspects of society, security becomes an important issue and a vital requirement for the software system (Salini and Kanmani, 2012a). Many security issues such as confidentiality, availability and integrity need to be preserved in order to consider software as secure (Khan and Zulkernine, 2009).

Non-secure software can cause serious problems for an organisation's reputation with customers, partners and investors; it increases costs as companies are forced to repair unreliable applications; and it delays other development efforts as limited resources are assigned to address current software deficiencies (Khan, 2011). In addition, vulnerable software can be invaded and modified to cause damage to previously working software, and infected software can replicate itself and be carried across networks to cause damage in other systems. Equally, effective security can protect a business from the problems associated with crashes, or allow the business to move faster and be more agile. Software security vulnerabilities are not like other software defects and need to be treated separately and differently (Wysopal, 2008).

As a consequence of this importance and according to Gartner (2016), worldwide spending on IT security products and services will reach $81.6 billion in 2016, an increase of 7.9% over 2015. Software security is currently accounting for more than 10% of global IT security revenue worldwide (McGraw, 2016). The importance of software security in the IT panorama was labelled by McGraw (2006) as critical and central. In spite of this importance, many cybersecurity practitioners focus on the promise of network security as the silver bullet (Garfinkel, 2012), ignoring fundamental problems caused by software vulnerabilities.

According to Bellovin (2015), the biggest security problem cybersecurity face stems from one simple fact: software is often buggy. Bugs are the common traps for attackers, and these traps should be closed before software is delivered. The quest for software security should start sooner and attack its root causes: software development processes. It is important to adopt an approach in which security concerns are integrated in all software development processes towards built-in security instead of batching security afterwards (Ramachandran, 2016). As a consequence of this, software security management has pushed hard in the overall software engineering panorama. From static analysis tools (check Kupsch et al., 2016, for an up-to-date list of tools) to security maturity models mapping security into software processes like OpenSAMM (SAMM, 2016) or Build Security In Maturity Model (McGraw, 2006), several initiatives have been taken to improve the integration of these two worlds. However, the most ambitious initiatives are designed for experts leading to a pale adoption by the software community while the static analysis is just covering a small portion of the problems. Finally, new approaches like participatory security are trying to attract users to the security management and process from a different perspective.

However, not all software running in an organization is developed internally. First of all and even in purely development activities, new software can include COTS (commercial off the shelf) components. Second, there is the opportunity also to acquire a full software package to solve specific needs or rule the whole organization by means of an ERP package. Although and according to Daneshgar et al. (2013) software acquisition methods in organisations have progressed from the 'buy vs. build' scenarios to more complex models incorporating acquisition of system components on the web and building new systems using open source software and selective adoption of cloud computing, the basic options are still buy or build. The aim of this chapter is to provide an overview of the software security process needed in these two situations and to assist organizations to minimize and ideally prevent security vulnerabilities. To do so, the remainder of the chapter will be structured as follows. First, we review the evolution of the state of the art in the field of security procedures in software purchases. In what follows, we introduce security requirements engineering as a way to secure software development life cycle. Finally, we conclude with a brief summary, conclusions and outline of future works.

## 2 Buy software

In the scope of this chapter, 'buy' means that you purchase a system or subsystem and avoid a completely custom job. The mass market of software is flooding the bazaar with software products. Any software product is, initially, cheaper to buy than to build afresh (Brooks, F.P., 1987), and that is the reason behind the increasing importance of software market in the world.

Custom software can be based also on commercial components at least in part. Thus, new software can include COTS (commercial off the shelf) components developed to be sold and integrated this way (Cortellessa et al., 2008). Using COTS components from third-party providers is one key technology used to develop systems quickly and cost-efficiently (Vale et al., 2016). The process of COTS software selection is difficult due to the large number of existing COTS components (Konys, 2015). As a consequence of this fact, literature has reported a panoply of approaches on COTS selection (Ayala et al., 2011; Gupta et al., 2010; Jadhav and Sonar, 2011; Jha et al., 2014; Mehlawat and Gupta, 2014). In spite of these efforts, COTS selection is still a complicated task that led us to the problem of certification of systems made up of components and subsystems, analysed in detail in the review by Nair et al. (2014). However, and in spite of the importance of COTS components, we will focus our analysis on the purchase of bigger software solutions intended to operate by themselves in a given technological ecosystem.

Thus, there is the opportunity also to acquire a full software package to solve specific needs or to rule the whole organization by means of an ERP package. Again, literature is full of examples on software package selection from different perspectives including traditional and highly cited works (e.g. Al-Mudimigh et al., 2002; Bernroider and Koch, 2001; Chau, 1995; Franch and Carvallo, 2003; Montazemi et al., 1996) and more recent and innovative approaches (e.g. Ayala and Franch, 2014; Azadeh et al., 2014; Colomo-Palacios and Rodríguez, 2014; Kaur and Tomar, 2015).

Cloud computing is also paying a role in the buy scenario. Cloud computing is technology that evolved from distributed, grid and utility computing (Shiau and Chau, 2016), and now has grown from being a promising business concept to one of the fastest growing segments of the IT industry. According to Stratistics MRC, the Global Cloud Computing Market is accounted for $103.35 billion in 2015 and is poised to reach $512.81 billion by 2022 growing 25.7% yearly during the forecast period (Stratistics MRC, 2016). According to Chang and Ramachandran (2016; Ramachandran, 2016), security, trust and privacy remain challenges for organizations that adopt cloud computing. In this scenario, the Cloud Service Measurement Index Consortium (CSMIC) proposed the Service Measurement Index (SMI), a framework based on common characteristics of cloud services. This is a set of business-relevant key performance indicators (KPIs) that provide a standardized method for measuring and comparing a business service regardless of whether that service is internally provided or sourced from an outside company (CSMIC, 2014). Security and privacy was one of the seven top level categories inside the initiative. Inside this broad category, several indicators were defined: access control and privilege management, data geographic/political, data integrity, data privacy and data loss, physical and environmental security, proactive threat and vulnerability management, retention/disposition and security management. For each of the indicators, a matric is proposed to measure each indicator. However, it is also important to note that in cloud settings, security compliance is a shared responsibility among organizations and service providers; it involves service providers, service brokers, customers and auditors (Yimam and Fernandez, 2016). This fact is making security a complicate aspect in cloud regardless of the delivery model adopted (public, private, hybrid or community).

Other important input in the field is coming from the process improvement perspective. CMMI (Capability Maturity Model Integration) is a collection of best practices that helps organizations improve their processes. The CMMI for Acquisition (CMMI-ACQ) model provides guidance for applying CMMI best practices in an acquiring organization (CMMI Product Team, 2011). The emphasis of the model is on the processes of the acquirer, more precisely on activities for initiating and managing the acquisition of products and services to meet the needs of customers and end users. CMMI-ACQ includes 22 process areas; 16 of these process areas are CMMI Model Foundation (CMF) process areas, while the remaining six areas focus on practices specific to acquisition:

- Agreement management
- Acquisition requirements development
- Acquisition technical management
- Acquisition validation
- Acquisition verification
- Solicitation and supplier agreement development.

Security is an aspect pervasive in the model. Focusing on the product or service to be acquired (and not in the internal support process), security is treated as a non-functional property of a product or service to be identified in the acquisition requirements development (process area at maturity level 2) from multiple stakeholders (e.g., the acquirer, multiple suppliers, customers, end users) perspective. It is also present in organizational process focus (process area at maturity level 3) suggesting interfaces with relevant standards like ISO/IEC 27001:2005 Information technology – Security techniques – Information Security Management Systems – Requirements. It is also present in the process area at maturity level 2, solicitation and supplier agreement development. There security is listed as one of the due diligence activities and also as part of the security and legal penalty recoveries. Anyhow, none of the CMMI models is explaining how to implement specific practices, in this case, security practices.

Another big initiative to take into account is ISO/IEC 27001:2013 (ISO, 2013). This standard contains the requirements for planning, implementing, operating and improving an information security management system. The requirements set out in ISO/IEC 27001:2013 are generic and are intended to be applicable to all organizations, regardless of type, size or nature. The importance of ISO/IEC 27001 and CMMI-ACQ has been highlighted and their mapping (Pino et al., 2008) has been considered of interest. In this work, authors discovered that the support provided in ISO/IEC 27001 to CMMI-ACQ is suitable for agreement management, acquisition verification, acquisition validation, acquisition requirements development and, although to a lesser extent, solicitation and supplier agreement development. Conversely, the support provided to the acquisition technical management is stumpy.

In this scenario, and given that the aim of this chapter is to give a view on security practices, in this case in the purchase of software, in what follows a compilation of security practices will be provided to guide software acquirers in their efforts. The approach is based on previous works on quality attributes on for software and services selection (Ameller et al., 2015; Ayala and Franch, 2014; Carvallo et al., 2007; Franch and Carvallo, 2003) along with initiatives introduced previously in the chapter (CMMI Product Team, 2011; CSMIC, 2014; ISO, 2013). The methodology suggested to check security matters in software or service acquisition is based on previous works (Franch and Carvallo, 2003) and includes the following steps:

1 Domain definition
2 Define security attributes
3 Determining metrics for attribute
4 Measure each attribute.

In what follows, several recommendations for each of the steps will be provided.

## 2.1 Domain definition

It is necessary to define the domain of the system. This includes possible candidates, information about the supplier, independent reports, experiences on the field, test of tools and systems and other information. Some existing resources have been listed in Ayala and Franch (2014). In the list, one can find reports from independent consultants (Gartner and Forrester) along with catalogues and other sources. The authors would like to add other consultants, such as Ovum. Apart from that, several user reviews sites can be helpful too, for instance Trustradious, Capterra, IT Central Station, Experts Exchange, Software Advice or G2 Crowd. There are also dozens of websites devoted to specific packages that can be useful in the documentation process. Thus, in focusing in the ERP scenario one can find www.erpfocus.com/, www.top10erp.org/ and www.erpsoftwareblog.com/, naming just some of the most important sites. However, it is also important to note that in some cases, the independence of the given information is not as assured as it is in the case of independent consultants.

## 2.2 Define security attributes

The second step is the identification of security attributes valid for the organization. Although every organization can present its own set of attributes, the ones defined in SMI under the security category (CSMIC, 2014), can be valid as a start set of factors. These are as follows:

- Access control and privilege management. Policies and processes in use by the manufacturer/service provider to ensure that only the personnel granted appropriate privileges can make use of or modify data/work products.
- Data geographic/political. The client's constraints on service location based on geographical or political risk.
- Data integrity. Keeping the data that is created, used and stored in its correct form so that clients may be confident that it is accurate and valid.
- Data privacy and data loss. Client restrictions on use and sharing of client data are enforced by the provider or vendor.
- Physical and environmental security. Polices and processes in use by the provider or vendor to protect the facilities from unauthorized physical access, damage or inference.
- Proactive threat and vulnerability management. Mechanisms in place to ensure that the service or product is protected against known recurring threats as well as vulnerabilities.
- Retention/disposition. Service provider's data retention and disposition meet the customers' requirements.
- Security management. Capabilities of the provider or vendor to ensure application, data and infrastructure security based on the requirements of the client.

It is also possible to define a hierarchy of attributes, as defined in Franch and Carvallo (2003) or a weighted scale following a request for proposals approach.

## *2.3 Determining metrics for attribute*

Once attributes are defined, the next step is the definition of quantitative metrics. In Table 16.1, authors present the set of metrics defined under SMI for the previous attributes are presented (CSMIC, 2014) and later adapted in Colomo-Palacios and Rodríguez (2014).

## *2.4 Measure each attribute*

The final step is aimed to provide a final score to each of the attributes following the metrics defined in the previous step. This could be the foundation for a possible comparison among different options or just a sound way to provide information on security aspects for software products and services.

*Table 16.1* Example of metrics for quality attributes

| | |
|---|---|
| Access Control & Privilege Management | $\frac{\textit{number of secured components}}{\textit{number of contracted components}}$ |
| Data Geographic/Political | Likert Scale 1–10 |
| Data Integrity | Likert Scale 1–10 |
| Data Privacy & Data Loss | Likert Scale 1–10 |
| Physical & Environmental Security | Likert Scale 1–10 |
| Proactive Threat & Vulnerability Management | $\frac{\textit{number of contracted components}}{\textit{number of components that can be managed under potential threats}}$ |
| Retention/Disposition | Likert Scale 1–10 |
| Security Management | Likert Scale 1–10 |

## 3 Build software

The previous section dealt with the choice to purchase a system or subsystem. This section deals with the decision to develop a custom or bespoke software system, that is the 'Build' aspect of the 'Build vs. Buy' decision, where an awareness of security requirements becomes of significant importance in the software development process. The purpose of this section is to present the domain of security engineering, explain its importance and introduce the key software development life cycle process to improve software security and standards that assist with the development of secure and trusted software systems.

Software developers have to cope with the complexity (Clarke et al., 2016) of insecure operating environments by considering potential threats. However, security requirements are rarely at the forefront of stakeholders' concerns, apart from the need to comply with basic legal requirements. Traditionally, software security is considered only in the later stages of software development, by incorporating security concerns as an afterthought (Khan and Zulkernine, 2009). As a consequence, the risk of introducing new security vulnerabilities into various stages of software development life cycles is increased. Following the traditional method of securing software has led to the 'Penetrate and Patch' approach, in which the security specialist tries to assess the software by breaking it from its environment via exploiting common security vulnerabilities. Successful penetration leads to patch development and deployment of the identified vulnerabilities. Security is mostly treated as an add-on feature in the software development life cycle, and is addressed by security professionals using antivirus, platform security, proxies, firewalls and intrusion prevention systems (McGraw, 2006).

Such security concerns should be taken into account as early as possible and not added to systems as an afterthought. However, a significant issue facing information systems designers and software developers is that in the majority of information systems projects security is dealt with when the system has already been designed and put into operation. This is generally a result of requirements work being primarily focused on eliciting tangible business requirements, whilst designers and engineers often fail to pay sufficient attention to security concerns. Compounding this problem is the fact that the actual security requirements themselves are often not well understood.

Security concerns should therefore be an integral part of the entire planning, design development, testing and ongoing maintenance of all software-intensive systems. Inadequate attention to security considerations in these key software development life cycle phases is frequently the source of security vulnerabilities associated with software systems. Accordingly to improve software security, effort and resources should be concentrated on security aspects of the SDLC in order to ensure security is built into software systems from the beginning. This can be achieved by ensuring that security safeguards are planned, designed, developed and tested in a manner that is consistent with the sensitivity of the data and/or software application.

The field of security engineering is broad and encompasses many activities for secure software or a trusted system addressing the complete life cycle of concept definition, analysis of customer's requirements, high-level and low-level design, development, integration, installation and generation, operation, maintenance and de-commissioning. Software or product developers must use security engineering techniques and best practices to gain an understanding of the customer's security needs and formally capture customer security requirements early in the development life cycle (Hwang, 2007).

Secure software is becoming more and more important. However, most of the time security is dealt with in a reactive manner, where it is incorporated in a software after its development.

Unfortunately, a reactive approach increases software development costs and may leave security loopholes in the software. A less common although more cost-effective approach is a proactive way, where security concerns are addressed throughout the software development life cycle (SDLC) (Khan and Zulkernine, 2009).

### *3.1 Security management*

When you consider security issues, you have to consider both the application software (the control system, the information system, etc.) and the infrastructure on which this system is built (see Figure 16.1). In practice, there is an important distinction between application security and infrastructure security (Sommerville, 2016):

- Application security is a software engineering issue where software developers should ensure that the system is designed to resist attacks.
- Infrastructure security is an IT management problem where system managers configure the infrastructure to resist attacks.

The majority of external attacks focus on system infrastructures because infrastructure components (e.g., web browsers) are well known and widely available. Attackers can probe these systems for weaknesses and share information about vulnerabilities that they have discovered. As many people use the same software, attacks have wide applicability. Infrastructure vulnerabilities may lead to attackers gaining unauthorized access to an application system and its data.

Security management is vitally important, but it is not usually considered to be part of application security engineering (Sommerville, 2016). Rather, application security engineering is concerned with designing a system so that it is as secure as possible, given budget and usability constraints. Part of this process is 'design for management', where you design systems to minimize the chance of security management errors leading to successful attacks on the system.

Pfleeger et al. (2015) characterize threats under four headings, which may be used as a starting point for identifying possible misuse cases. These headings are as follows:

- Interception threats that allow an attacker to gain access to an asset.
- Interruption threats that allow an attacker to make part of the system unavailable.
- Modification threats that allow an attacker to tamper with a system asset.
- Fabrication threats that allow an attacker to insert false information into a system.

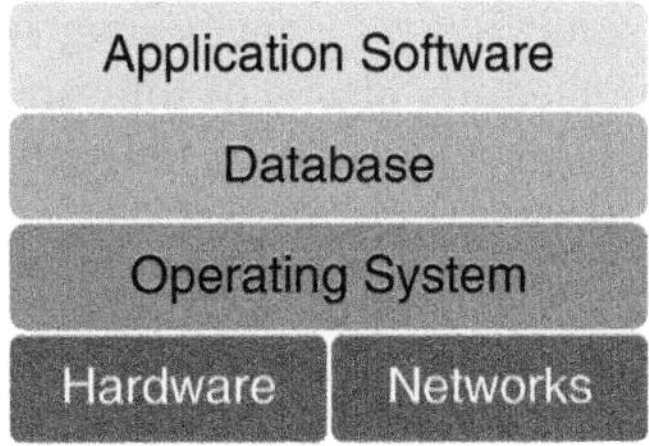


*Figure 16.1* IT system layers

### 3.2 Security risk management

Security risk assessment and management is essential for effective security engineering. Risk management is concerned with assessing the possible losses that might ensue from attacks on assets in the system, and balancing these losses against the costs of security procedures that may reduce these losses.

Risk management is a business issue rather than a technical issue, so software engineers should not decide what controls should be included in a system (Sommerville, 2016). It is up to senior management to decide whether or not to accept the cost of security or the exposure that results from a lack of security procedures. Rather, the role of software engineers is to provide informed technical guidance and judgment on security issues. They are, therefore, essential participants in the risk management process.

Risk assessment starts before the decision to acquire the system has been made and should continue throughout the system development process and after the system has gone into use (Alberts and Dorofee, 2002) and has three major stages:

- *Preliminary risk assessment*: At this stage, decisions on the detailed system requirements, the system design, or the implementation technology have not been made. The aim of this assessment process is to decide if an adequate level of security can be achieved at a reasonable cost. If this is the case, you can then derive specific security requirements for the system. You do not have information about potential vulnerabilities in the system or the controls that are included in reused system components or middleware.
- *Life-cycle risk assessment*: This risk assessment takes place during the system development life cycle and is informed by the technical system design and implementation decisions. The results of the assessment may lead to changes to the security requirements and the addition of new requirements. Known and potential vulnerabilities are identified and this knowledge is used to inform decision making about the system functionality and how it is to be implemented, tested and deployed.
- *Operational risk assessment*: After a system has been deployed and put into use, risk assessment should continue to take account of how the system is used and proposals for new and changed requirements. Assumptions about the operating requirement made when the system was specified may be incorrect. Organizational changes may mean that the system is used in different ways from those originally planned. Operational risk assessment therefore leads to new security requirements that have to be implemented as the system evolves.

A key aspect underpinning life-cycle risk assessment is the concept of secure software engineering. The idea behind secure software engineering is to implement well-structured processes and mechanisms from the early phases of software development. Secure software engineering starts from the requirements phase and is reflected in the entire stage of the SDLC (Sindre and Opdahl, 2004).

### 3.3 Security requirements engineering

It is well recognized in the software industry that requirements engineering is critical to the success of any major development projects. The requirements for a system are the descriptions of what the system should do – the services that it provides and the constraints on its operation – and reflect the needs of the customer. The process of finding out, analyzing, documenting and checking these services and constraints is called requirements engineering

It is important to ensure that software systems are developed according to the user needs and equal importance is given to ensure that the systems are secure. A common approach towards the inclusion of security within a software system is to identify security requirements after the definition of a system (Salini and Kanmani, 2012a), which has led to serious design challenges that usually translate into the emergence of computer systems badly affected with security vulnerabilities. Instead it is argued that security requirements should be considered from the early stages of the development process and it should be defined alongside the system requirements specifications.

Security requirements engineering is the process of eliciting, specifying and analyzing the security requirements for system fundamental ideas like 'what' of security requirements is, it is concerned with the prevention of harm in the real world and considering them as constraints upon functional requirements.

Security requirements (Haley et al., 2008) can be defined as "constraints on the functions of the system, where these constraints operationalize one or more security goals." In this definition, security requirements operationalize the security goals as follows:

- They are constraints on the system's functional requirements, rather than being themselves functional requirements.
- They express the system's security goals in operational terms, precise enough to be given to a designer or architect. Security requirements, like functional requirements, are prescriptive, providing a specification (behaviour in terms of phenomena) to achieve the desired effect.

The modelling and analysis of security requirements are a key challenge for software engineering (Devanbu and Stubblebine, 2000). According to Firesmith (2003), most requirement engineers are poorly trained to extract, analyze and specify security requirements and often confusing security requirements with the architectural security mechanisms that are traditionally used to fulfil. Thus, they end up specifying architecture and design constraints rather than true security requirements. Whilst some requirements engineers extract and analyze some quality requirements such as interoperability, availability, performance, reliability, portability and usability, many requirements engineers lack the skills to extract and analyze security requirements. The common problem with security requirements, when they are specified, is that they tend to be accidentally replaced with security-specific architectural constraints that may unnecessarily constrain the security team from using the most appropriate security mechanisms for meeting the true underlying security requirements. There are also many recent works done in the area of security mechanism like authentication, signatures, encryption and access (Salini and Kanmani, 2012a) rather than analysis of security requirements, which lead to poor security requirements specification.

Firesmith (2003) suggests that security requirements be organized into 12 categories. Among them, 10 of them are for Web applications:

1 Identification: any security requirement that specifies the extent to which a business, application, component or centre shall identify its before interacting with them.
2 Authentication: any security requirement that specifies the extent to which a business, application, component or centre shall verify the identity of its externals before interacting with them.

3 Authorization: any security requirement that specifies the access and usage privileges of authenticated users and client applications.
4 Immunity: any security requirement that specifies the extent to which an application or component shall protect itself from infection by unauthorized undesirable programs.
5 Integrity: any security requirement that specifies the extent to which an application or component shall ensure that its data and communications are not intentionally corrupted via unauthorized creation, modification or deletion.
6 Intrusion detection: any security requirement that specifies the extent to which an application or component shall detect and record attempted access or modification by unauthorized individuals.
7 Non-repudiation: any security requirement that specifies the extent to which a business, application or component shall prevent a party to one of its interactions from denying having participated in all or part of the interaction.
8 Privacy: any security requirement that specifies the extent to which a business, application, component or centre shall keep its sensitive data and communications private from unauthorized individuals and programs.
9 Audit: any security requirement that specifies the extent to which a business, application, component or centre shall enable security personnel to audit the status and use of its security mechanisms.
10 Maintenance: any security requirement that specifies the extent to which an application, component or centre shall prevent authorized from accidentally defeating its security mechanisms.
11 Physical protection requirements: a security requirement that specifies the extent to which an application or centre shall protect itself from physical assault.
12 Survivability requirement: a security requirement that specifies the extent to which an application or centre shall survive the intentional loss or destruction of a component.

### 3.4 Security requirements engineering methods

A method or a process is needed to derive security requirements. Such a process is called a security requirements engineering process and has multiple activities. As the idea of incorporating security into software from the very beginning of development has gained acceptance, various security requirements engineering methods were suggested. In the security requirements engineering phase the following important activities should be included (Salini and Kanmani, 2012b):

- Assets, threats and vulnerabilities should be identified.
- Threat modelling to depict the possible threats to the software so that appropriate security features and mechanisms can be specified.
- Risk analysis to prioritize the identified security requirements and security assessment to evaluate the security state of the requirement specifications.
- Security requirements specification using a security requirements specification language or modelling to remove the identified errors.
- Requirements specification review/inspection to find security errors by possibly using a checklist of potential requirements specification security errors.

There has been much research projects undertaken in requirements engineering in recent years have resulted in the development of methods and processes that can be used in identifying security requirements. The following section explains three popular security requirements engineering methods: multilateral security requirements analysis (MSRA), security quality requirements engineering methodology (SQUARE) and goal-based requirements analysis method (GBRAM) (Fabian et al., 2009).

The multilateral security requirements analysis (MSRA) method (Gürses et al., 2006) applies the principles of multilateral security (Rannenberg et al., 1999) during the requirements engineering phase of systems development. This is done by analysing security and privacy needs of all the stakeholders of a system to be, identifying conflicts and consolidating the different stakeholder views. The method borrows both from theories on multilateral security and viewpoint-oriented requirements engineering. The following are the main steps of the multilateral security requirements analysis method, once an initial functional requirements analysis for the main functionalities of the system is concluded:

- Identify stakeholders: Stakeholders are all parties that have functional, security, privacy or information interests in the system to be.
- Identify episodes: Episodes are similar to scenarios, but are of a lower granularity, identifying sets of functionalities as would be meaningful to users. Episodes are used to partition the security goals and are later useful in identifying conflicts between multiple security goals.
- Elaborate security goals: Identify and describe the security goals of the different security stakeholders for each of the episodes.
- Identify facts and assumptions: These are the properties of the environment that are relevant for stating security goals.
- Refine stakeholder views on episodes: Elaborate the stakeholder views taking facts, assumptions and the relationships between episodes into account.
- Reconcile security goals: Identify conflicts between security goals, find compromises between conflicting goals and establish a consistent set of security system requirements.
- Reconcile security and functional requirements: Trade functionality for security and vice versa in case of conflicting functional and security requirements.

The security quality requirements engineering methodology (SQUARE) (Mead and Stehney, 2005) is a comprehensive methodology for security requirements engineering. Its aim is to integrate security requirements engineering into software development processes (Mead et al., 2008). SQUARE stresses applicability in real software development projects and thus provides an organizational framework for carrying out security requirements engineering activities. It is assumed that SQUARE is carried out jointly by requirements engineers and stakeholders. It consists of nine steps:

- Agree on definitions: This step serves to enable a clear communication between requirements engineers and stakeholders.
- Identify security goals: Initially, the stakeholders will state different security goals. In this step, the goals are aligned and conflicts are resolved.
- Develop artifacts: The authors name the following artifacts that should be collected: system architecture diagram, use case scenarios/diagrams, misuse case scenarios/diagrams, attack trees, and standardized templates and forms. These artifacts form the basis for the subsequent steps of the method.
- Perform risk assessment: In this step, the vulnerabilities and threats related to the system are identified, as well as the likelihood that the threats will lead to attacks. The authors propose to apply existing risk assessment methods.

- Select elicitation technique: The method selected in this step will be applied in the next step to perform the actual security requirements elicitation. Again, SQUARE recommends to apply an existing technique to be chosen for the project at hand.
- Elicit security requirements: A crucial point in this step is to ensure that the requirements are verifiable and that they are not implementations or architectural constraints instead of requirements.
- Categorize requirements: The elicited requirements are categorized (at least) according to the following criteria: essential, non-essential, system-level, software-level architectural constraint. Since the latter are not considered as requirements, their existence indicates that the previous steps should be executed again.
- Prioritize requirements: It is assumed that not all requirements can be implemented; hence, the most important requirements must be identified.
- Requirements inspection: In this last step, the requirements are checked for ambiguities, inconsistencies, mistaken assumptions and the like. Its result is the final security requirements documents for the stakeholders.

The objective of the goal-based requirements analysis method (GBRAM) (Anton and Earp, 2000) is to utilize goal- and scenario-driven requirements engineering methods to formulate privacy and security policies, as well as requirements for e-commerce systems. Furthermore, the method targets change management in organizational privacy and security policies, and system requirements. Lastly, the method is used to assure compliance of these system requirements to the privacy and security policies. GBRAM contains a number of heuristics that can be applied to the various activities to identify, refine and operationalize security and privacy goals. These are:

- Identification heuristics are used by the requirements analyst to study existing security and privacy policies, requirements analysis and design documentation in order to identify both strategic and tactical goals related to the organizational assets. These goals are annotated, including information about stakeholders and responsibilities.
- Classification heuristics are used to classify the identified goals according to their type and dependencies.
- Elaboration heuristics are used to further analyze the classified goals by studying scenarios, goal obstacles, constraints, preconditions, postconditions, questions and the underlying rationale.
- Refinement heuristics are used to remove synonymous and redundant goals. Inconsistencies among goals are solved, and the goals are operationalized into a requirements specification.

## 4 Concluding remarks

To assure safe and secure products and services, good development practice must be used from the beginning. Safety and security should be viewed as enablers, not constraints because they impact an organization's goals and reputation. One general principle that facilitates stakeholders to focus on safety and security throughout the software life cycle is to use iterative, continuous and evolutionary approaches to direct product acquisition, development and delivery. Such approaches provide developmental agility, which is helpful to effectively address high uncertainty and to respond to unanticipated change.

Good development practice that is specific to safety and security includes (Chrissis et al., 2013):

- Provide early and careful consideration to quality attributes. Experience shows that safety and security cannot be added at the end of the development life cycle. Rather, products need to be developed with safety and security in mind from inception through disposal.
- Provide early and careful attention to an architecture that effectively addresses trade-offs among quality attributes and product functionality.
- Use processes that encourage careful consideration of how errors may be introduced, detected, removed and prevented. For example, explicit task kick-off and inspection checklists can be incorporated at multiple points in the SDLC to sustain attention on common error patterns affecting quality. Also, requirements elicitation, architecture, risk management and decision analysis processes (and thus software development teams) should encourage explicit attention to safety and security (as well as other critical quality attributes).
- View safety and security as enablers of the organization's core mission and objectives and not as constraints on creativity and innovation. Make sure these attributes are commonplace in the development of all products and services.
- Use reviews and code analysis tools to reduce code-induced vulnerabilities, thereby developing higher quality code.
- Be informed. Most exploitable errors are not the result of a lack of creativity or motivation but the lack of knowledge about vulnerabilities and human oversights. Better knowledge, processes and technology can help overcome these weaknesses and the limits of our self-awareness.

Only by increasing security-oriented effort throughout the software development life cycle can robust, secure software be designed. The early integration of security activities into the development life cycle leads to cheaper software development. Adding appropriate security later is difficult, if not impossible, because the design itself may be fundamentally insecure. Moreover, it can also cause changes to features and application interfaces affecting backwards compatibility. A successful incorporation of security-related activities in each SDLC phase reduces effort and time while delivering secure software.

By incorporating security activities into the SDLC, organizations will benefit from stronger security, reducing the likelihood and/or impact of exploited vulnerabilities. In addition, by considering security concepts during the correct SDLC phase, the integration of security into the system will be seamless and benefit from a reduction in cost. In contrast, retrofitting a system with security requirements can be a very costly process.

As a starting point, organizations should identify the policies, standards and business objectives that will drive excellence in your organization. Software life cycle standards (e.g., CMMI and ISO/IEEE 15288) provide the foundation and flexibility to build safety and security into an organization's life cycle processes (Chrissis et al., 2013).

## References


Alberts, C., Dorofee, A., 2002. *Managing Information Security Risks: The OCTAVE (SM) Approach*, 1st edition. Addison-Wesley Professional, Boston.

Al-Mudimigh, A., Zairi, M., Al-Mashari, M., 2002. ERP software implementation: an integrative framework. *Eur. J. Inf. Syst.* 10, 216–226. https:/doi.org/10.1057/palgrave.ejis.3000406.

Ameller, D., Galster, M., Avgeriou, P., Franch, X., 2015. A survey on quality attributes in service-based systems. *Softw. Qual. J.* 24, 271–299. https:/doi.org/10.1007/s11219-015-9268-4.

Anton, A. I., Earp, J. B., 2000. *Strategies for Developing Policies and Requirements for Secure Electronic Commerce Systems*. North Carolina State University at Raleigh, Raleigh, NC.

Ayala, C., Franch, X., 2014. Dealing with information quality in software package selection: an empirically based approach. *IET Softw*. 8, 204–218. https:/doi.org/10.1049/iet-sen.2013.0180.

Ayala, C., Hauge, Ø., Conradi, R., Franch, X., Li, J., 2011. Selection of third party software in Off-The-Shelf-based software development – An interview study with industrial practitioners. *J. Syst. Softw., The Ninth International Conference on Quality Software* 84, 620–637. https:/doi.org/10.1016/j.jss.2010.10.019.

Azadeh, A., Nazari-Shirkouhi, S., Samadi, H., Nazari-Shirkouhi, A., 2014. An integrated fuzzy group decision making approach for evaluation and selection of best simulation software packages. *Int. J. Ind. Syst. Eng.* 18, 256–282. https:/doi.org/10.1504/IJISE.2014.064709.

Bellovin, S.M., 2015. What a real cybersecurity bill should address. *IEEE Secur. Priv*. 13, 92–92. https:/doi.org/10.1109/MSP.2015.52.

Bernroider, E., Koch, S., 2001. ERP selection process in midsize and large organizations. *Bus. Process Manag. J.* 7, 251–257. https:/doi.org/10.1108/14637150110392746.

Brooks, F.P., J., 1987. No silver bullet essence and accidents of software engineering. *Computer* 20, 10–19. https:/doi.org/10.1109/MC.1987.1663532.

Carvallo, J.P., Franch, X., Quer, C., 2007. Determining criteria for selecting software components: lessons learned. *IEEE Softw*. 24, 84–94. https:/doi.org/10.1109/MS.2007.70.

Chang, V., Ramachandran, M., 2016. Towards achieving data security with the cloud computing adoption framework. *IEEE Trans. Serv. Comput.* 9, 138–151. https:/doi.org/10.1109/TSC.2015.2491281.

Chau, P.Y.K., 1995. Factors used in the selection of packaged software in small businesses: views of owners and managers. *Inf. Manage*. 29, 71–78. https:/doi.org/10.1016/0378–7206(95)00016-P.

Chrissis, M.B., Konrad, M., Moss, M., 2013. Ensuring your development processes meet today's cyber challenges. *CrossTalk* March–April, 29–33.

Clarke, P., O'Connor, R.V., Leavy, B., 2016. A Complexity Theory Viewpoint on the Software Development Process and Situational Context, in: *Proceedings of the International Workshop on Software and Systems Process*. ACM, New York, pp. 86–90.

CMMI Product Team, 2011. CMMI for Acquisition Version 1.3. Software Engineering Institute.

Colomo-Palacios, R., Rodríguez, J.M.Á., 2014. Semantic Representation and Computation of Cloud-Based Customer Relationship Management Solutions, in: Meersman, R., Panetto, H., Mishra, A., Valencia-García, R., Soares, A.L., Ciuciu, I., Ferri, F., Weichhart, G., Moser, T., Bezzi, M., Chan, H. (Eds.), *On the Move to Meaningful Internet Systems: OTM 2014 Workshops, Lecture Notes in Computer Science*. Springer, Berlin Heidelberg, pp. 347–357.

Cortellessa, V., Marinelli, F., Potena, P., 2008. An optimization framework for "build-or-buy" decisions in software architecture. *Comput. Oper. Res., Part Special Issue: Search-based Software Engineering* 35, 3090–3106. https:/doi.org/10.1016/j.cor.2007.01.011.

CSMIC, 2014. Service Measurement Index Framework Version 2.0.

Daneshgar, F., Low, G.C., Worasinchai, L., 2013. An investigation of "build vs. buy" decision for software acquisition by small to medium enterprises. *Inf. Softw. Technol.* 55, 1741–1750. https:/doi.org/10.1016/j.infsof.2013.03.009.

Devanbu, P.T., Stubblebine, S., 2000. Software engineering for security: a roadmap, in: *Proceedings of the Conference on the Future of Software Engineering*. ACM, New York, pp. 227–239. https:/doi.org/10.1145/336512.336559.

Fabian, B., Gürses, S., Heisel, M., Santen, T., Schmidt, H., 2009. A comparison of security requirements engineering methods. *Requir. Eng*. 15, 7–40. https:/doi.org/10.1007/s00766–009–0092-x.

Firesmith, D.G., 2003. Security use cases. *J. Object Technol.* 2.

Franch, X., Carvallo, J.P., 2003. Using quality models in software package selection. *IEEE Softw*. 20, 34–41. https:/doi.org/10.1109/MS.2003.1159027.

Garfinkel, S. L., 2012. The cybersecurity risk. *Commun ACM* 55, 29–32. https:/doi.org/10.1145/2184319.2184330.

Gartner, 2016. Gartner says worldwide information security spending will grow 7.9 Percent to Reach $81.6 Billion in 2016 [WWW Document]. URL www.gartner.com/newsroom/id/3404817 (accessed September 22, 2016).

Gupta, P., Mehlawat, M. K., Verma, S., 2010. COTS selection using fuzzy interactive approach. *Optim. Lett.* 6, 273–289. https:/doi.org/10.1007/s11590-010-0243-5.

Gürses, S., Berendt, B., Santen, T., 2006. Multilateral Security Requirements Analysis for Preserving Privacy in Ubiquitous Environments, in: *Proceedings of the UKDU Workshop*. pp. 51–64.

Haley, C., Laney, R., Moffett, J., Nuseibeh, B., 2008. Security requirements engineering: A framework for representation and analysis. *IEEE Trans. Softw. Eng.* 34, 133–153. https:/doi.org/10.1109/TSE.2007.70754.

Hwang, S. m, 2007. Intelligent methods and procedures of countermeasure design, in: *International Conference on Multimedia and Ubiquitous Engineering* (MUE'07). Presented at the 2007 International Conference on Multimedia and Ubiquitous Engineering (MUE'07), pp. 1168–1171. https:/doi.org/10.1109/MUE.2007.139.

ISO, 2013. ISO/IEC 27001:2013 – Information Technology – Security Techniques – Information Security Management Systems – Requirements.

Jadhav, A. S., Sonar, R. M., 2011. Framework for evaluation and selection of the software packages: a hybrid knowledge based system approach. *J. Syst. Softw.* 84, 1394–1407. https:/doi.org/10.1016/j.jss.2011.03.034.

Jha, P. C., Bali, V., Narula, S., Kalra, M., 2014. Optimal component selection based on cohesion & coupling for component based software system under build-or-buy scheme. *J. Comput. Sci., Empowering Science through Computing + BioInspired Computing* 5, 233–242. https:/doi.org/10.1016/j.jocs.2013.07.003.

Kaur, J., Tomar, P., 2015. Four tier architecture of component selection process using clustering. *Int. J. Softw. Eng. Technol. Appl.* 1, 155–171. https:/doi.org/10.1504/IJSETA.2015.075611.

Khan, M.U.A., Zulkernine, M., 2009. On Selecting Appropriate Development Processes and Requirements Engineering Methods for Secure Software, in: *33rd Annual IEEE International Computer Software and Applications Conference*. Presented at the 2009 33rd Annual IEEE International Computer Software and Applications Conference, pp. 353–358. https:/doi.org/10.1109/COMPSAC.2009.206.

Khan, R., 2011. Secure software development: a prescriptive framework. *Comput. Fraud Secur.* 2011, 12–20. https:/doi.org/10.1016/S1361–3723(11)70083–5

Konys, A., 2015. Knowledge-Based Approach to COTS Software Selection Processes, in: Wiliński, A., Fray, I. E., Pejaś, J. (Eds.), *Soft Computing in Computer and Information Science, Advances in Intelligent Systems and Computing*. Springer International Publishing, Berlin Heidelberg, pp. 191–205. https:/doi.org/10.1007/978-3-319-15147-2_17.

Kupsch, J.A., Heymann, E., Miller, B., Basupalli, V., 2016. Bad and good news about using software assurance tools. *Softw. Pract. Exp.* https:/doi.org/10.1002/spe.2401.

McGraw, G., 2016. Four software security findings. *Computer* 49, 84–87. https:/doi.org/10.1109/MC.2016.30

McGraw, G. R., 2006. *Software Security: Building Security In*. 1st edition. Addison-Wesley Professional, Upper Saddle River, NJ.

Mead, N. R., Stehney, T., 2005. Security quality requirements engineering (SQUARE) methodology, in: *Proceedings of the 2005 Workshop on Software Engineering for Secure Systems – Building Trustworthy Applications*. ACM, New York, pp. 1–7. https:/doi.org/10.1145/1082983.1083214.

Mead, N. R., Viswanathan, V., Padmanabhan, D., Raveendran, A., 2008. Incorporating security quality requirements engineering (SQUARE) into standard life-cycle models (No. CMU/SEI-2008-TN-006). Carnegie-Mellon University, Pittsburgh, PA, Software Engineering Institute.

Mehlawat, M. K., Gupta, P., 2014. Multiobjective credibilistic model for COTS products selection of modular software systems under uncertainty. *Appl. Intell.* 42, 353–368. https:/doi.org/10.1007/s10489-014-0602-5.

Montazemi, A.R., Cameron, D.A., Gupta, K.M., 1996. An empirical study of factors affecting software package selection. *J. Manag. Inf. Syst.* 13, 89–105. https:/doi.org/10.1080/07421222.1996.11518113.

Nair, S., de la Vara, J.L., Sabetzadeh, M., Briand, L., 2014. An extended systematic literature review on provision of evidence for safety certification. *Inf. Softw. Technol.* 56, 689–717. https:/doi.org/10.1016/j.infsof.2014.03.001.

Pfleeger, C.P., Pfleeger, S.L., Margulies, J., 2015. *Security in Computing*, 5th edition. Prentice Hall, Upper Saddle River, NJ.

Pino, F.J., Baldassarre, M.T., Piattini, M., Visaggio, G., Caivano, D., 2008. Mapping Software Acquisition Practices From ISO 12207 and CMMI, in: Maciaszek, L.A., González-Pérez, C., Jablonski, S. (Eds.), *Evaluation of Novel Approaches to Software Engineering, Communications in Computer and Information Science*. Springer, Berlin Heidelberg, pp. 234–247. https:/doi.org/10.1007/978-3-642-14819-4_17.

Ramachandran, M., 2016. Software security requirements management as an emerging cloud computing service. *Int. J. Inf. Manag.* 36, 580–590. https:/doi.org/10.1016/j.ijinfomgt.2016.03.008.

Rannenberg, K., Pfitzmann, A., Müller, G., 1999. IT security and multilateral security. *Multilater. Secur. Commun. Infrastruct. Econ.* 21–29.

Salini, P., Kanmani, S., 2012a. Survey and analysis on security requirements engineering. *Comput. Electr. Eng.* 38, 1785–1797. https:/doi.org/10.1016/j.compeleceng.2012.08.008.

Salini, P., Kanmani, S., 2012b. Security requirements engineering process for web applications. *Procedia Eng.* 38, 2799–2807. https:/doi.org/10.1016/j.proeng.2012.06.328.

SAMM, 2016. Software Assurance Maturity Model (SAMM): A guide to building security into software development [WWW Document]. URL www.opensamm.org/ (accessed 9.24.16).

Shiau, W.-L., Chau, P.Y.K., 2016. Understanding behavioral intention to use a cloud computing classroom: a multiple model comparison approach. *Inf. Manage., Information Technology and Innovation: Drivers, Challenges and Impacts* 53, 355–365. https:/doi.org/10.1016/j.im.2015.10.004.

Sindre, G., Opdahl, A.L., 2004. Eliciting security requirements with misuse cases. *Requir. Eng.* 10, 34–44. https:/doi.org/10.1007/s00766-004-0194-4.

Sommerville, I., 2016. *Software Engineering*, 10th edition. Pearson, Boston, MA.

Stratistics MRC, 2016. Cloud Computing – Global Market Outlook (2015–2022) [WWW Document]. URL www.strategymrc.com/report/cloud-computing-market (accessed September 30, 2016).

Vale, T., Crnkovic, I., de Almeida, E.S., Silveira Neto, P.A. da M., Cavalcanti, Y.C., Meira, S.R. de L., 2016. Twenty-eight years of component-based software engineering. *J. Syst. Softw.* 111, 128–148. https:/doi.org/10.1016/j.jss.2015.09.019.

Wysopal, C., 2008. Building security into your software-development lifecycle. *SC Mag.* 30.

Yimam, D., Fernandez, E.B., 2016. A survey of compliance issues in cloud computing. *J. Internet Serv. Appl.* 7, 5. https:/doi.org/10.1186/s13174-016-0046-8.

# 17

# Information security in an ever-changing threat landscape

*Matthew Lagana*

> The threat landscape in Security is in a constant state of flux, with new threats emerging and existing threats becoming ever more sophisticated.
>
> —*Steve Wright and Nick Frost*

> To improve is to change; to be perfect is to change often.
>
> —*Winston Churchill*

## 1 Introduction

> Technology changes faster than most business can keep up with. The proliferation of mobile technology, the Internet of Things (IoT) and cloud computing has changed the types of "assets" connected to networks. Implementing cybersecurity "best practices" across an increasingly unstructured and decentralized network is one of the most vexing challenges facing companies today.
>
> (Forbes, 2017)

In today's computing world, security concerns follow us everywhere and as such should be paramount to all, not just corporations or government entities. Whether you are driving in a smart car or are utilizing some type of medical technology to manage a condition, the question of "how secure is this?" should be part of our thinking. For an organization, information security protects both the brand and bottom line financial results.

In 2016, 89% of all attacks involved financial motivations (Verizon DBIR, 2016). Of those attacks, surprisingly or not, most were successfully conducted exploiting known vulnerabilities that were never addressed by organizations or individuals (i.e. in our own homes). Surprisingly, basic defences continue to be sorely lacking! So let's start off by exploring the role people, process, and technology play in the security equation.

*People*: Having the right staff with the right mix of skill sets is essential. Not only do security personnel have to be talented technically, they also need strong analytical skills. To that end, these individuals must be willing to question anything that either doesn't make sense, or is out of pattern. Throughout my career, I refer to this character trait as "native intellectual curiosity." As we all know, not everyone is wired the same way; therefore, not everyone is cut out to be an information security professional.

*Process*: An organization must have the proper structure in place to support their security program. This entails having strong policies, protocols and procedures in place as the foundation for an enterprise security architecture. These must be clearly defined and must also evolve with the times through mandatory annual reviews. These elements span areas such as technology use, operational risk, vendor management, data classification, cybersecurity and incident response.

*Technology*: Last but not least is the technology deployed to secure our information assets. A successful security architecture deploys and optimally configures the right mix of technology solutions from strong vendor partners. Having said that, the due diligence process employed in selecting these security tools is paramount for success. Today's security technology market is flooded with solutions, as cyber events have become regularly recurring headline news. It seems like every day, another company falls victim to some type of hacking. Whether it's a data breach or a denial of service attack, cyber events are a regular occurrence in today's reality.

It's also important to discuss the philosophy and corporate culture of an organization and how it supports the adoption, enforcement, and evolution of a sound security program. With this in mind, security policies should be driven by the needs of the business and in turn, those policies, should drive the security standards and guidelines used throughout the organization.

In today's security ecosystem, policies govern areas such as technology use, records retention, vendor management, internal controls, operational risk, and intellectual property. Moreover, a specific policy is now needed to govern cybersecurity and incident response. To help illustrate and provide additional context, I've included a sample purpose statement for a cybersecurity policy (see below).

## *Purpose*

The protection of Information Assets against unauthorized access, theft, and misuse is a critical issue for the Company. These assets are those used by Covered Persons to perform their duties on behalf of the Company, and include business and technology applications, networks, computing platform(s), and the data stored therein. The Cybersecurity Policy establishes the framework of the Company's controls to mitigate risks from malicious and unauthorized use of, and cybersecurity threats or attacks against, the Company's Information Assets.

Policies are designed to establish the framework for protecting critical Information Assets through an evolving, multi-tiered security approach. The cybersecurity program governed by this Policy applies to people, processes and technology. The Company has established a security team, which is comprised of representatives of different groups within the Company who are responsible for the security program and related policies. The purpose of this policy is to help ensure the Company has implemented the necessary policies, protocols and controls related to the security of its Information Assets and has tested the effectiveness of such controls and properly assessed risks related to the security of its Information Assets.

At the end of the day, the field of information security can be broken down into knowledge domains and for the purposes of this chapter, we will primarily follow an outline or model defined by a leading international security consortium (ISC2, 2017).

## 2 Security and risk management

So how much security do we actually need, and how much should we be spending on the program. Well, that brings us squarely into the area of risk management. You wouldn't ever spend $5,000 to insure a car that's only worth $3,000, would you? The level of security needed and the budget that supports it is primarily predicated by an organization's risk profile. While it is difficult to estimate the actual cost of a security breach since so many factors are at play, suffice to say it can be significant. Financial loss can typically be attributed to areas such as forensics, breach notification, credit monitoring, business income interruption, legal defence, legal settlement, regulator defence and regulatory fines. The sad news it that this hard dollar reality doesn't even speak to the reputational impact on a product or service's brand. That's why public relations is now one of the focal points in an incident response plan. Organizations recognize that this type of damage in turn can materialize in financial losses derived from decreased sales or even a drop in share price for publicly traded organizations. Just imagine the impact of customers, clients or business partners losing faith or confidence in your brand due to an unfortunate data breach. The pendulum has also swung where organizations who used to be portrayed as victims are now being publicly shamed as negligent. This is most felt and seen in both the court of public opinion, federal inquiries or recent legal judgements, where companies can and are being found guilty of simply not doing the basics. Take the 2016 Bangladesh Bank $81 million cyber heist, where a government panel conducting the investigation found five officials at the bank were guilty of negligence and carelessness, according to Reuters (2016). Former central bank governor Mohammed Farashuddin said the officials were "negligent, careless and indirect accomplices."

From a legal viewpoint, it doesn't come down to creating an environment that is 100% impenetrable, because everyone recognizes that is not a reality. However, there is an expectation of a minimum baseline of security. This threshold is what is expected and being demanded by the courts, regulators, customers and business partners.

So let's talk about how to go about assessing risk. Risks need to be first identified across the organization, then ranked by severity and frequency of a potential event.

Standards for assessing risk can vary, but for the most part recognized entities such as the Institute of Internal Auditors North America (IIA, 2017) are consistent in their respective approaches. For purposes of this chapter, we'll break this into five risk factors that can be applied to the various business processes throughout a company. These factors are intended to address the majority of risks; however, other factors may exist based on uniqueness of an organizations business processes. Each risk factor is normally assessed using a high, moderate, and low rating system with values assigned along a spectrum (e.g. 5, 4, 3, 2 and 1) for the correlating assessments. The risk assessment of each process should also be directly impacted by the ratings received. The ratings for all processes are then calculated and plotted on a risk map.

The five risk factors to consider when assessing risk to an organization are as follows.

### *Financial impact on organization*

Factors to consider in assessing the financial impact of a business process are:

- Size of portfolio
- Impact on revenue
- Potential for loss
- Volume/size of transactions.

### Complexity of a product, service or process

The complexity of a product, service or process is usually an indicator of risk. Complex business processes where intimate knowledge of the entire process and its impact on the company is difficult to understand present a higher level of risk to the organization.

Factors to consider in assessing the complexity of a business process include:

- Skill levels needed to perform job duties
- Complexity of transactions
- Amount of manual intervention needed to complete a function
- Complexity of IT systems supporting the business process
- Number of laws/regulations governing the function
- Impact of foreign operations on process.

### External factors

External factors are risks related to compliance with laws and regulations, reputation and market pressures. For the most part, the company has minimal or no control over these factors.

Specific factors include:

- Compliance with and understanding of applicable laws and regulations
- Potential amount of legal/regulatory fines
- Publicity and reputational impact of media attention
- Competitive pressures such as new entrants and/or products to the market, superior competitor performance, changing customer needs and wants
- Reliance on key business partners
- Changes in industry/potential obsolescence.

### Overall environment

The environment is the foundation that provides discipline and structure to the organization and its business processes/functions. It starts at the top with the moral climate set by the board of directors, chief executive and company officers and extends to each employee. It includes integrity and ethical values of management and staff, and their methods of authority and accountability. In a good environment, risk assessment and management are not external processes; they are part of everyday behaviour. Known control deficiencies, history of past audits and management's willingness to embrace processes and controls should be considered as part of the overall evaluation.

### Information systems

Information system risks impact overall risk to the extent that there is reliance on the applications and infrastructure. These risks should be considered when assessing the overall risk to the various business processes within the organization, including the IT area.

Specifically, information system risks can be summarized as the following factors:

*Access*: Failure to adequately restrict access to information (data or programs) may result in unauthorized knowledge and use of confidential information, or fraud. Excessive restriction of access to information may preclude personnel from performing their assigned responsibilities effectively and efficiently.

*Infrastructure*: Deficiencies in the IT infrastructure (i.e., hardware, networks, software, IT operations and processes) could impair the ability to meet current and future business needs in an efficient, cost-effective and well-controlled fashion.

*Availability*: Availability focuses on whether information will be available when needed. This includes risks such as the loss of communications (i.e., cut cables, telephone system outage and satellite loss), the loss of basic processing capabilities (i.e., disaster, application errors) and operational difficulties (i.e., disk drive breakdown, operator errors). Business interruption can also arise from natural disasters, vandalism, sabotage and accidents.

*Integrity*: Loss of integrity of data produced by the information systems infrastructure due to inappropriate aggregated data, irrelevant data or untimely delivery of data.

*Relevance*: Relevance is the risk that information is not relevant to the purpose for which it is collected, maintained or distributed. This risk relates to the usability and timeliness of information that is either created or summarized by an application system.

## 3 Security operations

The area of security operations has also seen much change in recent years, as security offerings to outsource this function are now widely available. The key functions can be broken down and explained as follows:

- Logging and monitoring activities
- Patch and vulnerability management
- Change management processes
- Incident management and response
- Investigations support and requirements.

Many of us may be familiar with hit TV shows like *CSI* (CSI, 2017), whose storyline is based on crime scene investigations. We have become fascinated with forensic investigations and how intriguing they are in being able to piece together all of the breadcrumbs left behind by criminals. Well, in the world of computer security, a security operations team handles this essential role. In today's security operations environment, robust logging and monitoring are key in being able to both early detect potential hacking activity and in being able to determine the extent of an attack. Many security experts have acknowledged that we must also be able to effectively 'detect, isolate and mitigate' an attack. Organizations cannot continue to focus a majority of their time and resources on prevention alone. It's just not realistic based on the sophistication and resources today's cyber criminals have at their disposal. We need to acknowledge that cybercrime is big business and has been commoditized in many respects. As stated earlier, 89% of all attacks in 2016 involved some form of financial motivation.

Attackers will attempt to exploit both well-known and newly discovered vulnerabilities. This means that our security operations team must be ready to handle both. To do so, the foundational elements of security operations must be in place, which start off by understanding the importance of a disciplined change management and vulnerability management program. This is an area that cannot be overstated and will help defend the organization from the majority of attacks being seen day in and day out. The known universe of attacks is the low-hanging fruit for attackers. In fact, the top 10 known vulnerabilities, as reported in Verizon's 2016 Data Breach Investigations Report, accounted for 85% of successful exploits.

To help better illustrate this point, imagine someone trying to steal a car. Will that criminal go after a car that simply has their doors locked or one that is equipped with a state-of-the-art security system? The known vulnerability universe is vast; however, the good news is that hardware and software manufacturers are actively remediating issues and delivering security patches or fixes. These patches are risk ranked (low, medium, high and critical) and are released on a scheduled or emergency basis. A phrase I use often with my security team is, "you are only as good as the latest security patch you've installed." So, you may be thinking, why wouldn't an organization simply apply these security updates to their environment as soon as they are made available? Well, this is not as easy as it sounds and is exactly where change management discipline squarely comes into the discussion. A systematic process must be in place which begins with being able to assess the update to confirm whether or not you are actually at risk (i.e. you may have already disabled a feature that is the basis of the vulnerability). Once you have completed your assessment and determined that you in fact need the update, you must assure it will not break some element of your technology environment. The level of integration between systems throughout an organization brings complexity to what would seem a very straightforward process. At the end of the day, it gets back to risk management. Unfortunately, you can sometimes take on more risk by prematurely applying an update if impacts the availability or integrity of a system or application. This potential havoc on your environment can sometimes be more risky than the probability of an attacker actually exploiting that vulnerability. Organizations need to strike a balance between adequate testing and the need to address vulnerabilities in a timely manner.

Now, let's turn our attention to vulnerabilities that that do not have available software fixes, sometimes referred to as 'zero' day. In this case, detecting and defending against attacks that utilize unknown or understood vulnerabilities is much harder. These exploits are unfortunately part of the attacker's tool kit and are being sold on the dark web, a criminal's version of a goods and services marketplace like Amazon.com. In the area of security operations, the team must be equipped with advanced technologies and strong analytic capabilities, which we'll discuss more in the security engineering section of this chapter.

Analytics and machine learning are quickly changing the face of security operations. Being able to correlate the breadcrumbs generated by the vast number of logging systems, provide better threat detection and allow for higher productivity of the security staff.

Advanced analytics complement traditional signature-based prevention systems which have been losing the battle in recent years. Security analytics include detection of external threats, insider threats and the act of data exfiltration from the organization.

Today's predictive security analytics have full visibility into the network, down to an organization's endpoint devices, and are able to correlate the volumes of data being generated across the technology environment. Decisions can then be made by the security team on how to stop or at the very least isolate an attack.

The last area we'll cover on the topic of security operations is incident management and response. To the earlier point on the shift to a 'detection, isolation and remediation' strategy, this has become one of the hottest topics in the security conversation. An organization must have a well-structured, documented and tested incident response plan which includes the following components:

- Incident reporting and communications plan (internal and external)
- First responders/key stakeholders (names, contact details and roles)

- Clear definition of roles and responsibilities within the team
- Incident assessment/forensics investigation
- Incident countermeasures (e.g. network isolation, disaster recovery or business continuity plan)
- Remediation strategy/identifying corrective actions.

## Key Definitions

*Security event*: The occurrence of an event in an information system or network that is detected and may ultimately be considered 'benign' if security controls effectively identify and prevent any damage or disruption of services or unauthorized access. Security events include, for example, the suspicion or presence of a malicious application or program, such as a virus, or a 'phishing' email.

*Data breach*: An incident that results in the confirmed disclosure of data to an unauthorized party.

## 4 Asset security

This discipline involves the practices of asset classification, ownership (e.g. data owners, system owners), security controls, data retention and data privacy. So let's start with the foundational basics: an organization data classification program. Data classification begins the identification of information assets. Data owners must be identified as the individuals who created or have custodial responsibility for that data. Once these assets are known and proper owners have been identified, the stratification process can begin to risk classify the data. For purposes of this chapter, we'll simply classify data as either public, private or confidential.

- *Public*: Data should be classified as public when the unauthorized disclosure, alteration or destruction of that data would results in little or no risk to the company and its affiliates. Examples of public data include press releases and research publications. While little or no controls are required to protect the confidentiality of public data, some level of control is required to prevent unauthorized modification or destruction of public data.
- *Private*: Data should be classified as private when the unauthorized disclosure, alteration or destruction of that data could result in a moderate level of risk to the company or its affiliates, By default, all institutional data that is not explicitly classified as restricted or public data should be treated as private data. Examples of private data are internal memos or email communications. A reasonable level of security control should be applied to private data.
- *Confidential*: Data should be classified as restricted when the unauthorized disclosure, alteration or destruction of that data could cause a significant level of risk to the company or its affiliates. Examples of restricted data include data protected by state or federal privacy regulations, data protected by confidentiality agreements (HR data) and key financial data (loss reserves, earnings). The highest level of security controls should be applied to restricted data.

Now that we have transparency on what data assets we have and who owns or is responsible for the data, we can properly define the level of security needed to protect it.

## 5 Security engineering

In this area, we will cover the security capabilities of our information systems. We'll discuss security architectures and solution elements like cryptography. Further, we'll review the key areas of vulnerability that an organizations security architecture is protecting against. This can range from internal applications to mobile systems vulnerabilities.

The area of security engineering has also seen much change in recent years, as solutions cover a wide range of security concerns in a very competitive marketplace. The picture below is a simple illustration of the areas covered by today's security technology vendors.

Security engineering is in and of itself an orchestration of technologies that have been architected to optimize their protection capabilities. This can be as simple as configuration and as complicated as the integration of different security technologies with our systems and data. In the end, security practitioners must have a methodology in place that addresses the security needs of the organization and the due care needed to select and implement the right architecture components. It should also be noted that many external resources are available to help with evaluating, building and evolving the security architecture. "Information security, network and communications practitioners must implement specific best practices to prevent,

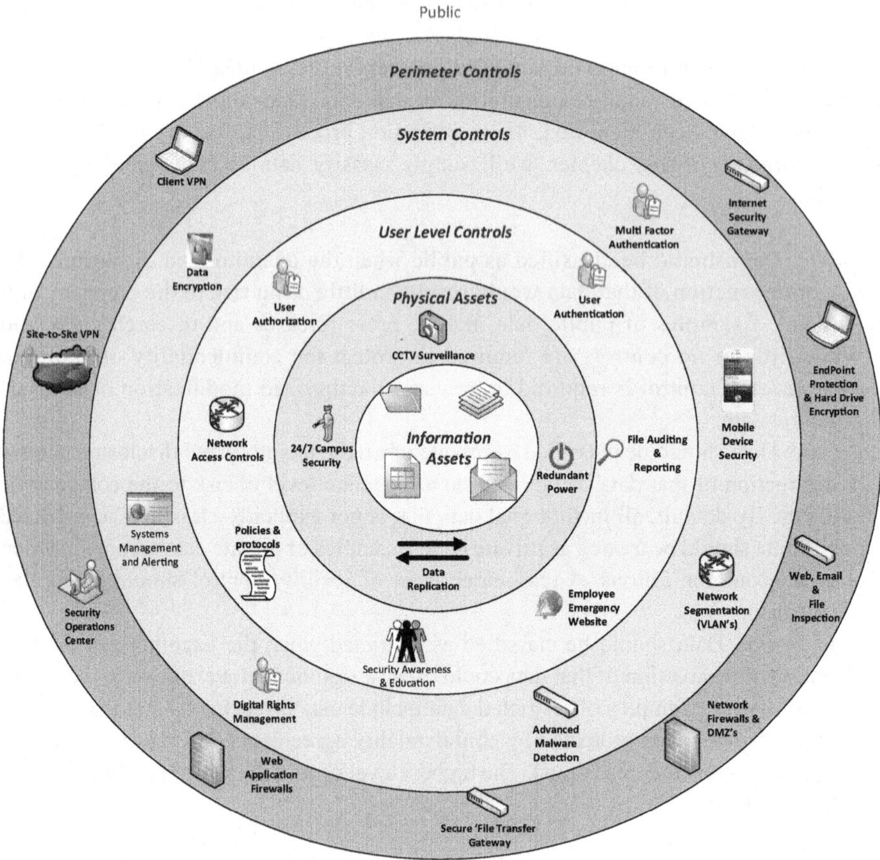


*Figure 17.1* Multi-layered defence

detect and mitigate advanced threats. These practitioners should leverage both existing and emerging security technologies in their security architectures" (Gartner, 2017).

## 6 Network security

Network security is now most commonly discussed in the context of cybersecurity, since it represents a key security discipline that is foundational to any security architecture. In the Internet of Things era, the network has no boundaries, so network security has become increasingly difficult to truly achieve. This section will give an overview of a wide range of network security technologies and approaches that span secure communications channels, network or web-based gateways and secure network architecture design.

Today's security architecture's continue to revolve around firewalls. Yes, firewalls are still essential and continue to control what network traffic is allowed into and out of the organization. This is accomplished by the creation of rules which govern different network elements. I like to think of this is as the 'who, what and how' model.

The 'who' is accomplished by network addresses (e.g. 192.168.1.1) that are allowed or denied from accessing the network or specific parts of the network. The 'what' is defined by the protocols (e.g. IP, UDP) encapsulating the traffic, and the 'how' is defined by the ports being traversed to deliver the traffic (e.g. port 80: HTTP).

The big difference, however, in modern firewalls, is that they have become much more intelligent. This is achieved primarily through the use of 'behavioural' analysis and community-based intelligence.

Behavioural analysis is very complicated, but at its essence identifies the intended action of the initiating traffic by executing in a virtual world often referred to as a 'sandbox'. A great example would take the action of a user clicking on a link within an email or directly from a web browser. The link can take that allowable HTTP (port 80) traffic and deliver a much different result such as redirecting your computer to an IP address of an attacker website. The attacker's site now has a direct connection established to your computer's browser and can now attempt to execute various hacking techniques like downloading malicious software. If infected, the unsuspecting computer can now be manipulated by the attacker (referred to as command and control) and initiate outward bound network traffic from your network (referred to as a call-back). In this scenario, instructions are given to the computer based on the type of attack being mounted. One of these later instructions can result in sending back your private information or data (referred to as data exfiltration).

By using behavioural analysis conducted in a secure virtual sandbox, we can play out the attacker's intent and the firewall can learn that this is not expected or good behaviour. The other important element in modern-day firewall technology is what I referred to earlier as community-based intelligence. In this same scenario, the firewall would also rely on information learned from the broader internet community. We can learn many things that may have been seen or experienced by the community. Has the IP address of an attacker's website already been reported as a malicious site? Has the software attempting to pass through your network already been seen and reported as malicious? As we know in the world of social media, the community can have great power and information can be disseminated at lightning speed. This power is brilliantly harnessed to achieve additional network security. Lastly, there are now more platform-specific uses of firewall technology. In today's arsenal, network security companies have created different purpose built firewalls to protect computing resources. In this regard, database firewalls or Web application firewalls have become popular network security control points. These firewalls can be configured in a much more granular fashion to determine what and how specific computing resources can be communicated with. These firewalls can also be trained to learn exactly how custom software has been programmed and what a valid transaction looks like.

Another great network security technique we'll learn is network segmentation. Networks can be broken into different parts. Each specific segment can then be treated as a virtual local ara network (VLAN). Now that the network has been broken into different pieces, we can now apply different levels of security based on what is residing in that segment. Another term that is important to understand in the area of network segmentation is a DMZ (demilitarized zone). DMZs are VLANs that have been earmarked as areas of a network that an organization wishes to expose to the internet. Think of a bank which allows its customers to login to a web portal to access their account information. Well, in order to facilitate this transaction, the website must be able to securely communicate to computing resources within the banks network (e.g. database server). The DMZ isolates the end users' connection from the website and will only allow the web server to initiate a connection to an authorized part of the bank's network. A series of DMZs can be created to further restrict and create layers between the external web connection and the bank's critical systems and data.

The other business problem that network security solves is the valid need for personnel, suppliers and/or business partners to access our networks remotely. Virtual private networks (VPNs) have broad application and can be used in many different ways. For instance, employees today need to perform their jobs remotely for many different reasons. VPNs are also used to connect geographically dispersed offices of an organization using nothing more than the public internet as a transport medium. In the past, this could only be accomplished by expensive dedicated private network connections purchased from global telecommunications carriers.

> A virtual private network (VPN) extends a private network across a public network, and enables users to send and receive data across shared or public networks as if their computing devices were directly connected to the private network. Applications running across the VPN may therefore benefit from the functionality, security, and management of the private network.
>
> *(Wikipedia, 2017)*

This virtual 'point-to-point' connection is encrypted to assure anything traversing it remains secure.

Keep in mind, what's been described are basic explanations of very complex and intricate network engineering practices. So as we've seen, a network security architecture in and of itself utilizes a layered defence strategy.

## 7 Identity and access management

Identity and access management is the ability to control access and manage identity. Access to physical and logical assets and associated facilities should be limited to authorized users, processes and devices and be consistent with the assessed risk of unauthorized access. Key elements of an identity and access management program include:

- Physical and logical assets control
- Identification and authentication of people and devices
- Access control
- Privileged account management

- Identity and access provisioning review
- Data leakage prevention.

For purposes of this chapter, we'll cover the following concepts.

## *Authentication*

From an authentication perspective, passwords still represent a major challenge and potential weakness for organizations. When considering traditional passwords, it is essential to set a strong policy which governs their use. This includes enforcing settings such as password length, password expiration, password history, password lockout (failed attempts) and password complexity.

Whenever talking about the password conundrum, it's important to talk about other forms of authentication such as multi-factor. The key to multi-factor is the theory of something you have and something you know. In today's marketplace this can take on many forms. A well-known example that's been around for decades is token technology. Today's tokens can be emailed, sent as text messages, be displayed on a mobile device app or even issued as a physical key fob (e.g. RSA SecurID). The token represents 'something you have' and the PIN and/or password represent 'something you know'. Use of multi-factor authentication can thwart more sophisticated hacking techniques used to break passwords such as a 'man-in-the-middle' attack. The fact that the token is always changing presents yet another challenge than an attacker must overcome.

More advanced systems can also leverage risk-based authentication. This is an authentication technique which intelligently interprets risk by detecting anomalies or changes in normal use patterns. The system can then require additional verification of identity when such deviations or changes are detected. A risk based authentication system can prompt for the use of challenge questions or a one time use PIN that can be sent to a mobile device. Most of us have probably experienced risk-based authentication when performing online banking. Have you ever tried to login to your bank account from a new computer or mobile device? Well, if you have, you've surely run into a risk-based authentication system. If you ever wondered why the bank was really asking you to provide more than just your normal ID and password, now you know that they deployed technology that supports this security principle. The anomaly the system detected is the fact that you are attempting to login from a new device. Until you provide additional verification of your identity, the system will assume someone else may be trying to use your credentials. That's why most systems will allow you the option of 'trusting' the device. Once the system gets positive affirmation that this is a device you wish to continue using, you can go back to simply using an ID and password to authenticate. Some risk-based authentication systems can employ much more complex algorithms and techniques to assess risk, but the basic premise remains the same.

## *Data leakage prevention (DLP)*

According to (ISACA, 2017), an international professional association focused on IT governance, DLP is defined as

> a suite of technologies aimed at stemming the loss of sensitive information that occurs in enterprises across the globe. By focusing on the location, classification and monitoring of information at rest, in use and in motion, this solution can go far in helping an enterprise

> get a handle on what information it has, and in stopping the numerous leaks of information that occur each day. DLP is not a plug-and-play solution. The successful implementation of this technology requires significant preparation and diligent ongoing maintenance. Enterprises seeking to integrate and implement DLP should be prepared for a significant effort that, if done correctly, can greatly reduce risk to the organization. Those implementing the solution must take a strategic approach that addresses risks, impacts and mitigation steps, along with appropriate governance and assurance measures.

While it may be true that implementing a successful DLP strategy can be a complex undertaking requiring significant effort, there are simple ways to begin to incorporate this strategy. For example, restricting the use of external media devices on a company computer can be a very effective control or at least a deterrent in preventing data from leaving the organization. While there may be many other ways data can be exfiltrated, it doesn't mean we've got to make it easy! A good DLP program requires the ability to identify, detect and control data. Data classified and tagged as confidential or privileged will certainly have stronger DLP rules applied. These technologies will scan data to determine whether or not it can leave the organization. DLP is also widely used to comply with regulatory mandates, such as PCI and HIPAA, which are focused on the protection of personal and health care data (e.g. social security number). Just think, an employee shouldn't be allowed to transmit a customer's social security number via an unencrypted email. In this instance, the DLP system would identify that the message contains a social security string and thereby block the transmission because the minimum data security standard was not being met.

### *Privileged accounts*

Privileged accounts, unlike standard user accounts, are created to perform advanced system functions such as running system processes on servers. Each of these accounts provides a substantial amount of authority and access to a system; therefore use of these privileges must be closely monitored and reported on.

### *Digital rights management (DRM)*

Digital rights management is also a key access management technique which is very specific to protecting data. The security in essence attaches itself to the digital asset. In today's day and age, where data is being consumed anywhere, anytime and on any device, the rollout of a DRM strategy is key. Consumers are exposed to DRM technology almost every day. Have you ever rented a movie or purchased music from Amazon or Apple? If you have, you've experienced DRM firsthand. In an example where someone rents a movie, DRM is placed on the content to ensure that it is only playable for a specific period of time. The security has been attached directly onto the content itself which enforces the prescribed security control to restrict play or reproduction of the media. In a corporate environment, DRM can be applied to an email attachment which is leaving the organization. Restrictions can be placed on the file to prevent actions such as printing or copy/paste functions. DRM is yet another useful tool in the information security arsenal.

At the end of the day, identity and access management can utilize many different technologies and can employ an array of techniques to protect data. The level of protection, as always, should be based on the level of risk or value of the data or digital asset.

## 8 Security assessment and vulnerability testing

In an era where cyberattacks are happening every moment of every day and can range from financially motivated hackers to nation state–sponsored threat actors, security assessments and vulnerability testing is no longer considered a nice to have, but rather a must have. Security teams must be able to understand their organization's security posture and potential weaknesses in order to have a chance of staying protected. Attacks today run the gamut from ransomware to denial of service all the way through to advanced persistent threats (APTs).

> Data breaches are complex affairs often involving some combination of human factors, hardware devices, exploited configurations or malicious software. As can be expected, data breach response activities – investigation, containment, eradication, notification, and recovery are proportionately complex.
>
> *(Verizon, 2017)*

Let's first spend some time talking about the most common types of attacks being defended against today.

*Ransomware*: Delivery of malicious software that can encrypt data and render it useless until a decryption key is applied. Ransomware is evolving every day and can cause an individual (at home) or an organization a great deal of harm.

*APTs*: Attacks in which a cyber criminal gains access to a network and may stay undetected for long periods of time until its next move is formulated. The intention of an APT can vary, but it is primarily used to steal data rather than to cause damage.

*Denial of service*: On the other side of the attack spectrum, we have attacks focused on causing destruction or harm to an organization's IT systems or networks. The most common denial of service example is where an attacker targets a company's website, either looking to bring the site completely down or making the site virtually unusable.

With that primer, you can begin to see why vulnerability assessments and testing are so important. The whole area of security assessment and testing has also been transformative in approach and sophistication. Irrespective of what level of sophistication an organization thinks it has in the area of security controls, something can always be missed. The human factor is always at play, and you must consider that every time a piece of hardware or software is introduced or changed in an IT environment, a vulnerability may come with it. Sure, testing and quality assurance practices are put in place to minimize this risk, however, it is far from perfect. With that said, a disciplined security team will always test for weaknesses in their environments. This practice is commonly referred to as penetration testing. Within the testing space, there are many tools and methods for identifying vulnerabilities. Ethical hacking is one which utilizes individuals who have very sophisticated skills in finding weakness in software, databases, networks and – let's not forget the human factor – 'social engineering'. Social engineering has become a go-to method for attackers to gain entry into an organization's network. Why try and break through many sophisticated layers of security when someone can basically just hand you the keys to the kingdom. A good example within the social engineering space is phishing attacks. A phishing attack in the context of email is when someone attempts to impersonate identity in the interest of having the receiver of the message take an action. The range of phishing attacks is limitless and the attacks have grown in sophistication. An illegitimate message may contain links to malicious websites or attachments with hidden executables aimed to infect the target computer. Attackers are well aware of the human physiology and how to leverage our instinctive nature against us. Social engineering is a fascinating area and one that forces security practitioners to think differently about defence. Implementing great security technology and having robust controls is not enough. Therefore, part of our strategy must incorporate testing focused on bringing up the awareness level of the user community we've granted access to our systems and data. Today's testing strategy should include regularly scheduled company-sponsored 'phishing' attacks. When a user clicks on a link they shouldn't have, it is an opportunity to provide in context and real-time training. To better illustrate, just imagine you've fallen for the trap and clicked on that link you thought was going to bring you to the Internal Revenue Service website, and all of a sudden you are brought to a company-sponsored web page that tells you exactly what you did wrong, explains the dangers had this been a real phishing attack and educates you on how to detect the illegitimacy of a link. Studies show that organizations can reduce their probability of social engineering attacks by up to 75% after rolling out a formal training program (knowb4, 2017).

There are also many resources on the internet that are entirely focused on reporting new vulnerabilities to the security community at large. Organizations like the National Institute of Standards and Technology (NIST) feature a Computer Security Resource Center that hosts a national vulnerability database (NIST, 2017). The Department of Homeland Security also hosts a website called US-CERT (United States Computer Emergency Readiness Team; US-Cert, 2017), where you can get information on the latest vulnerabilities. Many sites will also allow you to subscribe, so information security teams can sign up to receive these valuable and timely updates. There are many resources on the internet, but keep in mind that it is important to conduct proper due diligence in assessing the quality and timeliness of the information. A rule of thumb would suggest that a security professional subscribe to multiple community-based resources and/or government-sponsored agencies to assure broad enough coverage has been achieved.

## 9 Software development security

As a guiding principle, code should never be designed to perform a malicious activity or to deliberately work around security restrictions. With that, code should also always go through an independent review before being promoted to a production environment.

The following are guidelines that will help avoid unintentional security-related issues.

### *General security guidelines*

#### *Authentication*

Usernames and passwords should not be embedded in the code. If the code authenticates, it should use known authentication standards by the respective providers (e.g. code should not send unencrypted passwords).

#### *File access*

No code should change file permissions unless explicitly required to perform its function.

### *Minimum privilege*

Code should prevent abuse of required access privileges and always subscribe to the 'least privilege' model. Secure code should never request more than the minimum privileges necessary to perform its function.

### *Bounds and buffer checks*

Adequate bounds and parameter checks should be performed for all input data. All arguments should be current and valid for system calls. There should be no use of unbounded string copies/arguments which may be vulnerable to buffer overflows.

### *Connection strings*

Secure code should always use an encrypted connection string.

## *Logging and exception handling*

All application security events should be logged, with sufficient context information to be able to conduct proper forensics if needed. Security event notifications should also automatically be sent to the security team for investigation.

### *Documentation*

Every program, function, class, method and so forth should be properly documented to describe the purpose and, where warranted, the workings of the program/function/class/method and so on. This description should give a reviewer an adequate understanding of that piece of code. Within the code, comments should also be provided wherever required to explain the logic. This is especially important when you have to use complex or unusual logic for any reason.

### *Methods*

Avoid writing very long methods. A method should do only one 'job'. Do not combine more than one job in a single method, even if these jobs are very small.

Share data between methods by relying on method parameters rather than relying on member variables. If you share a member variable between methods, it becomes difficult to track which method changed the value (and when).

### *Constant values*

Avoid hardcoding numbers or strings within the code. Use constants, or rely on resource files instead.

### *Runtime environment*

A diagnostic page should be included as part of every application. The diagnostic page should be customized to reflect all runtime environment settings, and perform any necessary validation to indicate whether the runtime environment settings are correctly set.

## 10 Chapter summary and learning objectives

- Gain an understanding of the concepts of risk assessment, risk analysis, data classification and security awareness.
- Learn how an organization structures security processes, information security systems and personnel so that these practices and processes align with the organization's core goals and strategic direction.
- Understand the structures and security measures used to provide confidentiality, integrity and availability.
- Learn what actions organizations take to protect their valuable assets, and how to better understand the state of their security postures.
- Offer greater visibility into today's approaches on determining intrusion.
- Understand the basics of the software development life cycle (SDLC).

In summary, this chapter aimed to show that an information security program starts and ends with people, process and technology. The stronger the linkage and alignment between these three elements will determine the success of an organization's overall security program and defence posture. Another key takeaway that cannot be overstated is the need for a security program to be a living, breathing organism that evolves and continually learns. The bad guys are evolving the threats and clearly understand the need to stay one step ahead of defences. Therefore, if we fully acknowledge that the threat landscape is changing at a feverish pace, we too must take this same approach. From a people perspective, that means our security teams must continue to develop their skill sets and stay tied into the broader security community to keep abreast of new threats. This does not exclude the rest of the organization. While someone in finance may not directly have formal responsibility for security, their role in the creation of a 'human shield' is paramount to overall success. From a process perspective, organizational policies, protocols and procedures must adapt and stay in line with changes to the organization's risk profile (e.g. new business processes) and the threats it is being targeted with (directly or indirectly). A good example to help illustrate this point is an organization's stance on the use of social media at work.

Last, but certainly not least, is technology. As we learned, the ability to select and maintain the right mix of security platforms and the tools needed to properly capture and correlate data for analytics is the new game. Big data, machine learning and artificial intelligence are very powerful weapons in today's security arsenal. At the end of the day, all of these elements come together in a delicate orchestration that results in a beautiful harmony of defences.

## References

CSI, 2017. Crime Scene Investigations (WWW) URL www.cbs.com/shows/csi/ (accessed 3/14/17).

Forbes, 2017. How To Build A Cybersecurity Strategy For 2017 (WWW) URL www.forbes.com/sites/christieterrill/2017/02/14/how-to-build-a-cybersecurity-strategy-for-2017/#72f634e426cd (accessed 3/19/17).

Gartner, 2017. Best Practices for Detecting and Mitigating Advanced Threats (WWW Document) URL www.gartner.com/document/3266630?ref=solrAll&refval=183632805&qid=3e16355f1f09bb2b91df773390a30b63 (accessed 4/5/17).

IIA, 2017. Institute of Internal Auditors (WWW) URL https://na.theiia.org/Pages/IIAHome.aspx (accessed 3/14/17).

International Security Consortium, 2017, ISC2 CISSP Domains (WWW) URL www.isc2.org/cissp-domains/default.aspx (accessed 03/12/17).

ISACA, 2017. Risk Management Framework (WWW Document) URL www.isaca.org (accessed 3/14/17).

Knowb4, 2017. Phishing study (WWW) URL www.knowbe4.com/press/security-awareness-training-reduces-phishing-susceptibility-by-75 (accessed 4/2/17).

NIST, 2017. Computer Security Resource Center (WWW) URL https://nvd.nist.gov/ (accessed 3/1/17).

Reuters, 2016. Bangladesh Bank Cyber-Heist (WWW) URL www.reuters.com/article/us-cyber-heist-bangladesh-exclusive-idUSKBN13X1S4

US-CERT, 2017. Vulnerability Database (WWW) URL www.us-cert.gov/) (accessed 3/1/17).

Verizon, 2016. Data Breach Investigations Report (WWW Document) URL www.verizonenterprise.com/verizon-insights-lab/dbir/2016/ (accessed 3/1/17).

Verizon, 2017. Data Breach Digest (WWW Document) URL www.verizonenterprise.com/resources/reports/rp_data-breach-digest-2017-perspective-is-reality_xg_en.pdf (accessed 4/2/2017).

# 18

# Business continuity and e-business

## Towards an "always-on" e-business

*Nijaz Bajgoric*

### Introduction

Modern history of business computing started some 60 years ago by introducing accounting applications. For more than six decades information technologies (IT) have been used in business but with different focuses in different times. Several concepts of information systems have been developed during this time. With first business applications aiming at faster data processing and introducing transaction processing systems (TPS, in the 1950s), then moving towards managerial reporting support (MIS, or management information systems, in the '70s), better decision support (DSS, or decision support systems, in the '80s), office automation and personal productivity systems (the '90s), all these concepts and technologies were indended to be used primarily for improving efficiency of data processing (TPS) and enhancing effectiveness of decision making (MIS, DSS).

Up until the late nineties, information systems were developed around traditional computer centers organized as "behind-the-scenes" organizational units. Such computer centers were responsible for running data-intensive business applications such as the ledger, payroll, accounts payable and receivable, fixed assets, payments and providing reporting capabilities. Most business operations were based on traditional computer center logic with a combination of batch/online applications.

With the introduction of enterprise servers, client server computing, internet/Web/e-business technologies, SaaS/utility/cloud computing, businesses started to become more IT-dependent – in many segments, many of them started to become partially electronic business (e-business). In today's e-business world, the whole business is IT dependent and data driven. Business computing has evolved into an organizational engine that drives business and provides a powerful source for competitive advantage.

From the very first years of the e-business era, it turned out that the availability of information system platforms significantly determines e-business success. For example, in June 1999, Dembeck (1999) noted that financial losses to eBay were estimated at $3 million to $5 million after its site crashed. Fifteen years ago, the Contingency Planning Research Report (Eagle Rock Alliance, 2001) quoted that average hourly downtime costs ranged from $28,000/hr to $5.4 million/hr, depending on the industry. In a report issued in late 2002, IDC stated that

IT security and business continuity are both number one priorities of business professionals (IDC, 2002).

Today, some 15 years later, we are witnessing similar stories, even with higher figures. For instance, the London Stock Exchange suffered a trading downtime of several hours (Computer Weekly, 2007). The New York Stock Exchange was closed for 4 hours due to a computer glitch, according to NY Times (2015). CNBC (2015) reported that United Airlines' US flights were grounded for two hours in July 2015 due to IT issues, it turned out that a "bad router caused [the] outage." Examples of cloud computing providers' outages are that of Amazon in April 2011 (Maitland, 2011) and in January 2013. Butler (2013) reported that a 49-minute failure of Amazon's services on January 31, 2013, resulted in close to $5 million in missed revenue. Similar failures happened in 2015 and 2016 to Dropbox, Facebook, Microsoft, Google Drive and Twitter.

According to IDC (IDC, 2016), businesses cannot tolerate the same levels of planned and unplanned downtime that they could before they started on their digital transformation journey. While transactional systems once represented the business-critical aspects of an organization, in the modern digital era systems of engagement are equally important, and employees need to be able to access their productivity tools (email, file shares, and analytics), transactional systems and communication channels with customers and partners to create value and support success. The mean costs of 1 hour of downtime for an organization with between 1,000 and 4,999 employees is approximately $225,000.

This chapter aims at investigating the major perspectives for transforming modern business towards an "always-on" e-business and identifying major continous computing technologies as "always-on" business drivers. By the term "e-business" we refer to all kinds of businesses, not only "dot-com" organizations, that use information technologies in performing or supporting their business operations. With regard to this term, we use the definition provided by Srinivasan et al. (2002, p. 53): "We define e-business as the use of Internet-based systems to share business information, maintain business relationships, and/or conduct business transactions." They argued that e-business adoption ranges from simply using e-mail to communicate within the organization to developing entirely new business models.

The methodology is based on a comprehensive literature review to develop an understanding of the drivers and enablers that determine a framework for further research directions related to business continuity in the e-business era. As for the literature review, a primary focus was on articles published in peer-reviewed journals. The search was applied on the online databases: ProQuest, Emerald, Science Direct, ABI/Inform, JSTOR, ACM Digital Library, Wiley, IEEE, Springer and EBSCO in June/July 2016. The keywords used were as follows: business continuity, e-business, continuous computing and downtime.

## Downtime costs and business continuity: literature review

The eBay story quoted in the introduction (Dembeck, 1999) is an example of the downtime story which demonstrates how hardware/software glitches on modern information infrastructures can easily be transformed into financial losses.

Since the early 1990s, business continuity has been treated together with organizational strategy, information strategy, enterprise information systems, information management and disaster recovery/management. The term of "business continuance" (business continuity, or BC) was introduced in order to emphasize the ability of a business to continue with its operations even if some sort of disaster on its computing resources occurs (Bajgoric, 2006). Herbane

(2010) argued that business continuity management as a discipline has evolved since the 1970s in response to the technical and operational risks.

Aberdeen Report (2014) quoted the average cost of downtime for large companies as $686,250/hr, $215,638/hr for medium companies and $8,581/hr for small companies. Clancy (2013) noted that it takes an average of 30 hours to recover from failures, which can be devastating for a business of any size. Butler (2013) reported that a 49-minute failure of Amazon's services on January 31, 2013 resulted close to $5 million in missed revenue. Venkatraman (2013) found that more than a third of respondents viewed human error as the most likely cause of downtime. Forrester Report (2013) argued that there is less and less tolerance for any kind of downtime. Gartner (2014a) noted that "Based on industry surveys, the number we typically cite is $5,600 p/minute, the cost of improving availability remains high and downtime is less acceptable, making rightsizing network availability the key goal for enterprise network designers" (Gartner, 2014b). According to IDC Report (2015), "for a large firm, the mean cost of downtime per hour is nearly $1.7 million, with some specific industries approaching $10 million per hour of downtime." For the Fortune 1000, the average total cost of unplanned application downtime per year is $1.25 billion to $2.5 billion (IDC, 2014). Ponemon Institute and Emerson Network Power (Ponemon Institute Report, 2016) reported that the average cost of a data center outage has steadily increased from $505,502 in 2010 to $740,357 today (or a 38% net change). The analysis is derived from 63 data centers located in the United States. According to this report, the cost range, median and mean all consistently show substantial increases in cost over time, as reported in 2010, 2013 and 2016. The maximum cost has more than doubled over 6 years from just over $1 million to $2.4 million. On average, the cost of an unplanned outage per minute is nearly $9,000 per incident.

Leitch (2016) argued that downtime has reached an estimated cost of $700 billion per year to US businesses in 2016. He quoted Amazon which recently suffered downtime of around 15 minutes with a cost of $66,240 per minute. According to Martin (2011) the average data center downtime event lasts 90 minutes, and every minute the data center remains down, a company is effectively losing $5,600. The Veeam Report (2014) claimed that "there are clear demands for 24/7 access to IT services and applications, with over 90 percent of enterprises increasing their requirements for minimizing downtime and guaranteeing access to data." The report revealed that 68% of business modernizing their data centers are doing so in order to enable 24/7, always-on business operations. Emerson Report (2014) revealed that the most frequently unplanned outages include: VIT equipment failure, cyber crime, UPS system failure, water and accidental/human error. Table 18.1 presents a summary of reports that drmonstrate the downtime costs.

All these reports reveal that some sort of redefinition or re-engineering of modern information systems is needed. They indicate that today's business/enterprise information systems are much more than standard TPS, MIS or DSS, although their role in efficient data processing and effective decision support still remains very important. The key point here is that modern business information systems are needed on continuous basis, up and running, not only when some sort of data processing occurs or decision making is done. Modern information systems are expexted to be always on from a business perspective, in order to support modern e-business, which in turn is also expected by customers to be always on. Niemimaa (2015) reviewed articles addresing business continuity from information systems perspective and concluded that leading information systems journals provide little contributions on this perspective. Therefore, he identified the IS-BC relationship as "a timely question."

Hamraz et al. (2013) highlighted the importance of information availability while creating the models of engineering changes. Chalupnik, Wynn, and Clarkson (2013) suggested a framework for examining the relationships among reliability, robustness, adaptability and resilience

*Table 18.1* Reports on downtime costs

| *Report* | *Findings* |
|---|---|
| Butler (2013) | A 49 minutes failure of Amazon's services on January 31, 2013 resulted close to $5 million in missed revenue. |
| Aberdeen Report (2014) | The average cost of downtime for large companies is $686,250 per hour, $215,638/hour for medium companies and $8,581/ hour for small companies. |
| Gartner (2014, a) | Based on industry surveys, average downtime is $5,600 p/minute. |
| Avaya Report (2014) | 80% of companies lose revenue when the network goes down. |
| IDC (2014) | For the Fortune 1000, the average total cost of unplanned application downtime per year is $1.25 billion to $2.5 billion. |
| Veeam Data Availability Report (2014) | 68% of those organizations modernizing their data centers are doing so in order to enable 24/7, always-on business operations. |
| IDC Report (2015) | For a large firm, the mean cost of downtime per hour is nearly $1.7 million, with some specific industries approaching $10 million lost per hour of downtime. |
| Ponemon Institute Report (2016) | The average cost of a data center outage has steadily increased from $505,502 in 2010 to $740,357 today (or a 38% net change). |

in the context of system design. Bharosa, Lee, and Jansen (2010) investigated issues in sharing information during disasters, within the framework of disaster management. Lee, Thomas, and Baskerville (2015) recommended to restore the idea that the study of design in IS needs to attend to the design of the entire IS artifact, not just the IT artifact. A framework for aligning IT infrastructure and business model is presented in (Kuk and Janssen, 2013), while Ashurst et al. (2012) presented a new paradigm for IT-enabled innovation.

Gibb and Buchanan (2006) suggested a framework for a business continuity management program within an information strategy. Butler and Gray (2006) review relationships between system reliability and reliable organizational performance. Availability analysis of enterprise information system architectures is presented in Narman et al. (2014). Walker (2006) addressed outsourcing options for business continuity. Avery Gomez (2011) presented a model for alignment of business continuity and sustainable business processes. Lumpp et al. (2008) presented a high-availability (HA) clustering on distributed platform and mainframe systems as architectures for continuous availability.

King (2003) introduced a term of "business continuity culture" and noted "If you fail to plan, you will be planning to fail." Botha and Von Solms (2004) proposed a BCP methodology scalable for small and medium organizations. Herbane et al. (2004) investigated the organizational antecedents of BCM. Pitt and Goyal (2004) presented BCM as a tool for facilities management. Cerullo and Cerullo (2004) identified guidelines for developing and improving business continuity plan. Bertrand (2005) addresses the relationships between business continuity and mission-critical applications and focused on replication point objective (RPO) and replication time objective (RTO). Walker (2006) addressed outsourcing options for business continuity. Gibb and Buchanan (2006) defined a framework for a BCM program within an information strategy. Lumpp et al. (2008) investigated relationships among high availability, disaster recovery and business continuity. Wan (2008) argued that the continuity plan needs to be integrated with IT service continuity management. Nollau (2009) introduced the term of "enterprise business continuity," while Kadam (2010) introduced the concept of personal business continuity management. Speight (2011) defined business continuity as "a management process that identifies potential factors that threaten an organization and provides a framework for building resilience and the capability for an effective response." Avery Gomez (2011) presented a model for alignment of business continuity and sustainable business processes. Broder and Tucker (2012) focused on the differences between the continuity planning and a continuity plan. Craighead et al. (2007) studied business continuity issues within the supply chain mitigation capabilities and supply chain disruption severity. Bartel and Rutkowski (2006) argued that IT service continuity management is typically part of a larger BCM program, which expands beyond IT to include all business services within an organization. Bhatt et al. (2010) considered IT infrastructure as "enabler of organizational responsiveness and competitive advantage." Versteeg and Bouwman (2006) defined the components of a business architecture as a business domain within the relations between IT and business strategy. Jarvelainen (2013) focused on business continuity management in the context of information systems. A method for availability analysis is presented in Narman et al. (2014). Torabi, Soufi, and Sahebjamnia (2014) proposed a framework for conducting the business impact analysis by using MADM techniques. Venters and Whitley (2012) argued that successful cloud services must be able to match, if not exceed, the availability of local data centres and their disaster prevention and recovery systems. Aktas (2010) presented some principles and experiences in designing and building enterprise information systems from the always-on perspective. Bayram, Kirlidog and Vayvay (2010) presented a model of an always-on enterprise information systems with service-oriented architecture and load balancing. Delic and Riley (2009) argued that high availability and dependability are necessary engineering features for such global, always-on, always-available systems. Saha (2013) noted that enterprises are no longer grappling to have access to the latest technologies; harnessing technology to enable business outcomes is given. Chang et al. (2014) presented an example of how a continuous computing technology can be used on enhancing scalability and reliability. Miller and Engemann (2014) proposed reliability and simulation models in business continuity planning. Table 18.2 presents main contributions in the fields of BC and BCM since 2000.

Table 18.3 contains a summary of major works with regard to research streams, topics, outcomes and solutions.

## Towards an always-on e-business

The literature review revealed that today's information infrastructures represent a mission critical factor for business continuity. Figure 18.1 depicts typical client-server or client-cloud information architecture implemented in most business information systems today, while Figure 18.2 shows possible downtime points in such infrastructures. These downtime points could be mission critical as they can cause disruptions in mission critical business applications.

Turban et al. (2000) introduced a set of "business pressures" in the modern business environment, namely market pressures, technology pressures and societal pressures. They argue that organizations use IT in order to provide responses to business pressures.

However, in both modern e-business and its environment, there exists an additional "pressure" which reflects the requirement for continuous data access and data availability. In other words, modern business seeks an always-on application platform and consequently always-on information system (Figure 18.3). It requires an information system with zero or near-zero downtime. Not only availability, but scalability and reliability of e-business application platforms are business critical as well. Such businesses tend to provide products and services on continuous basis as each minute of downtime brings financial losses.

*Table 18.2* A review of literature related to business continuity

| *Article Year* | *Authors* | *Focus/contribution* |
|---|---|---|
| 2001 | Rick | Found that only 6% of companies suffering from a catastrophic data loss survive, while 43% never reopen and 51% close within 2 years. |
| 2002 | Barraza | Quoted that, simply put, the global economy runs on information. More importantly, it runs on available information. |
| 2003 | Lewis and Pickren | Presented a technique that can be used to assess the relative risk for different causes of IT disruptions. |
| 2003 | King | Introduced a term of "Business Continuity Culture." Underscored the fact "If you fail to plan, you will be planning to fail." |
| 2004 | Botha and Von Solms | Proposed a BCP methodology that is scalable for small and medium organizations. |
| 2004 | Herbane, Elliott and Swartz | Developed a conceptual approach to posit that BCM, in actively ensuring operational continuity, has a role in preserving competitive advantage. |
| 2004 | Finch | Revealed that large companies' exposure to risk increased by inter-organizational networking and that having SMEs as partners further increased the risk exposure. |
| 2004 | Wu, Chiag, Wu and Tu | Identified continuity as the most important behavioral factor on business process integration in SCM. |
| 2004 | Pitt and Goyal | Considered BCM as a tool for facilities management. |
| 2004 | Cerullo and Cerullo | Provided guidelinesfor developing and improving a firm's business continuity plan. |
| 2005 | Bertrand | Estimated the relationships between business continuity and mission-critical applications. Emphasized the role of RPO and RTO in recovering from disasters. |
| 2005 | Yeh | Identified the factors affecting continuity of cooperative electronic supply chain relationships with empirical case of the Taiwanese motor industry. |
| 2005 | Gerber and Solms | Presented a holistic approach with carefully planned security policy, the use of technology and well-trained staff. |
| 2005 | Umar | Investigated the role of several business servers in designing an IT infrastructure for "next generation enterprises." |
| 2006 | Walker | Considered outsourcing options for business continuity. |
| 2006 | Bartel and Rutkowski | Argued that IT service continuity management (ITSC) is typically part of a larger BCM program, which expands beyond IT to include all business services. |
| 2006 | Butler and Gray | Underscored the question on how system reliability translates into reliable organizational performance. |
| 2006 | Gibb and Buchanan | Defined a framework for the design, implementation and monitoring of a business continuity management program within an information strategy. |
| 2007 | Williamson | Found that in business continuity planning, financial organizations are ahead of other types of businesses. |
| 2007 | Craighead et al. | Proposed a multiple-source empirical research method and presented six propositions that relate the severity of supply chain disruptions. |

(*Continued*)

*Table 18.2* (Continued)

| *Article Year* | *Authors* | *Focus/contribution* |
|---|---|---|
| 2008 | Vatanasombut et al. | Argued that proliferation of internet has not only allowed businesses to offer their products and services, but has also undermined their ability to retain customers. |
| 2008 | Bielski | Considered business continuity as doing what is necessary to set up a "shadow" organization from incident response through various phases of recovery. |
| 2008 | Turetken | Developed a decision model for locating redundant facilities (IT-backup facility location) within the activities of business continuity planning. |
| 2008 | Lumpp et al. | Investigated several aspects and relationships among high availability, disaster recovery and business continuity solutions. |
| 2009 | Wan | Argued that in current business-aligned IT operations, the continuity plan needs to be integrated with IT service continuity management. |
| 2009 | Boehman | Presented a model for evaluating the performance of a BCM System according to BS 25999 standard. |
| 2009 | Nollau | Introduced the term of "enterprise business continuity." |
| 2010 | Adeshiyan et al. | Argued that HA-DR solutions require complex configurations, application specific logic, highly skilled personnel, and a rigorous testing process. |
| 2010 | Ipe, Raghu, Vinze | Explored the challenges specific to developing and institutionalizing an IT system for emergency preparedness. |
| 2010 | Singhal, Bokare and Pawar | Presented a solution for optimal BC based on the IP-SAN storage for enterprise applications used for data management without burdening application server. |
| 2010 | Kuhn and Sutton | Suggested alternative architectures for continuous auditing by focusing on the strengths and weaknesses of each architectural form of ERP implementation. |
| 2010 | Tammineedi | Categorized the key BCM tasks into three phases of business continuity: Pre-event Preparation, Event Management, and Post-event Continuity. |
| 2010 | Lindstrom, Samuelson, and Hagerfors | Proposed a multi-usable business continuity planning methodology based on using a staircase or capability maturity model. |
| 2010 | Kadlec | Reported on the IT DR planning practices of 154 banks in the United States. |
| 2010 | Arduini and Morabito | Argued that the financial sector sees business continuity not only astechnical or risk management issue, but as a driver towards discussion on mergers and acquisitions. |
| 2010 | Winkler et al. | Proposed a model-driven framework for BCM which integrates business process modelling and IT management. |
| 2010 | Kadam | Introduced the concept of personal business continuity management |
| 2011 | Tan and Takakuwa | Demonstrated how the computer-based simulation technique could be utilized in order to establish the business continuity plan for a factory. |
| 2011 | Zobel | Presented an approach in representing the relationship between two measures of disaster resilience: the initial impact of and the subsequent time to recovery. |

| *Article Year* | *Authors* | *Focus/contribution* |
|---|---|---|
| 2011 | Omar, A., Alijani, D., Mason, R. | Presented a framework for disaster recovery plan based on the Oracle's DataGuard solution that includes remote site, data replication, and standby database. |
| 2011 | Greening, P., Rutherford, C. | Proposed a conceptual framework based on network theories to ensure business continuity in the context of a supply network disruption. |
| 2011 | Brenes, E.R., Madrigal, K, Requena, B. | Focused on assessing the impact of business continuity-related governance structures on family business performances. |
| 2011 | Avery Gomez, E. | Presented a model for alignment of business continuity and sustainable business processes with regard to ICT usage behavior and response readiness. |
| 2011 | Sapateiro et al. | Designed a mobile collaborative tool that helps teams managing critical computing infrastructures in organizations. |
| 2011 | Blackhurst et al. | Provided a framework that can be used to assess the level of resiliency and a supply resiliency matrix. |
| 2012 | Broder and Tucker | Made the difference between the meaning of continuity planning and of a continuity plan. |
| 2012 | Lavastre, O., Gunasekaran, A., Spalanzani, A. | Considered business continuity planning within the "supply chain continuity planning framework." Introduced the concept of Supply Chain Risk Management. |
| 2012 | Kim, Y.G. and Cha, S. | Presented the improved scenario-based Security Risk Analysis method which can create SRA reports using scenario templates and manage security risk in IS. |
| 2013 | Jarvelainen | Focused on a framework for business continuity management and extended it to the context of information systems. |
| 2014 | Miller and Engemann | Proposed using reliability and simulation models in business continuity planning. |
| 2015 | Neimmiaa | Identified the information system-business continuity relationship as "a timely question." |

As shown in Figure. 18.3, "always-on" e-business relies on continuous computing technologies that are implemented as an "always-on" information system. Two trends (outcomes) based on business continuity paradigm can be identified as follows:

- New e-business model: always-on e-business (Figure 18.4)
- New model of business information systems: always-on IS (Figure 18.5).

The following technology enablers can be identified, in the same time, business continuity enablers:

- Continuous computing technologies
- Downtime costs
- Compliance regulations
- Disaster recovery technologies
- Security technologies.

*Table 18.3* Summary of major research streams, topics/outcomes/solutions and references

| *Business Continuity – Literature Review* | *Topics/Outcome-Framework-Solution* |
|---|---|
| *BC: Conceptual/Methodology Issues*<br>Herbane (2010), Speight (2011), King (2003), Herbane, Elliott and Swartz (2004), Nollau (2009), Kadam (2010), Boehman (2009), Greening and Rutherford (2011), Broder and Tucker (2012), Botha and Von Solms (2004), Lindstrom, Samuelson, and Hagerfors (2010), Jarvelainen (2013), Gibb and Buchanan (2006), Gerber and Solms (2005), Cerullo and Cerullo (2004) | – BCM in preserving competitive advantage<br>– BCP methodology for small and medium organizations<br>– The concept of Business Continuity Culture<br>– The concept of Enterprise business continuity<br>– Multi-usable BCP methodology<br>– Framework based on network theories for BC<br>– . . . |
| *BC and Organizational/IS strategy*<br>Herbane et al. (2004), Gibb and Buchanan (2006), Butler and Gray (2006), Brenes, Madrigal, Requena (2011), Walker (2006), Avery Gomez (2011), Swartz et al. (2003), Versteeg and Bouwman (2006), Kiyamoto et al. (2013), Chow and Wai (2009), Corey and Deitch (2011) | – Framework for BCM as part of information strategy<br>– Aligning of BC and sustainable business processes<br>– Outsourcing options for BC<br>– System reliability and reliable organizational performance<br>– . . . |
| *BC and Disaster Recovery/Disaster Management*<br>Herbane et al. (1997), Kadlec (2010), Zobel (2011), Galindo and Batta (2013), Singhal, Pawar and Bokare (2010), Lewis and Pickren (2003), Bielski (2008), Omar et al. (2011), Altay and Green (2006), Rebman et al. (2013), Hristidis et al. (2010), Lodree and Taskin (2008), Ipe, Raghu, and Vinze (2010), Stanton (2005), Sumner (2009), Lin et al. (2012), Karim (2011), Liu et al. (2012), Omar et al. (2011), Brett et al. (2006) | – Technique for assessing the risk of IT disruptions<br>– Framework for DR plan based on Oracle's DataGuard<br>– IT system for emergency preparedness<br>– Relationship between two primary measures of disaster resilience<br>– Solution for optimal business continuity based on the IP SAN storage<br>– . . . |
| *Business Continuity Planning*<br>Cerullo and Cerullo (2004), Bartel and Rutkowski (2006), Tammineedi (2010), Winkler et al. (2010), Lindstrom (2012), Tan and Takakuwa (2011), Asgary and Naini (2011), Martens and Teuteberg (2011), Marten et al. (2010), Ojha and Gokhale (2009) | – Developing and improving a firm's BC plan<br>– Business Continuity Maturity Model of Virtual Corporation<br>– Multi-usable BCP methodology<br>– Computer-based simulation to establish BCP<br>– . . . |
| *BC and Mission-critical applications*<br>Bertrand (2005), Wu et al. (2004), Craighead et al. (2007), Yan (2005), Kuhn and Sutton (2010), Blackhurst, Dunn, and Craighead (2011), Lavastre, Gunasekaran, and Spalanzani (2012), Park et al. (2013), Butler and Gray (2006), Loveland et al. (2008), Kistijantoro et al. (2008), Smith et al. (2008), Yan (2005), Goyal and Lavenberg (1987), Franke et al. (2012), Minhas et al. (2013), Kolowitz et al. (2011) | – Relationships between BC and mission-critical applications<br>– Relationships among high availability, disaster recovery and BC solutions<br>– BC as a behavioural factor on business process integration in SCM<br>– Role of RPO and RTO<br>– Factors affecting continuity of cooperative electronic supply chain<br>– Framework for assessing the level of resiliency and a supply resiliency |
| *BC and IT Infrastructure*<br>Umar (2005), Turetken (2008), Adeshiyan et al. (2010), Singhal, Pawar, and Bokare (2010), Gerber and Solms (2005), Walker (2006), Bartel and Rutkowski (2006), Brenes et al. (2011), Avery Gomez (2011), Mansoori et al. (2013), Lumpp et al. (2008), Radhakrishnan et al. (2008), Matos et al. (2012), Immonen and Niemela (2008), Sapateiro et al. (2011), Egwutuoha et al. (2013), Balabko and Wegmann (2006) | – Business servers in designing an IT infrastructure for "next generation enterprises."<br>– Decision model for locating redundant facilities within the activities of BCP<br>– Mobile collaborative tool that helps managing critical computing infrastructures<br>– Outsourcing options for BC<br>– . . . |

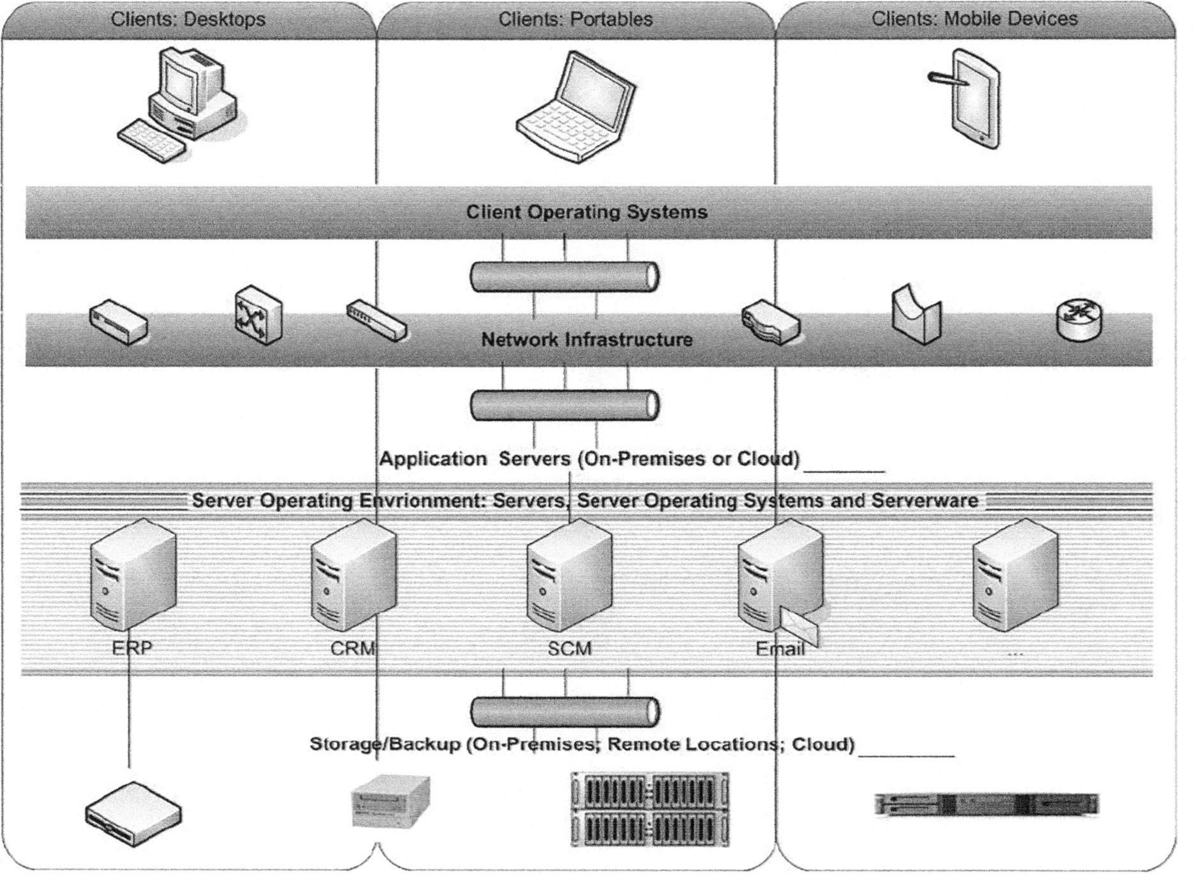


*Figure 18.1* Client-server/client-cloud information architecture

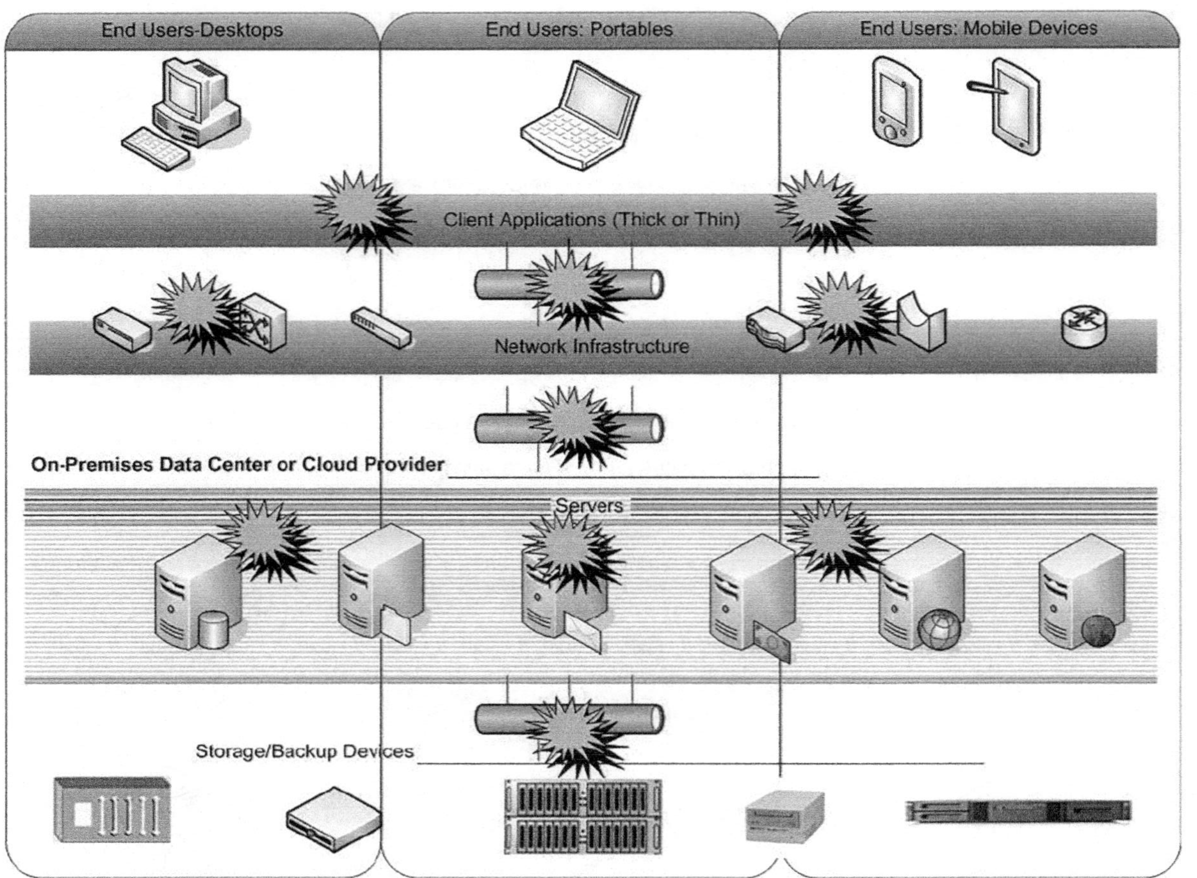


*Figure 18.2* Possible downtime points

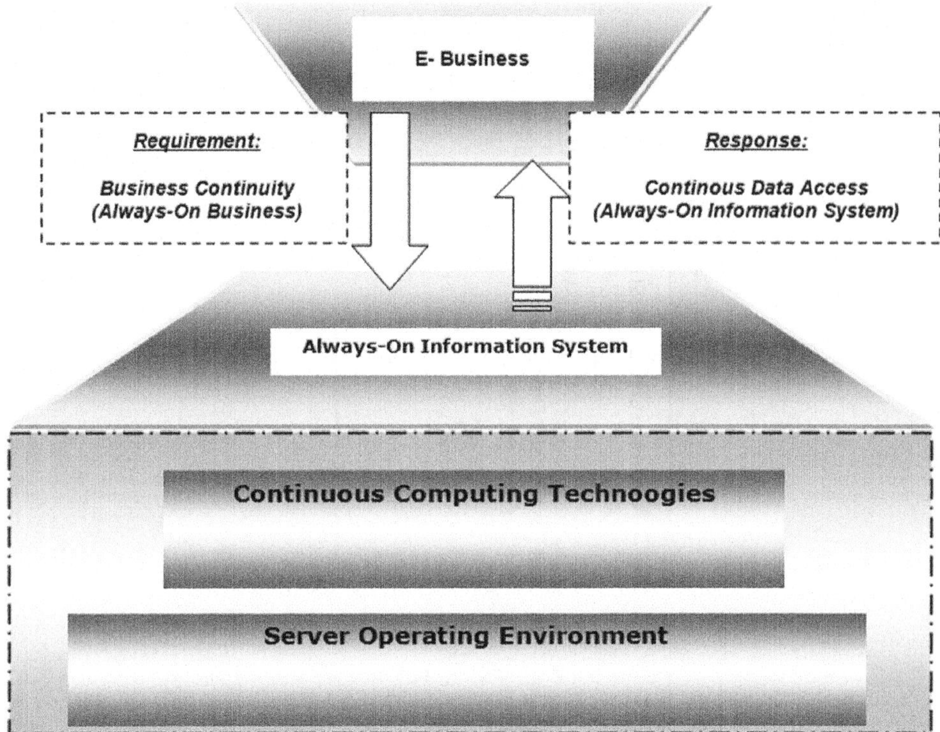


*Figure 18.3* Business continuity (always-on business): pressure and response

## Continuous computing technologies as business continuity drivers and enablers of always-on transformation

The technology enablers critical for implementation of always-on systems are presented in Figure 18.6.

The technologies include several high availability features implemented on servers, server operating systems, application servers, networks and storage. They are implemented and administered by system and network administrators. Such an infrastructure can be organized "on premises" (standard client-server architecture) or within the cloud computing provider's premises (client-cloud architecture). Figure 18.7 presents some of these technologies.

## Case analysis – server operating platforms for "always-on" information systems

In order to support the conceptual model of an always-on information system as a main prerequisite for always-on e-business, the following IT vendors and their main server operating platforms are presented: HP, IBM, Microsoft, SUSE and Oracle.

Among several versions of operating systems created and supported by selected vendors, the following server operating platforms are analyzed:

- HP-UX (www.hp.com)
- Microsoft Windows Server (www.microsoft.com)

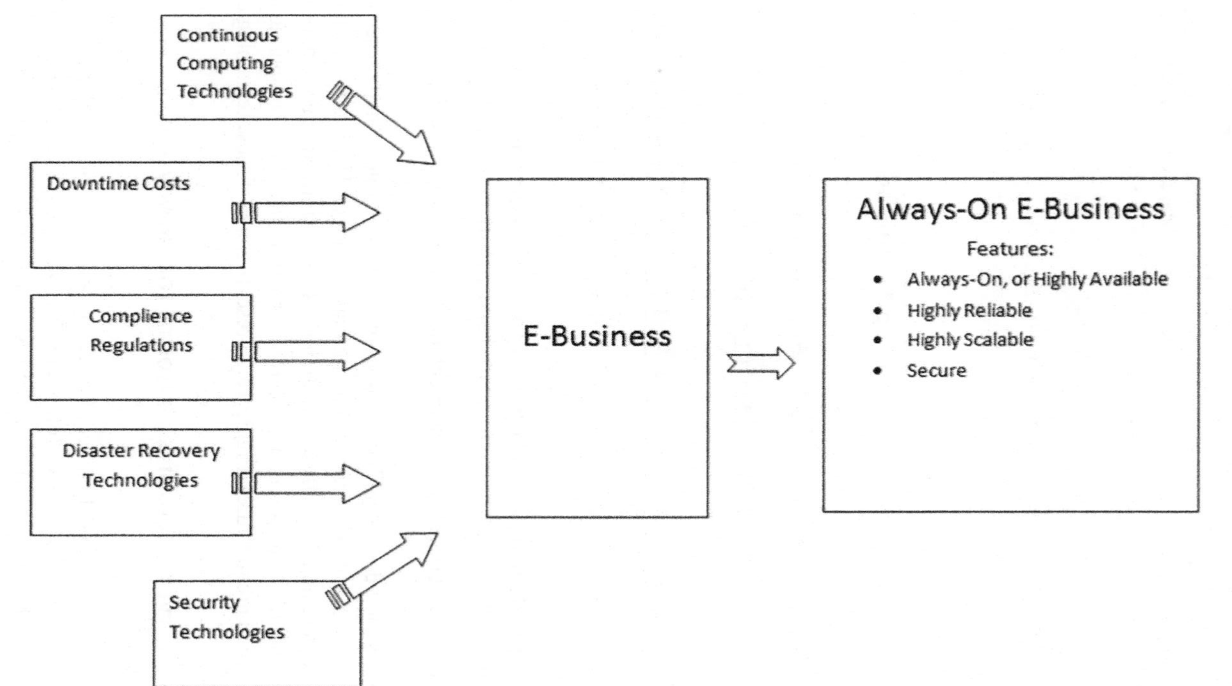


*Figure 18.4* Always-on e-business

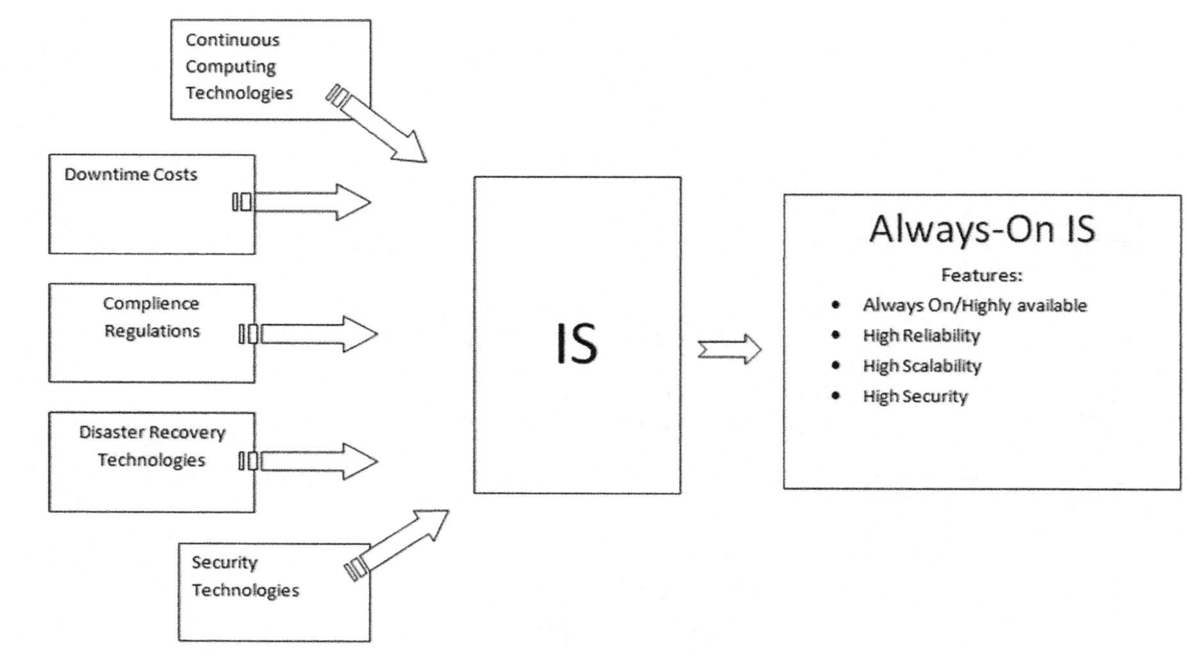


*Figure 18.5* Always-on information system

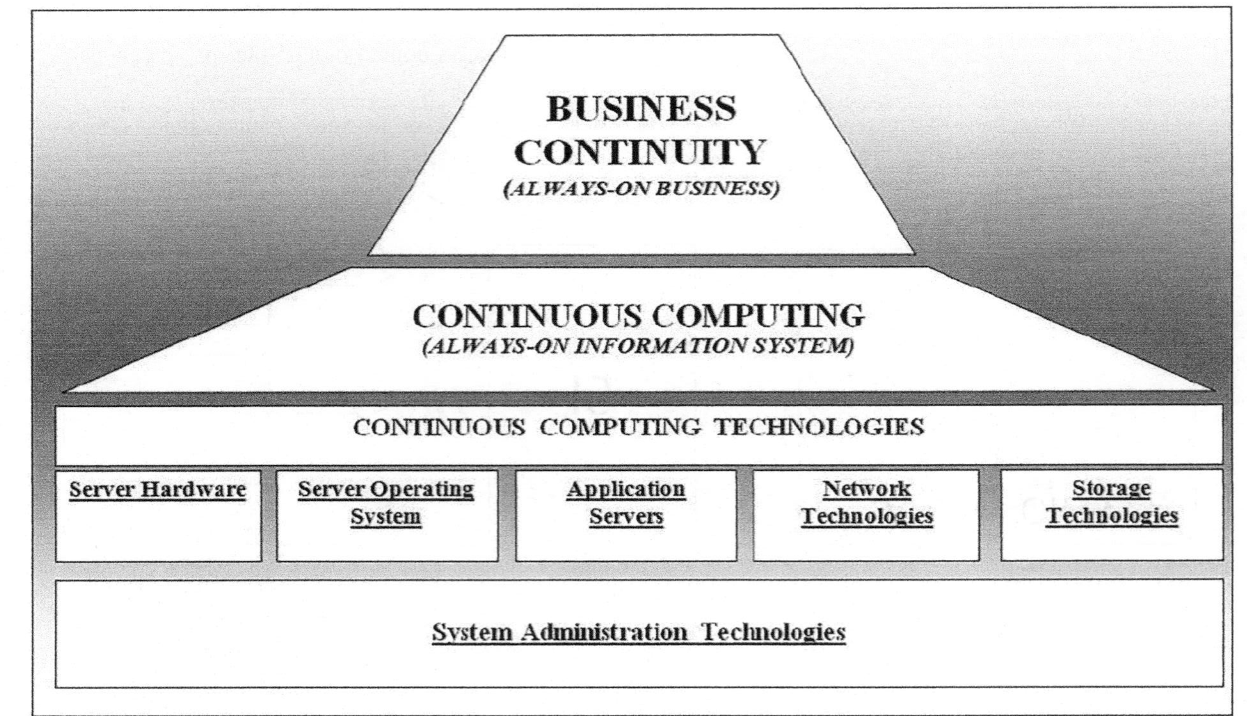


*Figure 18.6* Continuous computing technologies – several forms of high availability features

CONTINUOUS COMPUTING TECHNOLOGIES

| *Server Hardware* | *Server Operating System* | *Application Serv ers* | *Network T ethnologies* | *Storage Technologies* | *System Administration Technologies (HP-UX)* |
|---|---|---|---|---|---|
| • 64-bit processors | • 64-bit OS | • 64-bit applications | • Virtual networks | • RAID | • High availability monitors |
| • L1.L2. L3 cache | • Reloadable kernel | • VLDB | • SAN; NAS | • Storage arrays | • Compartments |
| • Online upgrade | • Online upgrade | • In-memory database | • Resilience-to-link-failures | • Unified St orage Systems | • Fine-Grained privileges |
| • Crash-handling | • Crash-handling | • Online upgrade | • Fibre channel failover | • Online backup | • Role-based Access Control |
| • Hardware mirroring | • Mirroring | • Crash-handling | • Software-defined networking | • Virtual tapes | • Hardware mirroring |
| • HA clustering | • HA clustering | • Application Recovery | • Redundant components | • Data vaulting | • Software mirroring |
| • Dvnamic Root Disk | • Dynamic Root Disk | * Virtualization | • Redundant paths | • Mirroring | • Veritas'VxFS JFS/Online JFS |
| • Automatic Failover | • Automatic Failover | • Oracle MAA | • IP multipath | • Shadowing | • Bastille security tool |
| • Fault-tolerance | • System Recovery | • Oracle RAC | • VPN devices | • Snapshoot | • Dynamic Root Disk (DRD |
| • ECC. MEC | • Fault-tolerance | * Recovery Manager | • Dual Home Link | • Hot sites | • Serviceguard |
| • RAID | • Virtualization | * IBMHADR | • Cluster Switching | • Clustering | • Extensions |
| • RAIM | • Snapshot | • MySQL DRBD | * IDS,IPS | • Disaster recovery sites | |
| • Hot-swappable hardware | • HA Filesystems. LVM; JFS | • SAP HANA | • ICMP failover | • Storage virtualization | |
| • Redundant unit s | • NFS. CIFS/SMB | • ........ ... | • ... | • OLARD | |
| ... | • ... | | | | |

*Figure 18.7* Continuous computing technologies

- SuSE Linux (www.suse.com)
- IBM AIX (www.ibm.com)
- Oracle Solaris (www.oracle.com).

Table 18.4 presents a SWOT analysis of these five server operating systems as to their general features, while Table 18.5 briefly explains the strengths of these SOS platforms as to their business continuity and system administration perspectives considered through additional high-availability (HA) features such as:

- Built-in server hardware HA features (processors, RAM, etc.)
- Core server operating system HA features
- Serverware and application servers
- Network HA features
- Storage HA features
- System administration suites.

HP's HP-UX includes several HA technologies and advanced system administration tools, routines and utilities that can be used to ensure higher levels of availability. Most of them are supported by HP's "HA operating environment" module including advanced system administration options for high availability and availability suites such as Ignite-UX, Bastille and HP Serviceguard.

IBM offers a set of integrated HA solutions including those related to hardware, systems and application software, storage and networking. IBM server configurations running include several advanced built-in HA technologies such as: PowerHA, Availability Factory, HA Clustering, Power HA System Mirror and DB2 HADR (High Availability Disaster Recovery).

Oracle supports a number of solutions such as: MAA (Maximum Availability Architecture), Application Continuity, Online System Reconfiguration, Recovery Manager, Oracle Secure Backup, Data Recovery Advisor, Zero Data Loss Appliance and Database shadowing features.

Microsoft Windows Server, particularly the latest version (2012), provides several features related to continuous availability such as recovery procedures and assistance for high IT service uptime and recovery, NIC failover, Cluster Failover Manager, Hyper-V Replica, Support for SQL Server Mirroring and AlwaysOn, Online Corruption Repairs, support for NUMA-aware scalability, Online Corruption Repairs and AlwaysOn Dashboard.

SuSE Linux operating platform provides high availability features by including the "SuSE Linux Enterprise High Availability Extension" as an add-on product which includes the following features: Cluster-aware file system and volume management, virtual high-availability clusters, Distributed Replicated Block Device, IP Load Balancing, Support for Relax and Recover (ReaR) as an open source tool for creating disaster recovery images.

As can be seen from Table 18.5, three vendors (HP, IBM and Oracle) provide integrated solutions that include hardware, system software, network, storage and administration features for high availability, while Microsoft and SUSE offer server operating system and serverware solutions that run mainly on Intel and AMD hardware platforms.

## Conclusions/lessons learned, and future research directions

Modern e-business has been analyzed from business continuity perspective. Conceptual framework has been proposed for transforming (migration) of traditional e-business into "always-on" e-business, supported by an always-on information system that enables continuous computing and business continuity.

*Table 18.4* SWOT analysis

| | *HP HP-UX* | *Microsoft Windows Server* | *SUSE Linux* | *IBM AIX* | *Oracle Solaris* |
|---|---|---|---|---|---|
| Strengths | • Stable UNIX platform<br>• 30 years in use<br>• Integrated with powerful HP server family<br>• High availability features<br>• HA Features of System<br>• Administration | • Strong integration with Microsoft Back Office<br>• Strong Appl. Base<br>• Rich Set of App. Dev. Tools<br>• High availability features<br>• HA Features of System Administration | • Open platform<br>• Scalability (available for IBM System z)<br>• High availability features<br>• HA Features of System Administration<br>• Strong partnerships with SAP and VMW | • Stable UNIX platform<br>• 30 years in use<br>• Integrated with IBM server line (RS/6000, POWER)<br>• High availability features<br>• HA Features of System Administration | • Stable UNIX platform<br>• More than 20 years in use<br>• Sun Server platforms (SPARC, x86)<br>• Oracle DBMS<br>• MySQL DBMS<br>• HA Features of System Administration |
| Weaknesses | • Runs only on HP servers<br>• Vendor lock-in<br>• License costs<br>• TCO<br>• App. Dev. Environm. | • Reliability and stability<br>• License costs<br>• TCO<br>• Costs of aplication servers<br>• Costs of application development tools | • Application Development Environment<br>• Vendor viability<br>• Maintenance and support lifetime<br>• Pricing confusion | • Runs only on IBM servers<br>• Vendor lock-in<br>• License costs<br>• TCO<br>• App. Dev. Environm. | • Runs only on SPARC servers<br>• Vendor lock-in<br>• License costs<br>• TCO<br>• App. Dev. Environm. |
| Opportunities | • Virtualization<br>• Cloud Computing | • Virtualization<br>• Cloud Computing | • Virtualization<br>• Cloud Computing | • Virtualization<br>• Cloud Computing | • Virtualization<br>• Cloud Computing |
| Threats | • Free Open/Linux<br>• Other Commercial UNIX (AIX, IRIX, Solaris, . . .)<br>• Free UNIX (Free BSD)<br>• Proprietary- OS (Open VMS, zOS, . . .)<br>• Windows Server<br>• . . . | • Free Open. Linux<br>• Commercial UNIX (AIX, HP-UX, IRIX, Solaris, . . .)<br>• Free UNIX (Free BSD)<br>• Proprietary OS (Open VMS, z/OS, . . .)<br>• OS X Server<br>• . . . | • Other Linux flavors (RedHat, Ubuntu, . . .)<br>• Commercial UNIX (AIX, HP-UX, IRIX, Solaris, . . .)<br>• Free UNIX (Free BSD)<br>• Proprietary OS (Open VMS, z/OS, . . .)<br>• Window's Server<br>• . . . | • Free Open/Linux<br>• Other Commercial<br>• UNIX (HP-UX, IRIX, Solaris, . . .)<br>• Free UNIX (Free BSD)<br>• Proprietary OS (Open VMS, z/OS, . . .)<br>• Windows Server<br>• . . . | • Free Open/Linux<br>• Other Commercial UNIX (AIX, HP-UX, IRIX. . .)<br>• Free UNIX (Free BSD)<br>• Proprietary OS (Open VMS, z'OS, . . .)<br>• Windows Server<br>• . . . |

*Table 18.5* Major high availability features of the five server operating systems

| *VENDOR/FEATURES* | *HP (HP-UX)* | *IBM (AIX)* | *MICROSOFT (Windows Server)* | *SUSE (SUSE Linux)* | *ORACLE (Solaris)* |
|---|---|---|---|---|---|
| HA-HARDWARE | + | + | | | + |
| HA-CORE SOS | + | + | + | + | + |
| HA-APPL-SERVERS | + | + | + | + | + |
| HA-NETWORK | + | + | | | + |
| HA-STORAGE | + | + | | | + |
| HA-SYS-ADMIN | + | + | + | + | + |

Conclusions/lessons learned are as follows:

- Traditional top-priority business requirements towards business information system in the e-business age are replaced by business continuity and always-on business.
- Information systems in the e-business age are expected to be up and running on continuous basis and with zero downtime. They must be “always-on,” or at least with “near-zero” downtime.
- Both e-business and business are expected to become always on.

Presented framework can be used in the projects of transforming or migrating:

- Business information systems into “always-on information systems”
- E-business systems into “always-on e-business”
- Business systems into “always-on business.”

Future research directions are identified around the following research topics:

- Assessing contribution of several information technologies as business continuity drivers, with regard to availability, scalability and reliability.
- Implementing “always-on IS” in different models of IT-architectures: on-site premises versus cloud computing.
- Positioning the concept of “always-on IS” within the IT-compliance regulations and standards.
- Developing “always-on e-business” and “always-on business” models for different e-business/e-commerce models and industries.
- Addressing managerial issues in integrating system/network administration, BC management, risk management, security management, disaster recovery management and organizational management.

## References

Aberdeen Report (2014). Preventing Virtual Application Downtime, available at: www.aberdeen.com, accessed on November 21, 2014.

Adeshiyan, T. et al. (2010). Using Virtualization for High Availability and Disaster Recovery, *IBM Journal of Research and Development*, 53(4), 587–597.

Aktas, M.S. (2010). Principles and Experiences: Designing and Building Enterprise Information Systems, in: Bajgoric, N. (Ed.), *Always-On Enterprise Information Systems for BusinessContinuance: Technologies for Reliable and Scalable Operations*, IGI – Global, Hershey, PA, pp. 58–77.

Asgary, A., Naini, A. S. (2011). Modeling the Adaptation of Business Continuity Planning By Businesses Using Neural Networks, *Intelligent Systems in Accounting, Finance and Management*, 18, 89–104.

Ashurst, C., Freer, A., Ekdahl, J., Gibbons, C. (2012). Exploring IT-Enabled Innovation: A New Paradigm? *International Journal of Information Management*, 32(4), 326–336.

Avaya Report (2014). Network Downtime Results in Job, Revenue Loss, March 2014, available at: www.avaya.com/usa/about-avaya/newsroom/news-releases/2014/pr-140305/.

Avery Gomez, E. (2011). Towards Sensor Networks: Improved ICT UsageBehavior for Business Continuity, *Proceedings of SIGGreen Workshop, Sprouts: Working Papers on Information Systems*, 11(13), available at: http://sprouts.aisnet.org/11-13.

Bajgoric, N. (2006). Continuous Computing Technologies for Improving Performances ofEnterprise Information Systems, *International Journal of Enterprise Information Systems*, 1(4), 70–89, October–December 2005.

Balabko, P., Wegmann, A. (2006). Systemic Classification of Concern-Based Design Methods in the Context of Enterprise Architecture, *Information Systems Frontiers*, 8, 115–131.

Barraza, O. (2002). Achieving 99,9998% ţ Storage Uptime and Availability, White Paper, DotHill Systems, available at: www.dothill.com/pdfs/5-9s_wp.pdf, accessed on December 12, 2005.

Bartel, V.W., Rutkowski, A.F. (2006). A Fuzzy Decision Support System for IT Service Continuity Threat Assessment, *Decision Support Systems*, 42(3), 1931–1943.

Bayram, S., Kirlidog, M., Vayvay, O. (2010). Always-On Enterprise Information Systems With Service Oriented Architecture and Load Balancing, in: Bajgoric, N. (Ed.), *Always-On Enterprise Information Systems for BusinessContinuance: Technologies for Reliable and Scalable Operations*, IGI – Global, Hershey, PA, pp. 91–108.

Bertrand, C. (2005). Business Continuity and Mission Critical Applications, *Network Security*, 20(8), 9–11.

Bharosa, N., Lee, J.K., Jansen, M. (2010). Challenges and Obstacles in Sharing and Coordinating Information During Multi-Agency Disaster Response: Propositions From Field Exercises, *Informatio Systems Frontiers*, 12, 49–65.

Bhatt, G., Emdad, A., Roberts, N., Grover, V. (2010). Building and Leveraging Information in Dynamic Environments: The Role of IT Infrastructure Flexibility as Enabler of Organizational Responsiveness and Competitive Advantage, *Information & Management*, 47(7–8), 341–349.

Bielski, R. (2008). Extreme Risks, American Bankers Association, *ABA Banking Journal*, Mar 2008, 100(3). ABI/INFORM Global, pp. 29–44.

Blackhurst, J., Dunn, K.S., Craighead, C.W. (2011). An Empirically Derived Framework of Global Supply Resiliency. *Journal of Business Logistics*, 32, 374–391.

Boehman, W. (2009). Survivability and Business Continuity Management System According to BS 25999, Proceedings of the 2009 Third International Conference on Emerging Security Information, Systems and Technologies, pp. 142–147.

Botha, J., Von Solms, R. (2004). A Cyclic Approach to Business Continuity Planning, *Information Management & Computer Security*, 12(4), 328–337.

Brenes, E.R., Madrigal, K., Requena, B. (2011). Corporate Governance and Family Business Performance, *Journal of Business Research*, 64, 280–285.

Brett, J.L., Landry, B.J.L., Koger, M.S. (2006). Dispelling 10 Common Disaster Recovery Myths: Lessons Learned from Hurricane Katrina and Other Disasters, *ACM Journal on Educational Resources in Computing*, 6(4), 1–14.

Broder, J.F., Tucker, E. (2012). *Business Continuity Planning, Risk Analysis and the Security Survey* (4th Edition), Elsevier, Oxford.

Butler, B. (2013). Amazon.com Suffers Outage: Nearly $5M Down the Drain?, Network World, January 31, 2013, available at: www.networkworld.com/article/2163191/cloud-computing/update – amazon-com-suffers-outage – nearly – 5m-down-the-drain-.html, accessed on July 25, 2016.

Butler, B.S., Gray, P.H. (2006). Reliability, Mindfulness, and Information Systems, *MIS Quarterly*, 30(2), 211–224.

Cerullo, V., Cerullo, R. (2004). Business Continuity Planning: A Comprehensive Approach, *Information Systems Management*, 2004, 70–78.

Chalupnik, M.J., Wynn, D.C., Clarkson, P.J. (2013). Comparison of Ilities for Protection Against Uncertainty in System Design, *Journal of Engineering Design*, 24(12), 814–829.

Chang, H.-T., Chang, Y.-M., Hsiao, S.-Y. (2014). Scalable Network File Systems With Load Balancing and Fault Tolerance for Web Services, *Journal of Systems and Software*, 93, 102–109.

Chow, W.S., Wai, O.H. (2009). Determinants of the Critical Success Factor of Disaster Recovery Planning for Information Systems, *Information Management & Computer Security*, 17(3), 248–275.

Clancy, H. (2013). Most Common Cause of SMB Downtime? The Answer May Surprise You, *ZDNET*, available at: www.zdnet.com/most-common-cause-of-smb-downtime-the-answer-may-surprise-you-7000011137, accessed on September 11, 2013.

CNBC (2015). United Airlines Flights Restored After Worldwide Groundstop, available at: www.cnbc.com/2015/07/08/, accessed on July 22, 2016.

ComputerWeekly (2007), London Stock Exchange Suffers Trading Downtime, available at: www.computerweekly.com/news/2240083830/London-Stock-Exchange-suffers-trading-downtime, accessed on July 22, 2016.

Corey, C.M., Deitch, E.A. (2011). Factors Affecting Business Recovery Immediately After Hurricane Katrina, *Journal of Contingencies and Crisis Management*, 19(3).

Craighead, C.W., Blackhurst, J., Rungtusanatham, M.J., Handfield, R.B. (2007). The Severity of Supply Chain Disruptions: Design Characteristics and Mitigation Capabilities, *Decision Sciences*, 38(1), 131–151.

Delic, K.A., Riley, J.A. (2009), Enterprise Knowledge Clouds: Next Generation KM Systems?, *International Conference on Information, Process, and Knowledge Management, IEEE Computer Society*, 49–53.

Dembeck, C. (1999). Yahoo Cashes in on Ebay's Outage, *E-commerce Times*, June 18, 1999, available at: www.ecommercetimes.com/perl/story/545.html, accessed on July 20, 2016.

Eagle Rock Alliance (2001). Costs of downtime, available at: www.contingencyplanningresearch.com/2001%20Survey.pdf, accessed on December 12, 2005.

Egwutuoha, I.P. et al. (2013). A Survey of Fault Tolerance Mechanisms and Checkpoint/Restart Implementations for High Performance Computing Systems, *Journal of Supercomputing*, 65, 1302–1326.

Emerson Report (2014). The Lowdown on Data Center Downtime: Frequency, Root Causes and Costs, available at: www.emersonnetworkpower.com/en-US/Solutions/ByApplication/DataCenterNetworking/Data-Center-Insights/Pages/Causes_of_Downtime_Study.aspx, accessed on November 21, 2014.

Forrester Report (2013). How Organizations Are Improving Business Resiliency With Continuous IT Availability, February 2013, available at: www.emc.com/collateral/analyst-report/forrester-improve-bus-resiliency-continuous-it-avail-ar.pdf, accessed on November 11, 2013.

Franke, U. et al. (2012). Availability of Enterprise IT Systems: An Expert-Based Bayesian Framework, *Software Quality Journal*, 20, 369–394.

Galindo, G., Batta, R. (2013). Review of Recent Developments in OR/MS Research in Disaster Operations Management, *European Journal of Operational Research*, 201–211.

Gartner (2014a). Network Downtime, July 2014, available at: http://blogs.gartner.com/andrew-lerner/2014/07/11/network-downtime/, accessed on November 19, 2014.

Gartner (2014b). The Costs of Downtime, July 2014, available at: http://blogs.gartner.com/andrew-lerner/2014/07/16/the-cost-of-downtime.

Gerber, M., Solms, R. (2005). Management of Risk in the Information Age, *Computers & Security*, 24, 16–30.

Gibb, F., Buchanan, S. (2006). A Framework for Business Continuity Management, *International Journal of Information Management*, 26, 128–141.

Goyal, A., Lavenberg, S.S. (1987). Modelingand Analysisof Computersystem Availability, *IBM Journal of Research and Development,* 31(6), 651–664.

Greening, P., Rutherford, C. (2011). Disruptions and Supply Networks: A Multi-Level, Multi-Theoretical Relational Perspective, *The International Journal of Logistics Management*, 22(1), 104–126.

Herbane, B. (2010). The Evolution of Business Continuity Management: A Historical Review of Practices and Drivers, *Business History*, 52(6), 978–1002.

Herbane, B., Elliott, D., Swartz, E.M. (2004). Business Continuity Management: Time for a Strategic Role?, *Long Range Planning*, 37, 435–457.

Hristidis, V., Chen, S-C., Li, T., Luis, S., Deng, Y. (2010). Survey of Data Management and Analysis in Disaster Situations, *The Journal of Systems and Software*, 83, 1701–1714.

IDC Report (2002). Available to: www.hp.com/hps/news/news_072303.html.

IDC Report (2015). High-Value Business Applications on x86: The Need for True Fault -Tolerant Systems, May 2015, available at: http://www8.hp.com/h20195/v2/GetPDF.aspx/4AA5-8631ENW.pdf, accessed on December 14, 2015

IDC Report (2016). Cut Costs, Reduce Complexity and Drive Availability for the Always-On Enterprise, available at: https://go.veeam.com/wp-2016-idc-executive-brief.html, accessed on August 10, 2016.

IDC White paper (2014). Devops and the Cost of Downtime: Fortune 1000 Best Practice Metrics Quantified, available at: www.idc.com/getdoc.jsp?containerId=253155, accessed on December 14, 2015.

Ipe, M., Raghu, T. S., Vinze, A. (2010). Information Intermediaries for Emergency Preparedness and Response: A Case Study From Public Health, *Information Systems Frontiers*, 12, 67–79.

Jarvelainen, J. (2013). IT Incidents and Business Impacts: Validating a Framework for Continuity Management in Information Systems, *International Journal of Information Management*, 33, 583–590.

Kadam, A. (2010). Personal Business Continuity Planning, *Information Security Journal: A Global Perspective*, 19(1), 4–10.

Kadlec, C. (2010). Best Practices in IT Disaster Recovery Planning Among US Banks, *Journal of Internet Banking and Commerce*, 15(1), 1–11.

Karim, A. J. (2011). Business Disaster Preparedness: An Empirical Study for Measuring the Factors of Business Continuity to Face Business Disaster, *International Journal of Business and Social Science*, 2(18).

King, D. L. (2003). Moving Towards a Business Continuity Culture, *Network Security*, Oxford: Elsevier, 12–17.

Kistijantoro, A. I., Morgan, G., Shrivastava, S. K., Little, M. C. (2008). Enhancing an Application Server to Support Available Components, *IEEE Transactions on Software Engineering*, 34(4).

Kiyamoto, S. et al. (2013). Security Issues on IT Systems During Disasters: A Survey, *Journal of Ambient Intelligence and Humanized Computing*, Springer, Berlin Heidelberg.

Kolowitz, B. J. et al. (2011). Workflow Continuity – Moving Beyond Business Continuity in a Multisite 24–7 Healthcare Organization, *Journal of Digital Imaging*, 25, 744–750.

Kuhn, J. R., Jr., Sutton, S. G. (2010). Continuous Auditing in ERP System Environments: The Current State and Future Directions, *Journal of Information Systems*, 24(1), 91–112.

Kuk, G., & Janssen, M. (2013). Assembling infrastructures and business models for service design and innovation. *Information Systems Journal*, 23(5), 445–469..

Lavastre, O., Gunasekaran, A., Spalanzani, A. (2012). Supply Chain Risk Management in French Companies, *Decision Support Systems*, 52, 828–838.

Lee, A. S., Thomas, M., Baskerville, R. L. (2015). Going Back to Basics in Design Science: From the Information Technology Artifact to the Information Systems Artifact, *Information Systems Journal*, 25, 5–21.

Leitch, G. (2016). The True Cost of Downtime in 2016, available at: http://flexitcenter.dataresolution.net/index.php/2016/06/09/true-cost-downtime-2016/, accessed on July 21, 2016.

Lewis, W. R., Pickren, A. (2003). An Empirical Assessment of IT Disaster Risk, *Communication of ACM*, 46(9), 201–206.

Lin., C. S., Kao, S., Chen, L. S. (2012). A Proactive Operational Framework for Business Continuity in the Semiconductor Industry, *Quality and Reliability Enginering International*, 28, 307–320.

Lindstrom, J. (2012). A Model to Explain a Business Contingency Process, *Disaster Prevention and Management*, 21, 2, 269–281.

Lindstrom, J., Samuelson, S., Hagerfors, A. (2010). Business Continuity Planning Methodology, *Disaster Prevention and Management*, 19(2), 243–255.

Liu, C., Black, W. C., Lawrence, F. C., Garrison, M.E.B. (2012). Post-Disaster Coping and Recovery: The Role of Perceived Changes in the Retail Facilities, *Journal of Business Research*, 65, 641–647.

Lodree, E. J., Taskin, S. (2008). An Insurance Risk Management Framework for Disaster Relief and Supply Chain DisruptionInventory Planning, *The Journal of the Operational Research Society*, 59(5), 674–684.

Loveland, S. et al. (2008). Leveraging Virtualization to Optimize High-Availability System Configurations, *IBM Systems Journal*, 47(4), 591–604.
Lumpp, T. et al. (2008). From High Availability and Disaster Recovery to Business Continuity Solutions, *IBM Systems Journal*, 47(4), 605–619.
Maitland, J. (2011). A Really Bad Week for Google and Amazon, available at: http://searchcloudcomputing.techtarget.com/news/2240035039/A-really-bad-week-for-Google-and-Amazon?asrc=EM_NLN_13718724&track=NL-1324&ad=826828, accessed on July 25, 2016.
Mansoori, B. et al. (2013). Design and Implementation of Disaster Recovery and Business Continuity Solution for Radiology PACS, *Journal of Digit Imaging*, August 2013.
Marten. S., Pontus, J, Mathias, E. (2010). The Effect of IT Governance Maturity on IT Governance Performance, *Information Systems Management*, 27(1), 10–24.
Martens, B., Teuteberg, F. (2011). Decision-Making in Cloud Computing Environments: A Cost and Risk Based Approach, *Information Systems Frontiers*, 14(4), 871–893.
Martin, N. (2011). The True Costs of Data Center Downtime, available at: http://itknowledgeexchange.techtarget.com/data-center/the-true-costs-of-data-center-downtime/, accessed on January 8, 2012.
Matos, R. S. et al. (2012). Sensitivity Analysis of Server Virtualized System Availability, *IEEE Transactions on Reliability*, 61(4), 994–1006.
Miller, H. E., Engemann, K. J. (2014). Using Reliability and Simulation Models in Business Continuity Planning, *International Journal of Business Continuity and Risk Management*, 5(1), 43–56.
Minhas, U. M. et al. (2013). RemusDB: Transparent High Availability for Database Systems, *The VLDB Journal*, 22, 29–45.
Narman, P., Franke, U., Konig, J., Buschle, M., Ekstedt, M. (2014). Enterprise Architecture Availability Analysis Using Fault Trees and Stakeholder Interviews, *Enterprise Information Systems*, 8(1), 1–25.
Niemimaa, M. (2015). Interdisciplinary Review of Business Continuity From an Information Systems Perspective: Toward an Integrative Framework, *Communications of the Association for Information Systems*, Vol. 37, pp. 69–102.
Nollau, B. (2009). Disaster Recovery and Business Continuity, *Journal of GXP Compliance*, 13(3), 51.
NYTimes (2015). The Stock Market Bell Rings, Computers Fail, Wall Street Cringes, available at: www.nytimes.com/2015/07/09/business/dealbook/new-york-stock-exchange-suspends-trading.html?_r=0, accesses on July 22, 2016.
Ojha, D., Gokhale, D. A. (2009). Logistical Business Continuity Planning-Scale Development and Validation, *The International Journal of Logistics Management*, 20(3), 342–359.
Omar, A., Alijani, D., Mason, R. (2011). Information Technology Disaster Recovery Plan: Case Study, *Academy of Strategic Management Journal*, 10(2), 127–141.
Park, Y. W., Hong, P., Roh, J. J. (2013). Supply Chain Lessons From the Catastrophic Natural Disaster in Japan, *Business Horizons*, 56(1), 75–85.
Pitt, M., Goyal, S. (2004). Business Continuity Planning as a Facilities Management Tool, *Facilities*, 22(3–4), 87–99.
Ponemon Institute Report (2016). Cost of Data Center Outages, available at: www.emersonnetworkpower.com/en-US/Resources/Market/Data-Center/Latest-Thinking/Ponemon/Documents/2016-Cost-of-Data-Center-Outages-FINAL-2.pdf, accessed on July 21, 2016.
Radhakrishnan, R., Mark, K., Powell, B. (2008). IT Service Management for High Availability, *IBM Systems Journal*, 47(4), 549–561.
Rebman, T., Wang, J., Swick, Z., Reddick, D., delRosario, J. L. (2013). Business Continuity and Pandemic Preparedness: US Health Care Versus Non-Health Care Agencies, *American Journal of Infection Control*, 41(4), 27–33.
Rick St. Cyr (2001). Firms Pay More Attention to Data Protection, *Disaster Recovery Journal*, 14(4), 22, Fall 2001.
Saha, P. (2013). Preface, Systemic Enterprise Architecture as Future: Tackling Complexity in Governments in the Cusp of Change, in: Saha, P. (Ed.), *A Systemic Perspective to Managing Complexity With Enterprise Architecture*, IGI – Global, Hershey, PA, pp. XIX–XXIV.

Sapateiro, C., Baloian, N., Antunes, P., Zurita, G. (2011). Developing a Mobile Collaborative Tool for Business Continuity Management, *Journal of Universal Computer Science*, 17(2), 164–182.

Singhal, R., Pawar, P., Bokare, S. (2010). Enterprise Storage Architecture for Optimal Business Continuity, *Proceedings of the 2010 International Conference on Data Storage and Data Engineering*, Bangalore, India, pp. 73–77.

Smith, W. E. et al. (2008). Availability Analysis of Blade Server Systems, *IBM Systems Journal*, 47(4), 621–640.

Speight, P. (2011). Business Continuity, *Journal of Applied Security Research*, 6, 529–554.

Srinivasan, R., Lilien, G. L., Rangaswamy, A. (2002). Technological Opportunism and Radical Technology Adoption: An Application to E-Business, *Journal of Marketing*, 66(3), 47–60, July 2002.

Sumner, M., (2009), Information Security Threats: A Comparative Analysis of Impact, Probability, and Preparedness, *Information Systems Management*, 26, 2–11.

Swartz, E., Elliott, D., and Herbane, B. (2003). Greater than the Sum of Its Parts: Business Continuity Management in the UK Finance Sector, *Risk Management*, 5(1), 65–80.

Tammineedi, R. L. (2010). Business Continuity Management: A Standards-Based Approach, *Information Security Journal: A Global Perspective*, 19(1), 36–50.

Tan, Y., Takakuwa, S. (2011). Use of Simulation in a Factory forBusiness Continuity Planning, *International Journal of Simulation Modelling (IJSIMM)*, 10(1), 17–26.

Torabi, S. A., Rezaei Soufi, H., Sahebjamnia, N. (2014). A New Framework for Business Impact Analysis in Business Continuity Management (With a Case Study). *Safety Science*, 68, 309–323.

Turban, E., Rainer, R. K., Potter, R. E. (2000). *Introduction to Information Technology*, Wiley, Hoboken, NJ.

Turetken, O. (2008). Is Your Backup IT-Infrastructure in a Safe Location – A Multi-Criteria Approach to Location Analysis for Business Continuity Facilities, *Information Systems Frontiers*, 10, 375–383.

Umar, A. (2005). IT Infrastructure to Enable Next Generation Enterprises, *Information Systems Frontiers,* 7(3), 217–256.

Veeam Report (2014). The Veeam Data Center Availability Report 2014, available at: www.veeam.com/wp-availability-report-2014.html, accessed on December 14, 2015.

Venkatraman, A. (2013). Human Error Most Likely Cause of Datacentre Downtime, Finds Study, *Computerweekly*, available at: www.computerweekly.com/news/2240179651/Human-error-most-likely-cause-of-datacentre-downtime-finds-study, accessed on September 11, 2013.

Venters, W., Whitley, E.A. (2012). A Critical Review of Cloud Computing: Researching Desires and Realities, *Journal of Information Technology*, 27(3), 179–197.

Versteeg, G., Bouwman, H. (2006). Business architecture: A new paradigm to relate business strategy to ICT, *Information Systems Frontiers* (2006) 8, 91–102.

Walker, A. (2006). Business Continuity and Outsourcing – Moves to ake Out the Risk, *Network Security*, May 2006, 15–17.

Wan, S. (2009). Service impact analysis using business continuity planning processes, *Campus-Wide Information Systems*, 26(1), 20–42.

Winkler, U, Fritzsche, M., Gilani, W., Marshall, A. (2010). A Model-Driven Framework for Process-centric Business Continuity Management, *Proceedings of the 2010 Seventh International Conference on the Quality of Information and Communications Technology*, Porto, Portugal, pp. 248–252.

Wu, W. Y., Chiag, C.Y., Wu, Y.J. and Tu, H. J. (2004). The influencing factors of commitment and business integration on supply chain management, *Industrial Management & Data Systems*, 104(4), 322–333.

Yan, H. (2005). An Integrated High Availability Computing Platform, *The Electronic Library*; 23(6); ABI/INFORM Complet, pp. 631–640.

Zobel, C. (2011). Representing perceived tradeoffs in defining disaster resilience, *Decision Support Systems*, 50(2), 394–403.

# 19

# Using location *k*-anonymity models for protecting location privacy

*Eric Di Carlo, Heechang Shin and Haibing Lu*

## 1 Introduction

Location-based services (LBS) are an increasingly growing market since they are a good way for a user to know about information around him/her. Also, in a push-based LBS environment, companies can market their goods to nearby users. LBS provide services based on the user's current location, and services can be constantly provided as the user moves. During 2016–2020, LBS is expected to grow with a minimum of 35.2% compound annual growth rate, which will lead to $54.95 billion revenue (Basiri et al., 2016). The main cause of growth is because more and more number of people use smartphone devices with GPS capability such as Apple's iPhone or Google's Android devices. In 2012, 46% of Americans have such devices, and 74% of those users use LBS (Andres et al., 2013). LBS is used for useful services including store locations, proximity-based marketing, location awareness, future traffic and weather, personalized dating services and so forth. Due to these useful features, LBS have had tremendous growth all around the world. However, a big negative for LBS would be its consequences on privacy because using LBS requires a user to provide his/her current location to a LBS service provider. An adversary can find out a person's location through an LBS service provider, and users have legitimate concerns on their personal safety and privacy.

In order to address such privacy threats, the idea of location *k*-anonymity (Gruteser and Grunwald, 2003) was introduced. Location *k*-anonymity is satisfied if a user is indistinguishable from at least $k - 1$ other users with respect to certain identifying attributes (Kalnis et al., 2007). The identifying attributes when linked with external data can uniquely identify someone are called quasi-identifiers. One example of quasi-identifiers would be three attributes (i.e., gender, zip code and date of birth), which are used to identify around 87% of over 200 million Americans (Sweeney, 2000). In LBS environment, most researchers consider the location and time acting as quasi-identifiers (Bettini et al., 2007). Location *k*-anonymity is defined as the state in which location information of a mobile user is indistinguishable from the location information of at least $k - 1$ other mobile users (Shin et al., 2011). More specifically, the location is generalized into a region such that the actual query issuer within the region cannot be distinguished from at least $k - 1$ other users (Shin et al., 2011). This generalized region is called as GR, and adversaries cannot assign probability of no more than $1/k$ to an individual user in it, thus achieving anonymity with those users located within it (Shin et al., 2011). In addition to generalization of the location, in order to achieve location *k*-anonymity, given an LBS query, the identifying information such as user ID should be removed (Gruteser and Grunwald, 2003; Mokbel et al., 2006). The main limitation of the original location *k*-anonymity model is that it assumes that all the users are using the same level of privacy, or *k*. Gedik and Liu (2005) provide personalized location *k*-anonymity model, allowing each user to specify their own level of *k*. Mokbel et al. (2006) utilize a similar model but propose a different implementation based on a multi-level grid-based index structure to allow more efficient anonymization and nearest neighbor queries (Shin et al., 2011).

While all these contributions to LBS privacy preservation via location *k*-anonymity are interesting and promising, the above contributions assume that spatiotemporal location is the only information acting as quasi-identifiers. Some researchers identify that background knowledge such as user's profile (Shin et al., 2011), movement information (Shin et al., 2010), historical trajectory (Bettini et al., 2005) and anonymization algorithms (Chow and Mokbel, 2007) can also act as quasi-identifiers. In order to defend against background knowledge of user profiles, Shin et al. (2011) introduce a set of anonymization models that are suitable for such environment. In case of movement information, Shin et al. (2010) extend the notion of location *k*-anonymity by incorporating user's moving direction into the anonymization process. There are some efforts to preserve the privacy even when the historical trajectory information is available. Bettini et al. (2005) extend location *k*-anonymity to include historical traces of location information. Xu and Cai (2007) address the issues of privacy in the context of continuous LBS that requires continuous location updates from users. Simply ensuring each cloaking area contains at least *k* users does not provide location *k*-anonymity protection as the intersection of users within subsequent GRs would result in smaller number of users, which will lead to privacy breaches. Chow and Mokbel (2007) also address the issue of privacy protection under the continuous LBS environment by forming a dynamic group such that the GR for each mobile user in a group is the spatial region that includes all users in the group. Kalnis et al. (2007) pointed out a possible problem with the proposed anonymization algorithms of Chow and Mokbel (2007) and Gruteser and Grunwald (2003) when the algorithm is revealed, and presented a possible solution.

This chapter introduces the concept of location *k*-anonymity for protecting location privacy. There are several location *k*-anonymity models with different assumptions, and this chapter introduces those models with possible shortcomings. The organization of the chapter is as follows: Section 2 introduces location *k*-anonymity. Various implementations of location *k*-anonymity are discussed in Section 3. Discussions and related work are discussed in Section 4 and Section 5 respectively. Section 6 presents conclusions and future work.

## 2 Location *k*-anonymity

Gruteser and Grunwald (2003) first propose the concept of location *k*-anonymity. Under the location *k*-anonymity scheme, instead of revealing the exact location, a bounding box, called generalized region (GR), is reported containing at least *k* people (Shin et al., 2011). If all the LBS requests satisfy location *k*-anonymity, the privacy of mobile users is assumed to be preserved because one cannot be individually identified among *k* other users (Shin et al., 2011). To achieve this, a user must submit his/her privacy requirement (i.e. the minimum level of *k*).

A generally accepted system architecture model in location *k*-anonymity community is based on the trusted third-party model (Shin et al., 2011). A mobile user uses a mobile device to send requests to a LBS provider using wireless technologies (Shin et al., 2011). Instead of sending them directly to a LBS provider, it is assumed that there exists a trusted location server (LS), which maintains the locations of mobile users (Shin et al., 2011). Although some proposals, such as Ardagna et al. (2007) and Duckham and Kulik (2006) assume users communicate with LBS providers directly, the architecture similar to the above has been employed by most of the proposals in this area (Gruteser and Grunwald, 2003; Bettini et al., 2005; Mokbel et al., 2006). LS is considered as a trusted party (Shin et al., 2011), and LS can be implemented as a globally distributed service to minimize single point of failure and being attractive to hacking attacks (Shin et al., 2011). The location and velocity information can be acquired either by locally using GPS or by network-based approach where the network infrastructure is responsible for computing a mobile user's location (Duckham and Kulik, 2006). For example, a cellular phone's location is computed using cell global identity (Shin et al., 2011). In this case, the locations and velocities of mobile users can be tracked by the system in the form of log files (Bettini et al., 2005), and need to be communicated to the LBS provider to obtain a service (Shin et al., 2011).

LS is responsible for anonymization based on users' privacy requirements that anonymize the original request to be forwarded to the LBS (Shin et al., 2011). The anonymization step includes both clustering of locations as well as anonymizing them. On receiving the candidate results from the LBS, LS sends the result back to the user requesting the service (Shin et al., 2011). It is assumed that LS uses a single pseudo ID throughout a request session's lifetime to maintain service continuity as in Xu and Cai (2007).

## 3 Implementation of location *k*-anonymity

This section introduces several approaches that implement location *k*-anonymity and discuss their shortcomings.

### *3.1 Anonymization based on quad-tree*

Gruteser and Grunwald (2003) present the idea of location *k*-anonymity model using quad-tree (Finkel and J. Bentley, 1974) for spatial generalization. The spatial generalization algorithm subdivides the area around the mobile user's position until the number of users in the area falls below the privacy level, i.e. $k$, and the previous quadrant, which meets the constraint of $k$, is then returned (Gruteser and Grunwald, 2003). For example, suppose that the minimum size of $k$ is 2 and the space is subdived into four. There are four users, $o_1$, $o_2$, $o_3$ and $o_4$ where $o_1$, $o_2$, and $o_3$ are located in the first quadrant, and $o_4$ is located in the third quadrant. When $o_4$ submits an LBS request, the number of users in the third quadrant that belongs to the requester, $o_4$, is less than the minimum size of $k$, 2, which results in merging with the other quadrants, of which space includes four users. In this case, the number of users is greater than the minimum size of $k$, thus satisfying location *k*-anonymity. In this case, the spatial generalization algorithm creates the spatial region of the whole region, and the anonymity set includes four mobile users (i.e. $o_1$, $o_2$, $o_3$ and $o_4$), which satisfies the minimum size of $k$, 2. Similar to Gruteser and Grunwald (2003), the anonymization algorithm by Mokbel et al. (2006) is based on a quad-tree structure.

Kalnis et al. (2007) address the privacy leakage problem of existing work (Gruteser and Grunwald, 2003) when outliers exist. The following example elaborates this problem. Here, $o_4$ is an outlier because the generated GR includes the whole region while the generated GR by other users such as $o_1$, $o_2$ and $o_3$ would include only the first quadrant of the whole region. Therefore, when the whole region is submitted as a part of anonymized request, the adversary is pretty sure that $o_4$ is the actual query submitter. The main reason for this privacy leakage is due to the fact that the computation of GR is fixed based on the region. In other words, the anonymization algorithm divides the region in a pre-determined way (in this case, four equal-sized regions), and therefore, the node structure of the tree is based on the distribution of the moving objects on the given space. Therefore, it is susceptible to the privacy attack based on the outliers.

## 3.2 Anonymization based on k-nearest neighbors

The *k*-nearest neighbor grouping strategy finds $k - 1$ nearest neighbors from the location of the query issuer, and sets the GR as MBR (minimum bounding rectangle) that encloses such locations. Although *k*-nearest neighbor search may generate a smaller sized GR, but it is likely to disclose the location of the query issuer under the center-of-ASR attack (Kalnis et al., 2007). The center-of-ASR attack is successful if the probability of *u* being the closest user to the center exceeds $1/k$. Kalnis et al. (2007) experimentally show that, in most cases, *u* is close to the center of the GR. Hence, an attacker with knowledge of the generalization algorithm may easily pinpoint *u* as the query issuer.

The problem of using the *k*-nearest neighbor approach is that the resulting objects of *k*-nearest neighbors do not include the query issuer as the their *k*-nearest neighbor. For example, if any of the objects in the *k*-nearest neighbor does not include the query issuer as a *k*-nearest neighbor, in other words, the reverse *k*-nearest neighbor of an object within the GR does not include the query issuer as the reverse *k*-nearest neighbor, it would be the problem. Therefore, a new anonymization model can be advanced in a way that at least *k* number of users are included in the anonymity set, and at the same time, at least *m* number of users must be included as the reverse *k*-nearest neighbors. An efficient search algorithm to check this property still needs to be developed.

## 3.3 Profile-based anonymization models

The integration of location data with personal and public information such as user profiles allows personalized LBS (Liu and Wilde, 2011). In a personalized mobile service environment, the adversary, with the knowledge of profiles, can prune out some of the users successfully from the anonymity set because their profiles are not identical (Shin et al., 2011). Thus, the adversary may identify the query issuer. First, the concept of user profile will be introduced, and then, profile-based anonymization models that enhance the traditional notion of location *k*-anonymity by Shin et al. (2011) will be discussed.

*User Profile*: A user profile represents a set of attributes associated with a mobile user (Atluri and Shin, 2007). These attributes may include (1) demographic information, (2) contact information, (3) personal preferences, and (4) behavioral profile (Shin et al., 2011). Given a set of user profile attributes $A = \{a_1, a_2, \ldots, a_m\}$ under consideration in the system, each user's profile is represented as $\{a_1: v_1, a_2: v_2, \ldots, a_m: v_m\}$, where $v_i$ is the value of $a_i$ (Shin et al., 2011). Suppose $A$ = {*gender, work_class*} where *gender* has two values of "male" and "female," and *work_class* has four values of "private," "self-employed," "government," and "never_employed." Each attribute can be represented using a string of binary bits. The length of the bit representation corresponds to the number of discrete values the attribute can have. For example, *gender* is represented with two bits since it has two values, and *work_class* has four bits. Then, the value of 1 is used in the appropriate place to indicate the attribute value. For example, for male, *gender* bit string can be represented as "10" and "female" is represented with "01" if the first bit represents male, and the second bit represents female. Similarly, since *work_class* has four different values, 4 bits are used to represent it. If the last bit corresponds to "never_employed," the bit string is 0001. In case of continuous attributes such as age or salary, discretization of values can be applied. The granular level of discretization is determined based on the application requirement. For more detailed information, refer to Shin et al. (2011).

Given two profiles represented with bit strings, the weighted profile vector distance measures their distance, and profile bounding vector is used to group a set of profiles, which is defined as follows (Shin et al., 2011). Profile bounding (PB) vector is a bitwise OR operation of a set of string representations of profile attributes. For example, suppose string representation of Tom's profile attribute is $\boldsymbol{p}_{\text{Tom}}$ [*gender*] = 10, and $\boldsymbol{p}_{\text{Tom}}$ [*work_class*] = 1000. Also, suppose Jane's profile attribute is $\boldsymbol{p}_{\text{Jane}}$[*gender*] = 10, and $\boldsymbol{p}_{\text{Jane}}$[*work_class*] = 0100. Then, for $\boldsymbol{P} = \{\boldsymbol{p}_{\text{Tom}}, \boldsymbol{p}_{\text{Jane}}\}$, profile bounding vector is {11, 1100} because for *gender*, $10 \vee 10 = 11$ and for *work_class*, $1000 \vee 0100 = 1100$. Similar to the GR that is used to generalize a set of locations, PB is used to generalize a set of profiles. Profile generalization is achieved by generating PB of all the users located within GR (Shin et al., 2011). Suppose Tom and Jane are located within GR, and their profiles need to be generalized. First, let us look at the attribute, *gender*. Because David's and Jane's genders are male and female respectively, their profile generalization should include both genders, which corresponds to the result PB(*P*[*gender*]) = 11. Similarly, profile generalization of two users for the attribute '*work_class*' should include the values of "private" and "self-employed," the resultant profile attribute generalization is PB(*P*[*work_class*]) = 1100. In the following, profile-based anonymization models by Shin et al. (2011) will be discussed.

*Profile-based Location Anonymity Models*: There are three anonymization models for profile-based LBS environments (Shin et al., 2011):

- *Location and Profile k-anonymity*: This is a direct application of location *k*-anonymity to a personalized LBS environment. A user request is generalized by converting a location into a GR that at least additional $k-1$ users with the identical profiles of the user. Because the profiles of mobile users within the GR are identical, an adversary cannot individually identify a person among them (Shin et al., 2011). However, ensuring that there exist at least *k* users that match the requesting user profile depends on the profile distributions of the users (Shin et al., 2011). As a result, to meet this requirement, the location may need to be generalized to a large extent so that it may render the LBS that is specific to a user's request useless as it could be far off from that of the user (Shin et al., 2011). For example, the spatiotemporal coverage may include the whole town to achieve this anonymity model. The next two models (Constrained Location and Profile *k*-anonymity and Constrained Location and Constrained Profile *k*-anonymity) are introduced to address this issue.
- *Constrained Location and Profile k-anonymity*: In case of constrained location and profile *k*-anonymity, the location is generalized so that GR does not exceed a user specified spatiotemporal extent, and at the same time contain at least additional $k-1$ users with identical profiles of the user (Shin et al., 2011). If one cannot find $k-1$ such users within the user specified spatiotemporal extent, then the profile is generalized as well within the user specified spatiotemporal extent (Shin et al., 2011). In order to do so, a user must submit his/her privacy requirement (i.e. the minimum level of *k*) as well as the maximum spatiotemporal region (i.e. the maximum size of spatiotemporal region that guarantees the LBS quality) (Shin et al., 2011). Profile generalization is achieved by

computing the profile bounding vector of the users within the GR. In this case, although an adversary can gain access to the requested information, it cannot distinguish the real requester from other $k - 1$ users because each user included in the location and profile generalization has the same probability of submitting a query (Shin et al., 2011). However, a random generalization of the user profiles may result in the decreased quality of service (Shin et al., 2011). For example, the profile attribute "gender" should not be generalized for a person looking for a dating service (Shin et al., 2011). For this reason, profile generalization should be done in a way that utility loss of profile generalization is minimized. The next model, Constrained Location and Constrained Profile *k*-anonymity, addresses this issue.

- *Constrained Location and Constrained Profile k-anonymity*: Under constrained location and constrained profile *k*-anonymity, location and profile are generalized at the same time, but both the location generalization as well as the profile generalization are constrained by the limit set by the user (Shin et al., 2011). The user specifies the level of generalization preference for each specific profile attribute, which is denoted as profile tolerance (Shin et al., 2011). The profile tolerance is the user specified generalization allowed for each profile attribute in the profile vector during anonymization (Shin et al., 2011). In the previous example of dating services, profile tolerance can be specified as 0 for the attribute of *gender* and 1 for the attribute of *work_class* so that generalization can be done only for the attribute of *work_class*.

Since the Location and Profile *k*-anonymity model achieves minimum information loss in terms of profile generalization, both Constrained Location and Profile *k*-anonymity model and Constrained Location and Constrained Profile k-anonymity model are used only if Location and Profile *k*-anonymity model generates the spatiotemporal coverage that exceeds the location tolerance level. However, this situation may cause a privacy leak. If $o_1$ is the only woman within the GR, and the profile is generalized, she is more likely to be the query issuer. In order to address this issue, the anonymization process can be independent of the profile distribution.

## 3.4 Anonymization based on space-filling curve

Kalnis et al. (2007) utilize the Hilbert space-filling curve to generate small size of GRs for variable values of *k*. The Hilbert space filling curve transforms the 2D coordinates of a location into a 1D value (Sagan, 1994). With high probability, if two points are in close proximity in the 2D space, they will also be close in the 1D transformation: thus, a major benefit of Hilbert curves, is that they permit the indexing of multidimensional objects through one-dimensional structures such as B-trees curve (Kalnis et al., 2007).

Given a query from user $u_1$ with minimum anonymity level *k*, Hilbert Cloak sorts the Hilbert values and splits them into buckets of size *k* except the last one which may contain up to $2k - 1$ users (Kalnis et al., 2007). The users in the same bucket become the corresponding anonymity set. When any of $u_1$, $u_2$ or $u_3$ issues a query, Hilbert Cloak returns those three users as the anonymity set, and the MBR of that bucket becomes the GR (Kalnis et al., 2007).

The Hilbert Cloak is considered to preserve the privacy against the background attack using anonymization algorithms because all users in the same bucket share the same anonymity set; therefore, spatial anonymity is considered to be guaranteed (Bettini et al., 2007). However, if the value of individual *k* is known to the adversary, this cannot guarantee the privacy. The individual value of *k* can be known by observing the historical bucket size of the users. For example, if $u_1$ is observed with bucket size $k_1$ over the last 10 anonymized request, $u_1$'s $k$ value is more likely to be $k_1$. For example, if the intersection of anonymity set is very smaller than it is more likely to reveal the privacy of that user.

### 3.5 Personalized location k-anonymity model

Gedik and Liu (2005) describe a personalized location k-anonymity model which enables each mobile user to specify the minimum level of location anonymity, *k*, as well as the maximum spatiotemporal resolutions it is willing to tolerate (Shin et al., 2011). The personalized location *k*-anonymity model is an important concept since more fine-grained quality of service can be provided to mobile users while meeting their privacy requirements. Because of the inverse relationship between the service quality and the level of privacy, in order to meet all the mobile users' privacy requirements, we may use the maximum value of minimum *k* of all the users. However, this approach may deteriorate the service quality for those who requires smaller level of anonymity because of applying the uniform level of minimum *k*. Therefore, a personalized location *k*-anonymity model can provide better quality of service while meeting each user's privacy requirement. Also, personalized location *k*-anonymity solves the privacy leakage of other approaches. It is because an attacker does not have the knowledge of the minimum level of *k*, it is possible that the given spatiotemporal region can be the result of high level of privacy requirement.

The main challenge is how to provide personalized location *k*-anonymity model efficiently. This challenge can be summarized into two sub-problems: (1) how to find the set of service requests that can be anonymized together, and (2) given a set of service requests that can be anonymized together, how to find the minimum spatiotemporal region that can include all the requests. Gedik and Liu (2005) tries to solve the first sub-problem by modeling the anonymization constraints of all messages as a constraint graph, and finding cliques that satisfy certain conditions in the constraint graph (Gedik and Liu, 2005).

Creating GRs from using the constraint graph can solve the second sub-problem. Suppose there are three users $o_1$, $o_2$ and $o_3$ in the system, and there exists only one edge between $o_1$ and $o_2$. Then, both $o_1$ and $o_2$ are anonymized, but $o_3$ is required to wait for another request which can create a connected sub-graph whose element is greater than the maximum level of *k* of all the connected components (Gedik and Liu, 2005).

### 3.6 Anonymization for directional location-based services

Location *k*-anonymity ignores the movement information of mobile users, assuming that it has no impact on privacy. Directional LBS is an advanced type of LBS that requires information about direction as well as speed of motion to process (Shin et al., 2010). For example, in a directional LBS, a user can ask to find the nearest restaurant in the north direction based on his/her current location. One observation is that the query direction may be different from his/her movement direction. Shin et al. (2010) discuss the details of such examples. In most GPS traces, in addition to location information, directional information is computed from the location tracking devices (Hoh et al., 2007). Therefore, in addition to the user's location, the user's movement direction should be considered to ensure privacy (Shin, et al., 2010). The following two models (Location and direction *k*-Anonymity and Relaxed location and direction *k*-Anonymity) extend the notion of location *k*-anonymity by incorporating user's moving direction into the anonymization process while serving directional LBS (Shin et al., 2010). These models are explained in the following:

- *Location and Direction k-Anonymity*: Given a user request, location and direction $k$-anonymity is satisfied by finding $k - 1$ users whose moving directions are identical with the query issuer. For example, assume that John is heading north. His LBS request is to find the nearest restaurant(s) heading north from his current location. In order to preserve the privacy of John, LS removes all the identifying information and replaces location information with GR that covers the locations of three other users (Tom, Kim, Rob) of whose direction is the same as Tom. The issue of this model is that the area of GR can be significantly larger than the utility threshold of the application (Shin et al., 2010). For example, for a sparsely populated area, the anonymization based on location and direction $k$-anonymity can cover the whole area, which is not desirable (Shin et al., 2010).
- *Relaxed Location and Direction k-Anonymity*: Relaxed location and direction $k$-anonymity is ensured if there are a group of users whose probability distribution of submitting a query is less than or equal to $1/k$ so that adversaries cannot differentiate between the actual query requester and the other users (Shin et al., 2010). This satisfies the underlying assumption of the location $k$-anonymity by ensuring that the probability of each user's submitting a query is less than or equals to $1/k$. Suppose that John is heading north. His LBS request is to find the nearest restaurant(s) heading north from his current location. In order to preserve the privacy of John, LS replaces location information with GR that covers the locations of three users (Harry, Marry, Tom, and John) of whose probability distribution of submitting a query is less than or equals to $1/k$. In order to explain the concept of Relaxed location and direction $k$-anonymity, concepts of anonymity measured by entropy and local anonymity need to be introduced. A user is anonymous within a group of other users called an anonymity set, denoted as $S$. Let $P(Q = u)$ be the probability of a user $u$ in $S$ submitting an LBS query. Quantifying the level of anonymity inherent in $S$ is calculated by Shannon entropy (Shin et al., 2011):

$$H(S) = -\sum_{u \in S} P(Q=u) log_2 P(Q=u)$$

The anonymity level of location $k$-anonymity is assumed to be $H(S) = -\log(\frac{1}{|S|})$ because of the uniform distribution among the users in the anonymity set, $S$, that is $P(Q = u) = 1/k$ for all $u \in S$ (Shin et al., 2010). However, in case of directional LBS environments, the moving directions of the mobile users in $S$ change the query probability distribution: more specifically, the posterior probability distribution given the query direction is not the same as the prior uniform query distribution assumed in location $k$-anonymity, i.e., $P(Q = u \backslash D = r.d) \neq P(Q = u)$ where $r.d$ is the query direction, and $P(D = d)$ is the probability that the moving direction of a user request matches $d$ (Shin et al., 2010). Under directional LBS environment, the anonymity level is measured by a conditional entropy $H(S \mid D = r.d) = -\log_2 \max_{u \in S} P(Q = u \mid D = r.d)$ (Shin et al., 2010). This notion of anonymity is integrated with the local anonymity measure proposed by Toth et al. (2004). Then, the following inequality holds (Shin et al., 2010):

$$H_{\cdot}(S) \geq H(S) \geq -\log \varepsilon$$

where $H_\Theta(S)$ is the local anonymity of $S$. The above equation implies that any system preserving local anonymity with parameter ε is at least as strong as a system with $1/\varepsilon$ users and uniformly distributed probabilities (Toth et al., 2004). For example, if local anonymity of parameter $\varepsilon = 0.1$ is preserved, the anonymity level would be at least greater than or equal to the anonymity level of 10 users with uniformly distributed probabilities (Shin et al., 2010). Therefore, in order to achieve the privacy level of $k$, as long as $-\log_2 \max_{u \in S} P(Q=u \mid D=r.d) \leq 1/k$ holds in the anonymity set $S$, the desired level of privacy is ensured.

Relaxed location and direction $k$-anonymity model selects an anonymity set such that the posterior probability distribution given the query direction is less than $1/k$ for all the users within the anonymity set (Shin et al., 2010). Efficient processing of finding such anonymity set is discussed in Shin et al. (2010).

## 4 Discussion

No anonymization algorithm discusses how to defend the attack based on the value of $k$. Only Gedik and Liu (2005) can protect from this kind of attack because each user's preference can be different. Hilbert Cloak may be susceptible to this attack. For example, if the minimum privacy level (i.e., $k$) of a user in the same bucket in Hilbert Cloak algorithm is larger than the bucket size, this user is definitely not the one who submits the query. The risk is being increased if $k$ of the query issuer is significantly smaller than any other user in the bucket, the privacy of the users is being breached. The maximum level of $k$ for the bucket size can be used, but this may overkill for generating the anonymity set.

## 5 Related work

The privacy issue of LBS, due to its increasing significance in modern society, has been researched because of the possible privacy violation. A privacy violation is when an individual identity and personal information is stolen by a third party without consent of the original user (Bettini and Riboni, 2015). Many personal information can be stolen because of LBS including phone number, social security number, address, or medical issues. In order to protect against an adversary stealing information, one would have to make the mobile user indistinguishable from other users. In order to be indistinguishable, location $k$-anonymity generates a GR and makes sure it is not distinguishable from $k - 1$ other users within the GR. Even though this considerably reduces the possibility of the user's location being discovered by the adversary, there are still risks. A possible privacy risk is revealing of the trajectory information (Nergiz et al., 2008). Even with remaining personal information from trajectories, peoples' information can still be discovered by linking common attributes, quasi-identifiers, in released databases to public databases. This is possible because in fixed locations are vulnerable to intersection attacks, which is when two equality groups containing a specific individual is intersected to find the identity of the individual. Different models of trajectory $k$-anonymity have been made by generalizing each location in the trajectory (Abul et al., 2008).

Obfuscation is another way to protect and preserve personal information of a user by adding noises to the user's location (Iyer and Shanthi 2013: 296). There are number of obfuscation models that have been proposed including ID shuffler, exchanging location information without contacting the server, and mobile networks that actively collect and disseminate location to others.

Privacy models suitable for mobile urban traffic monitoring have been introduced by Wang et al. (2015). Two problems with traditional sensory network was the sensor was too small and were power constrained. In order to fix this issue, Wang et al. (2015) proposed people-centric sensing at larger scales, and it provides privacy by allowing just enough information back to the server. Kumar and Dawra (2016) researched on how to protect the privacy of monitored objects in 3D space. They considered the scenarios of protecting privacy information of users in multi-floor, multi-section buildings. The 3D spatial histograms were used to calculate the number of people in a multi-floor building and tested their estimated distribution on a large range of queries.

## 6 Conclusion

The idea of location *k*-anonymity was proposed to protect location privacy. In location *k*-anonymity, it is harder for the adversary to distinguish between users within the GR. Thus, the users' privacy is protected. This chapter covers several different models of location *k*-anonymity with various background information such as user profiles, movement information, historical data, and anonymization algorithms. Since no anonymization algorithm discusses how to defend the attack based on the value of *k*, it would be interesting to propose a model that addresses such attack.

## References


Abul, O., Bonchi, F. and Nanni, M., 2008, April. Never walk alone: Uncertainty for anonymity in moving objects databases. In *2008 IEEE 24th International Conference on Data Engineering* (pp. 376–385). IEEE.

Ardagna, C.A., Cremonini, M., Damiani, E., Di Vimercati, S.D.C. and Samarati, P., 2007, July. Location privacy protection through obfuscation-based techniques. In *IFIP Annual Conference on Data and Applications Security and Privacy* (pp. 47–60). Springer, Berlin Heidelberg.

Atluri, Vijayalakshmi and Shin, Heechang., 2007. "Efficient security policy enforcement in a location based service environment." In *IFIP Annual Conference on Data and Applications Security and Privacy*. Springer, Berlin Heidelberg.

Basiri, A., Moore, T., Hill, C. and Bhatia, P., 2016, June. The non-technical challenges of Location Based Services markets: Are the users' concerns being ignored?. In *Localization and GNSS (ICL-GNSS), 2016 International Conference on* (pp. 1–5). IEEE.

Bettini, C., Mascetti, S., Wang, X.S. and Jajodia, S., 2007, May. Anonymity in location-based services: Towards a general framework. In *2007 International Conference on Mobile Data Management* (pp. 69–76). IEEE.

Bettini, C., Wang, X. S. and Jajodia, S., 2005. Protecting privacy against location-based personal identification. In *Workshop on Secure Data Management* (pp. 185–199). Springer, Berlin Heidelberg.

Bettini, C. and Riboni, D., 2015. Privacy protection in pervasive systems: State of the art and technical challenges. *Pervasive and Mobile Computing, 17*, pp. 159–174.

Chow, C. Y. and Mokbel, M. F. 2007. Enabling private continuous queries for revealed user locations. In *International Symposium on Spatial and Temporal Databases* (pp. 258–275). Springer, Berlin Heidelberg.

Duckham, M. and Kulik, L., 2006. Location privacy and location-aware computing. *Dynamic & Mobile GIS: Investigating Change in Space and Time, 3*, pp. 35–51.

Finkel, R. and Bentley J., 1974, Quad trees a data structure for retrieval on composite keys. *Acta Informatica, 4*(1), pp. 1–9.

Gedik, B. and Liu, L., 2005, June. Location privacy in mobile systems: A personalized anonymization model. In *25th IEEE International Conference on Distributed Computing Systems (ICDCS'05)* (pp. 620–629). IEEE.

Gruteser, M. and Grunwald, D., 2003, May. Anonymous usage of location-based services through spatial and temporal cloaking. In *Proceedings of the 1st International Conference on Mobile Systems, Applications and Services* (pp. 31–42). ACM.

Hoh, B., Gruteser, M., Xiong, H. and Alrabady, A., 2007, October. Preserving privacy in gps traces via uncertainty-aware path cloaking. In *Proceedings of the 14th ACM Conference on Computer and Communications Security* (pp. 161–171). ACM.

Iyer, K.P. and Shanthi, V., 2013. Study on privacy aware location based service. *Journal of Scientific & Industrial Research, 72*, pp. 294–299.

Kalnis P., Ghinita, G., Mouratidis, K., and Papadias, D., 2007, February. Preventing location-based identity inference in anonymous spatial queries. *IEEE Transactions on Knowledge and Data Engineering* (pp. 1719–1733).

Kumar, R. and Dawra, S., 2016. Simulation of 3D privacy preservation and location monitoring approach. *International Research Journal of Engineering and Technology*, 3(5), pp. 1099–1103.

Liu, Y. and Wilde, E., 2011, February. Personalized location-based services. In *Proceedings of the 2011 iConference* (pp. 496–502). ACM.

Mokbel, M.F., Chow, C.Y. and Aref, W.G., 2006, September. The new Casper: Query processing for location services without compromising privacy. In *Proceedings of the 32nd International Conference on Very Large Data Bases* (pp. 763–774). VLDB Endowment.

Nergiz, M.E., Atzori, M. and Saygin, Y., 2008, November. Towards trajectory anonymization: A generalization-based approach. In *Proceedings of the SIGSPATIAL ACM GIS 2008 International Workshop on Security and Privacy in GIS and LBS* (pp. 52–61). ACM.

Sagan, H., 1994. Hilbert's space-filling curve. In *Space-Filling Curves* (pp. 9–30). Springer, New York.

Shin, H., Vaidya, J. and Atluri, V., 2010. Anonymization models for directional location based service environments. *Computers & Security, 29*(1), pp. 59–73.

Shin, H., Vaidya, J. and Atluri, V., 2011. A profile anonymization model for location-based services. *Journal of Computer Security, 19*(5), pp. 795–833.

Sweeney, L., 2000. Simple demographics often identify people uniquely. *Health (San Francisco), 671*, pp. 1–34.

Tóth, G., Hornák, Z. and Vajda, F., 2004, November. Measuring anonymity revisited. In *Proceedings of the Ninth Nordic Workshop on Secure IT Systems* (pp. 85–90).

Wang, C., Liu, H., Wright, K.L., Krishnamachari, B. and Annavaram, M., 2015. A privacy mechanism for mobile-based urban traffic monitoring. *Pervasive and Mobile Computing, 20*, pp. 1–12.

Xu, T. and Cai, Y., 2007, November. Location anonymity in continuous location-based services. In *Proceedings of the 15th annual ACM International Symposium on Advances in Geographic Information Systems* (p. 39). ACM.

# Part V
# Risk in business sectors

# 20

# Accounting information systems

## Opportunity and risk

*Shoshana Altschuller and Shaya (Isaiah) Altschuller*

---

### Introduction

The "information revolution" is upon us and there is no industry or business function that is untouched. In recent years, advances in technology have caused organizations to consider and reconsider the implications that these fast-paced changes have on their business operations and environment. Sometimes it is helpful to pause and take stock of our surroundings as they change. The purpose of this chapter is to introduce some of the risks and opportunities surrounding the use of information systems for the processing of accounting and finance data within today's ever-advancing business organizations. After reading this chapter, the reader is expected to have a better understanding of the purpose of accounting information systems (AIS) within an organization and be able to identify the roles that they play within business operation and management. The chapter will explore the some of the opportunities presented by using technology to enhance business processing as well as the risks that are involved. It will also examine some ways to mitigate the risks associated with AIS.

### Opportunity and risk

The parallel between risk and opportunity has long been noticed. As T. S. Eliot pointed out close to a century ago, "Only those who will risk going too far can possibly find out how far it is possible to go." History has shown us repeatedly that success in business is often borne of risk-taking. However, executives and shareholders, as well as industry regulators, seem wary. After several misfortunes in recent years, both physical and financial, leaders of complex organizations have become increasingly aware of the necessity to understand and mitigate the risks facing their companies. Consequently, enterprise risk management has taken center stage in corporate planning.

While risk management includes the analysis of a wide gamut of sources of risk, this focus comes at a time when accounting information systems (AIS) are revolutionizing business processes with rapid speed. Over the past several decades, information systems have been developed and implemented to process, collect, and distill data and transactions as they flow through the company's operations. Investment in these systems has opened up worlds of opportunity for organizations, benefitting them by facilitating cost savings through implementation of operational efficiencies and adding value through differentiation of offerings and advanced data analysis. Information technology (IT) capabilities have even been credited with the creation of competitive advantage. However, as IT-based solutions continue to evolve, they get ever more sophisticated and integral to the operational processes of a company. With these changes comes exposure to risk. This chapter navigates the realm of accounting information systems during this time of rapid technological development, highlighting some of the opportunities gained and the risks encountered by growing IT capabilities, perhaps serving as a guide for those looking to balance their portfolio of opportunities and risks associated with the use of AIS.

## Information systems

If an organization is compared to a living thing, the information that flows through it is the lifeblood of the organization. Information continuously flows laterally and vertically throughout the organization, bringing with it opportunity to survive and grow. In the early days of business, information flowed manually throughout the organization. Today, firms have varying degrees of technology intervention to speed up and enhance this movement of information. An *information system* (IS) is typically defined as the interrelated set of technology-based components that pumps the information through the organization, collecting, storing, processing, and reporting on data to create usable information for the firm. The field of information systems addresses the application of these information technology-based solutions to create value for a firm (see Figure 20.1).

It is also important to note that the field of IS goes well beyond the study of technology and data analysis. While technological capabilities are at the core of an IS solution, IS addresses the combination of technology, the data resources and information needs of an organization, and people who are developers, stakeholders, and users of the systems. If all of these things don't come together in a productive way, IS solutions will fail, producing no added value to the firm, perhaps even losing value for the firm (see Figure 20.2). For example, an IS-based business solution for cutting back on expenditure on resources could involve a sophisticated set of technologies to track employees' usage of company resources. Implementation of this IS would be technologically advanced and create operational efficiency. However, perhaps it ignores the employees impacted by the system who can become disgruntled at the invasion of their privacy caused by constant monitoring, and their performance suffers in other ways. While the technology and data analysis in this example is sound, the implementation of the solution does not create value for the firm, so the IS solution is not successful.

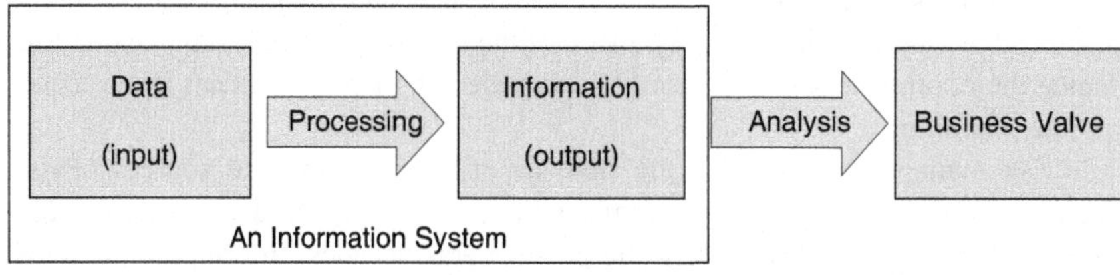


*Figure 20.1* Study of information systems

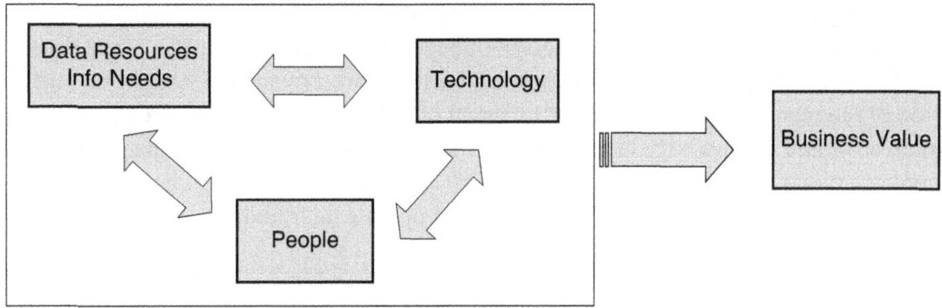


*Figure 20.2* Components of an information system

## Accounting information systems

The term *accounting information system* (AIS) most often refers not to a specific physical information system. Rather, it refers, conceptually, to the interrelated set of systems that are used within an organization to support all of the activities included in running and managing the accounting functions of a business organization. In simple terms, the accounting function can be thought of as responsible for three major activities: transaction processing, financial reporting, and management reporting. Accounting information systems are the subset of systems that automate and support these activities. These functions might be supported by multiple separate physical systems, or they might be supported by one or a few broad-ranging systems.

- *Transactions*: The accounting function of the business is charged with recording and managing the day-to-day operations of a business such as sales and expenditures. *Transaction processing systems* (TPS) are the (conceptual) systems that allow a business to convert economic events into financial transactions that can be recorded in journals and ledgers, and distributed to the personnel who run the daily operations of the business.
- *Financial (non-discretionary) reporting*: Transaction activity and other events also need to be summarized and reported to external stakeholders as financial reports, tax returns, and other reports required by law. *General ledger* and *financial reporting systems* are used to support this aspect of the accounting function.
- *Management (discretionary) reporting*: In order to control, manage, and plan business operations, information must also be shared internally with managers and decision makers. Reports such as budgets, variance reports, and cost-volume-profit analyses help management understand the status of the operations, respond to business challenges, and control the day-to-day and strategic activities of the business. *Management reporting systems* are used to support this area of the accounting function.

Together, these systems make up the AIS that a firm depends on for the accuracy of its financial transactions and reporting. In light of this dependency, AIS are a potential gateway for risk. Thus, they are subject to government regulation and the guidelines put forth by legislation, such as the Sarbanes-Oxley Act of 2002, which mandates such things as internal control of financial reporting and management certification and external audit opinion thereof. In order to accomplish this, management and auditors alike are required to have a full and deep understanding of a company's information systems as they pertain to the accounting function.

Increasingly, the processing of the above accounting functions has become automated by technology. What was once a manual process of data capture, recording, calculation, reporting, and analysis has become an automated activity. Furthermore, beyond the straightforward automation of the reporting processes, chief financial officers are increasingly becoming adopters of innovative and cutting-edge technology to manage the finances of a company. Blockchain technology, cloud computing, and the Internet of Things are just a few of the innovative technologies that are changing the way that companies operate their finances. These changes, too, introduce new potential for risk to the organization.

## Roles of AIS

To further navigate some of the potential impacts of AIS, we organize the applications into four main roles. For each role, we discuss the opportunities afforded, the risks that are encountered, and some solutions to potentially mitigate the risks. We also include some examples to illustrate.

### *To automate processes*

As mentioned, one of the main roles of an AIS is to eliminate the manual activities of gathering data, processing transactions, and producing reports. Information systems, by definition, apply technology to a set of data (*input*), *process* that data, and produce *output* (see Figure 20.1). For example, a large set of employee data can easily be utilized to systematically calculate compensation expense and related payroll taxes to be reported to company management as well as to outside regulatory agencies. In this scenario, great opportunity arises from the substitution of technology for human effort. In particular, the opportunity provided here is the acquired efficiency in time, power, and accuracy. Using computer programs, calculations can easily happen in a fraction of the time, can be much more complex, and are not subject to human error. Further, complex mathematical models and computerized simulations have been applied in many industries to help better understand the implications of various circumstances affecting a business. For example, in the insurance industry, modeling might be used to help determine the appropriate premiums to be charged based on historical data and trends. Without sophisticated computer systems to collect relevant data and simulate all possible scenarios, such analyses would not be possible. Taken even further, large volumes of data (often referred to as "big data") can be mined and analyzed to uncover useful correlations and unique insights that would otherwise have gone undetected. A company can capitalize on this business intelligence to create business opportunities and gain competitive advantage.

However, at each step of the way, risk is also introduced.

- *Input risk*: The value of the information produced by a system is only as good as the data provided to the system. No matter how powerful and fast a system's calculations are, if the data provided to the system is not accurate or appropriate, the value of the output is compromised. The input risk is related to the "people" component of the system (referenced in Figure 20.2), particularly the users of the system. It involves the possibility that the users of the system don't understand exactly how the system works, how they should best use it, or what data to provide as input. Consequently, even if the automation is sophisticated, fast, and efficient, the results produced will not be beneficial.
- *Processing/design risk*: Once the data is input into the system, predefined calculations are programmatically applied. The risk involved here is that the programmer who designed the system did not completely or accurately understand the calculations that needed to

be done in any given condition or, perhaps, an error of logic is included in the program. Because the calculations are hidden from the user, the output that results is assumed to be correct and any calculation or design error is difficult to detect. Furthermore, if a mistake does become embedded in the processing, the impact of that mistake is amplified by the volume, speed, and power of the processing. Additionally, even when processing is initially designed and implemented correctly, continuously changing business environments can be ahead of previously built calculations and might not anticipate changing conditions. Processing methods need to be consistently reviewed and new models and calculations considered to keep the design of the systems up to date and accurate.

- *Output risk*: Once the system has automatically produced output, that output has to be appropriately understood and applied by the user. Output risk includes the possibility that the user doesn't quite understand what information has been produced by the program and misinterprets or misrepresents the information that he/she has received.
- *Control risk*: One of the most important practices in addressing each of these risks is the use of *application controls* within a system and *internal controls* of financial processes. Application controls are tests that can be built into the system to indicate and ensure accuracy and appropriateness of all processing. Internal controls are additional measures that should be taken to check that input, processing, and output are accurate. Systems should also include the production of an *audit trail*. An audit trail is the creation of a record of the intermediate steps within the data processing that would otherwise be hidden. Using an audit trail, errors in processing can be identified. While it is the job of internal accounting managers to set up and use controls to ensure accuracy of data processing, external auditors are tasked with evaluation of those controls to make sure that they are working. One of the things that external auditors will be assessing is *control risk* which involves the possibility that material misstatements will not be prevented or detected by the firm's internal controls.

User education is also an extremely important step in mitigating these risks. The better that the users of the system understand the role of the system, the more likely they will be to enter the correct data and understand the output of the system.

### *To integrate data and processes throughout the organization*

In addition to automation, many relatively recent technology innovations in business systems have focused on integrating data and transaction processing throughout the organization, often unifying all processing into one *enterprise system*. With an enterprise system, previously isolated information processing instances are redesigned and integrated with one another, to streamline the processes and integrate data and processing from all parts of the business. Implementation of enterprise systems provides tremendous opportunity in terms of agility and decision making. Integrating all data processing into one system gives decision makers a real-time, bird's-eye view of the operations of the organization. Consolidated information is available without extra overhead allowing for swifter decisions based on more meaningful information. From an accounting perspective, having all data in one place without redundancy simplifies the possibility of monitoring and controlling its accuracy. In fact, *enterprise resource planning* systems (ERPs) have been shown to take advantage of built in controls, reducing reports of internal control weaknesses (Morris, 2011).

However, enterprise systems have been known to involve very complex technology implementations. At both the implementation and operational stages, the complexity of these systems poses several risks to which adopters should be attentive. A few examples of these risks follow.

- *Change management risk*: Implementing a system with an enterprise level scope is no simple task. The process is so complex that companies have even been known to abandon the project despite the large investment. Careful planning and the help of consultant experts can ease the process of implementing new systems of a large scope. Also, change management controls can be implemented to help ensure that changes are made in a structured and testable way.

  Designing the new system involves reviewing every single business process and redesigning many of them to streamline and integrate them and create uniformity. In doing so, businesses run the risk of improperly translating business activities to the new system. During the initial implementation, the act of moving data from legacy systems to the new systems is a complex activity that must be carefully planned to avoid the risk of data errors or loss. Switching over to the new mode of processing also must be done methodically to address the risks of processing errors. Implementation strategies include running both old and new systems in parallel until the new system is solidly up and running, or switching over one module or one department at a time to the new system. In either case, testing is the most crucial activity in ensuring that data and processing are operating correctly in the new environment.

  From the "people" perspective, another risk is that the users of the system will reject or have difficulty with the immense change involved in using the new system. Getting users involved in the design and implementation of the system is one tactic that can be taken to mitigate this risk. When the users are involved and take ownership of some part of the design and implementation, they are more likely to adjust positively to the change.
- *Audit risk*: Anecdotally, the complexity of ERP implementations has been known to result in material misstatements (Clark et al., 2006). Audit risk is the possibility that financial statements are incorrect even though auditors have not expressed concern over material misstatements. In a business that relies heavily on complex technology systems, it is incumbent upon the auditor to be very well-versed in the system and the technology it uses in order to confidently give an audit opinion. Audit teams will often include or hire IT specialists to help them navigate the system to make sure that they are getting a full understanding of the processes and the controls over them.
- *Business interruption risk*: With a consolidated system design such as an enterprise system, there is a risk that if something malfunctions in one part of the system the impact could be much more widespread, even interrupting the operation of the entire system. Likewise for a data error made in one area, the impact of the error is greater as the erroneous data flows through the system to all other business areas.

### To consolidate data from outside sources

In addition to automating and integrating business processing within the boundaries of the firm, business systems have been developed to gather and share information from beyond the firm as well. Additionally, current and developing technologies and platforms are having profound effects on the way that business information systems retrieve and handle data.

### Interfaces

Direct interfaces can be built between companies' internal systems and those of their vendors or clients helping to reduce processing time, reduce travel costs, and ease reporting efforts. These interfaces can utilize specially designed tools to import data and download information, providing flexibility to easily meet various reporting requirements for internal and external stakeholders, as well as opportunities for streamlined reporting. The currently emerging Internet of Things (IoT) has also presented new opportunities by collecting data in unconventional ways from unconventional sources. For example, the auto insurance industry might collect data about a customer's driving habits via a device embedded within a car to report on and inform the management and pricing of a particular driver's policy or the structure of products in general. Inventory could also be potentially controlled and managed by data delivered via sensors and tracking devices.

### Cloud computing

Even when data does not originate at an external source, the extremely common practice of storing proprietary data using third-party resources, or *cloud computing*, extends the reach of companies' internal systems beyond the boundaries of the firm. Cloud computing hosts some or all information processing and data storage to the hardware and software platforms of third-party companies. This practice reduces costs for companies and shifts the load of responsibility over the maintenance of the hardware and software to an outside vendor as well as drastically cutting down the time-to-readiness of the technology platform.

### User-generated content platforms

In a similar vein, the prevalence of internet capabilities and Web 2.0 technology enables systems to incorporate data from outside sources. E-commerce capabilities, social technologies, and user-generated information all contribute to expanding the scope of information processing, thereby broadening the purview and reach of a company's information systems. These cutting-edge platforms provide companies with opportunities to enrich their resources and enhance their offerings and analysis in new and innovative ways.

The inclusion of data and information from all these various sources does not come without risk.

- *Access risk*: When the data being processed by an AIS is not internally stored, there are numerous risks that arise. These risks include the possibility that external parties are able to gain access to the data. This has significant ramifications in terms of accuracy and confidentiality of the data as well as to the security of the systems. Without having direct control over who does and doesn't access the data, we cannot be sure that the data is not being read, copied, or altered (intentionally or accidentally) by unauthorized users who can abuse the data or the system. In cases of the IoT, numerous input points create many potential points of failure or unauthorized access. This risk of potential intentional or unintentional manipulation of data might be difficult to detect and control.

  Furthermore, an additional risk comes into play by virtue of the fact that the company and its auditors don't necessarily have access to data or systems that are in the domain of a host company. They therefore are forced to rely upon the security measures and policies of those companies. When the host companies' policies do not adequately satisfy the company's standards, that fact could potentially be overlooked. If multiple entities are involved, information and system management and audits become even more complicated.

- *Control risk:* Risk also arises when neither a company's management nor its auditors can control the data that is produced or the controls of the processes that manipulate it. Incoming data that is generated by users or originated from another company can lack integrity and are not subject to the company's internal controls. Similarly, the internal controls that keep a company's systems in line cannot apply to externally hosted systems. Therefore, managers and auditors can come to overrely on the controls of the third party.
- *Reliability risk*: In scenarios where business functions are being outsourced to outside vendors, we worry that lapses in availability of those systems will impact the success of the business.
- *Legal risk*: Finally, in interorganizational systems collaborations such as cloud computing, systems will also span national borders. Risks related to varying security and privacy laws among the various countries can become activated and complicate compliance. Accountability for any privacy breaches or inappropriate content or activities carried out on a cloud platform will also be confusing to resolve.

In response to some of these risks, it is recommended for companies to develop strict standards and guidelines regarding the security and control practices of the companies that they choose to share data with and the platforms that they choose to integrate with their own. Carefully crafted and reviewed service level agreements with the vendors can help ensure that system failures will be restored within an acceptable time frame. Clear and explicit contracts about the responsibility of each of the parties going into an agreement can help clear up any accountability ambiguities.

### To bring technology to the user

In prior eras, interfacing with data and systems was reserved for data specialists and programmers. One of the features of the new technology platforms that run today's accounting information systems is that data is readily available to a multitude of different types of users, even those with little to no special training and often with no special tools other than a browser. Business systems are increasingly internet ready and accessible directly to decision makers and managers on an interactive basis at both the operational and management levels of the organization. This allows for ad hoc requests for data and reports, eliminating the middleman and the wait time. Increasingly accessible and sophisticated tools for data analysis bring better analytics to the daily realm of managers and decision makers. Ultimately, these availabilities result in the ability to make more sophisticated, informed, and timely decisions, which help to successfully capitalize on opportunities, make strategic and operational decisions, and allocate resources efficiently.

However, bringing the data directly into the hands of the users has some significant risks. Most prominent among these is the concern for security.

- *Cybersecurity risk*: As non-technical users interface with technology-based tools, they open the company to the risk that their lack of knowledge will cause damage to its technology infrastructure. Hackers have become increasingly adept at targeting such users to cause damage to networks, steal passwords and information, and even identities. Some examples of common tactics that have cropped up are:

- *Phishing*. Phishing occurs when cyber criminals send e-mails or other messages that appear to have come from a legitimate source to entice recipients to click on a fraudulent link through which they might enter sensitive personal data such as account numbers and passwords. Users at any level of the organization are susceptible to this hoax, including senior management. The higher the level of the victim, the greater the potential is for damage.
- *Stolen identities*. Business users are often targets for stolen identities. Using information, even from generic corporate websites that include title and location, cyber criminals gather enough identifying information to impersonate transaction approvals or other damaging deceptions.
- *Network break-ins*. Sometimes non-technical business users are the cause of hackers gaining unauthorized access to corporate networks. This can happen if individuals have liberties to plug physical drives into corporate networks, allowance to install applications freely, or download unknown or untested applications. Unauthorized access to the network could potentially be very damaging to a company if critical financial, customer, or other proprietary business data is accessed.
- *Ransomware*. Recently, unauthorized access to a network or devices connected to a network has resulted in malware called ransomware being installed on the system or device. Ransomware encrypts the owner's data using a very strong encryption protocol such that it cannot be decrypted without paying large sums of money to the perpetrator of the hack. This relatively new and growing form of blackmail is a very dangerous attack as it could impact an entire company's collection of data leaving no choice but to pay the ransom. This encourages further attacks.

In order to prevent these and other such attacks, companies need to have aggressive education programs for their employees so that they have the basic knowledge of safe information system practices at all levels of the organization. They might also think about implementing strong and effective security measures and practices, such as:

- Not sharing login information among users
- Enforcing challenging password requirements, biometric and/or multifactor authentication
- General awareness and training through live sessions, webinars, corporate required sessions
- "Tone at the top": if senior management displays appreciation of the risks, better practices will filter down
- Testing and monitoring of compliance with security best practices
- Implementation of outside vendor protections
- Continuous communication with employees of the latest threats and examples of risks
- Update applications and apply software patches; automate or take control of software updates
- Internal stress testing.

## Conclusion

No matter the industry or company size, technology developments have been and will continue to create significant shifts in the way business data is collected, managed, and analyzed. As illustrated by daily business reports and some of the examples above, these shifts have resulted in powerful advances and opportunities for businesses to accomplish new and unprecedented things. With continued momentum in the application of technology, the future holds untold developments for the business environment. The opportunities are exciting. However, with change must come a thorough investigation of the potential risks associated with new implementations and changing business practices. Only with careful consideration of all the implications can new developments possibly succeed. This chapter serves to introduce a foundational understanding in this area and perhaps inspire continuous analysis by business managers of opportunity versus risk using accounting information systems.

## Bibliography

Alali, F.A., & Yeh, C.-L. (2012). Cloud computing: Overview and risk analysis. *Journal of Information Systems*, 26(2), 13–33.

Axson, David A. J. 2017. *CFOs Are the New Digital Apostles*. Accenture.

Burge, Dan. (2009, July). Cloud Computing – The Legal Risks. *Computer Weekly*. www.computerweekly.com/opinion/Cloud-computing-the-legal-risks, accessed: June 23, 2017.

Clark, T.D., Jones, M.C., & Zmud, R.W. (2006). Post adoptive ERP use behaviors: A dynamic conceptualization. Paper presented at the Proceedings of the 27th International Conference of the System Dynamics Society. Albuquerque, New Mexico, USA.

Curtis, M.B., Jenkins, G.J., Bedard, J.C., & Deis, D.R. (2009). Auditors' training and proficiency in information systems: A research synthesis. *Journal of Information Systems*, 23(1), 79–96.

Davenport, T.H. (1998). Putting the enterprise into the enterprise system. *Harvard Business Review*, 76(4).

Grabski, S.V., Leech, S.A., & Schmidt, P.J. (2011). A review of ERP research: A future agenda for accounting information systems. *Journal of Information Systems*, 25(1), 37–78.

Hall, James A. 2016. *Accounting Information Systems*, 9th edition. Cengage Learning.

Hunton, J.E., Wright, A.M., & Wright, S. (2004). Are financial auditors overconfident in their ability to assess risks associated with enterprise resource planning systems? *Journal of Information Systems*, 18(2), 7–28.

Morris, J.J. (2011). The impact of enterprise resource planning (ERP) systems on the effectiveness of internal controls over financial reporting. *Journal of Information Systems*, 25(1), 129–157.

Saharia, A., Koch, B., & Tucker, R. (2008). ERP systems and internal audit. *Issues in Information Systems*, 9(2), 578–89.

# 21

# Transcending beyond finance for managing foreign exchange risk

*George A. Zsidisin and Barbara Gaudenzi*

## Introduction

Almost every business organization is affected, either directly or indirectly, by global supply chains. Organizations have experienced the benefits and risks of global supply chains for decades. Besides the opportunities related to global markets and cheaper production costs in emerging countries, there are several risks that global organizations need to manage. For example, during the summer of 1997, Indonesia, South Korea and then a larger part of Asia experienced a strong, unexpected devaluation of their currencies (Pesenti and Tille, 2000). In another example concerning the toy industry, some producers discovered that their supply chain partners were not able to pay debts for supply due to the currency appreciation (Johnson, 2001). As alluded in these examples, financial market dynamics may impact the cost structure of products and logistics services in global supply chains. For these reasons, companies need to improve the capability to analyze, forecast and manage the operational and financial effects foreign exchange (FX) risk may have on performance.

FX risk and its management should transcend beyond the accounting and financing functions. Beside the traditional accounting and financial approaches for managing currency risk, organizations should consider adopting operating and contracting strategies extending beyond the firm to the customer and supply base. Purchasing and marketing serves a critical function in bridging firms with their global operations, both upstream and downstream in their supply chains respectively, while legal often serves a critical role in protecting firms contractually both domestically and internationally. Currency rate volatility poses a risk – and opportunity – for firms managing their global supply chains.

Currency (FX) risk is defined as the risk of an investment's value fluctuation due to the changes in currency exchange rate, and can significantly affect profitability, organizational cash flow and the ability to competitively price products (Burnside, 2012). Buyer-supplier negotiations and relationships are also influenced by issues related to currency dynamics and should be considered as structural determinants of a currency risk mitigation strategy – hence the importance of including purchasing and marketing in creating approaches for managing FX.

The purpose of this chapter is to investigate the role of the boundary spanning functions of purchasing and marketing, as well as legal, in developing and implementing strategies firms pursue in managing currency/foreign exchange risk. Our overall goal is to provide an initial framework for examining strategies to adopt for managing the effects of currency rate volatility, transcending beyond the traditional instruments developed by the finance function of organizations. As shown in our framework, financing strategies are a key set of tools and approaches for managing FX risk. However, with the complexity of global supply chains today, we believe organizations and businesses should take a more holistic approach in developing an array of approaches for managing FX risk exposure.

## Background

There are various perspectives of risk in business. These perspectives are summarized into strategic, corporate governance, financial and supply chains (Borghesi and Gaudenzi, 2013). The strategic perspective allows observing if and how the risk linked to the adoption of long-term strategies, new product development and internal processes may hinder the pursuit of strategic objectives, such as revenues and profitability. The corporate governance perspective concerns if and how risk management procedures are able to guarantee stakeholders corporate risk exposure falls within a certain risk tolerance and conforms to the organization's risk appetite. The financial perspective aims at observing the implications the risk system may have on business liquidity, both in the short and long term (Horcher, 2005). Finally, from a supply chain perspective, we observe if and how the management of all the processes related to purchasing, production, storage and distribution may hinder the pursuit of effectiveness and efficiency in managing the entire supply network.

Risk should be simultaneously observed and managed from different perspectives due to the interrelationships existing from a multitude of perspectives. For example, new product development, considered from a strategic perspective, also has financial implications associated with cash flows, corporate governance elements such as ownership of propriety knowledge and processes (Zsidisin and Smith, 2005), and the supply chain with regard to supplier capabilities and distribution capacities, to name a few. Therefore, risk management tools need to address the cross-functional influences among strategic, financial and supply chain risks. However, while there is a robust knowledge about 'ad hoc' risk management tools for different risks – from the strategic, financial, governance and supply chain perspectives – there is a lack of awareness of the potential cross-relationships.

Currency/FX risk is one form of risk where organizations may garner leverage in managing this risk from a multitude of perspectives, particularly those operating within emerging countries, where these currency fluctuations could disrupt supply and change cost structures. Firms may suffer an increase in operating costs due to changes in exchange rates, with the consequence of selling their products at an uncompetitive price, or purchasing components or materials at uncompetitive prices. In specific sectors, such as the transport and shipping industry, FX risk is particularly exacerbated by the quotations of freight rates that are fixed in US dollars, and then exchanged in other currencies (Leggate, 1999). FX risk is also well known in energy markets, where there is a prevalence of commodity exposures denominated in foreign currencies.

Although the finance literature is rich in developing approaches for hedging FX risk, few studies are available in the supply chain management literature on operational and financial approaches to manage this risk (Bandaly et al., 2014). We do strongly support the notion that firms exposed to FX risk should still use financial derivatives to manage the short-term impact of transaction risk, but these tools may be limited with regard to the long-term effects of competitive risk. Therefore, from this long-term perspective, we believe there are other tools and approaches in managing supply chains where companies should be able to manage currency fluctuations more holistically by creating flexible systems to quickly adapt to currency volatility. For these reasons, it seem that financial tools and supply chain approaches should be carefully integrated for both short- and long-term FX risk exposure.

The supply chain management literature has recently dedicated significant attention to the topic of supply chain risk management (SCRM), whose full description is beyond the scope of this chapter. However, as summarized by Jüttner et al. (2003), supply chain risk should be properly identified and managed by following some key steps:

- Assessing the risk sources for the supply chain, for example the functions of procurement, production, warehousing, research and development, transport and distribution;
- Defining the potential adverse consequences and risk drivers on the supply chain, which means the risk to be identified and measured at each source;
- Mitigating supply chain risk, on the basis of the global risk exposition, the amount of the budget available and the level of risk tolerance (for single risk sources and for the entire portfolio).

Related to FX risk, which has traditionally been an area of focus with finance, we have recently seen more linkages of supply chain management practices being analyzed from a supply chain finance (SCF) perspective (Gelsomino et al., 2016; Trent, 2016). This can represent a key step for developing future SCRM tools from a financial perspective. For example, the SCF literature identified finance-oriented supply chain decisions in areas such as inventory optimization, financial solutions and a structured focus on payables and receivables (Wuttke et al., 2013). More specifically to risk, Chen and Hu (2011) explicitly refer to the need to managing risk related to supply and demand in the financial flow, creating value for supply chain with capital constraints.

FX risk and its management cross these literature streams of supply chain risk management and finance (and specifically supply chain finance). Currency rate volatility (FX) risk assessment represents the first phase of a risk management process. Managers should then identify the appropriate set of risk mitigation strategies (ISO 31.000, 2009). From this assessment, several measurement techniques have been described in the literature, which mainly refer to financial analyses, currency portfolio maximization, measurement of abnormal returns in foreign exchange markets or currency risk factors explaining excess returns (Burnside, 2012). Although there are well-known financial models and metrics, there are few studies investigating the role of supply chain boundary spanning functions, and specifically purchasing and marketing, in assessing and managing FX risk. The reminder of the chapter will explore various strategies and business functions, including and going beyond finance, in how firms can manage FX risk in their supply chains.

## A supply chain framework for managing FX risk

The purpose of the chapter is to begin examining how organizations manage the effects of FX risk caused by currency exchange volatility, as part of an overall supply chain risk management strategy. We also aim at investigating how organizations integrate financial, operation and contractual strategies to manage foreign exchange risk using a more holistic perspective by understanding the influence of other business functions in this process. A conceptual model

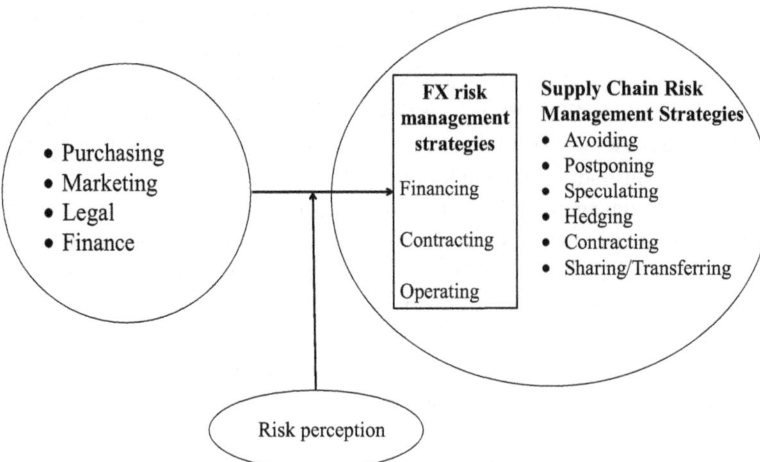


*Figure 21.1* FX risk management model

is shown in Figure 21.1. Each of the functional areas, strategies and the role of perception in the model is discussed below.

## *Functional roles, expertise and involvement*

There are several business functions that can be involved in creating and pursuing FX risk management strategies. Finance is one function traditionally tasked to create financial hedging strategies (Brown, 2001). However, marketing and purchasing serve as boundary spanning functions respectively for integrating with customers and suppliers, especially in developing and managing global supply chains. Due to their boundary spanning coordination with customers and suppliers from other countries, these business functions should serve a critical role incorporating various risk elements in business transactions, including FX. In addition, legal serves a significant role in mitigating this form of risk, particularly regarding the laws and treaties within and among countries in conducting business transactions (Aggarwal and Goodell, 2009).

These business functions should contribute to the discussion of risk related to foreign investing that is broader than the FX risk itself. For example, political risk and local tax implications should be monitored from a country risk perspective (Lievenbrück and Schmid, 2014). The functional roles serving in managing global supply chains, their level of expertise in managing these supply chains (and particularly with FX), and the extent of involvement in these efforts may have a direct effect on the successes or failures in managing currency rate volatility and FX. Although we argue finance, marketing, legal and purchasing serve important roles in creating and executing a FX risk mitigation strategy, each of these business functions must have the requisite expertise and involvement in managing this form of risk in global supply chains. Further, the motivation to manage this form of risk may be severely limited if currency rate volatility and its inherent risk is perceived to be low, and heightened under circumstances when risk is perceived as significant.

## *Risk perceptions*

There have been extensive studies in understanding how individuals perceive risk in general terms (Slovic, 2000), and specifically in the context of supply chain risk (Zsidisin and Wagner,

2010). With specific regard to FX risk, most of the available studies refer to the risk perceptions and risk decisions made by banks and investors, while very few studies focus on industries.

In the maritime sector, for example, Akatsuka and Leggate (2001) analyze risk perceptions in the shipping industry, comparing major shipping companies from Japan and Norway. The different exchange dynamics between the yen and the US dollar, and between the krone and the US dollar, allow for identifying different preferred mitigation strategies, country by country. To the best of our knowledge, there is a lack of studies regarding the level of risk appetite and risk perception towards the FX risk in private companies. Since the risk appetite determines the awareness about risk and hence the management strategies, this investigation seems to be relevant for future investigation. However, we believe that when FX risk is perceived as being significant, such as during times of political turmoil, firms, given the capability and wherewithal to do so, should consider a range of strategies, including and going beyond financing strategies, for managing FX risk.

## *Supply chain risk management strategies*

There are different studies that describe techniques and approaches for preventing and managing supply chain risk, which could be developed and various elements distilled in order to systematically manage FX volatility. For example, changing suppliers or relocating operations in other regions have a direct impact on FX risk exposure. Most of the strategies are often related to each other and, in several cases, the selection of one strategy can determine/influence the use of another one. From an operating perspective, risk sources have been typically categorized into demand and supply (Johnson, 2001). Risk related to product demand includes – for example – seasonality, volatility of fads, new product adoptions, safety and security, and short product life cycles. Risk related to product supply includes purchasing, manufacturing and logistics vulnerabilities. When organizations operate in global supply chains, there may be substantial currency risk, commodity price risk and political risk that can detrimentally affect product cost or disrupt supply.

Manuj and Mentzer (2008) categorized SCRM strategies into avoiding, postponing, speculating, hedging, controlling and sharing/transferring. Avoiding is a strategy adopted when the risk is considered unacceptable. This strategy can be adopted also with regard to FX risk, when for example the organization decides not to operate in emerging countries or where the geopolitical instability may generate unacceptable currency volatility. In these cases, for example, managers will either divest assets or business units, or delay/renounce the entry in a given market or the collaboration with a given actor.

Postponing means delaying the actual commitment of resources to maintain flexibility and delay the incurring of costs. The extent of postponement and decoupling points depends on strategic factors, such as demand customization, product costs and life cycle. The location of buffers and inventories will in part also influence the financial aspects related to the foreign exchange negotiations.

Speculating, from a supply chain perspective, can be also called assumption or selective risk taking, and is the opposite of postponement. In speculating, production and storage decisions are made on the base of a make-to stock strategy. This approach is most prevalent when production is customer driven and the level of customer service is well defined and stable. In these cases, supply chain managers can allocate resources to specific customers and/or projects, depending on their value, profits margin and cost objectives.

Hedging, in a supply-chain context, is a strategy for reducing the entire supply chain risk profile. The scope is to implement specific actions in the portfolio of suppliers, customers and facilities such that a single event (such as currency fluctuations, business interruption or a natural disaster) does not affect all the assets at the same time and/or with the same gravity. For example, multiple sourcing can be used as a "hedge" against risks of quality, delays, disruption or price. Maintaining two interchangeable production sites, in different locations, can be a hedge against risk of production shortages or increased volumes. Multiple contracting represents moreover a hedge to reduce variability in performance and supplier dependency.

With respect to controlling, considering the multiple actors operating in the supply chain, there are evident risks related to the loss of transparency and visibility of information related to key aspects of the supply chain such as products, demand and forecasts. Vertical integration may represent a controlling strategy by reducing the risk of supply or demand failures in the supply chain. This strategy changes variable costs into fixed costs. For this reason, organizations should selectively integrate those activities, which can create high value, transferring less strategic activities to other firms. This strategy is called partial or tapered integration. Similarly, in the relationships with suppliers, organizations should try to obtain the full utilization of their equipment, designing flexible contracts, which consider possible changes in products/service standards, and control mechanism, which might allow for some risk to be absorbed by the supplier.

The transferring and/or sharing of risks in a supply chain can be achieved through outsourcing, offshoring and contracting to other third parties. The term "off-shoring" is typically related to global supply chains, where sourcing operates across borders. The location of third-party actors in different countries and regions influence the currency risk exposure. In outsourcing and offshoring strategies there is a transfer of risk to (or sharing with) suppliers, but the collective risk of offshoring should be evaluated for the potential effect on the final customer, in terms of a product's quality, service levels and the organization's image and reputation. Moreover, a portfolio of contracts can be used in supply chains to induce, for example, retailers with different levels of risk aversion to select unique contracts. This portfolio approach may induce the retailers in the supply chain to order quantities that maximize the expected value for the organization. From these overall supply chain risk management strategies, we can further hone our analysis and strategies for managing one specific form of risk: FX risk.

## FX risk mitigation strategies

There are various strategies and approaches firms can further distill for purposes of managing one specific form of risk – FX risk – in their global supply chains. From the overall list of strategies addressing supply chain risk management in general, we propose firms consider financing, operating, and contracting strategies specifically when managing FX risk. *Financing strategies* are typically considered as a prevalent currency risk mitigation approach. There is a large use of foreign currency purchased option contracts and forward contracts, particularly with the scope to reduce the exposure to currency volatility, involving probable anticipated transactions and transactions with firm foreign currency commitments (Brown, 2001). Organizations typically invest in financial hedging strategies for increasing the certainty of operating margins, reducing negative impacts from currency movements on competitiveness, and facilitating internal contracting. In these cases, a robust FX risk management policy is essential for mitigating unexpected losses in foreign currency derivatives transactions. Examples of financial approaches include currency futures or swaps, foreign exchange binary options, foreign exchange options or swaps and forward exchange rates. Besides these financing tools, cross-hedging approaches may be used in circumstances where there are no hedging instruments between the home and foreign currencies are available. In these circumstances, a third country with a well-developed currency can serve to financially hedge FX risk. Hedging with futures or options and cross-hedging are complex processes, which usually requires working with finance for designing and implementing hedging strategies. However, other organizational functions, including purchasing, marketing and legal, may also have an influence in implementing this strategy.

There are *operating strategies* for managing FX risk. These strategies primarily involve decisions related to production flexibility, sourcing flexibility and natural hedging. Production flexibility allows the firm to alter their mix of supply sources by switching production between plants per observed changes in the currency exchange rate. Sourcing flexibility allows the firm to choose and diversify the firm's currency mix. Prior studies have examined the role of production flexibility for hedging foreign currency cash flows (Chowdhry and Howe 1999), while Hommel (2003) identified both the strategies of diversification and flexibility in response to currency rate volatility. Organizations can also adopt a natural hedge, which is a method of reducing financial risk by investing in two different financial instruments whose performance tends to cancel each other out (Hagelin and Pramborg, 2004). One advantage of natural hedges is that it does not require the use of sophisticated financial products such as forwards or derivatives, although close coordination among marketing, supply chain and finance may be necessary. For this reason it can be categorized as an operational strategy.

Financial and operational hedging strategies cannot eliminate risk (Hagelin and Pramborg, 2004; Makar et al., 1999). For this reason, contracting strategies may also be needed for further protecting organizations from volatile currency rate fluctuations.

*Contracting strategies* managing FX risk include escalation/de-escalation clauses, shorting an overvalued currency and building in financial slack. Escalation clauses in contractual agreements with suppliers and customers represent an effective approach for sharing the effects of currency price volatility. Managers should define how often the prices are reviewed and changed, the base cost/price, if past or future prices will be changed, and if there are upper and lower limits in which no price adjustments will be used. For organizations with a large base of customers or suppliers, these contracting strategies can become very complex if different customers and/or suppliers have different contractual clauses in various countries. The experience and know-how of purchasing, marketing and legal professionals is therefore crucial to perform an effective risk management strategy. Organizations can also short the currencies susceptible to FX risk. Two examples include requiring payments in a currency going to appreciate, and requiring prompt payments. Buying in a currency for a predetermined price on a specific date in the future represents a sophisticated contractual strategy that may cover against a currency risk. In addition, firms may simply build in contingencies in the sales prices of their products to account for currency volatility. However, this may be a difficult approach to execute when pursuing a cost leadership strategy.

## *Not a one-size-fits-all approach*

There may be additional factors influencing the ability of firms to use a more holistic array of approaches for managing FX risk. These influencing factors include industry, the form of currency and firm size. With regard to *industry*, there are sectors particularly exposed to FX risk. The aforementioned case of the transport and shipping industry and the energy market are examples. More in general, in industries where there is a prevalence of commodity exposures denominated in foreign currencies, organizations need to be more aware and proactive in managing this risk with ad hoc tools. In addition, the international logistics industry can manage FX risks and interest rate risks when operating in mature and emerging nations with different currencies (Gerald, 2014).

In conjunction with industry, we also recognize *currency* may influence FX risk mitigation approaches. Companies are typically exposed to FX risk when they buy materials often purchased in U.S. dollars, and then sell product in local currency. This is particularly true for energy markets and commodities (Lievenbrück and Schmid, 2014). These authors also noted that utilities, for example, have a risk exposure to commodity prices on both supply and demand sides because they buy primary energy sources such as oil or gas and sell power. The currency can also influence the opportunity to adopt cross-currency swaps (Chang and Wong, 2003). In these cases the organization could swap a loan denominated in U.S. dollars, for example, for a loan denominated in other currency to reduce interest rates and foreign exchange risk, typically in short-term time frame contractual agreements. In general, the depreciating (appreciating) of a currency against foreign currencies may have a net negative (positive) impact on organizations' returns. Risk exposure may be also influenced by the time frame of the currency fluctuation. For all the currencies, it seems that in a short-term time frame, the FX risk can be better hedged (Pantzalis et al., 2001).

Examining the influence of *firm size*, Vaaland and Heide (2007) stated that the size is positively correlated with the use of risk management approaches, and SMEs pay less attention to risk-reducing and control methods than large firms. Studies (Lievenbrück and Schmid, 2014) have noted the larger the size of a firm the more likely it is to use derivative instruments in hedging its exchange rate risk exposure. Allen (2012) also highlights these risks could damage profitability and market value of all the firms, the use of various risk mitigation approaches depends, all else being equal, on the size of the firm, but further clarifies smaller-size organizations have become increasingly proactive in managing these risks.

## Concluding thoughts

This chapter highlights currency rate volatility and its resulting FX risk exposure is truly a supply chain challenge – and opportunity – for today's organizations and businesses. We believe FX risk should be managed beyond the financing function of firms, and instead be addressed in a more holistic manner by including the boundardy-spanning functions of purchasing and marketing, as well as the risk management expertise of legal. Going beyond utilizing financing strategies, firms should likewise consider various operating and contracting strategies for managing this truly global supply chain problem of FX risk. It is by implementing more holistic approaches that firms may be able to truly leverage their supply chain expertise in creating greater predictability of outcomes, and overall improving firm financial performance, by better managing FX risk.

## References

Aggarwal, R. and Goodell, J.W., 2009. Markets and institutions in financial intermediation: National characteristics as determinants. *Journal of Banking & Finance*, *33*(10), pp. 1770–1780.

Akatsuka, K. and Leggate, K., 2001. Perceptions of foreign exchange rate risk in the shipping industry. *Maritime Policy & Management*, *28*(3), pp. 235–249.

Allen, S.L., 2012. *Financial risk management: A practitioner's guide to managing market and credit risk* (Vol. 721). John Wiley & Sons, Hoboken, NJ.

Bandaly, D., Satir, A. and Shanker, L., 2014. Integrated supply chain risk management via operational methods and financial instruments. *International Journal of Production Research*, *52*(7), pp. 2007–2025.

Borghesi, A. and Gaudenzi, B., 2013. *Risk management, how to assess, transfer and communicate critical risks*, Springer, Berlin Heidelberg.

Brown, G.W., 2001. Managing foreign exchange risk with derivatives. *Journal of Financial Economics, 60*(2), pp. 401–448.

Burnside, C., 2012. Carry trades and risk, in *Handbook of exchange rates* (eds. J.James, I. Marsh, and L. Sarno), Vol. 2. John Wiley & Sons, Inc. Hoboken, NJ.

Chang, E.C. and Wong, K.P., 2003. Cross-hedging with currency options and futures. *Journal of Financial and Quantitative Analysis, 38*(03), pp. 555–574.

Chen, X. and Hu, C., 2011. The value of supply chain finance, in Habib, M. (Ed.), *Supply chain management – applications and simulations*, InTech, Rijeka, pp. 111–132.

Chowdhry, B. and Howe, J.T., 1999. Corporate risk management for multinational corporations: Financial and operational hedging policies. *European Finance Review, 2*(2), pp. 229–246.

Gelsomino, L.M., Mangiaracina, R., Perego, A. and Tumino, A., 2016. Supply chain finance: A literature review. *International Journal of Physical Distribution & Logistics Management, 46*(4), pp. 348–366.

Gerald, R.V., 2014. United Parcel Service Financial Challenges in a Developed or Developing Nations. *Strategic Management Quarterly*, 2(1), pp. 1–10.

Hagelin, N. and Pramborg, B., 2004. Hedging foreign exchange exposure: Risk reduction from transaction and translation hedging. *Journal of International Financial Management & Accounting, 15*(1), pp. 1–20.

Horcher, K.A., 2005. *Essentials of financial risk management*. Wiley, New York.

Hommel, U., 2003. Financial versus operative hedging of currency risk. *Global Finance Journal, 14*(1), pp. 1–18.

ISO 31.000, 2009. *Risk management standard*, available at: www.iso.org/iso/home/standards/iso31000.htm.

Johnson, M.E., 2001. Learning from toys: Lessons in managing supply chain risk from the toy industry. *California Management Review, 43*(3), pp. 106–124.

Jüttner, U., Peck, H. and Christopher, M., 2003. Supply chain risk management: outlining an agenda for future research. *International Journal of Logistics: Research and Applications*, 6(4), pp. 197–210.

Leggate, H.K., 1999. Norwegian shipping: Measuring foreign exchange risk. *Maritime Policy & Management, 26*(1), pp. 81–91.

Lievenbrück, M. and Schmid, T., 2014. Why do firms (not) hedge? – Novel evidence on cultural influence. *Journal of Corporate Finance, 25*, pp. 92–106.

Makar, S.D., DeBruin, J. and Huffman, S.P., 1999. The management of foreign currency risk: Derivatives use and the natural hedge of geographic diversification. *Accounting and Business Research, 29*(3), pp. 229–237.

Manuj, I. and Mentzer, J. T., 2008. Global supply chain risk management strategies. *International Journal of Physical Distribution & Logistics Management*, 38(3), pp. 192–223.

Pantzalis, C., Simkins, B.J. and Laux, P.A., 2001. Operational hedges and the foreign exchange exposure of US multinational corporations. *Journal of International Business Studies, 32*(4), pp. 793–812.

Pesenti, P. and Tille, C., 2000. *The economics of currency crises and contagion: An Introduction Economic Policy Review*, September, available at: www.jamus.name/teaching/460or6a.pdf.

Slovic, P.E., 2000. *The perception of risk*. Earthscan Publications, London.

Trent, R.J., 2016. *Supply chain financial management: Best practices, tools and applications for improved performance*, J. Ross Publishing, Plantation, FL.

Vaaland, T.I. and Heide, M., 2007. Can the SME survive the supply chain challenges?. *Supply chain management: An International Journal, 12*(1), pp. 20–31.

Wuttke, D.A., Blome, C., Foerstl, K. and Henke, M., 2013. Managing the innovation adoption of supply chain finance – empirical evidence from six European case studies. *Journal of Business Logistics, 34*(2), pp. 148–166.

Zsidisin, G.A. and Smith, M.E., 2005. Managing supply risk with early supplier involvement: A case study and research propositions. *Journal of Supply Chain Management, 41*(4), pp. 44–57.

Zsidisin, G.A. and Wagner, S.M., 2010. Do perceptions become reality? The moderating role of supply chain resiliency on disruption occurrence. *Journal of Business Logistics, 31*(2), pp. 1–20.

# 22

# Financial risk inherent in oil fracking

*Roy Nersesian*

## Adam Smith and Karl Marx

The central economic problem associated with Marxism is that production is based on quotas. In the Soviet Union, quotas were determined by Gosplan, where prices were arbitrary with little or no association with costs. Gosplan-administered prices allowed a Soviet company to have a checking account to pay for supplies and wages and deposit receipts. If prices generated a negative cash flow, the company received an injection of cash to keep it solvent (100% subsidized). If by chance funds were accumulating in the checking account, the excess was removed (100% taxed). Obviously there was no incentive to be efficient. Moreover, without prices related to costs, Marxist society was robbed of a vital signal of when and where to invest in new capacity. A capitalist society operates on profits which do provide an incentive to be efficient. And if price is primarily set by supply and demand, then it becomes a vital signal of when and where capital should be employed to expand productive capacity.

## In the world of Adam Smith

My first exposure to the free market was probably in the freest market of them all: shipping. Tanker rates are extremely sensitive to the relationship between supply and demand both globally and locally. In a global setting where supply exceeds demand and rates are low, a shortage of capacity at a particular load area would cause a spike in local rates. This then becomes a signal for tanker owners to divert their vessels to earn a higher return, which they do. Rates remain high until enough tankers show up for supply to again exceed demand, suppressing rates. While higher rates indicate that ships are in short supply, they do not let owners know the degree of the shortage. Owners have no idea how many ships are needed. They learn "how many" when too many show up at the load area. Even if owners knew how many ships were needed, which they don't, too many owners would deploy their vessels to fill that need in a race to be first. Despite this weakness, the "invisible hand" of price assures that the distribution of tankers is responsive to fluctuations in global oil movements with no external assistance whatsoever.

After graduating with a MBA in 1971, my first civilian job was in the planning division of a shipping company. The planning division was composed of three individuals, two recently hired graduates as analysts with no previous experience in shipping, and our supervisor. Our first assignment was to answer the question whether the shipping company, active in both dry bulk carriers (iron ore, coal, grain) and tankers, should order a very large crude carrier (VLCC). Typical VLCCs were about 250,000 deadweight tons (dwt), meaning they could carry crude oil cargoes of about 240,000 tons. The two of us took different tacks to address this issue.

The late 1960s and early 1970s was a time of rapidly expanding demand for VLCCs because of growing oil demand in Europe and Japan, and most importantly, the transition of the US from self-sufficiency to import dependency. Having rapidly exhausted available supplies from nearby sources in South America and west Africa, most of the incremental demand for crude oil was from the far-off Middle East. This gave an enormous impetus to VLCC demand. Rates rose as demand absorbed supply, igniting an ordering spree for new vessels when rates cleared that necessary to financially support building a new vessel.

There were two chief constraints on how many vessels can be ordered. One is available financing. If banks are acting conservatively, they would require a multi-year charter (preferably 5 years) from a creditworthy charterer such as a major oil company. Then the constraint, under these circumstances, would be the availability of suitable charters. The second constraint is the capacity of the world's shipyards to build VLCCs. This constraint becomes controlling when shipyards accept orders with nothing more than a down payment, which they are tempted to do when rates are high. With high rates, shipyards perceive that there will be little difficulty for owners to attract permanent financing to fund the sequence of payments while the vessel is under construction. Shipyards are hesitant to start construction of a vessel without an owner lining up permanent financing such as a commercial bank loan or government supported shipyard credit.

There were two VLCC (business) cycles in the years prior to our being hired. In both cases, when rates rose, owners collectively ordered too many VLCCs. There is a saying in shipping that if there is a need for one new vessel, 10 owners will order it. When the VLCCs were delivered after a lapse of 1–2 years after placing their orders, the market was flooded with excess capacity causing a rate collapse, cessation of further orders, and financial distress for those who were too aggressive in ordering new capacity. But bad times did not last long because the underlying demand for VLCCs was rapidly expanding absorbing excess capacity. We were then in the third VLCC cycle. Rates were very high and rising higher. My co-worker, an economist working towards his doctorate, looked at the previous VLCC cycles and noted that the number of VLCCs already on order far, far exceeded the total of the previous two cycles. Shipyard capacity in the interim had been vastly expanded as part of the economic development of Japan (and other nations) to foster employment and exports. Now the fondest dreams of owners to increase the size of their fleets could be accommodated. Based on his analysis of the size of the existing order book compared to past levels, he concluded that the company should not order any tankers.

My approach was different. I calculated the crude oil growth rates necessary in key consuming areas to absorb VLCCs already on order. Even allowing for further growth in oil consumption, which was already at historically high levels, and taking into account the exponential effect oil growth had on tanker demand emanating from the Middle East, more than enough tankers were on order to fulfill record oil growth for years to come. My conclusion was not to order any tankers.

So what happened when the president of the shipping company got off the plane in Japan after reading our two reports? He immediately made a down payment for three ULCCs – ultra large crude carriers of 350,000 dwt – the largest at that time – which represented a mammoth expansion of the company's tanker fleet. Why? He was mesmerized by VLCC rates being so high that an investment in a new vessel with a 20-year life could be recouped during its first year of operation. The problem was that the president did not have these three vessels immediately available to be employed in a peak market. He would have to wait 3 years before the shipyard, already stuffed with orders, could get around to building his vessels. By that time the peak market, by historical standards, would have been long gone.

It turned out that his orders were among the last to be placed. Shortly after his return to the US, the 1973 oil crisis struck and cheap oil was gone forever. Oil consumption collapsed along with demand for existing vessels. Not only did this mean that tankers operating without oil company charters were left bereft of revenue sufficient to sustain operations, but it also meant that all those VLCCs on order were no longer needed. With no subsequent recovery in oil demand, the VLCC market went into a prolonged two-decade-long depression. VLCCs delivered after the crisis without underlying charters were not to see a single day's profitable operation before they were scrapped. For some, scrapping occurred immediately upon delivery. The shipping company the two of us worked for was eventually liquidated even with the modification of the ULCC orders to smaller-sized tankers, which also were not needed. Luckily for us we found other jobs.

What did I learn? Price is a reliable signal of when to add capacity, but price does not tell you how much capacity to add. We invariably add too much capacity because those responsible for making investment decisions believe that high prices will last forever: there is no end to the good times. Unfortunately their fondest dreams can be realized by the eagerness of banks to finance capacity expansions when profits bloom. Forecasts aid and abet this behavior by supporting the contention that high prices will invariably last long enough to economically justify further capacity expansions. I've seen this story repeated over and over for industry after industry. While Marxism doesn't work – that has been clearly demonstrated – the free market is flawed because there are no controls over capacity expansion condemning industries to the ups and downs, the booms and busts, of the business cycle.

There seems to be no exceptions that I can think of other than monopolistic control over the market. In the world of oil, this was accomplished by Rockefeller's control over the refining industry. After Rockefeller, the mantle of controlling oil prices passed to a cartel of major oil companies headed by Shell Oil that parceled out geographic spheres of influence among major oil companies limiting competition. When that failed, control of oil prices passed to the Texas Railroad Commission that authorized the output for all oil wells in Texas and Oklahoma. The Texas Railroad Commission lost control of price via production quotas in the early 1970s when it was forced to authorize full production of all wells under its jurisdiction to meet demand. Shortly after, the 1973 oil crisis struck and OPEC gained the upper hand. OPEC mimicked the Texas Railroad Commission of influencing price by controlling volume. Rockefeller, Shell, and the Texas Railroad Commission succeeded in keeping stable (and low) oil prices, but OPEC was not interested in low prices. Rockefeller failed when he could no longer control global refining capacity; Shell Oil cartel and Texas Railroad Commission failed because they could not control non-cartel oil production.

For OPEC or any cartel to work, its members must be willing to cut production when price weakens. Under OPEC, the only major swing producer was Saudi Arabia. In 2015 Saudi Arabia gave up its role to cut production for the benefit of others and increased production to regain its historical market share. This should not be looked at as a monument of permanence. There may come a day when Saudi Arabia becomes more concerned over price than market share.

## Is there such a thing as stable oil prices?

A simulation was created to analyze the challenges faced by an oil cartel managing volume to control price.[1] The simulation involved an oil cartel whose output is large enough to affect global prices. The cartel desires to maximize its revenue over the long haul. Maximizing price does maximize revenue in the short haul, but not for the long haul. Maintaining high prices has long term consequences on cartel volume, which ultimately affects revenue. A high oil price:

- Puts a drag on economic activity reducing energy consumption;
- Induces energy users to switch from oil to natural gas or coal or alternative energy sources reducing oil demand;
- Incentivizes motor vehicle owners to consider alternative fuels or hybrid models or smaller-sized vehicles with improved mileage and to drive fewer miles, reducing gasoline demand;
- Creates an incentive for non-cartel owners to upgrade existing oil production facilities and invest in new capital projects increasing oil output.

The combination of lower crude oil growth, better maintenance of existing production capacity, and most importantly, investments in new incremental sources of oil by non-cartel producers reduces the market for the oil cartel. Eventually supply exceeds demand and prices fall. A low oil price:

- Diverts money away from buying oil to buying goods and services that enhance economic activity, which encourages energy consumption;
- Acts as an incentive to buy larger-sized motor vehicles that get lower gasoline mileage and encourage people to drive greater distances, increasing gasoline consumption;
- Discourages other forms of conservation and encourages more wasteful or excessive levels of energy consumption (e.g. flying cargoes of flowers from New Zealand to Europe and the US);
- Provides little incentive to maintain oil flow in existing wells and to drill new wells.

These are the classic economic conditions for creating cyclicality in a free market – high prices increase supply and suppress demand, and low prices increase demand and suppress supply. Similar to prices for other businesses and industries operating in a competitive environment, oil prices cycle between extremes depending how supply lines up with demand plus the perception by buyers and sellers to a possible change to that relationship.

## The simulation model

### *Oil cartel controlling price*

In the simulation, the oil cartel does not issue an edict to control price. The control mechanism is indirect through production volume as it influences inventory. If production volume is too high in relation to demand, inventory begins to climb. Oil consumers in a world of plentiful inventory play one competing producer off another to obtain their supplies for the lowest possible price. The oil market reacts to excess inventory by price discounting. At some point, the cartel is forced to cut prices to remain competitive.

Falling prices tend to increase demand, but low prices also cut back on maintenance of wells and drilling for new oil, both of which adversely affect future oil production. Rising demand coupled with declining supply causes demand to exceed supply, leading to inventory drawdowns. As inventories fall, oil consumers lose their negotiating strength. Now it is the turn of the oil producers to play one competing consumer off another to obtain the highest possible price for what has become a scarce resource. As the cartel reacts to falling inventories by increasing prices, a corrective reaction sets in. Higher oil prices adversely affect economic activity depressing energy consumption. Oil consumers reduce wasteful consumption and tend to buy fuel-efficient smaller-sized motor vehicles and drive less. Non-cartel oil producers spend money to increase production from their existing wells and make investments to bring on new production. What happens to oil prices with all the yin and yang, thesis and antithesis, up and down of a classic business cycle? Can the oil cartel adjust production to guide prices that would maximize their long-term revenue? Figure 22.1 is a large segment of the simulation spreadsheet.

Oil prices per barrel in column C are determined by the percent change in column D, which is a function of the level of inventory in column N. Global demand starts out at 85,000 barrels (bbls) per day and climbs or shrinks by the percentage change entries in column F, which is a function of price in column C with a lag of 1 year. As price climbs from $100 to $150 per barrel, the highest permissible level, annual demand growth shrinks from 1% to −1.5%. Non-cartel production starts at 60,000 bbls per day and is a function of price in column C. As price increases, percent growth for non-cartel oil production maxes out at 2% for oil at $150 per barrel with a 2-year delay between investing in new wells and their coming on stream. Cartel production in column I, which is determined by Evolver, maximizes aggregate revenue in column O. Column J totals cartel and non-cartel production and column K is the amount of production over demand, which is reflected in inventory in column L. Column M expresses inventory as a percentage of annual demand and column N in terms of months of inventory on hand. Cartel revenue is in column O.

## Caveats

It is not that the model is difficult to build; the challenge is in assessing relationships. The relationship between inventory and price changes can be constructed using historical data as a guide, but historical data does not provide complete coverage over the entire spectrum of possibilities. More distressing, historical data do not reflect the current or future relationship between inventory and price changes. Expert opinions may have to be sought. Thus there is a significant degree of uncertainty as to the exact relationship between price changes and inventory levels as well as other relationships assumed in the model.

Investments have to be continually made in existing oil production facilities to maintain oil flow. Without these investments, oil production declines as oil fields are depleted. These investments are made during times of high oil prices and may not be economically justified at low oil prices. Moreover the higher the oil price, the greater is the incentive to explore and develop new oil fields. Several issues complicate the relationship between oil prices and new production. One is that there is a 2-year hiatus between the decision to invest in developing a new oil field and its coming on stream (for deep water offshore fields, the hiatus may be over 10 years). Thus high oil prices do not immediately result in new oil field production. Revenues

| | B | C | D | E | F | G | H | I | J | K | L | M | N | O |
|---|---|---|---|---|---|---|---|---|---|---|---|---|---|---|
| 2 | | | | | | | | | | Production | | Inventory | Months | |
| 3 | | | | Global | Demand | Non-Cartel | % | Cartel | Total | less | Inventory | as % of | of | Cartel |
| 4 | Year | Price | % Change | Demand | Growth | Production | Growth | Production | Production | Demand | 10000 | Demand | Inventory | Revenue |
| 5 | 0 | $ 100.00 | | 85,000 | | 60,000 | 0.0% | 25,000 | 85,000 | - | 10,000 | 11.8% | 1.4 | $2,500,000 |
| 6 | 1 | $ 100.00 | 29% | 85,850 | 1.0% | 60,000 | 0.0% | 30,000 | 90,000 | 4,150 | 14,150 | 16.5% | 2.0 | $2,585,000 |
| 7 | 2 | $ 128.80 | 25% | 86,709 | 1.0% | 60,000 | 0.0% | 40,000 | 100,000 | 13,292 | 27,442 | 31.6% | 3.8 | $3,440,003 |
| 8 | 3 | $ 150.00 | 12% | 86,489 | -0.3% | 60,000 | 0.0% | 30,000 | 90,000 | 3,511 | 30,953 | 35.8% | 4.3 | $3,973,309 |
| 9 | 4 | $ 150.00 | 9% | 85,194 | -1.5% | 60,000 | 1.1% | 17,000 | 77,000 | (8,194) | 22,759 | 26.7% | 3.2 | $3,779,034 |
| 10 | 5 | $ 150.00 | 16% | 83,918 | -1.5% | 60,640 | 2.0% | 33,000 | 93,640 | 9,722 | 32,481 | 38.7% | 4.6 | $3,491,728 |

*Figure 22.1* Simulation spreadsheet

can be maximized in the short term by restricting cartel output since the repercussions of a shrinking oil market and expanding production are not immediately felt.

Another element of uncertainty is the difficulty to project the future output of an oil field under development. Sometimes production from a new field disappoints its investors. Other times it proves to be a bonanza, perhaps leading to other major discoveries. New oil fields, once developed, don't disappear. The "mistake" of having too high of an oil price for too long a period of time spurs development of new oil fields, which may be in excess of future demand. This cannot be undone during times of low oil prices. Oil fields developed in northern Alaska (North Slope) and in North Sea were started when oil prices were high in the late 1970s and early 1980s. Oil prices collapsing in the mid-1980s did not stem production: once in production, always in production. Unlike conventional wells, fracked oil wells have a short life of about 3–4 years. Cessation of new fracked wells means a fairly rapid depletion in fracked oil production, which is sure to impact oil prices within a shorter time frame. It also makes investments in fracked wells more risky than conventional wells in that the probability of a strong market reoccurring after it has weakened is much reduced for an asset with a productive life of not more than 4 years compared to one that has a productive life of 20–30 years.

Improved technology affects the relationship between present oil prices and future addition to oil production. For instance, developing oil fields in the North Sea during the late 1970s and early 1980s presented a challenge of drilling production wells in 1,000-foot water with 100-foot waves and 100-knot gales. This was accomplished by building gigantic "ocean scrapers" on shore that were towed, tipped, and lowered into place. These 1,000-foot plus ocean scrapers resting on the ocean bottom and extending above the ocean surface numbered among the world's tallest and costliest structures. Today technological advances in three-dimensional seismology have significantly cut the cost of developing new fields by reducing the chance of drilling a dry hole. Far less costly floating production platforms drilling wells from the ocean surface eliminate the need for ocean scrapers and have been successfully employed in waters 10 times deeper. Horizontal drilling significantly extends the area (reach) that can be served by a floating oil production platform along with productivity gains in drilling speed and well depth. Floating production platforms remain on station until the oil field is depleted. They are reusable and can be moved to another oil field, whereas ocean scrapers are fixed and must be abandoned or, worse yet, dismantled when an oil field is depleted.

In oil fracking, there are no exploration costs and no dry holes because wells are drilled in specific geological formations that cover wide areas of entire states. But knowing where to drill is still vital information, as there are sub-areas within these formations where fracked oil well productivity is higher. The breakeven price for oil fracking is falling from lower capital costs, shorter completion times, higher output volume, and longer productive life. This reduces the inherent risk in oil fracking projects and enhances their prospects.

### *Final steps in formulating the simulation*

The completed cash flow model needs a few more steps to get ready for Evolver to determine the optimal production for the cartel oil. Negative and excess inventory is to be avoided by incorporating punitive charges in the objective cell. The objective cell maximizes aggregate cartel revenue in column O less two punitive charges: 1,000 times the total of column Q that already has a punitive charge of 100 times negative inventory and 100 times the sum of excess inventory in column R. The would be achieved by by varying the adjustable cells in column P between integer values of 10 and 40, which represent cartel production between 10,000 and 40,000 barrels per day in column I. Actual cartel production starts out at 60,000 barrels per day and after that fills the gap between total oil demand and non-cartel production net of the indicated cycling. The simulation covers 85 years, and the solution was interesting to watch as Evolver worked with 85 variables where each could take on 30 distinct values.

### *Results of the Evolver optimization run*

In this mythical world, oil prices cycled between the lowest and highest price permitted with short periods of stability during price reversals seen in Figure 22.2.

We can now answer the question whether oil prices can be stabilized under a cartel that controls volume to influence price: the short answer is "No!" Even to keep prices within the extreme bounds in Figure 22.2, the variable portion of cartel oil production cycles between the permissible limits of 10,000 and 40,000 barrels per day (bpd) in Figure 22.3.

This is entirely unrealistic – OPEC production does not cycle between such extremes. Thus the cartel has its work cut out to "manage" price with volume with an eye on maximizing

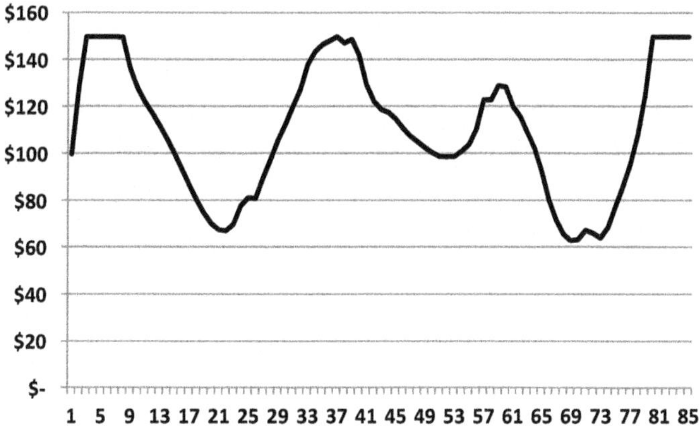


*Figure 22.2* Fluctuations in oil prices

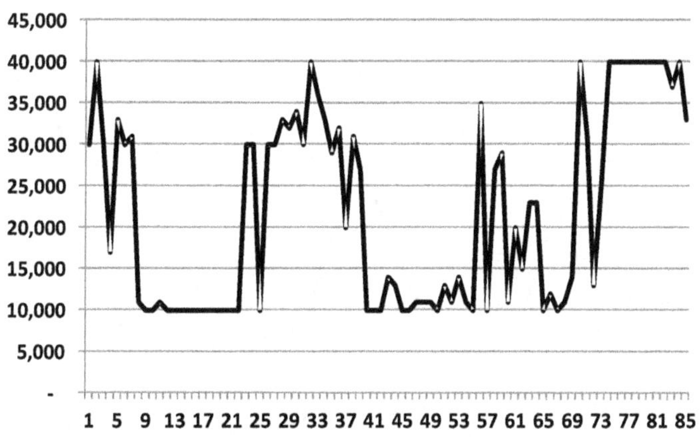


*Figure 22.3* Fluctuations in cartel oil output

aggregate revenue. Inventory in terms of months of annual demand remained within 4–7 months for the most part seen in Figure 22.4. The dive to zero at the end of the period is Evolver maximizing revenue – the period of analysis probably should not extend beyond 70 years to avoid this end play.

Cartel revenue in Figure 22.5 also oscillates considerably between high and low priced crude accompanied with large swings in production.

Again, the revenue spike at the end is Evolver attempting to maximize aggregate revenue by liquidating inventory. This attempt by Evolver to maximize revenues with a high price of oil near the end of the time horizon should be ignored. Thus in setting up a spreadsheet, extra years should be added beyond the desired time horizon to eliminate endgame moves by an optimization program.

While this model cannot be used to model reality as relationships were arbitrarily assumed, the conclusion of the model is still pertinent. The oil cartel has its hands full in attempting to maximize revenues by controlling market price via production quotas. Expanding or cutting

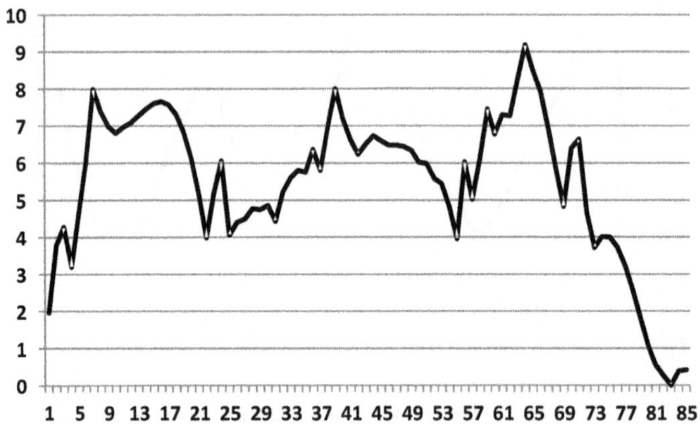


*Figure 22.4* Fluctuation in oil inventory

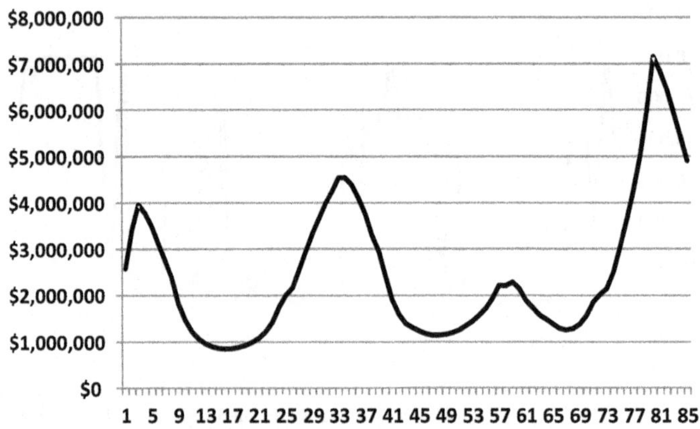


*Figure 22.5* Cartel revenue oscillations

back on production affects supply and consequently inventories, which in turn affects price. It takes a major shift in cartel volume to affect a price change sufficient in magnitude to influence supply and demand because the immediate impact is relatively small. But once a trend is set in motion, it is difficult to change its direction by steering the ship of oil with a rudder tied to production that indirectly influences price.

## History of oil prices

Other than the very beginning of the oil industry, prices were low in today's dollars up to 1973. Figure 22.6 is the history of oil prices since 1973 in constant 2015 dollars.[2]

Table 22.1 shows the periods of high, intermediate, and low prices. High prices are greater than $80 per barrel, low prices are less than $40 per barrel, and intermediate prices are between the two. One can argue about these demarcations. They were chosen because oil fracking costs have been reduced and productivity of fracked wells have been improved to the point where it is felt that sustained prices above $80 per barrel can turn the industry on – that is, begin fracking new wells in earnest. A price of $80–$100 encourages expansion of Canadian oil sand production and development of deep oil fields. A price of $100 per barrel or more is necessary to keep OPEC nations financially solvent to cover the cost of government-assumed societal responsibilities. Prices falling below $80 per barrel stops drilling of new fracked oil wells along with developing new deep oil fields and Canadian oil sand projects and puts OPEC nations in a financial bind. Table 22.1 also includes the inputs for triangle probability distributions for price and years duration for each market environment.

We can use Table 22.1 to judge the ability of OPEC to maintain high oil prices. With the exception of one year (1990), there was a 17-year slump in oil prices where OPEC was seemingly unable to cut production enough to sustain higher prices.

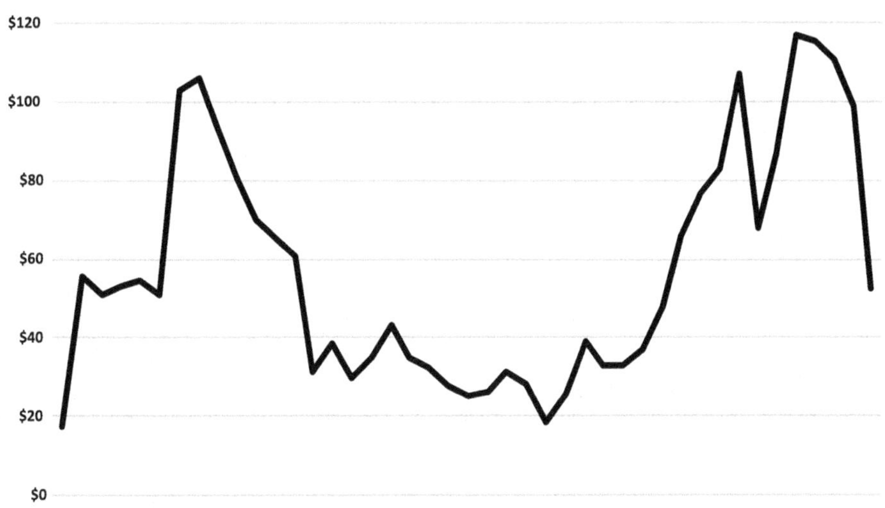


*Figure 22.6* Annual average oil prices in $ per barrel

*Table 22.1* Demarcation of market environments

| *Market Environment* | *Years* | *Duration (# Years)* | *Triangle Distribution Parameters for Oil Prices Low, Most Likely, High* | *Triangle Distribution Parameters for Duration Low, Most Likely, High* |
|---|---|---|---|---|
| High >$80/bbl | | | $80, $100, $120 | 3, 5, 7 |
| | 1979–1982 | 4 | | |
| | 2007–2008 | 2 | | |
| | 2010–2014 | 5 | | |
| Medium $40–$80/bbl | | | $40, $60, $80 | 1, 3, 6 |
| | 1974–1978 | 5 | | |
| | 1983–1985 | 3 | | |
| | 1990 | 1 | | |
| | 2004–2006 | 3 | | |
| | 2009 | 1 | | |
| | 2015–2016 | 2 | | |
| Low <$40/bbl | | | $25, $35, $40 | 3, 7, 12 |
| | 1973 | 1 | | |
| | 1986–1989 | 4 | | |
| | 1991–2003 | 12 | | |

## Establishing an $80 per barrel breakeven price

A spreadsheet set up a simulation to model oil fracking wells with the objective of maximizing revenue by varying the percentage of debt to support financing. But before that can be done, it is necessary to design the parameters of a "standard" fracked well to have an $80 per barrel breakeven price, which is derived in Figure 22.7.

The well is assumed to have a 4-year life with the percent of annual output given in column B along with the aggregate lifetime output of 200,000 barrels. While the breakeven price per barrel of oil is about $80 per barrel, an owner of a fracked well does not see this price. Transportation of fracked oil is very expensive as there are generally no major crude pipelines passing close to oil fracking areas and building permanent pipelines to wells with a short life time of 4 years or less would be quite expensive. Oil from fracked wells are gathered by local pipelines and shipped by truck to existing crude oil pipelines or to rail heads for transport by railroad tank cars to the nation's refineries. It is estimated that transportation along with the variable cost of operating a well plus some contribution to fixed costs consumes $20/bbl, over half being logistical costs. Thus an owner of a fracked well actually sees $60/bbl when the market price is $80/bbl at major refining centers. Figure 22.7 is the solution of a what-if analysis. The parameters are a fracked well costing $10 million producing a total of 200,000 barrels over its 4-year lifetime with 40% of its total production the first year, 30% the second, 20%

| | A | B | C | D |
|---|---|---|---|---|
| 32 | | Output | Price $/bbl | Cash flow |
| 33 | Years | 200,000 | $60 | -$9,961,615 |
| 34 | 1 | 40% | $4,800,000 | $4,800,000 |
| 35 | 2 | 30% | $3,600,000 | $3,600,000 |
| 36 | 3 | 20% | $2,400,000 | $2,400,000 |
| 37 | 4 | 10% | $1,200,000 | $1,200,000 |

*Figure 22.7* Economic analysis of $80/bbl breakeven price

| | A | B | C |
|---|---|---|---|
| 2 | Market | | |
| 3 | 1-Low | | |
| 4 | 2-Medium | Duration | Cumulative |
| 5 | 3-High | in Years | Years |
| 6 | 3 | 6 | 6 |
| 7 | 2 | 6 | 12 |
| 8 | 1 | 9 | 21 |
| 9 | 2 | 4 | 25 |
| 10 | 3 | 5 | 30 |
| 11 | 2 | 4 | 34 |
| 12 | 1 | 10 | 44 |

*Figure 22.8* Spreadsheet showing market condition and duration

the third, and 10% the fourth, will breakeven with a net price of $60/bbl, which corresponds to a market price of $80/bbl. The breakeven price includes a 10% discount factor. One could argue that perhaps the breakeven price should have a discount rate of 0%, but most wells have associated debt and thus there has to be some return built into the breakeven rate in order to pay interest on the debt. While the breakeven price can vary considerably for each well, verification that $80/bbl or more as the industry breakeven price was the cessation of drilling new fracked wells when crude prices fell below $80/bbl.

Figure 22.8 shows that the simulation starts out with a strong market with the subsequent market being intermediate, then low, then intermediate, then high again. Duration in column B is determined by triangle distributions whose parameters are listed in Table 22.1. Column C cumulates these durations, which are incorporated in the simulation to determine market conditions for each year of an iteration.

Since each iteration starts with a strong market, this creates a period of zero cash flows in the simulation from the end of the first period of high oil prices and the subsequent intermediate-weak-intermediate market environments before a strong market emerges again. This interim exceeds the 4-year life for the last wells drilled. This "dead" period occurs in about the same time frame for all iterations. While this could be "fixed" by having the first market condition randomly determined, it would not affect the conclusions of a simulation. The benefit of setting the spreadsheet up this way clearly demonstrates the risk of fracked wells over conventional wells. A concern whose only assets are fracked wells may well experience extensive periods of no activity and no revenue. This is hardly a mark of an ongoing concern. Figure 22.9 shows the spreadsheet for the first 5 years.

| | E | F | G | H | I | J | K | L |
|---|---|---|---|---|---|---|---|---|
| 1 | | | Equity | 25.0% | | Debt Repayment | | 0.29523 |
| 2 | | | | | | | | |
| 3 | | | Total Cash Flow | $ (25,000) | $ 30,458 | $ 52,416 | $ 40,045 | $ 42,003 |
| 4 | | | Cum Cash | $ (25,000) | $ 5,458 | $ 57,874 | $ 97,918 | $ 139,921 |
| 5 | | | | | | | | |
| 6 | Ending Cum Cash Position | | Year | 1 | 2 | 3 | 4 | 5 |
| 7 | $106,668 | | | 3 | 3 | 3 | 3 | 3 |
| 8 | | | | | | | | |
| 9 | Min Cash Flow | | Oil Price | $ 113 | $ 117 | $ 98 | $ 106 | $ 105 |
| 10 | ($34,684) | | | | | | | |
| 11 | | | Expansion | | | | | |
| 12 | Min Cum Cash Position | | of Wells | 10 | 10 | 5 | 10 | 10 |
| 13 | ($25,000) | | | | | | | |
| 14 | | | Year 1 | | 10 | 10 | 10 | 10 |
| 15 | Years Neg Cum Cash | | Investment | $ 100,000 | | | | |
| 16 | 1 | | Equity | $ 25,000 | | | | |
| 17 | | | Debt | $ 75,000 | $ 75,000 | $ 75,000 | $ 75,000 | $ 75,000 |
| 18 | Total Wells | | Debt Payments | | $ 22,142 | $ 22,142 | $ 22,142 | $ 22,142 |
| 19 | 85 | | | | | | | |
| 20 | | | Revenue | | $ 77,600 | $ 46,800 | $ 34,400 | $ 17,000 |
| 21 | Objective Cell | | | | | | | |
| 22 | $106,668 | | Cash Flow | $ (25,000) | $ 55,458 | $ 24,658 | $ 12,258 | $ (5,142) |

*Figure 22.9* Spreadsheet showing simulation for the first 5 years

Cell H1 contains the equity investment for all fracked wells. Cell L1 is the capital charge to be placed on the debt portion of the financing for a 4-year loan at 7% interest. This capital charge, derived by the PMT function, is applied against the loan amount and is sufficient to both pay off the loan in 4 years and provide 7% interest on the amount outstanding. Row 3 is the cash flow over 35 years and row 4 accumulates annual cash flows. Row 7 starting at column H is the market condition reflected in column C. Oil price in row 9 is determined by triangle probability distributions whose parameters for the applicable market condition are contained in Table 22.1.

Expansion of capital capacity in any year follows the rule that 10 wells will be authorized to be built if oil prices are above $100 per barrel and 5 wells if oil prices are between $80 and $100 per barrel and none if oil prices are below $80 per barrel. Ten wells are the presumed maximum capacity of the owner to increase capacity. Five wells reflect reluctance of financial institutions to support new wells when oil prices approach breakeven. Since $80 per barrel is the minimum oil price in a strong market, either 5 or 10 wells will be authorized to be built in the first year and for each of the subsequent years of a strong market. Wells are completed 1 year after authorization and have a production life of 4 years.

The financial analysis starts in row 14. The number of wells authorized for construction in year 1 in cell H12 is repeated in cells I14:L14 in order that the year 1 financial results are "replicable" for the remaining 34 years. The investment in cell H15 is the number of wells multiplied by $10 million expressed as thousands of dollars. Equity is assumed to be 25% of the investment. Debt is investment less equity and is repeated in cells I17:K17, again for ease of replication. Debt payments is the capital charge applied against the amount of debt. Revenue in row 20 is the price of oil less $20 per barrel for logistic and variable costs plus a contribution to overhead expenses multiplied by the step-downs in production volume. Cash flow in row 22 is revenue less equity and operating costs. The financial analysis of year 1 is replicated for year 2 and so forth for 35 years of financial results. The ending cumulative cash position after 35 years is in cell E7, the minimum cash flow over the 35-year span of the simulation is in cell E10, the minimum cumulative cash position over the 35-year span is in cell E13, the number of years when the cumulative cash position is negative is in cell E16. The minimum number is 1 since the first year starts with a negative value for the cumulative cash position from the initial equity investment. The total number of wells drilled is in cell E19 and the objective function is in cell E22.

The objective function contained a punitive charge of $10,000 times the number of negative cumulative cash positions exceeding. RISKOptimizer result was an optimal value for equity of 20.7% and the probability of occurrences of negative cash positions above 1 shown in Figure 22.10.

This is the cumulative ascending probability distribution. The chance of the number of years of negative cumulative cash positions being over 1 year from 80% to 60% (40.6% for 1 or less), 11.5% for greater than 2 occurrences, and therefore 47.9% chance for 2 occurrences (remember that a value of 1 is acceptable as it represents the initial equity investment). Cash flows over 35 years in Figure 22.11 reveal the consequences of always starting an iteration with a strong market. The starting cash position is either $10 or $20 million reflecting the first year investment of 20% × $10 million × 5 or 10 wells.

The cash flow is initially positive, but turns negative when oil prices fall below $80 with the start of the intermediate market. Prices falling below breakeven generates negative cash flows for 4 years after completion of the last set of 5 or 10 wells. After that there is no revenue. A period of zero revenue occurred mostly twice. Once after the completion of the first strong market and then again near the end of the simulation. The timing of the start of the second strong market had enough variation built into its starting year to mask the intensity of periods

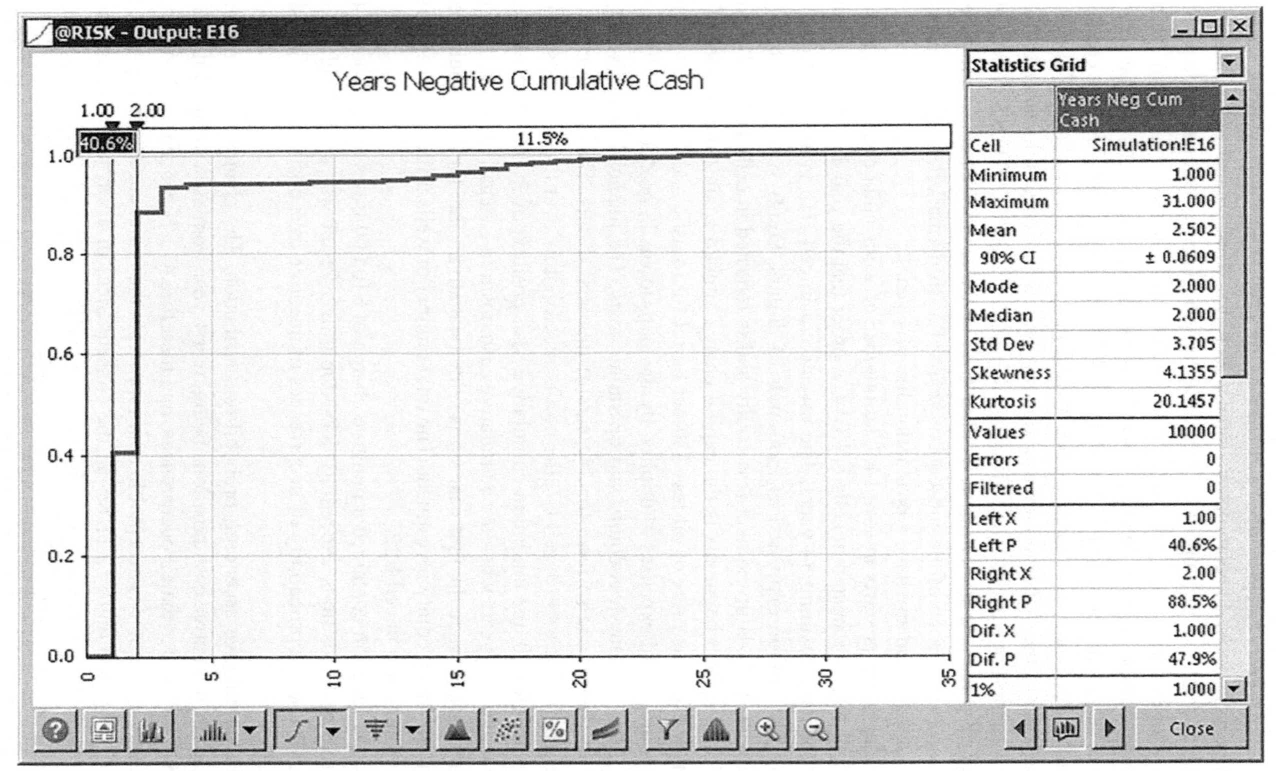


*Figure 22.10* Revised years of negative cumulative cash

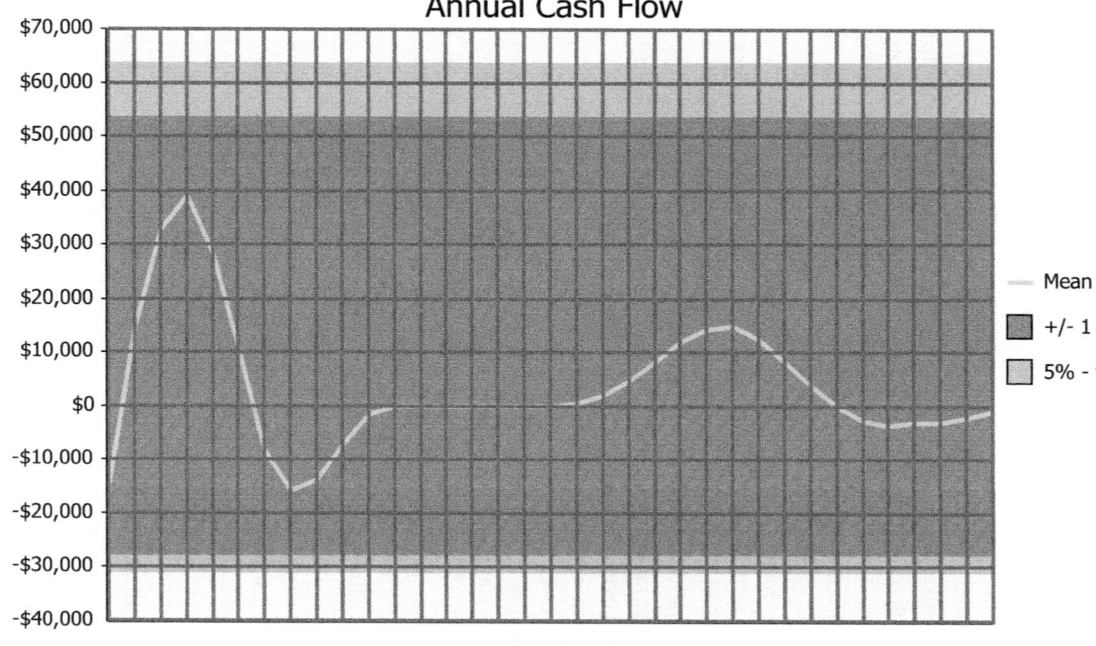


*Figure 22.11* Cash flow over 35 years

of zero cash flows; but on individual iterations, they still occur as seen by striking the F9 key in random mode.

Maximum negative cash flows can be as large as $30 million per year. Generally speaking this is not fatal if the cumulative cash position is large enough to fund the deficits, which it is most of the time as seen in Figure 22.10. Figure 22.12 reinforces this point that cumulative cash positions are sufficient to fund a cash outflow most of the time.

It appears that other than year 1 where the initial negative cash flow is either $10 or $20 million, the cumulative cash position is positive growing during the initial strong market. It levels off during the subsequent intermediate-weak-intermediate markets when cash flow is zero and then subsequently resumes growing with the start of the next strong market. The cumulative cash position levels off again during the end period of the simulation when cash flow is again zero.

Although it appears that the cumulative cash position is always positive, this is not quite true as the entire band represents 95% of all values. Thus there is a small chance that there may be negative cumulative cash position illustrated in Figure 22.10. The low probability stretches of negative cumulative cash extending over a number of years are those periods of no revenue that happen to start out with a negative cash position. Figure 22.13 is the ending cumulative cash position after 35 years of fracking activity.

The initial investment is either 5 or 10 wells costing $50 or $100 million ($50,000 or $100,000). The chance of the ending cumulative cash position being less than $100,000 is 33.9% including a 0.9% chance of being less than zero. The mean is $130 million. The maximum ending cumulative cash position of $433 million reflects a string of short duration weak and intermediate markets coupled with long duration strong markets. Figure 22.14 is the number of wells drilled over 35 years.

The total number varies between 40 and 125 wells with an average of 81 wells. There is a 1.9% chance that fewer than 60 wells would be drilled over the 35-year span and 4.7% that they will number over 100. Thus there is a 93.4% chance that the number of wells drilled will be between 60 and 100 wells. As a point of reference, drilling the maximum of 10 wells per year would result in 350 wells, but oil prices prohibit this from happening. The 81 wells represent a total investment of $810 million. The ending cumulative cash position is money free and clear as normal operations amortized the investment in the wells.

Table 22.2 shows the respective long-term returns. If the initial investment is limited to the cash required to drill the wells ($10 or $20 million), then the return on the ending cumulative cash position looks attractive. If the total investment in the initial wells are used for evaluating returns, then the investment is not attractive. Business people often prefer to evaluate investments in terms of a leveraged basis of cash outlay, but financial analysts prefer to evaluate projects on a non-leveraged basis. The choice is an important one in evaluating competing projects.

The probability of achieving the maximum cumulative cash position is very low. If the average cumulative cash position is used for evaluation purposes, then the return is relatively modest if the project is evaluated on a cash investment basis (leveraged). On a non-leveraged basis, the return is quite low.

## Managing risk for an oil fracker

This simulation models reality in that owners of fracked wells drill as many wells as possible as long as oil prices are high enough for them to attract necessary capital. Where are the sources of this capital? Financial managers of pension and insurance companies have huge

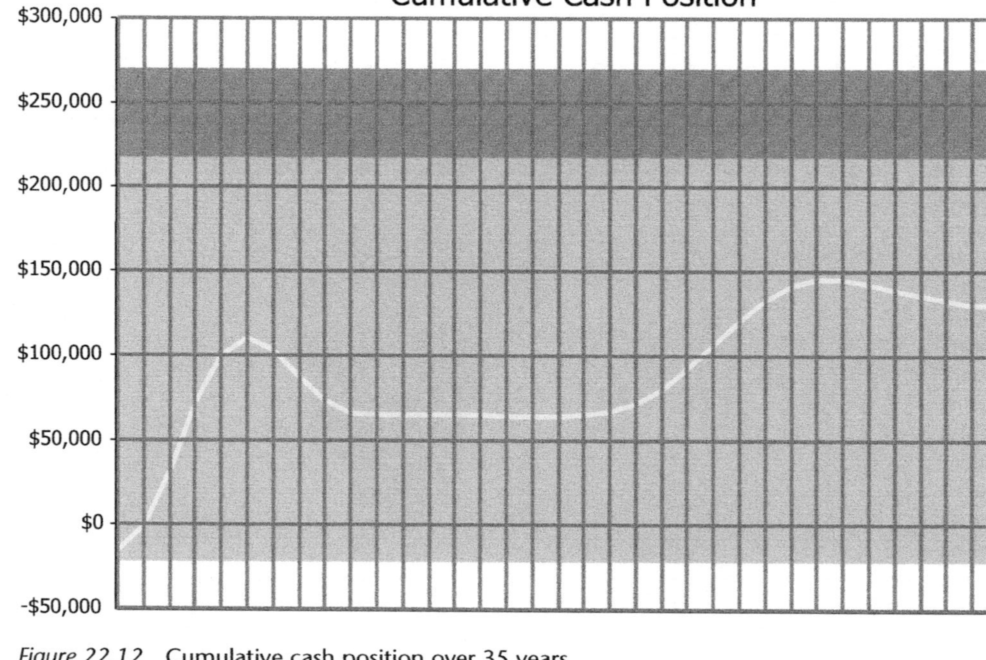


*Figure 22.12* Cumulative cash position over 35 years

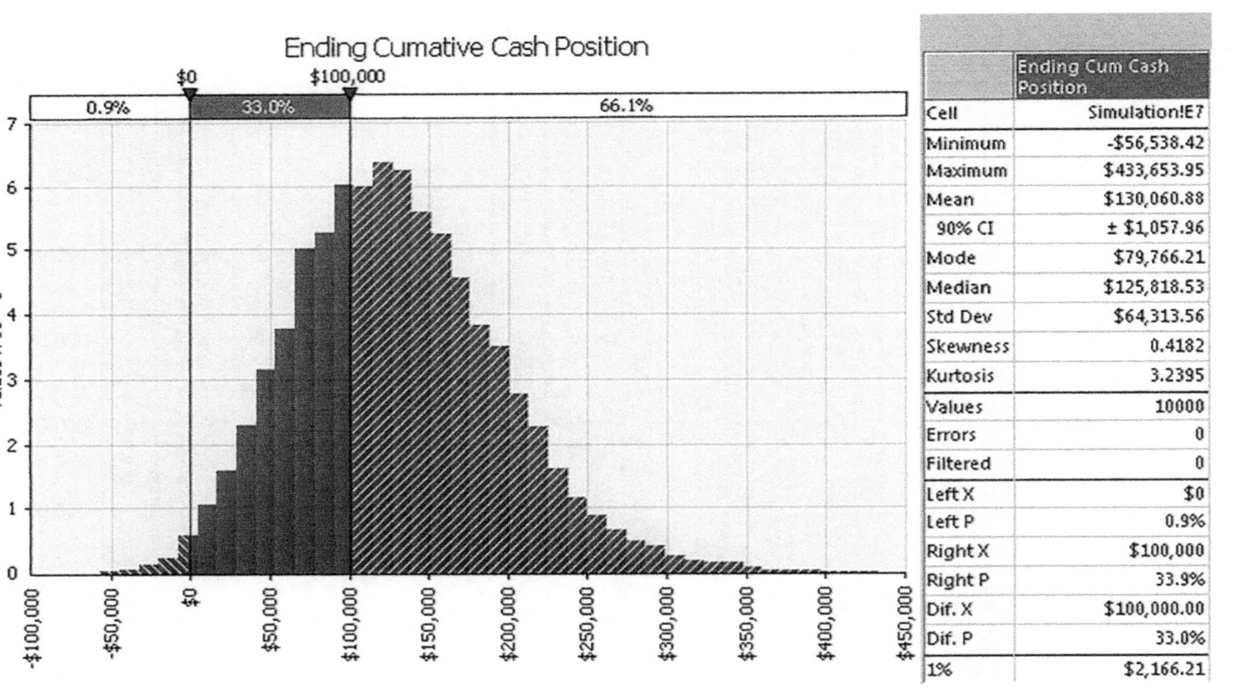


| | Ending Cum Cash Position |
|---|---|
| Cell | Simulation!E7 |
| Minimum | -$56,538.42 |
| Maximum | $433,653.95 |
| Mean | $130,060.88 |
| 90% CI | ± $1,057.96 |
| Mode | $79,766.21 |
| Median | $125,818.53 |
| Std Dev | $64,313.56 |
| Skewness | 0.4182 |
| Kurtosis | 3.2395 |
| Values | 10000 |
| Errors | 0 |
| Filtered | 0 |
| Left X | $0 |
| Left P | 0.9% |
| Right X | $100,000 |
| Right P | 33.9% |
| Dif. X | $100,000.00 |
| Dif. P | 33.0% |
| 1% | $2,166.21 |

*Figure 22.13* Ending cumulative cash position

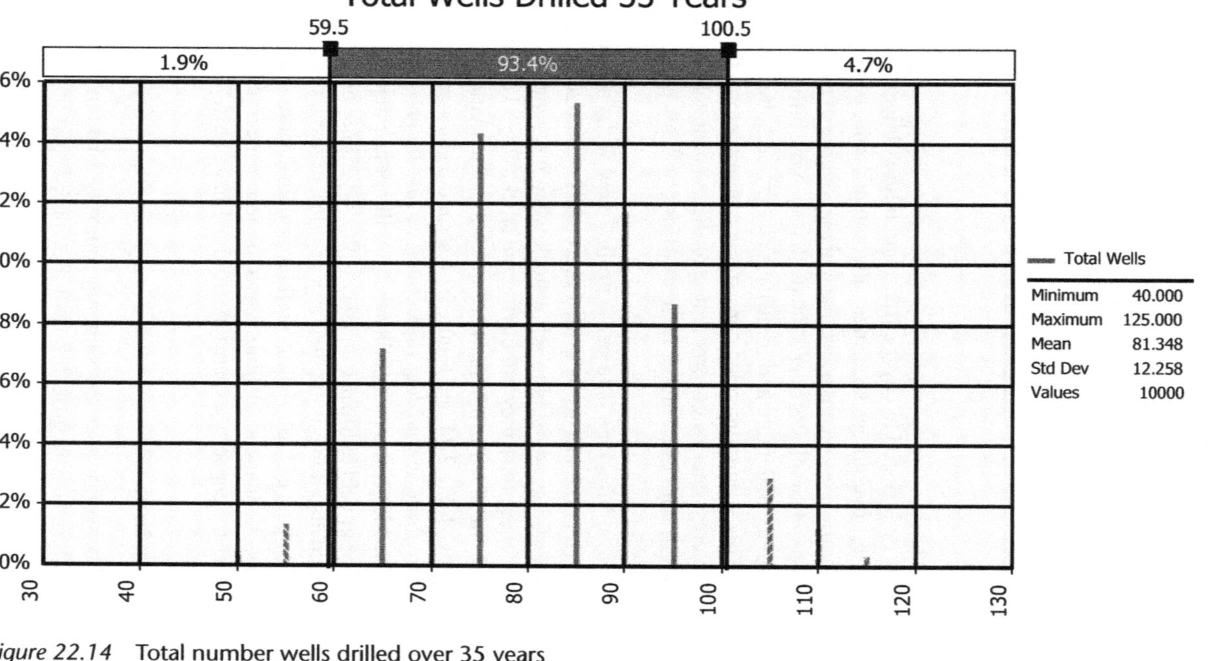


*Figure 22.14* Total number wells drilled over 35 years

*Table 22.2* Long-term returns

| *Initial Investment* | *Rate of Return over 35 Years* | *Rate of Return over 35 Years* |
|---|---|---|
| | Average End Cum Cash Position $130 mm | Maximum End Cum Cash Position $433 mm |
| Leveraged | | |
| $10 mm | 7.6% | 11.4% |
| $20 mm | 5.5% | 9.2% |
| Non-leveraged | | |
| $50 mm | 2.8% | 6.4% |
| $100 mm | 0.8% | 4.3% |

cash reserves that must be invested to cover current and future obligations. In an environment of zero interest rates on government securities, alternative forms of investment have to be sought that do earn a return. This means accepting a higher degree of risk. Investing in fracked wells was very attractive when oil was over $100 per barrel. Now billions of dollars of fracked oil debentures are in danger of default, and some have already defaulted in 2016 with oil prices far below breakeven. This is an unintended consequence of not letting the market set interest rates; that is, forcing interest rates of government securities to near zero levels fuels the search for higher returns fraught with even higher degrees of risk perhaps perpetuating a junk bond bubble.

The simple advice to oil frackers is to cease drilling new wells about 3–4 years before a strong market lapses. Thus the last wells drilled are mostly amortized before oil prices fall. This advice is just as useful as advising to sell a stock when it reaches its historical high. For many individuals, this is the time they are buying the stock, why else would it be at a high? The best advice that can be given is that markets are cyclical no matter how short-term thinking an individual may be. Table 22.1 and Figure 22.6 should be burned into a manager's mind. *Good times do not last forever; and bad times seem to last longer*. Moreover, the longer a strong market exists, the higher the probability that it will not last that much longer. Financial institutions buying 10-year debt to finance an asset with a 4-year life on the basis of an ongoing fracking program should also think about their risk profiles. Investors of tens of billion dollars of debt had a few good years of high returns *on* their principal, now they can worry about the return *of* their principal. If financial institutions were more concerned about risk, maybe the most aggressive dreams for capacity expansion could not have been realized.

## Difficulty of forecasting

Back in the early 1970s, working for the shipping company, I had in my hand all I needed to know to predict an oil crisis. The growth rates I assumed, based on actual rates, would not only make the Middle East the primary source of world oil, but would also tax their capacity to produce oil. Unbeknownst to me at that time, the oil market had already made the transition from a buyers' to a sellers' market. Oil companies had lost control of pricing, but they and the oil producers had not yet realized it. The situation needed only a trigger event for the era of low oil prices to end. I missed this point entirely. I could have written a paper on the "Coming Oil Crisis," but would the *New York Times* or *Wall Street Journal* publish such an outlandish assertion after a century of low oil prices as an op-ed? The trigger event that changed the oil market forever was the Saudi oil embargo of oil shipped to the US and Netherlands for support of Israel during the Yom Kippur War. The resulting shortfall in supply caused oil prices to spike, taking Big Oil and oil producers entirely by surprise. I mention this to demonstrate the difficulty in forecasting prices even for those most immerged in an industry. Unforeseen and unforeseeable events have repeatedly made mish-mash of logically constructed forecasts based on a continuation of existing trends.

I remember when oil prices were at $100 per barrel in the years prior to 2015. A well-known oil expert, after traveling the world talking to oil producers and oil company executives and who knows who else, came to the logically arrived conclusion that $100 per barrel oil was here to stay: it would never end. Why? World oil consumption was rising and incremental oil was mainly from unconventional and costly sources: oil fracking, Canadian oil sands, and deep well drilling in 10,000 foot waters, all of which required $100 per barrel oil to be exploited. Moreover there was every incentive for OPEC to maintain high prices because the cost of free medical, housing, education, and guaranteed income coupled with a huge growth in their populations required high oil prices to prevent societal breakdown. Despite my life-long experience in watching forecasts fail, I bought into this argument hook, line, and sinker. How wrong could I have been? Within a year this forecast was proven to be entirely wrong.

The wild card that brought about lower oil prices far below that to sustain incremental sources of production in the face of growing world oil consumption was Saudi Arabia giving up its role of being a swing producer. Rather they desired to punish Russia for supporting Assad in Syria, to starve Iran of funds to prevent or at least slow down its nuclear weapon development, and last thought of, to bankrupt the US oil fracking industry. All Saudi Arabia had to do to lower prices was open up the oil spigot and flood the market with unneeded oil. It was thought that the US State Department had a part in this decision for the first two reasons. The prognosis at this time (summer 2016) is for lower prices for a whole set of logical reasoning built around bloated inventories even in the face of continued growing demand for oil. But low prices may not remain forever if Saudi Arabia believes that it has achieved its objectives or that it is facing societal disruption over cuts in public spending or its record production levels cannot be sustained. This latter point is the basis for those forecasting higher oil prices. But even this forecast is fraught with uncertainty depending on future production in Iraq and Iran, where plenty of extra capacity of cheaply produced oil can be developed in a relatively short time. It may be beyond Saudi Arabia's ability to act on its own volition if, for instance, an outbreak of war between Iran and Saudi Arabia closes the Arabian Gulf to oil exports. Then the frackers will be back in business overnight. Those who invest in the oil industry have a wide assortment of forecasts on oil prices to choose from, one of which may actually turn out to be true. This is what makes investing in oil so challenging.

## One final observation

If fracking company investment decision makers would only think in terms of the transience and impermanence of business conditions (oil markets), then they would conduct themselves in such a way to always be ready to face a market reversal. This would subdue the overall temptation of gross overexpansion; the pit bull that inevitably turns around and bites its owner. Banks insisting on swaps being arranged to protect revenue of fracked wells for some time into the future was an excellent example of risk mitigation. Simulation can be employed to determine the degree of swap coverage to reduce risk to a manageable level without unduly affecting potential profitability.[3] Unfortunately these swaps were generally too short in duration to provide full coverage for the underlying debentures, but they did delay the onslaught of the vicissitudes of low oil prices on corporate solvency for certain companies. Perhaps the next time around, they will provide adequate coverage for all.

## Notes

1 Nersesian, R. (2011). Energy risk modeling. Ithaca, NY: Palisade. "An Oil Price Model" (Section 23) provides detailed spreadsheet formulation on an oil cartel attempting to control price via production. @RISK software contains two optimization programs Evolver and RISKOptimizer described on the provider's web site (www.palisade.com).

2 *British Petroleum Energy Statistics* 2016 available at www.bp.com.

3 Further information on the use of simulation to obtain the optimal level of swaps can be obtained from Nersesian (2011), "Mitigating Risk with Swaps" (Section 15).

# 23

# Cause-related marketing and disaster management

## Opportunities from tourism-related initiatives

*Giuseppe Aliperti, Francesco Rizzi and Marco Frey*

## 1 Introduction

Disasters may generate several negative effects. According to the Munich RE, economic losses from internationally reported disasters have increased steadily since 1990, reaching in 2013 an estimated annual average of US$200 billion (UN GAR, 2015). The victims of disasters need help, and it is fundamental to collect funds in order to support the hazard-exposed communities and facilitate the pre-disaster mitigation (He and Zhuang, 2016) or the recovering operations (Oosterhof et al., 2008). Cause-related marketing (CrM) is a form of fundraising that may contribute to increasing the resilience of these communities. An increasing number of firms are currently adopting CrM campaigns through promoting disaster-related causes. This trend is confirmed within the tourism industry.

However, studies on the links between CrM, tourism and disaster management seem to be weak. Our study aims at (a) investigating the current academic contributions on the topic, (b) analyzing the main case studies of tourism firms promoting disaster-related fundraising campaign and (c) identifying suggestions for a future research agenda able to support these fundraising activities.

After describing the conceptual background (section 2), in section 3, we provide information on the methodology that has been adopted to carry out the study. In section 4, we highlight some evidence from the literature on CrM and we describe the state of the art of the current academic contributions focused on the link between CrM, tourism and disaster management. We then propose an analysis of disaster-related CrM initiatives in the tourism industry with the aim to identify a bridge between academic contribution and currently existing initiatives. The last section includes conclusions, suggests a new research agenda and describes limitations of the study.

## 2 Conceptual background

Disasters refer to "situations where an organization is confronted with sudden unpredictable catastrophic changes over which it has little control" (Faulkner, 2001 p. 36). Disaster generates costs in terms of human life, physical environment, economic and social impact. Tourism-related organizations are also strongly influenced by the effects generated by disasters (Huang et al., 2007).

The link between tourism firms and disaster management may be analyzed from two different perspectives: one negative and one positive. The negative one refers to the fact that disasters have the potential to threaten the organizations' survival (Duncan et al., 2011). On the other hand, the positive one refers to the new opportunities that disasters may offer to the companies in order to enhance their brand image and increase the consumers' perception regarding the firm's corporate social responsibility (CSR) through promoting disaster-related CrM campaigns.

CrM is a particular typology of CSR initiatives (Nan and Heo, 2007; Brønn and Vrioni, 2001) and it has been categorized among CSR initiatives that "Do Better by Doing Good" (Varadarajan and Menon, 1988). CSR activities are now promoted by a large number of firms (Pirsch et al., 2007). The tourism industry is also involved in this trend (Coles et al., 2013). Within these CSR activities, CrM is increasingly becoming a meaningful part of corporate marketing plans (Gupta and Pirsch, 2006) This marketing strategy is able to influence consumers' perception of brand image (Westberg and Pope, 2014; Bigné-Alcañiz et al., 2012; Codogni, 2012; Myers et al., 2012; Kim and Lee, 2009; Samu and Wymer, 2009) and enhance CSR itself. At the same time, it results to be a very useful integrative tool in order to collect money to be used in the disaster management context.

These are the reasons why an increasing number of tourism firms are currently promoting disaster-related CrM campaigns. Academic studies are needed in order to support these activities through providing insights and suggestions able to maximize the effectiveness of these marketing campaigns. Due to this motivation, we have felt the necessity to investigate more in-depth the academic contributions focused on CrM with the aim to evaluate their applicability within the tourism industry in presence of disaster-related causes. In order to do that, we developed a systematic literature review with the goal to describe the current body of knowledge of the CrM-oriented studies. Later, we identified links between CrM and tourism, and CrM and disaster management.

## 3 Research method

The literature review includes articles up to May 2016. Following Coles et al. (2013), a series of systematic and connected searches were undertaken. SCOPUS has been used as the source. The search has been developed in two main stages.

The first step of the search was mainly focused on the concept of "cause-related marketing." A number of 275 articles were including the keyword in the title, abstract or keywords. Only papers included in the area "business, management and accounting" were considered. The list has been reduced to 207. Considering only peer-reviewed journals, the number decreases to 158. These articles have been analyzed in order to define section 3 and therefore describe the general body of knowledge on CrM.

In the following stage, we reviewed the existing links between CrM and tourism. Using Fenclova and Coles's (2011) approach, we included the tourism industry in the search considering keywords referring to tour operators, cruise companies, airlines, and hotels. Using the keywords "cause-related marketing" AND travel, "cause-related marketing" AND tourism and "cause-related marketing" AND airlines, two papers were identified. Using the keywords "cause-related marketing" AND hotel, one paper was identified. Using the keywords "cause-related marketing" AND hospitality, "cause-related marketing" AND tour, "cause-related marketing" AND tour operator, and "cause-related marketing" AND cruise, no papers were identified. All three articles have been included in the analysis.

The further step consisted on the identification of the existing links between CrM and disaster management. Using the keywords "cause-related marketing" AND relief, two papers were identified. Using the keywords "cause-related marketing" AND aid, two papers were identified. Using the keywords "cause-related marketing" AND disaster, one paper was identified. Using the keywords "cause-related marketing" AND disaster management, no paper was identified. Comparing the results and eliminating the duplicates, we were able to identify three papers.

Each article was accurately filtered in order to check potential links between CrM, tourism and disaster management. Additional gray literature has been consulted in order to better describe disaster-related initiatives among tourism industry (Section 4.4.).

## 4 Results

### *4.1 Evidence from the literature on CrM*

CrM is part of CSR (Nan and Heo, 2007; Brønn and Vrioni, 2001) and has to be considered as a marketing strategy different from corporate giving and strategic philanthropy (Fenclova and Coles, 2011). Corporate giving is linked to a voluntary donation to a charity that has no specific marketing interests. Strategic philanthropy is only linked to brand reputation and visibility. CrM is principally used in order to increase sales. It consists on a promise to donate a certain amount of money to a non-profit organization or a social cause when customers purchase a company's products or services (Nan and Heo, 2007; Lafferty and Goldsmith, 2005; Pracejus et al., 2003; Varadarajan and Menon, 1988).

According to Berglind and Nakata (2005), the classical transactional programs, the message promotion programs and the licensing programs can be considered as CrM activities. Transactional programs and licensing programs need the existence of a transaction (e.g. product selling or credit card transaction). Message promotion programs identify and support a cause. However, the presence of a previous transaction is not necessary and the donation is not necessarily monetary (Berglind and Nakata, 2005).

A CrM campaign's success depends on several factors. First, the selection of the cause seems to be fundamental. According to Kim and Lee (2009), the choice of the cause is strictly related to the nature of the firm. If the firm is more associated to social responsibility, it is preferred a high fit between brand and cause. If the firm is more associated to corporate ability, it is preferred a low fit between brand and cause. In addition, hedonic products request complementary-fit cause; utilitarian/functional products request high-related fit cause (Chang and Liu, 2012).

CrM studies are divided into two main research streams. One, more consistent, tends to put in evidence the positive effects generated by a higher cause/brand fit (Westberg and Pope, 2014; Buil et al., 2012a; Chang and Liu, 2012; Manuel et al., 2014; Samu and Wymer, 2009). The other one supports the necessity to develop a lower cause/brand fit (Moosmayer and Fuljahn, 2013). Despite these opposite perspectives, the majority of the scholars agree that the credibility (Galan-Ladero et al., 2013; Pérez and Bosque, 2013; Buil et al., 2012b; Kim and Lee, 2009; Lafferty, 2007; Barone et al., 2000) and the ethical behavior (Bodkin et al., 2015; Kwarciński, 2012; Doster and Tyrrel, 2011; Berglind and Nakata, 2005; Creyer and Ross, 1996) of the firm are the most important factors in order to promote a successful CrM campaign.

Cause-brand alliance (CBA) influences the perception of the CrM campaign (Baghi and Gabrielli, 2013) and its success. The choice of the right partner (Bennett et al., 2008; Hou et al., 2008) and the further consumer's perception are crucial elements (Trimble and Holmes, 2013; Lafferty et al., 2004). Socio-ethical aspects should be considered (Berglind and Nakata, 2005). Relationship with local community is also important as the resident's perception of the brand image may influence the CrM campaign success (Brønn, 2006). In addition, CrM can be very effective to involve employees in corporate values (Papasolomou and Kitchen, 2011; Larson et al., 2008; Berger et al., 2006).

A successful CrM campaign is supported by a strong ability in public relations (Nelson et al., 2007), and a clear (Westberg and Pope, 2014) and vivid message (Baghi et al., 2009) should be communicated to the market. According to Lafferty and Edmondson (2009), a positive (Grau and Folse, 2007) message with a prominent brand photo is more efficient than a message with a prominent cause photo. In addition, Kuo and Rice (2015) reveal that perceptual attributes such as color (i.e., perceptual congruence) can also enhance the effectiveness of CRM campaigns. Structural elements as donation quantification, donation size compared to product price, donation deadlines and caps and level of promotion do influence consumers' perception of the CRM campaign (Landreth et al., 2007).

Regarding donation, firms may decide to provide cash donations or product donations. The latter is perceived as less favorable (Folse et al., 2014). The cash donation may refer to an abstract, estimable and calculable amount (Pracejus et al., 2003). If donation magnitude is constant and a firm is selling low-priced products, a donation amount framed by a dollar value results to be more effective than a percentage. On the contrary, in the case of high-priced products, the percentage term is more effective (Chang, 2008).

### *4.2 CrM and tourism*

Due to the limited number of academic studies that have analyzed CrM application in the tourism industry, we propose to start the analysis from an overview of the main contributions that have linked CSR and tourism.

Fenclova and Coles (2011) report CSR initiatives promoted by tour operators (e.g. Gurney and Humphreys, 2006; Van Wijk and Persoon, 2006), cruise companies (e.g. Weaver and Duval, 2008), airlines (e.g. Gupta and Saxena, 2006; Philips, 2006; Lynes and Andrachuk, 2008; Tsai and Hsu, 2008) and hotels (e.g. Holcomb et al., 2007; Tsai et al., 2010). At a later time, Coles et al. (2013) offer a critical review and develop a research agenda focusing on the link between tourism and CSR. According to the authors, CSR has become a very popular field of study in business and management studies (Blowfield and Murray, 2008; Burchell, 2008; Crane et al., 2008). However, in travel and tourism, it is at a relatively early stage (Coles et al., 2013).

Studies on CrM initiatives are particularly weak. Fenclova and Coles (2011) report the example of two low fare airlines (LFAs) promoting CrM campaign: EasyJet and Ryanair. The companies declared to make a donation of an unspecified percentage of profits derived from selling scratch cards. However, a negative effect was generated when an investigation promoted by the *Times* revealed that EasyJet was donating just the 1% of scratch card profits and Ryanair declined to communicate the amount of their donation (Fenclova and Coles, 2011).

Chen et al. (2008) investigates the causal relationship among relational selling behaviors (RSB), CrM and consumer value (CV) in resort hotels based in Hualien, Taiwan. According to the author, CrM significantly affects service brand image and perceived service quality (Chen, et al. 2008).

Turner et al. (2001) refer to several initiatives adopted within the tourism industry in order to promote a fundraising campaign. No links to disaster management emerged. However, the study highlights the important role played by travel-related events as fundraising facilitators.

## *4.3 CrM and disaster management*

According to Petty et al. (1983), disasters are perceived as more personally involving by consumers. This aspect results to be very important considering that a higher importance of the cause generates a higher consumers' purchase intention (Nejati et al., 2015; Hou et al., 2008). However, the academic contribution related to the specific link between CrM and disaster management seems also to be weak.

The selection of the cause results to be a fundamental step in order to guarantee the success of the CrM campaign. Focusing on the disaster-related cause, it has been demonstrated that CrM can be fruitfully used in order to support hunger relief (Berglind and Nakata, 2005). Andreasen (1996) refers about one of the most successful CrM campaign launched by American Express in 1993 and linked to hunger relief. This case study supports the necessity to develop a high fit between cause and product. A large proportion of the American Express credit card business was coming from the use of the cards in restaurants. This food-related link (hunger relief/restaurants) seemed to be fundamental in order to facilitate the success of the campaign (Andreasen, 1996).

Ellen et al. (2000) provide a different example. They analyzed a grocery store and a building supply store "as familiar retail environments that sell products that can meet primary needs of communities during natural disasters as well as the needs of numerous ongoing humanitarian causes" (Ellen et al., 2000). They demonstrated that consumers' positive evaluation was significantly higher in presence of disaster-related causes compared to ongoing causes. In addition, when referring to disaster-related causes, consumers seemed to prefer product rather than cash contributions (Ellen et al., 2000).

Studies on disaster-related CrM campaigns also focus on the question of brand/cause congruence and brand reputation. Referring to this topic, Bodkin et al. (2015) explored the British Petroleum (BP) Deepwater Horizon oil spill. The expression "natural disaster" has long been considered a misnomer (Alexander, 1997; Schipper et al., 2006), as main causes of disasters are related to human actions (Schipper et al., 2006). The examined case study is specifically focused on the negative environmental effects generated by human activities. The authors demonstrated that the consumer-company identification and the consumer-brand identification could be influenced by CrM campaigns. However, these correlations are usually mediated by a firm's CSR reputation (Lii and Lee, 2012). Consumers' skepticism may be reduced if the firm has a good reputation and if there is a high fit between a company and CSR domain (Elving, 2013). However, the oil spill in the Gulf of Mexico had a bad effect on company's reputation as it revealed BP's extensive greenwashing (Bodkin et al., 2015). Findings emerging from this study highlight that once the incongruence between environmental cause and CrM strategies occurs, there is a high probability of negative irreparable change in consumers' perception (Bodkin et al., 2015).

## *4.4 Disaster-related CrM initiatives among tourism industry*

Despite the limited academic contributions on the topic, it is possible to identify several firms adopting disaster-related CrM initiatives among the tourism industry.

On 25 April 2015, a Mw 7.8 earthquake hit central Nepal, killing more than 8,700 people (Jones et al., 2016). Hilton Worldwide Responds Funds have supported charities as

MercyCorps, Oxfam and Save the Children, promoting an online fundraising campaign (Hilton Worldwide, 2015). Intercontinental Hotels Group, through the program Shelter in a Storm, collected more than $30,000 from 27 April 2015 to 15 May 2015 (IHG Shelter in a Storm, 2015). Exodus Travel UK organized a fundraising campaign supporting several recovery-related actions (Exodus, 2016). Marriott, its associates, and guests are constantly contributing to the American Red Cross (ARC) and to the International Federation of Red Cross and Red Crescent (IFRC) disaster relief funds to help to provide shelter, food, emotional support and other assistance to victims of disasters (Marriot Sustainability Report, 2010). In 2013, the Carlson Family Foundation, in partnership with global travel and hospitality company Carlson, announced a $20,000 pledge to Typhoon Haiyan relief groups to aid recovery in the devastated region of the Philippines. In addition, Carlson Wagonlit Travel (CWT) announced a donation of $25,000 to the IFRC. CWT constantly encourages employees to donate personally to relief organizations. Regarding the same disaster event in the Philippines, TGI Friday's restaurants encouraged team members to donate directly to the American Red Cross Typhoon Appeal or Red Cross Philippines (CWT, 2013).

International big-size companies seem to prefer to invest on strategic philanthropy considering CrM as a tool to reach the final target of "enhanced brand reputation and visibility." In order to do that, they use CrM message promotion programs including monetary donations facilitated by the fundraising campaign. Donations are not usually related to the product selling. Firms usually invite (real and potential) customers and employees to make free donations.

At the same time, the majority of the tourism firms embracing classical CrM campaigns (transactional) seems to be composed by SMEs. They operate in different areas of the tourism industry as well as tour operation (i.e. Uniline, Croatia), private accommodation (i.e. WildSpring Guest Habitat, Oregon) or luxury hotel reservations (i.e. Suiteness, California). However, we found examples of big-size companies from LFAs adopting transactional CrM programs (Fenclova and Coles, 2011).

Bookdifferent seems to be a hybrid case. The CrM initiatives are developed by this company in collaboration with Booking.com, and this example demonstrates that transactional CrM initiatives can be fruitfully adopted also by international big-size companies. Bookdifferent is using the reservation system from Booking.com. They get a commission from Booking.com for each reservation. Fifty percent of that commission is donated to a charity organization. Customers choose the charity organization and they are informed about the amount of the donation realized by the firm (Bookdifferent, 2016).

In the following paragraphs, we offer a special focus on two important disaster-related initiatives promoted by the Intercontinental Hotel Group (IHG) and the Hilton Hotels and Resorts. These two case studies can be considered as significant due to the importance of the promoted disaster-related initiatives and due to the international size of the companies. We developed an analysis of their projects considering the online information provided by the companies. This step enables a more in-depth investigation of the initiatives promoted by the tourism industry and to better identify the opportunities and necessity for further academic research.

### *The IHG Shelter in a Storm project*

Every year IHG publishes the Responsible Business Report. A huge part of the report is dedicated to the description of disaster relief activities. The responsible business approach aims to reduce environmental impacts and to leverage the economic and social contribution of the hotels. Offering support and shelter when disaster strikes is part of this general strategy. Governance and leadership are led by the company board that is supported by six committees. The

Corporate Responsibility Committee is in charge to enhance disaster preparedness efforts in IHG hotels and local communities. The final aim consists on increasing community resilience in the destinations where IHG hotels are located.

According to the IHG Foundation (IHG, 2015), the main targets of their projects focus on helping communities to develop hospitality skills, ensuring support for those impacted by the disaster, facilitating local community investment and protecting the environment. The foundation aims at empowering the IHG hotels to support guests, colleagues and the local community. They want to be able to guarantee financial support, vital suppliers and accommodation. At the same time, they try to guide hotels to enhance their preparedness and enrich community resilience. In order to reach these targets, the IHG Shelter in a Storm project has been realized.

It is a disaster relief program. The approach seems to be related to strategic philanthropy. We can classify the realized actions as part of a CrM message promotion programs developed with the aim to facilitate fundraising campaigns. IHG signed a global partnership with CARE International, a humanitarian agency founded in 1945 and based in the US. CARE supports IHG in order to find appropriate partners in the area when disaster strikes. According to IHG (2015), CARE International is characterized by a high level of expertise regarding disaster preparedness and relief. On the other side, the head of the Emergency Shelter Team at CARE International underlines the importance of the partnership with IHG, as they are able to provide rapid and scalable assistance for communities in times of need (IHG, 2015).

The IHG Shelter in a Storm project benefits from the support of IHG Academy. This institution is used in order to prepare future employees within the tourism industry. Disaster management topics are also identified and investigated by the Academy.

The Shelter in a Storm project includes fundraising activities over the years in order to define a designated disaster relief fund. This approach allows being prepared in case of a disaster occurrence. They don't have to wait for a fundraising campaign to take effect. The involvement of colleagues and guests allows collecting a considerable amount of funds. In 2015, IHG collected more than $775,000. IHG responded to 27 disasters in 17 countries.

The biggest ever contribution was given in order to support relief work after Nepal's earthquake of April 2015. They provided help to different types of needy people, and through CARE International they were able to support the local community. Additional funds were allocated in order to help colleagues working at the Crowne Plaza Soaltee Kathmandu. Further funds were allocated in order to help Nepalese colleagues, working in IHG hotels around the world, whose homes and families had been affected. IHG was also involved in disaster relief after the flooding of October 2015 in South Carolina. IHG aimed to support local hotels and help colleagues. This attitude to create a network of employees is supported by the "global community fundraising week." It is an example of fundraising travel event (Turner et al., 2001). A huge amount of team building activities (e.g., bike sales, bike rides, water rafting) were organized in order to share company's attitude toward disaster relief.

According to IHG, a priority for future activities regards the promotion of further partnerships with humanitarian agencies and like-minded companies. Regarding this latter point, in 2009 IHG joined the community Business in the Community (BITC) and BITC Human Rights Working Group. The members of these communities aim to develop best practices to manage environmental resources and generate positive impact in the destinations where the hotels are based.

### *The Hilton Worldwide Responds Fund*

Every year Hilton Worldwide publishes a Corporate Responsibility Report (CRR). It is divided into several main areas. One section is dedicated to the internal stakeholders' engagement.

Hilton Worldwide University (HWU) supports this strategy and provides a learning process through organizing courses and lectures. According to the report, the company aims to promote a multicultural approach and defend human rights. An eco-friendly strategy is also supported. In particular, the Hilton Worldwide CRR 2014–2015 focuses on energy, water, waste, carbon and suppliers' management issues. Finally, a special section is dedicated to fundraising initiatives related to disaster management.

The Hilton Worldwide Responds Fund (HWRF) is the main tool that the company uses to collect funds in order to support communities where disaster strikes. The selection of territories that will be supported is realized by Hilton Worldwide and it depends on the portfolio of brands' presence. The HWRF aims at increasing the resilience of the communities in order to prepare for and respond to disasters. Donations to the fund may be provided by companies or individuals. A donor-advised fund (DAF) has been created. This is a philanthropic vehicle established at a public charity where donations may be made by company or individuals. The DAF is managed by a non-profit organization named Global Impact. A list of organizations and local disaster response organization are included in the fund list. The Red Cross and Red Crescent Society are not included in the list but they are considered as partners. The organizations are selected by Global Impact and Hilton Worldwide. Hilton Worldwide guarantees transparency and accountability. The financed charity organizations have to certify that they will use the funds to the specific disaster-related cause indicated by Hilton Worldwide. The Corporate Responsibility team monitors disasters on daily basis. Criteria set by FEMA (Federal Emergency Management Agency) and OCHA (Office for the Coordination of Humanitarian Affairs) support the identification and selection of disasters.

Regarding the donation's process, donors are able to make the donation to a general disaster-related fund or to select a fundraising campaign related to a specific shock event. However, funds may only be distributed to the partners designated in the DAF.

## 5 Discussion and conclusions

After reviewing the main academic contributions on CrM, we were able to identify different typologies of CrM strategies. The current body of knowledge on the topic suggests that several elements may influence the success of CrM campaigns. The role of cause/brand fit and the cause-brand alliance seem to be influenced by the context and seem to vary depending on the cause. In addition, firms should engage local communities and employees in order to maximize the positive effect of the campaigns.

Disaster-related CrM campaigns promoted within the tourism industry are sometimes matching with the findings emerged from the CrM literature. For instance, tourism enterprises tend to involve local communities and employees in order to promote effective CrM campaigns. In addition, some of them recognize the importance of product/cause fit in order to increase the efficacy of their CRM campaigns. An example is provided by the Intercontinental Hotel Group that enhances the role that the hotels may play in case of disaster occurrence:

> When disasters strike, people naturally come to hotels to seek shelter in a storm. This is a key role of hotels in society, and one that is really important to all the communities in which they operate.
>
> *(IHG Shelter in a Storm, 2016)*

However, the number of studies focusing on tourism and disaster management is dramatically low. A new research agenda is needed to offer a concrete support to tourism firms that have decided to promote disaster-related CrM campaigns.

Our chapter highlights the necessity to develop further tourism-oriented studies. We, therefore, conclude by proposing a few themes that could be investigated more in the future.

Considering the direct connection between employees and clients within the tourism industry (Fenclova and Coles, 2011), the ability to manage relationships and to properly communicate to the stakeholders play a key role in the success of the firm. Several tourism enterprises aim at involving local communities, customers and team members in order to increase the effectiveness of disaster-related fundraising campaign. Further studies could focus on the processes able to facilitate consumers and employees' involvement in order to identify the most effective strategies to be adopted to increase their engagement. In addition, targeting the communities affected by disasters, firms should consider their local attitude toward multinationals or small-medium enterprises (SMEs) (La Ferle et al., 2013) in order to avoid failures.

Consumers' attitude seems to change in case of utilitarian or hedonic products (Chang and Liu, 2012). The tourism industry is composed of different types of tourists. The comparison between business travelers and leisure travelers may reveal very interesting findings, as the first category of consumers could be linked to a utilitarian need and the second category to a hedonic need. Further investigations may focus on this aspect.

Previous findings reveal that psychological and socio-demographic consumers' characteristics influence CrM's success (Vaidyanathan et al., 2013; Winterich and Barone, 2011; Corbishley and Mason, 2011; Arnold et al., 2010; Hyllegard et al., 2010; Demetriou et al., 2010; Starmer, 2007; Jacobs, 1995). Therefore, more in-depth studies on tourists' behavior are needed.

Finally, taking into consideration the few academic contributions focused on the tourism industry, additional case studies need to be developed within the specific setting characterized by disaster-related CrM campaigns promoted by tourism enterprises.

Our chapter shed light on the important disaster-related CrM initiatives promoted within the tourism industry and pointed out the necessity to develop additional studies able to support them. We provided some suggestions for further research with the final aim to promote additional tourism-oriented studies. The identification of a structured research agenda may help the tourism firms to increase the efficacy of currently adopted CrM campaigns. More efficient campaigns will be able to generate best performing fundraising activities and consequently, they will contribute to disaster risk reduction (DRR).

## References

Alexander, D.E. 1997, "The study of natural disasters", 1977–97: Some reflections on a changing field of knowledge. *Disasters*, vol. 21, no. 4, pp. 284–304.

Andreasen, A.R. 1996, "Profits for nonprofits: Find a corporate partner", *Harvard Business Review*, vol. 74, no. 6, pp. 47–50, 55–59.

Arnold, T.J., Landry, T.D. & Wood, C.M. 2010, "Prosocial effects in youth from involvement in an experiential, cause-related marketing event", *Journal of Marketing Theory and Practice*, vol. 18, no. 1, pp. 41–52.

Baghi, I. & Gabrielli, V. 2013, "Co-branded cause-related marketing campaigns: The importance of linking two strong brands", *International Review on Public and Nonprofit Marketing*, vol. 10, no. 1, pp. 13–29.

Baghi, I., Rubaltelli, E. & Tedeschi, M. 2009, "A strategy to communicate corporate social responsibility: Cause related marketing and its dark side", *Corporate Social Responsibility and Environmental Management*, vol. 16, no. 1, pp. 15–26.

Barone, M. J., Miyazaki, A. D. & Taylor, K. A. 2000, "The influence of cause-related marketing on consumer choice: Does one good turn deserve another?", *Journal of the Academy of Marketing Science*, vol. 28, no. 2, pp. 248–262.

Bennett, R., Mousley, W. & Ali-Choudhury, R. 2008, "Transfer of marketing knowledge within business-nonprofit collaborations", *Journal of Nonprofit and Public Sector Marketing*, vol. 20, no. 1, pp. 37–70.

Berger, I. E., Cunningham, P. H. & Drumwright, M. E. 2006, "Identity, identification, and relationship through social alliances", *Journal of the Academy of Marketing Science*, vol. 34, no. 2, pp. 128–137.

Berglind, M. & Nakata, C. 2005, "Cause-related marketing: More buck than bang?", *Business Horizons*, vol. 48, no. 5, pp. 443–453.

Bigné-Alcañiz, E., Currás-Pérez, R., Ruiz-Mafé, C. & Sanz-Blas, S. 2012, "Cause-related marketing influence on consumer responses: The moderating effect of cause-brand fit", *Journal of Marketing Communications*, vol. 18, no. 4, pp. 265–283.

Blowfield, M. & Murray, A. 2008, *Corporate responsibility. A critical introduction*, Oxford University Press, Oxford.

Bodkin, C. D., Amato, L. H. & Amato, C. H. 2015, "The influence of green advertising during a corporate disaster", *Corporate Communications*, vol. 20, no. 3, pp. 256–275.

Bookdifferent.com. 2016, www.bookdifferent.com/en/page/about-bookdifferent/nabn

Brønn, P. S. 2006, "Building corporate brands through community involvement: Is it exportable? The case of the Ronald McDonald house in Norway", *Journal of Marketing Communications*, vol. 12, no. 4, pp. 309–320.

Brønn, P. S. & Vrioni, A. B. 2001, "Corporate social responsibility and cause-related marketing: An overview", *International Journal of Advertising: The Review of Marketing Communications*, vol. 20, no. 2, pp. 207–222.

Buil, I., Martínez, E. & Montaner, T. 2012a, "The influence of cause-related marketing actions on brand attitude", *Cuadernos de Economia y Direccion de la Empresa*, vol. 15, no. 2, pp. 84–93.

Buil, I., Melero, I. & Montaner, T. 2012b, "Cause-related marketing strategy: Success factors", *Universia Business Review*, vol. 36, pp. 90–107.

Burchell, J. 2008, *The corporate social responsibility reader*, Routledge, London.

Chang, C. 2008, "To donate or not to donate? Product characteristics and framing effects of cause-related marketing on consumer purchase behavior", *Psychology and Marketing*, vol. 25, no. 12, pp. 1089–1110.

Chang, C. & Liu, H. 2012, "Goodwill hunting? Influences of product-cause fit, product type, and donation level in cause-related marketing", *Marketing Intelligence and Planning*, vol. 30, no. 6, pp. 634–652.

Chen, T., Sung, W., Chen, K. & Liang, G. 2008, "Investigating of the causal relationship among relational selling behaviors, cause-related marketing and consumer value in the resort hotel", *International Journal of Electronic Customer Relationship Management*, vol. 1, no. 4, pp. 402–420.

Codogni, I. 2012, "Marketing social engagement as a tool for creating benefits for non-profit and for-profit organizations", *Prakseologia*, no. 153, pp. 281–296.

Coles, T., Fenclova, E. & Dinan, C. 2013, Tourism and corporate social responsibility: A critical review and research agenda, *Tourism Management Perspectives*, vol. 6, pp. 122–141.

Corbishley, K. M. & Mason, R. B. 2011, "Selection of causes according to socio-demographic status in South Africa", *Journal of Promotion Management*, vol. 17, no. 2, pp. 228–240.

Crane, A., Matten, D. & Spence, L. J., 2008. *Corporate social responsibility. Readings and cases in a global context*, Routledge, London.

Creyer, E. H. & Ross, W. T., Jr. 1996, "The impact of corporate behavior on perceived product value", *Marketing Letters*, vol. 7, no. 2, pp. 173–185.

CWT. 2013, www.carlson.com/news-and-media/news-releases.do?article=7558632.

Demetriou, M., Papasolomou, I. & Vrontis, D. 2010, "Cause-related marketing: Building the corporate image while supporting worthwhile causes", *Journal of Brand Management*, vol. 17, no. 4, pp. 266–278.

Doster, L. & Tyrrell, J. M. 2011, "Marketing communications in the classroom: The parents' view", *Journal of Marketing Communications*, vol. 17, no. 1, pp. 1–15.

Duncan, W. J. et al. 2011, "Surviving organizational disasters", *Business Horizons*, vol. 54, no. 2, pp. 135–142.

Ellen, P. S., Mohr, L. A. & Webb, D. J., 2000. "Charitable programs and the retailer: Do they mix?", *Journal of Retailing*, vol. 76, no. 3, pp. 393–406.

Elving, W.J.L. 2013, "Scepticism and corporate social responsibility communications: The influence of fit and reputation", *Journal of Marketing Communications*, vol. 19, no. 4, pp. 277–292.

Exodus. 2016, www.exodus.co.uk/nepal-earthquake-news.

Faulkner, B. 2001, "Towards a framework for tourism disaster management", *Tourism Management*, vol. 22, pp. 135–147.

Fenclova, E. & Coles, T. 2011, "Charitable partnerships among travel and tourism businesses: Perspectives from low-fares airlines", *International Journal of Tourism Research*, vol. 13, no. 4, pp. 337–354.

Folse, J.A.G., Grau, S. L., Moulard, J. G. & Pounders, K. 2014, "Cause-related marketing: Factors promoting campaign evaluations", *Journal of Current Issues and Research in Advertising*, vol. 35, no. 1, pp. 50–70.

Galan-Ladero, M. M., Galera-Casquet, C. & Wymer, W. 2013, "Attitudes towards cause-related marketing: Determinants of satisfaction and loyalty", *International Review on Public and Nonprofit Marketing*, vol. 10, no. 3, pp. 253–269.

Grau, S. L. & Folse, J.A.G. 2007, "Cause-related marketing (CRM) the influence of donation proximity and message-framing cues on the less-involved consumer", *Journal of Advertising*, vol. 36, no. 4, pp. 19–33.

Gupta, D. K. & Saxena, S. 2006, "Corporate social responsibility in Indian service organisations: An empirical study", Paper presented at the International Conference on "CSR-Agendas for Asia", Kuala Lumpur, Malaysia (13–14 April 2006).

Gupta, S., & Pirsch, J. 2006, "The company-cause-customer fit decision in cause-related marketing", *Journal of Consumer Marketing*, vol. 23, no. 6, pp. 314–326.

Gurney, P. M. & Humphreys, M. 2006, "Consuming responsibility: The search for value at Laskarina Holidays", *Journal of Business Ethics*, vol. 64, pp. 83–100.

He, F., & Zhuang, J. 2016, "Balancing pre-disaster preparedness and post-disaster relief", *European Journal of Operational Research*, vol. 252, no. 1, pp. 246–256.

Hilton Worldwide. 2015, www.hiltonresponds.com/campaigns/42#about.

Holcomb, J. L., Upchurch, R. S. & Okumus, F. 2007, "Corporate social responsibility: What are top hotel companies reporting?", *International Journal of Contemporary Hospitality Management*, vol. 19, no. 6, pp. 461–475.

Hou, J., Du, L. & Li, J. 2008, "Cause's attributes influencing consumer's purchasing intention: Empirical evidence from china", *Qualitative Research in Organizations and Management*, vol. 20, no. 4, pp. 363–380.

Huang, Y. C., Tseng, Y. P. & Petrick, J. F. 2007, "Crisis management planning to restore tourism after disasters: A case study from Taiwan", *Journal of Travel & Tourism Marketing*, vol. 23, pp. 203–221.

Hyllegard, K. H., Ogle, J. P., Yan, R. & Attmann, J. 2010, "Exploring gen y responses to an apparel brand's use of cause-related marketing: Does message matter when it comes to support for the breast cancer cause?", *Clothing and Textiles Research Journal*, vol. 28, no. 1, pp. 19–34.

IHG Shelter in a storm. 2015, www.ihgshelterinastorm.com/fundraising-events/events/fundraising-for-nepal.aspx#sthash.8XDeKEOe.dpbs.

IHG Shelter in a Storm, 2016, www.ihgshelterinastorm.com/about.aspx.

Jacobs, G., Stutts, M.A. & Patterson, L.T. 1995, "The effects of cause-related marketing appeals on consumer purchase and donation behavior", *Journal of Promotion Management*, vol. 2, no. 3–4, pp. 105–120.

Jones, S., Oven, K.J. & Wisner, B. 2016, "A comparison of the governance landscape of earthquake risk reduction in Nepal and the Indian State of Bihar", *International Journal of Disaster Risk Reduction*, vol. 15, pp. 29–42.

Kim, Y.J. & Lee, W. 2009, "Overcoming consumer skepticism in cause-related marketing: The effects of corporate social responsibility and donation size claim objectivity", *Journal of Promotion Management*, vol. 15, no. 4, pp. 465–483.

Kuo, A. & Rice, D.H. 2015, "The impact of perceptual congruence on the effectiveness of cause-related marketing campaigns", *Journal of Consumer Psychology*, vol. 25, no. 1, pp. 78–88.

Kwarciński, T. 2012, "Market as "means" to help the poor. Ethical aspects of cause related marketing", *Prakseologia*, no. 153, pp. 297–314.

La Ferle, C., Kuber, G. & Edwards, S.M. 2013, "Factors impacting responses to cause-related marketing in India and the United States: Novelty, altruistic motives, and company origin", *Journal of Business Research*, vol. 66, no. 3, pp. 364–373.

Lafferty, B.A. 2007, "The relevance of fit in a cause-brand alliance when consumers evaluate corporate credibility", *Journal of Business Research*, vol. 60, no. 5, pp. 447–453.

Lafferty, B. A., & Edmondson, D. R. 2009, "Portraying the cause instead of the brand in cause-related marketing ads: does it really matter?", *Journal of Marketing Theory and Practice*, vol. 17, no. 2, pp. 129–144.

Lafferty, B.A. & Goldsmith, R.E. 2005, "Cause-brand alliances: Does the cause help the brand or does the brand help the cause?", *Journal of Business Research*, vol. 58, no. 4, pp. 423–429.

Lafferty, B.A., Goldsmith, R.E. & Hult, G.T.M. 2004, "The impact of the alliance on the partners: A look at cause-brand alliances", *Psychology and Marketing*, vol. 21, no. 7, pp. 509–531.

Landreth, S., Garretson, J.A. & Pirsch, J. 2007, "Cause-related marketing: An exploratory study of campaign donation structures issues", *Journal of Nonprofit and Public Sector Marketing*, vol. 18, no. 2, pp. 69–91.

Larson, B.V., Flaherty, K.E., Zablah, A.R., Brown, T.J. & Wiener, J.L. 2008, "Linking cause-related marketing to sales force responses and performance in a direct selling context", *Journal of the Academy of Marketing Science*, vol. 36, no. 2, pp. 271–277.

Lii, Y. & Lee, M. 2012, "Doing right leads to doing well: When the type of CSR and reputation interact to affect consumer evaluations of the firm", *Journal of Business Ethics*, vol. 105, no. 1, pp. 69–81.

Lynes, J.K. & Andrachuk, M. 2008, "Motivations for corporate social and environmental responsibility: A case study of Scandinavian Airlines", *Journal of International Management*, vol. 14, pp. 377–390.

Manuel, E., Youn, S. & Yoon, D. 2014, "Functional matching effect in CRM: Moderating roles of perceived message quality and skepticism", *Journal of Marketing Communications*, vol. 20, no. 6, pp. 397–418.

Marriot Sustainability Report, 2010.

Moosmayer, D.C. & Fuljahn, A. 2013, "Corporate motive and fit in cause related marketing", *Journal of Product and Brand Management*, vol. 22, no. 3, pp. 200–207.

Myers, B., Kwon, W. & Forsythe, S. 2012, "Creating effective cause-related marketing campaigns: The role of cause-brand fit, campaign news source, and perceived motivations", *Clothing and Textiles Research Journal*, vol. 30, no. 3, pp. 167–182.

Nan, X. & Heo, K. 2007, "Consumer responses to corporate social responsibility (CSR) initiatives: Examining the role of brand-cause fit in cause-related marketing", *Journal of Advertising*, vol. 36, no. 2, pp. 63–74.

Nejati, M., Amran, A. & Wen, G.T.Y. 2015, "Cause-related marketing: Uncovering the myth", *International Journal of Management Practice*, vol. 8, no. 1, pp. 57–69.

Nelson, R.A., Kanso, A.M. & Levitt, S.R. 2007, "Integrating public service and marketing differentiation: An analysis of the American Express Corporation's 'Charge Against Hunger' promotion program", *Service Business*, vol. 1, no. 4, pp. 275–293.

Oosterhof, L., Heuvelman, A., & Peters, O. 2009, "Donation to disaster relief campaigns: Underlying social cognitive factors exposed", *Evaluation and program planning*, vol. 32, no. 2, pp. 148–157.

Papasolomou, I. & Kitchen, P.J. 2011, "Cause related marketing: Developing a tripartite approach with BMW", *Corporate Reputation Review*, vol. 14, no. 1, pp. 63–75.

Pérez, A. & del Bosque, I.R. 2013, "Extending on the formation process of CSR image", *Social Marketing Quarterly*, vol. 19, no. 3, pp. 156–171.

Petty, R.E., Cacioppo, J.T. & Schumann, D. 1983, "Central and peripheral routes to advertising effectiveness: The moderating role of involvement", *Journal of Consumer Research*, vol. 10, pp. 135–146.

Philips, E.D. 2006, "Corporate social responsibility in aviation", *Journal of Air Transportation*, vol. 11, pp. 65–87.

Pirsch, J., Gupta, S. & Grau, S.L. 2007, "A framework for understanding corporate social responsibility programs as a continuum: An exploratory study", *Journal of Business Ethics*, vol. 70, no. 2, pp. 125–140.

Pracejus, J.W., Olsen, G.D. & Brown, N.R. 2003, "On the prevalence and impact of vague quantifiers in the advertising of cause-related marketing (CRM)", *Journal of Advertising*, vol. 32, no. 4, pp. 19–28.

Samu, S. & Wymer, W. 2009, "The effect of fit and dominance in cause marketing communications", *Journal of Business Research*, vol. 62, no. 4, pp. 432–440.

Schipper, L. & Pelling, M. 2006, "Disaster risk, climate change and international development: scope for, and challenges to, integration", *Disasters*, vol. 30, no. 1, pp. 19–38.

Starmer, A. 2007 "Gen Jones", Textile View Magazine, no. 78, pp. 252–259.

Trimble, C. & Holmes, G. 2013, "New thinking on antecedents to successful CRM campaigns: Consumer acceptance of an alliance", *Journal of Promotion Management*, vol. 19, no. 3, pp. 352–372.

Tsai, W.H. & Hsu, J.L. 2008, "Corporate social responsibility programs choice and costs assessment in the airline industry – a hybrid model", *Journal of Air Transport Management*, vol. 14, pp. 188–196.

Tsai, W.H., Hsu, J.-L., Chen, C.-H., Lin, W.-R. & Chen, S.-P. 2010, "An integrated approach for selecting corporate social responsibility programs and costs evaluation in the international tourist hotel", *International Journal of Hospitality Management*, vol. 29, no. 3, pp. 385–396.

Turner, R., Miller, G. & Gilbert, D. 2001, "The role of UK charities and the tourism industry", *Tourism Management*, vol. 22, no. 5, pp. 463–472.

UN. 2015, The pocket GAR 2015 making development sustainable: The future of disaster risk management, p. 28.

Vaidyanathan, R., Aggarwal, P. & Kozłowski, W. 2013, "Interdependent self-construal in collectivist cultures: Effects on compliance in a cause-related marketing context", *Journal of Marketing Communications*, vol. 19, no. 1, pp. 44–57.

Van Wijk, J. & Persoon, W. 2006, "A long-haul destination: Sustainability reporting among tour operators", *European Management Journal*, vol. 24, no. 6, pp. 381–395.

Varadarajan, P.R. & Menon, A. 1988, "Cause-related marketing: A coalignment of marketing strategy and corporate philanthropy", *Journal of Marketing*, vol. 52, no. 3, pp. 58–74, July 1988.

Weaver, A. & Duval, D.T. 2008, "International and transnational aspects of the global cruise industry", In *International business and tourism: Global issues, contemporary interactions*, Coles, T. & Hall, C.M. (eds). Routledge: Abingdon; 106–123.

Westberg, K. & Pope B, N. 2014, "Building brand equity with cause-related marketing: A comparison with sponsorship and sales promotion", *Journal of Marketing Communications*, vol. 20, no. 6, pp. 419–437.

Winterich, K.P. & Barone, M.J. 2011, "Warm glow or cold, hard cash? Social identify effects on consumer choice for donation versus discount promotions", *Journal of Marketing Research*, vol. 48, no. 5, pp. 855–868.

# 24

# Shared sorrow is half a sorrow

## The role of social capital in building resilient supply chains

*Mitchell J. van den Adel, Dirk Pieter van Donk and Kirstin Scholten*

### Introduction

Collaborative relationships in supply chains are known to be an important source of operational performance (Kamal & Irani 2014) that help supply chain partners to "achieve mutual advantages that are greater than the firms would achieve individually" (Cao et al. 2010: 6616). In particular, these inter-organizational relationships build social capital facilitating secure network ties, shared understanding, and trust (Nahapiet & Ghoshal 1998). While the relevance and importance of relationships for supply chain performance is evident for daily operations, little is known related to building and maintaining supply chain resilience (SCRes; Wieland & Wallenburg 2013). SCRes – the ability to prepare for, respond to, and recover from disruptions – is increasingly important (Tukamuhabwa et al. 2015) as events that harm the ability of an organization to bring finished products or services to the market are inevitable: in 2015, 74% of the companies experienced at least one disruption (Business Continuity Institute 2015). This chapter will explore whether and how social capital in inter-organizational relationships enables or limits SCRes.

It is well known that appropriate levels of social capital foster teamwork, reduce detrimental behaviour of partners, and ensure effective communication (Johnson et al. 2013; Nahapiet & Ghoshal 1998; Villena et al. 2011). However, at the same time, extensive levels of social capital may yield diminishing returns due to opportunistic behaviour, losses in flexibility, and latent lock-in effects by means of discriminating against new, potentially better suppliers (Gargiulo & Benassi 1999; Granovetter 1985; Kern 1998; Villena et al. 2011). Whereas the positive and negative implications of social capital for regular supply chain performance have been elaborated upon in literature, little is known about the implications of social capital for dealing with supply chain disruptions (Johnson et al. 2013). Wieland and Wallenburg (2013) recently acknowledged the usefulness of a relational perspective toward SCRes, but in-depth insights into the corresponding underlying mechanisms of inter-organizational relationships are missing. Therefore, this chapter sets out to explore the role of social capital in preparing for, responding to, and recovering from disruptions (i.e., SCRes), for which a multiple case study across three tiers in a single supply chain of a multinational technology corporation is seen as appropriate. Our results contribute new fine-grained details on the specificities and underlying mechanisms that explain whether and how relationships aid organizations in dealing with supply chain disruptions. Additionally, the exploration of these mechanisms provides guidance for supply chain managers in the allocation of resources in building relationships underpinned by social capital and how such efforts can enhance SCRes.

The remainder of this chapter is structured as follows. First, the concepts of SCRes and social capital will be explored and linked into a research framework. The methodological approach and examined relationships will be discussed in the third section. The fourth section will present the findings and consider them in relation to extant literature. Finally, the conclusion will explore theoretical and managerial implications.

## Theoretical background

### *Supply chain resilience*

SCRes evolves around the notion that not all risks can be foreseen or accounted for. Hence, supply chains need to be capable of absorbing the impact of disruptions – the manifestation of risks (Peck 2006). Accordingly, SCRes has been defined as the "adaptive capability of the supply chain to prepare for unexpected events, respond to disruptions, and recover from them by maintaining continuity of operations at the desired level of connectedness and control over structure and function" (Ponomarov & Holcomb 2009: 131).

While there is consensus on the definition of SCRes in literature, there is less agreement on the formative elements corresponding to the development of resilient supply chains (Tukamuhabwa et al. 2015). For example, Christopher and Peck (2004) specify a system perspective, in which supply chain (re-)engineering, collaboration, risk management culture, and agility enable SCRes. In contrast, Wieland and Wallenburg (2013) conceptualize SCRes via the capabilities of robustness and agility, and Jüttner and Maklan (2011) refer to flexibility, visibility, velocity, and collaboration. Reflecting upon their confirmed instrumental value (Johnson et al. 2013; Scholten & Schilder 2015), this chapter follows Jüttner and Maklan's (2011) conceptualization of SCRes.

*Flexibility* enables a supply chain to effectively detect, manage, and exploit unexpected disruptions (Skipper & Hanna 2009) via, for example, dual or multiple sourcing, control systems, and slack resources and capacity (Sheffi & Rice 2005). Whereas flexibility emphasizes the effectiveness of response and recovery, *velocity* places more emphasis on the efficiency (i.e., speed of recovery; Jüttner & Maklan 2011). Velocity is seen as complementary to flexibility as it relates to the rate at which (flexible) adjustments can be realized (Stevenson & Spring 2007; Wieland & Wallenburg 2013). The implementation of these adjustments requires *visibility*, which is the ability to see from one end of the supply chain to the other (Van der Vorst & Beulens 2002) through the timely availability of, and access to, crucial information (Jüttner & Maklan 2011). The subsequent awareness of potential and actual disturbances throughout the supply chain (Pettit et al. 2013) ensures confidence, prevents overreactions, and avoids unnecessary interventions (Christopher & Lee 2004). Finally, *collaboration* refers to "a long-term partnership process where supply chain partners with common goals work closely together to achieve mutual advantages that are greater than the firms would achieve individually" (Cao et al. 2010: 6616). Collaboration is imperative for SCRes as it enhances joint relationship effort and knowledge creation, as well as the willingness to share sensitive, yet potentially important information (Scholten & Schilder 2015). Table 24.1 summarizes the four SCRes capabilities and their associated aspects.

Table 24.1 An overview of the four SCRes capabilities

| Dimension | Conceptual definition | Associated aspects |
|---|---|---|
| Flexibility | Ability to detect, manage, and exploit unexpected disruptions (adapted from Scholten and Schilder (2015)). | – Dual or multiple sourcing<br>– Reallocation of capacity and resources<br>– Modifiable contracts<br>– Redundancy in capacity and resources |
| Velocity | Speed of flexible adjustments (adapted from Jüttner and Maklan (2011)). | – Rate at which a disruption unfolds<br>– Rate at which losses are incurred<br>– Rate at which a disruption is discovered<br>– Rate at which a supply chain can recover |
| Visibility | Ability to see from one end of the supply chain to the other (adapted from Jüttner and Maklan (2011)). | – Monitoring suppliers<br>– Access to (sensitive) information<br>– Accuracy of information<br>– Timely availability of information<br>– Awareness of (potential) disruptions |
| Collaboration | Configuration of joint efforts prior, during, and after a disruption (Scholten and Schilder (2015)). | – Information-sharing<br>– Decision synchronization<br>– Incentive alignment<br>– Resource-sharing<br>– Collaborative communication<br>– Joint knowledge creation |

In terms of the importance of inter-organizational relationships for SCRes, collaboration and collaborative relationships have recurrently been identified among the most employed and important resilience strategies (Hohenstein et al. 2015; Kamalahmadi & Parast 2016; Tukamuhabwa et al. 2015). However, the role of the social capital embedded in these relationships has remained largely unexplored in contemporary SCRes literature (Johnson et al. 2013; Scholten & Schilder 2015; Wieland & Wallenburg 2013). As such, the following section will elaborate on the main aspects of social capital and further explore whether and how these may relate to SCRes.

## Social capital

Nahapiet and Ghoshal (1998: 243) propose that deeply embedded social capital – "the sum of the actual and potential resources embedded within, available through, and derived from the network of relationships possessed by an individual or social unit" – improves a firm's value creation and performance. These gains result from higher efficiency (e.g., decreased costs) and increased creativity (e.g., enhanced new product development) through cooperative behaviour. Partners in relationships that are characterized by higher levels of social capital are more inclined to work together, communicate more effectively, and are less prone to engage in detrimental behaviour (Johnson et al. 2013; Nahapiet & Ghoshal 1998; Villena et al. 2011). However, the relationship between social capital and these returns from inter-organizational synergies is curvilinear. That is, as a result of extensive levels of social capital, diminishing returns may arise due to possibilities for opportunistic behaviour, losses in flexibility, and latent lock-in effects by means of discriminating against new, potentially better suppliers (Gargiulo & Benassi 1999; Granovetter 1985; Kern 1998; Villena et al. 2011). Such curvilinear relationship can be observed in the three dimensions of social capital as conceptualized by Nahapiet and Ghoshal (1998) in their seminal work.

### *Structural social capital*

Structural social capital (henceforth structural capital) refers to the existence and configuration of inter-organizational connections and the subsequent frequency and quality of information sharing between supply chain partners (Villena et al. 2011). It thus concerns the flow of information (Johnson et al. 2013) and the properties of the information and resource sharing network (Nahapiet & Ghoshal 1998). Carey et al. (2011) and Roden and Lawson (2014) conceptualize structural capital as the strength and number of social interactions between a buyer and a supplier. As such, structural capital embeds, rather than integrates, a buying firm with its key suppliers, fostering reciprocated communication and information sharing (Carey et al. 2011), which are subsequently reflected in relational norms (Liu et al. 2009) and competencies (Wieland & Wallenburg 2013). Together, these enable the timely exchange of reliable information that, in turn, increases the velocity of reaction processes across organizational boundaries (Ergun et al. 2010).

### *Cognitive social capital*

Shared visions, interpretations, and representations between two or more organizations stemming from a commonality in resources are characteristic for the cognitive dimension of social capital (henceforth cognitive capital; Nahapiet & Ghoshal 1998; Tsai & Ghoshal 1998). The resulting shared language and culture, as well as congruency in goals (Inkpen & Tsang 2005), form the basis for interpretation (Johnson et al. 2013) and collective understanding (Villena et al. 2011), "outlining appropriate ways for buyers and suppliers to coordinate their exchange" (Roden & Lawson 2014: 90) and improve the supply chain (Krause et al. 2007). Partners subsequently have "a deeper understanding of *why* the relationship exists and *how* they can contribute to the attainment of compatible goals" (Villena et al. 2011: 562, italics in original). In contrast, the absence of a shared understanding may trigger conflicts and have detrimental effects on performance (Inkpen & Tsang 2005).

### *Relational social capital*

The relational dimension of social capital (henceforth relational capital) is often associated with a reciprocity in obligations and mutual trust, respect, and friendship nurtured by personal relationships between representatives of partnering firms (Cousins et al. 2006; Nahapiet & Ghoshal 1998; Villena et al. 2011). Each of these aspects, which develops as a consequence of recurring transactions between a buyer and a supplier, reduces the concern for opportunistic behaviour, fosters open communication, and increases behavioural transparency (Blau 2009; Kale et al. 2000). Norms of cooperation, which are an integral aspect of relational capital, induce the identification of supply chain members with the broader supply chain and foster supply chain visibility and velocity (Wieland & Wallenburg 2013). Table 24.2 summarizes the three dimensions of social capital and their associated aspects.

*Table 24.2* An overview of the three dimensions of social capital (based on the conceptualization of Villena et al. (2011))

| *Dimension* | *Conceptual definition* | *Associated aspects* |
|---|---|---|
| Structural capital | The strength and number of social interactions between a buyer and a supplier. | - Access to information<br>- Timely availability of information<br>- Frequency/intensity of interactions (density)<br>- Diversity of points of contact (across levels/functions) |
| Cognitive capital | The degree to which goals are congruent and a shared understanding and culture persists between a buyer and a supplier. | - Similar corporate culture and management style<br>- Compatible goals and objectives<br>- Shared understanding, narratives, and interpretations<br>- Joint problem solving |
| Relational capital | A reciprocity in obligations and the mutual trust, respect, and friendship nurtured by personal relationships between representatives of partnering firms. | - (Mutual) respect and trust<br>- Personal friendship<br>- Identification with the supply chain<br>- Reciprocity (in obligations/expectations) |

### *Social capital and resilience*

Considering the acknowledged importance of collaborative relationships for SCRes, the literature review above reveals several potential linkages between the four resilience capabilities and the three dimensions of social capital. Johnson et al. (2013) were the first to empirically accentuate these potential relationships. Their single case study suggests that established relationships and frequent interactions between a buyer and a supplier enables velocity in responding to disruptions. Likewise, prevailing shared understanding and narratives foster visibility and the exchange of information. Relational capital, in turn, was found to enhance flexibility and collaboration as a result of established norms of trust and reciprocity. However, while showing the potential value of social capital, Johnson et al. (2013) base their findings on a rather specific case and did not consider the potential curvilinear relationship between social capital and supply chain performance as postulated by Villena et al. (2011). Accordingly, this chapter will more closely explore whether and how social capital in inter-organizational relationships enables or limits SCRes.

## Methodology

Considering the underexplored relationship between social capital and SCRes, as well as the rather contemporary and complex nature of general supply chain topics, a multiple case study was conducted (Eisenhardt 1989; Voss et al. 2002; Yin 2009). In line with the research question and aim of this study, the unit of analysis is the intra- or inter-organizational relationship between two members of the supply chain.

## *Case context and selection*

The study took place within the network of a multinational corporation (MNC), headquartered in Europe. The MNC is a leading global supplier in the engineering and technology industry, which is characterized by high capital intensity, technological know-how, and competitive pressures for a wide variety of products and services, all of which contribute to the importance of SCRes. Recently, the MNC introduced a state-of-the-art appliance that is the first project within its division to encompass multi-subsidiary development and production. This project involves both established intra- and inter-organizational relationships, as well as new inter-organizational relationships, allowing for the careful exploration of the relationship between social capital within an intra- or inter-organizational relationship and SCRes.

The new appliance is set to be modularly produced at Subsidiaries A (lead developer) and B (both high-cost locations) and, once the appliance is successfully launched, also in Subsidiary C (low-cost production location). At the time of the case study, however, Subsidiary C had not yet been involved and hence will not be further considered. At the supply side, Supplier D (preferred supplier of the MNC for several years), and Supplier E (new to the MNC) are involved in the production of the new appliance. Besides delivering components to Subsidiaries A and B, Supplier D also supplies equipment to Supplier E. We therefore focus on six relationships (see Table 24.3) within the supply chain of the new state-of-the-art appliance (depicted in Figure 24.1). Evident from Table 24.3 is that the six relationships differ in terms of duration and the level of social capital, making them appropriate for the purpose of our

*Table 24.3* Overview of cases

| *Case* | *Relationship* | *Duration* | *Nationality* | *Social capital* |
|---|---|---|---|---|
| A | Subsidiary A – Subsidiary B | 13 years | Different | Moderate (3,6) |
| B | Subsidiary A – Supplier D | More than 20 years | Same | High (4,4) |
| C | Subsidiary A – Supplier E | New | Different | Low (2,6) |
| D | Subsidiary B – Supplier D | 13 years | Different | High (4,1) |
| E | Subsidiary B – Supplier E | New | Same | Moderate (3,1) |
| F | Supplier D – Supplier E | New | Different | Moderate (3,7) |

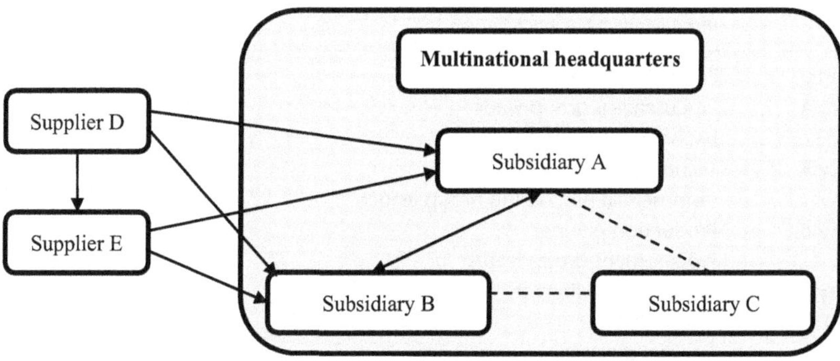


*Figure 24.1* Graphical representation of the considered supply chain

study. The social capital scores are based on survey questions among the interview respondents adapted from Villena et al. (2011), using 5-point Likert scales (1 = strongly disagree; 5 = strongly agree) and have an illustrative, rather than statistical, purpose.

### *Data collection and analysis*

We decided to focus on a specific disruption for data collection to get firsthand insights into the potential influence of social capital on SCRes. The considered disruption put significant stress on the newly formed supply chain as inaccurate forecasts required preliminary production lines to run at maximum capacity. The push for more products put severe strain on the suppliers and led to considerable tensions between the subsidiaries. When, in a later stage, the forecasts were discovered to have grossly overestimated initial demand, production was completely stopped because of high levels of finished products and raw material in inventory.

Data on the described disruption was primarily collected by means of seven semi-structured interviews with knowledgeable informants, including an appropriate diversity in functional perspectives (see Table 24.4) (Voss et al. 2002). The interview protocol was grounded in existing literature and contained questions on relationship characteristics and mitigation approaches toward the disruptive event. The interviews lasted on average 60 minutes and were conducted by two researchers. The interviews were recorded and transcribed verbatim. Subsequently, the interviewees were provided with the opportunity to review the transcribed interviews and provide feedback.

In order to ensure data triangulation and construct validity (Voss et al. 2002; Yin 2009), additional data was obtained from three informal meetings, company documentation, and documented email correspondence between the involved organizations (see Table 24.5). All of the collected data was systematically analysed using coding procedures and guidelines outlined by Miles and Huberman (1994), Yin (2009), and Eisenhardt (1989).

## Findings and discussion

The analysis of the data enabled the identification of underlying mechanisms that explain how social capital in inter-organizational relationships enables or limits SCRes. In particular, we

*Table 24.4* Overview of interview respondents

| *Company* | *Interviewees' business functions* | *Duration* |
|---|---|---|
| Headquarters | Production director Europe | 42 min. |
| Subsidiary A | Procurement group leader<br>Logistics manager | 58 min. |
| Subsidiary A | Technical purchaser<br>Commercial purchasing group leader | 99 min. |
| Subsidiary B | Production planner<br>Procurement group leader | 79 min. |
| Subsidiary B | Value stream director | 40 min. |
| Supplier D | Sales manager<br>General director | 104 min. |
| Supplier E | Account manager (general)<br>Account manager (specific relationship) | 61 min. |

*Table 24.5* Overview of supplementary data sources

| *Source* | *Type* | *Length* | *Year* |
|---|---|---|---|
| Procurement group leader and logistics manager at Subsidiary A | Informal meeting | 40 minutes | 2016 |
| Customer logistics planning at Subsidiary A | Informal meeting | 60 minutes | 2016 |
| Procurement group leader and logistics manager at Subsidiary A | Informal meeting | 45 minutes | 2016 |
| Company websites | Website | n.a. | 2016 |
| Headquarters – Annual reports | Report | 226 pages | 2014 and 2015 |
| Headquarters – Company information (incl. organizational charts) | Report | 50 pages | 2015 |
| Headquarters – Contract with Supplier D | Contract | 18 pages | 2006 |
| Headquarters – Supplier evaluations | Report | 46 pages | 2016 |
| Subsidiary A – Production meeting presentations | Presentation | 22 slides | 2015 and 2016 |
| Subsidiary A – Detailed production plan | Excel | n.a. | 2015 and 2016 |
| Subsidiary A – Documented email correspondence | Email | n.a. | 2015 and 2016 |
| Supplier D – Detailed production plan | Excel | n.a. | 2015 |
| Supplier E – Facts and figures | Report | 16 pages | 2016 |
| Supplier E – Company information | Report | 24 pages | 2016 |

found that structural capital contributes to SCRes via increased bidirectional communication and the subsequent improved access to (sensitive) information, cognitive capital via flexibility in supplier attitudes, understanding and acceptance of cultural differences, and a sense of ownership, and relational capital via supplier development, (mutual) respect and trust, and close personal interaction. At the same time, we also found that the rotation of interacting personnel in order to promote objectivity in terms of relational capital can be counterproductive for SCRes. Following, we will discuss our in-depth findings in light of extant literature following the three social capital elements.

## *Structural capital*

The interviews reveal that structural capital predominantly promotes SCRes through increased bidirectional communication and the subsequent improved access to (sensitive) information. In particular, we found that the failure within the considered supply chain to coordinate activities arose from constrained interactions between its (newly introduced) member organizations, hampering *visibility* and increasing complexity in line with findings from Durach et al. (2015). As structural capital is not yet evident in newly formed organizational relationships, non-existing direct communication lines between organizations impede successful *collaboration*: "I don't want to be talking through Subsidiary B with Supplier E, that doesn't make sense. [. . .] We need to be able to make our own arrangements, we need to have feeling with them, what's happening there" (Subsidiary A – Procurement group leader). Moreover, the limited integration in terms of structural capital restricted *flexibility*, allowing the disruption to affect and harm other members by means of a rippling effect (Jüttner 2005): "even suppliers were saying 'OK, I will just do like I can deliver 800 parts, I know that I cannot, but I hope that someone else is failing worse than me, therefore my problem doesn't show'" (Subsidiary A – Logistics manager).

Partially because of communication through Subsidiary B and infrequent own site visits, structural capital was lacking for the relationship between Subsidiary A and Supplier E: "this relationship, communication, and mutual understanding of processes is not in place. Therefore, [Supplier E] is much more of a 'black box'" (Subsidiary A – Procurement group leader). In contrast, Subsidiary A acknowledges that because of a higher density of (bidirectional) interactions, Supplier D "has a good feeling for what is happening here." This shows that the restricted development of structural capital in the former relationship, in terms of loose interactions, particularly impeded SCRes through limited *visibility* and *flexibility*. *Visibility* was further restricted because of ineffective and limited interactions across functions. While such interactions can enhance the speed of problem solving and synchronize interfirm processes (Dyer & Nobeoka 2003; Heide & Miner 1992), promoting the sharing of sensitive information, potentially leading to strategic benefits (Villena et al. 2011), that was not the case in the examined relationship.

The analysis of the data correspondingly points toward the need for a substantial number of periodically scheduled (i.e., dense) interactions, such as telephone and videoconferences, especially when time pressures are high. As the general director of Supplier D postulates: "if we don't do that [i.e., schedule meetings], we need even more time to make corrections." The subsequent coordination of business processes necessitates the use of communication media beyond those that are considered formal (e.g., emails) in order to further develop the respective inter-organizational relationship and build structural capital. Richer and less formal communication channels (e.g., face-to-face meetings), in contrast to more formal channels such as electronic data interchanges (EDIs), allow for more and quicker feedback, thereby promoting collaborative communication (Ambrose et al. 2008). That is, periodically scheduling personal meetings and site visits is imperative considering that "it opens doors and eyes. And then things are discussed in a more personal way than in a formal way. [. . .] We experienced that it is necessary to have these conversations in person or eye-to-eye, even if you don't have time for it" (Subsidiary A – Technical purchaser). Li et al. (2014) propose that initially formal communication channels should be established and, only in a later stage, informal communication channels as these necessitate established relationships characterized by shared understanding and trust. However, in contrast to Li et al. (2014), the present findings reveal a need for informal communication even when formal communication channels are not fully integrated in order to enhance *collaboration*, supporting the observations by Scholten and Schilder (2015).

To summarize, our study suggests that structural capital facilitates SCRes as a result of direct and bidirectional (i.e., dense) communication between member organizations, necessitating the use of informal communication channels. The above discussion additionally reveals that disruptive events, but especially the inability to deal with them, may limit the further development of structural capital.

## Cognitive capital

The data reveals that cognitive capital promotes SCRes through an understanding and acceptance of cultural differences, flexibility in supplier attitudes, and a sense of ownership. Prior to the introduction of the new appliance, product development approaches differed between Subsidiaries A and B. We found that this affected resilience during the disruption as there was a limited understanding between the subsidiaries about the diverse operational and corporate processes. For instance, when Subsidiary B needed further information on the standard "imposed" by the lead-plant Subsidiary A, "it was hard to get this information because there was not an understanding why this information is needed because in [Subsidiary A] it is working without this information" (Subsidiary B – Production planner). In contrast, an awareness and understanding about different corporate cultures and business processes was present within the relationship between Subsidiary A and the less hierarchical Supplier D, which subsequently displayed substantial *flexibility* and *velocity*. These contrasting relationships of Subsidiary A characterized by distinct levels of cognitive capital illustrate the role of a shared understanding in facilitating supply chain *visibility* and *collaboration*. More specifically, the present observations reveal that differences in (corporate) culture might not necessarily impede resilience as long as a shared awareness, understanding, and acceptance endure regarding these differences. Albeit these differences were relatively minor and need further exploration in future research, our case study provides initial support for the role of cognitive capital in bridging cultural differences and subsequently enhancing SCRes.

In addition to an understanding about cultural differences, shared norms that emphasize cooperation rather than competition promote exchanges of knowledge and the creation of intellectual capital (Nahapiet & Ghoshal 1998). Competition, on the other hand, may inhibit members' willingness to cooperate or share information (Johnson et al. 2013). Multiple times during the disruption, the subsidiaries competed with each other for the limited capacity that was available at suppliers, claiming to be more efficient, and "accusing" each other of not operating in the best interests of the supply chain. This behaviour strengthened the impact of the disruption, led to incongruent objectives, and further reduced mutual understanding, additionally affecting *collaboration* with external organizations: "I don't understand how that should have happened. We are [the business unit], we are not [Subsidiary A] and we are not [Subsidiary B] towards a supplier. We should be [the business unit]" (Headquarters – Production director Europe). Hence, our observations show that within the considered supply chain, goals and objectives were neither aligned, nor congruent, which inhibited the (timely) availability of information and the forming of a common identity, further limiting *visibility* and *collaboration*.

The analysis of the data additionally suggests that the willingness to engage in joint problem solving and goal alignment, which is an important aspect of cognitive capital, is important for fostering SCRes. "We tend to change our systems, for instance, or processes, so we have to have a good relationship with them in order to change that, to make sure that they are helpful" (Subsidiary A – Logistics manager), which is particularly true for the relationship between Subsidiary A and Supplier D. In contrast, the limited engagement in joint problem solving and goal alignment with Supplier B ultimately "was too much for the supply chain to react. Especially for [Supplier B], they had to close down their production lines completely for weeks" (Subsidiary B – Procurement group leader). Hence, our observations support the notion that mutually committed parties are more inclined to adopt *flexible* approaches and have a deeper understanding about "*how* they can contribute to the attainment of compatible goals" (Villena et al. 2011: 562, italics in original).

Johnson et al. (2013: 330) propose that by giving a sense of ownership to supply chain members, a focal company creates "conditions conducive to shaping cognitions, i.e., shared codes," thereby reducing the requirements for strict monitoring and control. A sense of ownership enhances an entity's willingness to contribute to the overall network's well-being, to assume personal risk or sacrifices, and to proactively assume responsibility (Pierce et al. 2001, 2003; Wieland & Wallenburg 2013). A sense of ownership and willingness to engage in joint problem solving were absent between the two suppliers in our study considering that their cooperation was "forced" by the MNC. As a result of not selecting their own partner, both suppliers did not feel responsible and perceived the other party lacking the appropriate capabilities and only reluctantly engaged in information-sharing. The account manager (general) at Supplier E acknowledged that "if we would have had the choice we would have chosen another supplier instead of [Supplier D]." Thus, a sense of ownership, as an important characteristic of cognitive capital, facilitates commitment, a shared understanding, and congruency in goals, thereby increasing supply chain *visibility* and *collaboration.*

In conclusion, our case study revealed the potential of cognitive capital for enhancing SCRes by means of an understanding and acceptance of (corporate) cultural differences, subsequent shared norms of cooperation, increased willingness of supply chain partners to adopt flexible approaches, and an enduring sense of ownership.

## *Relational capital*

Although relational capital may reduce the ability to remain objective and critical, our study reveals that it enhances information-sharing and collaborative efforts in response to a disruption, as well as promotes desirable behaviour and open communication by means of supplier development. Similar to the other dimensions of social capital, the observations show that more developed supply chain relationships allow for proactive suppliers, which are more inclined to share important, yet potentially sensitive information, in a timely manner. Nevertheless, the procurement group leader at Subsidiary B acknowledged that although an established relationship with more mutual respect and trust would have helped to solve the emerging problems quicker, "it would not have avoided the problems." He further identified the absence of an established relationship not as "a cause, but it made the situation worse because the information sharing did not work well all the time." Hence, the absence of relational capital in response to a disruption reduces the *flexibility* and *velocity* at which a supply chain can respond and recover.

Reflecting upon the decreased objectivity of individuals as relationships mature, which Villena et al. (2011) term the "dark side" of social capital, the MNC implemented a policy in which every 5 years different lead buyers are assigned to suppliers. This periodic circulation promotes objectivity and the ability to remain critical toward current processes. However, a disadvantage of the circulation is that longer periods in which the same persons interact establish stronger relationships in terms of respect, trust, and access to sensitive issues. From the perspective of the supplier, the circulation of personnel frequently necessitates the adaptation of processes and business approaches: "if somebody is doing a new job, for us it's the same of course, then you have somebody quite different to communicate with and they take their own new ideas and how they want things to change" (Supplier D – General director).

As an aspect of relational capital, trust may ensure confidence, prevent overreactions, and avoid unnecessary interventions (Christopher & Lee 2004). Villena et al. (2011: 564) describe improved relationship strength and the "willingness to cooperate beyond contractual provisions" as outcomes of relational capital, both of which are of paramount importance in response to a disruptions. Furthermore, the absence of relational capital introduces uncertainty in the relationship and the withholding of potentially important information (Perrone et al. 2003), which is partially reflected in the considered supply chain. Thus, relational capital may be a necessary, but insufficient condition for preventing the occurrence of disruptions, yet a primary condition for mitigating the impact of disruptions. Furthermore, understanding and knowing a colleague at a personal level increases *visibility* due to more effective formal communication and fewer misunderstandings: "We are talking almost to everybody. If you need to do that only in mailing, you can write one sentence which is positive and negative. And one reads him positive, because he knows me, and the other one thinks: 'Who is that guy? What does he think?'" (Supplier D – General director). Hence, in terms of fostering the development of relational capital in the context of *visibility*, there is a trade-off between objective judgement and more effective (formal) communication, allowing for the timely access to sensitive issues. These findings are similar to Scholten and Schilder's (2015) proposition that new, potentially more valuable suppliers reduce SCRes because of diminished *visibility* as a result of less developed and collaborative relationships.

Similar to the case examined by Johnson et al. (2013), supplier development in our case study was an important manifestation of relational capital, involving aspects such as joint knowledge creation and resource-sharing, both of which are important features of *collaboration*. For example, Supplier D is a member of the self-learning group that includes the preferred suppliers of the MNC: "We have a long-term relationship. We know what they can do, we are very happy with them. And we grow with them and they grow with us. We learn from each other, we help them in investments, so it's like a good corporation" (Subsidiary A – Commercial purchasing group leader). Hence, supplier development reduced concerns for opportunistic behaviour and fostered open communication (Blau 2009; Kale et al. 2000). Rather than terminating the relationship when problems arise with Supplier D, Subsidiary A educates them and "punishes" underperformance by selecting different suppliers in other areas. As such, undesirable behaviour is constrained, norms of trust and reciprocity are fostered, and incentives are aligned. In accordance, Supplier D was actively involved in, and committed to, the design of the new appliance and proactively monitored and communicated production difficulties. In contrast, the relationship between Subsidiary A and Supplier E, which is not part of the supplier development program, is "superficial and distant [. . .] and a risk for problems in the chain in the future" (Subsidiary A – Procurement group leader). The limited time frame in which this respective relationship had to develop, as well as the experienced problems, did not allow for building norms of trust and reciprocity. At this point, Supplier E is "much more of 'black box'. We do not know what is done with the input we give it and are not certain the output is as expected" (Subsidiary A – Procurement group leader). Hence, our findings support the observations by Blackhurst et al. (2011) and Johnson et al. (2013) regarding the positive relationship between supplier development programs and SCRes.

In summary, the findings of our case study show that improved speed and reliability of information sharing after a disruption has occurred, more efficient open and personal communication, and supplier development programs are essential features of relational capital that enhance SCRes. Overall, our interviews suggest that frequent face-to-face meetings, in which rich and diverse information is shared (structural capital), allow for the alignment of goals and understanding (cognitive capital) and the development of strong relationships characterized by mutual trust and respect (relational capital). Notwithstanding the fact that the interrelatedness of the three dimensions of social capital should be further explored in the context of SCRes, these observations lend support to earlier social capital literature (e.g., Inkpen & Tsang 2005; Tsai & Ghoshal 1998; Roden & Lawson 2014).

## Conclusion

This chapter set out to explore the role of social capital, via the three dimensions of relational, structural, and cognitive capital (Nahapiet & Ghoshal 1998), in building and maintaining SCRes, defined by flexibility, velocity, visibility, and collaboration (Jüttner & Maklan 2011). Figure 24.2 summarizes our findings on the relationship. The feedback loop included between SCRes and social capital acknowledges the importance of the context in which social action is embedded (Giddens 1984; Johnson et al. 2013). In particular, the perceived resilience will

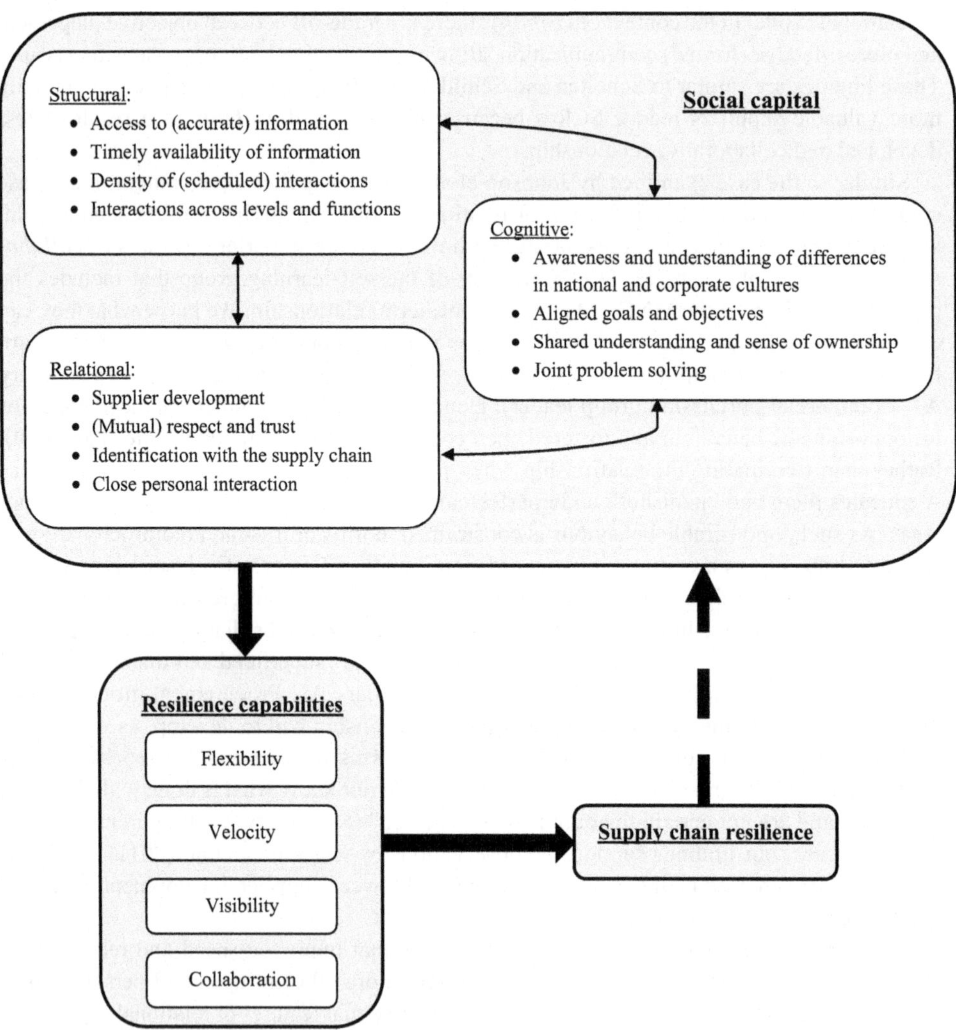


*Figure 24.2* Relationship between social capital and supply chain resilience

influence the desired and displayed behaviour of partners in intra- and inter-organizational relationships.

Several contributions emerge from our study. First, regarding structural capital, the case study revealed the importance of informal interactions across supply chain partners, even if formal interactions and communication are not fully integrated. Our examples show that loose interactions and the absence of direct communication lines reduce *flexibility* and *velocity* by means of lock-in effects due to the inaccessibility of information. In terms of managerial implications, managers should thus proactively engage in developing a network of dense interactions across the supply chain in order to allow for timely and flexible responses toward emerging disruptions.

Second, our findings provide initial support for the role of cognitive capital in bridging cultural differences and subsequently enhancing SCRes. This contrasts extant literature that shows that considerable differences in national and corporate cultures may trigger conflicts that result in frustration (Inkpen & Tsang 2005), as well as generate transaction costs that are incurred when resolving these disputes (Holcomb & Hitt 2007). Our findings indicate that these differences might not necessarily impede SCRes as long as a shared awareness, understanding, and acceptance endure regarding these differences. This seems to open up new avenues for future research.

Third, this chapter is among the first to underscore and further explore the role of a sense of ownership as an important aspect of cognitive capital. Specifically, a lack of ownership across a supply chain may cause reluctance among member organizations to proactively assume personal risk and responsibility, which both hamper *visibility* and *collaboration*. A sense of ownership rationalizes cooperative behaviour and promotes the development of a common identity, facilitating commitment, a shared understanding, and congruency in goals. This theoretical insight is especially significant for managers in assigning responsibilities across a supply chain. For instance, involving supply chain partners early in the design and development of new products accords these partners a sense of ownership and the willingness to contribute to the overall chain's well-being. These implications of a sense of ownership for cognitive capital should be further examined within the context of resilience, as well as in the context of regular operational activities.

Finally, in line with Blackhurst et al. (2011) and Johnson et al. (2013), further support was provided for the role of supplier development programs in enhancing resilience through improved relational capital. The observations show that, due to supplier development, partners in these relationships, which are subsequently characterized by higher levels of trust and respect, are more inclined to share sensitive information in a timely manner after a disruption has occurred. The use of supplier development programs further nurtures mutual commitment toward long-term relationships and the identification with the broader supply chain. As such, managers should strive to proactively develop relational competencies with suppliers in order to allow for rapid and flexible approaches toward emerging disruptions. Although these relational investments may reduce objectivity and potentially result in lock-in effects, the subsequently developed relational tenability is of significant importance for SCRes. In addition, our study revealed that maintaining objectivity by means of periodically rotating personnel is traded off against a loss in established relationships that promote visibility and collaboration. Along with the emerging attention for this "dark side" of social capital, in terms of reduced flexibility, opportunistic behaviour, and latent lock-in effects (Villena et al. 2011), this trade-off should also be further examined in the context of resilience. Specifically considering that Scholten and Schilder (2015) recently found a similar trade-off between the superior efficiency of new suppliers and the loss in the level of collaborative activities.

Furthermore, additional avenues of future research can be derived from some of the limitations of this study. First, we examined a newly introduced appliance that relied upon an emerging network of intra- and inter-organizational relationships. Accordingly, social capital for several of the considered relationships was incompletely developed and was still evolving. Future studies may wish to consider the role of social capital for SCRes in more established networks of intra- and inter-organizational relationships. Second, the examined disruption originated from within the supply chain, potentially inducing diverse organizational responses compared to external disruptions that emerge as a result of, for example, natural hazards. Hence, the effect of the origin of a disruption for SCRes and the role of social capital should be further reflected upon in future research. Finally, although the absence of social capital in our case study led to a stronger impact of the disruption, it remains unclear whether the presence of social capital would have the opposite effect. That is, future research should explore whether the presence of more gradually developed social capital reduces the impact of a disruption.

## Bibliography


Ambrose, E. et al., 2008. Communication media selection in buyer-supplier relationships. *International Journal of Operations and Production Management*, 28(4), pp. 360–379.

Blackhurst, J., Dunn, K. S. & Craighead, C. W., 2011. An empirically derived framework of global supply resiliency. *Journal of Business Logistics*, 32(4), pp. 374–391.

Blau, P. M., 2009. *Exchange and power in social life*, 13th ed., New Brunswick: Transaction Publishers.

Business Continuity Institute, 2015. *Supply chain resilience report 2015*, Caversham.

Cao, M. et al., 2010. Supply chain collaboration: Conceptualisation and instrument development. *International Journal of Production Research*, 48(22), pp. 6613–6635.

Carey, S., Lawson, B. & Krause, D. R., 2011. Social capital configuration, legal bonds and performance in buyer-supplier relationships. *Journal of Operations Management*, 29(4), pp. 277–288.

Christopher, M. & Lee, H., 2004. Mitigating supply chain risk through improved confidence. *International Journal of Physical Distribution and Logistics Management*, 34(5), pp. 386–396.

Christopher, M. & Peck, H., 2004. Building the resilient supply chain. *International Journal of Logistics Management*, 15(2), pp. 1–13.

Cousins, P. D. et al., 2006. Creating supply chain relational capital: The impact of formal and informal socialization processes. *Journal of Operations Management*, 24(6), pp. 851–863.

Durach, C. F., Wieland, A. & Machuca, J.A.D., 2015. Antecedents and dimensions of supply chain robustness: A systematic literature review. *International Jounal of Physical Distribution and Logistics Management*, 45(1/2), pp. 118–137.

Dyer, J. H. & Nobeoka, K., 2003. Creating and managing a high-performance knowledge-sharing network: The Toyota case. *Strategic Management Journal*, 21(3), pp. 345–367.

Eisenhardt, K. M., 1989. Building theories from case study research. *The Academy of Management Review*, 14(4), pp. 532–550.

Ergun, Ö. et al., 2010. Waffle house restaurants hurricane response: A case study. *International Journal of Production Economics*, 126(1), pp. 111–120.

Gargiulo, M. & Benassi, M., 1999. The dark side of social capital. In R. Leenders & S. M. Gabbay, eds. *Corporate social capital and liability*. Boston: Kluwer, pp. 298–322.

Giddens, A., 1984. *The constitution of society: Outline of a theory of structuration*, Berkeley: University of California Press.

Granovetter, M., 1985. Economic action and social structure: The problem of embeddedness. *American Journal of Sociology*, 91(3), pp. 481–510.

Heide, J. B. & Miner, A., 1992. The shadow of the future: Effects of anticipated interaction and frequency of contact on buy-seller cooperation. *Academy of Management Journal*, 35(2), pp. 265–291.

Hohenstein, N.-O. et al., 2015. Research on the phenomenon of supply chain resilience: A systematic review and paths for further investigation. *International Jounal of Physical Distribution and Logistics Management*, 45(1/2), pp. 90–117.

Holcomb, T. R. & Hitt, M.A., 2007. Toward a model of strategic outsourcing. *Journal of Operations Management*, 25(2), pp. 464–481.

Inkpen, A. C. & Tsang, E., 2005. Social capital, networks, and knowledge transfer. *Academy of Management Review*, 30(1), pp. 146–165.

Johnson, N., Elliott, D. & Drake, P., 2013. Exploring the role of social capital in facilitating supply chain resilience. *Supply Chain Management: An International Journal*, 18(3), pp. 324–336.

Jüttner, U., 2005. Supply chain risk management: Understanding the business requirements from a practitioner perspective. *The International Journal of Logistics Management*, 16(1), pp. 120–141.

Jüttner, U. & Maklan, S., 2011. Supply chain resilience in the global financial crisis: An empirical study. *Supply Chain Management: An International Journal*, 16(4), pp. 246–259.

Kale, P., Singh, H. & Perlmutter, H., 2000. Learning and protection of proprietary assets in strategic alliances: Building relational capital. *Strategic Management Journal*, 21(3), pp. 217–228.

Kamal, M.M. & Irani, Z., 2014. Analysing supply chain integration through a systematic literature review: A normative perspective. *Supply Chain Management: An International Journal*, 19(5/6), pp. 523–557.

Kamalahmadi, M. & Parast, M.M., 2016. A review of the literature on the principles of enterprise and supply chain resilience: Major findings and directions for future research. *International Journal of Production Economics*, 171(1), pp. 116–133.

Kern, H., 1998. Lack of trust, surfeit of trust: Some causes of the innovation crisis in German industry. In C. Lane & R. Bachmann, eds. *Trust within and between organizations*. New York: Oxford University Press, pp. 203–213.

Krause, D.R., Handfield, R.B. & Tyler, B.B., 2007. The relationships between supplier development, commitment, social capital accumulation and performance improvement. *Journal of Operations Management*, 25(2), pp. 528–545.

Li, Y., Ye, F. & Sheu, C., 2014. Social capital, information sharing and performance: Evidence from China. *International Journal of Operations and Production Management*, 34(11), pp. 1440–1462.

Liu, Y., Luo, Y. & Liu, T., 2009. Governing buyer-supplier relationships through transactional and relational mechanisms: Evidence from China. *Journal of Operations Management*, 27(4), pp. 294–309.

Miles, M.B. & Huberman, M.A., 1994. *Qualitative data analysis*, 2nd ed., Thousand Oaks: Sage Publications.

Nahapiet, J. & Ghoshal, S., 1998. Social capital, intellectual capital, and the organizational advantage. *Academy of Management Review*, 23(2), pp. 242–266.

Peck, H., 2006. Reconciling supply chain vulnerability, risk and supply chain management. *International Journal of Logistics Research and Applications*, 9(2), pp. 127–142.

Perrone, V., Zaheer, A. & McEvily, B., 2003. Free to be trusted? Organizational constraints on trust in boundary spanners. *Organization Science*, 14(4), pp. 422–439.

Pettit, T.J., Croxton, K.L. & Fiksel, J., 2013. Ensuring supply chain resilience: Development and implementation of an assessment tool. *Journal of Business Logistics*, 34(1), pp. 46–76.

Pierce, J.L., Kostova, T. & Dirks, K.T., 2001. Toward a theory of psychological ownership in organizations. *Academy of Management Review*, 26(2), pp. 298–310.

Ponomarov, S.Y. & Holcomb, M.C., 2009. Understanding the concept of supply chain resilience. *The International Journal of Logistics Management*, 20(1), pp. 124–143.

Roden, S. & Lawson, B., 2014. Developing social capital in buyer-supplier relationships: The contingent effect of relationship-specific adaptations. *International Journal of Production Economics*, 151, pp. 89–99.

Scholten, K. & Schilder, S., 2015. The role of collaboration in supply chain resilience. *Supply Chain Management: An International Journal*, 20(4), pp. 471–484.

Sheffi, Y. & Rice, J.B., Jr., 2005. A supply chain view of the resilient enterprise. *MIT Sloan Management Review*, 47(1), pp. 41–48.

Skipper, J.B. & Hanna, J.B., 2009. Minimizing supply chain disruption risk through enhanced flexibility. *International Journal of Physical Distribution and Logistics Management*, 39(5), pp. 404–427.

Stevenson, M. & Spring, M., 2007. Flexibility from a supply chain perspective: definition and review. *International Journal of Operations and Production Management*, 27(7), pp. 685–713.

Tsai, W. & Ghoshal, S., 1998. Social capital and value creation: The role of intrafirm networks. *Academy of Management Journal*, 41(4), pp. 464–476.

Tukamuhabwa, B.R. et al., 2015. Supply chain resilience: Definition, review and theoretical foundations for further study. *International Journal of Production Research*, 53(18), pp. 5592–5623.

Villena, V.H., Revilla, E. & Choi, T.Y., 2011. The dark side of buyer-supplier relationships: A social capital perspective. *Journal of Operations Management*, 29(6), pp. 561–576.

Van der Vorst, J. & Beulens, A., 2002. Identifying sources of uncertainty to generate supply chain redesign strategies. *International Journal of Physical Distribution and Logistics Management.*, 32(6), pp. 409–430.

Voss, C., Tsikriktsis, N. & Frohlich, M., 2002. Case research in operations management. *International Journal of Operations and Production Management*, 22(2), pp. 195–219.

Wieland, A. & Wallenburg, C.M., 2013. The influence of relational competencies on supply chain resilience: A relational view. *International Jounal of Physical Distribution and Logistics Management*, 43(4), pp. 300–320.

Yin, R.K., 2009. *Case study research: Design and methods*, 4th ed., London: Sage Publications.

# 25

# Risk management and auditing of technology incubators/ science parks

## Innovation enabler to drive capacity of tech ventures

*Jarunee Wonglimpiyarat and Mark Billington*

## 1 Introduction

Technology incubators and science parks play an important role to support economic growth and sustainable development. Policy makers around the world establish them to improve innovation commercialisation, a path to improve national innovative capacity. Given the high-risk nature of technology-based firms which need an incubation scheme, this chapter discusses the application of risk management and auditing to technology incubators/science parks, based on the Committee of Sponsoring Organizations of the Treadway Commission (COSO) framework. The proposed audit plan and performance analysis can be used as a risk management tool to improve effective operation of the incubator programs.

The structure of this chapter is as follows. Section 2 reviews the concept of technology incubators, the Committee of Sponsoring Organizations of the Treadway Commission (COSO) framework, the auditing approach as well as the national innovation system (NIS). Section 3 discusses the role of government policies as well as technology incubators/science parks as an important engine to support innovation development in the United States and China. Section 4 discusses the risk management and auditing of technology incubators/science parks are discussed, and the audit plan focused on the risk assessment using the Committee of Sponsoring Organizations of the Treadway Commission (COSO) framework is sketched. Section 5 provides the performance analysis tool to help perform risk assessments across various aspects of incubation operation. Conclusions and recommendations are drawn in Section 6.

## 2 Theoretical framework

### *2.1 Technology incubators*

A technology incubator is a kind of infrastructure playing a critical role of supporting and nurturing small and medium-sized enterprises (SMEs) and entrepreneurial development (Barrow,

*Table 25.1* Characteristics of technology incubators

| *Host institution* | *University* | *Research facilities* | *Production facilities* | *Technology transfer office* | *Park facilities* | *Incubator* | *Venture capital* |
|---|---|---|---|---|---|---|---|
| Science and research parks | x | x | o | x | x | x | o |
| Innovation centre | o | o | x | x | o | x | o |
| Technology park | x | x | x | x | x | x | x |

*Source*: The Working Group on Innovation and Technology Policy (TIP) of the OECD Committee for Scientific and Technological Policy (CSTP).

Notes:

x = Essential feature of technology incubator

o = Desirable feature of technology incubator

2001; Bøllingtof and Ulhøi, 2005, Wonglimpiyarat, 2014; Pauwels et al., 2016). The incubator program provides business assistance to firms in the early stages of development to increase firm survival rates (Bøllingtof and Ulhøi, 2005; Bøllingtof, 2012). The characteristics of technology incubators are shown in Table 25.1. The incubators provide value-added services such as laboratories and equipment, management and technical support, legal advice and networking to incubating companies (OECD, 1997, 2010, 2015). The incubator resources could help young entrepreneurial firms access new knowledge, expertise and industrial networks (Barrow, 2001; Rothschild and Darr, 2005). By increasing access to financial resources, the business incubation program assists in the process of technology commercialization, leading to new job creation and wealth of the nation (Lewrick, Omar, Raeside and Sailer, 2011; Wonglimpiyarat, 2014; Mas-Verdú, Albort-Morant and Oghazi, 2016).

A technology incubator functions as part of the ecosystem to foster entrepreneurship and sustainable economic development. Technology incubators are generally known under various names such as research transitional labs, innovation centres, science parks, accelerators, technology centres, venture labs and company builders. Figure 25.1 demonstrates a schematic presentation of a technology incubator/science park. Given the high risks associated with the formation of new enterprises, many governments attempt to use a technology incubator/science park as a vehicle for linking technology, entrepreneurs, small and large firms and sources of capital to support technology development and commercialisation (OECD, 1997, 2010, 2015; Lofsten and Lindelof, 2005; McAdam and McAdam, 2008; Wonglimpiyarat, 2010; Murthy, 2012; Khan, 2013; Pauwels et al., 2016).

## 2.2 Committee of Sponsoring Organizations of the Treadway Commission (COSO) framework

The important role of the business incubator in the ecosystem challenges the model of performance measurement. Interestingly, the performance of business incubators can be assessed in various dimensions. From the literature review, the indicators of incubator performance are, for example, the occupancy rate, the number or proportion of firms graduated, the number of business spin-offs, the number of jobs created, the number of patent applications per firm and so forth (Colombo and Delmastro, 2002; Chan and Lau, 2005; Hackett and Dilts, 2008; Schwartz and Hornych, 2010). In the recent study by Özdemir and Şehitoğlu (2013),

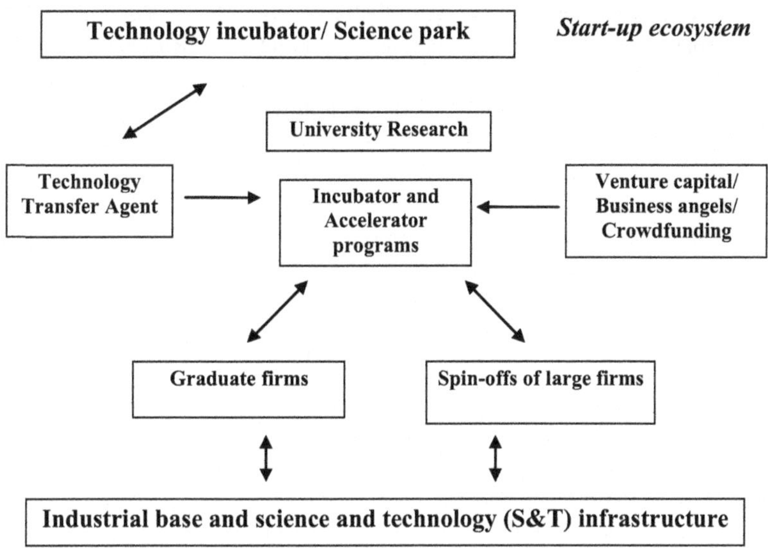


*Figure 25.1* Schematic presentation of technology incubator/science park

*Source*: The author's design, adapted from OECD (1997, 2010, 2015)

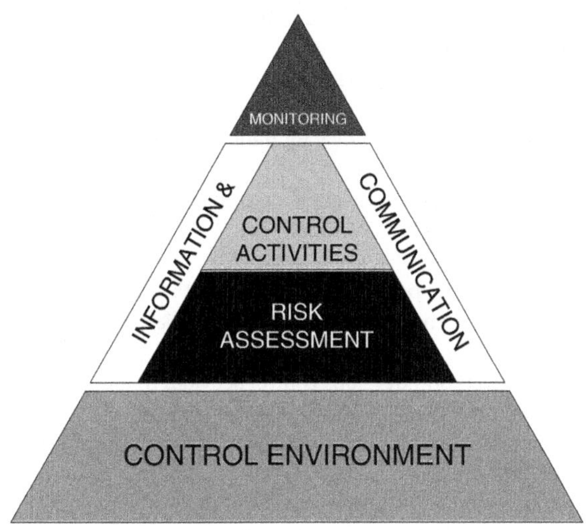


*Figure 25.2* The COSO integrated framework

*Source*: Internal Control COSO Framework 2013 (COSO, 2013)

risk management is one of the important dimensions to measure the performance of business incubation programs.

The Committee of Sponsoring Organizations of the Treadway Commission (COSO) issued the internal control framework to improve efficiency and effectiveness of enterprise risk management (COSO, 2013). The COSO integrated framework (Figure 25.2) consists of five components and 17 relevant principles and serves as an integrated guidance on internal control.

The 2013 framework components are (1) control environment, (2) risk assessment, (3) control activities, (4) information and communication and (5) monitoring (Rittenberg, 2013; Wright, 2013; Clinton et al., 2014).

The COSO Framework 2013 (COSO, 2013) is as follows:

---

**I. Control environment**

The control environment covers the policies, procedures, organization structure and serves as a basis to carry out organization activities.

The control environment comprises principles 1–5 as follows:

(1) The organization demonstrates a commitment to integrity and ethical values.
(2) The board of directors demonstrates independence from management and exercises oversight of the development and performance of internal control.
(3) Management establishes, with board oversight, structures, reporting lines, and appropriate authorities and responsibilities in the pursuit of objectives.
(4) The organization demonstrates a commitment to attract, develop, and retain competent individuals in alignment with objectives.
(5) The organization holds individuals accountable for their internal control responsibilities in the pursuit of objectives.

**II. Risk assessment**

Risk assessment is the analysis of risks and potential impacts on the achievement of organization goals and objectives.

The risk assessment comprises principles 6–9 as follows:

(6) The organization specifies objectives with sufficient clarity to enable the identification and assessment of risks relating to objectives.
(7) The organization identifies risks to the achievement of its objectives across the entity and analyzes risks as a basis for determining how the risks should be managed.
(8) The organization considers the potential for fraud in assessing risks to the achievement of objectives.
(9) The organization identifies and assesses changes that could significantly impact the system of internal control.

**III. Control activities**

Control activities include control policies and procedures to ensure that the organization actions are effectively carried out to meet its objectives for financial reporting.

The control activities comprise principles 10–12 as follows:

(10) The organization selects and develops control activities that contribute to the mitigation of risks to the achievement of objectives to acceptable levels.
(11) The organization selects and develops general control activities over technology to support the achievement of objectives.
(12) The organization deploys control activities through policies that establish what is expected and in procedures that put policies into action.

**IV. Information and communication**

Information and communication provide an information exchange system to assist systematic sharing and dissemination of information across the organization.

The information and communication comprise principles 13–15 as follows:

(13) The organization obtains or generates and uses relevant, quality information to support the functioning of internal control.
(14) The organization internally communicates information, including objectives and responsibilities for internal control, necessary to support the functioning of internal control.
(15) The organization communicates with external parties about matters affecting the functioning of internal control.

**V. Monitoring**

Monitoring is the process of assessing the adequacy and effectiveness of internal controls underlying the organization's activities.

The monitoring comprises principles 16–17 as follows:

(16) The organization selects, develops, and performs ongoing and/or separate evaluations to ascertain whether the components of internal control are present and functioning.

(17) The organization evaluates and communicates internal control deficiencies in a timely manner to those parties responsible for taking corrective action, including senior management and the board of directors, as appropriate.

## *2.3 Auditing approach*

There is a growing realisation for many countries to adopt international accounting standards (IAS) and international financial reporting standards (IFRS), as these standards would make financial statements comparable and prevent financial instability (Dumontier and Raffournier, 1998; Meall, 2004). The International Federation of Accountants (IFAC) is a key organisation influencing the development of global accounting standards. IFAC is an organisation serving the global public interest. The mission of IFAC is to strengthen the worldwide accountancy profession and contribute to the development of strong international economies by establishing and promoting adherence to high-quality professional standards. Many governments suggest the use of IAS and IFRS standards to strengthen the financial system and increase market efficiencies (Street et al., 1999; Street and Bryant, 2000; Ball et al., 2003; Brown and Tarca, 2005; Humphrey et al., 2009; Perera and Chand, 2015).

Financial auditing is an audit of the financial reporting process comprising the annual financial statements, the company's internal controls over the process and all related financial information. The financial auditing approach can be seen as a standard – surveillance – compliance system to achieve transparency of accounts (Carmichael, 2003; Wade, 2007; Rikhardsson and Dull, 2016). Certified public accountants (CPAs, with the CPA licensing adaptive to local economic conditions) are authorised under the law to audit and certify the accounts. In financial auditing approach, the responsibility of CPAs is to examine and analyse the accounting and financial records to ensure compliance with accounting standards and applicable laws and express an opinion on the financial statements based on the audit. The true and fair view based on the generally accepted accounting principles adopted by the accounting profession aims to achieve the objective of assurance and public expectations so that the investors and users in the world's capital markets can use the audited financial information for making economic decisions (Rutherford, 1985; Wade, 2007).

The tax auditing is an important aspect of financial auditing approach in public finance. The possibility of non-compliance with tax laws and loss of tax revenue are issues of critical interest to tax policy makers and enforcement agencies. Currently, many countries have placed importance on the public concern over issues of tax issues and fraud in economic activities. The government aims to use tax auditing to prevent and suppress tax evasion which would adversely affect the economy. However, the scope of tax auditing tends to have a narrower functional focus of obtaining compliance with existing laws and the revenue code (compared to the broader scope of financial auditing to examine the compliance with the accounting act, the companies act and a number of tax laws). Tax compliance includes the examination of activities relating to tax calculations and evaluating whether they are in line with the firm's audit policy (Cuccia, 1994; Mata and Call, 2010; Bayer and Cowell, 2016).

The auditor has a responsibility to apply sufficient procedures to audit the financial statements according to the Generally Accepted Auditing Standards (GAAS). The auditor needs to plan and perform the audit to obtain reasonable assurance that the financial statements are free from material misstatements and faithfully represent the financial performance (a true and fair view of the financial statements in accordance with the Generally Accepted Accounting Principles, or GAAP). An audit also includes evaluating the appropriateness of accounting policies and the adequacy of effective internal controls. The auditor plays an important role in enterprise risk management by performing internal control evaluations and making recommendations to improve the organization's governance. Table 25.2 and Table 25.3 list the respective international accounting standards (IAS) and international financial reporting standards (IFRS) that can be used to apply when preparing a risk-based audit plan.

## 2.4 National innovation system

The concept of the national innovation system (NIS) stresses the importance of networkings among the actors and institutions. In other words, NIS is the interactive system of existing institutions, private and public firms (either large or small), universities and government

*Table 25.2* The international accounting standards (IAS)

| *No.* | *Standard particulars* |
|---|---|
| IAS 1 | Presentation of Financial Statements |
| IAS 2 | Inventories |
| IAS 7 | Statement of Cash Flows |
| IAS 8 | Accounting Policies, Changes in Accounting Estimates and Errors |
| IAS 10 | Events After the Reporting Period |
| IAS 11 | Construction Contracts |
| IAS 12 | Income Taxes |
| IAS 16 | Property, Plant and Equipment |
| IAS 17 | Leases |
| IAS 18 | Revenue |
| IAS 19 | Employee Benefits |
| IAS 20 | Accounting for Government Grants and Disclosure of Government Assistance |
| IAS 21 | The Effects of Changes in Foreign Exchange Rates |
| IAS 23 | Borrowing Costs |
| IAS 24 | Related Party Disclosures |
| IAS 26 | Accounting and Reporting by Retirement Benefit Plans |
| IAS 29 | Financial Reporting in Hyperinflationary Economies |
| IAS 32 | Financial Instruments: Presentation |
| IAS 33 | Earnings Per Share |
| IAS 34 | Interim Financial Reporting |
| IAS 36 | Impairment of Assets |
| IAS 37 | Provisions, Contingent Liabilities and Contingent Assets |
| IAS 38 | Intangible Assets |
| IAS 39 | Financial Instruments: Recognition and Measurement |
| IAS 40 | Investment Property |
| IAS 41 | Agriculture |

*Source*: Deloitte

*Table 25.3* The international financial reporting standards (IFRS)

| *No.* | *Standard particulars* |
|---|---|
| IFRS 1 | First-time Adoption of International Financial Reporting Standards |
| IFRS 2 | Share-based Payment |
| IFRS 3 | Business Combinations |
| IFRS 4 | Insurance Contracts |
| IFRS 5 | Non-current Assets Held for Sale and Discontinued Operations |
| IFRS 6 | Exploration for and Evaluation of Mineral Assets |
| IFRS 7 | Financial Instruments: Disclosures |
| IFRS 8 | Operating Segments |
| IFRS 9 | Financial Instruments |
| IFRS 10 | Consolidated Financial Statements |
| IFRS 11 | Joint Arrangements |
| IFRS 12 | Disclosure of Interests in Other Entities |
| IFRS 13 | Fair Value Measurement |
| IFRS 14 | Regulatory Deferral Accounts |
| IFRS 15 | Revenue from Contracts with Customers |
| IFRS 16 | Leases |

*Source*: Deloitte

agencies aiming at the production, diffusion and exploitation of knowledge within national borders (Lundvall, 1992, 1993, 1998, 1999, 2003; Freeman, 1987; Nelson, 1988, 1993; Fagerberg and Srholec, 2008; Guan and Chen, 2012). Interactions can be achieved by both market mechanism and non-market mechanisms such as collaboration and long-term network arrangements. The NIS concept is a dynamic tool to investigate, formulate, plan and position the national economic and social development by using technology and innovation as the main driving force (Lundvall, 1992, 1993, 1998, 1999, 2003).

An understanding of NIS can help policy makers develop approaches to enhance the nation's innovation performance. The NIS studies explore the interrelations between technological development and the institutional embeddedness of innovative organizations (Freeman, 1987, 1988, 1992; Lundvall, 1992, 1993, 1998, 1999, 2003; Nelson, 1988, 1993, Fagerberg and Srholec, 2008; Guan and Chen, 2012 among others). The level of resources devoted by each nation to research and development (R&D) and innovative activities represents a basic characteristic of the NIS (Lundvall, 1992; Nelson, 1993; MjØset, 1992). Determinants of national economic performance and technological capabilities are the size of a country, R&D intensity and market structure (Freeman, 1987; Archibugi and Michie, 1997).

Schumpeter (1939, 1967) argues that finance and financial institutions are the mainstream of innovation system as well as crucial determinants of the entrepreneurial ability to develop the new economy. The entrepreneurial firms play a crucial role to the economy in terms of creating jobs contributing to economic growth. The financial innovation system provides specific institutional frameworks and interlinkages with financial markets, government agencies, financial institutions, regulatory authorities and research organizations to support innovation activities and strengthen technological capabilities at sectoral and national levels (Pavitt, 1984; Patel and Pavitt, 1994; Archibugi et al., 1999; Malerba, 2002). The financial innovation system thus provides necessary resources required for financing enterprises to enhance economic performance within the national innovation system (Mani, 2004; Hyytinen and Toivanen, 2005).

## 3 Technology incubators/science parks – the engine of high-tech innovation

This section discusses the role of government policies as well as technology incubators/science parks as an important engine to support innovation development in the United States and China. The case of the United States represents the Western country and the world's most innovative economy whereas the case of China represents the influential Asian country and one of the world's fastest growing economy (with average growth rate of 10% per annum). In 2015, the United States and China were in 1st and 22nd position, respectively, according to the International Institute for Management Development (IMD) world competitiveness ranking. According the Global Competitiveness Report 2015–2016 by the World Economic Forum (WEF), the United States was ranked 3rd whereas China was ranked 28th. A comparative case of the United States and China would provide better understanding on the public policies and mechanisms to support high-tech entrepreneurship.

### *3.1 Case of the USA*

The high-technology regions of Silicon Valley and Boston Route 128 (New England) are the centres of innovation and commercialization where the growth of these high-tech economies are a result of government programs and effective technology transfer. Silicon Valley is the world's most dynamic economic region as it is a habitat for innovation and entrepreneurship. This economic region begins in the northwest of the valley in Palo Alto, California, where the theoretical and practical technological research in the area occurs at Stanford University and the Stanford University Research Park (Lee et al., 2000; Wonglimpiyarat, 2010). The rapid industrial development at Silicon Valley comes from the entrepreneurs who have taken aggressive professional and technical risks to create successful companies.

Boston Route 128 is a technologically sophisticated region in the US. The success of Boston is mainly attributable to the business start-ups by Massachusetts Institute of Technology (MIT) graduates to capture the benefits of proximity to MIT and other local institutions. This has fueled the growth of technology-based industries along Boston Route 128. The setup of industrial park and business incubators within the universities in Route 128 is an effective tool for creating jobs, encouraging technology transfer and launching new business ventures. As the corporations are located at university-based incubators or science parks, the physical proximity makes it is easier to withdraw knowledge from the universities to the industries and create new technology spin-offs.

Figure 25.3 portrays the public policies and mechanisms to support innovation system development in the US. The technology incubators/science parks play an important role behind the progress of US economic growth. The successful technology commercialization reflects effective risk management in transferring research results from the research lab to the marketplace. Arguably, the success of US economic growth is a result of its entrepreneur's risk-taking culture to drive the innovation system. The US government has launched various policy initiatives to fill the funding gap. In particular, the federal policy initiatives of the Bayh-Dole Act of 1980 and the Federal Technology Transfer Act of 1986 help facilitate the commercialization of early stage technology. There are many government programs to support the financing of innovations. The major programs to support the firm in early stages are, for example, the Small Business Innovative Research (SBIR) and the Small Business Technology Transfer Program (STTR). The major programs to support the firm in later stages are, for

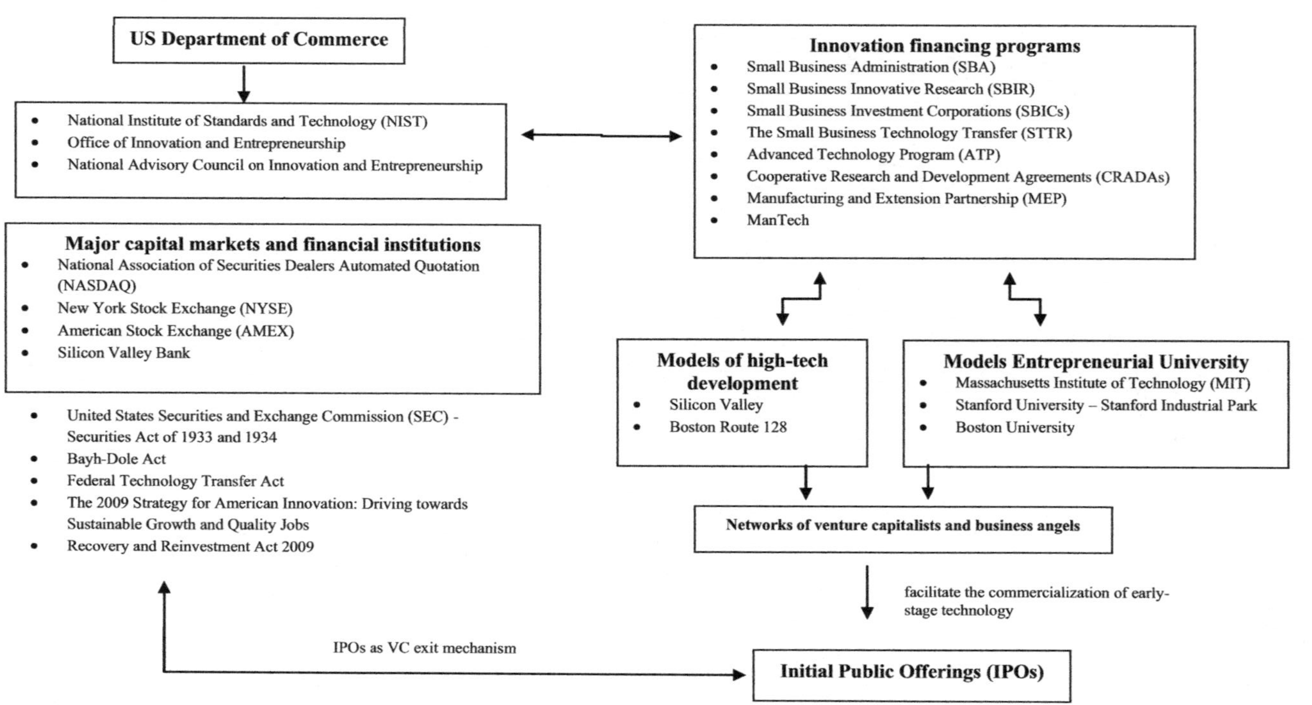


*Figure 25.3* Public policies and mechanisms to support innovation system development in the US

*Source*: The author's design

example, the Advanced Technology Program (ATP), the Defense Advanced Research Projects Agency (DARPA) and Dual Use (Wonglimpiyarat, 2009).

Silicon Valley and Boston Route 128 represent the dynamic model of high-tech innovation and have become symbols of technopreneurship. The economic transformation is the result of collaborative networks between the scientists of the high-tech industries and entrepreneurs to bring new ideas to market. The Hewlett-Packard is an important high-tech entrepreneurship model among others (such as General Electric, Cisco, Yahoo, Google, Charles Schwab, Netflix) that brings about regeneration of Silicon Valley. The presence of strong science and technology-based research institutions in Cambridge like Massachusetts Institute of Technology (MIT), Harvard University and Boston University helps form the high-tech industries and support the proliferation of technology spin-offs. MIT has focused its policy towards cooperation with industry to develop spin-off firms; Harvard University has set up the Harvard Innovation Lab (i-lab) as a venture incubation program to support entrepreneurial ventures; Boston University has set up the Photonics Center as an incubator to bring business and academia closer together for commercial exploitation. These incubation programs are important resources in bridging the culture gap between the academic and industrial world.

It is argued that the economic transformation of Silicon Valley and Boston Route 128 is the result of collaborative networks between the scientists of the high-tech industries and entrepreneurs to bring new ideas to market. The dense industrial networks, knowledge intensity and community dynamics between the government and industrial sectors as well as the supply of venture capital provide effective mechanisms to encourage entrepreneurship and innovation. Further, the US government provides favorable tax policies, such as tax-exempt capital gains and pension funds as investment incentives to facilitate the development of high-tech industry. The US government under President Obama administration simplified the research and experimentation tax credit in attempts to spur productive entrepreneurship and economic performance of the innovation system.

### *3.2 Case of China*

China has tried to remodel itself into an innovation-driven economy since joining the World Trade Organization (WTO) in 2001. China has launched various innovation policies to catch up with leading-edge countries. At present, it is one of the fastest growing economies in the world whereby the Chinese government has adopted trade liberalization policies and various government policies to drive the innovation system. Realizing the importance of small- and medium-sized enterprises (SMEs) in economic development as SMEs account for 90% of the total number of companies in China, the Chinese government has implemented SME policies to drive the innovation system. The 12th National Economic and Social Development Plan (5-year plan) is the major government policy that places a specific emphasis on supporting SMEs in terms of creating an environment conducive to entrepreneurship and innovation for SMEs.

Figure 25.4 depicts the public policies and mechanisms to support innovation system development in China. The Chinese government plays an important role in developing policies and strategies to support the innovation system, for example, the Decision on Developing High-Tech and Realizing Industrialization (CCCP) sets forth the tenth plan (2001–2005) to promote S&T based innovation commercialization. The Guideline for Developing National University Science Parks provides a plan to promote the development of university science parks. The government policy in encouraging R&D can be seen a result of adopting Deng Xiaoping's open-door policy to encourage foreign investments and attract new technologies. The

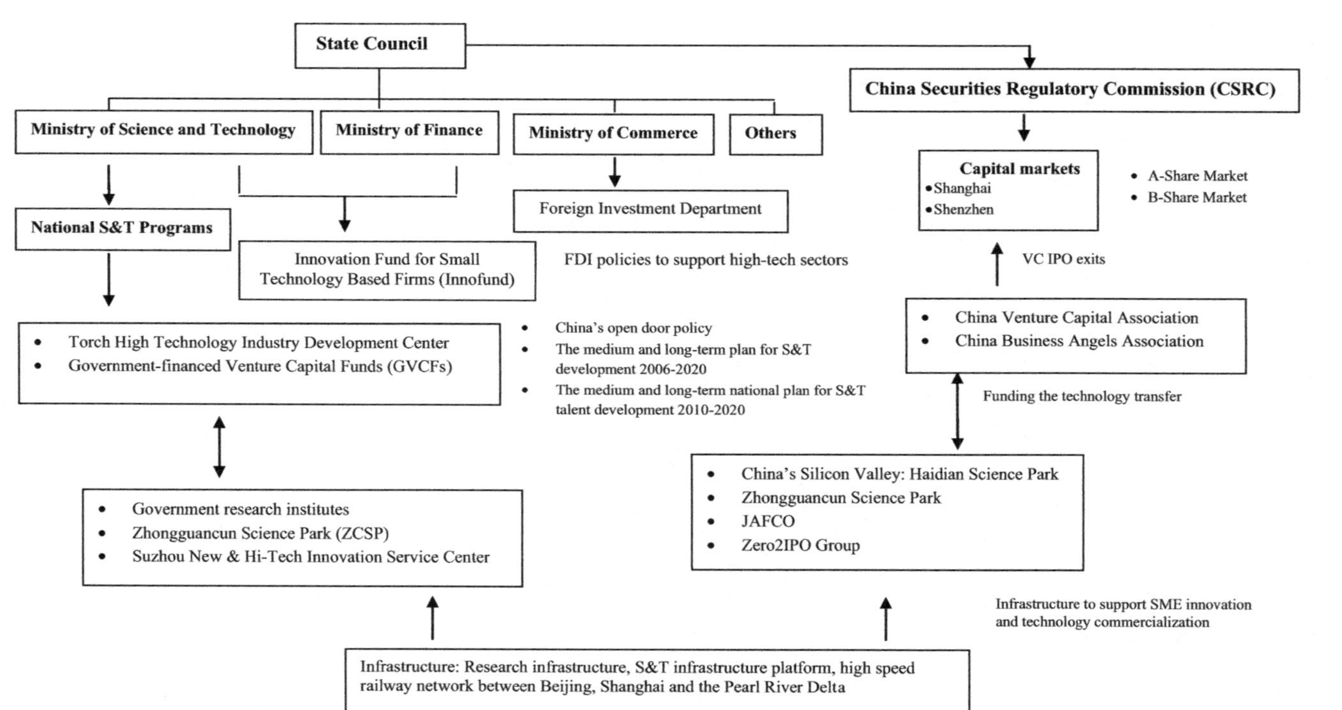


*Figure 25.4* Public policies and mechanisms to support innovation system development in China

*Source*: The author's design

major policy of the Ministry of Science and Technology includes the guidelines on national medium- and long-term program for science and technology development during the period of 2006–2020.

Currently, the national industrial policy has placed a greater emphasis on strengthening clusters of special economics and high technology zones as the government realizes their crucial role in offering infrastructure for implementing the innovation strategies. The Ministry of Science and Technology also assumes a significant role in the design and implementation of national innovation policies. The special economic zones (SEZs) and Science Parks were established to foster new technology development. In particular, the Torch Program was developed to support the creation of industrial clusters. The national Science and Technology Industrial Parks (STIPs) were also established to support high-technology enterprises. The national STIPs were missioned by the Torch Program to promote the development of innovation clusters and advance upgrades in high technologies. Zhongguancun Science Park (ZCSP) is a major technology incubator/science park established to emulate the success of Silicon Valley in the US. It is situated in Beijing's Haidian District and near Tsinghua and Peking Universities. It is the home to high-tech start-ups which grow into global firms like Lenovo, Baidu and Xiaomi. Zhongguancun Science Park is thus recognized as China's Silicon Valley.

The Chinese government provides grants, loans and other incentives (such as tax incentives for R&D, low income tax rates for high-technology enterprises) to drive innovation and growth. These programs are a result of government intervention to fill SME financing gap. Taking into account the public policy, President Xi Jinping's open-door policies have emphasized the innovative SMEs development (President Xi Jinping's open-door policies to build national innovative capacity comprise patriotism (or *aiguo*), innovation (or *chuangxin*), inclusiveness (or *baorong*) and morality (or *houde*)). Moreover, the Chinese government has reduced the corporate income tax rate and value-added tax (VAT) to promote high-technology enterprises. The Chinese government has also intensified its effort to attract foreign direct investment (FDI) to support the industries. To put it another way, the FDI policies have helped the country access foreign capital and technologies. Interestingly, the open-door policy has enabled China to remodel itself from an agriculture-based economy towards an innovation-driven economy.

## 4 Risk management and auditing of technology incubators/science parks

Technology incubators/science parks are used as a strategy and tool by policy makers around the world to support entrepreneurial development and increase innovative capacity of nations. However, there are no particular standards to assist technology auditing. The traditional audit approach has the limitations for application to auditing of technology incubators/science parks. The following audit plan thus attempts to address the risks associated with technology incubators/science parks using the Committee of Sponsoring Organizations of the Treadway Commission (COSO) framework. It serves as a risk-based audit plan to help assess risk and improve security of incubation operation.

## 5 Performance analysis tool for the incubator programs

In evaluating and monitoring the performance of technology incubators and science parks, the performance analysis tool as shown below provides a non-exhaustive list of aspects that should be taken into account in auditing. The performance analysis is measured on a scale of 0–5 along the spectrum of activities performed by the technology incubators/science parks.

*Technology Incubators/Science Parks Risk-based Audit Plan*

**1. Audit objectives**

To examine the operation and performance of technology incubators/science parks in meeting the goals and objectives outlined in the organization strategy. The audit work includes assessment of the program efficiency and effectiveness in line with the organization policy.

**2. Scope of audit**

The auditing scope includes testing to assess adequacy of internal control designs and operating control effectiveness.

**3. Auditors assuming the audit responsibilities**

(Internal Audit Department and. . . . . . . . . . )

**4. Period of audit**

(No. of days. . . . . . . . . . . . . . . . . .)

**5. Budgeted expenses for auditing**

(Budget amount USD. . . . . . . . . . . . . . . . . .)

| **6. Detailed audit plan** | **Working paper reference** | **Prepared by/Date** |
|---|---|---|
| *6.1 Infrastructure* | | |
| 6.1.1 Check the period of setting up the incubator programs with a building contract | | |
| 6.1.2 Determine if the developmental milestones of building infrastructure are in line with the action plan | | |
| 6.1.3 Examine, on a test basis, the activities taken to bring the incubator plan into practice | | |
| 6.1.4 Assess and evaluate the continuity of funding to support the operation of technology incubators/science parks (the going concern principle) | | |
| 6.1.5 Examine the overall readiness of infrastructure and facilities to assist incubating companies (e.g. laboratory equipment, computer facilities, etc.) to verify the existence and completeness | | |
| 6.1.6 Examine the structural layout of setting up technology incubators/science parks<br>• Organization structure<br>• Employment status (directors, managers, employees, workers, staffs, etc.)<br>• Status of the specialists working for technology incubators/science parks<br>• Sources for recruiting staffs to operate the incubation programs | | |
| 6.1.7 Calculate the breakeven point of technology incubators/science parks (the payback period that would generate excess returns to cover its fixed and variable costs) | | |

*(Continued)*

(Continued)

| *6.2 Management of technology incubators/science parks* |
|---|
| 6.2.1 Assess the ability of technology incubators/science parks in serving the incubating companies according to the incubation goals<br>6.2.2 Analyse the ability of technology incubators/science parks in functioning as innovation enabler/innovation accelerators to support technology-based firms<br>6.2.3 Analyse the success of setting up technology incubators/science parks<br>• Success in terms of job creation, increased employment, creation of new tech ventures<br>• Success in terms of transferring technology from the laboratory to commercialisation<br>• The number of technology spin-offs<br>• The number of technology patents<br>• Success in financial terms (return on investment (ROI), internal rate of return (IRR), economic value added (EVA), etc.)<br>6.2.4 Evaluate the efficiency in managing space rented to tenants in the technology incubators/science parks<br>6.2.5 Calculate the utilization rate of providing office area and manufacturing space to support start-up businesses<br>• Analyse the utilization rate of providing space and incubating services to support in-house projects, spin-off projects and other programs<br>6.2.6 Review the residency fees charged to tenants on the basis of reasonableness<br>• Rental fee (charged as a fixed rate or variable rates)<br>• Other service fees (expenses charged based on the flat rate percentage or variable rate according to the rental area)<br>• Consultancy service fees (expenses charged based on the flat rate percentage or variable rate according to the rental area)<br>6.2.7 Examine the rules/regulations for approval as an incubating company and assess the basis of incubator's selection criteria to ensure that they are in line with the policy and objectives of technology incubators/science parks<br>6.2.8 Examine if the rules/regulations for exiting companies are in line with the policy and objectives of technology incubators/science parks<br>6.2.9 Review the actions taken to address risks and uncertainties in operating the technology incubators/science parks<br>6.2.10 Assess the effectiveness of establishing collaborative partnership with other organizations at the national and international levels in promoting the process of technology transfer and commercialisation |

***6.3 Management of venture capital (VC) financing***

6.2.11 Examine the rules of VC financing to ensure that they are in line with the policies of technology incubators/ science parks

6.2.12 Review the VC investments if they could finally create new tech ventures, increase exports, make value-added contribution to the industrial sector (evaluation can be performed by computing the aggregate value)

6.2.13 Examine sources of finance for tech ventures (e.g. grants, special rate loans etc.) and determine whether they are in line with the control objectives

6.2.14 Assess the effectiveness of transferring lab results to industry
(Assessment can be made using the ratios of VC investments to the total budget)

6.2.15 Review the size of VC-backed finance to ensure that the deals are in line with the policy to support entrepreneurial development

6.2.16 Evaluate efficiency of investments through VC funds and their functions to support high-potential entrepreneurs and SMEs

6.2.17 Evaluate the VC investment ratio by comparing the portion of VC financing with the authorized share capital and determine whether the ratio is in line with the investment policy

Prepared by ______________________
Signature

Examined by ______________________
Signature

Approved by ______________________
Signature

The scale of quantitative measurement would help decrease subjective judgement. The proposed performance analysis tool would provide confidence to determine whether the operation of incubating programs meets their objectives. The audit areas covered in the performance analysis tool include the following aspects.

- Entrepreneurial development
- Product/process innovations
- Production
- Marketing
- Management
- Finance and investments

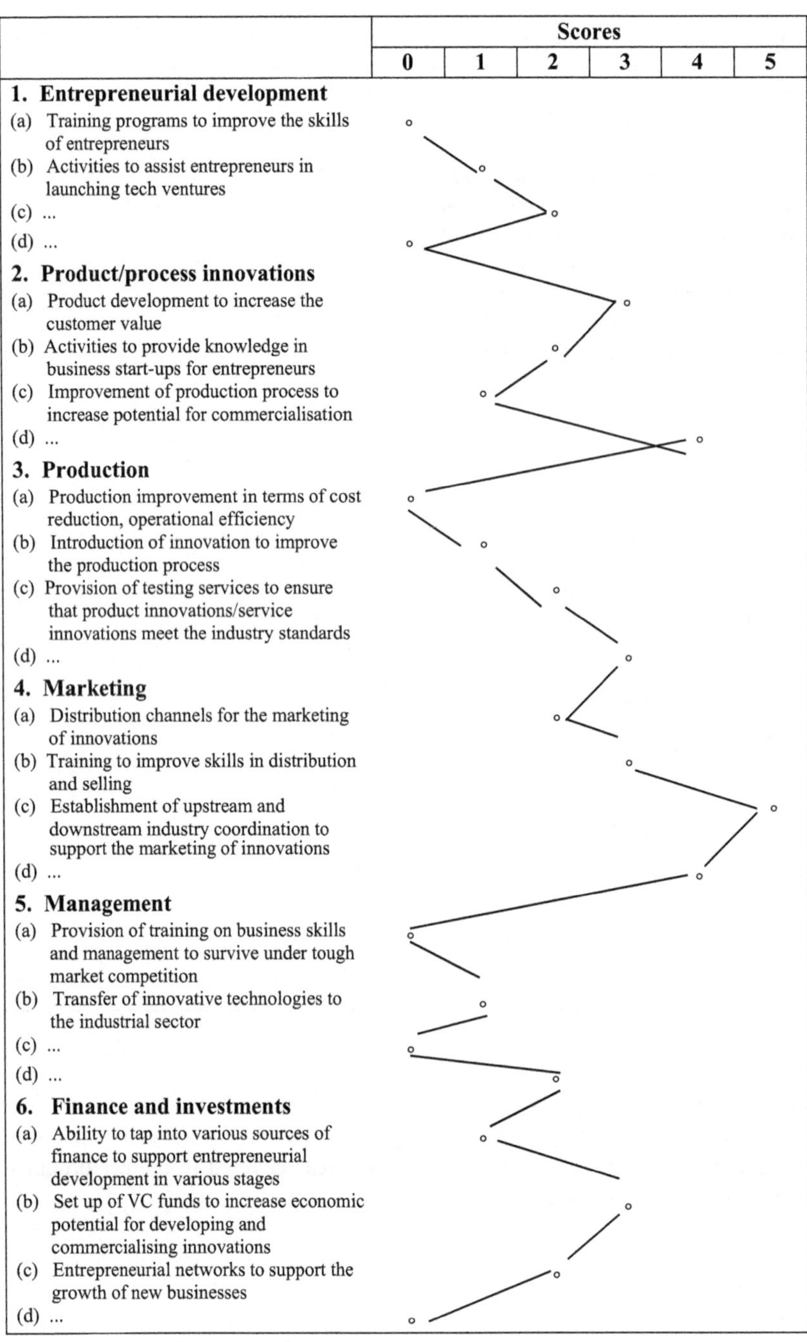

Scores
0
1
2
3
4
5
1. Entrepreneurial development
(a) Training programs to improve the skills of entrepreneurs
(b) Activities to assist entrepreneurs in launching tech ventures
(c) ...
(d) ...
2. Product/process innovations
(a) Product development to increase the customer value
(b) Activities to provide knowledge in business start-ups for entrepreneurs
(c) Improvement of production process to increase potential for commercialisation
(d) ...
3. Production
(a) Production improvement in terms of cost reduction, operational efficiency
(b) Introduction of innovation to improve the production process
(c) Provision of testing services to ensure that product innovations/service innovations meet the industry standards
(d) ...
4. Marketing
(a) Distribution channels for the marketing of innovations
(b) Training to improve skills in distribution and selling
(c) Establishment of upstream and downstream industry coordination to support the marketing of innovations
(d) ...
5. Management
(a) Provision of training on business skills and management to survive under tough market competition
(b) Transfer of innovative technologies to the industrial sector
(c) ...
(d) ...
6. Finance and investments
(a) Ability to tap into various sources of finance to support entrepreneurial development in various stages
(b) Set up of VC funds to increase economic potential for developing and commercialising innovations
(c) Entrepreneurial networks to support the growth of new businesses
(d) ...


By scoring the activities of the incubator programs in details as shown in the graph above, it will help identify the strengths and weaknesses of operation. By combining the risk-based audit plan and performance analysis tool in technology auditing, this form of gap analysis would provide an overall picture to understand which areas need to be improved and which areas perform well. Furthermore, the performance analysis tool can help the management gain insights of relevant risks and potential impacts along the incubator program activities and plan for the risk management approach effectively.

## 6 Conclusions and recommendations

Technology incubators and science parks are seen as an important mechanism to foster innovations. Policy makers around the world establish the incubator programs to promote technology transfer and commercialisation – a path to improve technological innovations. This chapter proposes the audit plan and performance analysis tool to assist risk assessments across the aspects of entrepreneurial development, product/process innovations, production, marketing, management as well as finance and investments. The application of risk management and auditing to technology incubators/science parks is based on the Committee of Sponsoring Organizations of the Treadway Commission (COSO) framework. Under the rising challenges of technology incubators/science parks in fostering innovations, the proposed audit plan and performance analysis tool can be used as a risk management approach to improve effective operation of the incubator programs and maximize the success of emerging businesses.

## References

Albort-Morant, G. and Oghazi, P. (2016), 'How useful are incubators for new entrepreneurs?', *Journal of Business Research*, Vol. 69(6), pp. 2125–2129.

Archibugi, D., Howells, J. and Michie, J. (1999), 'Innovation systems in a global economy', *Technology Analysis and Strategic Management*, Vol. 11(4), pp. 527–539.

Archibugi, D. and Michie, J. (1997), 'Technological globalisation or national systems of innovation', *Futures*, Vol. 29(2), pp. 121–137.

Ball, R., Robin, A., and Wu, J. S. (2003), 'Incentives versus standards: Properties of accounting income in four east Asian countries', *Journal of Accounting and Economics*, Vol. 36(1–3), pp. 235–270.

Barrow, C. (2001), *Incubators: A Realist's Guide to the World's Business Accelerators*, Wiley, Chichester.

Bayer, R. and Cowell, F. (2016), 'Tax compliance by firms and audit policy', *Research in Economics*, Vol. 70(1), pp. 38–52.

Brown, R. and Tarca, A. (2005), 'A commentary on issues relating to the enforcement of international financial reporting standards in the EU', *European Accounting Review*, Vol. 14(1), pp. 181–212.

Carmichael, D. R. (2003), *Professionalism is primary*. Prepared remarks for the AICPA National Conference, December 12, 2003, Washington, DC.

Chan, K. and Lau, T. (2005), 'Assessing technology incubator programs in the science park: The good, the bad and the ugly', *Technovation*, Vol. 25(10), pp. 1215–1228.

Colombo, M. G. and Delmastro, M. (2002), 'How effective are technology business incubators: Evidence from Italy', *Research Policy*, Vol. 31(7), pp. 1103–1122.

Cuccia, A. D. (1994), 'The economics of tax compliance: What do we know and where do we go?', *Journal of Accounting Literature*, Vol. 13, pp. 81–116.

Dumontier, P. and Raffournier, B. (1998), 'Why firms comply voluntarily with IAS: An empirical analysis with Swiss data', *Journal of International Financial Management and Accounting*, Vol. 9(3), pp. 216–245.

Fagerberg, J. and Srholec, M. (2008), 'National innovation systems, capabilities and economic development', *Research Policy*, Vol. 37(9), pp. 1417–1435.

Freeman, C. (1987), *National Systems of Innovation: The Case of Japan Technology Policy and Economics Performance: Lessons from Japan*, Pinter Publishers, London.

Freeman, C. (1988), Japan: A new national system of innovation. In: Dosi, G., Freeman, C., Nelson, R., Silverberg, G., and Soete, L. (Eds.), *Technical Change and Economic Theory*, Pinter, London.

Freeman, C. (1992), Formal Scientific and Technical Institutions in the National System of Innovation. In: Lundvall, B. (Ed.), *National Systems of Innovation: Towards a Theory of Innovation and Interactive Learning*, Pinter, London.

Guan, J. and Chen, K. (2012), 'Modeling the relative efficiency of national innovation systems', *Research Policy*, Vol. 41(1), pp. 102–115.

Hackett, S.M. and Dilts, D.M. (2008), 'Inside the black box of business incubation: Study B scale assessment, model refinement, and incubation outcomes, *Journal of Technology Transfer*, Vol. 33(5), pp. 439–471.

Humphrey, C., Loft, A., and Woods, M. (2009), 'The global audit profession and the international financial architecture: Understanding regulatory relationships at a time of financial crisis', *Accounting, Organizations and Society*, Vol. 34, pp. 810–825.

Hyytinen, A. and Toivanen, O. (2005), 'Do financial constraints hold back innovation and growth? Evidence on the role of public policy', *Research Policy*, Vol. 34(9), pp. 1385–1403.

Khan, M.R. (2013), 'Mapping entrepreneurship ecosystem of Saudi Arabia', *World Journal of Entrepreneurship, Management and Sustainable Development*, Vol. 9(1), pp. 28–54.

Lewrick, M., Omar, M., Raeside, R. and Sailer, K. (2011), 'Education for entrepreneurship and innovation: Management capabilities for sustainable growth and success', *World Journal of Entrepreneurship, Management and Sustainable Development*, Vol. 6(1/2), pp. 1–18.

Lofsten, H. and Lindelof, P. (2005), 'R&D networks and product innovation patterns academic and non-academic new technology-based firms on science parks', *Technovation*, Vol. 28, pp. 277–290.

Lundvall, B. (1992), *National Systems of Innovation: Towards a Theory of Innovation and Interactive Learning*, Pinter, London.

Lundvall, B. (1993), User-producer relationships, national systems of innovation and internationalization. In: Foray, D. and Freeman, C. (Eds.), *Technology and the Wealth of Nations*, Pinter, London.

Lundvall, B. (1998), 'Why study national systems and national styles of innovation?', *Technology Analysis & Strategic Management*, Vol. 10(4), pp. 407–422.

Lundvall, B. (1999), *National Business Systems and National Systems of Innovation*, Special Issue on Business Systems, International Studies of Management and Organisation.

Lundvall, B. (2003), *National Innovation System: History and Theory*, Aalborg University, Aalborg, Denmark.

Malerba, F. (2002), 'Sectoral Systems of Innovation and Production', *Research Policy*, Vol. 31, pp. 247–264.

Mani, S. (2004), 'Financing of Innovation – A survey of various institutional mechanisms in Malaysia and Singapore', *Journal of Technology Innovation*, Vol. 12(2), pp. 185–208.

Mata, P. and Call, R.C. (2010), 'Best practices for creating, maintaining, and protecting state income tax audit files', *Tax Executive*, Vol. 62(1), pp. 25–31.

McAdam, M. and McAdam, R. (2008), 'High-tech start-ups in university science park incubators: The relationship between the start-up's lifecycle progression and use of the incubator's resources', *Technovation*, Vol. 28, pp. 277–290.

Meall, L. (2004), 'Technology: IAS/IFRS – Can you comply?', *Accountancy*, Vol. 133(1329), pp. 73–74.

Mjøset, L. (1992), *The Irish Economy in a Comparative International Perspective*, National Economic and Social Council, Dublin.

Murthy, V.P. (2012), 'Integrating corporate sustainability and strategy for business performance', *World Journal of Entrepreneurship, Management and Sustainable Development*, Vol. 8(1), pp. 5–17.

Nelson, R. (1988), Institutions Supporting Technical Change in the United States. In: Dosi, G., Freeman, C., Nelson, R., Silverberg, G. and Soete, L. (Eds.), *Technical Change and Economic Theory*, Pinter, London.

Nelson, R. (1993), *National Systems of Innovation: A Comparative Study*, Oxford University Press, Oxford.Organisation for Economic Co-operation and Development (OECD) (1997), *Technology Incubators: Nurturing Small Firms*, OECD Publishing, Paris.

Organisation for Economic Co-operation and Development (OECD) (2010), *High-Growth Enterprises: What Governments Can Do to Make a Difference*, OECD studies on SMEs and entrepreneurship, OECD Publishing, Paris.

Organisation for Economic Co-operation and Development (OECD) (2015), *OECD Studies on SMEs and Entrepreneurship Russian Federation: Key Issues and Policies*, OECD studies on SMEs and entrepreneurship, OECD Publishing, Paris.

Özdemir, O. C. and Şehitoğlu, Y. (2013), 'Assessing the Impacts of Technology Business Incubators: A framework for Technology Development Centers in Turkey', *Procedia – Social and Behavioral Sciences*, Vol. 75, pp. 282–291.Patel, P. and Pavitt, K. (1994), 'National innovation systems: Why they are important, and how they might be measured and compared', *Economics of Innovation and New Technology*, Vol. 3(1), pp. 77–95.

Pauwels, C., Clarysse, B., Wright, M. and Van Hove, J. (2016), 'Understanding a new generation incubation model: The accelerator', *Technovation*, Vol. 50–51, pp. 13–24.

Pavitt, K. (1984), 'Sectoral patterns of technical change: Towards a taxonomy and a theory', *Research Policy*, Vol. 13(6), pp. 343–373.

Perera, D. and Chand, P. (2015), 'Issues in the adoption of international financial reporting standards (IFRS) for small and medium-sized enterprises (SMES)', *Advances in Accounting*, Vol. 31(1), pp. 165–178.

Rikhardsson, P. and Dull, R. (2016), 'An exploratory study of the adoption, application and impacts of continuous auditingtechnologies in small businesses', *International Journal of Accounting Information Systems*, Vol. 20, pp. 26–37.

Rothschild, L. and Darr, A. (2005) 'Technological incubators and the social construction of innovation networks: an Israeli case study', *Technovation*, Vol. 25(1), pp. 59–67.

Rutherford, B.A. (1985), 'The true and fair view doctrine: A search for explication', *Journal of Business Finance & Accounting*, Vol. 12, pp. 483–494.

Schumpeter, J.A. (1939), *Business Cycles: A Theoretical, Historical and Statistical Analysis of the Capitalist Process*, 2 Vols., McGraw-Hill, New York.

Schumpeter, J.A. (1967), *The Theory of Economic Development*, 5th edn., Oxford University Press, New York.

Schwartz, M. and Hornych, C. (2010), 'Cooperation patterns of incubator firms and the impact of incubator specialization: Empirical evidence from Germany', *Technovation*, Vol. 30(9/10), pp. 485–495.

Street, D.L. and Bryant, S.M. (2000), 'Disclosure level and compliance with IASs: A comparison of companies with and without US listings and filings, *International Journal of Accounting*, Vol. 35(3), pp. 305–329.

Street, D.L., Gray, S.J. and Bryant, S.M. (1999), 'Acceptance and observance of International Accounting Standards: An empirical study of companies claiming to comply with IASs', *International Journal of Accounting*, Vol. 34(1), pp. 11–48.

Wade, R. (2007), 'A new global financial architecture?, *New Left Review*, Vol. 46, pp. 113–129.

Wonglimpiyarat, J. (2009), 'Strategies for technology commercialization – Silicon Valley as model of venture capital financing', *International Journal of Technology, Policy and Management*, Vol. 9(3), pp. 222–234.

Wonglimpiyarat, J. (2010), 'Commercialisation strategies of technology: Lessons from silicon valley', *Journal of Technology Transfer*, Vol. 35(2), pp. 225–236.

Wonglimpiyarat, J. (2014), 'Incubator policy to support entrepreneurial development, technology transfer and commercialization', *World Journal of Entrepreneurship, Management and Sustainable Development*, Vol. 10(4), pp. 334–351.

# Part VI

# Qualitative and quantitative risk modeling

# 26

# What's in a name?

*Kate Boothroyd*

> Whatever words we utter should be chosen with care for people will hear them and be influenced by them for good or ill.
>
> —*Buddha (Goodreads 2016)*

This quote from Buddha is as valid in the risk management process as in any personal or business situation. Words are the way we communicate information and ideas, and can be powerful, moving and suggestive. They can also be, and often are, misused, misunderstood and mistaken. Words have the ability to heal and the ability to harm and they can make situations better or worse, "Because even the smallest of words can be the ones to hurt you, or save you" (Natsuki Takaya, Goodreads 2016).

With the spoken word, there is better understanding of what is said as you can hear inflections and meaning, and if being said face-to-face, you can see people's body language, all of which does not often come across in the written word. There is also a much quicker reaction to the spoken word as you can sense whether the words are being understood through the reactions and challenges that are being put forward.

Once words are committed to print, a lot of that meaning and understanding is lost. So the way we talk about risk and the words that we use to describe risks and the management of them is more fundamental to the successful and effective implementation of risk management than many people realise.

Over the following pages, I will explore words within the sphere of risk management, considering their use and interpretation, and how, when used well, they can help make risk management a valuable tool within our organisations, or if used incorrectly can provide no value at all or can destroy value.

First, let's consider the word 'risk': it is used or understood in many different ways. A quick internet search for the definition of 'risk' always generates terms such as peril, hazard or harm. At the same time words such as probability, chance, likelihood or possibility are also provided. However, peril, hazard and harm all point to effect, and a bad one at that, whereas probability, chance, likelihood or possibility are all related to uncertainty. So what is 'risk'?

## Key concepts

The International Standard on risk management, ISO 31000, defines risk as the 'effect of uncertainty on objectives' (ISO 2018:1), which covers both points above; effect and uncertainty. In the project arena, the definition of risk is often shortened even further to 'an uncertainty that matters'. In that context, not all uncertainties are risks; if an uncertain event were to occur, but it would not affect the objectives, then it should not be considered a risk, as it would not matter. On the other hand, all risks are uncertainties (Hillson 2009:10). The ISO goes further in relation to effect, stating that it is a deviation from the expected – either positive or negative (ISO 2018:1). This means that, as far as the ISO is concerned, a risk can be a threat or an opportunity.

This definition of the word risk can be difficult for some people and organisations to grasp, because it doesn't tie in with the dictionary definitions shown previously, or with some of the common uses of risk assessment, such as insurance or health and safety, where risk is considered a hazard or harm. However, the ISO definition has been used for some time by many different professional associations and institutions, such as the Project Management Institute (PMI). Some people feel quite strongly about the alteration of the definition of risk, with one admonishing the PMI, stating that "such an odd deviation from the general use of a common word can happen only in an insular group that feels it has to reinvent such concepts" (Hubbard 2009:90). As such, some people or organisations consider risk as only the downside, or negative or threat aspect, and do not recognise opportunity in the definition of risk. The upside or positive aspect, if considered at all, is kept separate using the word opportunity, so you would have risks and opportunities.

However, as stated earlier, ISO 31000 defines risk as both an opportunity or a threat. The British Standard on risk management, BS 31100, uses the same definition (BS 2011:6). Even the COSO definition of risk is changing. The 2004 version of the Enterprise Risk Management framework considers uncertainty that presents both risk and opportunity. These risks and opportunities are defined as 'events with a negative impact represent risks, which can prevent value creation or erode existing value. Events with positive impact may offset negative impacts or represent opportunities' (COSO 2004:2). In June 2017, COSO updated the Framework and re-issued it with a new title – Enterprise Risk Management – Integrating with Strategy and Performance, which highlights the importance of considering risk in both the strategy-setting process and in driving performance. The updated publication contains a slightly new definition of risk: 'the possibility that events will occur and affect the achievement of strategy and business objectives', where an event is 'an occurrence of set of occurrences'. In addition, the publication states that 'Organizations commonly focus on those risks that may result in a negative outcome . . . However, events can also have positive outcomes' (COSO:17%). So with just a slight change in words, the meaning of the word risk has changed as it is now 'considering all reasonable possibilities – both positive and negative aspects of risk' (COSO 2017:14%).

It seems that despite some opposition to the linkage between opportunity and threat in the definition of risk it is becoming part of the standard risk language. However, it is entirely up to each organisation to decide how they are going to define risk.

Whatever that decision, it should be defined clearly and consistently used throughout all risk communication, both internally and externally.

## Words

As can been seen from the definition of the word 'risk' above, words can mean different things to different people:

- Words are used to describe risks and management actions in risk registers or risk logs; words that are usually read with no other explanation, so they need to say everything you want the reader to understand
- Words and their structure and order can very easily be misunderstood by the reader. Not everyone will read the same message you are trying to impart. The order of the words and the grammar used can change the meaning of a sentence entirely. The book *Eats, Shoots and Leaves* (Truss 2009) bemoans the misuse of punctuation in the English language. Even the title of the book is confusing: by using one comma, the title conveys a picture of someone eating, shooting and leaving; whereas the actual picture on the front cover of the book is of a panda in a bamboo forest where it would eat shoots and leaves (although it does hold a gun, just to add to the confusion).
- Words can have different meanings in different countries, and even within different areas of the same country. For example, the luggage compartment in a car in England is called a 'boot', whereas in America it is called a 'trunk'. 'Chips' in the UK mean sliced fried potatoes served hot, and in the US they are called 'fries'. In the UK, more thinly sliced potatoes that are fried and served hot are called 'French fries', but in France they are called '*pommes frites*'. Very thinly sliced potatoes, fried (or baked) and served cold are called 'crisps' in the UK, and in the US and Europe they are called 'potato chips'. Confused? And this is in some countries where English is the native language. Consider the difficulties where the reader is not fluent in the language used, and where a lot of information is being given which can sometimes be complex or technical, and where translation is required.

  A case in point is the definition of the word 'likelihood' in ISO 31000. Note 2 in the definition states that 'the English term "likelihood" does not have a direct equivalent in some languages; instead, the equivalent of the term "probability" is often used. However, in English, "probability" is often narrowly interpreted as a mathematical term. Therefore, in risk management terminology, "likelihood" is used with the intent that it should have the same broad interpretation that the term "probability" has in many languages other than English' (ISO 2018:5).
- Words can sound the same but have completely different meanings. For example: they're (they are), their (belonging to) and there (place or position); you're (you are) and your (belonging to); site (location) and sight (vision); or bread (food) and bred (reared).

  Similar sounding words can also mean very different things. Often mistaken in the risk management arena are the words 'averse' and 'adverse', which seem to be used interchangeably. You can be averse to taking risks, but you can't be adverse to taking them, whereas you can have adverse impacts from risks occurring. Averse is an adjective that means strongly against or opposed to, and is usually related to people, where adverse is an adjective that means harmful or unfavourable, and usually relates to an objective or situation.

The Institute of Risk Management in the North West of England held a meeting in June 2016, called 'Risk Management – the KISS Principle (Keep It Simple Stupid)'. It was felt by the organisers that risk management is becoming too complex to be effectively implemented, which is also true for the risks themselves. We all work in an ever-increasing global environment, communicating with people whose first language is not English, and yet they must often communicate in this business language, which is littered with jargon and acronyms.

Students starting university strive to improve their written work to ensure it includes more management and advanced words so that they can be seen to meet academic criteria. Meanwhile, those of us in the business environment are trying to reduce the use of these more advanced words in report writing. "Don't use words too big for the subject. Don't say infinitely when you mean very; otherwise you'll have no word left when you want to talk about something really infinite" (C. S. Lewis, Goodreads 2016).

Risk management is all about finding, creating, communicating and using information to help us make decisions in times of uncertainty. In this day and age, with the massive global and local changes that are occurring, it seems that all times are uncertain.

This means that we need to clearly understand the risks that face us so that we can proactively manage them, and perhaps actively pursue them. We will then not only be prepared for what lies ahead, but also ready to seek out new challenges and opportunities.

This sounds quite reasonable, and many, if not most, organizations are taking steps to introduce, implement or improve risk management. However, there are too many examples of problems and catastrophes in organizations where their risk management process should have made a difference, but didn't. There are many reasons why risk management did not help, but often the causes relate to people, perceptions and culture and their effect on the process and the way risk information has been captured and communicated.

## People

People can quite profoundly influence, and can be influenced by, the risk management process. Using the ISO 31000 eight-step risk management process, we can briefly examine how people interact with the risk management process (ISO 2018:9):

- Scope, Context, Criteria – people within an organisation set objectives, whether at corporate, business, functional, project or activity levels. People then tailor the risk management process to suit their particular situations, and set the risk criteria; the terms of reference against which the significance of risk is evaluated (for example, likelihood and impact scales and risk thresholds.
- Risk identification (risk assessment) – people use information gathered from internal or external sources, and their knowledge and experience to identify risks, both upside opportunities and downside threats.
- Risk analysis (risk assessment) – people consider those identified risks to assess the likelihood of risks occurring and impact if they did occur; to measure the significance of and to prioritise the risks, whether qualitatively, quantitatively or both.
- Risk evaluation (risk assessment) – people decide whether or not these assessed risks are significant in line with the risk thresholds.
- Risk treatment – people decide what to do to manage the risks, hopefully in order of priority, and then they implement those actions (or at least, they should!).

- Monitoring and review – people put the effort in to keeping the risk management process alive and the risk information up to date, to ensure that it is relevant and supports decision making.
- Communication and consultation – people communicate risk information, to ensure expert knowledge is shared, views are considered and risk information is used in decision-making.
- Recording and reporting – people need to capture and disseminate risk information internally and externally, to ensure lessons are learnt, to inform decisions and to ensure that relevant stakeholders are appropriately risk aware.

Through all of those interactions with the risk management process, people are fundamental to its success or failure.

## *Risk type*

We all have different opinions and attitudes about risk arising from our inbuilt risk 'type' and from the different influences and experiences we faced throughout our lives. As mentioned earlier, some people are thought of as risk averse, and some perhaps risk seeking. The basis of this is our risk type.

A personality profiling tool has been developed by Psychological Consultancy Ltd that focuses on a person's propensity or tendency to take risk, and their capacity to manage risks. The Risk-Type Compass is a personality assessment focusing on differences in the way individuals perceive, manage and make decisions about risk. The first set of questions used in the assessment place individuals into one of eight distinctive risk types, which reflect how comfortable and willing the person is to take risk and their resilience in the face of risks occurring.

The following are the eight risk types of the compass with a very brief explanation of the type. The first four types are more risk averse, with people in this area of types being less comfortable in taking risk, and the last four types are more risk seeking, and more comfortable in taking risk (Psychological Consultancy Ltd n.d.):

- Intense – apprehensive, risk aware, dedicated people
- Wary – includes people who are more shrewd, vigilant, controlling
- Prudent – people with a tendency towards being systematic, orthodox, detailed
- Deliberate – people who display confidence, thoroughness and toughness
- Composed – people who are seen as calm, resilient, undaunted
- Adventurous – intrepid, enterprising, optimistic people
- Carefree – those who are seen as more audacious, curious, unconventional
- Excitable – people who tend to be more enthusiastic, anxious, committed.

No risk type is any better than the other, and none should be used in isolation to consider the capacity of a person to undertake their role. However, it is clear that some people may be better suited to particular roles, and a person's risk type can affect decision making and management in risky situations.

The second set of questions in the Risk-Type Compass assessment provide an indication of a person's risk behaviour, or in other words how they can flex their risk type in different situations. Although each risk type is set and will change very little, if at all, over the years, a person's risk behaviour often depends on the situation and can be at odds to their risk type. For example, people who are a risk wary type might be more adventurous in certain situations, and the more adventurous type might be cautious in other situations. A person's ability to flex their behaviour, sometimes outside of their risk type and comfort zone, is valued by leaders and managers in organizations.

Therefore, a person's risk type is not an accurate reflection of the way they will behave in every situation, but does help understand how natural tendencies influence judgements made in different situations, such as how much risk to tolerate, whether the situation is risky and to what degree either positively or negatively, how much preparation is needed before taking risks, how much management is required and how much effort is needed to monitor the situation.

It is not suggested that this tool is used to assess every person's predisposition towards risk within an organisation. However, it has been used successfully to better balance teams within organisations, whether at the project, business, functional or corporate level. If most or all team members are more risk-averse types, then more threat will be recognised, and those more risk seeking will often see fewer threats and more opportunities.

It is healthy for any team to have a certain amount of challenge to ensure the right risks have been identified, both threats and opportunities, and that the appropriate management of those risks is in place. As William Wrigley Jr. (from the chewing gum industry) once said, "When two men in business always agree, one of them is unnecessary" (Goodreads 2016).

## Perceptions – uncertainty and impact

It is clear from the previous sections on words and people that there will be different perceptions regarding risk. Going back to the shortened definition of risk as an uncertainty that matters, perception of what uncertainty is and what matters goes to the heart of some of the problems with risk management.

For this chapter, we can use the COSO definition of uncertainty as being 'the state of not knowing how potential events may or may not manifest' (COSO 2017:17%). Many books have been written about uncertainty, especially in relation to future variability, which is defined here as a range of possible outcomes of a given situation and also as a measure of a spread of a data set.

These definitions move uncertainty more towards the realm of statistical analysis. Statistical analysis underpins many areas of risk management, such as the banking and health sectors and weather forecasting, as a way of forecasting or predicting the future and communicating that information, often to lay people.

However, statistical analysis relies on data, usually historical, which can help in forecasting most situations, but not all. It also relies upon the ability or capability of people to input the right information into the statistical calculations and then to interpret the outputs, which can often leave a lot to be desired.

Let's consider the perceptions we have concerning uncertainty, and what matters, across three important areas that affect us all – our wealth, our health and the weather – and how words used in these areas make such a huge difference in our ability to understand and manage risk.

### *Wealth*

When considering our relative wealth, many will think about the economic crisis that manifested itself in 2008. There are several views regarding the collapse in the banking sector. Some blame the company and board culture. Others blame the use of and dependence on complex mathematical models used to measure risk in the banking sector. A lot of complex statistical models were used to measure complex risks, both of which were understood by very few people. The models were assessing risks that could be predicted and measured using data from the previous few years, covering a boom time. This was an optimistic view of the risks, with insufficient account taken of rare, catastrophic events, meaning it was not very reliable for forecasting. The models also produced single point measures of the risks rather than ranges to reflect uncertainty, giving a false sense of security to the users of the information.

Many blame both culture and mathematical models: 'The outputs came from "black box" computer models and were hard to subject to a commonsense [*sic*] smell test . . . The managers, who made the actual calls, lacked the math skills to understand what the models were doing or how they worked' (Salmon 2009).

On reading some of the numerous sources of information on the economic crisis, it is clear that many people did not understand, or chose not to understand the risks involved in the approaches taken by the banking sector, the impact of which was enormous for the global economy.

Due to the huge sums of money, involved there is a certain amount of detachment in the world of banking and finance from the real impact to the general public when considering. In an interview with the BBC's *Today* programme in 2012, Stephen Hester, the chief executive of Royal Bank of Scotland (RBS), admitted that 'the [banking] industry became a bit detached from society [and that] the cultural change is what, of course, is front and centre in all of our minds. We need to make sure the banking industry reconnects with its customers' (Hester 2012).

The impact on the public, however, is not detached; it is a personal matter. At the end of the day it was individual people's money, houses and livelihoods at risk and at stake, which mattered very much.

### Health

When talking about our health and risk in the medical/health sector, the impact is an even more personal matter. Being told you have a 1 in 12 chance of having cancer (here we are using frequency), or that you were one of the unlucky 7% people who have ocular migraines that develop into a stroke (here we are using probabilities), doesn't really mean much if you are the person being spoken to. In fact, the mere mention of the word cancer or stroke can make any further conversation or discussion on the chances of developing these diseases meaningless for some patients, depending on their experiences, understanding and perceptions.

It becomes a little more disconcerting when you realise that it is not just the general public who don't understand medical statistics, but also some of the medical practitioners who have to communicate risk information to their patients. In a small test conducted by Gerd Gigerenzer and a colleague, they found that 'when the information was presented in probabilities, the majority of physicians in our study grossly overestimated the risk'. When the information was presented in frequencies, 'the majority of physicians . . . responded with the correct answer, or close to it' (Gigerenzer 2002:44).

As stated on the back cover of Gigerenzer's book, 'every day, millions of us confront statistical information that may influence our health decisions, even life-or-death events. How we interpret this information can make a critical difference' (Gigerenzer 2002).

### Weather

When considering the weather, the impact is felt by everybody to different extents, depending on what kind of weather we are talking about and when. To some people weather can pose a threat and to others an opportunity. In flood situations, households and businesses can be waterlogged and even destroyed, but other businesses will benefit from the clean-up operations. Severe cold and snow can bring infrastructure to a standstill, but can be perfect for those testing 4x4 vehicles or children who have a day off from school and can go tobogganing.

Weather forecasting has been undertaken informally for thousands of years with more formal, scientific methods being introduced in the 1800s. Nowadays, statistical analysis and meteorology is used to project how the atmosphere will change within a given time frame.

Usually, forecasts provide the range of predicted temperatures from minimum to maximum and a precipitation probability. The UK's Met Office explains the probability of precipitation (PoP) a little further:

> [A PoP of 10%] means that there is a 1 in 10 chance that precipitation will fall during this period. Another way of looking at this probability is that there is a 9 in 10 chance that it will stay dry. Similarly, a PoP of 80% means an 8 in 10 chance that precipitation will fall, and only a 2 in 10 chance that it will remain dry.
>
> *(Met Office 2014)*

Remember, in Gigerenzer's test with physicians, it was found that physicians understood statistics more readily if they were explained in frequencies rather than probabilities, and the Met Office follows this thinking by providing both explanations of PoP on their website.

In most cases, the longer the time frame, the less reliable the weather forecast, mainly due to the unpredictability of the atmosphere. However, in the early hours of 16 October 1987, southern England and France suffered from a storm bringing hurricane force winds that caused billions of pounds' worth of damage and killed 22 people. The day's weather forecasts had failed to predict the severity of the storm. Earlier, on 15 October, the British weather forecaster Michael Fish said during a televised forecast, "Earlier on today, apparently, a woman rang the BBC and said she heard there was a hurricane on the way . . . well, if you're watching, don't worry, there isn't!" (TV insider 1 2007). Apparently, this related to a different storm over Florida, USA, but was misquoted so often in the British press that the public perceived it to be related to the storm over Europe. Since then, there have been a lot of improvements in weather forecasting, including training for forecasters.

Knowing the unpredictability of the weather does not help individuals or organizations protect their property and livelihoods if probability were the only consideration. In the UK, the Environment Agency provides flood risk information for England and Wales, with national, regional and specific flood risk information and warnings.

In 2005, people in Cumbria, North West England, understood there was a 1 in 100-year chance of flooding. So when there were severe floods in Cumbria that year, many people thought they had encountered their share of flooding for their lifetime. However, 1 in 100-year chance does not mean that there will be a flood once every hundred years. The information provided by the Environment Agency about flooding has changed more recently, and according to the Environment Agency website, the Glenridding area of Cumbria currently has a low flood risk from rivers or the sea, which equates to a chance of flooding of between 0.1% and 1% each year in this area (Environment Agency 2016). This statement is essentially the same as the 1 in 100-year chance, but they can and have been perceived completely differently by people in the area.

The website also states for the same area that there is a high flood risk from surface water; "each year this area has a chance of flooding of greater than 3.3%" (Environment Agency 2016). So there is low flood risk from rivers or the sea, and a high risk from surface water each year, both in the same vicinity and with no more than a 4 in 100 chance. Following the floods in 2005, Cumbria also suffered from flooding in 2009, and in 2015 the Glenridding community was flooded three times in 1 month.

In a presentation to the North West England Regional Group of the Institute of Risk Management (IRM), a principal scientist with the Environment Agency stated that the agency had consulted further with the public, and that the way they were communicating with the public about flood risk was changing again. It was explained that the likelihood of flooding was often misunderstood by the people who were at risk of being flooded, but communication about which areas had flooded in the past, which areas may flood in the future and how deep the flooding will it be, if it does flood, is much more meaningful. This helps people consider what actions they can take to reduce impacts and gives a better understanding of what authorities are also doing to help.

It clear from the three example sectors discussed above that the communication about risk is paramount for proper understanding of the real risks, and the effective actions that can or should be put in place to manage them.

## Culture

As mentioned earlier, the Risk-Type Compass tool helps to better understand the tendency of individuals and groups within an organization to take risk, and their ability to cope with the occurrence of risk. As can be seen in any walk of life 'types' of people often seem to be attracted to each other, forming groups that can develop different behaviours and that hold different perceptions, especially in relation to risk. We have also seen how our perceptions of risk can be hugely influenced by what we are told and what we read.

The IRM has considered behaviours relating to and perceptions of risk in one of its thought leadership papers on risk culture (IRM 2012:7). The paper has suggested a simple ABC approach to risk culture, comprising risk *attitude*, risk *behaviour* and risk *culture*:

- Risk attitude is the position adopted by an individual or group to a risk based on their risk type and risk perception.
- Risk behaviour covers the actions taken in relation to risk, such as decision making, communication, processes, etc.
- Risk culture is defined as 'the values, beliefs, knowledge and understanding about risk shared by a group of people with a common purpose, in particular the employee of an organisation or teams of groups within an organisation'.

Different cultures have already been mentioned when thinking about the words we use to describe a risk, in that different words have different meanings in different countries and in different cultures. The cultures within our work environments are equally important, especially when considering organizational risks.

Culture has been blamed for failures in many organisations and many industries. "It is widely agreed that failures of culture, which permitted excessive and uncontrolled risk-taking and a loss of focus on end clients, were at the heart of the financial crisis" (Power n.d.: 4).

It is clear that even some of the best policies, procedures, frameworks and standards on risk management have not been enough to prevent some catastrophic organizational failures. Some of these failures have been caused by individuals and groups within these organizations who have behaved and been allowed to behave in ways that have put the organizations in harm's way.

Therefore, having a better understanding of the different cultures within your organization will help with plans for effectively implementing risk management and also the capturing and communication of risk information to be used in decision making at any level within the organization.

## Communication

According to ISO Guide 73, communication is the "continual and iterative processes that an organization conducts to provide, share or obtain information, and to engage in dialogue with stakeholders regarding the management of risk" (ISO 2009a:3).

George Bernard Shaw (Goodreads 2016) is quoted as saying "The single biggest problem in communication is the illusion that it has taken place." When communicating risk management information, careful consideration should always be given to the what, when, why, how and to whom questions. A risk register or a risk report are often the only form of risk communication that some audiences see. The words used in those documents must be chosen wisely to ensure that those audiences properly understand the information that is being given.

The main reasons for writing words down are to impart knowledge or to ask permission for action. The person who reads these words must be able to understand quite clearly what was meant by them. Putting words to print (whether on paper or electronically):

- Focuses attention
- Means things are less likely to be forgotten
- Requires the writer to clearly and articulately form meaningful statements or sentences, which helps the writer process the information/situation more thoroughly in a detailed and ordered way
- Can be the basis for better decision making as the reader better understands the situation, and what is being required of them.

If this is the case, the risk register should be a powerful management tool that can be understood by anyone who picks it up. However, they are often used as proof that risk management has been undertaken – a tick-in-the box exercise. The word management is key here; this is not risk register writing, but the proactive management of risks which is extremely difficult if the risks are not clearly and unambiguously named.

## Naming risks

All of the previous 'words' bring us back to the title of this chapter – 'What's in a Name?' As can be seen in the examples above, the failure of risk management in many sectors or organisations is due to complex models or culture. I would like to take this a step further back, to the basics of what the identified risks are and how they have been named. If risks are properly understood in the first instance, the complex models might make more sense, and the some of the cultural issues might be overcome.

The most common proof that risk management is being implemented in an organisation is the existence of a risk register or risk log. These registers can contain many risks covering all areas of an organisation, from admin to audit, from unions to utilities and all categories of risk between. However, when reviewing risk registers, there is often confusion over what the risks really mean.

Going back again to the shortened definition of risk as an uncertainty that matters, it is clear that some risks are not uncertainties and others don't really matter. What makes this understanding more difficult is that many organisations shorten their risks to 'risk names', which are then used for reporting and reviewing purposes. The problem with this is that if the risk has been shortened (even if it had been well written in the first place), how can the people who read this condensed information really understand what the risk is about, where it has come from, why it is a risk or what the impact could be.

To fully understand the risks on a risk register, the risk should be linked to its causes and consequences. ISO 31000 notes in its definition of risk, that 'risk is usually expressed in terms of risk sources, potential events, their consequences and their likelihood' (ISO 2018:1).

### *Causes*

The risk sources, or causes, are facts; things that have occurred or are in place, which could give rise to a risk. For example, we currently have a lack of skilled staff in a particular area of the organization, or our recruitment procedures are out of date, or we don't have sufficient information about a certain part of the design, or we are working in a new country and so forth. These are all facts, but are often logged as risks.

Sometimes, these causes are more than just statements of fact, and are actually issues; being unplanned events that have occurred and that need action to manage them. It is often not until qualitatively rating the likelihood of the item that they are recognised as issues because it is realised that they have already occurred. If this is the case, then the item will have to be considered further to see if there are any risks related to it, or whether they should be captured as issues separately.

It is important to understand the causes, as these are the things that are looked at first to manage the risk. If the causes can be managed, that is more skilled staff are recruited or the procedures are updated, or more information is gathered, then the likelihood of the risk occurring will be affected.

Care should be taking when writing the causes down, as they must be factually correct. For example, saying that there are no skilled staff, or that all procedures are out of date or there is no information, can cause a lot of problems for an organization. At the least, those who read the risk could be offended, for example "NO skilled staff; are they saying I'm not skilled?" At the most, the cause could be used as proof in a potential prosecution or sanction in the event of a risk occurring, for example "But your risk register says that you have no skilled staff. It says nothing about a specific part of the organizationor a particular skill, it just says that you have no skilled staff, at all!"

### *Risks*

The risks are uncertainties; things that might or might not happen. For example, interest rates might go down (or up), we might not be able to effectively resource a project, staff might not comply correctly with requirements and so forth. These are all uncertainties, with the use of words such as may, might or possibly to indicate they are uncertain statements.

If risks are named without these 'uncertain' words when using the cause, risk, consequence concept, then they sound and will be read as facts. 'We can't effectively resource a project' or 'staff won't comply correctly', don't sound like uncertain statements; they sound like factual statements.

## *Consequences*

ISO 31000 defines consequences as 'the outcome of an event affecting objectives' (ISO 2018: 2). For example, the project will be late, the organization will be prosecuted or fined, our reputation will be damaged, we will lose money and so forth. These are all impacts, and should be impacts that reflect one or more objectives. Remember, risks are uncertainties that matter. If they do not affect the one or more objectives, then the risk doesn't matter, right?

That is essentially true, however, there are cases where the objectives are not correct or complete. Here, further work would be needed to ensure that the objectives themselves really reflect what is important to an organisation. There are other situations where the risk does not matter to the objectives for that particular project, department or function within an organization, but does matter to another project, department or function or to the organization as a whole. In these cases, the risks should be moved to the relevant risk register where the risk can be effectively managed.

## *Cause, risk, consequence*

One further challenge when describing causes and consequences is the ability to be honest about what these are. Some people and organizations don't seem willing or able to recognize existing issues in their businesses or to have them discussed. Some are not willing or able to consider the extent of the consequences should risks occur. The difficulty here is being reasonable about how big the impact will be; it's not that all threats will destroy the organization, but if one or more risks could irreparably damage the organization, it should be recognised. The same applies to opportunities; not all will mean the organization is going to exceed all objectives, but if an opportunity could propel the organization to the best in class, then that should be acknowledged. This ability to be reasonable and to recognise the relevant extremes that risks can reach, is interconnected with the people, culture and perceptions that have been examined earlier.

When drawing out the cause, risk and consequence, there is often more than one cause and more than one impact related to a risk. It is important to capture as much information as possible so that the risk is clearly understood, while at the same time making sure that the information captured is not overwhelming.

In the first instance, it can be enough just to note the main causes and consequences. One tool for the facilitator of a risk identification session is to ask 'why' five times (the five whys technique). This technique suggests asking 'why' a number of times (not necessarily five) in order to get to the root cause of a situation. It also helps where consequences have been raised as risks, for example, we could go over budget. Keeping to budget is often an objective, and as such this is a consequence or impact, so asking why we could go over budget usually brings out the risk(s).

A further technique is to ask the question, 'so what?' This is a useful technique if it is felt that causes are being raised as risks, for example, we are going to work in a new country. Asking 'so what?' will prompt the identification of the risk(s) that might come from that fact.

The International Standard on risk assessment techniques, ISO 31010, notes many different techniques for risk assessment, some of which are specifically related to the better understanding of causes and consequences, for example:

- Root cause analysis – analysis of a single loss in order to better understand the causes
- Business impact analysis – analysis of the effect that risks could have on an organisation should they occur, (part of business continuity planning)

- Fault trees – analysis of how faults or risks could occur
- Event trees – evaluation of the likelihood of different outcomes from risks occurring
- Cause/consequence analysis – combination of the fault tree and event tree with the risk in the middle
- Cause-and-effect analysis – evaluation of broad categories of causes that relate to a specific effect
- Failure modes and effects analysis (FMEA) – technical assessment to identify ways in which components, systems, processes or can fail to meet their design target, looking at both what can fail and what the effects would be
- Bow tie analysis – a simple way of considering the causes that could lead to a risk occurring and the consequences following the occurrence. It is a basic combination of the fault tree and event tree with the risk in the middle, with the focus in this method being on the barriers between the cause and risk, and then between the risk and consequence. (ISO 2009b: 42–66).

### *Risk meta-language*

If less detailed and technical methods are being used to identify risks than those noted above, for example structured brainstorming sessions, the three parts of the risk – cause, risk, consequence – can be better understood if they are put together to form the full risk name. However, trying to distinguish between cause, risk and consequence can be difficult. For example, we don't have all the information, so we could be late, which would lead to penalties. In this case, 'we don't' have all of the information' is the cause, whereas 'we could be late' is actually a consequence or impact as it relates to a common objective to complete work on time, with the penalties being a further consequence; there is no risk in this statement.

A method that has been used to name risks successfully in the project environment for many years, is risk meta-language (Hillson 2004: 73–75). Risk meta-language is a way of writing risks in a sentence format that brings out the cause, risk and consequence sequentially. This structured sentence takes the form of:

> As a result of, or due to, or because of a cause(s) [FACT/S] a risk [UNCERTAINTY] may occur which would have an effect(s) [IMPACT/S] on objectives.

An example of a threat (downside risk) written using the risk meta-language:

> Because our communication policy is out of date and our induction training is not being completed by all new employees especially in the research department, employees may post sensitive information about the organisation through social media, which would lead to a negative impact on our brand, loss of intellectual property, and loss of competitive advantage.

An example of an opportunity (upside risk) written using the risk meta-language:

> Due to the allegiances and partnerships with suppliers and subcontractors X, Y and Z, we might be able to develop collaboration clubs through social media leading to additional publicity, improved loyalty and improved relationships,

As can be seen in both examples, the causes are clear and quite precise and the consequences take us to a reasonable extreme.

It is further suggested that particular language or words are used for each part of the risk meta-language:

- For causes, factual words should be used, such as 'is', 'do', 'has' and 'has not'.
- For risks, uncertain words should be used as mentioned previously, such as 'may', 'might' and 'possibly'.
- For consequences, the words used for a future state or the impact (conditional on the risk occurring) should be 'would' or 'will'. Some texts suggest the use of the word 'could' when describing the consequences (Hillson 2004:75). However, in practice this has generated problems as some people associate the word 'could' quite strongly with uncertainty and feel it should only be used for risks (uncertainties).

The risk-meta language method is not an easy concept to grasp at first, but is fundamental to a well worded risk, and, as noted at the beginning of this chapter, the value of naming a risk properly is profound and essential to the effective management of risk.

## Conclusion

This might seem quite a long chapter to cover what seems to be quite a simple concept; the proper use of words in the risk management process. The proper use of words is important in any context, but when considering risk, it becomes slightly more important because we are dealing with uncertainty, and all the baggage, in terms of perceptions and understanding, that comes with trying to predict or describe the future.

First, define risk management terms that work best for you and your organization and use them consistently to give clear direction and understanding across the organization.

Second, think carefully about the words you are using to describe risks and their actions in whichever format is applicable, such as risk registers and risk reports. If you get the risk name right, there will be fewer challenges and greater understanding of your risk information, and a lot of the other risk management steps fall automatically from that information:

- Knowing the specific causes, can lead you to the first management actions to affect how likely a risk is to occur.
- Knowing the causes will provide some guidance on how likely the risk is to occur.
- Knowing the risk and the impacts, will give some substance to how much the risk matters for impact rating.
- Knowing the impacts will lead you to the first management actions to put in place to help manage the risk should it occur.

I have tried to use the right words to describe the concepts throughout this chapter, but as the author Stephen King (Goodreads 2016) is quoted as saying, "Any word you have to hunt for in a thesaurus is the wrong word." I must admit that I have resorted to the use of a thesaurus at times, but only to try and find words that are easier to understand. Without wanting to offend anyone, I have tried to keep it simple . . . stupid (the KISS principle).

## References

British Standards Institute (2011) *BS 31100:2011 Risk Management Code of Practice for the Implementation of BS ISO 31000*, Milton Keynes: BSI.

COSO (2004) Enterprise Risk Management – Integrated Framework, North Carolina: COSO.

COSO (2017) Enterprise Risk Management – Integrated.

Environment Agency (2016) Detailed Flood Risk Information for Glenridding, Cumbria [online]: Environment Agency's official website. Available at https://flood-warning-information.service.gov.uk/long-term-flood-risk/risk-detail?address=10070538252 [Accessed 4 August 2016].

Gigerenzer, G. (2002) *Calculated Risks How to Know When Numbers Deceive You*, New York: Simon & Schuster.

Goodreads (2016) Popular quotes [online]: Goodreads official website. Available at www.goodreads.com/quotes [Accessed 20 May 2016].

Hester, S. (2012) Interview on the Today programme, Interviewed by James Naughtie [radio] BBC Radio 4, 3 August 2012.

Hillson, D. (2004) *Effective Opportunity Management for Projects*, Florida: Taylor & Francis.

Hillson, D. (2009) *Managing Risk in Projects*, Surrey: Gower Publishing Limited.

Hubbard, W. (2009) *The Failure of Risk Management*, New Jersey: John Wiley & Sons, Inc.

International Standard Office (2009a) ISO 73:2009 *Risk Management – Vocabulary*.

International Standard Office (2009b) *ISO 31010:2009 Risk Management Risk Assessment Techniques*, Geneva: ISO.

International Standard Office (2018) *ISO 31000:2009 Risk Management Principles and Guidelines*, Geneva: ISO.

IRM (2012) *Risk Culture Under the Microscope Guidance for Boards*, London: IRM.

Met Office (2014) The Science of 'Probability of Precipitation' [online]: Met Office's official website. Available at www.metoffice.gov.uk/news/in-depth/science-behind-probability-of-precipitation [Accessed 10 June 2016].

Power, M. Ashby, S. & Palermo, T. (n.d.) Risk Culture in Financial Organisations A Research Report [online]: London School of Economics. Available at www.lse.ac.uk/accounting/CARR/pdf/final-risk-culture-report.pdf [Accessed 10 June 2016].

Psychological Consultancy Ltd, Risk Type Compass [online]: PCL's official website. Available at www.psychological-consultancy.com/products/risk-type-compass/ [Accessed 10 June 2016].

Salmon, F. (2009) Recipe for Disaster: The Formula That Killed Wall Street [online]: Wired. Available at www.wired.com/2009/02/wp-quant/ [Accessed 10 June 2016].

Truss, L. (2009) *Eats, Shoots and Leaves a Zero Tolerance Approach to Punctuation*, 4th edn, London: HarperCollins

TV insider 1 (2007) BBC Weather Blooper by Michael Fish Storm of 1987 [video online]. Available at www.youtube.com/watch?v=uqs1YXfdtGE [Accessed 10 June 2016].

# 27
# Leading through uncertainty

*Cesar Marolla*

Our lives are shaped by threats and uncertainty. These events and situations represent the risks we face of gaining or losing something of value (such as property, money, health, and life) and are universal. Risk indicates that some present or future event may endanger an asset or something else of value. Any risk inherent in a situation relates mainly to the uncertainty and variability that results from specific actions. A system that aims to follow the rules of risk management in crisis situations must take into account prevention or mitigation strategies for possible threat effects (Ostrowska, 2014).

Managing business risk is a complex task that has as its ultimate goal minimizing the damage *a crisis can inflict on an enterprise's operations, services, and stakeholders*. Businesses face a variety of challenges in monitoring and managing the consequences of risks. Thus, it is important to understand the business impact and to prepare contingency plans to reduce the effect of an event and to cope effectively with its detrimental outcomes. Potentially catastrophic risks are not always apparent to governing boards; and guidance is needed to develop and implement a risk management strategy deserves particular attention. Any risk that might hav large negative impacts on investors, stakeholders, taxpayers, or the environment needs urgent attention and definitive action to minimize the damage to business operations. The importance of preparing and responding to crisis can make the difference between closing and surviving.

A comprehensive and all inclusive risk management framework can also create the conditions for the business to flourish when the circumstances are right.

Businesses need to recognize that crises are fertile opportunities for learning and changing, if an enterprise is well prepared to cope with the hazards that it confronts. Risk management frameworks create an environment that enables a business to manage external and internal threats, anticipate the possibility of a crisis, and prepare properly. With the proper framework, the company or agency will be better equipped to manage such situations or avoid them altogether. Three questions are key to guiding plans for risk management and crisis response:

1 What could go wrong?
2 What will you do to prevent things from going wrong?
3 What will you do if something goes wrong?

*(Managing Crisis: Risk Management and Crisis Response Planning, 2015)*

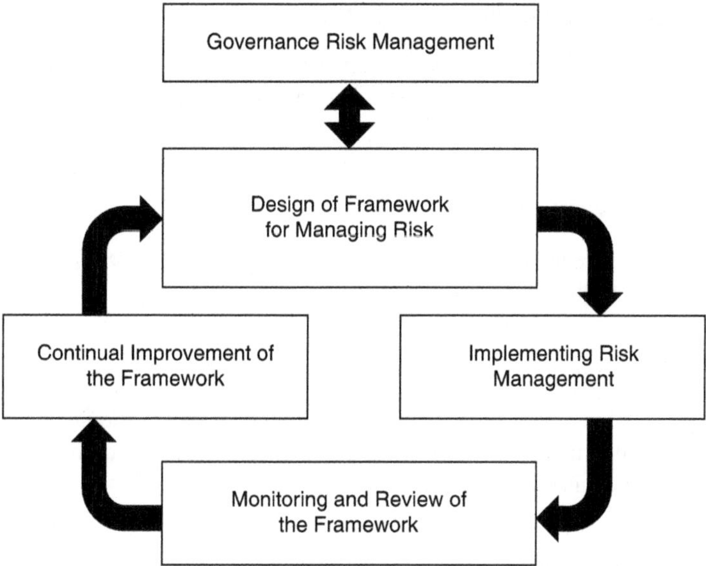


*Figure 27.1* Risk management 31000 framework for managing risk

*Source*: Pojasek (2011)

## Managing risks

Risk management frameworks help businesses and organisations to specify and prioritize what needs further attention, and they establish a process for ensuring that these higher priority risks are managed effectively.

ISO 31000 for managing risk follows a typical plan-do-check-act cycle. The elements of the framework are described in Figure 27.1.

### *Governance of risk management*

A company or an agency board of directors represents the center of its risk management governance structure. The board presents the mandate and commitment to risk management.

### *Design of the risk management program*

The process of designing or planning the company's risk management program includes the following components:

- Understanding how it is organized and its context
- Establishing risk management policy
- Creating accountability associated with the management of risk
- Integrating risk management into your processes
- Providing adequate resources for risk management
- Establishing internal and external communication
- Reporting mechanisms.

*(Pojasek, 2011)*

### Implementation of the risk management program

The company puts its risk management program into effect by carrying out the elements specified during the program's design phase. This action is accompanied by implementing a risk management process.

### Monitoring and review

Management at all levels in the company should be involved in monitoring and reviewing the parts of the framework that they control.

### Continual improvement

Each person involved in governance at any level of the organisation should be responsible for continually improving the risk management framework. Judicious use of the risk management process helps to drive this improvement.

### Risk management process

ISO 31001 articulates a clear process for managing risk.

- Establishing context: It is important to view every risk in the context of the organisation and the interests of the stakeholders.
- Risk identification, analysis, and evaluation: The organisation assesses key business risks using risk identification, analysis, and evaluation methods.
- Risk treatment: The company "treats" unacceptable risks in an effort to lower the risk threshold.
- Communication and consultation: The organisation communicates all these activities to stakeholders in order to provide a proper level of engagement and consultation with company management.
- Monitoring and review: The organisation carries out extensive monitoring and review to determine how its risk profile is changing over time.
- Further risk assessment: The organisation needs to carry out additional contextual analysis and further risk assessment and treatment when appropriate (Pojasek, 2011).

ISO 31000 can be used to establish a risk management policy, ensure that risk is managed properly and manage and control risk. Furthermore, it can explain how risk should be managed and controlled and provide a framework to develop risk management procedures and guides. Therefore, the risk management framework can reduce uncertainty in how to deal with crisis and threats to the organisation by improving knowledge and understanding of risk.

### Analysis of risk

The assessment framework is developed to methodically study the risks. Then, risk is evaluated by identifying the consequences and probabilities in the context of existing controls. In this way the framework sets risk priorities and enables assigning a priority to each risk. The source of risk is important and must be emphasized to understand the positive and negative effects and probabilities. A qualitative risk assessment requires an individual analysis of the consequences and likelihood of a particular outcome. An effective analysis uses past events, practices and relevant information, as well as applicable published literature in its development. The level of risk is studied in relation to existing controls, if any. The key questions used to assess risks include:

- What are the current controls or actions which may identify or avert potential risks?
- What is the likelihood of the risks addressed by the organisation?
- What are the possible consequences of the risks if they impact the organisation?

*(EAM Risk Management Framework, 2009)*

## *The risk analysis stages*

- Stage 1. Identify existing controls to minimize the consequences and likelihood of each risk. Only existing controls that are funded and require no further work to implement should be measured at this stage. Assuming the risk scenario is occurring, reducing the consequences and likelihoods of risk should be evaluated.
- Stage 2. Determine the event's magnitude of consequence and likelihood. Establish the phase of an event in which consequences occur and also the likelihood of their occurrence.
- Stage 3. Assign the risk priority rating. Use the risk priority table presented in Table 27.1 to obtain the risk rating. Each risk requires its own analysis (Risk assessment, 2011).

## *Level of risk: likelihood X consequence*

ISO 31000:2009 provides the level of risk, expressed as the product of the consequence and likelihood. Therefore, a description of these elements is fundamental to developing a risk management strategy for the organisation (Rollason, 2010).

## *Evaluate risks*

ISO 31000:2009 risk evaluation framework compares the results of the risk analysis against risk criteria to determine if the level is acceptable, allowable or intolerable. The latter risks receive top priority. It is not possible to lessen every risk, and the cost of implementing some mitigation strategies could offset the benefits of action. The methods of risk-level reduction are evaluated, and then steps follow to investigate new management measures. The combination of likelihood and consequence presents the "unmitigated risk." These are the risks that are not diminished or moderated in intensity or severity. After implementing existing management

*Table 27.1* Risk priority ratings example given that a scenario arises. Adapted from NHS Scotland model for organisational risk management (Gov.scot, 2016).

| *CONSEQUENCE* | | | | | |
|---|---|---|---|---|---|
| **Likelihood** | Insignificant | Minor | Moderate | Major | Catastrophic |
| Almost certain | Medium | Medium | High | Extreme | Extreme |
| Likely | Low | Medium | High | High | Extreme |
| Possible | Low | Medium | Medium | High | High |
| Unlikely | Low | Low | Medium | Medium | Medium |
| Rare | Low | Low | Low | Low | Medium |

measures in the assessment, identifying risk priorities occurs. Monitoring and reviewing the process allows following all types of risk to make certain that they remain within a tolerable level (Rollason, 2010).

## *Are you prepared?*

To address any impact (positive or negative) that an event might have requires significant time and resources. However, the unpredictability of business threats can create a crisis. An enterprise not only must avert or minimize risks but also have a comprehensive plan for continuing operations after disaster strikes. Having a business continuity management system (BCMS) in place is a vital part of a corporation's function (Preparing your business for disaster, 2013).

## *Response time is critical*

The basic actions are prepare, respond and recover. They summarize the ongoing management and governance processes that a business must provide to identify the impact of potential losses, maintain viable recovery strategies, and plan for various emergencies and interruptions (Preparing your business for disaster, 2013). BCMS follows the "plan-do-check-act" process and is the building block of a management system. It is used for "planning, establishing, implementing, operating, monitoring, reviewing, maintaining and continually improving the effectiveness of an organization's [*sic*] BCMS" (ISO.org., 2012).

## *Recover to a better position*

Risks can never be entirely eliminated. Residual risks always remain, and a BCMS involves measures to safeguard the normal procedures of a business and its critical processes and to ensure the effectiveness of its operations. Having a resiliency strategy in a BCMS helps to mitigate the negative effects on an organisation and can significantly reduce interruptions created or exacerbated by unpredictable events. Resilience is the foundational competency for a business.

An enterprise faces varied issues, but some of the most important ones are as follows:

- Surprise
- Time-pressured decision making
- Disruption to strategic objectives
- Demands from multiple, diverse stakeholders
- Intense and immediate public exposure
- Overload on existing or remaining infrastructure and resources, especially people
- Escalation of severity
- Organisational paralysis
- Loss of control.

*(Business resilience and crisis management, 2016)*

A wide range of events or triggers can escalate already devastating levels of interruption, losses, and delays to business operations. Such events can worsen the adverse effects and extend the damage to undermining trust in the organisation's reputation and capability to act (Business resilience and crisis management, 2016). The business community plan must understand the qualitative distinctions among the types of risks that enterprises face if it is to effectively manage them. A risk management plan creates and protects value. And it must be an integral part of all organisational processes. The plan must explicitly address uncertainty with measures that are systematic, structured, timely, transparent and inclusive. Furthermore, it must be based on the best available information to be dynamic and responsive to change (Björnsdóttir, 2015).

## Identifying business risks

Many events can affect your business depending on specific and sometimes variable conditions. Geographical location, economic instability, extreme weather events, local and global financial crisis, environmental degradation and more can all have a destabilizing impact on an organisation. Natural disasters such as flooding, theft or vandalism, fire, electrical power outage, failure of IT systems caused by computer virus, pandemics, significant loss of utilities, financial crises, accidents, and incidents that threaten your reputation in addition to hackers that can affect severely the ability to perform. A natural or man-made disaster can block access to the premises and interrupt operations. Moreover, the loss or illness of key staff who are in charge of running the business must be considered. Other factors to keep in mind include:

- Disease outbreak can affect the workforce in some regions of the world.
- Terrorist attacks pose a threat to employees' lives.
- Geographical distance (within the country of origin or internationally) between locations means that the longer-term effects on the particular market or sector must be given thought.

Crisis affects the reputation of your business, customers, and suppliers. Sourcing alternative supplies in addition to insurance plans or customer guarantees that offset a client's inability to take your goods or services are important considerations.

All the scenarios described are possible impacts. Leaders need to assess every possible outcome and prepare a continuity plan if any these risks are possible. Indirect risks to your business are commonly overlooked because business leaders don't think certain events directly impact the organisation. A severe weather event might impact another region that is affecting your suppliers and therefore your business will be also impacted (British Standards Institution, 2014).

## Learning how to prioritize risks

Risks that affect your business can have different dimensions. The challenge we face is that risk and the practice of risk management is seldom receives attention. Implementing a risk management strategy that is both sustainable and efficient must fit into a three-dimensional risk program: likelihood, severity and level of control.

It is important to evaluate and determine the level of potential threats your enterprise faces. Think of the levels of likelihood as frequency values or signals of how easily a business can make use of a threat. Under likelihood scenarios, some threats can be categorized by frequency or probability. Others can be classified by how liable an event can occur by misuse or mistake, or to motivation for performing a malicious action. The main purpose of Table 27.2 is to decide the most appropriate rating or the column that is easiest to use to estimate the likelihood of the threat (Watson, 2010). The table describes the likelihood of occurrence, the rating and the description of the risk.

*Table 27.2* Risk likelihood and consequence descriptors

| *Rating* | *Description* | *Likelihood of occurrence* |
|---|---|---|
| 1 | Rare | Highly unlikely, but it may occur in exceptional circumstances. It could happen, but probably never will. |
| 2 | Unlikely | Not expected, but there's a slight possibility it may occur at some time. |
| 3 | Possible | The event might occur at some time as there is a history of casual occurrence at the University &/or similar institutions. |
| 4 | Likely | There is a strong possibility the event will occur as there is a history of frequent occurrence at the University &/or similar institutions. |
| 5 | Almost Certain | Very likely. The event is expected to occur in most circumstances as there is a history of regular occurrence at the University &/or similar institutions. |

Risk is an event that "may" occur and the likelihood of it occurring can range widely from no possibility of occurrence to a high possibility. When an event is inevitable it becomes a certainty, not a risk. The next step is to analyze the probability and consequences of crisis. Determining the likelihood and possible frequency of any incident assists in identifying the primary business functions that need to keep running or be brought back to operational status quickly when a crisis happens. You must also define the vital roles within your business that are needed to function and determine which roles are not critical in a disaster.

Your management plan will identify and assess risks and develop strategies to manage them. This plan is essential part of any business because it helps you to understand potential risks and identify ways to minimize them or recover from their impacts to a "normal" level of operations.

Not all risks are avoidable and some are certainties. For those risks, it is important to have a plan to minimize them and protect your business function from them. The following section shows some examples in how you can manage risks and develop a strategy to deal with crisis.

## Business continuity management plan

Business continuity management is defined as a holistic management process that identifies potential impacts that threaten an enterprise and provide a framework for building resilience, enabling you to effectively safeguard the interests of key stakeholders, the reputation of the business, and its value-creating activities. The business must be prepared to function efficiently under adverse circumstances. Here is an example of the plan's outline:

1 **Chain of authority**

Determine the overall responsibility for the business continuity plan, and designate leadership successors in case of team absences.

2 **Crisis management group**

Create a crisis management group to effectively coordinate and implement response and relief measures.

3 **Documentation and location**

Store documents in a properly secured location within the business. This action allows management, key team members, and staff to access the documents easily. Make the appropriate personnel aware of its location. Take special care to include access to electronic files; for example, using a remote access server.

4 **Review of business continuity plan**

Undertake a concise assessment of risks. The management team can plan revisions to occur annually, semi-annually, and so on, and then present them to a higher authority for improvement, development, implementation and testing.

5 **Training**

Make roles and responsibilities part of the training program for a continuity plan under a crisis or major event. Include procedures, key policies, and implementation guidance in the plan.

Become familiar with the content of the plan; and use regular drills and plan different scenarios to test awareness.

6 **Coordinated responses**

Coordinate efforts with local, regional and federal authorities. This important step to solidifies efforts for an efficient and effective execution. The business continuity plan must be tailored to the existing authorities' strategy within your local or national jurisdiction.

7 **Risk assessment and response**

Identify main risks, their likely level of impact on operations and the planned responses to address these risks.

8 **Recording incidents**

Take note of incidents and major events impaction the business. This documentation assists with any further investigation and help to be well informed of potential impacts for future business continuity planning.

9 **Key contacts**

Identify key contacts such as stakeholders, landlord, utility companies, service users, suppliers and insurers. Furthermore, make contact information available of executive and risk management team, responsible personnel and after hours key employees in charge of emergencies.

## Managing crisis

The core of managing crisis is preparation and response. After identifying the key risks your business faces, the next step should be to protect your business functions against them. Categorize the key business functions needed to get up and running as quickly as possible after a disaster and specify the resources required to efficiently operate under adverse conditions. Identify the role each person plays in a crisis and make sure they are prepared to act in an emergency.

The first hour of a crisis is essential to minimizing its effects on the business. Consequently, the business continuity plan needs to define the actions immediately required in that first hour and also to specify the training that responsible personnel need to succeed in their roles. Your premises' map must be available to everyone to help emergency services, showing fire escapes, sprinklers and other safety equipment. Furthermore, communicating with the media in an effective way helps avoid chaos and misinformation that would lead to confusion for employees, customers and the general public. Appoint a single company spokesperson to handle questions and encourage a positive tone in any statements given to the company's workforce and the public. However, make sure staff, customers and suppliers are informed before they find out in the media. As a final point, keep hard copies of your business continuity plan at a secure, offsite location that more than one key employee can access.

We live in shifting business climate that is influenced by local and global events. Risks come as opportunities or threats requiring your immediate attention. The timing of the approach to threats is crucial to determine the outcome desired. Not all risks can be avoided but the main goal should be to minimize, as much possible, the negative impact to the organisation. Business resilience is always a concern for a CEO and the executive team. A business resilience framework should focus on continuity of operations and preparedness. Its contents should be anticipatory, adaptive, and robust. The framework should also highlight regulatory compliance issues, particularly new and changing government rules and regulations. Including compliance information will provide a competitive advantage and avoid legal ramification that are detrimental to the business. An integrated risk management plan enables a company to minimize costs and stay competitive. It must address security, privacy and data protection to safeguard the organisation from internal and external threats and to help develop a critical information management policy. The risk management and continuity plan can be combined into a single, integrated strategy. The framework should address the following key areas:

- Going beyond disaster recovery to become a resilient business
- Accessing to expertise and skills (via outsourcing or training)
- Developing the infrastructure to support the easy acquisition and management of expert assistance in maintaining continuous business operations
- Anticipating and responding to changing marketplace conditions and accelerating research and development as necessary to get the right products to the right buyers at the right time (Cocchiara, 2007).

In the past, businesses typically have addressed these concerns separately. However, many companies now recognize that a single, integrated strategy is more cost-effective. A holistic approach can help minimize risks, maximize opportunities and address compliance needs – all at the same time.

## Risk management governance and its relation to your risk management plan

Comprehensive risk management governance is crucial to the success of your program. Executive responsibilities must include a chief risk officer who becomes the evangelist delivering and communicating the values and best practices of the risk management for the entire enterprise. It is important to understand this role because it can assure the success of the program. External and internal forces affect the business and that drive the need for this valuable role.

Internal forces are those that create changes to the business and entail evaluation, and risks that need to be assessed. External forces affecting the business include regulatory changes and initiatives from your competitors. And as a company crosses the $1B revenue mark, these forces include buyout offers and increased regulatory scrutiny.

Corporate governance plays an important role in setting the organisation's tolerance for risk, establishing key risk indicators and determining what resources to allocate to mitigation. As you assess current practices for continual improvement, train the workforce so they are more risk-minded and create a clear path for everyone to communicate risk (Lam, 2015). These steps can make significant changes and create the pathway to understanding what the enterprise must do to access more resources and technology to mitigate risk.

## Business continuity management framework

An organisation needs to be adaptable and flexible not only to compete and win in different and challenging markets, but also to meet customers' demands and new technological trends. A framework helps to capitalize on opportunities created by the disruptive event and provides adaptive capability that builds high-level resilience and increases security awareness. A business continuity framework improves understanding of functions and opportunities for improvement and helps identify the need for change. A strategy must be developed that indicates which steps in the process are broken, why and how they should be improved and then identify any financial and resource implications. Answering how the process can be improved is a catalyst to develop and implement your improvement objectives. It is recommended that you set realistic and measurable objectives that align with your overall strategic goals. It is important to seek feedback from stakeholders and learn from each disruptive event to ensure that the organisation is better prepared to respond to future events.

## Managing crisis and avoiding silos

Often a business operates its programs in silos that lead to disruptive activities despite improvement in its ability to plan for and predict disasters. Silos promote the lack of an effective response. In fact, the biggest issue in business continuity today is how to make different departments and levels of managers work together and communicate effectively for a common goal. A successful program leverages its integrated governance to promote effective communication among the organisation, between the business teams, and the decision-making executives.

## Create a culture of quick change adoption

A business continuity plan is never finished, and the planning activities should keep up with the ever-changing needs of your business. The governance model should support a change management process to navigate the quick transitions these changes demand. Change management helps ensure that changes are identified, risks are revisited and essential modifications are made to the business continuity and disaster recovery plans. A sustainable continuity program constantly identifies and manages its organisation's risks. The strategic approach requires regular comprehensive assessments of the proposed plan so that risks are addressed appropriately according to their level of impact. Governance function should be fully integrated across the business and support a hands-on risk management approach.

The challenge to perform business processes effectively and to guarantee their continuous operation is greater when companies are without a concise risk management and business continuity plan. Thus companies need to apply process management concepts to meet the economic requirements and successfully address risks. Consequently, an integrated consideration of economic, risk and security concerns delivers enormous value to meeting these requirements.

## The plan-do-check-act cycle

Continuity management plans apply the 'plan-do-check-act' (PDCA) cycle. This involves planning, establishing, implementing, operating, monitoring, reviewing, maintaining and continually improving the effectiveness of operations (Societal security, 2011). Assessing the risks that affect operations is critical to preparing different departments and jurisdictions against the potential impact of disruptions (i.e. flooding, fires, power outages infrastructure collapse) that ultimately interrupt the business' ability to function and recover to the previous state of operations (Business Continuity, 2009).

Assessing a business continuity management plan should include the following considerations:

- Historical: What types of threats to the business have occurred?
- Geographic: What could happen to the well-being of your business considering its geographical location and vulnerabilities to any type of crisis?
- Structural: What could affect the functional ability of business operations?
- Human Factors: Human-caused emergencies can result from inadequate training, supervision or negligence (Business Continuity, 2009).

## Societal security: ISO 22301 – continuity management approach

What would happen if your business were involved in a severe disruption? Would the business survive the crisis? How would you ensure that your business endures the disaster?

Business continuity management (BCM) is about preparing an organisation to deal with disruptive incidents that might otherwise prevent it from achieving its objectives. The international standard ISO 22301 specifies requirements to plan, establish, implement, operate, monitor, review, maintain and continually improve a documented management system to protect against, reduce the likelihood of, prepare for, respond to, and recover from disruptive incidents when they arise (ISO 22301 societal security, 2012). This international standard can significantly reduce risk, particularly when a lack of awareness and a concrete strategy in a continuity management planning after a disaster or impact is present. It also provides flexibility of implementation, identifying what is most relevant to minimize deaths and injuries, financial loss, infrastructure damage, communications failures and other harm to overall operations.

Managing a business's overall continuity of operation becomes a priority in any type of crisis. Any number of events can bring the business grinding to a halt and business continuity management planning will ensure the organisation's leaders will respond judiciously to the circumstances. A continuity management approach contributes to a more resilient business. The following key components should be part of the plan:

- Policy
- People with defined responsibilities

- Management processes relating to:
  - Policy
  - Planning
  - Implementation and operation
  - Performance assessment
  - Management review
  - Improvement
- Documentation providing auditable evidence
- Any business continuity management processes relevant to the organisation (Societal security, 2011).

## Resuming "normal operations" after the disaster

Ten important points of action determine how the business will preserve or restore its critical functions. The business's quick resumption of normal operations after an event will affect the entire recovery process. Ten important points of action determine how the business will preserve or restore its critical functions. Quickly resuming normal operations after an event will affect the entire recovery process.

1 Establish an emergency planning team. Workers from all levels and departments must be included on the team, focusing on those with expertise vital to the daily business operations.
2 Announce who is in charge. Having a clear chain-of-command during a disaster and communicating it to all employees is an essential part of your plan. Also, establish a succession plan in case a leader is not available at the time of the crisis.
3 Examine the business's operations and activities: Identify internal and external processes and services that are essential to the recovery and continuation of the enterprise's departments.
4 Identify an alternate location from which to run operations. Include locations for the various jurisdictions within your operations. Moreover, develop collaboration and viable assistance with "like" departments or the public building commission/department to share facilities if necessary.
5 Plan for employees with special needs. Include in your plan specifics about how to meet the requirements of employees and others with special needs or disabilities.
6 Develop an evacuation plan. Account for every site address your business has. It is important to determine how notice will be given whether by alarm, intercom, phone call, siren or other means. All employees and staff must be aware of where to assemble in the event of an evacuation or emergency occurrence.
7 Create a shelter-in place plan for everyone of your business's buildings. This shelter must be a safe area within each building where employees and others are protected from outside harm. All employees should know where the shelter is located and know how to reach it safely.
8 Create a communication plan that defines how employees will be advised of the emergency plan and what communication devices will be used if an event occurs. List the communication tools in order of preference, emphasizing the most effective way for communication to the least effective according to the type of disaster the business is facing.

9 Obtain emergency contact information. An emergency contact list identifies how to contact staff in the event of a crisis. This will include the technical means where the employees may receive different types of communication, so they can respond and act to restore operations and act to ensure the safety of others in the workforce.
10 Keep the plan current. Document and update your business' continuity management plan at least once a year (Business Continuity, 2009).

It is forecast which activities that will be interrupted during a crisis and how events will affect the function of the organisation. A continuity management plan draws attention to the impact of disruption and identifies those activities where a business needs to focus for its recovery. A continuity management system plan assists the business's leaders in recognizing what needs to be done to protect its employees and infrastructure. ISO 22301 business continuity management system may also be able to take advantage of opportunities that might otherwise be overlooked or considered to be too high risk (Societal security, 2011).

## Adapting and using the framework

Effective response to and recovery from crisis involves advance readiness. A proactive approach must be established along with planning for the likelihood of an event and its capacity to interrupt a business' operations. It is necessary to emphasize the personal commitment of the organization's leaders to dismissing the "it can't happen here."

Disruptions happen on a daily basis and, as previously mentioned, preparedness means being proactive and planning. That is the essence of efficient business continuity planning (Building Business Resilience, 2009).

## Impact analysis

Organisations of any size have overall functions that are important for maintaining normal operations but only a percentage of those vital for a business to continue its normal level of functionality. Executive leaders and operation managers need to gather information to determine basic recovery requirements in the event of a disaster. Identifying which areas and departments of operations of the business will be most affected by a crisis is crucial in order to develop a plan and to determine what effect it will have on the business as a whole (Building Business Resilience, 2009). The risk management impact analysis will be used to establish the business' critical activities, the resources required to support such activities and the impact of ceasing to perform these activities.

## Recovery time objectives, planning and strategies

Recovery time objectives (RTO) should be part of your risk management impact analysis and assigned to each activity. It identifies the time from which you declare a crisis or disaster to the time that the critical business activity must be fully operational in order to prevent serious infrastructure damages, health risks, financial losses and loss of life (Building Business Resilience, 2009).

The response phase of the business continuity planning takes place as the event happens and immediately after it occurs. This phase minimizes the loss of life and property and insures that the event will not create a chain reaction of incidents that will be more difficult to deter. Response to an incident generally involves a response from management, operational and communication departments. An incident response management team mainly takes care of the response phase of the plan. Responding quickly to a negative impact on the business infrastructure, people and so forth becomes vital to reduce negative impacts; although many events are often unpredictable, they are not always unexpected. If the effects of risks are not dealt with promptly and effectively, they are likely to have detrimental consequences on the enterprise's financial situation, government and workforce welfare (Building Business Resilience, 2009).

Some actions to recover from a devastating event may not always be possible. These actions can be generally identified as:

- Resumption (continuity) of business activities
- Restoration (recovery) of resources (Building Business Resilience, 2009).

Recovery planning is a proactive approach to restore operations in a prompt manner after an event hits the business. This is a crucial task to implement because a serious incident can occur at any time. To ensure personnel are prepared and in the right mindset, business leaders must assure the staff is well trained and rehearsed throughout the planning process.

The recovery plan focuses on how to bring back important activities after the crisis has taken place. The business leaders must assemble teams dedicated to the following tasks:

- Recovery team sets goals needed to demonstrate a clear understanding of the recovery planning that reflects what is needed to continue operating the business. A recovery team must be set up with the allocation of backups to ensure awareness of their functions in the recovery process.
- Disaster recovery team establishes an offsite location where the organisation's vital staff can work to access significant backup systems, records and supplies. Identify essential assets that need to be recovered and required special protection. Safety storage areas off-site and fireproof cabinets are needed.
- Communication strategies team outlines how to communicate with other with other organisations in the region affected (e.g., community centers, church and schools) as well as other cities and states where the business operates. This effort enables gathering relevant information and aid to cooperate, manage the crisis, provide health care assistance if necessary and mobilize the people affected by the event to allocate them to a safe area for treatment and temporary housing assistance, particularly in international locations affected by natural disasters.
- Planning for disruptions team identifies backup systems and other alternatives for electricity, water, sewerage and telecommunications. These systems need to be available and when an event occurs (Building Business Resilience, 2009).

Assembling a business impact analysis and defining recovery time objectives (RTO) for your activities is closely related to your business continuity plan's success and execution. It is clear that business leaders need to understand and identify the 'maximum tolerable period of disruption' for the activity in question as it is fundamental for the effectiveness of the process.

## Conclusion

It's only a matter of time before your company experiences a crisis. It is highly important to develop and implement a cohesive plan to be prepared and to cope with crisis and disruptions to your operations. This imperative turns out to be vital for the long-term success and endurance of your enterprise. Severe consequences can result if a company does not have a solid plan because no one is immune to adverse events. Therefore, the most effective steps are the ones taken before times get tough. Developing a risk management framework and business continuity plan are strategic moves that help to safeguard critical operations in the event of a crisis. Organisations of any size must have the ability to provide the services they offer and efficiently function at level that satisfies the needs of customers, suppliers and markets. Knowing your capabilities and the strength of your resiliency plans enables your business to minimize the impact of crisis and makes it possible to return to normal operations or *near normal operations* as quickly as possible.

## References


Björnsdóttir, S. (2015). *Managing Risks – A New Framework*. Federation of Icelandic Industries.

British Standards Institution. (2014). *Adapting to Climate Change Using your Business Continuity Management System*.

Building Business Resilience – Business Continuity Planning Guide. (2009). The State of Queensland, Department of Employment, Economic Development and Innovation, 12–18.

Business Resilience and Crisis Management. (2016). *Deloitte Touche Tohmatsu Limited. Crisis Management and Solutions*.

Cocchiara, R. (2007). *Beyond Disaster Recovery: Becoming a Resilient Business*. [online] An object-oriented framework and methodology.

EAM Risk Management Framework. (2009). Available at: www.gbrmpa.gov.au/__data/assets/pdf_file/0008/4949/gbrmpa_EAMRiskManagementFramework.pdf

Gov.scot. (2016). *The Risk Management of HAI: A Methodology for NHSscotland*. [online] Available at: www.gov.scot/Publications/2008/11/24160623/3 [Accessed 29 Aug. 2016].

ISO 31000:2009. Risk management principles and guidelines. (2009), 'International Organization for Standardization', Ed 1, rev:2018. ISO/TC 262 Risk management.

ISO.org. (2012). *Societal Security – Business Continuity Management Systems – Guidance*. [online] Available at: www.iso.org/obp/ui/#iso:std:iso:22313:ed-1:v1:en [Accessed 31 Aug. 2016].

Lam, J. (2015). *Implementing an Effective Risk Appetite*. Institute of Management Accountants.

Managing Crisis: Risk Management and Crisis Response Planning. (2015). The Compassion Capital Fund (CCF), U.S. Department of Health and Human Services. Availabe at: http://strengtheningnonprofits.org/resources/guidebooks/Managing_Crisis.pdf [Accessed 27 Aug. 2016].

Ostrowska, M. (2014). Risk Management in Crisis Situations. *Forum Scientiae Oeconomia*, 2(2).

Pojasek, R.B. (2011). Linking Sustainability to Risk Management. *Environmental Quality Management*, 21(2), 85–96. https:/doi.org/10.1002/tqem.20320.

Preparing your business for disaster. (2013). *Patmos, LLC*. Available at: www.nashvillechamber.com/docs/default-source/disaster-preparedness-pdfs/a_basic_guide_for_business_continuity_planning.pdf?sfvrsn=2 [Accessed 29 Aug. 2016].

Risk assessment. (2011). State of NSW and Office of Environment and Heritage, 1, 23–26.

Risk Likelihood and Consequence Descriptors. (2009). *Risk Management. AS/NZS ISO 31000:2009 Risk Management – Principles and Guidelines*.

Rollason, V. (2010). Applying the ISO 31000 Risk Assessment Framework to Coastal Zone Management. *NSW Government's Sea Level Rise Policy Statement, Coastal Planning Guideline: Adapting to Sea Level Rise*, 4–13.

Societal security — Business continuity management systems — Guidance. (2011). Draft International Standard ISO/DIS 22313. ISO/TC 223. International Organization for Standardization.

Watson, C. (2010). Risk Assessment Using the Three Dimensions of Probability: Likelihood, Severity, and Level of Control. *NASA System Safety*.

## Terms

Crisis – a risk characterized by an "event, revelation, allegation, or set of circumstances that threatens the integrity, reputation, or survival of an individual or an institution."

Crisis response – an approach to dealing with an event in a professional manner that addresses the critical needs of the time. The focus is on surviving the crisis in progress and easing the effects of the crisis as much as possible. Also referred to as crisis management.

Maximum tolerable period of disruption (MTPOD) – the maximum amount of time that an enterprise's key products or services can be unavailable or undeliverable after an event that causes disruption to operations, before its stakeholders perceive unacceptable consequences.

Risk – any factor that might hinder an organisation achieving its goals. Risks can be related to an organisation's programs, finances, management, infrastructure or susceptibility to natural disasters.

Risk management – a process for identifying an organisation's risks, assessing their significance, and preparing for and treating those deemed significant in a measured, professional manner. Risk management enables organisations to cope with uncertainty by taking steps to protect their vital assets and resources.

# 28

# Safety and economic activity

*Eirik B. Abrahamsen, Frank Asche and Roy E. Dahl*

## 1 Introduction

Are wealthier societies safer? It is well known that the opportunity cost of a worker depends on the worker's skill set or human capital. Moreover, there is a trade-off between compensation and risk (Viscusi and Moore, 1987), so that a worker can be induced to take on riskier occupations if sufficiently compensated. Different countries have substantially different wealth and wage levels, suggesting that the human capital associated with each worker and possibly each citizen varies. This argument entails that the accident risk a person is exposed for to be smaller in wealthier countries as these will undertake larger investments in safety measures. However, there is also literature emphasizing new risks associated with new technologies and increased complexity (Pronovost et al., 2016; WHO, 2010; Yu et al., 2016; Weinger and Gaba, 2014), suggesting that risk increase with more economic activity, making these societies less safe.

In this chapter we will investigate the relationship between safety and economic activity for 48 large cities. The approach is inspired by the "environmental Kuznetz curve" literature where an inverted U relationship is hypothesized to exist between pollution and economic activity (Grossman and Krueger, 1995). This relationship is explained by the fact that pollution first tends to increase with increased economic activity. However, development also leads to a structural transformation in what is produced and how, and with increased wealth natural amenities increase their value, giving stronger incentives to protect and thereby limit pollution. If the changes in technology as well as regulations that clean up or drive the most polluting industries out of the country are strong enough, the pollution will decrease at higher wealth levels. While controversial, there is substantial empirical support for this hypothesis.

There are a number of similarities between pollution and safety in that there are drivers that potentially can make both worse with increased economic activity, but that increased wealth also gives stronger incentives and ability to address the issues. We will apply the relatively simple model used by Grossman and Krueger (1995) due to the available data and since our motivation is to investigate if there is evidence of such a relationship. However, we recognize that there exist a number of extensions of Grossman and Krueger (1995), including building a firmer theoretical foundation, a substantial focus on the importance of trade and a decomposition of the total effect to scale, technology and composition of economic activity (Antweiler et al., 2001). These are extensions that are of interest in future research provided that there is a relationship between economic activity and safety, and if it has an inverted U shape.

## 2 Data

The key data series for this analysis is the Safe City Index produced by the Economist's Intelligence Unit (EIU, 2015), who were collecting the data in 2014. The index is composed of more than 40 quantitative and qualitative indicators, split across four thematic categories: digital security, health security, infrastructure safety and personal safety. All the 50 cities in the Index are scored across these four categories. However, we will have to exclude Doha and Teheran due to lack of gross domestic product (GDP) data. Hence, our data set contains 48 observations.

The index ranges between 0 and 100, with 100 as best. Hence, the higher the index the safer a city. Hence, if the relationship studied here is to resemble the environmental Kuznetz curve, it is U shaped, and not inverted U shaped as in Grossman and Krueger (1995). The 48 cities are spread around the world, as there are seven cities in North America, six in South America, six in the Middle East and Africa, 13 in Europe and 16 in the Asia-Pacific region. All cities are listed in Table 28.1.

*Table 28.1* Cities, safety index and GDP/capita

| *City* | *GDP/ capita* | *Safety index* | *City* | *GDP/ capita* | *Safety index* |
|---|---|---|---|---|---|
| Tokyo | 43,664 | 85,63 | Abu Dhabi | 61,009 | 69,83 |
| Singapore | 66,864 | 84,61 | Milan | 41,147 | 69,64 |
| Osaka | 35,902 | 82,36 | Rome | 38,025 | 67,13 |
| Stockholm | 56,25 | 80,02 | Santiago | 23,929 | 66,98 |
| Amsterdam | 45,265 | 79,19 | Shanghai | 24,065 | 65,93 |
| Sydney | 46,344 | 78,91 | Buenos Aires | 23,606 | 65,88 |
| Zurich | 56,666 | 78,84 | Shenzhen | 33,731 | 65,76 |
| Toronto | 45,771 | 78,81 | Lima | 16,53 | 65,01 |
| Melbourne | 40,244 | 78,67 | Tianjin | 24,224 | 63,55 |
| New York | 69,915 | 78,08 | Rio de Janeiro | 14,176 | 63,52 |
| Hong Kong | 57,244 | 77,24 | Kuwait City | 55,171 | 63,47 |
| San Francisco | 72,39 | 76,63 | Beijing | 23,39 | 63,25 |
| Taipei | 46,102 | 76,51 | Guangzhou | 29,014 | 62,79 |
| Montreal | 38,867 | 75,6 | Bangkok | 19,705 | 62,69 |
| Barcelona | 36,157 | 75,16 | Sao Paulo | 20,65 | 62,33 |
| Chicago | 58,861 | 74,89 | Istanbul | 24,867 | 62,25 |
| Los Angeles | 65,082 | 74,24 | Delhi | 12,747 | 61,88 |
| London | 57,157 | 73,83 | Moscow | 45,803 | 61,6 |
| Washington DC | 73,017 | 73,37 | Mumbai | 7,005 | 60,72 |
| Frankfurt | 51,645 | 73,05 | Mexico City | 19,239 | 59,46 |
| Madrid | 39,288 | 72,35 | Riyadh | 22,139 | 57,09 |
| Brussels | 46,298 | 71,72 | Johannesburg | 16,37 | 56,26 |
| Paris | 57,241 | 71,21 | Ho Chi Minh City | 8,66 | 54,93 |
| Seoul | 34,355 | 70,9 | Jakarta | 9,984 | 53,71 |

Data on GDP/capita is obtained from the 2014 Global Metro Monitor Map, and this is listed as well in Table 28.1. We have the same challenge as Grossman and Krueger (1995) in that GDP per capita for the individual cities are not readily available and/or comparable for all cities. However, the argument for using country data is even stronger here as regulations and legal system are the same within each country.

## 3 Empirical approach

Grossman and Krueger (1995) estimate a cubic relationship between pollution and GDP. Given the panel structure of their data, they also have an income smoothing term, as well as a set of regressors, mostly dummies, addressing specific data issues. We use a cross-section data set, and will only estimate the basic cubic relationship. That is, the most general relationship motivated by Grossman and Krueger (1995) to be estimated is given as:

$$S_i = a + b_1 * GDP_i + b_2 * GDP_i^2 + b_3 * GDP_i^3 + e_i \tag{1}$$

Here, $S_i$ is the safety index for city $i$, and $GDP_i$ is the GDP for the country of city $i$ and $e_i$ is an error term assumed to be white noise.

We will estimate three Grossman and Krueger style models with increased degree of flexibility. The first model (Model 1) will be a linear model. This is of interest as it will provide an indication of whether the general trend in the data is increased or reduced safety with increasing income levels. The second model (Model 2) is a quadratic model, which allow for a concave as well as a convex relationship. The final model (Model 3) is a cubic model allowing for the additional flexibility inherent in the cubic term.

## 4 Empirical results, U shaped relationships

With standard errors in the parenthesis, Model 1 gives the following result:

$$\begin{aligned} S_i = \ & 57.110 + 0.326 * GDP_i \\ & (1.886) \quad (0.044) \qquad R^2 = 0.543 \end{aligned} \tag{2}$$

With an $R^2$ of 0.543, the explanatory power of the model is reasonably good. Both the constant term and the parameter on the *GDP* variable are statistically significant at a 5% level. The fitted regression line is also shown in Figure 28.1. Hence, there is a statistically significant positive relationship between *GDP* and higher safety, providing a strong indication that there is a positive correlation between wealth and safety.

Next we turn to Model 2, the quadratic model. The results from this estimation is:

$$\begin{aligned} S_i = \ & 48.953 + 0.850 * GDP_i - 0.006 * GDP_i^2 \\ & (3.334) \quad (0.186) \qquad (0.002) \qquad R^2 = 0.614 \end{aligned} \tag{3}$$

The explanatory power of the Model 2 improves substantially relatively to model 1 as the reported $R^2$ is 0.614. Both the slope parameters as well as the constant term are statistically significant at a 5% level. Hence, there is strong statistical support for the quadratic model relatively

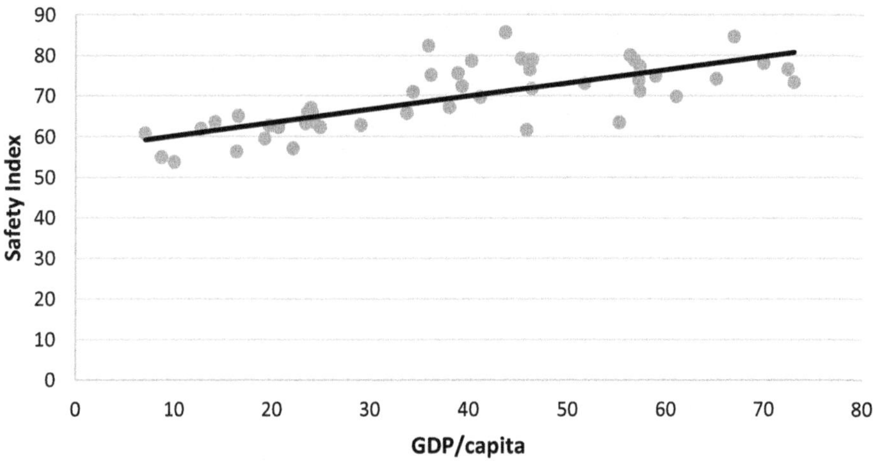


*Figure 28.1* Safety index vs. GDP/capita – model 1

to the linear model. The estimated parameter at 0.850 on the linear *GDP* term shows a much steeper slope than the slope parameter in the linear model, while the estimated parameter on the quadratic *GDP* term is negative, indicating an inverted U shape for the relationship. This is clearly evident in Figure 28.2 where the fitted regression line is shown together with the data.

The inverted U shape of the relationship is fundamentally different from the environmental Kuznets curve, as the safety index indicate improved safety with a higher value. Hence, with the initial positive slope, for poorer cities safety improves rapidly with increased income levels. However, the willingness to invest or the returns on additional investments or regulations to improve safety is diminishing with higher wealth levels. Taking the derivative of the relationship in equation (3) locates the peak at the relatively high income level of 70,800 USD/capita, but the curve is fairly flat at this point. Hence, the fact that there is a peak may well be an artifact of the functional form. The fact that the regression line is always increasing suggests that there is no period or level of economic activity where reduced safety facilitate economic growth.

Finally, we report the results for Model 3, the cubic model. The results from this estimation is:

$$\begin{aligned} S_i = \; & 51.182 + \quad 0.611 * GDP_i + \quad 0.0002 * GDP_i^2 - \quad 0.00005 * GDP_i^3 \\ & (6.088) \qquad (0.577) \qquad\qquad (0.015) \qquad\qquad\quad (0.0001) \\ & R^2 = 0.616 \end{aligned} \tag{4}$$

The explanatory power of the Model 3 barely improves relatively to Model 2 with a gain of 0.2%. Moreover, all the parameters on the GDP terms are statistically insignificant at any conventional significance level. However, the $F$-test that all the slope parameters are zero is clearly rejected with a $p$-value $< 0.001$. Hence, there is a strong indication of multicollinearity. Hence, Model 3 performs much poorer statistically than the other two models. The fitted regression line is shown in Figure 28.3 together with the data. Even though the slope parameters are statistically insignificant, it is striking how similar the fitted line is to the one in Model 2. This is despite the fact that the parameter on the quadratic term is now positive, and it is first the cubic term that provides the curve with a negative parameter.

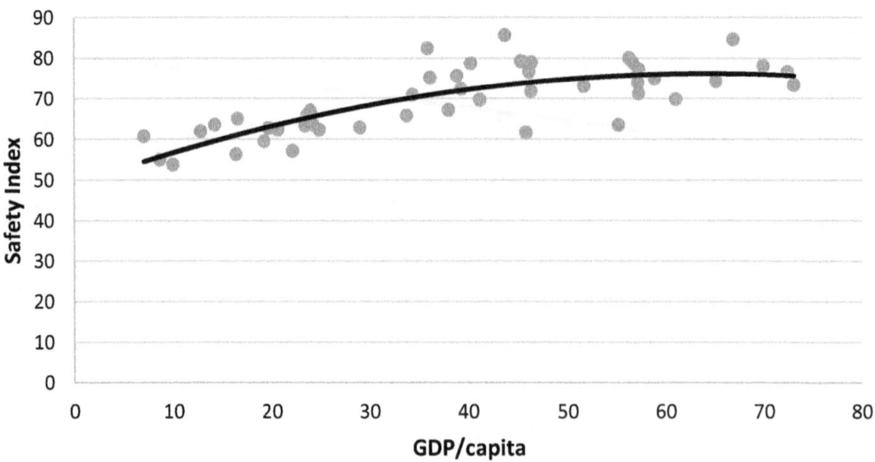


*Figure 28.2* Safety index vs. GDP/capita – model 2

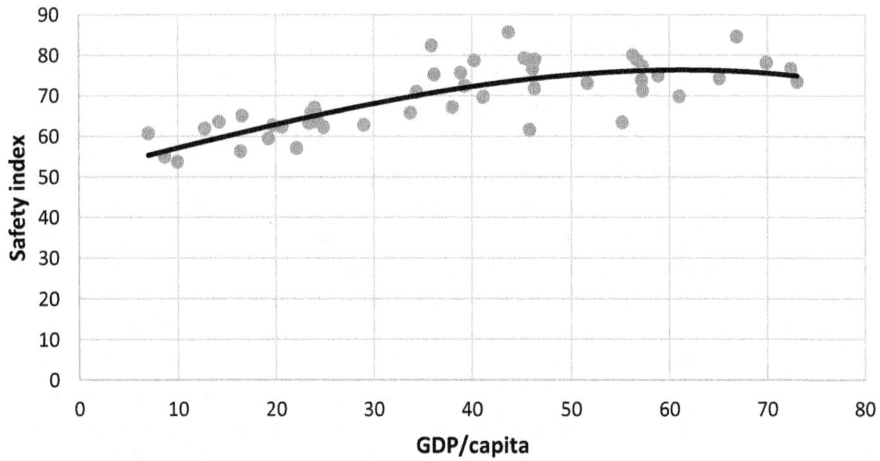


*Figure 28.3* Safety index vs. GDP/capita – model 3

## 5 Other functional forms

The poor performance of Model 3 suggests that a cubic functional form is not a good choice for this data set. The results in Models 1–3 suggest that the reason may be that there do not seem to a where safety deteriorates as economic growth commences. Rather, it seems like safety improves with economic growth, but at a declining rate. We will therefore estimate to relationships were the functional form implies asymptotic convergence.

Our Model 4 will add the term 1/*GDP* to the linear Model 1. This equation gives the following result:

$$\begin{array}{llll} S_i = 63.744 & + \; 0.230 * GDP_i & - \; 80.405 * 1/GDP_i & \\ \quad\;\; (4.584) & \quad (0.075) & \quad (50.801) & R^2 = 0.567 \end{array} \tag{5}$$

The fitted regression line is shown in Figure 28.4 together with the data. As one can see, this model only has a marginally better fit than Model 1, and the $1/GDP$ term is not statistically significant. Hence, this model specification also seems to be a poorer representation than the quadratic specification.

Our final model, Model 5, will also include the term $1/GDP_i^2$. The results from this model are given as:

$$\begin{aligned} S_i = {} & \underset{(11.261)}{89.224} - \underset{(0.135)}{0.053} * GDP_i - \underset{(244.64)}{668.72} * 1/GDP_i + \underset{(1353.95)}{3321.06} * 1/GDP_i^2 \\ & R^2 = 0.619 \end{aligned} \tag{6}$$

The fitted regression line is shown in Figure 28.5 together with the data. Here, the linear term is not statistically significant, but both the terms with GDP in the denominator is. The

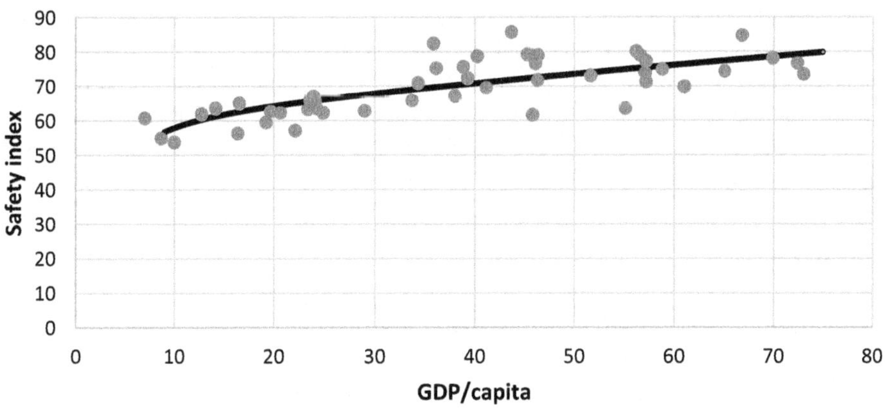


*Figure 28.4* Safety index vs. GDP/capita – model 4

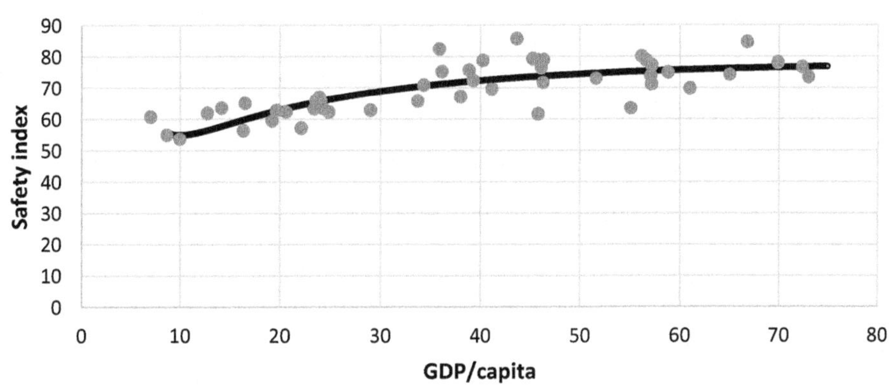


*Figure 28.5* Safety index vs. GDP/capita – model 5

negative parameter on the first order term ensures that the regression line is increasing, while the positive parameter on the second order term in the relevant range is just bending the curve down slightly. The $R^2$ at 0.619 is slightly higher than in the quadratic and also the cubic model, but providing essentially the same fit.

## 5 Concluding remarks

In this chapter we have applied the concept of an environmental Kuznetz curve to relate safety to economic growth. In an analogue fashion as for environmental impact, the literature indicates that increased economic activity introduce new risks that possibly may reduce safety levels. However, with enough resources available, societies are expected to spend more resources to reduce risk.

Overall, results indicate a strong positive relationship between safety and economic growth, but where safety is growing with GDP at a declining rate. Hence, there is no evidence in this data of increased activity reducing safety. However, it should be noted that our data is all recent, and from large and relatively wealthy cities. We can therefore not rule out that such a relationship exist in poorer economies. We have estimated the relationship between safety and economic activity with a number of functional forms. The cubic form of Grossman and Krueger (1995) does not work very well, presumably because there is no inflexion point or U-shaped relationship in our data. Within the range of our data, there is only evidence that societies with higher economic activity are safer, but that economic activity increase at a faster rate than safety. This is not very surprising, as one would expect that the law of diminishing marginal returns applies also to safety.

## References

Antweiler, Werner, Copeland, Brian, R. and Taylor, M. Scott. 2001. Is Free Trade Good for the Environment? *The American Economic Review* 91(4): 877–908.

The Economist Intelligence Unit (EIU). 2015. The Safest Cities Index 2015 – Assessing Urban Security in the Digital Age. http://safecities.economist.com/report/safe-cities-index-white-paper/ (Accessed 19 October 2016).

Grossman, Gene M. and Krueger, Alan B. 1995. Economic Growth and the Environment. *The Quarterly Journal of Economics* 110(2): 353–377.

Pronovost, P.J., Powers, J. and Jin, W. 2016. Technology Development in Health Care Is Broken. *American Journal of Medical Quality*, August 25 (Epub ahead of print) https:/doi.org/10.1177/1062860616666165.

Viscusi, W. Kip. and Moore, Michael J. 1987. Workers' Compensation: Wage Effects, Benefit Inadequacies, and the Value of Health Losses. *The Review of Economics and Statistics* 69(2): 249–261.

Weinger, M.B. and Gaba, D.M. 2014. Human Factors Engineering in Patient Safety. *Anesthesiology* 120: 801–806.

WHO (World Health Organization). Increasing Complexity of Medical Technology and Consequences for Training and Outcome of Care. Background paper 4. August 2010.

Yu, A., Flott, K., Chainani, et al. 2016. *Patient Safety 2030*. London, UK: NIHR Imperial Patient Safety Translational Research Centre.

# 29

# The role of decision-making support systems in risk management

*Manuel Mora, Gloria Phillips-Wren and Fen Wang*

## 1 Introduction

Every business organization is exposed daily to a set of unwanted events caused by natural or artificial (intentional or non-intentional) sources that can produce damage on human beings and organizational assets (Leven, 2016). To cope with such negative events and their potential consequences, the field of risk management has emerged as a scientific discipline in the last 40 years. In a few words, risk management refers to anticipating the occurrence of potential negative events, estimating their effects, and elaborating and implementing suitable actions against them. Risk management methods are used in several relevant fields such as project management (Raz and Michael, 2001), financial investments (Aebi et al., 2011), hazards management (Liu et al., 2016) and business continuity (Torabi et al., 2014), among others.

In this chapter, we introduce and review the characteristics of a set of specialized computer-based systems called Decision-Making Support Systems (DMSS) (Forgionne et al., 2000) as valuable tools for supporting a risk management process. Our aim is to provide a brief but well-structured introduction to DMSS, the risk management process, linkages between DMSS and risk management, and illustrative applications in order to promote awareness of the usefulness and value of DMSS to risk managers. Toward this goal, we summarize the main concepts and characteristics of the risk management process in section 2; we review the types and characteristics of DMSS in section 3; we report six illustrative application examples of DMSS in several risk management domains in section 4; we present a discussion of implications for risk managers on the availability of DMSS to support a risk management process in section 5; and finally we close this chapter with conclusions, limitations and final recommendations.

## 2 Review of risk management process

Risk management is the overall process of identifying, analyzing and monitoring risks as well as designing and implementing risk treatments for those risks (NIST, 2002). Risk management (Aven, 2016) is a field of study and practice established and matured over the last 40 years with the overall aim of conceptualizing, assessing and managing risks. The concept of risk has been defined in several qualitative and quantitative forms, but all of them share the notion of an undesirable uncertainty event which would cause damage on humans and/or assets valued by humans (Aven, 2016). The risk management field has permeated and influenced other domains such as project management (Raz and Michael, 2001), financial investments (Aebi et al., 2011), hazards management (Liu et al., 2016) and business continuity (Torabi et al., 2014), among others. The impact of risk management on other fields shows that it has high practical value.

For instance, Raz and Michael (2001) reported that risk management is an essential process that accompanies the whole project life cycle through planning, execution, control and completion phases. Furthermore, the body of knowledge from the Project Management Institute (PMI, 1996) includes the risk management process as one of their eight core areas. Aebi et al. (2011) reported the criticality of the risk management function exercised by a chief risk officer (CRO) in banks. In particular, they found that banks with adequate governance structures for risk management had better performance than those with weak governance structures. Liu et al. (2016) highlighted the usefulness of a risk management process to address natural hazards such as earthquakes, hurricanes, volcanic eruption, river flood, and landslide among others. They elaborated a classification of hazard interactions to complement the current Multi-Hazard Risk Management (MHRA) method (Marzocchi et al., 2009). Torabi et al. (2014) supported the implicit and required utilization of risk management techniques as well as of the Business Impact Analysis (BIA), as part of the Business Continuity Management (BCM) process with the aim of increasing business organizational resilience after disruptions caused by the realization of risks. These authors elaborated a comprehensive BIA framework supported with multi-attribute decision making (MADM) methods based on the notion of the concept risk appetite defined as "the amount of risk that an organization is willing to pursue or retain" (Torabi et al., 2014, p. 314).

A risk management process usually covers three sub-processes: Risk Assessment, Risk Mitigation, and Risk Evaluation (NIST, 2002). An updated concept of risk management in the context of Information Technology standards (NIST, 2012) covers the following phases: Risk Framing, Risk Assessment, Risk Responses, and Risk Monitoring. Both traditional and updated concepts can be mapped as follows: traditional Risk Assessment sub-process includes updated Risk Framing and Assessment sub-processes; traditional Risk Mitigation sub-process corresponds to updated Risk Responses; and traditional Risk Evaluation sub-process corresponds to Risk Monitoring.

The purpose of the Risk Framing sub-process (NIST, 2012) is to establish the high-level organizational context for implementing the right level, neither under nor over, of a risk management process. A risk management strategy is delineated and decisional boundaries are established. A high-level analysis of the organizational context including priorities, assumptions, trade-offs, as well as selection of risk approaches, models and methods are established. In particular, a risk model is a core operational concept because it defines the specific elements to be included in the analysis of risks and their interrelationships. In NIST (2002, 2012) the expected elements are: threats, sources of threats, threats scenarios, threats shifting, assets vulnerabilities, severities of vulnerabilities, likelihood of threat exploitation on vulnerabilities, harm impact on assets, likelihood of occurrence of harm impact, final organizational risk as the product of the harm impact and its likelihood of occurrence, and risk uncertainty level. This first sub-process is critical to establish a formal risk management process in the organization and is executed as a preparation sub-process for the next one of risk management.

The purpose of the Risk Assessment sub-process (NIST, 2002, 2012) is to determine the specific organizational risks through the detailed analysis of threats, vulnerabilities, impacts, likelihoods and uncertainties (i.e. by using the agreed risk model). To achieve the goal, a specific and agreed risk management approach, method and type of analysis (i.e. qualitative, quantitative or hybrid) is used. This sub-process can be considered the core essential sub-process because a wrong analysis of organizational risks will lead to failed actions and countermeasures for risk treatments with potential severe economic and organizational impacts. In some cases, the harm can be also on human beings, thus, this sub-process becomes critical.

The next sub-process is Risk Mitigation/Risk Responses (NIST, 2002, 2012). Its purpose can be stated as "prioritizing, evaluating, and implementing the appropriate risk-reducing controls recommended from the risk assessment process" (NIST, 2002, p. 27). For each organizational risk, the selected alternative courses of action for coping with the risk in consistency with the organizational risk strategy must be developed, evaluated and implemented (NIST, 2012). This third sub-process is also very important because it is usually economically impractical or impossible to eliminate organizational risks, and thus, adequate and economically viable countermeasures must be proposed and implemented in the organization (NIST, 2002, 2012). The risk mitigation countermeasures can be one of the following according to NIST (2002): (1) risk acceptance; (2) risk avoidance; (3) risk limitation; (4) risk planning; (5) risk acknowledgement and research treatment; and (6) risk transference. Naturally, every organization must be treated with different risk mitigation actions based on their economic and impact analysis.

The final sub-process is Risk Evaluation/Risk Monitoring (NIST, 2002, 2012). The purpose of this sub-process is to conduct an ongoing evaluation and monitoring of the implemented risk mitigation countermeasures, as well as to watch over organizational and external changes that may reduce the effectiveness of the current mitigation actions. In this sub-process, also the compliance or adherence analysis to best risk management practices and external regulations is conducted.

Table 29.1 summarizes the essential characteristics of the risk management sub-processes as reported in the consulted sources (NIST, 2002, 2012).

## 3 A review of decision-making process and decision-making support systems (DMSS)

Decision-Making Support Systems (DMSS) are computer-based systems designed to support some or all phases of a decision-making process (Forgionne et al., 2000). A high-level generic decision-making process (Forgionne et al., 2000; Mora et al., 2014) can be defined as a managerial process of five phases: *intelligence, design, choice, implementation* and *learning*.

In the *intelligence* phase, the decision maker gains a fundamental understanding of, and acquires the general information needed to address, the organization's problems or opportunities. In the *design* phase, the decision maker develops a specific and precise model that can be used to systematically examine the discovered problem or opportunity. Using the explicit model to logically evaluate the specified alternatives and to generate recommended actions constitute the ensuing *choice* phase. During the subsequent *implementation* phase, the decision maker ponders the analyses and recommendations, weighs the consequences, gains sufficient confidence in the decision, and implements a final decision. In the final *learning* phase, the decision maker or decision team reviews the process and outcomes with learning purposes (e.g. for reinforcing good practices and discouraging bad ones).

Figure 29.1 (adapted from Mora et al., 2014) illustrates this high-level generic decision-making process with their phases, inputs and outputs.

DMSS have been available since the early 1980s, and they have evolved during these last 45 years (Shim et al., 2002). We can report the existence of classic and modern DMSS

*Table 29.1* Risk management process and sub-processes profile

| *RISK MANAGEMENT PROCESS PROFILE* | | | |
|---|---|---|---|
| *SUB-PROCESS* | *INPUTS* | *TASKS* | *OUTPUTS* |
| Risk Assessment (NIST, 2002) / Risk Framing (NIST, 2012) | • Risk Context (assumptions, constraints, priorities and tradeoffs, tolerance and uncertainty levels) | • Identify the purpose of the assessment<br>• Identify the scope of the assessment<br>• Identify the assumptions and constraints associated with the assessment<br>• Identify the sources of information to be used as inputs to the assessment<br>• Identify the risk model and analytic approaches to be employed during the assessment | • Risk management strategy<br>• Risk assessment methodology (risk steps, risk model, assessment approach, and analysis approach). |
| Risk Assessment (NIST, 2002) / Risk Assessment (NIST, 2012) | • Inventory of assets<br>• History of attacks<br>• Data from intelligence on attacks<br>• Reports from prior risk managements<br>• Current Controls<br>• Security Requirements<br>• Threats-Sources Profiles<br>• Criticality of assets | • Identify threat sources that are relevant to organizations<br>• Identify threat events that could be produced by those sources<br>• Identify vulnerabilities within organizations that could be exploited by threat sources<br>• Determine the likelihood of identified threat sources<br>• Determine the adverse impacts to organizational operations and assets<br>• Determine information security risks including any uncertainties associated with the risk determinations | • System boundaries<br>• List of Threats-Sources<br>• List of Potential Vulnerabilities<br>• Current and Potential Controls<br>• Likelihood Rating<br>• Impact Rating<br>• Risks and Risks Levels<br>• Recommended Controls |
| Risk Mitigation (NIST, 2002)/Risk Responses (NIST, 2012) | • Risk Management Report | • Prioritize actions<br>• Evaluate recommended control actions<br>• Conduct Cost-Benefit analysis<br>• Select control<br>• Assign responsibility<br>• Develop a safeguard implementation plan<br>• Implement selected controls | • Actions ranking from High to Low<br>• List of possible Controls<br>• Cost-Benefit Analysis<br>• Selected Controls<br>• List of Responsible Persons<br>• Safeguard Implementation Plan<br>• Residual Risks |
| Risk Evaluation (NIST, 2002)/Risk Monitoring (NIST, 2012) | • Risk Management Report<br>• Risk Mitigation/ Responses Report<br>• Risk Management Regulations<br>• Best Practices on Risk Management Reports | • Determine the ongoing effectiveness of risk responses<br>• Identify risk-impacting changes to organizational assets and the environments<br>• Conduct audit evaluations<br>• Trace risk management best practices and new regulations | • Risk Evaluation/ Monitoring Report |

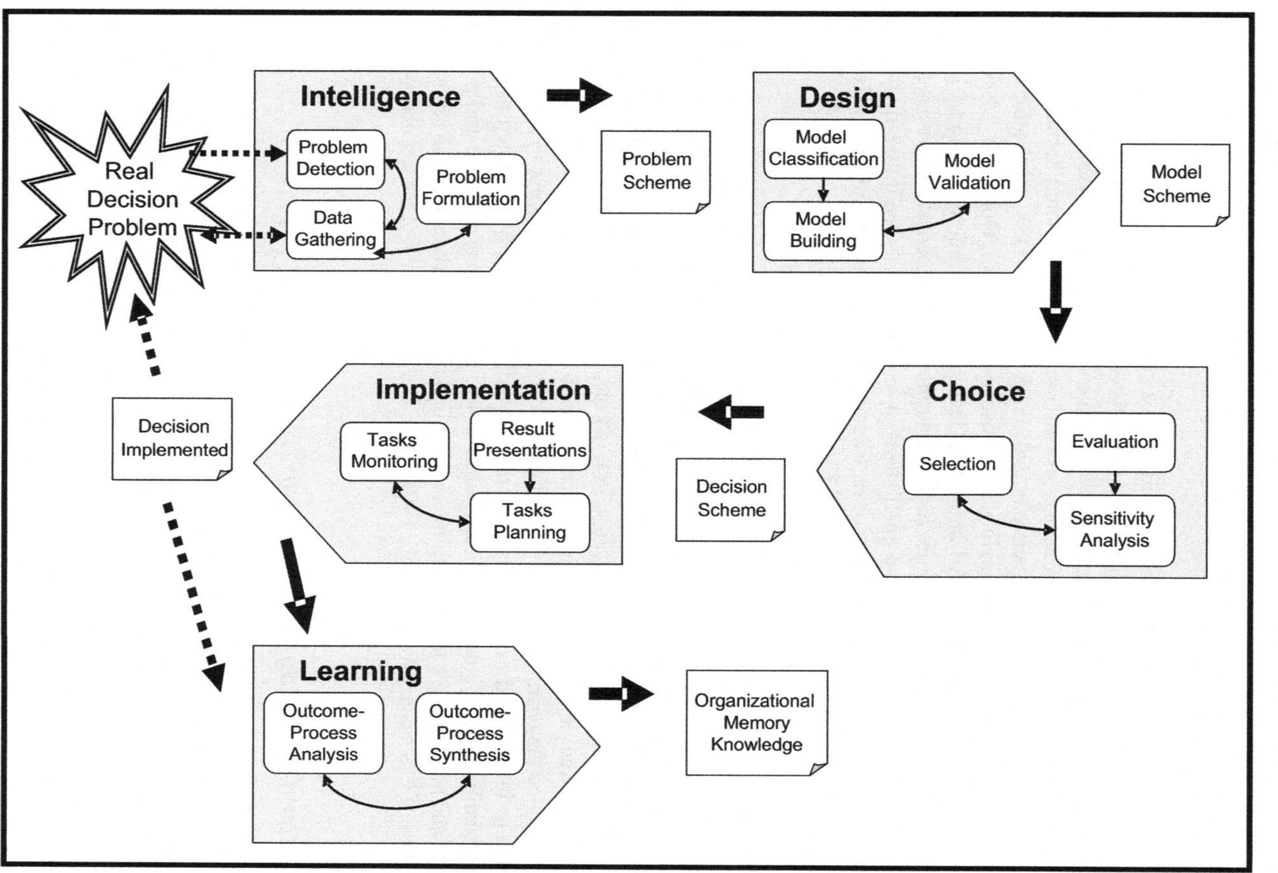


*Figure 29.1* A high-level generic decision-making process

*Source*: Mora et al. (2014)

(Forgionne et al., 2005). Classic DMSS are Decision Support Systems (DSS), Executive Information Systems (EIS), and Expert Systems/Knowledge-based Systems (ES/KBS). Modern DMSS are Data Warehouse-based Business Intelligence tools (DW/BI) and Data Mining-based and Business Analytics DMSS (DM/BA), and intelligent DMSS (i-DMSS).

### *Decision support systems (DSS)*

According to Sprague (1980), "a DSS is an interactive computer-based system which helps decision makers utilizing data and quantitative models to solve semi-structured problems." A DSS offers the following capabilities: what-if analysis of scenarios, goal-seeking analysis, and sensitivity analysis of variables. A DSS is usually used by staff personal in the organizations, top managers, and executive decisions makers. A survey of DSS applications (Eom and Kim, 2006), pointed out that the main areas of use are Production/Operation, Marketing, Finance and Strategic Management. An interesting fact is that the underlying model in DSS was initially totally quantitative in nature (either deterministic or stochastic), but has shifted to a hybrid nature (i.e. quantitative and qualitative) in modern times. Qualitative models are now based on Artificial Intelligence techniques. Literature reports successful cases of the use of DSS (Sprague and Carlson, 1982; Eom and Kim, 2006).

### *Executive information systems (EIS)*

An Executive Information Systems (EIS) according to Rockart and Treacy (1982) "is a computer based system which let to access a common core of data covering key internal and external business variables by time and by business unit." Rockart and Tracy discovered in the early '80s that some top executives (i.e. CEOs, CFOs) were using special information systems, which allowed them to monitor and track key performance indicators of the company. Thus, they coined the term: EIS. The capabilities typical of an EIS are access to summarized information as internal and external key performance indicators usually presented as graphical and text-tables displays, analysis through drill-down, roll-up, slice and dice and pivoting operations, and networking communications to bulletin boards. The literature also reports successful cases of EIS usage (Watson et al., 1991; Elam and Leidner, 1995; Rainer and Watson, 1995).

### *Expert systems/knowledge-based systems (ES/KBS)*

An ES/KBS, according to several researchers in the field (Feigenbaum et al., 1988; Liebowitz, 1990) is a computer based system that exhibits, in a specific domain, a high degree of expertise in problem solving that is comparable to that of a human expert. An ES/KBS contains three main components: a knowledge base specialized in a specific domain, an inference algorithm, and a user interface. Two types of problems are usually addressed: classification (e.g. diagnosing, repairing, prediction, interpretation, monitoring and control) or construction (e.g. scheduling, configuration, planning or designing). An ES/KBS offers the following capabilities: intelligent advice, qualitative reasoning, problem-solving assistance, and explanation of advices. Successful cases of ES/KBS are reported from several sources (Feigenbaum et al., 1988; Eom, 1996). The difference between an ES and a KBS is that the former contains the knowledge of a recognized expert in the field and the second contains only knowledge valuable for the organization.

## *Data warehouse-based and business intelligence tools (DW/BI)*

A Data Warehouse is a specialized organizational macro data base usually composed of a large number of dimensions and containing a huge quantity of records (Wixom and Watson, 2001). A Data Warehouse is defined as "subject-oriented, integrated, time-invariant, non-updatable collection of data used to support management decision-making processes and business intelligence" (March and Hevner, 2007, p. 1031). A Data Warehouse is the organizational repository of relevant data sets which can be exploited through computer-based systems named Business Intelligence (BI) tools. BI tools aim to support Business Intelligence activities in an organization. BI activities refers essentially to scanning environmental and organizationally relevant data and interpreting those data to produce organizational knowledge (i.e. interpreted information useful for a specific organizational context) (March and Hevner, 2007). BI tools emerged as the evolution of EIS (Adam and Pomerol, 2002) to reach all organizational levels in addition to the top management level addressed by EIS. BI tools, thus, provide the same capabilities as EIS (i.e. graph and text-tables displays, analysis through drill-down, roll-up, slice and dice and pivoting operations, and networking communications to bulletin boards, among others) but they are released to end-users through the concept of Dashboards. Dashboards are systems that present a controlled display of the main indicators of interest for a decision maker, and their name comes as an analogy of the car dashboards for drivers.

Similar to classic DMSS, DW/BI tools have provided several benefits to users such as a better understanding of the decision context, increased decision-making productivity, positive change on how people perform tasks, effective decision support, improved on-line analytical processing, availability of high quality/accurate/secure data, high payback, and low cost access (Wixom and Watson, 2001; March and Hevner, 2007; Ramamurthy et al., 2008).

## *Data mining and business analytics tools (DM/BA)*

These types of DMSS are based on the application of classical and modern statistical algorithms and heuristic intelligent, both numerical and logical, techniques that discover useful relationships among (usually) a vast quantity of heterogonous sources of data mainly for classification and prediction purposes (Davenport, 2006; Delen and Demirkan, 2013; Watson, 2014). Data Mining (also called Knowledge Discovery in Databases) emerged from the Artificial Intelligence research community (Fayyad et al., 1996) with the aim of coping with the massive quantity of heterogeneous sources of data available from new information and communication technologies (i.e. massive use of internet, cloud computing, social web tools, RFID devices, mobile phones and tablets, and so on). This technological availability also enabled the convergence of advanced visually oriented tools. Analytics, then, encompasses a set of statistical and intelligent heuristics algorithms for exploring, analyzing and visualizing huge quantities of heterogeneous sources of data.

According to Delen and Demirkan (2013), and Watson (2014), analytics can be classified as one of three types: descriptive, predictive, and prescriptive. Descriptive analytics refers to the already well-known reporting, OLAP, dashboards/scorecards, and data visualization techniques (i.e. DW/BI DMSS tools). Predictive analytics covers techniques such as regression analysis, machine learning, and neural networks, with the aim of providing forecasts based on historical data. Finally, prescriptive analytics includes techniques such as optimization modeling, simulation modeling, multi-criteria decision modeling, expert systems and group support systems with the aim of obtaining optimal or near-optimal solutions (i.e. decisional courses of action) for complex problems.

### *Intelligent and integrated DMSS (i-DMSS)*

These types of DMSS emerged by the need to combine the capabilities of single DMSS (i.e. a DSS, an EIS or an ES/KBS) and add human-like intelligent capabilities to traditional DMSS. Several research efforts were conducted toward this goal (Turban and Watkins, 1986; DeLong and Rockart, 1986; Elam and Konsynski, 1987; Turban and Watson, 1989; Klein and Methie, 1990; Forgionne, 1991; King, 1992; Forgionne and Kohli, 1996; and Turban and Aronson, 1998).

For instance, Turban and Watkins (1986) proposed to integrate DSS and ES/KBS to add the qualitative modeling capabilities of an ES/KBS to enhance a DSS. Delong and Rockart (1986), proposed the integration of a DSS with an EIS to add analytical capabilities to EIS, and to extend the time frame of analysis from past and present to future forecasted data. Elam and Konsynski (1987) developed the first prototypes to improve the management model modules of DSS by using intelligent techniques. Turban and Watson (1989), Forgionne (1991) and Forgionne and Kohli (1996), posed the integration of DSS, EIS and ES/KBS. The main aim was to support all the phases of the decision-making process that stand-alone systems are unable to do. Turban and Watson (1989), and Forgionne (1991) developed a conceptual model proposing how this integration could be developed. Forgionne and Kohli (1996), based on this model, developed an intelligent integrated DMSS and tested its effectiveness and efficiency versus stand-alone systems in an experimental setting. King (1992) suggested the addition of why-analysis to traditional DSS. Why-analysis consists of explanation facilities in quantitative models to track how a numerical variable in the model reached a particular value. Klein and Methie (1990) suggested this integration to access data and knowledge bases in order to effectively support decision makers in complex and ill-structured tasks. Finally, Turban and Aronson (1998) surveyed the potential usage of other intelligent-based technologies including Genetic Algorithms, Fuzzy Logic Systems, Neural Networks, Case-Based Reasoning, and Knowledge-Management Systems (KMS). Most modern efforts are oriented to ontology-based systems (Chandrasekaran et al., 1999). Instances of these integrations and successful cases of intelligent DMSS were reported in Gupta et al. (2005).

Classical and modern DMSS have been widely used in organizations because when they are successfully implemented, they provide benefits such as improved organizational performance, better decision quality, improved communication, enhanced mental models, amplified analytical skills of decision makers, and reduced decision times among others (Turban and Aronson, 1998; Forgionne and Kohli, 2000; Eom and Kim, 2006; March and Hevner, 2007; Davenport, 2006; Delen and Demirkan, 2013; Watson, 2014). Table 29.2 summarizes the main capabilities provided by the different types of DMSS tools regarding the phases conducted in a generic decision-making process.

Hence, we propose that classical and modern DMSS can be very adequate tools for supporting a risk management process in all domains of application. However, the design and utilization of DMSS in general are not seamless organizational implementations despite the benefits of deploying them. Technical and organizational challenges must be addressed and solved to achieve a successful DMSS design, build and implementation (Setzekorn et al., 2002; Mora et al., 2013).

## 4 Utilization of DMSS in risk management – six illustrative cases

Six illustrative cases are reviewed to indicate the ways that DMSS have been utilized in risk management, and their highlights are summarized in Table 29.3. The purpose of this section

*Table 29.2* Decision-making process vs. DMSS capabilities by DMSS type

| *Decision-making process phase* | *DMSS Type* | | | | |
|---|---|---|---|---|---|
| | *DSS* | *EIS* | *ES/KBS* | *DW/BI* | *DM/BA* |
| Intelligence | — | Drill-Down, Roll-Out, Pivoting, Executive Dashboards on Data warehouses | Conceptual knowledge stored and logical inferences for analysis and synthesis tasks | Drill-Down, Roll-Out, Pivoting, Visual Reporting, Multiple Dashboards on Data warehouses | Descriptive Analytics for reporting and visualizing past facts |
| Design | — | — | | — | Predictive Analytics for exploring and elaborating forecasts models |
| Choice | What-if, Goal-Seeking, Sensitivity Analysis on Quantitative Models | — | | — | Prescriptive Analytics for searching optimal or satisfactory solutions on Quantitative Models |
| Implementation | — | Drill-Down, Roll-Out, Pivoting, Executive Dashboards on Data warehouses | | Drill-Down, Roll-Out, Pivoting, Visual Reporting, Multiple Dashboards on Data warehouses | Descriptive Analytics for reporting and visualizing past facts |
| Learning | — | — | | — | Predictive Analytics for exploring and elaborating predictive models |

is to provide evidence that DMSS have improved decision making involving risky decisions by capturing risk factors in a quantitative and qualitative manner, thereby mitigating risk in real applications.

Areas such as life insurance are driven as part of their business strategy to provide fast, accurate decisions as a competitive advantage. Meyer et al. (1992) diagnosed the flow of information and the process of making a determination on life insurance underwriting and found signification opportunities to improve the decision-making process. They evaluated two expert systems at two companies, John Hancock and Lincoln National. John Hancock approved 43% of applications within 24 hours, reducing expenses and permitting underwriters to focus on more complex cases. Lincoln National formed a new organizational unit and a product that could be sold to other insurance companies. Both expert systems supported the companies' strategic plans and improved decision making in risky situations.

Deshmulch and Millet (1999) used previous research on groupings and subgroupings of red flags for management fraud to create a three-level Analytic Hierarchy Process (AHP) model as part of a DMSS that could be used by independent auditors. Rather than a relative measurement scale, risk factors were rated by an absolute scale of intensity allowing each auditor to express the extent to which the risk factor is present on the lowest level. Weights were assigned to criteria based on the user's preferences. The authors demonstrated the method in a generalized case study.

A scenario-based approach was proposed by Li et al. (2009) to involve decision makers and stakeholders in each step of the process to assess risk in emergency management. A value tree was developed that includes key assets and impact. Several methods were proposed to develop an integrative value of impact such as AHP for a preliminary assessment of relative preferences. Value functions for performance measures were generated, and consistency between decision makers was assessed. A performance index for a scenario was then developed. The authors ranked 80 scenarios of random failures based on their performance indices. A major difficulty, however, was the uncertainty associated with the probability of occurrence of an adverse event, although these uncertainties can be reduced through more information.

Dey (2010) used AHP to identify project level risks and select the least risky project. The method was applied to a cross-country oil pipeline project in western India comparing four pipeline routes. Dey attempted to capture both business risks and operational risks as determined by a team of experts. The author noted that although the method is tedious and time-consuming, the combined AHP and risk map was a useful technique for risk analysis and potential response planning.

Wu (2014) surveyed risk analysis tools and application areas. The author classified risks as either field based or property based. Field-based risks are those associated with the context; for example, financial risk includes market risk, credit risk, liquidity risk and so forth. Property-based risk are those associated with the four properties that the author states as uncertainty, dynamics, interconnection and dependence and complexity. The author reviewed risk management tools at a high level to be computational intelligence (e.g. artificial intelligence methods and data mining) and optimization (e.g. forecasting and automatic control).

Choi et al. (2016) discussed challenges in applying big data analytics to business applications. The authors presented an extensive references list and review of the literature to conclude that there are a myriad of opportunities. However, there are also significant challenges including cost, value, data quality, and systems security.

The six studies reviewed are summarized in Table 29.3.

## 5 Discussions and implications on the linkage between DMSS and risk management

In the previous sections, we have summarized the main concepts and characteristics of the risk management process, reviewed the types and characteristics of DMSS tools, and reported six illustrative application examples of DMSS tools in several risk management domains. Throughout the discussion, we have identified the theoretical as well as practical linkages between DMSS and risk management processes. Figure 29.2 below illustrates the theoretical

*Table 29.3* Case studies of risk management applications

| *Authors* | *Publication Date* | *Industry Area* | *Brief Description* |
|---|---|---|---|
| Meyer et al. | 1992 | Underwriting life insurance | Linkage between business strategy and development of large-scale expert systems in the context of project selection and evolution |
| Deshmulch and Millet | 1999 | Management fraud | Identify significant red flags to independent auditors using AHP |
| Li et al. | 2009 | Pre-disaster planning and actions applied to university campus | Systematic methodology to assess and rank the risks from multiple hazards in a community |
| Dey | 2010 | Oil pipeline construction project | Integrated framework using AHP and risk map for managing project risks |
| Wu et al. | 2014 | Survey of risk analysis tools and application areas | Introduction to special issue on business intelligence in risk management |
| Choi et al. | 2016 | Industrial-based business systems, reliability and security of industrial systems, and operational risk management | Challenges and opportunities of big data analytics in industrial systems |

mapping framework between the generic decision-making processes and risk management processes in the context of Information Technology standards.

As illustrated in Figure 29.2 above, the essential risk management process and its sub-processes can be naturally mapped to the established generic decision-making process and the five phases therein. For instance, the *intelligence* phase of the generic decision-making process, when mapped to the essential risk management sub process of Risk Framing, involves acquiring risk relevant contextual information and identifying possible risks in the identified organizational and/or project context. Next, in the *design* phase of the generic decision-making process, which is mapped to the essential risk management sub-process of risk management, decision makers or managers would identify or develop a relevant risk model to analyze and assess the identified risks in terms of their probabilities and consequences. Following that, generating recommended actions and responses and putting that into final decisions and strategies correspond to the *choice* phase and *implementation* phase respectively of the generic decision-making process, which are mapped to the essential risk management sub-process of Risk Responses and Risk Mitigation. Finally, in the *learning* phase of the generic decision-making process, which is mapped to the essential risk management sub-process of Risk Evaluation and Monitoring, decision makers or managers review, evaluate, and monitor the process and outcomes of implemented risk mitigation strategies for future organizational learning.

Accordingly, DMSS, which are designed to support some or all phases of a decision-making process, can be considered as valuable and pertinent tools for supporting a risk management process. Table 29.4 illustrates the application framework of applying relevant DMSS tools and capabilities to the specific risk management sub processes.

From an applied perspective, executives and decision makers of worldwide organizations are facing challenges of effective risk management in the current era and they look for

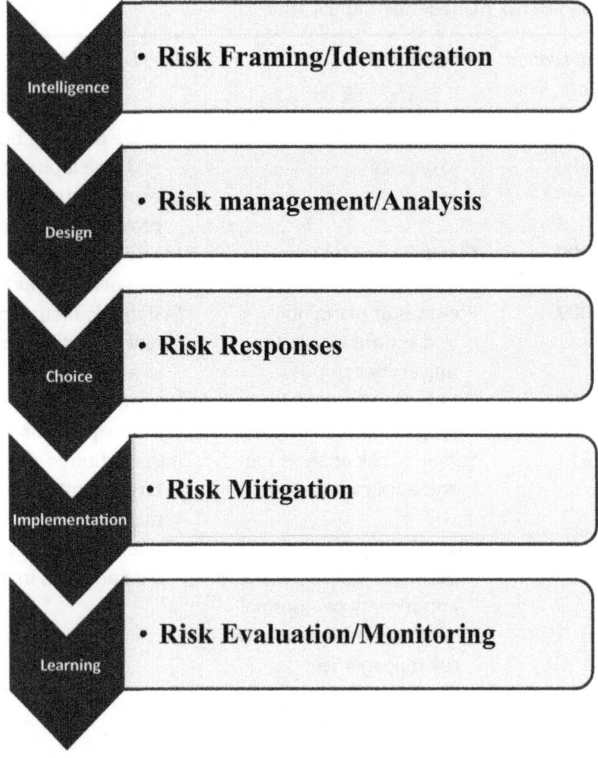


*Figure 29.2* Theoretical mapping framework of Decision-Making Process and Risk Management

practical DMSS solutions that can help them better identify, assess, mitigate, and monitor organizational risks. This integrative review paper adds to this body of knowledge and helps facilitate additional research and practical endeavors.

Based on the richness and variety of risk management application and research findings, we can present the following recommendations and cautions to executives and decision makers interested in applying relevant DMSS tools to managing organizational risks:

- All industry fields face the challenges of effective and efficient risk management and both classical and modern DMSS solutions can help them better identify, assess, mitigate, and monitor organizational risks.
- To effectively address risk management challenges, classic DMSS solutions need to be equipped with modern and advanced techniques depending on the data types, sources, structures, constraints, priorities, uncertainty levels, and other organizational characteristics involved.
- Practitioners across different industries can utilize the presented application framework to adopt or develop appropriate DMSS techniques and solutions to reduce risks and derive the intended benefits of making well-informed decisions and risk strategies.
- Big data brings a new culture and way of decision making and risk management. Besides technical challenges, managerial challenges of DMSS for risk management in the current era must be addressed to reap the full benefits of that transition.

*Table 29.4* The application framework of applying DMSS to risk management processes

| *Risk Management Sub-Process* | *Main Tasks* | *Suggested DMSS Tools* | *Relevant DMSS Capabilities* |
|---|---|---|---|
| Risk Management / Risk Framing | • Establish the high-level organizational context and decisional boundaries for risk management | • EIS<br>• ES/KBS<br>• DW/BI<br>• DM/BA | • Drill-Down, Roll-Out, Pivoting, & Executive Dashboards<br>• Visual, interactive, & real-time Reporting<br>• Descriptive Analytics for reporting and visualizing |
| Risk Management / Risk Analysis | • Determine the specific organizational risks through the detailed analysis of threats, vulnerabilities, impacts, likelihoods and uncertainties | • ES/KBS<br>• DM/BA | • Intelligent advice, qualitative reasoning, problem-solving assistance, and logical inferences<br>• Predictive Analytics for exploring and elaborating forecasts models |
| Risk Mitigation/Risk Responses | • Prioritize, evaluate, and implement the appropriate risk-reducing controls recommended from the risk assessment process | • DSS<br>• EIS<br>• ES/KBS<br>• DW/BI<br>• DM/BA | • What-if, Goal-Seeking, Sensitivity Analysis on Quantitative Models<br>• Prescriptive Analytics for searching optimal or satisfactory solutions on Quantitative Models |
| Risk Evaluation/Risk Monitoring | • Conduct an ongoing evaluation and monitoring of the implemented risk mitigation countermeasures, and watch over organizational and external changes | • ES/KBS<br>• DM/BA | • Intelligent advice, qualitative reasoning, problem-solving assistance, and explanation of advices<br>• Predictive Analytics for exploring and elaborating predictive models |

Our study reveals that the risk management process has experienced drastic changes in its execution by organizations, its theoretical conceptualization by researchers, and its practical implications in the current era. The main shift of the risk management process can be stated as an evolution from traditional analytical and statistical techniques with structured data sets in highly predictable and cooperative business environment, to data-driven discovery and highly proactive and creative decision making utilizing modern and advanced analytical techniques with unstructured and massive data sources to cope with a highly dynamic global business environment in the current era.

## Conclusions on contributions, limitations, trends and open challenges

Risk management has become a vital theme in both academia and practice over the past several decades (Wu et al., 2014). It refers to the overall process of identifying, analyzing and monitoring risks as well as designing and implementing risk strategies for such identified risks. In this chapter, we introduced and reviewed the characteristics of a set of DMSS as valuable tools to support the risk management process. We have also reported and analyzed six illustrative application examples of DMSS in several risk management domains. Along the way, we have identified the theoretical as well as practical linkages between the DMSS and risk management processes. A theoretical mapping framework between generic decision-making processes and risk management processes was identified and depicted. We also developed an integrated application framework for applying relevant DMSS tools and capabilities to the specific risk management sub-processes.

This study also elicits a set of practical recommendations to executives and decision makers in organizations worldwide for interpreting the risk management literature and applying the rich body of knowledge for business practitioners. Given the importance and complexity of risk management and big data phenomenon, we encourage and anticipate continued research efforts to investigate and establish advanced and updated conceptualizations and frameworks to understand this complex yet critical subject.

## References


Adam, F., and Pomerol, J. (2002). Critical Factors in the Development of Executive Systems-Leveraging the Dashboard Approach. In G. Forgionne, J. Gupta, and M. Mora (Eds.), *Decision-Making Support Systems: Achievements and Challenges for the New Decade* (pp. 305–330). Hershey, PA: IGI Global.

Aebi, V., Sabato G., and Schmid, M. (2011). Risk management, corporate governance, and bank performance in the financial crisis. *Journal of Banking & Finance*, 36, 3213–3226.

Aven, T. (2016). Risk assessment and risk management: Review of recent advances on their foundation. *European Journal of Operational Research*, 253(1), 1–13.

Chandrasekaran, B., Josephson, J.R., and Benjamins, V.R. (1999). What are ontologies, and why do we need them? *IEEE Intelligent Systems*, 14(1), 20–26.

Choi, T., Chan, H., and Yue, X. (2016). Recent development in big data analytics for business operations and risk management. *IEEE Transactions on Cybernetics*, Pre-print, pp 1–12.

Davenport, T.H. (2006). Competing on analytics. *Harvard Business Review*, 84(1), 1–8.

Delen, D., and Demirkan, H. (2013). Data, information and analytics as services. *Decision Support Systems*, 55(1), 359–363.

DeLong, D.W., and Rockart, J.F. (1986). Identifying the attributes of successful executive support system implementation (pp. 190–205). Center for Informations Systems Research, Sloan School of Management, MIT, USA.

Deshmulch, A., and Millet, I. (1999). An analytic hierarchy process approach to assessing the risk of management fraud. *The Journal of Applied Business Research*, 15(1), 87–102.

Dey, P. (2010) Managing project risk using combined analytic hierarchy process and risk map. *Applied Soft Computing*, 10(4), 990–1000.

Elam, J.J., and Konsynski, B. (1987). Using artificial intelligence techniques to enhance the capabilities of model management systems. *Decision Sciences*, 18(3), 487–502.

Elam, J., and Leidner, D. (1995). EIS adoption, use, and impact: The executive perspective. *Decision Support Systems*, 14(2), 89–103.

Eom, S. (1996). A survey of operational expert systems in business (1980–1993). *Interfaces*, 26(5), 50–70.

Eom, S., and Kim, E. (2006). A survey of decision support system applications (1995–2001). *Journal of the Operational Research Society*, 57(11), 1264–1278.

Fayyad, U., Piatetsky-Shapiro, G., and Smyth, P. (1996). The KDD process for extracting useful knowledge from volumes of data. *Communications of the ACM*, 39(11), 27–34.

Feigenbaum, E., McCorduck, P., and Nii, P. (1988). *The Rise of the Expert Company*, Alexandria, VA: Time Life.

Forgionne, G. (1991). Decision technology systems: A vehicle to consolidate decision making support. *Information Processing & Management*, 27(6), 679–697.

Forgionne, G.A., and Kohli, R. (1996). HMSS: A management support system for concurrent hospital decision making. *Decision Support Systems*, 16(3), 209–229.

Forgionne, G.A., and Kohli, R. (2000). Management support system effectiveness: Further empirical evidence. *Journal of the Association for Information Systems*, 1(1), 1–39.

Forgionne, G., Mora, M., Cervantes-Pérez, F., and Kohli, R. (2000). Development of integrated decision-making support systems: A practical approach. *AMCIS 2000 Proceedings*, 83.

Forgionne, G., Mora, M., Gupta, J.N., and Gelman, O. (2005). Decision-Making Support Systems. In M. Khosrow-Pour (Ed.), *Encyclopedia of Information Science and Technology*, First Edition (pp. 759–765). Hershey, PA: IGI Global.

Gupta, J., Forgionne, G., and Mora, M. (2005). *Intelligent Decision-Making Support Systems*. Germany: Springer.

King, D. (1992). Intelligent Support Systems: Art, Augmentation, and Agents. In: R. Sprague and H. Watson (Eds.), *Decision Support Systems* (pp. 137–159). Englewood Cliffs: Prentice-Hall, Inc.

Klein, M., and Methie, L. (1990). *Expert Systems: A Decision Support Approach: With Applications in Management and Finance*. New York: Addison Wesley Publishing Company.

Leven, T. (2016). Risk assessment and risk management: Review of recent advances on their foundation. *European Journal of Operational Research*, 253, 1–13.

Li, H., Apostolakis, G., Gifun, J., VanSchalkwyk, W., Leite, S. and Barber, D. (2009). Ranking the risks from multiple hazards in a small community. *Risk Analysis*, 29(3), 438–456.

Liebowitz, J. (1990). *Expert Systems for Business & Management*, Englewood Cliffs, NJ: Yourdon Press, 1990.

Liu, B., Siu, Y., and Mitchell, G. (2016). Hazard interaction an alysis for multi-hazard risk assessment: A systematic classification based on hazard-forming environment. *Natural Hazards Earth System Science*, 16, 629–642.

March, S.T., and Hevner, A.R. (2007). Integrated decision support systems: A data warehousing perspective. *Decision Support Systems*, 43(3), 1031–1043.

Marzocchi, W., Mastellone, M., Di Ruocco, A., Novelli, P., Romeo, E., and Gasparini, P. (2009). Principles of Multi-risk management: Interactions Amongst Natural and Man-Induced Risks, European Commission, Directorate-General for Research, Environment Directorate, Luxembourg, 72, 2009.

Meyer, M., DeTore, A., Siegel, S., and Curley, K. (1992). The strategic use of expert systems for risk management in the Insurance Industry. *Expert Systems with Applications*, 5(1–2), 15–24.

Mora, M., Phillips-Wren, G., Marx-Gomez, J., Wang, F., and Gelman, O. (2014). The role of decision-making support systems in IT service management processes. *Intelligent Decision Technologies*, 8(2), 147–163.

Mora, M., Wang, F., and Gelman, O. (2013). A comparative study on the implementation inhibitors and facilitators of management information systems and integrated decision support systems: A perception of IT practitioners in Mexico. *Information Technology for Development*, 19(4), 319–346.

NIST (2002). – NIST Special Publication 800–30 – risk management Guide for Information Technology Systems. National Institute of Standards and Technology Gaithersburg, MD, USA.

NIST (2012). Guide for Conducting risk management – NIST Special Publication 800–30 R1. National Institute of Standards and Technology Gaithersburg, MD, USA.

PMI (1996). A Guide to the Project Management Body of Knowledge. Project Management Institute, Upper Darby, USA.

Rainer, R.K., Jr., and Watson, H.J. (1995). The keys to executive information system success. *Journal of Management Information Systems*, 12(2), 83–98.

Ramamurthy, K., Sen, A., and Sinha, A.P. (2008). Data warehousing infusion and organizational effectiveness. *IEEE Transactions on Systems, Man, and Cybernetics-Part A: Systems and Humans*, 38(4), 976–994.

Raz, T., and Michael, E. (2001). Use and benefits of tools for project risk management. *International Journal of Project Management*, 19, 9–17.

Rockart, J., and Treacy, M. (1982). The CEO goes on-line. *Harvard Business Review*, 60(1), 82–89.

Setzekorn, K., Sugumaran, V., and Patnayakuni, N. (2002). A comparison of implementation resistance factors for DMSS versus other information systems. *Information Resources Management Journal*, 15(4), 48–63.

Shim, J. P., Warkentin, M., Courtney, J. F., Power, D. J., Sharda, R., and Carlsson, C. (2002). Past, present, and future of decision support technology. *Decision Support Systems*, 33(2), 111–126.

Sprague, R. H., Jr. (1980). A framework for the development of decision support systems. *MIS Quarterly*, 1–26.

Sprague, R. H., Jr., and Carlson, E. D. (1982). *Building Effective Decision Support Systems*. Prentice Hall Professional Technical Reference.

Torabi, S., Soufi, H., and Sahebjamnia, N. (2014). A new framework for business impact analysis in business continuity management (with a case study). *Safety Science*, 68, 329–323.

Turban, E., and Aronson, E. (1998). *Decision Support System and Intelligent System*. Prentice-Hall, Upper Saddle River, NJ.

Turban, E., and Watkins, P. R. (1986). Integrating expert systems and decision support systems. *MIS Quarterly*, 10(2), 121–136.

Turban, E., and Watson, P. (1989). Integrating Expert Systems, Executive Information Systems and Decisions Support Systems. DSS 89 Transactions, 74–82.

Watson, H. J. (2014). Tutorial: Big data analytics: Concepts, technologies, and applications. *Communications of the Association for Information Systems*, 34(1), 1247–1268.

Watson, H. J., Rainer, R. K., Jr., and Koh, C. E. (1991). Executive information systems: A framework for development and a survey of current practices. *MIS Quarterly*, 15(1), 13–30.

Wixom, B. H., and Watson, H. J. (2001). An empirical investigation of the factors affecting data warehousing success. *MIS Quarterly*, 25(1), 17–41.

Wu, D., Chen, S., and Olson, D. (2014). Business intelligence in risk management: Some recent Progresses. *Information Sciences*, 256, 1–7.

# 30

# Intelligent rule-based risk modeling for decision making

*Ronald R. Yager*

## 1 Introduction

Almost all domains of human experience are affected by risky decisions. The support of decisions involving risk in most cases require tools to address issues related to a desire to satisfy multiple, often conflicting, goals and a need to negotiate between numerous, often adversarial, constituencies. In addition choices must be made in the face of uncertainty and associated risks. Further compounding any formal attempt to support risky decisions is the imprecision in much of the information provided by the participating agents. In this work we introduce some tools to address issues related to uncertainty and risk management. We are particularly concerned with problems inherent in the imprecision of our knowledge of uncertainty and the imprecision in the characterization of the decision maker's risk tolerance.

The need for risk management arises when we have to make a choice involving a risky alternative. One component of a risky alternative is the uncertainty of the payoff (outcome) resulting from its selection, there are more than one possible outcome. Making decisions in the face of uncertain outcomes requires some of representation of our knowledge of uncertainties associated with the possible outcomes, for example probabilities. Often this information is impossible to obtain precisely and may require an imprecise and fuzzy characterization. Here we shall take advantage of Zadeh's work (1999, 2001a, 2001b, 2002) on perception-based probability information.

A fundamental difficulty that arises when making decisions involving alternatives with uncertain outcomes is the comparison of the alternatives. This is due to the fact that the multiplicity and complexity of these types of the alternatives makes their direct comparison almost impossible. Here we use rule-based valuation functions to circumvent this difficulty.

An additional feature that distinguishes a risky alternative from one that is simply uncertain is that at least one of its possible outcomes is bad, "undesirable" or "disturbing." The concept of undesirable is fuzzy and often involves aspects of human perception. Let us try to provide some intuition. Consider a financial decision in which we can make a profit of either \$50, \$100 or \$200. In this case while we have uncertainty with respect to the outcome and a preference for 200 over 100 over 50, we don't have a risky alternative because none of the payoffs are undesirable. On the other hand, consider an alternative with payoffs −\$10,000, \$50 or \$200. This can be considered as a risky alternative because in addition to there being an uncertainty with respect to the outcome, it has at least one undesirable outcome. As another example, we can consider a person who has a non-life-threatening medical disorder and is offered a treatment that can either cure his disorder or kill him. This can be clearly seen as a risky alternative. The determination of whether a particular outcome is undesirable is often subjective and context dependent. It is very much dependent on the current state of the decision maker, what in some situations would be considered as disturbing may in other situations not be considered disturbing.

A fundamental point that we want to make here is that the construction of decision functions involving these "risky" alternatives often involves some kind of categorization of outcomes with respect to their being undesirable or bad. From a formal point of view, decision making with risky alternatives requires that the possible outcomes be expressed on a scale that is richer than an ordinal scale. The scale used must be of a bivalent nature (Yager, 2002), having positive and negative members, and thereby enabling the capturing of concepts good and bad. An additional feature is that the concepts used to specify "bad" and "good" outcomes are generally fuzzy and imprecise.

We should note that in addition to comparing risky alternatives risk management involves another important aspect, the creation of new alternatives to better satisfy the needs of the participants. Since this process of alternative creation is generally domain dependent, we shall not focus on this important issue. However, the tools developed here can play a role in the part of risk management focusing on alternative creation.

## 2 Modeling the valuation function

One approach to addressing the problem of comparing alternatives having uncertain outcomes is to use a valuation function. These functions map the possible payoffs associated with an uncertain alternative into a single scalar value called its valuation. The association of a scalar value with an alternative allows us to easily compare alternatives. Conceptually these valuation functions can be viewed as a mechanism to enable the responsible decision maker to reflect their preferences among different uncertain situations. Statistics such as expected value, median and variance have historically been used to help provide valuation functions. With the consideration of risky alternatives, the nature of the decision makers' preferences between different uncertain situations becomes more complex than can be captured by these simple statistics. In order to capture the decision maker's preference in these situations, we need more sophisticated structures for modeling the valuation functions.

One approach to modeling a decision maker's preference structure, that is valuation function, is to use a rule base (Yager & Filev, 1994). A rule base consists of a collection of statements, rules, each of which expresses the decision maker's valuation (attitude) about a particular uncertain situation. The totality of these individual components constitutes the decision maker's preference function. The use of a rule base allows a decision maker to express their preferences in a modular fashion. The facility of using a modular expression of their valuation greatly eases the task of formulating the function.

We see how this rule base (knowledge base) is used. An alternative is presented to the rule base, which then provides a value for V for the alternative. The value of V is some score associated with the alternative.

Fuzzy system modeling (Yager & Filev, 1994; Takagi & Sugeno, 1985) provides a well-established framework for constructing these types of models used to capture the decision makers' valuation function in the form of a rule base. An individual component rule in the preference rule base is of the form

If **antecedent** then V *is* $S_i$

where the term **antecedent** describes some characterization of a risky alternative. An example could be "if an alternative has a very bad outcome with a substantial probability of occurrence then give it a very low value."

In this approach, we use predicates to construct the antecedent. Here we use $\text{Pred}_i$ to indicate a predicate corresponding to some property or feature of an alternative. For any alternative A we can calculate $\text{Pred}_i(A)$, the degree to which A satisfies the predicate. The antecedent of a rule may consist of a single predicate or a collection of predicates connected by some logical or other aggregation procedure. Typically the antecedent can be expressed in terms of properties associated with surrogate features of the uncertainty profile of an alternative. Things like variance, probability of particular situations, and expected values are examples of these features. The consequent of the rule, V *is* $S_i$ indicates a valuation of an alternative that satisfies this rule.

Given a collection of rules

$R_i$: If $\text{Pred}_i$ then V *is* $S_i$

the general procedure for working with these rules is as follows. For the alternative A we calculate $\text{Pred}_i(A)$, the degree $R_i$ is valid for this alternative. This gives us a collection of pairs $(\text{Pred}_i(A), S_i)$. We then aggregate these pairs to get an overall valuation for the alternative being valuated, $V(A) = \text{Agg}_i(\text{Pred}_i(A), S_i)$. The methodology used to aggregate these pairs depends upon the structure underlying the partitioning of the uncertainty profile space by the rules. We note in fuzzy systems modeling the most common aggregation is a weighted average

$$V(A) = \frac{\sum_i \text{Pr}ed_i(A) S_i}{\text{Pr}ed_i(A)}$$

Our focus here shall be on the formulation and evaluation of some types of predicates needed to describe antecedents in these rule-based models of valuation functions.

## 3 Valuation functions and uncertainty profiles

Formally a risky alternative is characterized by an **uncertainty profile**. In part an uncertainty profile consists of a collection of possible outcomes (payoffs) that can occur as a result of selecting this alternative. We shall denote this collection of possible payoffs as X. In addition an uncertainty profile usually contains information about the realizability of each of the payoffs. A general framework for expressing this information can be had in terms of a monotonic set measure $\mu: 2^X \rightarrow [0, 1]$ having the properties **1.** $\mu(\varnothing) = 0$, **2.** $\mu(X) = 1$ and **3.** $\mu(A) \geq \mu(B)$ if $B \subset A$ (Klir, 2006). Here $\mu$ provides a measure of the anticipation of finding the actual payoff in the subset A. If as is often the case in many applications we assume $\mu$ is additive, $\mu(A \cup B) = \mu(A) + \mu(B)$ for $A \cap B = \varnothing$ then $\mu$ is a probability measure.

In the following we assume that the measure associated with the uncertainty profile of an alternative is best captured by a probability model. Thus we are assuming that the payoff of a risky alternative is a random variable **R**. One of our concerns here is with the characterization of the features of this random variable that can be used as predicates in the antecedent of the rules used in the rule base definition of the valuation function. We must emphasize that the representation of the features used must be such that we can evaluate the degree of satisfaction of the associated predicate for an alternative given our knowledge of the uncertainty profile of the alternative. Well-established features associated with a random variable are expected value, variance, model and median. A typical example of the use of these features in a rule base is the form

*If the expected payoff is **high** then V is **good**.*

Here the expected value is the feature being used. The predicate here is "the expected payoff *is **high***." Thus for a given alternative we must determine the degree to which this is true. Specifically if we have the uncertainty profile of the alternative expressed in terms of a random variable with known probability distribution we can calculate the expected value. With ***high*** expressed as a fuzzy set we can calculate the degree to which the predicate is satisfied. Another example would be a rule of the form

*If the expected payoff is **high** and the variance is **small** then V is **very good**.*

Here our antecedent consists of two predicates connected by an "and." The second predicate, the "variance is **small**," uses as its feature the variance. Here then for a given alternative we would calculate its expected value and its variance from its uncertainty profile. We then calculate the satisfaction of each of the two predicates and then take the "anding" of these two values. Using results from multivalued logic (Klir & Yuan, 1995) we could use the minimum of these values as the "and." It important to emphasize that with the use of predicates and these rules we have circumvented the issue of combining expected values and variances.

In making decisions in which we have risky alternatives the responsible decision maker's mental preference structure is generally more complex than that which can expressed simply using the basic features such as expected value and variance. Making decisions in risky environments require us to use more sophisticated features of an alternatives uncertainty profile.

One feature of an uncertainty profile that can play an important role in the formulating decision rules in the face of risky alternatives is the probability of some subset of payoffs. An example of a rule using this type of feature is

*If the probability of having a severe loss is **low** then the value of the alternative is **high**.*

In this case the feature used in the rule is "the alternative's probability of having a severe loss." The predicate here is the degree to which this feature attains a value that is considered as **low**. The process of evaluating this antecedent predicate involves the following. We represent the concept "low probability" as a fuzzy subset, **LOW**, of the unit interval. If Prob(S) is the probability of having a severe loss under the alternative then the degree to which the predicate is satisfied is **LOW**(Prob(S)), the membership grade of value Prob(S) in the fuzzy subset **LOW**.

The issue now becomes that of obtaining Prob(S), the probability of having a severe loss under the alternative. The determination of this depends upon our definition of severe loss and our knowledge about the uncertainty profile associated with the alternative. Initially we shall assume complete information about the probability associated with the random variable, the uncertainty profile of the alternative. If **R** is a continuous random variable, we assume the availability of the probability density function f. If the random variable is discrete we assume the availability of the probability mass function. In addition to our knowledge of the uncertainty profile we need a definition of the concept of "severe loss." Here we can use fuzzy sets to help in the definition. More generally as we shall see the combined use of fuzzy sets with probabilistic information provides a very powerful way to express features that can play a role in constructing intelligent decision-making functions. Let us look at this closer.

Consider the payoff random variable whose uncertainty is captured by its probability density function f(x). Let us calculate the "probability of a severe loss." In order to obtain this, we first need a definition of the term "severe loss." We define the concept of a severe loss as a fuzzy subset S on X such that S(x) is the degree to which an outcome x satisfies the concept of being a severe loss. Using this definition and the probability density function f(x) we obtain the probability of a severe loss as (Zadeh, 1968):

$$Prob(S) = \int_R f(x)S(x)\,dx$$

We note if S is a crisp subset then this becomes $Prob(S) = \int_{x \in S} f(x)\,dx$. For example, if S is defined crisply as "any payoff less than or equal a" then $Prob(S) = \int_{-\infty}^{a} f(x)\,dx$.

In similar manner we can define the concept of a large payoff as the fuzzy subset L and obtain $Prob(Large\ Payoff) = \int_R f(x)L(x)\,dx$. More generally if $\mathcal{E}$ is any linguistically expressed description of the payoff space which can be represented as a fuzzy subset $\mathcal{E}$ then we can obtain Prob($\mathcal{E}$) = $Prob(\mathcal{E}) = \int_R f(x)E(x)\,dx$. We emphasize the subjective nature of the concept $\mathcal{E}$ and the related fuzzy subset $\mathcal{E}$. This situation comes with positives and negatives. While this allows a user to introduce the concepts needed to describing their preferences it requires a definition be supplied either by the user or via some default supplementary mechanism.

**Note**: In the case in which the random variable describing the payoffs is discrete and captured by a probability mass P, then Prob($\mathcal{E}$) = $\Sigma_i P(x_i)\, E(x_i)$.

## 4 Perception-based granular probability distributions

In the complex environment of decision making under risk the information needed to fully detail the probability measure associated with an alternative's uncertainty profile may only be partially or imprecisely available.

Techniques such as the Dempster-Shafer theory of evidence (Yager & Liu, forthcoming) provide useful structures for the representation of an alternative's uncertainty profile in the cases of lack of precise knowledge about the exact probability measure. Another approach developed by Zadeh (2002) is rooted in the observation that much of the information appearing in an alternative's uncertainty profile is based upon the perceptions of the decision maker. In the light of this understanding Zadeh (2002) has introduced the idea of Perception Based Granular (PBG) probability distributions to address situations in which we have less than perfect information about the uncertainty profile. We now consider the situation where this is the case.

Zadeh (2002) observed that the type of probability information associated with an uncertainty profile is generally a reflection of perceptions as well as measurements by the decision-making entity. He suggested that an appropriate way of representing this type of information is with a Perception Based Granular (PBG) probability distribution. With the aid of a PBG probability distribution the human can very naturally express their perceptions of an uncertainty profile. As we shall see, a PBG probability distribution generalizes the idea of ordinary probability distribution.

Let **R** be a random variable whose domain X is a subset of the real line. A PBG probability distribution consists of a collection of tuples $(A_i, Q_i)$. Within each of these tuples $A_i$ is an imprecise element from the domain X of **R** represented as a fuzzy subset of X. $Q_i$ is an amount of probability allocated to that range, generally having an imprecise linguistic nature and expressed as a fuzzy subset of the unit interval. For example, if **R** takes its values in the interval X = [−10 to 10] then an example of a such a PBG probability distribution is

(low, about 0.5), (near zero, about 0.3), (near 10, about 0.2)

In order to further discuss PBG probability distributions we must first distinguish between two types of situations regarding the underlying domains. The first is when X is a continuous subset of the real line, X = [a, b], and the second is when X is discrete $X = \{x_1, \ldots, x_n\}$.

We first consider the case in which X is discrete. Here the underlying measure is a probability distribution P, whose actual values are unknown. The PBG probability distribution is providing partial information about the underlying probability distribution. Let us look at this situation. First we recall with $X = \{x_1, \ldots, x_n\}$ then a valid probability distribution P on X is a collection $[p_1, .., p_n]$ such that $Prob(x_j) = p_j$ and $p_j \in [0, 1]$ $Prob(xj) \; = pj \; and \; pj\hat{I}\,[0,\, 1]$ and $\sum_{i=1}^{n} p_j = 1$. We shall let $\mathcal{P}_X$ be the set of all valid probability distributions on X.

Formally a PBG probability distribution induces a possibility distribution over all the valid probability distributions over X. Let $\mathcal{K} = \{(A_i, Q_i) | i = 1, \ldots, m\}$ be a PBG probability distribution on X. If $\prod_{\mathcal{K}}$ is the induced possibility distribution then for each valid probability distribution, $P \in \mathcal{P}_X$, $\prod_{\mathcal{K}}(P)$ indicates the possibility that P is the actual probability distribution on X.

With $P = [p_1, \ldots, p_n]$ in the following we describe one approach to determine $\prod_{\mathcal{K}}(P)$ given $\mathcal{K} = ((A_i, Q_i) | i = 1, \ldots, m\}$.

(1) For each $A_i$ calculate $Prob(A_i)$ using $P$: $Prob\left(A_i \,|\, P\right) \; = \sum_{j=1}^{n} A_i(x_j)\, p_j$

(2) For each i calculate, $\tau_i = Q_i(Prob(A_i|P))$. This is the compatibility of P with $Q_i$

(3) $\prod_{\mathcal{K}}(P) = Min_i[\tau_i]$

In the case in which X = [a, b], it is continuous, the random variable is characterized by a probability measure. Here the PBG probability distribution is only providing partial information about underlying probability measure. We note that a valid probability measure f associated with X is such that $f(x) \geq 0$ for all $x \in [a, b]$ and $\int_a^b f(x)\, dx = 1$. We let $\mathcal{F}_X$ be the collection of all valid probability measures on X. In this case a PBG probability induces a possibility distribution over the set $\mathcal{F}_X$. Again, we shall assume $\mathcal{K} = ((A_i, Q_i), i = 1, \ldots, m)$ is the PBG probability distribution corresponding to the uncertainty profile. We let $\prod_{\mathcal{K}}$ be the induced possibility distribution over $F_X$. Here $\prod_{\mathcal{K}}(f)$ indicates the possibility that f can be the actual probability measure given $\mathcal{K}$. We determine $\prod_{\mathcal{K}}(f)$ as follows:

(1) For each $A_i$ we calculate $Prob\left(A_i \,|\, f\right) \; = \int_a^b f(x)\, A_i(x)\, dx$.

(2) For each i calculate, $\tau_i = Q_i(Prob(A_i|p))$. This is the compatibility of f with Q

(3) $\prod_{\mathcal{K}}(f) = Min_i[t_i]$

Let us look at this nature of the PBG probability distribution in more detail. As we shall subsequently see a PBG probability distribution is essentially a generalization of the idea of an ordinary probability distribution. Consider the PBG probability distribution $((A_i, Q_i), i = 1, \ldots, m)$. First we note that each $Q_i$ is a fuzzy number drawn from the unit interval I, it is normal and unimodal. In particular, there exists an $r \in [0, 1]$ such that $Q_i(r) = 1$. In addition, since it is unimodal, there exist two values $a_i$ and $b_i \in I$ such that

1 $Q_i(r)$ is non-decreasing for $r \in [0, a_i]$
2 $Q_i(r) = 1$ for $r \in [a_i, b_i]$
3 $Q_i(r)$ is non-increasing for $r \in [b_i, 1]$

One implication of the unimodality of the granular probabilities is the interval nature of the associated level sets (Dubois & Prade, 1980). Thus if $Q_i^\alpha$ is the α-level set of $Q_i^\alpha = \{r \,/\, Qi(r) \bullet \alpha\}$, then $Q_i^\alpha = [l_i(\alpha), u_i(\alpha)]$. It is also the case that the unimodality of $Q_i$ implies that if $\alpha > \beta$ then $Q_i^\alpha \subseteq Q_i^\beta$ , the level sets are nested.

We should note two special cases of these granular probabilities. The first is the case when $Q_i$ is a precise value $q_i$ in I, $Q_i = \{q_i\}$. The second is when $Q_i$ is an interval, $Q_i = [a_i, b_i]$. Here $Q_i(r) = 1$ for $r \in [a_i, b_i]$ and $Q_i(r) = 0$ for $r \notin [a_i, b_i]$.

Generally, the $A_i$ are human comprehensible concepts associated with the space X. As discussed by Gardenfors (2000) concepts on a domain are expressed as convex subsets. Thus formally the $A_i$ are normal and unimodal, they are fuzzy numbers from the domain X. Two special cases of $A_i$ are singletons and crisp intervals.

## 5 Evaluating decision functions with PBG uncertainty profiles

Previously we indicated that the rule-based approach for modeling the decision maker's valuation function can involve rules in which we have antecedent terms of the form:

If Prob(Fuzzy Event) *is* Large then. . .  (I)

Here we shall investigate a method for evaluating the satisfaction of this type of antecedent by risky alternatives for this case in which an alternative's uncertainty profile is expressed in terms of a PBG probability distribution.

We first formalize the above antecedent. Let **R** indicate the payoff associated with the alternative being evaluated. Formally it is a random variable on real line. In order to formalize the antecedent in (I) we let F be a fuzzy subset of the domain of **R**, this corresponds to a general fuzzy event. In addition, we let Q be a fuzzy probability corresponding to what we generically denoted as Large in (I). Using these notations our rule becomes

If Prob(**R** *is* F) *is* Q then. . .

Let us use W to indicate the variable corresponding to the "probability of the event **R** *is* F." Using this notation, we can express our rule as

"If W *is* Q then. . . . "

The firing of this rule is determined by the compatibility of the value of W with the fuzzy subset Q.

We now consider a risky alternative whose uncertainty profile is expressed using the PBG probability distribution $\mathcal{K} = ((A_i, Q_i), i = 1, \ldots, m)$. Here $A_i$ is a fuzzy subset of X and $Q_i$ is a fuzzy subset corresponding to an amount of probability, a fuzzy number in the unit interval.

The task of evaluating the degree to which the risky alternative under consideration satisfies the rule can be formulated as follows. We need to determine the compatibility of the value of W, the probability of the event **R** *is* F with Q, given that all we know about **R** *is* $\mathcal{K}$, $((A_i, Q_i), i = 1, \ldots, m)$.

Consider the firing of the rule "If W *is* Q then. . . ." If we know that the probability of the event **R** *is* F is precisely equal to the value b, W = b, then the degree of firing $\tau$ is simply Q(b). More generally, if the value for W is a fuzzy probability B, then using the established procedure in fuzzy systems modeling we obtain as the firing level = $\text{Max}_y[Q(y) \wedge B(y)]$, we take the maximum of the intersection of Q and B.

The situation we are faced with is slightly different than either of these. Instead of knowing the value of W, the probability of **R** *is* F, all we have is the PBG probability distribution $\mathcal{K}$ on **R**. In this case our task becomes to calculate the value of W from our information about **R**.

If instead of having a PBG probability distribution we had an ordinary probability distribution $P = [(x_i, p_i)]$, $p_i$ being the probability that **R** = $x_i$ then to calculate W, probability that **R** *is* F, we use

$$W = \sum_{i=1}^{n} F(x_i)\, p_i$$

We must now extend this approach to our situation where we have the PBG probability distribution $\mathcal{K} = [(A_i, Q_i), i = 1, \ldots, m]$. With $\mathcal{K}$ we have that both $A_i$ and $Q_i$ are fuzzy subsets. The fact that $A_i$ is not crisp conceptually provides more difficulty than the fuzziness of $Q_i$.

If we temporarily consider the situation in which $Q_i$ is precise, $Q = q_i$ and $A_i$ is an interval we can get some insight into how to proceed. We shall also for simplicity assume that F is a crisp subset. In calculating W we are essentially obtaining the sum of the probabilities of the possible values of **R** that lies in F. When $A_i$ is an interval it is difficult to decide whether the probability is associated with element in F or not. To get around this problem we must obtain upper and lower bounds on W. The actual probability lies between these values.

Using this idea for the more general situation where all the objects are fuzzy we obtain

$$Upper_F = \sum_{i=1}^{n} Poss\left[F / A_i\right] Q_i$$

$$Lower_F = \sum_{i=1}^{n} (1 - Poss[\underset{\substack{x_j \ s.t \\ \Sigma_j \alpha_j x_j = z}}{Max} [A_i(x_i)] \overline{F} / A_i]\ )\ Q_i$$

where $\text{Poss}[F/A_i] = \text{Max}_x[F(x) \wedge A_i(x)]$ and $\text{Poss}[\overline{F}/A_i] = \text{Max}_x[(1 - F(x)) \wedge A_i(x)]$ Essentially we see that $\text{Poss}[F/A_i]$ is the degree of intersection of $A_i$ and F while $1 - \text{Poss}[\overline{F}/A_i]$ is the degree to which $A_i$ is included in $\overline{F}$. There values are closely related to the measures of plausibility and belief in Dempster-Shafer theory (Yager & Liu, forthcoming).

At this point we must draw upon some of results from fuzzy arithmetic (Dubois & Prade, 1987). We recall if A and B are two fuzzy numbers then their sum $D = A \oplus B$ is also a fuzzy number such that

$$D(z) = \underset{\substack{x, y s.t. \\ x+y=z}}{Max}[A(x)\hat{U}B(y)]$$

More generally if $D_1, \ldots, D_n$ are fuzzy numbers and $\alpha_1, \ldots, \alpha_n$ are nonnegative scalars then

$$D = \alpha_1 D_1 \oplus \alpha_2 D_2 \oplus \ldots \oplus \alpha_n D_n$$

is a fuzzy number such that $D(z) = \underset{\substack{x_i\ s.t \\ \Sigma_i \alpha_i x_i = z}}{Max}[A_i(x_i)]$

The point we can conclude from this digression is that we have available to us the facility to calculate the values $Upper_F$ or $Lower_F$. More specifically if we denote $\lambda_i = Poss[F/A_i] \in [0,1]$ then $Upper_F$ is a fuzzy number H defined on the unit interval such that for all $z \in [0, 1]$

$$H(z) = \underset{\substack{z_i\ s.t \\ \Sigma_i \lambda_i z_i = z}}{Max}[Min_i[Q_i(z_i)]]$$

If we denote $\gamma_i = 1 - Poss[\overline{F}/A_i] \in [0, 1]$ then $Lower_F$ is a fuzzy number L defined on the unit interval such that for all $z \in [0,1]$

$$L(z) = \underset{\substack{z_i\ s.t \\ \Sigma_i \gamma_i z_i = z}}{Max}[Min_i[Q_i(z_i)]]$$

We must now consider the relationship between the fuzzy subsets H and L. In anticipation of uncovering this we look at the relationship between $\lambda_i = Poss[F/A_i]$ and $\gamma_i = 1 - Poss[\overline{F}/A_i]$. Here we use the fact that F and $A_i$ are normal, they have at least one element with membership grade 1. Assume $\gamma_i = \alpha$, then $Max_x[(1 - F(x)) \wedge A_i(x)] = 1 - \alpha$. Since $A_i$ is normal, there exists some $x^*$ where $A_i(x^*) = 1$ and therefore $(1 - F(x^*)) \wedge 1 = (1 - F(x^*)) \leq 1 - \alpha$, hence $F(x^*) \geq \alpha$. Since $\lambda_i = Max_x[F(x) \wedge A_i(x)] \geq F(x^*) \wedge A_i(x^*) \geq \alpha$. Hence we get $\lambda_i \geq \gamma_i$ for all i. Thus we see that $L = \sum_{j=1}^{n} \gamma_j Q_j$ and $H = \sum_{j=1}^{n} \lambda_j Q_j$ where $\lambda_j \geq \gamma_j$ for all j.

Before proceeding we want to introduce a type of relationship between fuzzy numbers:
**Definition**: Let $G_1$ and $G_2$ be two fuzzy numbers such that

$G_j(x)$ is non-decreasing for $x \leq a_j$
$G_j(x) = 1$ for $x \in [a_j, b_j]$
$G_j(x)$ is non-increasing for $x \geq b_j$

where $a_1 \leq a_2$ and $b_2 \geq b_1$. If, in addition, we have

$G_1(x) \geq G_2(x)$ for all $x \leq a_1$
$G_2(x) \geq G_1(x)$. for all $x \geq a_2$

we shall say $G_2$ is to **the right of** $G_1$ and denote this as $G_2 \geq_R G_1$.

This relationship $G_2 \geq_R G_1$ can be equivalently expressed in terms of level sets. If $G_i(\alpha) = [a_i(\alpha), b_i(\alpha)]$ is the level set of $G_i$, then the relationship $G_2 \geq_R G_1$ is equivalent to the condition that for each $\alpha \in [0,1]$ we have $a_1(\alpha) \leq a_2(\alpha)$ and $b_1(\alpha) \leq b_2(\alpha)$.

It can be shown that if $G2=\sum_{i=1}^{n}\lambda_i Q_i \sum_{i=1}^{n}\lambda_i Q_i$ and $G1=\sum_{i=1}^{n}\gamma_i Q_i$ where $0 \leq \gamma_i \leq \lambda_i \leq 1$ for all i and the $Q_i$ are non-negative fuzzy number then $G_2 \geq_R G_1$. From this it follows that $H \geq_R L$, the upper bound is always to the right of the lower bound.

Earlier we indicated that the value of W, the probability that **R** is F, lies between the H and L. In particular, we have the following constraints on the value of W:

W is greater than or equal L
***and***
W is less than or equal H.

If we let L* indicate the fuzzy subset *greater than or equal L* and let H* indicate the fuzzy subset *less than or equal H* then W *is* E where $E = L^* \cap H^*$. It is the intersection of the fuzzy subsets L* and H*.

Let us now calculate L* and H* from L and H. L* is obtained as

$$L^*(x) = Max_y[GTE(x, y) \wedge L(y)]$$

where GTE is the relationship "greater then or equal" defined on $[0, 1] \times [0, 1]$ by

$$GTE(x, y) = 1 \text{ if } x \geq y$$
$$GTE(x, y) = 0 \text{ if } x < y$$

Here L(x) is non-decreasing for $x \leq a_1$ and $L(x) = 1$ for $x \in [a_1, b_1]$ it is non-increasing for $x \geq b_1$. It is easy to show that in this case that L* is such that

$$L^*(x) = L(x) \text{ for } x \leq a_1 \text{ and } L^*(x) = 1 \text{ for } x \geq a_1$$

Similarly for H* we have $H^*(x) = Max_y[LTE(x, y) \wedge H(y)]$ where LTE is the relationship "less then or equal" defined on $[0, 1] \times [0, 1]$ by

$$LTE(x, y) = 1 \text{ if } x \leq y$$
$$LTE(x, y) = 0 \text{ if } x > y$$

If H(x) is a fuzzy number with value one in the interval $[a_2, b_2]$ then H* is a fuzzy number such $H^*(x) = 1$ for $x \leq b_2$ and $H^*(x) = H(x)$ for $x > b_2$.

Combining L* and H* to get E, the possible values for W, we have $E = H^* \cap L^*$ hence $E(x) = H^*(x) \wedge L^*(x)$. From this we get

$$E(x) = L(x) \text{ for } x \in [0, a_1]$$
$$E(x) = 1 \text{ for } x \in [a_1, b_2]$$
$$E(x) = H(x) \text{ for } x \in [b_2, 1]$$

Returning to our concern with determining the firing level of the rule

If W *is* Q then

when our input is W = $\mathcal{K}$ we now use this E to calculate the firing level of the rule as $\tau = \text{Max}_x[Q(x) \wedge E(x)]$.

## 6 Conclusion

We focused on the issue of decision making in risky situations. We discussed the need for using decision functions to aid in capturing the decision maker's preference among these types of uncertain alternatives. The use of fuzzy rule-based formulations to model these functions was investigated. We discussed the role of Zadeh's perception-based granular probability distributions as a means of modeling the uncertainty profiles of the alternatives. We looked at various properties of this method of describing uncertainty and showed how they induced possibility distributions of the space of probability distributions. Tools for evaluating rule-based decision functions in the face of perception-based uncertainty profiles were presented.

## References


Dubois, D. and Prade, H., "Fuzzy numbers: An overview," in *Analysis of Fuzzy Information Vol 1: Mathematics and Logic*, Bezdek, J. C. (ed.), CRC Press: Boca Raton, FL, 3–39, 1987.

Dubois, D. and Prade, H., *Fuzzy Sets and Systems: Theory and Applications*, Academic Press: New York, 1980.

Gardenfors, P., *Conceptual Spaces: The Geometry of Thought*, MIT Press: Cambridge, MA, 2000.

Klir, G. J., *Uncertainty and Information*, John Wiley & Sons: New York, 2006.

Klir, G. J. and Yuan, B., *Fuzzy Sets and Fuzzy Logic: Theory and Applications*, Prentice Hall: Upper Saddle River, NJ, 1995.

Takagi, T. and Sugeno, M., "Fuzzy identification of systems and its application to modeling and control," *IEEE Transactions on Systems, Man and Cybernetics* 15, 116–132, 1985.

Yager, R. R., "Using a notion of acceptable in uncertain ordinal decision making," *International Journal of Uncertainty, Fuzziness and Knowledge-Based Systems* 10, 241–256, 2002.

Yager, R. R. and Filev, D. P., *Essentials of Fuzzy Modeling and Control*, John Wiley: New York, 1994.

Yager, R. R. and Liu, L., (A. P. Dempster and G. Shafer, Advisory Editors), *Classic Works of the Dempster-Shafer Theory of Belief Functions*, Springer: Heidelberg, 2008.

Zadeh, L. A., "Probability measures of fuzzy events," *Journal of Mathematical Analysis and Applications* 10, 421–427, 1968.

Zadeh, L. A., "From computing with numbers to computing with words-From manipulation of measurements to manipulations of perceptions," *IEEE Transactions on Circuits and Systems* 45, 105–119, 1999.

Zadeh, L. A., "A new direction in AI – toward a computational theory of perceptions," *AI Magazine* 22, No 1, 73–84, 2001a.

Zadeh, L. A., "Toward a logic of perceptions based on fuzzy logic," in *Discovering the World with Fuzzy Logic*, edited by Novak, W. and Perfilieva, I., Physica-Verlag: Heidelberg, 4–28, 2001b.

Zadeh, L. A., "Toward a perception-based theory of probabilistic reasoning with imprecise probabilities," *Journal of Statistical Planning and Inference* 105, 233–264, 2002.

# Index

Note: Page numbers in *italic* indicate figures; page numbers in **bold** indicate tables.